Professional Java Web Services

S. Jeelani Basha

Scott Cable

Ben Galbraith

Mack Hendricks

Romin Irani

James Milbery

Tarak Modi

Andre Tost

Alex Toussaint

Wrox Press Ltd. ®

Professional Java Web Services

Printing History

First published   January 2002

Published by Wrox Press Ltd,
Arden House, 1102 Warwick Road, Acocks Green,
Birmingham, B27 6BH, UK
Printed in the United States
ISBN 1-861003-75-7

Trademark Acknowledgements

Credits

Authors
S. Jeelani Basha
Scott Cable
Ben Galbraith
Mack Hendricks
Romin Irani
James Milbery
Tarak Modi
Andre Tost
Alex Toussaint

Technical Architect
Chanoch Wiggers

Technical Editors
Helen Callaghan
Mankee Cheng
Shivanand Nadkarni
Nick Manning
Robert FE Shaw

Managing Editor
Adam Maclean

Project Manager
Claire Robinson

Author Agent
Nicola Phillips

Index
Michael Brinkman

Technical Reviewers
Javad Abdollahi
Rahim Adatia
Kapil Apshankar
John Bell
Pete Clark
Cosmo di Fazio
Kevin Farnham
Barry Feigenbaum
Romin Irani
Damon Payne
Phil Powers de George
Vinay Menon
Judith Myerson
Larry Rodrigues
Purush Rudrakshala
David Whitney
Dave Writz

Production Project Coordinator
Abbie Forletta

Illustrations
Abbie Forletta
Emma Eato

Cover
Chris Morris

Proof Readers
Fiver Locker
Lisa Stephenson

Chris Smith

About the Authors

S.Jeelani Basha

Jeelani works as a Senior Software Engineer at Insync Information Systems, Fremont, California. He has a Bachelor's in Electrical Engineering and is a Sun Certified Java2 Programmer. His interest in programming led him from electrical engineering to software programming. He has more than 5 years of experience and has done various projects using J2EE technology.

His current subject of interest is web services and is putting his part of efforts in making web services a viable solution for enterprise applications.

Thanks to my wife, Tahaseen for her love.

Jeelani welcomes your comments at s_jeelani@yahoo.com

Jeelani contributed Chapter 14 to this book.

Scott Cable

Scott gained an MSc in Cognitive Science five years ago, and has been working with Internet technologies such as Java and XML ever since. He currently works as a consultant for a news and financial information provider. He can be reached at webservices@scottcable.com.

Scott contributed towards Chapter 6 to this book.

Ben Galbraith

Ben Galbraith started programming in BASIC on an Atari 800 when he was six years old. The years since have included forays brief and extended in Pascal, C, Perl, Delphi, and yes, even Visual Basic. Unimpressed with Java Applets, he nearly avoided the language altogether, were it not for his sudden and complete repentance in late 1999. An amateur historian and part-time businessman, Mr. Galbraith is currently free-lancing in the western United States.

"To my brother, Reed, for his example."

Ben contributed Chapter 12 to this book.

Mack Hendricks

Mack Hendricks currently works for Sun Microsystems within the iPlanet division as a Systems Engineer. He holds a B.S. and M.S. in Computer Science from Oakland University, located in Rochester, MI. He has eight years of experience working in a number of different areas of computing which consist of system administration, software development, and enterprise support. His technical interests include: distributing computing systems, XML, Java, datamining, object oriented design and operating systems. When not writing books or exploring with new technologies, he's spending time with his daughter, Courtney and his girlfriend, LaTorri McCray.

I would like to first thank God for allowing me to fulfill my dream of always wanting to publish a technical book. Next, I have to say thanks to my parents, McLevyonne and Barbara Hendricks for buying me a Commodore VIC 20 when I was eight – look at me now! Also, I would like to thank the iPlanet Enterprise Support Account Manager team for their support throughout the writing process. I also want to thank a good friend of mine, Eric Hamilton for providing me with encouragement throughout the whole writing process. Last but not least, I want to thank my girlfriend for her patience and support throughout the entire process. I will make it up to you :-)

The author can be reached via e-mail at mlhendri@oakland.edu

Mack contributed Chapter 2, 3, and 11 to this book.

Romin Irani

Romin Irani is a Senior Software Engineer with InSync Information Systems, Inc in Fremont, California. He graduated with a Bachelors degree in Computer Engineering from University of Bombay, India. Romin spends most of his time researching Web Services technologies and products and writing about them at www.webservicesarchitect.com. When he is not reading and writing about Web Services, he is still thinking about them. He firmly believes that Web Services will win the Nobel Peace Prize (for bringing the Microsoft and Java worlds together) and the Nobel Economics Prize (for bringing the cost of integration significantly down). He welcomes your comments at romin@rocketmail.com.

First and foremost to my wife Devyani for her support and understanding. To Peter Fletcher and Mark Waterhouse at www.webservicesarchitect.com for giving me so many opportunities to research and write about Web Services. To the wonderful folks at Wrox for giving me another opportunity to write. To my parents, Khushru and Gulrukh for all that they have taught me. Finally, I wish to devote the chapters that I wrote to my lovely sister Romana. Romana ... these chapters are for you !!!

Romin contributed Chapters 1, 7, and 8 to this book.

James Milbery

James Milbery is a Principal with Kuromaku Partners LLC. He has worked with a diverse group of clients such as Oracle Corporation, William Blair Capital Partners and Allied Capital. He spent many years as a sales consultant and sales consultant manager with Compuware, Ingres, and Compaq (Digital Equipment Corporation). He is also the Product Reviews Editor for SYS-CON Media's Java Developer's Journal, XML Developer's Journal and Wireless Business and Technology. He specializes in providing technology strategy to early and mid-stage software companies. He is well versed in deploying pre-sales technical teams and developing competitive-intelligence strategies.

James contributed Chapters 6 and 9 to this book.

Tarak Modi

Tarak Modi has been architecting scalable, high performance, distributed applications for over six years. His professional experience includes hardcore C++ and Java programming; working with Microsoft technologies such as COM, MTS, COM+, and experimenting with .NET; Java platforms including J2EE; and CORBA. His professional experience is built on a solid educational foundation that consists of a Bachelor's degree in Electrical Engineering, a Master's degree in Computer Engineering, and an MBA concentrating in Information Systems (with a 4.0 GPA in each one :)). He has written many articles in prominent software magazines including Dr. Dobbs Journal, Java Report, Java Developer's Journal, Java World, and Java Pro. When he is not keeping up with new technologies or working around his newly built house, Tarak enjoys working out, playing tennis and a good round of golf. Tarak lives in Atlanta, GA (USA) with his wife and a four-year-old son, who is quite a handful.

> *I would like to acknowledge all the hard work put in by mother in raising me. Having a son of my own has put everything in perspective. I also want to thank my wife for being so understanding and not just allowing but encouraging me to follow my dreams. Finally, I want to apologize to my son for all those times when he wanted to play with me and he was told, "Papa is working."*

Tarak contributed Chapter 13 to this book.

Andre Tost

Andre Tost works as a Solution Architect for IBM's WebSphere Software Group in Rochester, Minnesota. In his current assignment, he helps IBM's strategic software partners to integrate with IBM middleware products. Before that, he had various development and architecture roles in IBM's SanFrancisco and WebSphere Business Components development organizations. He started Java programming in early 1996 in the SanFrancisco project and has been developing in this language ever since. For the past year or so, he has been closely following the evolution of Web Services technologies and spends a large portion of his time consulting and teaching programming workshops about it.

He was born and raised in Northern Germany and moved with his family to (cold!) Minnesota in 1998. Being a big football fan (menaing the real football that Americans call soccer), he likes to play and watch the game. Fortunately, Rochester has a quite an active soccer scene with plenty of playing opportunities. Besides spending his time on programming and soccer, he likes to be with his wife and his two boys (they're two and five years old and think that being a programmer at IBM must be the biggest fun one can possibly have - oh well...).

Andre contributed Chapters 4 and 5 to this book.

Alex Toussaint

Alex Toussaint is Director of Engineering for Vignette Corporation in Austin, Texas. He has over 10 years of software development experience and has extensive experience with Java since 1996 and J2EE technologies since 1998. Alex has contributed articles on web application and electronic commerce to online journals, such as Microsoft MSDN and he was a contributing author to the Professional Site Server book by Wrox. Alex has also been invited to lecture at the University of Texas at Austin Red McCombs School of Business on topics such as Electronic Commerce and Enterprise Software Development. Alex now lives in Austin, Texas with his wife Danielle and their little dog Sasha. Alex welcomes your email at alex_toussaint@yahoo.com.

Alex contributed towards Chapter 6 to this book.

Table of Contents

Table of Contents

Table of Contents

Table of Contents

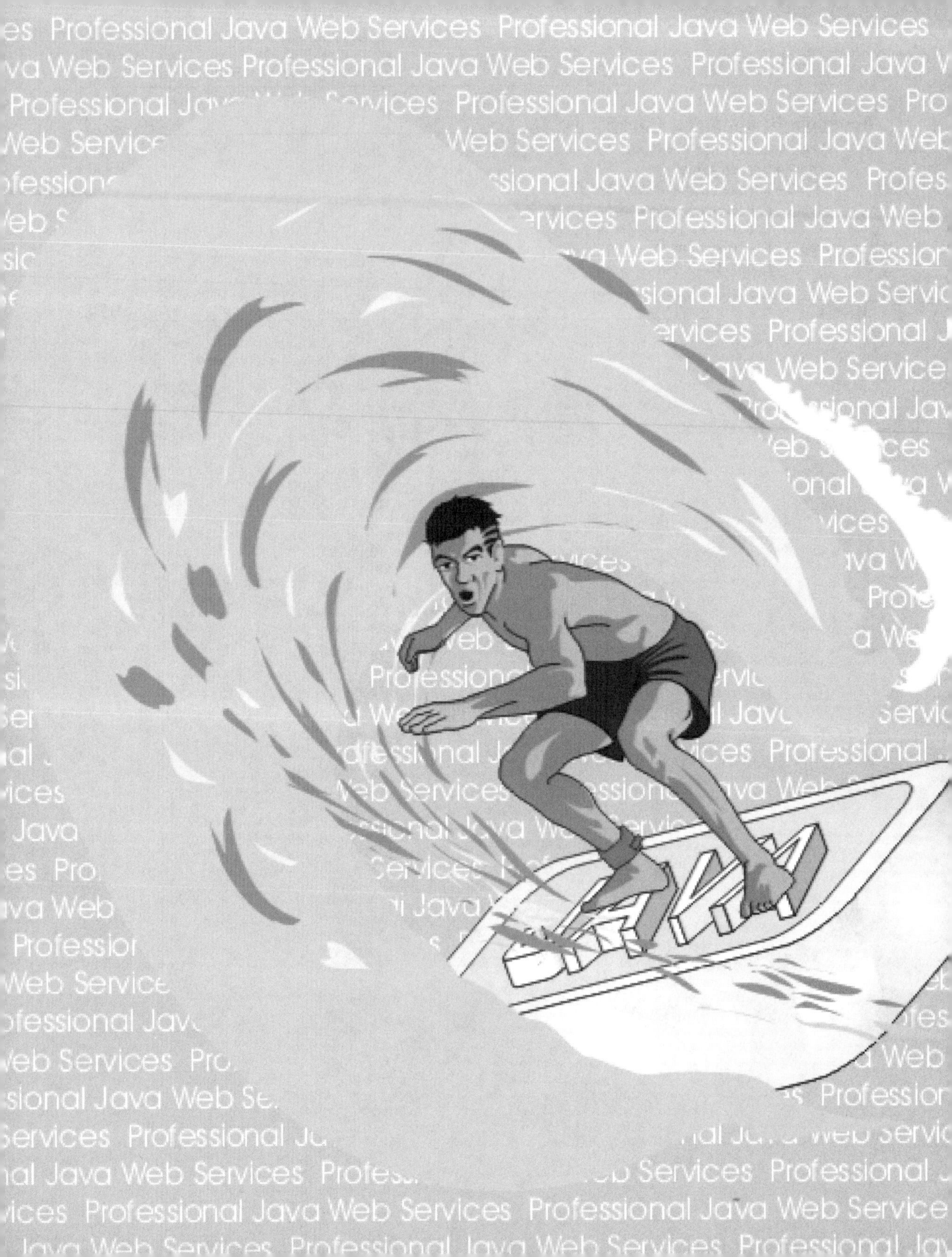
Professional Java Web Services

Introduction

What Are Web Services?

Web services are the latest thing in application development, and have attracted the interest of developers working on all platforms. The fundamental concept is simple – web services allow us to make Remote Procedure Calls (RPCs) against an object over the Internet or a network. Web services aren't the first technology to allow us to do this, but they differ from previous technologies in that their use of platform-neutral standards such as HTTP and XML allow us to hide the implementation details entirely from the client. The client needs to know the URL of the service, and the data types used for the method calls, but doesn't need to know whether the service was built in Java and is running on Linux, or is an ASP.NET web service running on Windows.

We will introduce many technologies in the course of this book: XML, XSL, XSLT, XML Schemas, SOAP, WSDL, and UDDI to name a few. This book is about sharing our experience in deploying SOAP-based, performance-minded distributed applications, however, because the field of web services is not mature and evolving quickly, you will find discussions about tools and utilities that are not quite production-worthy. We were careful not to depend on those tools for the mission-critical aspects of our sample application. A good example of experimental tools is our use of IBM's Web Service ToolKit (WSTK) to assist in the development of WSDL documents, which can be bypassed by manually writing the WSDL files.

This book looks at the different ways that we can build web services using the Java platform, and at the tools, technologies, and protocols that we will need to work with if we're to take advantage of this vital development.

Organization of this Book

The book is organized in three parts: Fundamentals, Practical Web Service Development, and The Future of Web Services.

In Chapter 1, Architecture for web services, we look at the way that web services are accessed and outline the various components of a web services system.

We then review the SOAP specification in detail in Chapter 2 – how it came to be, what its main purpose is, and what it is being used for now, followed by a closer look at the SOAP implementation that we will use in this book, Apache SOAP, in Chapter 3.

In Chapter 3, Apache SOAP v2.2, we get down to the details of downloading and configuring the necessary software to get your SOAP server up and running.

From this point onward, we move into the second part of the book. Web Services Description Language and its tools, including WSDL document structure (services, bindings, ports, operations, types) are covered in Chapter 4. UDDI – the Universal Description, Discovery, and Integration Registry, with its search engines for business applications is described in Chapter 5.

In Chapter 6, we will look at securing SOAP, Web Services, and XML Signatures. No discussion of application development is complete without coverage of Security and Personalization.

In Chapter 7, we show a case study that combines all the technologies for Web Services (SOAP, WSDL, and UDDI) into an integrated system.

Chapter 8 will show you how an existing J2EE application can have its functionality exposed as a web service.

We look at using Web Services with SAP to get access to SAPs functionality in Chapter 9.

Finally, in Chapter 10, IBM and Web Services, we will look at the tools available from IBM for the implementation of Web Services on your existing infrastructure.

In the third part of the book, we talk about what is happening at present for new technologies in the market. Chapter 11, JAXM and JAX-RPC, we introduce the reader to the Java APIs for XML Messaging and Remote Procedure Calls, with JAXM allowing the transmission of XML documents of any type and JAX-RPC focused on defining the mechanism for doing RPC method calls and responses using an XML-bases protocol, such as SOAP 1.1.

In Chapter 12 we discuss JAXR, Sun's official Java high-level abstraction layer for communicating with an XML registry via some form of XML messaging (like SOAP). The chapter will discuss the JAXR architecture and public API.

Chapters 13 and 14 will introduce you to Sun ONE and Axis. Sun ONE is Sun's specification describing a roadmap to creating a service-driven network based on open standards. Axis is the project name for version 3.0 of Apache SOAP with the goal of Axis to extend the functionality of the present Apache SOAP v2.0 specification.

Who Is This Book For?

This book is aimed at experienced developers, who have already some experience of developing or experimenting within the J2EE platform. We also assume some familiarity with web programming.

What You Need To Use This Book

To run the samples in this book you need to have the following:

- Java 2 Enterprise Edition (J2EE)
- Java 2 Standard Edition (J2SE)
- WebLogic Server 6.1
- Tomcat 3.2+
- IBM's Web Services ToolKit 2.4 (WSTK)
- CapeClear's Cape Connect 3.0 and Cape Studio 1.1

The complete source code for the samples is available for download from our web site at http://www.wrox.com/Books/Book_Details.asp?isbn=1861003757.

Conventions

To help you get the most from the text and keep track of what's happening, we've used a number of conventions throughout the book.

For instance:

> **These boxes hold important, not-to-be forgotten information, which is directly relevant to the surrounding text.**

While the background style is used for asides to the current discussion.

As for styles in the text:

- When we introduce them, we **highlight** important words.
- We show keyboard strokes like this: *Ctrl-A*.
- We show filenames and code within the text like so: doGet()
- Text on user interfaces and URLs are shown as: Menu.

We present code in three different ways. Definitions of methods and properties are shown as follows:

```
protected void doGet(HttpServletRequest req, HttpServletResponse resp)
                    throws ServletException, IOException
```

Example code is shown:

```
In our code examples, the code foreground style shows new, important,
    pertinent code
while code background shows code that's less important in the present context,
    or has been seen before.
```

Customer Support

We always value hearing from our readers, and we want to know what you think about this book: what you liked, what you didn't like, and what you think we can do better next time. You can send us your comments, either by returning the reply card in the back of the book, or by e-mail to feedback@wrox.com. Please be sure to mention the book title in your message.

How to Download the Sample Code for the Book

When you visit the Wrox site, http://www.wrox.com/, simply locate the title through our Search facility or by using one of the title lists. Click on Download in the Code column, or on Download Code on the book's detail page.

The files that are available for download from our site have been archived using WinZip. When you have saved the attachments to a folder on your hard-drive, you need to extract the files using a de-compression program such as WinZip or PKUnzip. When you extract the files, the code is usually extracted into chapter folders. When you start the extraction process, ensure your software (WinZip, PKUnzip, etc.) is set to use folder names.

Errata

We've made every effort to make sure that there are no errors in the text or in the code. However, no one is perfect and mistakes do occur. If you find an error in one of our books, like a spelling mistake or a faulty piece of code, we would be very grateful for feedback. By sending in errata you may save another reader hours of frustration, and of course, you will be helping us provide even higher quality information. Simply e-mail the information to support@wrox.com, your information will be checked and if correct, posted to the errata page for that title, or used in subsequent editions of the book.

To find errata on the web site, go to http://www.wrox.com/, and simply locate the title through our Advanced Search or title list. Click on the Book Errata link, which is below the cover graphic on the book's detail page.

E-mail Support

If you wish to directly query a problem in the book with an expert who knows the book in detail then e-mail support@wrox.com, with the title of the book and the last four numbers of the ISBN in the subject field of the e-mail. A typical e-mail should include the following things:

- ❑ The **title of the book, last four digits of the ISBN**, and **page number** of the problem in the Subject field.

- ❑ Your **name**, **contact information**, and the **problem** in the body of the message.

We *won't* send you junk mail. We need the details to save your time and ours. When you send an e-mail message, it will go through the following chain of support:

- ❑ Customer Support – Your message is delivered to our customer support staff, who are the first people to read it. They have files on most frequently asked questions and will answer anything general about the book or the web site immediately.

- ❑ Editorial – Deeper queries are forwarded to the technical editor responsible for that book. They have experience with the programming language or particular product, and are able to answer detailed technical questions on the subject.

- ❑ The Authors – Finally, in the unlikely event that the editor cannot answer your problem, he or she will forward the request to the author. We do try to protect the author from any distractions to their writing; however, we are quite happy to forward specific requests to them. All Wrox authors help with the support on their books. They will e-mail the customer and the editor with their response, and again all readers should benefit.

The Wrox Support process can only offer support to issues that are directly pertinent to the content of our published title. Support for questions that fall outside the scope of normal book support, is provided via the community lists of our http://p2p.wrox.com/ forum.

p2p.wrox.com

For author and peer discussion join the P2P mailing lists. Our unique system provides **programmer to programmer™** contact on mailing lists, forums, and newsgroups, all in addition to our one-to-one e-mail support system. If you post a query to P2P, you can be confident that it is being examined by the many Wrox authors and other industry experts who are present on our mailing lists. At p2p.wrox.com you will find a number of different lists that will help you, not only while you read this book, but also as you develop your own applications. Particularly appropriate to this book are the **xml_web_services**, **java_webservices**, and **java_xml** lists.

To subscribe to a mailing list just follow these steps:

1. Go to http://p2p.wrox.com/.

2. Choose the appropriate category from the left menu bar.

3. Click on the mailing list you wish to join.

4. Follow the instructions to subscribe and fill in your e-mail address and password.

5. Reply to the confirmation e-mail you receive.

6. Use the subscription manager to join more lists and set your e-mail preferences.

Why this System Offers the Best Support

You can choose to join the mailing lists or you can receive them as a weekly digest. If you don't have the time, or facility, to receive the mailing list, then you can search our online archives. Junk and spam mails are deleted, and your own e-mail address is protected by the unique Lyris system. Queries about joining or leaving lists, and any other general queries about lists, should be sent to listsupport@p2p.wrox.com.

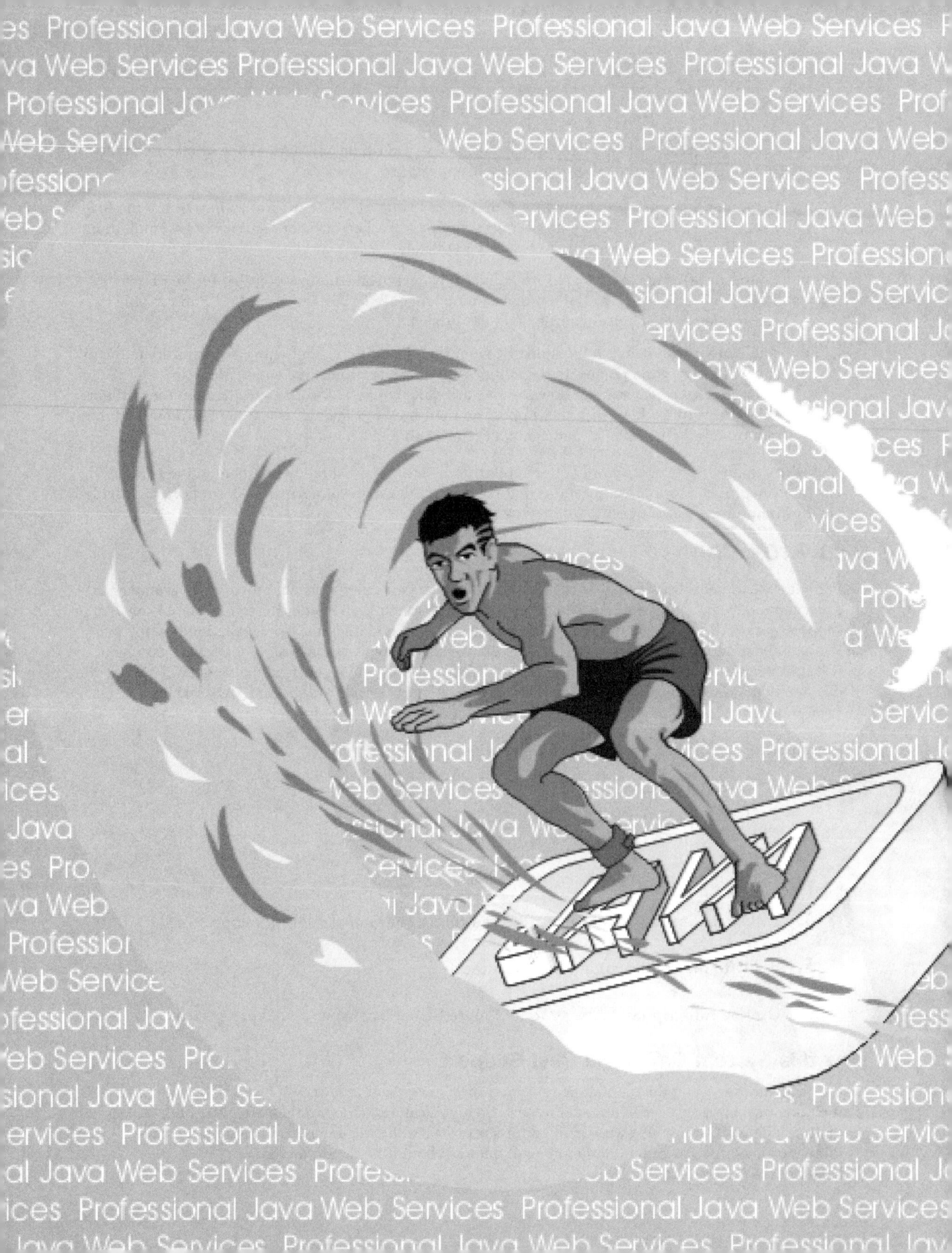
Professional Java Web Services

1

Architecture for Web Services

In this chapter, we will look at the concept of Web Services, their benefits, and how one would go about architecting a Web Services system. By architecture, we mean the different components or building blocks that would help us build a Web Services system. More specifically, in this chapter we will:

❑ Understand the Web Services model and identify the different roles and operations within a Web Services environment.

❑ Look at the basic Web Services stack and SOAP, WSDL, and UDDI.

❑ Learn the basic architecture of a Web Services in J2EE.

❑ Study the architecture of Web Services in detail.

❑ Discuss additional requirements for a Web Services system to address real world e-business issues like Transactions, Quality of Service (QoS), Web Services Management, and Security.

❑ Discuss the performance issues for Web Services.

Web Services Model

There can be tremendous benefits to Web Services. We have heard of interoperability among disparate platforms, ability to invoke a Web Service over ubiquitous network technologies, and so on. However, how does all that work? The answer is best given by looking at a conceptual Web Services model. The model will highlight two important artifacts of any system – roles and operations. By roles, we mean the different types of entities, and operations are the functions performed by these entities in order to make the Web Service work. Let's look at the following diagram to understand the Web Services model:

#### Chapter 1

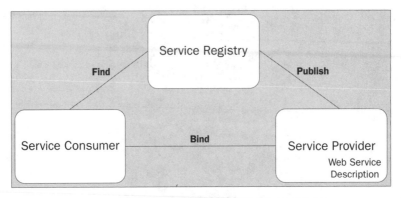

In this typical Web Services model diagram, we can identify three kinds of roles in a typical Web Services environment and the operations that they perform in order to make Web Services work. The roles shown in the diagram are as follows:

❑ **Service Provider** – A service provider is the entity that creates the Web Service. Typically, the service provider exposes certain business functionality in their organization as a Web Service for any organization to invoke. An example could be an online book seller who wishes to expose its online ordering service as a Web Service. The service provider needs to do two things to reach the full potential of a Web Service. First, it needs to **describe** the Web Service in a standard format, which is understandable by all organizations that will be using that Web Service. Secondly, to reach a wider audience, the service provider needs to **publish** the details about its Web Service in a central registry that is publicly available to everyone.

❑ **Service Consumer** – Any organization using the Web Service created by a service provider is called a service consumer. The service consumer can know the functionality of a Web Service from the description made available by the service provider. To retrieve these details, the service consumer does a **find** in the registry to which the service provider had published its Web Service description. More importantly, the service consumer is able to get from the service description, the mechanism to **bind** to the service provider's Web Service and in turn to invoke that Web Service.

❑ **Service Registry** – A service registry is a central location where the service provider can list its Web Services, and where a service consumer can search for Web Services. Service providers normally publish their Web Service capabilities in the service registry for service consumers to find and then bind to their Web Service. Typically, information like company details, the Web Services that it provides, and the details about each Web Service including technical details is stored in the service registry.

In our Web Services model, we can also identify three operations that are fundamental to making Web Services work – 'find', 'bind' and 'publish'. We need to achieve inter-application communication irrespective of the kind of language the application is written in, the platform the application is running on, and so on. To make this happen, we need the standards for each of these three operations and a standard way for a service provider to describe their Web Service irrespective of the language that it is written in:

❑ A standard way to describe Web Services – The Web Service Description Language (WSDL) is a standard that uses XML format to describe Web Services. Basically, the WSDL document for a Web Service would define the methods that are present in the Web Service, the input/output parameters for each of the methods, the data types, the transport protocol used, and the end point URL at which the Web Service will be hosted.

❑ A standard protocol to publish or find Web Services – The Universal Description, Discovery, and Integration (UDDI) standard provides a way for service providers to publish details about their organization and the Web Services that they provide to a central registry. This is the 'description' part in UDDI. It also provides a standard for service consumers to find service providers and details about their Web Services. This is the 'discovery' part in UDDI.

❑ A standard protocol for applications to bind to Web Services. The Simple Object Access Protocol (SOAP) is a lightweight XML mechanism used to exchange information between applications regardless of the operation system, programming language, or object model.

In the next section, let's review these three standards in detail.

Basic Web Services Stack

In this section, we will discuss the three standards – SOAP, WSDL, and UDDI, conceptually within the context of Web Services architecture. However, we will not be going into the full technical details each of the standards.

We discussed in the previous section the fundamental operations, publish, find, and bind, in a Web Services environment. In order to make that possible, what we need is a basic Web Services stack that will be present in each application that wishes to play a certain role in the Web Services system.

Such a basic Web Services stack is shown below:

Service Publication/Discovery	UDDI
Service Description	WSDL
XML Messaging	SOAP
Transport Network	HTTP, SMTP, FTP, HTTPs over TCP/IP

Concentrate for the moment on the left side of the above diagram, that is, the layered blocks. These layered blocks are conceptual, whereas the labels shown on the right of each of the layered blocks are the actual technologies that are present in each layer. Each of the blocks, as you can see from the diagram, builds upon the block beneath it.

Transport Network

This layer of the Web Services stack is responsible for making the Web Services accessible by using any of the transport protocols available, like HTTP, SMTP, FTP, and so on. Remember that Web Services are built on existing communication standards, which make them transport-independent. In the present scenario, HTTP is the most ubiquitous communication protocol. Most of the browsers support HTTP, and it is widely used across the Internet.

It is important to note that Web Services can be deployed both across the Internet and internally within an organization. If it is being implemented for access across the Internet, it makes sense to choose HTTP as the primary network protocol. On the other hand, if you are implementing Web Services within an organization, it is possible that you can also select different network technologies, like Messaging Standards (JMS).

XML Messaging – SOAP

The next layer in the basic Web Services stack is XML Messaging. This layer defines the message format that is used for application communication and the standard commonly used by Web Services is SOAP, an XML-based protocol for exchanging information between applications regardless of the operation system, programming environment, and object model.

Some of the characteristics of SOAP are:

❑ SOAP is a lightweight and simple protocol because all you need is XML data to be passed over HTTP. It does not attempt to define a programming model or implement specific APIs.

❑ SOAP is not bound to any particular transport protocol. This statement should be clear to you from the Web Services stack, since the XML Messaging layer is built on top on the Transport Network layer. One deduction can be that SOAP is XML over HTTP, which is perfectly fine. But at the same time, we can easily see that SOAP can be bound to any other transport protocol like SMTP, FTP, and so on.

❑ SOAP is easily extensible via XML. Though not present in the SOAP standard, we can easily extend it to incorporate enterprise level features like transactions, security, and so on. We shall take a look at these later on in the chapter.

A sample SOAP Message

To understand SOAP a little better, let us take a look at a simple SOAP message. A SOAP message is conceptually represented as shown below:

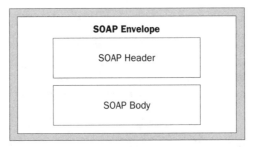

A SOAP message consists of a SOAP `Envelope` element that encloses an optional SOAP `Header` element and a mandatory SOAP `Body` element. The SOAP `Envelope` defines a framework for describing what is in the message and how to process it. The optional `Header` element can be used effectively by users to provide any extra data that is required. The `Body` element contains the XML payload that encodes either the procedure call, the response from calling the procedure, or fault reporting.

Let us a take a look at a sample SOAP message:

```
<?xml version="1.0"?>
<soap:Envelope xmlns:soap="http://schemas.xmlsoap.org/soap/envelope/"
               soap:encodingStyle="http://schemas.xmlsoap.org/soap/encoding/">
  <soap:Header>
    <h:identity xmlns:h="http://www.wrox.com/header">author@wrox.com</h:identity>
  </soap:Header>
  <soap:Body>
    <m:GetStockQuote  xmlns:m="http://www.wrox.com/getstockquote/">
      <m:ticker>WROX</m:ticker>
    </m:GetStockQuote>
  </soap:Body>
</soap:Envelope>
```

From the above SOAP message, we can see that the `Header` element, though it is optional, is being used to further extend SOAP by passing an additional parameter that is used to provide identity information.

The `Body` element contains an XML representation of a method call `GetStockQuote()`. You will also find that the method takes in a parameter called `ticker`, which is the stock symbol.

We have now seen two layers of the basic Web Services stack; the Transport Network layer and the XML Messaging layer. At the XML Messaging layer we will be using the SOAP protocol whereas at the Transport Network layer we can use any of the common transport protocols available. However, since we are interested in a wider reach for our web service, it is preferable to use the widely accepted HTTP protocol. Given these two layers, let us take a look at how this works:

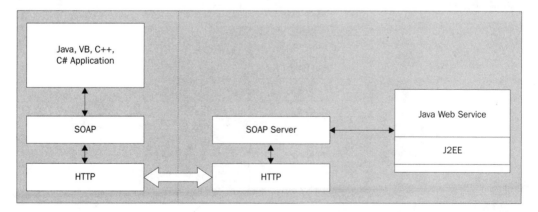

On the server side, for the purposes of this example, let's assume a standard J2EE application that's running in a Web Services-enabled app server. Now, consider the Java, VB, C++, or C# client program at the top left corner of the diagram. This application makes SOAP requests. The SOAP request envelops the Web Service operation into an XML payload that is then transported over the HTTP protocol. On the Web Service side, the transport layer then passes on the call to the SOAP server, which then invokes the appropriate J2EE functionality that has been exposed as a web service. Any response from the Web Service is encoded back into a SOAP response that is transported back over HTTP to the client.

From this diagram, it should now be clear to you how, by using the Messaging layer (SOAP) and the Transport Network layer (HTTP), we can achieve inter-application communication. Inter-application communication has been tackled before by several proprietary vendor technologies like CORBA, DCOM, and so on. These technologies have been cumbersome to work with and they cannot pass through firewalls, and so on. So, by using SOAP, we have effectively achieved inter-application communication via simple XML that is based on open-standards, without getting ourselves locked into any vendor-proprietary mechanism.

However, you will notice that there is a fairly tight coupling between the SOAP messages amid the two applications. It is absolutely essential that we achieve a fairly loose coupling between the calling application and the Web Service because by achieving loose coupling between components we have much more flexibility in making changes to the components without affecting the other components much. What we need is a higher-level description of the Web Service such that neither the caller nor the Web Service is aware of the underlying operating system, programming platform and the object model. This is the main objective of defining the next layer in our basic Web Services stack, the service description.

Service Description – WSDL

The Service Description layer, as we discussed, provides a mechanism for the service provider to describe the functionality that the Web Service provides. WSDL provides the mechanism for this by defining XML grammar for describing the Web Service. A WSDL document describes a Web Service as having a collection of endpoints or ports operating independently on both document-oriented and procedure-oriented messages. WSDL is to a Web Services what CORBA IDL is to CORBA or Microsoft MIDL is to COM components, and so on.

Conceptually, we can represent how to describe a Web Service according to the WSDL Specification as shown below:

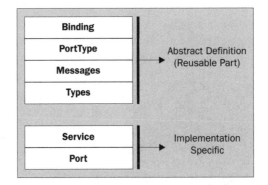

To better appreciate WSDL, it is important to note that it provides the definition of a Web Service in two parts. The first is a high-level, transport protocol-independent abstract definition of a Web Service and second is a transport network-specific binding description.

At the abstract high level, a Web Service definition contains the following elements:

- ❏ **Port Types** - The `portType` elements contain a set of **Operations**, represented as `operation` elements, that are present in a Web Service for example, `GetStockQuote`, `SellStock`, `BuyStock`, and so on. This is analogous to an interface in Java. An operation can thus have an input message and an output message. Also, it might have only an input or output message, just like a normal method call.

- ❏ **Messages** - A `message` element contains a definition of the data that is transmitted. This is similar to a parameter in the method call.

- ❏ **Types** - The `types` element contains the data types that are present in the message.

- ❏ **Bindings** - A `binding` element maps the `operation` elements in a `portType` element to a specific protocol.

This is the reusable part of the Web Service Definition since it represents only an abstract definition of the Service. We have learnt so far that for an operation to be executed over the network, it would be necessary to use a specific transport protocol to send the data across. This is what the `binding` element of the Web Service definition language captures for you. A `binding` element captures the particular protocol (SOAP, HTTP GET, HTTP POST, and so on) and the `portType`, `message`, and `types` elements outlined above. We can thus bind the abstract definition to several transport protocols. What this means is that a WSDL definition can allow us to define a Web Service independently of the transport protocol.

To quickly review, the WSDL description of a Web Service contains a collection of ports - each port associates an end Point where the Web Service can accept communications (such as a URL or an email address) with a particular `binding` element, which describes the supported messages for this port.

Let us look at how we can use the three layers that we have covered so far to see how it all works from an architectural perspective:

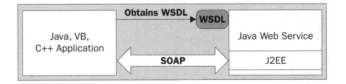

The figure shown above is a simple extension of the Web Services model diagram we saw before. In the previous diagram, there was a close coupling between the SOAP messages that needed to be passed between both applications. Now, with the additional Web Service description layer, the service provider describes the Web Service by creating and publishing a WSDL document. The WSDL document contains not only an abstract definition of the Web Service but also the implementation (binding) details for the Web Service. What this means is that the service consumer, in this case the client application needs to get hold of the WSDL document. From this document, it would not only get the different operations including messages/data types supported by the Web Service, but also it will be able to retrieve the end point (for example, URL) of the Web Service over which SOAP messages can be exchanged. If our sample J2EE services exposed functions via SMTP messaging, the WSDL document would describe this as well.

This would be sufficient to form an "Interoperable Web Services Stack". For more on WSDL, see Chapter 4, but for now let us move on to the next layer in our basic Web Services stack, the Service Publication and Discovery layer.

Service Publication & Discovery – UDDI

From a WSDL document, it is possible for a service consumer to determine the Web Service details like the different operations, data types, the end points, the binding protocols, and so on. However, there are more issues to be addressed. Let us look at what those issues are from the perspective of both the service provider and service consumer.

Firstly, instead of publishing the WSDL document to every possible client, a service provider would be well-served by publishing the information about their Web Service to a central registry that is publicly available to interested service consumers. In addition to just their Web Service description, it would be good if they could publish business related information like the name of their business, the different Web Services that they offer, and so on. Assuming that this would be published in the same central registry, it would help them in advertising their Web Service to a wider audience.

Similarly, service consumers would like to find out the different Web Services that are made available by service providers. They would like to evaluate them independently before integrating those Web Services into their application. Hence, it makes logical sense for them to search the same central registry in which the service providers have already published their details. Service consumers may also like to do a broader level search based on business categories to find the companies in that category and then drill down into further details about the Web Services that they offer.

There are many possibilities in addition to those above. However, what is underlined is a necessity for a central registry where service providers and service consumers work together to publish and retrieve the appropriate information. In other words, we need a specification for publishing and discovering business information. Instead of exchanging business information among them directly, a central registry introduces another level of indirection that further promotes loose-coupling among participating Web Services.

The specification for publishing and discovering business information is the Universal Discovery, Description, and Integration (UDDI) specification. The UDDI specification provides a business structure that is used to describe a particular business. The business structure, as shown below, will contain the following information:

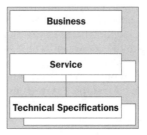

- ❑ **Business -** This contains the business information like business name, business contact, and so on. It will contain one or more instances of the service structure. The UDDI specification also allows a business definition to contain a classification code that will identify it as belonging to a certain category of business, for example, financial loan institution.

❑ **Service -** A service structure captures the different Web Services that this business provides. Each Web Service will contain one or more technical specification structures, for example an organization might have two Web Services; a sales order status and an inventory status Web Service. The UDDI specification also allows a service definition to contain a classification code that will identify it as belonging to a certain service category, for example, credit checking.

❑ **Technical Specifications -** The technical specifications contain technical details about a Web Service. One of the technical specifications is a WSDL specification, which a service consumer can refer to and determine the technical details about invoking the Web Service.

We will discuss the details of these structures in Chapter 5 on UDDI. Now, it is more important to conceptually understand the Web Services stack.

Now that we have covered our basic Web Services stack, let's take a look at how the three technologies (UDDI, WSDL, and SOAP) would work together from an architectural perspective:

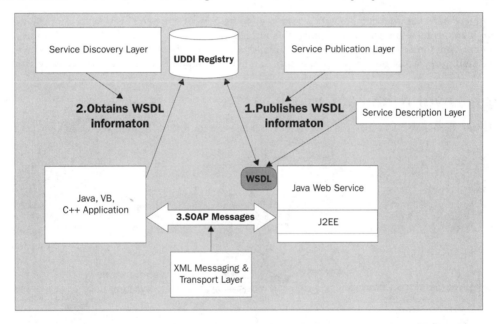

Before we discuss the above diagram, let us make an assumption. We shall assume that the service provider has made the decision to expose certain business functionality as a Web Service. This Web Service is residing in a Java-based Web Services system. Later in this chapter, we will go into the architectural details of what such a Web Services system would contain. With that assumption made, let us look at the entire mechanism through a sequence of steps as shown in the diagram:

1. The first step for the service provider would involve writing the WSDL file. There are several tools available in the market today that aid in generating the WSDL file from existing object definitions. Then it would need to publish information about itself that is the business and the Web Service technical specification as a WSDL file to the central UDDI Registry. Thus describing the Web Service by writing the WSDL file captures the *Service Description* layer, whereas publishing business information and the WSDL file represents the *Service Publication* layer that we saw in our Web Services stack.

2. The service consumer application can discover the Web Services that it is interested in using. Discovery would involve not only searching for the business and its services, but also downloading the technical specifications mentioned in the WSDL file. This discovery step corresponds to the *Service Discovery* layer in our basic Web Services stack.

3. Finally, the service consumer application uses the WSDL file to determine the messages that need to be passed to communicate with the service provider's Web Service. It also determines the binding information, which for our purposes will be SOAP over HTTP. It then sends across SOAP requests and receives appropriate SOAP responses. This step thus corresponds to the *XML Messaging and Transport* layer in our Web Services stack.

Basic Web Services Architecture in J2EE

Let us determine what components would need to be present in a Web Services system. We will follow an incremental approach to developing this instead of a big-bang approach. This will help us understand the architecture much better. In addition, by introducing the architecture in a layered fashion, we will also be in a position to mix and match components for a Web Services system.

High Level Architecture

Let us discuss an overview of Web Services architecture for a J2EE System shown below:

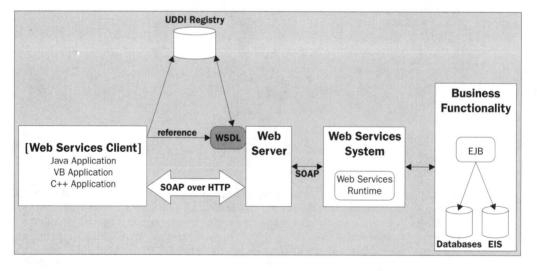

Let us talk about each area of the diagram now:

Business Functionality

This is the functionality that is exposed by the Web Service provider as a Web Service. It is important to understand that business organizations are not going to take their existing J2EE-based applications and expose their EJBs as Web Services. Though it is technically possible with the Web Services platforms or tools that are available in the market today, in a business it probably does not make much practical sense. The reason is that businesses do not expose method calls in some components. Instead, what they expose is a business functionality that will translate into a series of orchestrated actions required to execute the business functionality. This may or may not result in an immediate response back to the service consumer. It could execute over a period of days also. Businesses also develop the functionality in their systems via several layers, keeping in mind several levels of security, and use by different internal applications.

For example, consider business ABC that sells books over the Internet. Let us say that they have decided to expose an online ordering service as a Web Service over the Internet. When a customer places an order, the order information kicks off a business process inside business ABC. This business process will need to perform activities like checking the inventory for the books ordered, execute a financial transaction which will involve payment from the consumer to the business ABC and finally sending a message to the shipping department to ship the books. From a J2EE system perspective, this business process will need to possibly interact with various EJBs that in turn interact with Enterprise Information Systems or databases across the organization. During the course of all these transactions, transactional integrity needs to be preserved as well as any other standard requirements that one would expect from a serious enterprise level business process.

Web Services System

The Web Services System is similar to a container concept in J2EE. It will provide a runtime environment for the execution of Web Services. For the purpose of this discussion, it is sufficient to say that, at a higher level, the Web Services System would contain a Web Services runtime environment that would take in SOAP requests and map them to the appropriate Java component, that is, Java class or EJB that kicks in the business functionality. At the same time, it would be responsible for collecting any results from the business process, and encapsulating them within a SOAP response that is sent back to the Web Service client.

Web Server

The web server is the main gateway for the SOAP requests from the Web Service client to be received by the service provider. A web server communicates via the HTTP protocol and is normally listening on port 80. As a result of that, it fits quite well into our XML Messaging layer and Transport layer since our SOAP message needs to be transported over the HTTP protocol. A key thing that you should notice in the diagram is the fact that the WSDL file is located on the web server. The reason for this is that it provides a globally accessible mechanism for service consumers to refer to the WSDL specification. Hence, if we provide a WSDL file reference as a URL in the UDDI registry, service consumers can easily locate the WSDL through the URL, download the WSDL, and interpret it to determine the services supported by the organization and the end points for the same.

The web server also executes another important functionality in this whole system. It will forward the appropriate SOAP request to the Web Services System.

Web Service Client

The Web Service client is the consumer of the Web Service. Since Web Services are platform neutral, a client written in any of the mainstream programming languages available today can invoke them. For example, it can be a Java program, a Visual Basic program, or a C++ program. The first step that a Web Service client will do is to reference the UDDI information for the business providing the Web Service that they are interested in. From the UDDI information, they retrieve the WSDL URL reference and download the WSDL document from the publicly accessible URL. Normally this would be the web server as shown in the diagram. Once the WSDL file is obtained, the service consumer has the technical information needed to invoke the Web Service. By technical information we mean the methods in the Web Service, the parameters for the methods, the data types for the methods and the endpoint information. There are several tools available, as we shall see later in the book, which can be used to generate SOAP client code from a WSDL file. This SOAP client code can then be embedded into the client program to invoke the Web Service.

Detailed Architecture

Now that we have seen a Web Services System from a high level, it is time to get into the details of what really comprises a Web Services System, that is, the different components and their functions. We shall spread this discussion to two types of Web Services – Simple Web Services and Business Web Services. Simple Web Services are the predominant Web Services today. Most of the Web Services platforms/tools that are available in the market today address simple Web Services. Business Web Services, on the other hand, are representations of real world e-business scenarios where collaboration and multiple businesses are involved. A high level way of understanding the difference between Simple and Business Web Services is to consider the analogy of web servers vs. application servers. In the next few sections, we shall look at both these types of Web Services and identify the composition of a Web Services platform that would serve its needs appropriately.

Simple Web Services

Simple Web Services are the predominant Web Services that we see today. A look at the popular Web Services brokerage sites like http://www.salcentral.com or http://www.xmethods.com will present us with a directory listing of hundreds of Web Services that we can invoke today from our client program. Most of these are simple 'request-response' type of Web Services and are mostly informational in nature. A typical mechanism to implement Simple Web Services would be to take a look at the existing systems in the organization and determine if certain functionality of your system could be exposed as a Web Service. Let's consider the following examples:

❑ A credit card validating company is interested in exposing its already existing credit card checking functionality as a SOAP-based Web Service. Online merchants could be potential subscribers of this Web Service.

❑ A recruiting company is interested in publishing its latest job-openings as a SOAP-based Web Service. Job placement (contracting) companies could be potential subscribers of this Web Service.

❑ An airline reservation system is interested in publishing its latest airfares as a Web Service. Travel agencies could be potential subscribers of this Web Service.

The above examples should help in giving you an idea about the categories of Web Services that could be classified as simple Web Services. Keep in mind that the technical infrastructure needed to support the implied functionality at the backend may be very complex. However, the common theme in all the above examples and similar ones is that most of the functionalities are already present in their systems. For the sake of our discussion, we will consider that all the above organizations are Java-based, and these organizations already have the appropriate EJBs that encapsulate this functionality. Another common thread through these kinds of services is that they are devoid of any sort of collaboration or workflow. Once a request comes into the system, there is a simple flow to obtain the result and package it back as an appropriate response. There is no collaboration with multiple partner Web Services to achieve the end result. Complex issues like transactions, context, and so on are present within the enterprise application itself, and the simple Web Service that acts as an interface to this application need not worry about them.

Nevertheless, simple Web Services are prevalent today. The first step that most organizations should take is to evaluate new technologies like SOAP, WSDL, and UDDI within the context of Simple Web Services. Simple Web Services would also help in certain scenarios where they could be valuable alternatives to EAI. Organizations are increasingly looking at Web Services as a viable alternative to heavy-duty EAI solutions to connect applications within the enterprise. With the advent of Web Services, several small organizations are now in a position to implement low-cost XML-based interfaces around their applications and thereby take important steps towards participation in a global e-business communication that is rapidly adopting industry standards like RosettaNet, ebXML, aned so on.

Application Level View

Let us now take an application level look at simple Web Services. In the diagram shown below, you will find an application level flow that helps to achieve a simple Web Service:

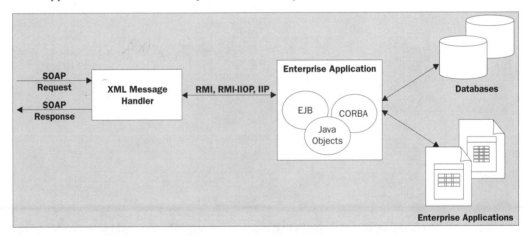

The first step that an organization could take would be to expose certain functionality in their enterprise system as a Web Service. Shown on the right of the diagram is a typical enterprise that has several applications and databases present throughout the enterprise. The organization has already implemented a J2EE-based system with EJBs encapsulating the core functionality. Alternately, it could have used CORBA or even simple Java objects to achieve some of the functionalities. Once they had that in place, they would expose some of these functionalities as a Web Service either by exposing existing EJBs or by writing a façade EJB that would provide more control over invoking internal functionality. Once they had the EJB ready, they would write a WSDL that maps out some of the methods of the EJB and make that available to a service consumer either from their web server or directly.

Now, let us concentrate on the flow, which is shown below as a series of steps:

1. The SOAP request comes in from the Web Service client and the XML Message Handler intercepts this request. The first thing it needs to do is to parse the SOAP request, which is in XML format. By parsing the SOAP request, the system will be able to obtain the operation that was invoked and also any particular parameters for that operation. It would also know from the SOAP request its intent, that is, for which unique object name the operation is intended. Hence, now our system has the object for which the operation was intended, the operation and its parameters. In short, it has all the information any client program would normally need to invoke a Java class or EJB.

2. When the Web Service was deployed, a mapping entry was present that mapped a unique object name to the actual Java component. This is how our Web Services system would know which Java object to invoke from the unique object name obtained from the SOAP request.

3. Finally, the Web Services system would use the appropriate communication protocol for example JNDI, to locate the object, EJB in our case, and invoke the operation on it by passing the parameters to the operation. The response from the EJB would then be wrapped back into a SOAP response and sent back to the client.

Simple Web Service Core Components

Based on the application level view, it is now easy for us to determine what kind of core components would be needed in a Web Services system to meet the needs of simple Web Services. The following diagram shows some of these components:

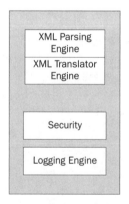

❑ **XML Parsing Engine**: Since the SOAP requests are in XML, we would need a XML parsing engine to parse the incoming SOAP request into the appropriate object name, operation name, parameters, and so on. The XML parsing engine can also double up as a XML validation engine to ensure that the XML adheres to the SOAP specification.

❑ **XML Translator Engine:** The response that we receive from our enterprise objects might not always be in a form that could serve all clients. For example, we could have different kinds of devices that are invoking the Web Service and it might be necessary to translate the XML into different forms before being passed back to the client. The XML translator engine would achieve this purpose.

❑ **Security**: We would need basic authentication and authorization services over here to check the validity of the user credentials invoking the Web Service. This is the function of the security component.

❑ **Logging Engine**: Finally, there should to be a logging service that logs all that is happening during the invocation call. A robust and well-designed logging engine would aid not only in debugging where the problem is but also for auditing and billing purposes.

In addition to the core components highlighted above, we would also need a bottom layer in our Web Services System which would provide **system services** which tackle communication protocols like RMI, IIOP, and so on. The system services are not directly exposed to the user level, they are more likely built into the system.

Let us now look at the complete architecture for our simple Web Services System shown below:

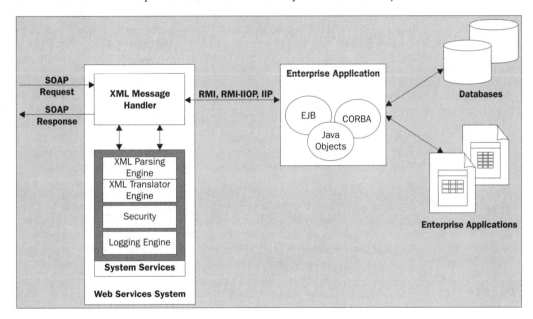

Simple Web Service

Let us briefly recap, from the above diagram, how it all works:

❑ The XML Message Handler first intercepts the SOAP request. It uses the XML parsing engine to parse this request.

❑ It uses the security engine to authenticate the user. If not authenticated, it sends back an appropriate SOAP response containing an error description.

❑ If authentication is successful then from its deployment settings it determines the object to be invoked. It uses the appropriate communications protocol from the system services and invokes the operation on the object.

❑ It uses the XML engine to appropriately translate the results returned from the call on the object and package it into a SOAP response, and sends it back to the client.

❑ During all the above steps, the logging engine is invoked appropriately to log all messages and operations for auditing and debugging purposes.

❑ Any exceptions that happen in the system are packaged as SOAP `Fault` elements and returned back as a SOAP response to the client.

Now that we have seen what simple Web Services are, and described the architecture to cater for it, let us go into the realm of real world business Web Services.

Business Web Services

The simple Web Services that we saw in the previous sections were a simple request-response type of Web Services. Business Web Services, on the other hand, address the real-world e-business, as we know today. Businesses are capable of supporting not only simple request-response type of services but also long-running and deeply collaborative business processes. These businesses do not function in isolation. Normally, a typical business process will involve several conversations with trading partners, exchange of data among trading partners, and so on. Sometimes these processes are short-lived, but they can last for several days, too.

For Web Services to capture these business processes there are several areas that need to be addressed. In the next few sections, we shall delve into each of the areas that need to be addressed by any platform that plans or claims to support Web Services. Once we have identified these issues, we shall map them onto a business Web Services system to understand it from an architectural perspective. In the later part of this chapter, we shall see what standards are evolving to address each of these issues so that the benefits of Web Services like interoperability are not lost.

The simple Web Services do not address real world e-business issues. Some of the issues that are of paramount importance in any business transaction are security, quality of service, transaction management, context/privacy, and so on. We will look at each of these issues in detail. It will become apparent to you that without some of the features being delivered as standards and accepted by organizations, conducting business via Web Services will take some time to gain widespread acceptance. We will also discuss the standards that are currently being developed to address each of these issues.

Security

Security is one of the most important issues to consider whenever any business transaction needs to be done. Any time you present a new technology to a company, one of the areas that they are most interested in addressing is security. Without a solid security model in your application or technology, it is not going to be accepted by any business that is committed to do business on the Internet. The same applies to Web Services. Unless Web Services address security adequately, there is not going to be much widespread acceptance of them among the business organizations.

Security normally includes the following three areas:

❑ **Privacy**: We need to ensure that the conversation between the client and the Web Service is encrypted so that no one can snoop in on the conversation.

❑ **Authentication**: It is important that the both the client and the Web Service need to confirm the identity of each other. This is really important if you are going to be charging for the use of your Web Service.

❑ **Non-repudiation**: It is important that the Web Service keeps a log of the invocations so that the client cannot deny at a later stage that they did not send the message.

So, how do you address security within Web Services? Web Services can address security at two levels:

❑ **Transport level security** – This is already available today in the form of HTTPS (HTTP Secure) and this should be sufficient for quite a few applications. However, when we consider intermediaries (discussed later in the chapter), we find a need for message level security.

❑ **Message level security** – Intermediaries are present between the client and the actual Web Service server on the network. Intermediaries provide an efficient way to reduce the load on the main server. The main point to note is that in such a scenario, it is possible that our message moves from one hop to another until it reaches its final destination. This means that we also need message level security so that it fosters an authentication mechanism between each of our intermediaries.

Now we know that security needs to be addressed at each level of the Web Services stack, we can take a look at a few of the standards that are currently being developed to address the issue of security in Web Services:

❑ **XKMS** – The XML Key Management Services (XKMS) standard will provide us with a standard to distribute and manage keys for secure communications between endpoints.

❑ **XML Encryption** – This standard will help us in encrypting the message from the sender, and decrypting the message at the receiver end. This will make the message unreadable by other elements during transport.

❑ **SAML** - Security Access Markup Language (SAML) will provide us with mechanism to determine access rights at endpoints.

More details on Web Services security please refer to Chapter 7 on Securing Web Services.

Reliable Messaging

Reliable messaging is an important component of any e-business system and caters to things like making sure that the message has been delivered to the intended recipient. It also handles situations where the message could not be delivered due to a problem. Depending on the features present, it will perform a resend accordingly.

Reliable messaging needs to be built into both the transport network layer and the messaging layer of the Web Services stack that we saw. It will need to address issues like message ordering, delivery time constraints, priorities, and so on.

HTTP is the primary protocol that is going to be used as the transport protocol and, as we all know, it is not a reliable protocol. Efforts are currently underway to provide a reliable extension to HTTP, such as the HTTP Reliable (HTTP-R) specification from IBM.

Quality of Service

Quality of Service (QoS) is very important in doing business between any two organizations. QoS lays down certain criteria about a particular Web Service and, if a particular Web Service provider documents its QoS, the service consumers can assume that those conditions will be met.

QoS addresses several different areas and some of them may be extremely important to certain service consumers while others may not - it is a relative thing. Let us look at some of the issues addressed by QoS:

❑ Different support options: gold service, economy service

❑ Guaranteed level of system performance

❑ Maximum downtime allowed

❑ Penalty clauses if any of the above are not met

❑ Network bandwidth

❑ Disaster scenarios

QoS is directly related to reliable messaging, which forms an important component of QoS. For example, a service provider can provide reliable messaging, and list down QoS levels in that section, like resending messages in case of delivery problems, delivering a message at least once, and so on.

QoS definitions will need to be present in the Web Service description layer. The binding information will need to provide information about the kind of QoS that it can offer. Normally, a **Service Level Agreement** (SLA) between two business organizations determines the quality of service and, as such, it's a legal agreement between the service provider and a service consumer.

There are currently no standards available to address the issue of QoS and SLAs. However, the **Web Services EndPoint Language** (WSEL) from IBM attempts to address the complex realm of SLAs.

Context/Privacy

The simple Web Services that we saw earlier were simple request-response services. Typically, in a business environment, we find that despite having the same business function, we need to change having behavior a little to fit the needs of the user. For example, a user can have specific preferences like device type, language, country of origin, and so on. Thus, we need to incorporate **context** into the execution of a particular Web Service.

Also, when a service consumer invokes a particular Web Service, it is very likely that the business Web Service is actually a composition of many other Web Services. These Web Services might be additional Web Services within the organization or they could also be from outside the organization. This gives a new dimension to the definition of context. What it means is that the context now needs to be passed (propagated) to various other Web Services that work in unison to complete the business process.

Since a Web Service context is usually related to user information, it is critical that we maintain the **privacy** of this information. For example, in a credit card validation Web Service we need to protect the credit card information. The same applies to monetary transactions that could happen via Web Services. Thus, context usage goes hand-in-hand with privacy.

As a side note, propagation of context information and privacy of that information not only has technical challenges but also legal ones. For example, for collaborative Web Services – if you have a server in Europe, the amount of information that can be sent from that server to a server in the USA is very restricted (European Union rules).

There are currently no standards available for propagating context information since context is strongly related to different industry domains. Context information with a business process in a particular industry might not fit well with others. Hence, the recommended approach is to do it within your site itself. However, it is important to stress that an extensible mechanism is necessary for context propagation so that different industries can build on top of that.

Transactions

Transactions are fundamental to any business. Roughly put, a transaction defines a unit of work that encapsulates a set of operations such that all of them succeed or all of them fail. If a single critical operation does not succeed then all the related operations are rolled back.

A Business Web Service would probability invoke other Web Services. Since the nature of transactions in a Business Web Service could involve long-running transactions, you would also have to co-ordinate transactions across the Web Services that you invoke. These are in contrast to the short transactions that we find in databases and typical transaction systems.

Currently there is no standard available that is able to define Web Services transactions within the context of activities and conversations between collaborating Web Services. However, one of the emerging standards is the Business Transaction Protocol (BTP).

Process Flow

As mentioned in prior sections, a Web Service can be composed of different Web Services. Let us take an example of an 'Order' Web Service that encapsulates a business Web Service which accepts an order. Now, let's examine a sample flow for this 'Order' Web Service:

❑   It invokes an external 'Credit Card Validation' Web Service to validate the payee information

❑   It invokes an internal 'Inventory' Web Service to check if items are present in a locally maintained inventory

❑   If items are not present, it places an order to an external 'Procurement' Web Service from which it usually orders items to replenish its inventory

❑   If items are present, then it invokes an internal 'Shipping' Web Service and then sends a message across to the shipping department to ship the Items to the buyer

❑   The internal 'Shipping' Web Service might invoke a 'Notification' Web Service that sends an email to the user informing them that their items have been shipped

The above series of actions does not comprise a complete order workflow because there could also be other scenarios and several error conditions that need to be tried. However, what it should have demonstrated to you is the fact that developing a Web Services workflow would be a core activity. You will also notice that a particular Web Service workflow can be of different types:

❑   It could be a simple workflow, that is, invoking just one internal Web Service:

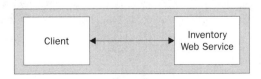

❏ It could be a composite workflow embedding within it both internal and external Web Services:

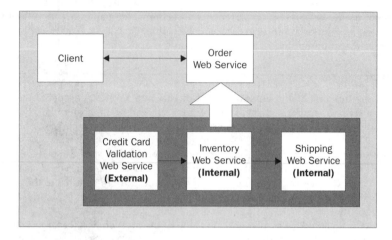

❏ It could be a composite workflow embedding within it not only internal and external Web Services, but also the external workflow:

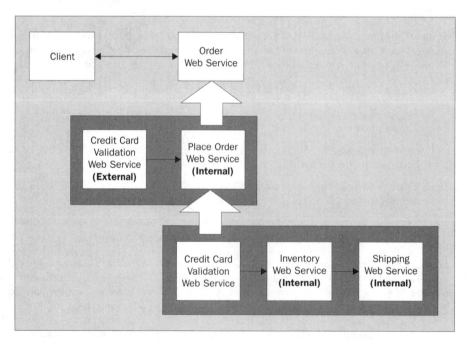

Currently, there are no standards for business workflow among Web Services, but IBM is fairly active in defining and promoting their Web Services Flow Language (WSFL) standard.

Extended Web Services Stack

Now that we have seen the various issues that need to be addressed within the realm of business Web Services, it is fair to say that the basic Web Services stack that we discussed before will not be sufficient for Business Web Services. The Web Services stack that we saw before containing HTTP, SOAP, WSDL, and UDDI present a perfectly sound interoperable Web Service stack, and is extremely well-suited to address development, deployment, and usage of Simple Web Services.

The issues that we discussed for Business Web Services, like security, reliable messaging, service context, transactions, and workflow, are currently done in proprietary ways across different platforms. Hence, it is perfectly valid to address these issues in a manner that your Web Services platform vendor has provided for. However, you should step back for a moment and look at the initial goals that Web Services were invented to address. Key among them was interoperability among diverse operation systems, programming platforms and object model frameworks. To achieve that, it is necessary that open and interoperable standards that address each of the issues should be developed. We have mentioned the current activities and standards being developed in each of the areas, and we are confident that in the coming months, we shall hear more about them. The onus is really on companies to drive these standards forcefully thereby resulting in widespread adoption of a Business Web Services stack.

To summarize, let us take a look at a diagram showing how a Business Web Services stack, also called an Extended Web Service stack, should look:

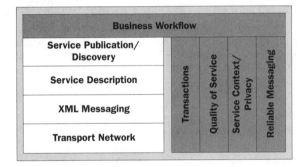

Business Web Service Application Level View

Even though there are no current standards to address each of the technical business issues that we covered earlier in the chapter, it is still useful for us to determine what would be the components of a Web Services System that would be able to satisfactorily capture what we discussed in the previous section.

We will follow the same pattern that we used to describe a Web Services System that addressed simple Web Services. We will first take a look at it from an application level, and then we will drill down into the different components that would be needed in such a platform. Let us first take a look at the Application Level view shown below:

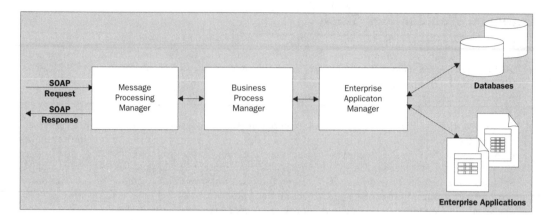

We will not go into the details of describing of the mechanism here, since it is more or less similar to the one described where the message processing manager receives an initial SOAP request, and so on. Let us describe each of the blocks to better understand their roles. At every required point, we will highlight the issues that we have discussed so far.

Message Processing Manager

The message process manager is responsible for receiving the SOAP requests and parsing the XML to determine the intent of the Web Service invocation. It will also be able to identify from the SOAP message the security credentials of the caller, and will authenticate the caller. It also identifies the context of the caller, which could be a particular device type or the geographical location, language, and so on. The message processing manager would also be responsible for enforcing the SLA thereby guaranteeing the QoS levels mentioned in the SLA. Finally, it passes on this information to the business process manager to start the business process.

Business Process Manager

This layer is responsible for initiating the workflow or business process. The business process manager also propagates the Web Service context, that is, the contextual information across the entire workflow. The state of the application is thus maintained at this layer. At each step in the business workflow, the business process manager will interact with the enterprise application manager to interact with the enterprise components that encapsulate certain business functionality. These enterprise components have access to other enterprise resources like databases, legacy applications, and so on. The business process manager would also need to propagate the transaction context to the appropriate enterprise activity.

Enterprise Application Manager

This layer is responsible for interacting with the enterprise resources in the system. The different resources in the enterprise could be EJBs as well as legacy systems that contain data. In addition to them, it could also be a composition of other Web Services, that is, a business process/workflow. The enterprise application manager will thus have to co-ordinate this activity, and ensure transactional and data integrity across different components and the data that these components access.

Business Web Service Core Components

From the previous section, it would now be clear to you that we need some additional components that need to be present in a business Web Services system in addition to the core components that we saw in the simple Web Services section.

The core components needed are shown below:

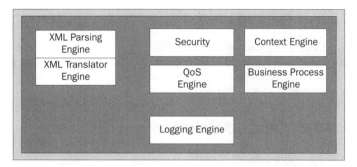

Let us now look at a business Web Services platform in its entirety. This is merely an extension of the one that we saw for the simple Web Services platform with the appropriate modules added:

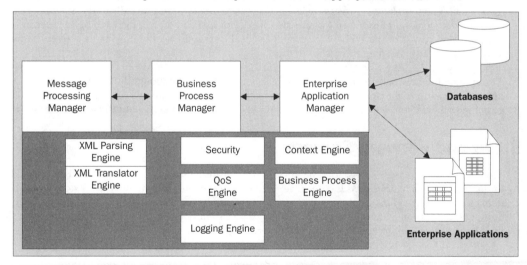

Let us now move on to the Performance.

Performance

In this section, we shall discuss different mechanisms for improving our Web Service performance.

A Web Service is, after all, accessible over the Internet via the ubiquitous HTTP protocol. Hence, in essence it would be a safe assumption to make that the performance of the Web Service would be related to performance considerations of web sites. The reason being that in most cases it is going to be the web server that is going to receive the SOAP Request over HTTP.

29

In general, we would need to address the issue of scalability in our Web Service too. By scalability we mean the ability of the Web Service to serve an increased demand for service. An ideal situation would be for a Web Service to provide a constant and acceptable response time irrespective of the request load. However, that is not practical. There have been several techniques that have been used for addressing Web site scalability over the Internet in the past few years. The same applies to within the realm of addressing Web Services scalability too.

Load-Balancing Servers

One of the techniques used to address the scalability of Web Services would be to replicate the Web Service across the multiple distributed servers on the Internet that would share the load appropriately. Having multiple such instances of the Web Service is a more efficient technique to address scalability than providing more resources to a Web Service on a single machine.

Caching Load-Balanced Servers

This is another way of making our load-balanced servers provide much faster response time to the Web Service consumers. Caching provides a means for storing frequently access data locally, so that instead of obtaining the same data from across servers/systems, you can deliver the data from the local cache, thereby improving the response time. Extending this concept to our load-balanced servers, we can make them caching load-balanced servers such that they make the appropriate calls to the Web Service and store the data locally. Thus, when a request comes in for a Web Service, the caching server can retrieve the execution results of the Web Service from its local storage instead of making calls over the Internet. This would greatly speed up the response time.

At the same time, we must note that a caching scheme needs to be thoughtfully implemented. It would be a good idea to cache, for example, news items that would not change frequently. It is also likely that a caching scheme could get complex, and would also involved a significant infrastructure cost.

Store and Forward Servers

This is another extension of our load-balanced servers where instead of sending messages across directly to the recipient, they are stored in a local repository and then are sent in an entire batch over a single network connection. This would greatly help in preventing expensive network calls for each request. Store and forward mechanisms would also need to be carefully designed to co-ordinate between the load balanced server and the Web Service server.

Role of Intermediaries

Before we conclude this chapter, it is important to take a look at an emerging entity that is bound to play an important role in providing valuable benefits to Web Services implementations. The role is that of an intermediary. An intermediary is a component that sits between the service consumer and the service provider. An intermediary's role gets activated during a Web Service invocation. By placing themselves between the service consumer and service provider, they have the potential to provide several value-added benefits to Web Services. In fact, an intermediary is well suited to address some of the concerns that we raised during our discussion of Business Web Services. The services that can be provided by the intermediaries can be thought of as being similar to the runtime APIs provided by J2EE containers.

Shown below is a diagram of how an intermediary may be positioned between the service consumer and service provider. Note that there could be one or more intermediaries between the service consumer and provider:

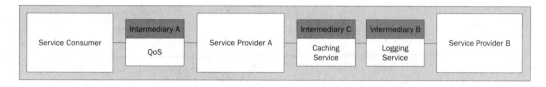

From the diagram, we can see that the service consumer is using a Web Service from service provider 'A'. An intermediary 'A' between these two organizations can serve the purpose of ensuring the SLA between the two organizations, thereby assuring the QoS levels mentioned in the SLA are conformed to.

Similarly, when service provider 'A' invokes a Web Service from service provider 'B', there are two Intermediaries 'B' and 'C' between them. Intermediary 'B' provides a logging service and intermediary 'C' provides a caching service for service provider 'B'. This is similar to our caching server discussion where we would have a server that would cache results locally and deliver them to the service consumer resulting in faster response time. The intermediary 'C' here provides exactly that kind of service. This type of division of functions into layers also helps in achieving additional scalability. Whenever there is a bottleneck, you simply add more servers to the layer.

It is easy to see that Intermediaries will play an increasingly important role within the Web Services system. Other areas that Intermediaries can provide support for are auditing services, non-repudiation services, and so on. There are several examples of intermediaries currently live, for example, Akamai (content caching), Microsoft (Passport Authentication), and so on.

Summary

In this chapter, we covered the following:

❑ Basic Web Services stack comprising of SOAP, WSDL, and UDDI technologies

❑ Simple Web Services and an architecture representing them

❑ Business Web Services and issues like security, transactions, context, business process workflow, and so on, which need to be addressed by standards before Business Web Services can gain widespread acceptance

❑ Aarchitecture for Business Web Services

❑ Performance issues for Web Services and the role of intermediaries in providing more value-added services

In the next chapter we will begin our look at SOAP.

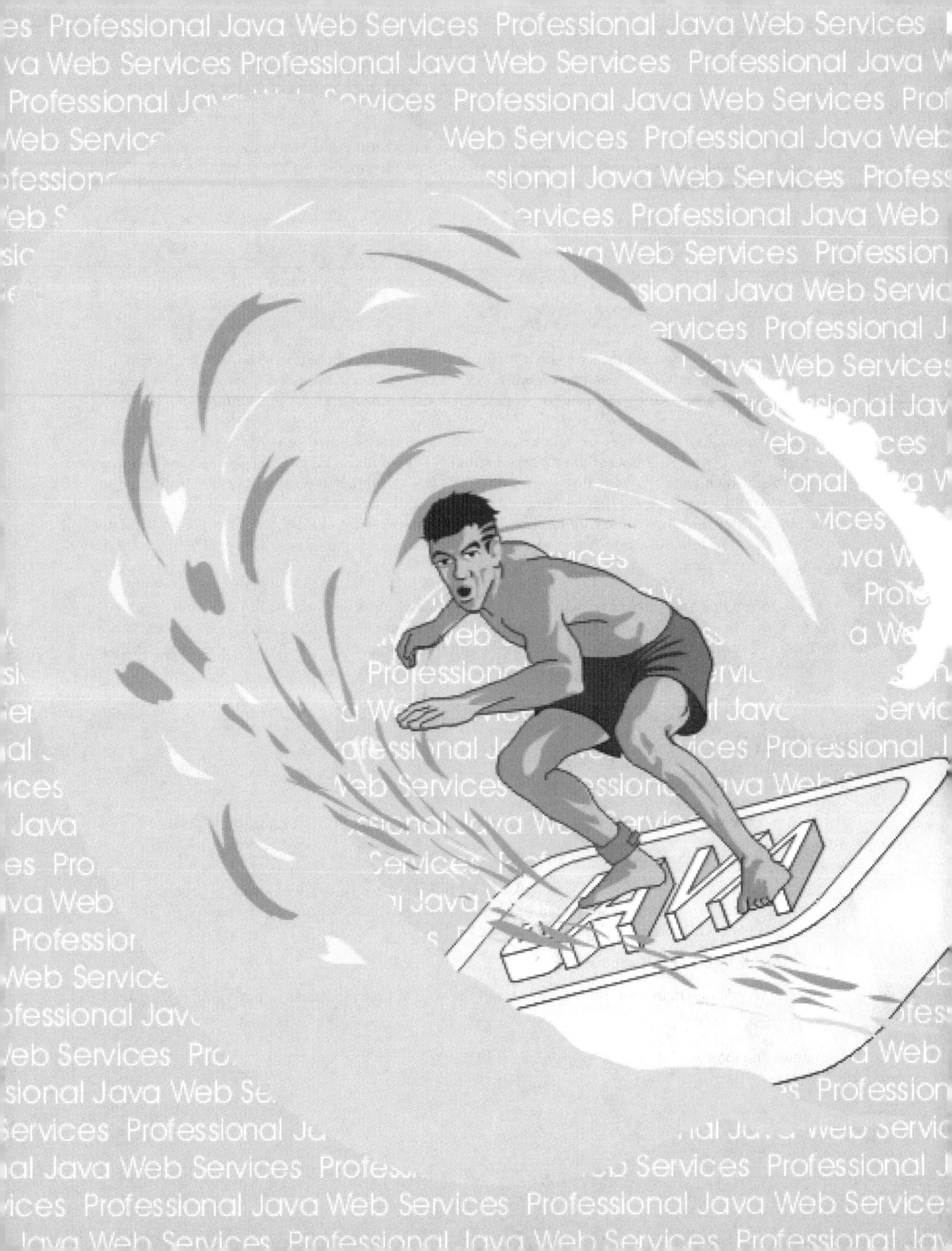
Professional Java Web Services

SOAP

Simple Object Access Protocol (SOAP) is a lightweight distributed computing protocol that allows information to be exchanged in a decentralized, distributed environment. The SOAP specification defines a framework for transmitting messages between distributed systems and conventions for handing remote procedure calls and responses. However, SOAP doesn't define the semantics of the messages, but simply provides the framework. Other specifications, such as ebXML, which utilizes SOAP as its transport mechanism, define the semantics of messages. In many cases these semantics will be application defined.

SOAP communicates with distributed systems using the text-based XML protocol instead of a binary format used by other distributed computing protocols such as CORBA, RMI, and DCOM. This makes SOAP highly interoperable across hardware platforms, operating systems, programming languages, and network hardware platforms. SOAP can be transported over HTTP, which allows it to capitalize on existing infrastructure investments, such as web servers, proxy servers, and firewalls. SOAP can also be transported using other protocols such as SMTP and JMS.

SOAP isn't the first distributed computing protocol, but it's the first to receive unprecedented industry backing from all of the major software and hardware vendors. This has never happened for other distributed computing protocols such as CORBA, RMI, and DCOM – causing the development community to become fragmented, with some developers implementing distributed systems using one protocol and others deciding to use another.

This has made it cumbersome to develop distributed applications that depend on software components (objects) that use different distributed computing protocols. SOAP can resolve this problem by residing on top of applications that utilize other distributing computing protocols – and thus making objects accessible from systems that would normally not have access to them. For example, adding SOAP support to three systems that use CORBA, RMI and DCOM respectively, would allow the systems to have access to one another's objects without having to deal with the particulars of each protocol.

In this chapter, the following topics will be covered:

- ❑ The history of SOAP
- ❑ SOAP 1.2
- ❑ The benefits and disadvantages of SOAP
- ❑ SOAP Messages with Attachments
- ❑ Design goals of SOAP
- ❑ Security concerns
- ❑ Common SOAP architectures
- ❑ SOAP Message Framework (envelope, header and body)
- ❑ Encoding of SOAP messages
- ❑ The transporting of SOAP messages using HTTP
- ❑ Remote procedure calls and responses within SOAP

Introducing SOAP

This section will serve as an introduction into the world of SOAP. First, we will define SOAP, and then we will review its history. We will also examine the current version of SOAP, version 1.2. The benefits and disadvantages of SOAP will also be discussed.

We will also consider a related specification, SOAP Messages with Attachments. This specification defines a mechanism for sending one or more attachments along with a SOAP message. We will also look at the design goals of SOAP, and finally, we will look at a basic SOAP example. This should serve as a primer for upcoming sections.

What is SOAP?

As mentioned above, the **Simple Object Access Protocol (SOAP)** is a lightweight distributed computing protocol that allows information to be exchanged in a decentralized, distributed environment. We will discuss the 1.1 version of the protocol because the 1.2 version of the protocol has only recently been released and is therefore very new and does not have widespread support as of yet. Furthermore, there were no major changes from 1.1 to 1.2.

SOAP is not bound to a hardware platform, operating system, programming language, or network hardware. Unlike other distributed computing systems, SOAP is built on top of open standards such as HTTP and XML. Using widely accepted and known standards makes it easier for developers to learn the new technology, and for existing infrastructure to support it.

The SOAP protocol is considered lightweight because it contains less features than other distributed computing protocols, making the protocol less complex. For example, unlike CORBA, SOAP doesn't depend on an Object Request Broker (ORB). This means that CORBA-enabled systems must communicate through the ORB. However, SOAP allows distributed systems to communicate directly without any intermediary. Also, SOAP doesn't define a mechanism for describing and locating objects on distributed systems. These mechanisms are being defined by the WSDL and UDDI specifications (discussed in Chapters 4 and 5), respectively.

The SOAP specification really consists of two parts: **messaging** and **Remote Procedure Call (RPC)** encapsulation. The messaging part of the specification defines a messaging framework for transmitting messages between distributed systems. The RPC part of the specification defines how to embed remote procedure calls and responses within the messages for the purpose of invoking procedures on remote systems.

The RPC encapsulation part of the specification allows SOAP to provide a protocol-layer abstraction for distributed computing protocols within an intranet or on the Internet. This abstraction provides remote systems with access to objects across otherwise incompatible platforms, operating systems, and environments. For example, a SOAP layer can be added to a Java and CORBA object. This layer creates a common distributed commuting environment between the two objects – making the CORBA objects accessible to Java objects and vice-versa without having to worry about the particulars of each distributed computing protocol. The following diagram depicts this:

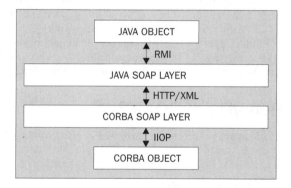

In the above example, the Java object communicates with a SOAP layer (Java SOAP Layer) using RMI and the CORBA object communicates with the SOAP layer (CORBA SOAP Layer). The SOAP layers communicate with one another by exchanging SOAP messages (encoded in XML) using HTTP.

The History of SOAP

A group of people from companies such as Microsoft, DevelopMentor and UserLand Software were involved in creating SOAP in 1998. The original intent of the protocol was to simply define a mechanism for transmitting XML documents that contained commands that would trigger operations or responses on remote systems, or RPC. In order to realize this goal, a schema language or type system for XML was needed. At the time, this didn't exist. So, they turned their focus to defining a type system. However, the type system was rather basic; it contained some primitive types, structs, and arrays.

According to an article written by Don Box, SOAP would have been released as a specification in 1998, but politics within Microsoft groups that were working on the specifications caused the specification to sit in limbo until the political issues were resolved. Unwilling to wait on this process, Dave Winer, president of UserLand Software and one of the people working on the SOAP specification, decided to produce a similar specification called XML-RPC. The XML-RPC specification uses a subset of the type system that was defined as the original type system for SOAP.

In the fourth quarter of 1999 the SOAP 1.0 specification shipped. However, the native type system was replaced by the "XML Schema Part 2 Datatypes" specification (http://www.w3.org/TR/xmlschema-2/), which defined XML datatypes. Most of the SOAP 1.0 specification illustrated how to model data using the new type system. There were no useful changes to the specification from SOAP 1.0 to SOAP 1.1.

The SOAP 1.1 specification was the first version to be submitted to the **World Wide Web Consortium (W3C)**. It was used for discussion purposes and to decide if a W3C working group would be established to shape the protocol into a formal standard. It was decided to create a working group for the protocol and the first working draft of the specification was SOAP 1.2, Working Draft 1.

SOAP 1.2

The current release of SOAP is version 1.2, Working Draft 2 and it's the second working draft of the specification, which means that SOAP is moving farther down the W3C review and approval process for eventual release as a formal standard. The specification has been split into two documents: **Messaging Frameworks** and **Adjuncts**. The Messaging Framework document discusses the SOAP envelope and transport-binding framework. The Adjuncts document describes the RPC convention and encoding rules along with a concrete HTTP binding specification. The specifications can be obtained from http://www.w3.org/TR/soap12-part1/ and http://www.w3.org/TR/soap12-part2/ respectively.

What are the Benefits of SOAP?

SOAP provides several advantages over other distributed systems, among them:

- ❑ SOAP can easily traverse firewalls

- ❑ SOAP data is structured using XML

- ❑ SOAP can potentially be used in combination with several transport protocols, such as HTTP, SMTP, and JMS

- ❑ SOAP maps nicely to the request/response pattern of HTTP and HTTP Extension Framework

- ❑ SOAP is fairly lightweight as a protocol

- ❑ There is SOAP support from many vendors, including Microsoft, IBM, and SUN

One major benefit of SOAP, which can also be viewed as a disadvantage, is that SOAP-enabled applications can easily traverse firewalls, since SOAP can be used with HTTP. This allows SOAP-enabled applications to be available internally (intranet) and externally (Internet) from initial deployment. However, this has the potential to become a major security problem, with SOAP applications being accessible to unauthorized parties.

Another benefit of SOAP is that messages are transmitted using the XML protocol, which is text-based. This means that messages can be understood by almost any hardware platform, operating system, programming language, or network hardware.

SOAP can also be used with other protocols besides HTTP, such as SMTP and Java Messaging Server (JMS). However, HTTP is the most commonly used protocol, because of its widespread support. In addition, the SOAP message model naturally maps to the request/response model of HTTP. The following diagram shows this:

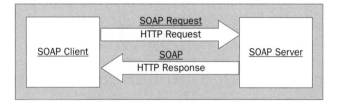

In the above example, a SOAP client makes a SOAP request embedded within a HTTP request message. In return, the SOAP server returns a SOAP response message embedded within a HTTP response message.

As mentioned previously, the SOAP protocol is considered lightweight because it contains less features than other distributed computing protocols. It's also receiving unprecedented support from many vendors, which means a large number of products will be SOAP-enabled, pushing the protocol into wide acceptance.

Disadvantages of SOAP

In the above section, we highlighted the benefits of SOAP. In this section we will highlight the disadvantages of SOAP, amongst which are:

❑ **Lack of interoperability between SOAP toolkits**
Even though SOAP has widespread support, there are still incompatibility issues between different SOAP implementations.

❑ **Security mechanisms are immature**
SOAP doesn't define a mechanism for authenticating a message before it's processed. It also doesn't define a mechanism for encrypting the contents of a SOAP message to prevent others from obtaining the contents of the message.

❑ **No guaranteed message delivery**
While a message is being transferred, if the system fails, a SOAP enabled system doesn't knows how to resend the message.

❑ **No publish and subscribe**
A SOAP client doesn't have the ability to send a request to multiple servers without sending the request to all of the servers.

SOAP Messages with Attachments

A related specification worth mentioning is the SOAP Messages with Attachments specification (http://www.w3.org/TR/SOAP-attachments). This specification defines a mechanism for sending one or more attachments along with a SOAP message. An attachment could be any type of binary data, such as facsimile images of legal documents, or non-binary data, such as engineering drawings. The specification doesn't define any new encoding mechanism. Instead it employs the MIME standard, which is an encoding mechanism used for sending e-mail attachments. The specification uses the MIME mechanisms to package a SOAP message and reference its attachments. The following diagram shows this:

SOAP Design Goals

The major design goals of the SOAP 1.1 specification were simplicity and extensibility. SOAP fulfilled the simplicity design goal by making the protocol a simple lightweight mechanism for exchanging structured and typed information between distributed systems. SOAP doesn't contain features that are in traditional messaging and distributed object systems such as:

- ❑   Distributed garbage collection
- ❑   Batching of messages
- ❑   Object-by-reference
- ❑   Activation

A distributed computing protocol that utilizes distributed garbage collection such as DCOM has the ability to locate clients that are no longer using a remote server object. Once located, the remote server object is destroyed and the memory is released. Since the SOAP specification doesn't define this, details of garbage collection are left to each SOAP implementation to handle.

SOAP also doesn't support batching of messages. Batching of messages is the ability to send multiple messages during a transmission instead of one. This minimizes network traffic and improves performance because it minimizes the number of round trips between the client and server. However, the implications to supporting this mean creating some sophisticated rules for handling how messages would be dealt with when received, such as which message should be processed and what happens if one of the message can't be processed. The complexity of this feature would conflict with the simplicity design goal.

CORBA uses object-by-reference to allow remote server objects to be manipulated by clients. This is done through the use of stubs. So, in order to manipulate a remote object, the stub has to be obtained, which is cumbersome. SOAP resolves this issue by allowing objects to be manipulated using the XML protocol instead of object-by-reference, making it easy to manipulate objects from almost any platform.

Activation is the ability to specify how the remote server object is invoked. Activation is also not supported by SOAP. SOAP leaves this detail up to the SOAP implementation to handle.

What Does SOAP Look Like?

Now that we've had an overview of SOAP, let's see what it looks like, without getting into the details. We will save this for a later section.

SOAP consists of messages being sent between a sender and receiver that are capable of processing SOAP messages. SOAP messages can be used to transmit data for many different reasons, but we will focus on discussing how SOAP can be used to transmit Remote Procedure Call (RPC) method calls and responses between a SOAP client and a SOAP server.

A SOAP message is an XML document that consists of a mandatory envelope, an optional header, and a mandatory body element. For simplicity, we will only discuss the mandatory components at this time. The <Envelope> element serves as the top element of the XML document representing the message. The <Body> element contains a RPC method call or response. The following code snippet illustrates this:

```
<SOAP-ENV:Envelope
  xmlns:SOAP-ENV="http://schemas.xmlsoap.org/soap/envelope/"
  <SOAP-ENV:encodingStyle="http://schemas.xmlsoap.org/soap/encoding/">
  <SOAP-ENV:Body>
  //RPC method Call or Response
  </SOAP-ENV:Body>
</SOAP-ENV:Envelope>
```

Let's assume that we want to invoke the RPC method GetDateTime, which simply returns the current date and time of a remote system. In order for this to happen the GetDateTime call has to be carried inside the <Body> element. The following code snippet illustrates this:

```
<SOAP-ENV:Envelope
  xmlns:SOAP-ENV="http://schemas.xmlsoap.org/soap/envelope/"
  <SOAP-ENV:encodingStyle="http://schemas.xmlsoap.org/soap/encoding/">
  <SOAP-ENV:Body>
    <ns1:GetDateTime xmlns:ns1="urn:TimeService">
      // Parameters go here (optional)
    </ns1:GetDateTime>
  </SOAP-ENV:Body>
</SOAP-ENV:Envelope>
```

Notice that GetDateTime is specified within the SOAP message as a fully qualified element name <ns1:GetDateTime>. The method requires one parameter called format. The format parameter specifies if the date and time should be returned in a short or long format. The format parameter is specified in the SOAP message as a sub-element of the <ns1:GetDateTime> element. The following code snippet illustrates this:

```
<SOAP-ENV:Envelope
   xmlns:SOAP-ENV="http://schemas.xmlsoap.org/soap/envelope/"
   <SOAP-ENV:encodingStyle="http://schemas.xmlsoap.org/soap/encoding/">
   <SOAP-ENV:Body>
      <ns1:GetDateTime xmlns:ns1="urn:TimeService">
         <format>long</format>
      </ns1:GetDateTime>
   </SOAP-ENV:Body>
</SOAP-ENV:Envelope>
```

Note that the value of the `<format>` element is `long`, which specifies that we want the date and time to be returned in a long format.

SOAP messages have to be embedded within a transport protocol such as HTTP in order for them to be transmitted between a SOAP client and a SOAP server. The following code snippet illustrates this:

```
POST /rpcrouter HTTP/1.1
Host: 127.0.0.1
Content-Type: text/xml; charset="utf-8"
Content-Length: 287
SOAPAction: "http://www.wrox.com/TimeService/GetDateTime"

<SOAP-ENV:Envelope
   xmlns:SOAP-ENV="http://schemas.xmlsoap.org/soap/envelope/"
   <SOAP-ENV:encodingStyle="http://schemas.xmlsoap.org/soap/encoding/">
   <SOAP-ENV:Body>
      <ns1:GetDateTime xmlns:ns1="urn:TimeService">
         <format>long</format>
      </ns1:GetDateTime>
   </SOAP-ENV:Body>
</SOAP-ENV:Envelope>
```

The above code snippet shows a SOAP message embedded within an HTTP request. The first five lines contain HTTP and SOAP header information, which we will discuss in detail later.

Once the SOAP server receives the request, it will be processed and a response will be sent back to the SOAP client. Like RPC method calls, RPC responses are sent using a SOAP message. However, the SOAP message is embedded within a HTTP response instead of a HTTP request. The following code snippet illustrates this:

```
HTTP/1.1 200 OK
Content-Type: text/xml; charset="utf-8"
Content-Length: 342

<SOAP-ENV:Envelope
   xmlns:SOAP-ENV="http://schemas.xmlsoap.org/soap/envelope/"
   SOAP-ENV:encodingStyle="http://schemas.xmlsoap.org/soap/encoding/">
   <SOAP-ENV:Body>
      <ns1:GetDateTimeResponse xmlns:ns1="urn:TimeService>
         <return xsi:type="xsd:string">Wed Jul 18 08:22:03 EDT 2001</return>
      </ns1:GetDateTimeResponse>
   </SOAP-ENV:Body>
</SOAP-ENV:Envelope>
```

The first three lines contain HTTP response headers. The format of the SOAP message is exactly the same as the SOAP message that contained the RPC method call, except that the `<Body>` element contains a `<ns1:GetDateTimeResponse>` element. It contains the return value of the method call, which is Wed Jul 18 08:22:03 EDT and its data type, which is a `String`.

Security Concerns

Unlike other distributed computing protocols, SOAP has the ability to utilize HTTP as a transport protocol.

Since the majority of corporate firewalls allow HTTP traffic we now have to be concerned about a new breed of security risks. The SOAP specification addresses the concern by defining a new HTTP request header field called `SOAPAction`. A SOAP client that uses the HTTP transport must use this field when issuing a SOAP request. The value of the field should be a **Uniform Resource Identifier (URI)** that identifies the intent of the SOAP message. This could be used by firewalls to appropriately filter SOAP request messages.

The following SOAP message illustrates this:

```
POST /rpcrouter HTTP/1.1
Host: 127.0.0.1
Content-Type: text/xml; charset="utf-8"
Content-Length: 287
SOAPAction: "http://www.wrox.com/TimeService/GetDateTime"

<SOAP-ENV:Envelope
  xmlns:SOAP-ENV="http://schemas.xmlsoap.org/soap/envelope/"
  <SOAP-ENV:encodingStyle="http://schemas.xmlsoap.org/soap/encoding/">
  <SOAP-ENV:Body>
    <ns1:GetDateTime xmlns:ns1="urn:TimeService">
      <format>long</format>
    </ns1:GetDateTime>
  </SOAP-ENV:Body>
</SOAP-ENV:Envelope>
```

In the above example, servers such as firewalls and proxies could use the `SOAPAction` header to either accept or deny the request. The URI can also be a value of empty string (`""`). The following example shows this:

```
POST /rpcrouter HTTP/1.1
Host: 127.0.0.1
Content-Type: text/xml; charset="utf-8"
Content-Length: 287
SOAPAction: ""

//SOAP Message
```

An empty string means that the HTTP Request-URI specifies the intent of the SOAP message. So, in this case, the firewall or proxy would use the /rpcrouter URI to decide whether to accept or deny the request. Lastly, a SOAPAction field can contain no value. The following example depicts this:

```
POST /rpcrouter HTTP/1.1
Host: 127.0.0.1
Content-Type: text/xml; charset="utf-8"
Content-Length: 287
SOAPAction:

//SOAP Message
```

A field that contains no value means that there is no indication of the intent of the message. Once again, the firewall or proxy server could be configured to accept or deny requests with anonymous intent. Since this may be considered a huge security gap, a firewall or proxy server could be configured to deny all requests that don't contain a value for the SOAPAction header.

SOAP Architecture in Java

This section discusses some common SOAP architectures that could be used as a basis for designing new or enhancing existing distributed applications using Java technologies. This section is not meant to be an exhaustive list of architectures, but is simply provided to help you to start thinking about where SOAP could fit into your applications. We will discuss each one of the architectures independently, but two or more architectures could be combined to design an application.

Standard Architecture

The first architecture that we are going to discuss is probably the most used SOAP architecture, so we will refer to it as the standard architecture from this point forward. It consists of making functionality within a Java object available to remote systems through the use of SOAP. In this architecture a Java object can access local or remote resources. The architecture is shown below:

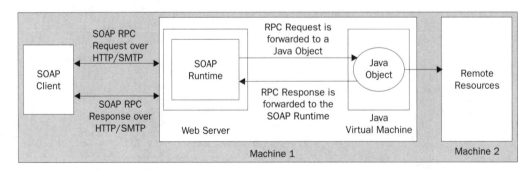

In the above diagram, a client application makes a remote procedure call (RPC) over HTTP or SMTP using SOAP. Upon receiving the RPC request the SOAP runtime (for instance, Apache SOAP) environment routes the request to the Java object that contains the requested method. In this architecture, the Java method could access local or remote resources. Examples of local resources are the system clock or the file system. Examples of remote resources are relational or object oriented databases, LDAP servers, or an ERP system. The return value of the method call is received by the SOAP runtime and forwarded back to the originating SOAP client as a SOAP response. This architecture will mostly be used in the following situations:

❑ The remote system uses a programming language other then Java, therefore preventing the use of Remote Method Invocations (RMI). In order to use RMI the client and the server have to be written in Java.

❑ The remote system is outside a firewall. Unlike RMI, SOAP doesn't have a problem traversing a firewall. This is usually the case when trying to make remote server objects available to other business entities such as suppliers and vendors.

Distributed Architecture

This architecture consists of using SOAP in combination with other distributed computing systems such as Enterprise JavaBeans (EJB) and CORBA. The architecture is exactly the same as the standard discussed above, except that the Java Object interacts with a distributed system instead of remote resources. The distributed system then accesses the remote resources. The following diagram illustrates this:

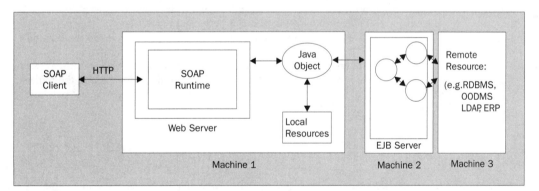

This architecture fosters the reuse of software components. For example, business logic that exists in a distributed system can be used by remote systems that are utilizing an alternative distributed computing protocol. It is also an effective way to allow an external organization to access business logic contained within distributed systems that have problems traversing a firewall. Similarly, it could be used for Enterprise Application Integration (EAI) projects.

Peer-to-Peer (P2P)

The third architecture that we are going to discuss consists of using SOAP to make remote procedure calls between nodes in a Peer-to-Peer (P2P) network. The architecture is depicted below:

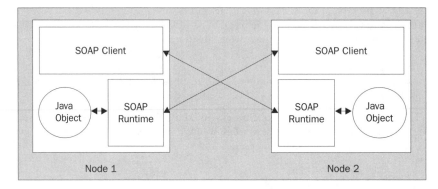

The P2P computing model has become popular due to the popularity of consumer file swapping services such as Napster. Even though the idea of accessing resources on remote computers is not new, Napster and other file-sharing services have shown the potential of P2P computing. P2P computing consists of one or more computers that can act as either a client or server depending on the scenario. We will refer to these computers as nodes from this point forward. As a client, a node is capable of accessing resources on other nodes. As a server, the node provides services to other nodes.

In the above architecture, Node 1 makes a request for a service; Node 2 receives the request and checks to see if it provides the service. If so, the request is fulfilled just as we saw in the standard architecture. If not, Node 2 could ignore the request or send back a message stating that the service is not available. Likewise, Node 2 could make a request for a service and Node 1 could fulfill or ignore the request. Here we are only discussing the interaction between two nodes. However, a true peer-to-peer network could contain hundreds or thousands of nodes.

The Protocol

In the *What Does SOAP Look Like* section we briefly discussed different aspects of SOAP without going into detail. In this section we will dig into the details. We will cover:

❑ The role of XML within SOAP

❑ The components of a SOAP message

❑ How SOAP encodes (serializes) data for transmission purposes

❑ How SOAP is transported using HTTP, HTTP Extension Framework and potentially any other transport language

❑ The conventions that SOAP uses in order to make remote procedure calls and responses

XML

SOAP utilizes XML to encode all messages. In keeping with the goal of simplicity SOAP messages cannot contain a DTD. A SOAP message must include the proper XML namespaces on all elements and attributes defined by SOAP. If the namespaces aren't specified then the SOAP application may not be able to process the SOAP message. The benefit of using namespaces within SOAP is that elements we define will not conflict with the default SOAP elements. All default SOAP elements and attributes are prefixed with the `SOAP-ENV` namespace identifier, which is associated with the http://schemas.xmlsoap.org/soap/envelope namespace.

SOAP Message

A SOAP message is an XML document that can contain a maximum of three parts: A SOAP envelope (mandatory), SOAP header (optional), and SOAP body (mandatory).

The following diagram provides a graphical representation of a SOAP message:

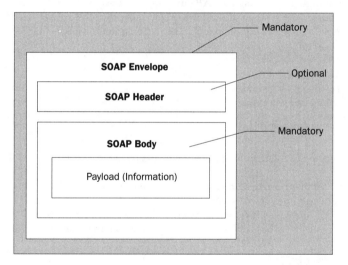

SOAP Envelope

The SOAP envelope is the top-level element of a SOAP message. It can be thought as being equivalent to an envelope that is used to send letters via the postal service. It contains an optional SOAP header and a mandatory SOAP body. The SOAP envelope is denoted in a SOAP message by the `<Envelope>` element. The following code snippet illustrates this:

```
<SOAP-ENV:Envelope
  <SOAP-ENV:Header>
    ... // Optional
  </SOAP-ENV:Header>
  <SOAP-ENV:Body>
    ...// Mandatory
  </SOAP-ENV:Body>
</SOAP-ENV:Envelope>
```

Notice that all elements are prefixed with the SOAP-ENV namespace identifier, which is associated with the http://schemas.xmlsoap.org/soap/envelope namespace. As mentioned previously, all SOAP elements are associated with the SOAP-ENV prefix to ensure that SOAP elements don't conflict with elements that we might define.

In our efforts to better understand the <Envelope> element, let's look at part of the http://schemas.xmlsoap.org/soap/envelope schema:

```
<xs:element name="Envelope" type="tns:Envelope" />
  <xs:complexType name="Envelope" >
  <xs:sequence>
    <xs:element ref="tns:Header" minOccurs="0" />
    <xs:element ref="tns:Body" minOccurs="1" />
    <xs:any namespace="##other" minOccurs="0" maxOccurs="unbounded"
      processContents="lax" />
  </xs:sequence>
```

The above code snippet shows that a SOAP envelope can have a SOAP header or not, but must contain only one SOAP body. The schema also allows other elements to be added to a SOAP envelope without explicit declaration. The following lines within the schema demonstrate this:

```
. . .
  <xs:sequence>
    <xs:element ref="tns:Header" minOccurs="0" />
    <xs:element ref="tns:Body" minOccurs="1" />
    <xs:any namespace="##other" minOccurs="0" maxOccurs="unbounded"
. . .
```

This allows vendors to add value to their implementation by creating extensions to the SOAP specification.

A SOAP application that receives a message with a namespace other than http://schemas.xmlsoap.org/soap/envelope should return a version error and disregard the message. The sending of error messages such as a version error is done using the SOAP <Fault> element. We will discuss the details later, but this is what a SOAP message that contains a version error looks like:

```
<SOAP-ENV:Envelope
  xmlns:SOAP-ENV="http://schemas.xmlsoap.org/soap/envelope/"
  SOAP-ENV:encodingStyle="http://schemas.xmlsoap.org/soap/encoding/">
  <SOAP-ENV:Body>
    <SOAP-ENV:Fault>
      <faultcode>VersionMismatch</faultcode>
    </SOAP-ENV:Fault>
  </SOAP-ENV:Body>
</SOAP-ENV:Envelope>
```

In the above example, the pre-defined error code, VersionMismatch, would be sent back to the SOAP application.

SOAP encodingStyle Attribute

The SOAP `encodingStyle` global attribute can be used to specify how information should be encoded. The SOAP specification encourages the value to be http://schemas.xmlsoap.org/soap/encoding, which is the namespace associated with the encoding rules defined by SOAP. A value of empty string ("") indicates that no decision has been made about the encoding style of the child elements. This could be used to allow child elements to define their own encoding rules. The attribute could also contain a value that points to a different namespace that specifies a different set of encoding rules.

A SOAP message using the `encodingStyle` attribute and the recommended SOAP encoding namespace would look like this:

```
<SOAP-ENV:Envelope
  xmlns:SOAP-ENV="http://schemas.xmlsoap.org/soap/envelope/"
  SOAP-ENV:encodingStyle="http://schemas.xmlsoap.org/soap/encoding/">
  <SOAP-ENV:Header>
    ...
  </SOAP-ENV:Header>
  <SOAP-ENV:Body>
    ...
  </SOAP-ENV:Body>
</SOAP-ENV:Envelope>
```

SOAP Header

The SOAP header is a generic and flexible way of adding features such as authentication, transaction management and payment services to a SOAP message. A SOAP header is specified in a SOAP message by the `SOAP-ENV:Header` element. A SOAP header is not mandatory, but if used, it must immediately come after the SOAP envelope element. A SOAP header can contain child elements, which are referred to as header entries within the SOAP specification. The following example shows how a SOAP header would be written.

```
<SOAP-ENV:Envelope
  xmlns:SOAP-ENV="http://schemas.xmlsoap.org/soap/envelope/"
  SOAP-ENV:encodingStyle="http://schemas.xmlsoap.org/soap/encoding/">
  <SOAP-ENV:Header>
    <a:authentication
      xmlns:a="http://www.wrox.com/soap/authentication">
      <a:username>mlhendri</a:username>
      <a:password>courtney</a:password>
    </a:authentication>
  </SOAP-ENV:Header>
  <SOAP-ENV:Body>
    ...
  </SOAP-ENV:Body>
</SOAP-ENV:Envelope>
```

The above example shows a SOAP header that contains authentication information. A SOAP application could use the information to disregard the message if the user name or password was incorrect. The authentication information is specified as a header entry. All first level header entries must be fully qualified, which means that every element must be associated with a namespace. This isn't necessary for child elements of header entries, but this example uses them anyway to fully qualify the child elements: <username> and <password>. The namespace space can be non-existent. It's just used to differentiate between SOAP elements. In the above example, the http://www.wrox.com/soap/authentication namespace is used, but doesn't really exist.

SOAP header entries can contain two attributes: actor and mustUnderstand. The actor attribute can be used to indicate who should process a header element. The mustUnderstand attribute can be used to indicate whether a header entry is mandatory for the SOAP message to be processed. If the SOAP application doesn't know how to process the header entry then the processing of the message should fail. Otherwise, the message should be processed.

A SOAP application must ignore all SOAP header attributes that aren't applied to an immediate child of a SOAP header element. The following code snippet illustrates this:

```
<SOAP-ENV:Envelope
  xmlns:SOAP-ENV="http://schemas.xmlsoap.org/soap/envelope/"
  SOAP-ENV:encodingStyle="http://schemas.xmlsoap.org/soap/encoding/">
  <SOAP-ENV:Header>
    <a:authentication
    xmlns:a="http://www.wrox.com/soap/authentication">
      <a:username SOAP-ENV:mustUnderstand="1">mlhendri</a:username>
        //Invalid
      <a:password>courtney</a:password>
    </a:authentication>
  </SOAP-ENV:Header>
  <SOAP-ENV:Body>
    ...
  </SOAP-ENV:Body>
</SOAP-ENV:Envelope>
```

Having the mustUnderstand attribute with the user name is invalid and will be ignored. The valid way is shown below:

```
<SOAP-ENV:Envelope
  xmlns:SOAP-ENV="http://schemas.xmlsoap.org/soap/envelope/"
  SOAP-ENV:encodingStyle="http://schemas.xmlsoap.org/soap/encoding/">
  <SOAP-ENV:Header>
    <a:authentication xmlns:a=http://www.wrox.com/soap/authentication
                      SOAP-ENV:mustUnderstand="1">
      <a:username>mlhendri</a:username> //Invalid
      <a:password>courtney</a:password>
    </a:authentication>
  </SOAP-ENV:Header>
  <SOAP-ENV:Body>
    ...
  </SOAP-ENV:Body>
</SOAP-ENV:Envelope>
```

In the above example, the `mustUnderstand` attribute is specified as part of the authentication element, which is the immediate child of the SOAP header element.

SOAP actor Attribute

A SOAP message can be potentially passed through multiple SOAP intermediaries before arriving at its final destination. The `actor` attribute can be used to indicate who should process a header element. The value of the `actor` attribute is based on the assumption that every SOAP processor will be associated with a URI. The following example shows this:

```
<SOAP-ENV:Envelope
  xmlns:SOAP-ENV="http://schemas.xmlsoap.org/soap/envelope/"
  SOAP-ENV:encodingStyle="http://schemas.xmlsoap.org/soap/encoding/">
  <SOAP-ENV:Header>
    <a:authentication
      xmlns:a="http://www.wrox.com/soap/authentication"
      SOAP-ENV:actor="http://www.wrox.com/soap/authenticator">
      <a:username>mlhendri</a:username>
      <a:password>courtney</a:password>
    </a:authentication>
  </SOAP-ENV:Header>
  <SOAP-ENV:Body>
    ...
  </SOAP-ENV:Body>
</SOAP-ENV:Envelope>
```

In the above example, the SOAP message is specifying that the recipient of the authentication header element should be a SOAP processor that is associated with the `http://www.wrox.com/soap/authenticator` URI.

The recipient of a SOAP header element cannot forward the header element to the next intermediary. The SOAP specification states that the role of a recipient of a header element is similar to that of accepting a contract, in that it cannot be extended beyond the recipient. However, the recipient can insert a similar header entry, but now the contract would be between that application and the recipient of the header actor. The following example depicts this:

```
<SOAP-ENV:Envelope
  xmlns:SOAP-ENV="http://schemas.xmlsoap.org/soap/envelope/"
  SOAP-ENV:encodingStyle="http://schemas.xmlsoap.org/soap/encoding/">
  <SOAP-ENV:Header>
    <a:authentication
      xmlns:a="http://www.wrox.com/soap/authentication">
      <a:token>Na73lak2da6dka6adaj72ana</a:token>
    </a:authentication>
  </SOAP-ENV:Header>
  <SOAP-ENV:Body>
    ...
  </SOAP-ENV:Body>
</SOAP-ENV:Envelope>
```

In the above example the original authentication header entry has been replaced with a similar header element, but it only contains a token header element. The token element contains a hashcode that represents the credentials of the user, which could be used to determine if and how the payload can be processed. For example, let's assume that the payload contains a RPC call. The token can be used to determine if the user is authorized to make the RPC call. Also notice that the `actor` attribute is not used. A header element without an actor attribute means that the recipient of the element should be the final destination of the SOAP element.

An `actor` attribute can also contain a URI value of `http://schemas.xmlsoap.org/soap/actor/next`. This URI indicates that the header element is intended for the first application that processes the message.

SOAP mustUnderstand Attribute

The `mustUnderstand` attribute indicates if a header entry is mandatory or optional. The value of the attribute is either 1 or 0. A value of 1 means that the recipient of the header must know how to process the element, or the processing of the message must fail. A value of 0 means that the recipient doesn't have to understand the element in order to process the message. A SOAP header without the `mustUnderstand` attribute is read as if the attribute was present with a value of 0. The following example uses the `mustUnderstand` attribute to specify that the `<authentication>` element has to be understood by the SOAP application in order to process the message.

```
<SOAP-ENV:Envelope
  xmlns:SOAP-ENV="http://schemas.xmlsoap.org/soap/envelope/"
  SOAP-ENV:encodingStyle="http://schemas.xmlsoap.org/soap/encoding/">
  <SOAP-ENV:Header>
    <a:authentication xmlns:a="http://www.wrox.com/soap/authentication"
      SOAP-ENV:mustUnderstand="1">
      <a:username>mlhendri</a:username>
      <a:password>courtney</a:password>
    </a:authentication>
  </SOAP-ENV:Header>
  <SOAP-ENV:Body>
    ...
  </SOAP-ENV:Body>
</SOAP-ENV:Envelope>
```

This feature is useful when the processing of a message depends on some information. In the above example, by setting the `mustUnderstand` attribute to 1 we are implying that the authentication information is necessary for processing the message. Likewise, the feature is useful to specify that the presence of some information is optional. The following example illustrates this:

```
<SOAP-ENV:Envelope
  xmlns:SOAP-ENV="http://schemas.xmlsoap.org/soap/envelope/"
  SOAP-ENV:encodingStyle="http://schemas.xmlsoap.org/soap/encoding/">
  <SOAP-ENV:Header>
    <a:authentication xmlns:a="http://www.wrox.com/soap/authentication"
      SOAP-ENV:mustUnderstand="0">
      <a:username>mlhendri</a:username>
      <a:password>courtney</a:password>
    </a:authentication>
  </SOAP-ENV:Header>
  <SOAP-ENV:Body>
    ...
  </SOAP-ENV:Body>
</SOAP-ENV:Envelope>
```

In the above example, the value of the `mustUnderstand` attribute is 0, which implies that the authentication information is not necessary to process the message.

SOAP Body

The SOAP body contains the payload (information) that must be received by the recipient of the message. The SOAP body of a message is specified using the `<Body>` element. In practice, the payload typically consists of a RPC call, RPC response, or error reporting. But, in theory a SOAP body can contain any type of information. If a header element is present the `<Body>` element must immediately follow the `<Header>` element. The following examples illustrates where the payload would reside:

```
<SOAP-ENV:Envelope
  xmlns:SOAP-ENV="http://schemas.xmlsoap.org/soap/envelope/"
  SOAP-ENV:encodingStyle="http://schemas.xmlsoap.org/soap/encoding/">
  <SOAP-ENV:Header>
    <a:authentication xmlns:a="http://www.wrox.com/soap/authentication"
      SOAP-ENV:mustUnderstand="1">
      <a:username>mlhendri</a:username>
      <a:password>courtney</a:password>
    </a:authentication>
  </SOAP-ENV:Header>
  <SOAP-ENV:Body>
    // Payload Goes Here
  </SOAP-ENV:Body>
</SOAP-ENV:Envelope>
```

Similar to a `<Header>` element, all immediate child elements of the SOAP `<Body>` element are called body entries. A body entry is identified by a fully qualified element name. Immediate child elements of a body entry don't have to be namespace-qualified. Optionally a body entry can contain an `encodingStyle` attribute that can be used to specify the encoding rules for that body entry. If specified, it would override the encoding rules specified in the SOAP `<Envelope>` element.

SOAP Fault

The SOAP `<Fault>` element is used for error handling within a SOAP application The `<Fault>` element can only exist once within a SOAP message. There cannot be multiple SOAP `<Fault>` elements. It is worth noting that the SOAP `<Fault>` element is the only body entry defined within the SOAP specification. The `<Fault>` element defines the following four sub-elements: `<faultcode>`, `<faultstring>`, `<faultactor>`, and `<detail>`.

The `<faultcode>` element is the only mandatory element. It was created to provide an easy mechanism for identifying a fault. The SOAP specification defines some generic `<faultcode>` values that must be used when a fault occurs. The `<faultcode>` values are defined in an extensible manner such that it allows a more specific `<faultcode>` to be defined while maintaining backwards compatibility with generic `<faultcode>` values. The notation for a more specific `<faultcode>` is:

```
GenericFaultCode.SpecificFaultCode
```

A dot "." is used as a separator of <faultcode> values indicating that what is to the left of the dot is a more generic fault value than the value to the right. An example of a more specific <faultcode> taken from the SOAP specification is:

```
Client.Authentication
```

This specifies that the SOAP message didn't contain the proper authentication. SOAP processors that understand this specific <faultcode> would process it accordingly, whereas SOAP processors that don't understand the specific <faultcode> would simply process the generic client <faultcode>.

The table below contains the fault codes and their meanings taken from the SOAP 1.1 specification:

FaultCode Name	Meaning
VersionMismatch	The processing party found an invalid namespace for the SOAP envelope element
MustUnderstand	An immediate child element of the SOAP header element that was either not understood or not obeyed by the processing party, and contained a SOAP mustUnderstand attribute with a value of 1.
Client	The Client class of errors indicate that the message was incorrectly formed or did not contain the appropriate information in order to succeed
Server	The Server class of errors indicate that the message could not be processed, for reasons not directly attributable to the contents of the message itself, but rather due to the processing of the message

The <faultstring> can be used to provide a human readable explanation of the fault. The following example illustrates this:

```
<SOAP-ENV:Envelope
  xmlns:SOAP-ENV="http://schemas.xmlsoap.org/soap/envelope/"
  SOAP-ENV:encodingStyle="http://schemas.xmlsoap.org/soap/encoding/">
  <SOAP-ENV:Body>
    <SOAP-ENV:Fault>
      <faultcode>Client.Authentication</faultcode>
      <faultstring>The username or password is invalid</faultstring>
    </SOAP-ENV:Fault>
  </SOAP-ENV:Body>
</SOAP-ENV:Envelope>
```

In this example, the <faultstring> is used in combination with the <faultcode> to describe the exact problem that was encountered, which in this case was an invalid user name or password.

The <faultactor> element is intended to specify information about what caused the fault to happen within a message. This is a useful element if a SOAP message passes through multiple SOAP applications before arriving at its final SOAP application. For example, let assumes that a SOAP message passes through SOAP application A and B in order to get its final destination, which is SOAP application C. If B generates a fault then the <faultactor> element can be used to specify B as the generator.

SOAP Encoding

The SOAP 1.1 specification defines how data within the payload of a SOAP message can be encoded. However, SOAP doesn't define a new type system, but adopts it from the "XML Schema Part 2: Datatypes" specification (http://www.w3.org/TR/xmlschema-2/). However, the SOAP encoding mechanism doesn't have to be used, we could define our own – though the SOAP specification encourages the use of the mechanism within the aforementioned specification.

The specification defines two groups of types: **simple types** and **complex types**. The difference between simple types and complex types is that simple types cannot have element children or attributes, whereas complex types may have element children and attributes. Within this section we will show how both simple types and complex types can be used to encode data within the payload of a SOAP message.

Simple Types

The "XML Schema Part 2: Datatypes" specification defines 44 built-in simple types that can be specified by using the `xsi-type` attribute within an element.

The following example shows how the `string` and `int` types can be encoded within a SOAP message:

```
<SOAP-ENV:Envelope
  xmlns:SOAP-ENV="http://schemas.xmlsoap.org/soap/envelope/"
  SOAP-ENV:encodingStyle="http://schemas.xmlsoap.org/soap/encoding/">
  <SOAP-ENV:Header>
    <a:authentication xmlns:a="http://www.wrox.com/soap/authentication"
      SOAP-ENV:mustUnderstand="1">
      <a:username>mlhendri</a:username>
      <a:password>courtney</a:password>
    </a:authentication>
  </SOAP-ENV:Header>
  <SOAP-ENV:Body>
    <cmd:processReboot xmlns:cmd="http://www.wrox.com/soap/cmd">
      <ip xsi:type="xsd:string">192.168.1.3</ip>
      <delay xsi:type="xsd:int">30000</delay>
    <cmd:processReboot>
  </SOAP-ENV:Body>
</SOAP-ENV:Envelope>
```

The payload of the above message contains a RPC call, `processReboot`. The purpose of the RPC call is to reboot a remote computer. It has two parameters: `ip` and `delay`, which are encoded using the `string` and `int` datatypes, respectively.

Alternatively, the payload could be encoded as:

```
<cmd:processReboot xmlns:cmd="http://www.wrox.com/soap/cmd">
  <SOAP-ENC:string id="ip">192.168.1.3</SOAP-ENC:string>
  <SOAP-ENC:int id="delay">30000</SOAP-ENC:int>
</cmd:processReboot>
```

The above syntax specifies the parameters using elements that are defined in the SOAP-ENC namespace. The SOAP-ENC namespace declares an element for every simple data type. Note that the id attribute is used to uniquely identify an element. Otherwise, if you had a parameter that had the same type, then there would be no way to distinguish between the two.

SOAP uses the concept of an accessor in order to obtain an encoded value. An accessor is either the element name that encloses a value or the value of the id attribute. So the accessor for the IP address would be "ip" if defined as:

```
<SOAP-ENC:string id="ip">192.168.1.3</SOAP-ENC:string>
```

or if defined as:

```
<ip xsi:type="xsd:string">192.168.1.3</ip>
```

In the above example, the IP address could be obtained by using the id attribute, which is "ip" or the <ip> element.

There are two types of values that can be used within a SOAP payload. The first type is called **single-reference**, which means that a value is only accessed by one accessor. The second type of value is called **multi-reference**, which means that one or more accessors can access a value. Let's examine the following XML fragment:

```
<cmd:processReboot xmlns:cmd="http://www.wrox.com/soap/cmd">
   <requester href="#ipaddress"/>
   <ip id="ipaddress">192.168.1.3</ip>
   <delay>30000</delay>
<cmd:processReboot>
```

In the above example, another parameter called requester has been added. The requester parameter is used to specify the IP address of the computer where the request originated. In this example the ipaddress of where the request originated and the ipaddress of the machine being rebooted is the same. Instead of specifying the IP address twice, the IP address was turned into a multi-reference value through the use of the id attribute. So, the IP address can be accessed using either the <ip> or <requester> element.

Compound Types

SOAP defines two types of compound types: struct and array. A struct compound type allows values of different types to be grouped together with each value being stored and received using a unique accessor name. An array compound type consists of values being stored and retrieved using an ordinal position number.

Structs

A `struct` compound type is very similar to a structure within the C programming language. The following `struct` of type `Book` is taken from the SOAP 1.1 specification:

```
<e:Book>
  <author>Henry Ford</author>
  <preface>Prefactory text</preface>
  <intro>This is a book.</intro>
</e:Book>
```

Like simple types, compound types can be multi-reference. The following example, also taken from the SOAP 1.1 specification, shows this:

```
<e:Book>
  <title>My Life and Work</title>:
  <author href="#Person-1"/>
</e:Book>
<e:Person id="Person-1">
  <name>Henry Ford</name>
  <address href="#Address-2"/>
</e:Person>
<e:Address id="Address-2">
  <e-mail>mailto:henryford@hotmail.com</e-mail>
  <web>http://www.henryford.com</web>
</e:Address>
```

The modularity of the data values above is especially handy if a value will be used more than once. The following example shows this:

```
<e:Book>
  <title>My Life and Work</title>:
  <firstauthor href="#Person-1"/>
  <secondauthor href="#Person-2"/>
</e:Book>
<e:Person id="Person-1">
  <name>Henry Ford</name>
  <address href="#Address-2"/>
</e:Person>
<e:Person id="Person-2">
  <name>Henry Ford Jr</name>
  <address href="#Address-2"/>
</e:Person>
<e:Address id="Address-2">
  <e-mail>mailto:henryford@hotmail.com</e-mail>
  <web>http://www.henryford.com</web>
</e:Address>
```

In the above example, the book has two authors where both are associated with the same address (`Address-2`) information.

#### Chapter 2

Arrays

Arrays can be defined as having a type of SOAP-ENC:Array or a type derived from there. The elements contained within an array can be of any type, including nested arrays. The following example taken from the SOAP 1.1 specification shows how an array would be defined:

```
<element name="myFavoriteNumbers" type="SOAP-ENC:Array"/>

<myFavoriteNumbers SOAP-ENC:arrayType="xsd:int[2]">
  <number>3</number>
  <number>4</number>
</myFavoriteNumbers>
```

The above example consists of a schema fragment that defines <myFavoriteNumbers> as an array and an instance of the <myFavoriteNumbers> array. The <myFavoriteNumbers> array is defined as type SOAP-ENC:Array. The SOAP-ENC:Array type allows unqualified element names without restriction, which doesn't convey any type information. Therefore, type information has to be specified within elements of the array using the xsi:type attribute or the containing element must have a SOAP-ENC:arrayType attribute. In the above example, the former method is used to specify that the elements of the array should be restricted to integers.

The elements of an array can contain any subtypes of the specified SOAP-ENC:arrayType attribute. So, elements within the <myFavoriteNumbers> array could contain elements that are derived from the int datatype. The following example depicts this:

```
<element name="myFavoriteNumbers" type="SOAP-ENC:Array"/>
  <simpleType name="myint" >
    <restriction base="xsd:int">
      <pattern value="0\[0-9]">
    </restriction>
  </simpleType>

<myFavoriteNumbers SOAP-ENC:arrayType="xsd:int[2]">
  <number xsi:type="myint">00</number>
  <number xsi:type="myint">09</number>
</myFavoriteNumbers>
```

In the above example, the elements within the <myFavoriteNumbers> array are of type myint, which is derived from the int datatype using the restriction element. The value of the type is also restricted by the pattern element. The value of a pattern element is a regular expression. The value in the above example specifies that a value of type myint can only contain two digits, where the first digit must be 0 and the second digit must be a valid value between zero and nine, making valid values between 00-09.

struct datatypes or other compound values can be values within an array. The following XML snippet shows this:

```
<BookArray SOAP-ENV:arrayType="e:Book[2]">
  <e:Book>
    <author>Henry Ford</author>
    <preface>Prefactory text</preface>
    <intro>This is a book.</intro>
  </e:Book>
```

```
  <e:Book>
    <author>Henry Ford Jr</author>
    <preface>Prefactory text Part II</preface>
    <intro>This is another book.</intro>
  </e:Book>
</BookArray>
```

In the above example, an array called <BookArray> has member values of type Book, which is a struct.

Arrays may have other arrays as member values. The following is an example of an array containing two arrays:

```
<Drinks SOAP-ENC:arrayType="xsd:string[][2]">
  <drink href="#drink-1"/>
  <drink href="#drink-2"/>
</Drinks>
<SoftDrinks id="drink-1" SOAP-ENC:arrayType="xsd:string[3]">
  <drink>Mountain Dew</drink>
  <drink>Coke</drink>
  <drink>Sprite</drink>
</SoftDrinks>
<Juices id="drink-2" SOAP-ENC:arrayType="xsd:string[3]">
  <drink>Cranberry</drink>
  <drink>Grape</drink>
  <drink>Orange</drink>
</Juices>
```

In the above example, the <Drinks> array contains two other arrays. We are assuming the member arrays will potentially be multi-reference so href tags were used to reference the member arrays, instead of embedding the arrays within the <Drinks> array.

Arrays may be multi-dimensional, which means that more then one size will appear in the arrayType attribute. The following example depicts this:

```
<MultiStrings SOAP-ENC:arrayType="xsd:string[2,3]">
  <item>Row 1, Column1</item>
  <item>Row 1, Column2</item>
  <item>Row 1, Column3</item>
  <item>Row 2, Column1</item>
  <item>Row 2, Column2</item>
  <item>Row 2, Column3</item>
</MultiStrings>
```

In the above example, [2,3] is specified as part of the arrayType attribute. This denotes the array consist of two rows and three columns.

SOAP provides support for partially transmitted arrays, which are used when wanting to transmit part of an array. The SOAP-ENC:offset attribute is used to indicate the zero-origin offset of the first element to be transmitted. If the attribute is omitted, the offset is taken as zero. The following is an example of an array of ten, but only the ninth and tenth elements were transmitted.

```
<ClassList SOAP-ENC:arrayType="xsd:string[10]" SOAP-ENC:offset="[8]">
  <student>Courtney Anderson</student>
  <student>Torri McCray</student>
</ClassList>
```

SOAP allows the position of an element within an array to be specified using the `SOAP-ENC:position` attribute. This type of array is known as a sparse array. The following is an example of a sparse array of ten, but position four and five are the only ones used:

```
<ClassList SOAP-ENC:arrayType="xsd:string[10]">
  <student SOAP-ENC:position="[4]">Courtney Anderson</student>
  <student SOAP-ENC:position="[5]">Torri McCray</student>
</ClassList>
```

SOAP in HTTP

In this section we will discuss how SOAP messages can be transported using the HTTP transport protocol. In practice, this is usually known as binding. In theory, a SOAP message can be bound to any transport protocol, but we will limit our discussion to the HTTP transport protocol since it's defined in the SOAP specification and it's the most widely used. SOAP fits nicely into the HTTP request/response message model. This allows a SOAP request to be transmitted via a HTTP request message and the SOAP response to be transmitted via a HTTP response message.

SOAP HTTP Request

A SOAP HTTP request is a HTTP request that contains a SOAP message. The SOAP message contains a SOAP request (for example, an RPC call). The SOAP HTTP request has to be transmitted using the HTTP POST method. A SOAPAction header field has to be used to indicate the intent of the SOAP HTTP request, which was discussed in the *Security Concerns* section. In the following example a SOAP-HTTP request is shown:

```
POST /rpcrouter HTTP/1.1
Host: 127.0.0.1
Content-Type: text/xml; charset="utf-8"
Content-Length: 559
SOAPAction:

<SOAP-ENV:Envelope
  xmlns:SOAP-ENV="http://schemas.xmlsoap.org/soap/envelope/"
  SOAP-ENV:encodingStyle="http://schemas.xmlsoap.org/soap/encoding/">
  <SOAP-ENV:Header>
    <a:authentication xmlns:a="http://www.wrox.com/soap/authentication"
      SOAP-ENV:mustUnderstand="1">
      <a:username>mlhendri</a:username>
      <a:password>courtney</a:password>
    </a:authentication>
  </SOAP-ENV:Header>
  <SOAP-ENV:Body>
    <cmd:processReboot xmlns:cmd="http://www.wrox.com/soap/cmd">
```

```
      <ip xsi:type="xsd:string">192.168.1.3</ip>
      <delay xsi:type="xsd:int">30000</delay>
   <cmd:processReboot>
 </SOAP-ENV:Body>
</SOAP-ENV:Envelope>
```

SOAP HTTP Response

A SOAP HTTP response is a HTTP response that contains a SOAP message. The SOAP message contains a SOAP response message. The HTTP status codes are used to communicate status information in HTTP. A status code of 2xx indicates that the client's request including the SOAP component was successfully received and understood. The following code snippet depicts this:

```
HTTP/1.1 200 OK
Content-Type: text/xml; charset="utf-8"
Content-Length: 320

<SOAP-ENV:Envelope>
  ...
</SOAP-ENV:Envelope>
```

If a SOAP error occurs while processing the request, the HTTP server must issue an HTTP 500 "Internal Server Error" response, which should also include a response containing a SOAP <Fault> element that indicates the processing error. The following example depicts this:

```
HTTP/1.1 500 Internal Server Error
Content-Type: text/xml; charset="utf-8"
Content-Length: 320

<SOAP-ENV:Envelope
  xmlns:SOAP-ENV="http://schemas.xmlsoap.org/soap/envelope/">
  <SOAP-ENV:Body>
    <SOAP-ENV:Fault>
      <faultcode>Client.Authentication</faultcode>
      <faultstring>The username or password is invalid</faultstring>
    </SOAP-ENV:Fault>
  </SOAP-ENV:Body>
</SOAP-ENV:Envelope>
```

RPC within SOAP

One of the major benefits of using SOAP is the ability to encapsulate RPC calls within the payload of a SOAP message. As mentioned before, a SOAP message can potentially be bound to any transport protocol. However, an RPC call maps naturally to an HTTP request and a RPC response maps naturally to an HTTP response. In order to create a method using HTTP or any other transport protocol the following information is needed:

❑   The request URI of the target object

❑   Header data (optional)

❑   A method name

❑   A method signature (optional)

❑   The parameters to the method

The request URI of the target object is not something handled by SOAP, but should be provided by the transport protocol. If HTTP is used as the transport protocol the request URI is used to indicate the resource that the invocation is being made against. SOAP doesn't put any restrictions on the form of the URI, except that the URI must be valid. The following SOAP message contains a RPC call:

```
POST /rpcrouter HTTP/1.1
Host: 127.0.0.1
Content-Type: text/xml; charset="utf-8"
Content-Length: 559
SOAPAction: "http://www.wrox.com/processReboot"

<SOAP-ENV:Envelope
   xmlns:SOAP-ENV="http://schemas.xmlsoap.org/soap/envelope/"
   SOAP-ENV:encodingStyle="http://schemas.xmlsoap.org/soap/encoding/">
   <SOAP-ENV:Header>
      <a:authentication xmlns:a="http://www.wrox.com/soap/authentication"
        SOAP-ENV:mustUnderstand="1">
         <a:username>mlhendri</a:username>
         <a:password>courtney</a:password>
      </a:authentication>
   </SOAP-ENV:Header>
   <SOAP-ENV:Body>
      <cmd:processReboot xmlns:cmd=http://www.wrox.com/soap/cmd>
         <ip xsi:type="xsd:string">192.168.1.3</ip>
         <delay xsi:type="xsd:int">30000</delay>
      <cmd:processReboot>
   </SOAP-ENV:Body>
</SOAP-ENV:Envelope>
```

In the above example, the /rpcrouter is the request URI, which denotes that the request should be processed by the runtime components that are mapped to it. The header data in this example contains authentication information, which we discussed in an earlier section. The method name is processReboot() and it has two parameters: ip and delay. As stated before, the purpose of the processReboot() method call is to allow remote hosts to be rebooted. The ip parameter contains the IP address of the computer that is being rebooted. The delay parameter is used to specify the amount of time to wait before the remote computer will be rebooted in milliseconds.

The following example contains the RPC response to the RPC request we described above:

```
HTTP/1.1 200 OK
Content-Type: text/xml; charset="utf-8"
Content-Length: 320

<SOAP-ENV:Envelope
   xmlns:SOAP-ENV="http://schemas.xmlsoap.org/soap/envelope/"
   SOAP-ENV:encodingStyle="http://schemas.xmlsoap.org/soap/encoding/">
   <SOAP-ENV:Body>
      <cmd:processRebootResponse
        xmlns:cmd="http://www.wrox.com/soap/cmd">
         <status>1</status>
      <cmd:processRebootResponse>
   </SOAP-ENV:Body>
</SOAP-ENV:Envelope>
```

In the above example, the response to the `processReboot` RPC call returned a 1, which indicates that the computer was rebooted successfully.

Summary

Within this chapter we explored the SOAP protocol. We started out with defining SOAP and discussing its history and origins. The chapter is based on SOAP 1.1, but we did briefly review the current version of SOAP, which is 1.2. As well as comparing and contrasting the benefits and disadvantages of using SOAP, we also discussed three SOAP architecture patterns that could be applied to new or existing applications. Finally, we discussed the underpinning of the SOAP protocol in more detail.

In the next chapter we will discuss how to use Apache SOAP to develop SOAP-aware applications.

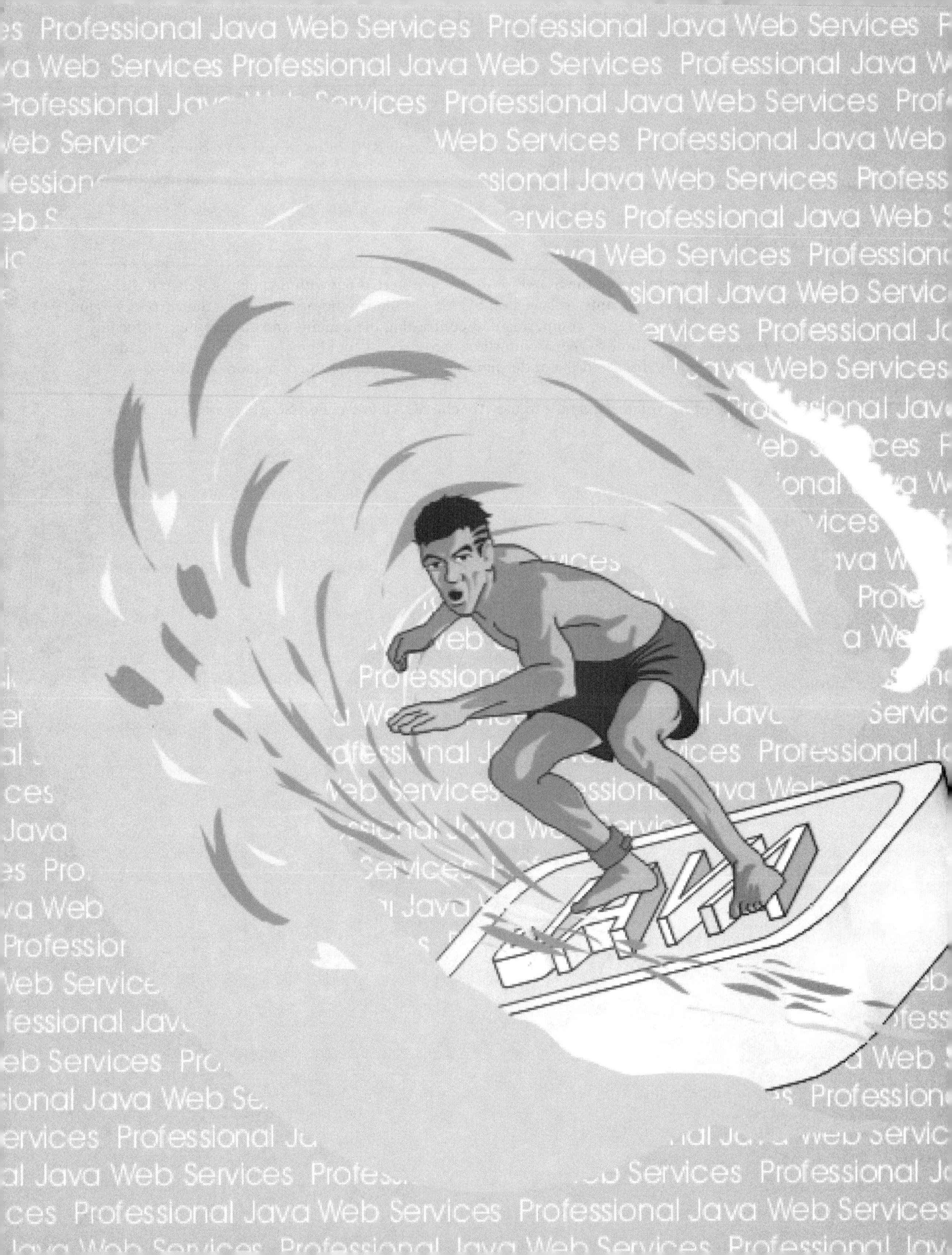
Professional Java Web Services

Apache SOAP 2.2

Introduction and What We Will Learn

In the previous chapter we discussed the internals of the SOAP 1.1 specification. In this chapter we will discuss Apache SOAP 2.2, an open source Java implementation of the SOAP 1.1 and SOAP with Attachments specifications. We will cover in this chapter:

- ❑ The history of the Apache SOAP project

- ❑ The future of Apache SOAP

- ❑ Installing Apache SOAP

- ❑ Developing a SOAP service using the facilities provided by Apache SOAP

- ❑ Deploying a SOAP service onto the Apache SOAP run-time environment

- ❑ Developing a SOAP client using the Apache SOAP client-side API

- ❑ Debugging SOAP clients and services

In order to illustrate the concepts discussed in this chapter we will use an example application called the "Job Resumé Repository System", which allows users to submit and retrieve their resumé.

History of Apache SOAP

Apache SOAP was originally developed by IBM and was known as IBM-SOAP. It was donated to the Apache Software Foundation's Apache XML initiative. What were the market forces that prompted IBM to take this action? The Microsoft SOAP toolkit was going very strong and IBM realized that it would be in the best interest of IBM-SOAP to provide it as an open source implementation for the Java Developer community. In June 2000, the first release of Apache SOAP was created based on the IBM-SOAP code base. The version number was 1.2.

The Apache Software Foundation is a nonprofit organization best known for facilitating the development of the most widely used web server on the Internet called the Apache Web Server. The organization has a number of projects with majority of the projects being focused on creating API's and applications for the development of web-based applications. The Apache XML Project is one of those projects. The goals of the project consists of:

❑ Providing commercial-quality standards-based XML solutions that are developed using the opensource programming paradigm.

❑ Providing feedback to standards bodies (for example, IETF and W3C) from an implementation perspective.

The Apache XML Project currently consists of seven sub-projects, each focused on a different aspect of XML, including a parser, a stylesheet processor, a web-publishing framework, and an implementation of the formatting objects specifications, among others.

More information about the Apache XML Project can be found at its web site, which is located at http://xml.apache.org.

Future of Apache SOAP

The next release of Apache SOAP will be called Axis. Axis is the third generation of the Apache SOAP API, IBM-SOAP being the first, Apache SOAP the second, and Axis the third. Axis is a total rewrite. One of the major changes to the architecture consists of using a Simple API for XML (SAX) parser to manipulate XML data streams internally instead of a Document Object Model (DOM) parser, which is used by Apache SOAP. This will improve performance since SAX parsers normally have reduced memory overhead compared to DOM parsers. The goals of the release are to create a SOAP implementation that is more modular, flexible, and provides higher-performance compared to Apache SOAP.

Apache SOAP can be used as a client to a SOAP server. It requires return values from RPC method calls to have explicit type information. The following SOAP message depicts this:

```
<SOAP-ENV:Envelope xmlns:xsd="http://www.w3.org/2001/XMLSchema"
                   xmlns:SOAP-ENV="http://schemas.xmlsoap.org/soap/envelope/"
                   xmlns:xsi="http://www.w3.org/2001/XMLSchema-instance">
  <SOAP-ENV:Body>
    <ns1:getMessageResponse xmlns:ns1="http://www.wrox.com/helloworld">
      <return xsi:type="xsd:string">Hello World!</return>
    </ns1:getMessageResponse>
  </SOAP-ENV:Body>
</SOAP-ENV:Envelope>
```

Notice that type information is declared using an attribute – this attribute is a XML schema declaration, which is used by Apache SOAP to figure out how to interpret the return values. In this case, the values will be interpreted as a Java `String` object. On the other hand, some SOAP toolkits such as the Microsoft SOAP toolkit don't provide this information (per the SOAP 1.1 specification they are not required to). The following SOAP message depicts this:

```
<SOAP-ENV:Envelope xmlns:xsd="http://www.w3.org/2001/XMLSchema"
                   xmlns:SOAP-ENV="http://schemas.xmlsoap.org/soap/envelope/"
                   xmlns:xsi="http://www.w3.org/2001/XMLSchema-instance">
  <SOAP-ENV:Body>
    <ns1:getMessageResponse xmlns:ns1="http://www.wrox.com/helloworld">
      <return>Hello World!</return>
    </ns1:getMessageResponse>
  </SOAP-ENV:Body>
</SOAP-ENV:Envelope>
```

Notice that there's no type information in the above message, so how do we know how to interpret the return value? We don't! Hence, this causes an interoperability issue. Apache SOAP has some workarounds to handle this situation, but Axis improves upon this by providing a mechanism for defining a default return type if the SOAP server doesn't return one.

Axis also provides support for more current standards such as WSDL. A WSDL document that describes a deployed service can be automatically generated by simply appending a "?WSDL" to the end of the URL that's defined as the endpoint for the service. For example, the WSDL document for a HelloWorld web service could be generated using the following URL: http://localhost:8080/axis/services/HelloWorld?wsdl. A WSDL to Java tool is also provided. This tool has the ability to create stubs. A stub is a Java class that has the same interface as a remote web service. It allows the service to be invoked exactly as if it were a local object.

More information on AXIS is available in Chapter 14. The third alpha release of Axis is available at http://xml.apache.org/axis/dist/alpha3/. Information about the project can be found at http://xml.apache.org/axis/.

Installing Apache SOAP

As mentioned before, Apache SOAP is an open source Java implementation of the SOAP 1.1 and SOAP with Attachments Specifications. It contains a client-side API for accessing SOAP services and facilities for implementing SOAP services. In order to implement SOAP services Apache SOAP has to be hosted within a servlet container such as Jakarta Tomcat (usually referred to as just Tomcat). Tomcat is an open source servlet engine that serves as the official Reference Implementation of the Java Servlet and Java Server Pages technologies. More information about Jakarta Tomcat can be found at http://jakarta.apache.org/tomcat/.

In order to install and configure Apache SOAP we need to do the following:

❑ Download and Unpack Tomcat

❑ Download and Unpack Apache SOAP Library

❑ Configure Tomcat for Apache SOAP

❑ Set up the CLASSPATH

❑ Testing the Configuration

Download and Unpack Tomcat 3.2.x

We can obtain a Tomcat 3.2.x from http://jakarta.apache.org/tomcat. After downloading, we need to unpack the distribution into a directory. If we unpack the files into C:\jakarta-tomcat-3.2.x we can then set the system variable TOMCAT_HOME, to this:

```
SET TOMCAT_HOME=C:\jakarta-tomcat-3.2.x
```

We will refer to TOMCAT_HOME for the rest of this chapter.

Download and Unpack Apache SOAP Library

Next, we can need to obtain Apache SOAP, which is available from http:/xml.apache.com/soap. After downloading, we need to unpack the distribution into a directory. If we unpack the files into C:\soap-2_2 we can then set the system variable SOAP_HOME to this as follows:

```
SET SOAP_HOME=C:\soap-2_2
```

We will refer to SOAP_HOME for the rest of this chapter.

Configure Tomcat for Apache SOAP

The Apache SOAP library must be made available from within Tomcat in order to develop Apache SOAP services or web-based Apache SOAP clients, or use the web based administration tool that's provided. In order to do this we must do the following:

❑   Copy soap.jar from <SOAP_HOME>\lib to %TOMCAT_HOME%\lib

❑   Copy soap.war from <SOAP_HOME>\lib to %TOMCAT_HOME%\webapps

The soap.jar file contains classes that implement the client-side API for developing SOAP clients and classes that allow services to be implemented. We will refer to the later as the Apache SOAP run-time environment. The soap.war file contains the Apache SOAP web-based administration tool that allows us to administer. When Tomcat is started the soap.war file will be extracted into a directory called soap in the %TOMCAT_HOME%\webapps\ directory.

Setup up the CLASSPATH

In order to develop Apache SOAP clients, execute Apache SOAP clients, and utilize tools that come with Apache SOAP from outside Tomcat (that is, console or GUI-based Java applications) we have to augment the CLASSPATH environmental variable to contain the following:

❑   %SOAP_HOME%\lib\soap.jar

❑   %TOMCAT_HOME%\lib\xerces.jar

❑   %TOMCAT_HOME%\lib\mail.jar

❑   %TOMCAT_HOME%\lib\activation.jar

Assuming that you installed Tomcat and Apache SOAP in the directories that we specified above your CLASSPATH variable should contain the following values:

> C:\soap-2_2\lib\soap.jar;C:\jakarta-tomcat-3.2.3\lib\xerces.jar;
> C:\jakarta-tomcat-3.2.3\lib\mail.jar;
> C:\jakarta-tomcat-3.2.3\lib\activation.jar

Testing the Configuration

Testing the Server-Side Configuration

In order to test the server-side configuration we first need to start Tomcat, by executing startup.bat, located in the %TOMCAT_HOME%\bin directory. The command line to start Tomcat looks like this:

Next, open a web browser and point it to the following URL:
http://localhost:8080/soap/servlet/rpcrouter. The following message should be displayed:

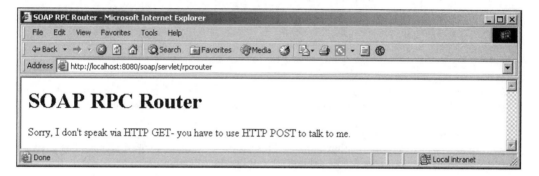

If the above message is not displayed then check your configuration to ensure that it is configured properly. This URL maps to the following servlet:
org.apache.soap.server.http.RPCRouterServlet. This servlet is responsible for processing SOAP messages that contain RPC method calls and dispatching them for processing. We will refer to this URL as Apache SOAP runtime endpoint for the rest of this chapter.

Testing the Client-Side Configuration

To ensure that the client-slide configuration is setup properly we can run the following command:

> ```
> > java org.apache.soap.server.ServiceManagerClient
> http://localhost:8080/soap/servlet/rpcrouter list
> ```

If it succeeds the output will only contain Deployed Services:. This command is used to list the services that are registered. In our case, no services will be registered since we just installed Apache SOAP. If you get any other output, then you need to check your configuration.

Deploying and Running a "Hello World" Service

Now that we have Apache SOAP installed and configured let's deploy and run a simple service called "Hello World". There are two ways a service can be deployed: via the Apache SOAP command line tool or via the web-based administration tool. We are going to discuss both methods within this section. We will also discuss how to use an Apache SOAP client to run the service. We will not dive into the details of implementing the service or the client, but will defer this discussion until the *Developing SOAP Services* and *Developing SOAP Clients* sections, respectively.

HelloWorld.java

The Java class that will implement the "Hello World" service is located in `HelloWorld.java`, which is listed below:

```
package com.wrox.helloworld.service;

public class HelloWorld {

  String getMessage() {
    return "Hello World!";
  }
}
```

Notice that this class only has one method, `getMessage()`. We will expose this method through the "Hello World" service. This means that SOAP clients will be able to invoke this method.

In order to utilize the `HelloWorld` class it must be accessible from the Apache SOAP run-time environment, which is hosted within Tomcat. This means that the `HelloWorld` class has to be accessible from Tomcat. This can be achieved by doing the following:

1. Create a JAR file called `helloworld.jar` with the contents containing the `com.wrox.helloworld.service.HelloWorld` class.

2. Copy the `helloworld.jar` file to `<TOMCAT_HOME>\lib\`

Deploying Via the Command Line

In order for the `getMessage()` method to be exposed a deployment descriptor for the service has to be created and registered with the Apache SOAP run-time environment. In this section we discuss the details of deployment descriptors and how to register the service using the Apache SOAP command line tool.

Deployment Descriptors

A deployment descriptor is an XML document that provides the details of the service to the Apache SOAP run-time environment. The format of a deployment descriptor depends on the type of **code artifact**. The term code artifact is usually used to refer to a software component that contains logic that can be invoked via methods or functions. A code artifact can be written in any language. Apache SOAP ships with support for the following code artifacts:

❏   Standard Java classes

❏   Enterprise Java Beans (EJB)

❏   Bean Scripting Framework (BSF)-supported script

Support for standard Java classes includes support for JavaBeans. Support for EJBs includes stateless session beans, stateful session beans, and entity beans. The BSF framework can be used to allow SOAP services to be written in any BSF-supported scripting language such as Rhino. Rhino is an opensource implementation of JavaScript that supports the BSF framework. Rhino is written completely in Java and is maintained by mozilla.org. More information about BSF and Rhino can be located at http://oss.software.ibm.com/developerworks/projects/bsf/ and http://www.mozilla.org/rhino/.

Apache SOAP defines a different deployment descriptor for each one the aforementioned code artifacts. We will discuss the deployment descriptor for a standard Java class. This is best done using an example, so we will discuss the deployment descriptor for the "Hello World" service, which is implemented as a standard Java class. The deployment descriptor for the "Hello World" service is located in a file called HelloWorldDD.xml. It's listed below:

```xml
<?xml version="1.0"?>
<isd:service xmlns:isd="http://xml.apache.org/xml-soap/deployment"
             id="urn:HelloWorldService">
  <isd:provider type="java"
                scope="Application"
                methods="getMessage">
  <isd:java class="com.wrox.helloworld.service.HelloWorld" static="false"/>
  </isd:provider>
  <isd:faultListener>org.apache.soap.server.DOMFaultListener</isd:faultListener>
</isd:service>
```

In order to understand this, we will go through each element to see how it is used.

Service Element

All elements within the deployment descriptor are prefixed with isd as a name identifier, which is associated with the http://xml.apache.org/xml-soap/deployment namespace. The service element is the root element.

```xml
<isd:service xmlns:isd="http://xml.apache.org/xml-soap/deployment"
                id="urn:HelloWorldService">

  ...
</isd:service>
```

All other elements are contained within the service element. The service element contains an id attribute, an optional type, and an optional checkMustUnderstands attribute. The id attribute is used to specify the name of the service. SOAP clients use the value of the id attribute to route requests to the service. In our case, we used the Uniform Resource Name (URN) syntax to specify the name of the service as "urn:HelloWorldService". However, this isn't required; the value of the id attribute can have any value and any format as long as the SOAP client uses the same value to refer to the service. With that being said, SOAP clients can specify "urn:HelloWorldService" for requests to be forwarded to the "Hello World" service.

The optional type attribute has a value of "message" if a service is message-oriented instead of RPC-based. In a message-oriented service, the service implementation is responsible for processing the contents of the SOAP Envelope. Therefore, it has full control of how the SOAP Envelope should be processed. So, any XML document may be passed as part of the envelope body. Also, a message-oriented service is responsible for sending responses back to a SOAP client. For example, if the message-oriented service is participating in a request-response protocol such as HTTP, then it is responsible for generating the appropriate response when a request is received. On the other hand, an RPC-based service doesn't have this type of granular control. When a SOAP message is received from a RPC-based service it's the responsibility of the Apache SOAP run-time environment to do the following: process the SOAP envelope, dispatch the RPC method call request to the service implementation class, and forward the response back to the SOAP client.

The optional checkMustUnderstands attribute can have a value of "true" or "false" depending upon whether or not we want the server to throw a fault if there are SOAP headers in a SOAP request message that have the MustUnderstand attribute set to "true". More information about the MustUnderstand attribute is located in the *The Protocol* section of Chapter 2.

Provider Element

The provider element contains attributes and sub-elements that specify the details of the code artifact that's implementing the service. The provider element for the "Hello World" service deployment descriptor is below:

```
<isd:provider type="java"
              scope="Application"
              methods="getMessage">
  <isd:java class="com.wrox.helloworld.service.HelloWorld" static="false"/>
</isd:provider>
```

The type attribute tells the Apache SOAP run-time environment which provider should be used to handle the code artifact. The type attribute is java for the above provider element since the code artifact for the "Hello World" service is a standard Java class. If the code artifact were an Enterprise JavaBean (EJB) then the value would be either "org.apache.soap.providers.StatelessEJBProvider", "org.apache.soap.providers.StatefulEJBProvider", or "org.apache.soap.providers.EntityEJBProvider", depending on whether or not the implementation is a stateless session bean, a stateful session bean, or an entity bean, respectively. If the code artifact were a BSF-supported script then the value would be "script".

The scope attribute indicates the lifetime of the instantiation of the implementing class. The attribute can contain three different values. The values are listed in the table below:

Value	Meaning
Request	Indicates that the object will be removed from memory after this request has completed
Session	Indicates that the object will last for the current lifetime of the HTTP session (Assuming that HTTP is used as the transport protocol)
Application	Indicates that the object will last until the servlet that is servicing the requests is terminated.

Note that the above values are the same as the scope options that are available when using JavaBeans with JavaServer Pages.

The methods attribute contains a space-separated list of methods we want to expose through the service. We want to expose the getMessage() method so it is specified as the value of the method attribute. A related attribute, contained within the java sub-element called class, should contain the fully qualified name of the class (that is, packagename.classname) that provides the methods being exposed.

The static attribute has a value of true or false depending upon whether or not the methods that are being exposed are static or not. In the above deployment descriptor, the static attribute has a value of "false" since the getMessage() method isn't defined as static.

Fault Listener Element

As discussed in the previous chapter, the SOAP specification defines the SOAP Fault element as a mechanism for reporting errors that occur when processing SOAP messages. Errors can arise for a number of reasons, for example, errors within the service implementation, malformed SOAP client request, network transmission problems, or a host of other problems. The Apache SOAP run-time will attempt to capture an error state and then construct a SOAP Fault message containing a base set of information about the error that occurred. In some cases it's useful to augment the fault information for a particular service or to perform one or more additional tasks when an error state arises. This type of fault handling mechanism is provided by Apache SOAP through the use of a pluggable fault handling mechanism into which one or more fault listeners may be registered to process faults. The pluggable fault handling mechanism is based on the event/listener model, which means that the fault listener remains idle until an event occurs.

The faultListener element is used to specify the fault listener that should be used with a service. The value has to be the fully qualified name of a class that implements the SOAPFaultListener interface. Apache SOAP provides two basic fault handlers; they are listed below:

❑ org.apache.soap.server.DOMFaultListener

❑ org.apache.soap.server.ExceptionFaultListner

The `org.apache.soap.server.DOMFaultListener` fault handler is usually used because it adds a DOM element representing the root exception that occurred, whereas the `org.apache.soap.server.ExceptionFaultListner` fault handler wraps the root exception in a parameter. Below is how the `faultListener` attribute would look with `org.apache.soap.server.DOMFaultListener` as the value:

```
<isd:faultListener>org.apache.soap.server.DOMFaultListener</isd:faultListener>
```

Registering the Service

After creating a deployment descriptor for the service, it has to be registered with the SOAP run-time environment. This is done through the use of the `ServiceManagerClient` class. The "Hello World" service can be registered by entering the following command:

```
> java org.apache.soap.server.ServiceManagerClient
http://localhost:8080/soap/servlet/rpcrouter deploy HelloWorldDD.xml
```

The first parameter specifies the URL of the Apache SOAP RPC router, which is responsible for routing client requests to the requested service. The second parameter specifies the operation that the client should do. The deploy operation consists of registering the service using the deployment information located in a file specified by the third parameter. In this case, the file is called `HelloWorldDD.xml` and it contains the deployment descriptor for the "Hello World" Service.

To see if the service was actually registered we ask the Apache SOAP runtime to provide us with a list registered services. This can be done using the following command line:

```
> java org.apache.soap.server.ServiceManagerClient
http://localhost:8080/soap/servlet/rpcrouter list
```

The first parameter is the same, but the operation is `list` instead of `deploy`. The output will be shown when running the above commands:

```
C:\javawebservices\Ch03\helloworld>java org.apache.soap.server.ServiceManagerClient
http://localhost:8080/soap/servlet/rpcrouter deploy HelloWorldDD.xml

C:\javawebservices\Ch03\helloworld>java org.apache.soap.server.ServiceManagerClient
http://localhost:8080/soap/servlet/rpcrouter list
Deployed Services:
     urn:HelloWorldService

C:\javawebservices\Ch03\helloworld>
```

The `ServiceManagerClient` can also be used to un-register a service. "Hello World" service can be un-registered by typing this:

```
> java org.apache.soap.server.ServiceManagerClient
http://localhost:8080/soap/servlet/rpcrouter undeploy "urn:HelloWorldService"
```

Notice that the operation is undeploy instead of deploy and that the third parameter is the name of the service defined by the id attribute of the service element within the deployment descriptor.

It's also worth mentioning that the ServiceManagerClient can be used for querying the attributes of a service. The following command can be used to query the attributes of the "Hello World" service:

```
> java org.apache.soap.server.ServiceManagerClient
  http://localhost:8080/soap/servlet/rpcrouter query "urn:HelloWorldService"
```

The parameters are the same as the undeploy version of the command, except that the undeploy operation is replaced by query. The following output will appear from running the above command:

```
C:\javawebservices\Ch03helloworld>java org.apache.soap.server.ServiceManagerClient
http://localhost:8080/soap/servlet/rpcrouter query "urn:HelloWorldService"
<isd:service xmlns:isd=http://xml.apache.org/xml-soap/deployment" id="urn:WorldService"
checkMustUnderstands="false">
  <isd:provider type="java" scope="Application" methods="getMessage">
    <isd:java class="com.wrox.helloworld.service.HelloWorld" static="false">
  </isd:provider>
  <isd:faultListener>org.apache.soap.server.DOMFaultListener</isd:faultListener>
</isd:service>

C:\javawebservices\Ch03helloworld>
```

Notice that the output from this command is just the contents of the deployment descriptor that we provided when we initially deployed the service.

It's worth noting, that by default, anyone can use the ServiceManagerClient to deploy a service, undeploy a service, list registered services, and query the attributes of a service. However, it does contain support for HTTP Basic Authentication. In order to enable security you would have to modify the web.xml file that's located in <TOMCAT_HOME>\webapps\soap\WEB-INF to secure the http://localhost:8080/soap/servlet/rpcrouter endpoint and include the -auth switch when executing the ServiceManagerClient. For example, if security were enabled the following command line would have to be specified in order to deploy the "Hello World" service:

```
> java org.apache.soap.server.ServiceManagerClient -auth deployer:password
  http://localhost:8080/soap/servlet/rpcrouter deploy HelloWorldDD.xml
```

The value that follows the -auth switch has a format of username:password. The value should consist of a valid username and password that has permissions to the http://localhost:8080/soap/servlet/rpcrouter endpoint. The undeploy, list, and query operations all work in a similar fashion.

Deploying via the Web-Based Administration Tool

An alternative to deploying a service via the command line is to deploy using the web-based administration tool that is provided by the Apache SOAP toolkit. We installed the tool when we installed Apache SOAP in the *Installing Apache SOAP* section. The admin tool doesn't use the deployment descriptor directly to register the service, but it uses the same data specified in the deployment descriptor. So, the deployment descriptor should be created even if the service is not going to be registered via the command line. It will be helpful in registering the service via the web-based tool. To access the administration tool point a browser to http://localhost:8080/soap/admin/index.html. The following screen will be shown:

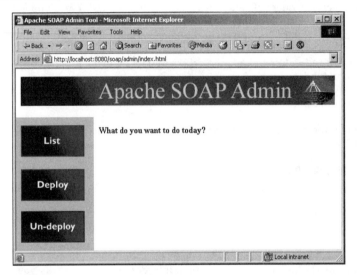

We can deploy the "Hello World" service by clicking the Deploy button. The following screen will be displayed:

Populate the form by entering values for fields (properties) that correspond with fields in the deployment descriptor. A list of the fields and their values are in the following table:

ID	urn:HelloWorldService
Scope	Application
Methods	getMessage
Provider Type	Java
Provider Class	com.wrox.helloworld.service.HelloWorld
Static	No
Default Mapping Registry Class	org.apache.soap.server.DOMFaultListener

Click Deploy at the bottom of the page to register the service. Once the service is registered it can be unregistered by clicking Un-deploy. A list of registered services will be displayed. To delete a service, click on its name.

Running the Service

Now that the "Hello World" service is deployed we will discuss a console-based Java application that uses the Apache SOAP client-side API for accessing the service. The name of the application is "HelloWorldClient". Running the application in a command prompt will give you:

```
> java -cp .;%CLASSPATH%; HelloWorldClient
Hello World!
```

Note that the service could also be accessed using other toolkits such as the Microsoft SOAP toolkit. This is not always a straightforward task because there are some interoperability issues that we may encounter when using a SOAP toolkit other than Apache SOAP to access an Apache SOAP service. As discussed in the *Future of Apache SOAP* section, this type of issues are being addressed by the next generation of Apache SOAP called Axis.

HelloWorldClient.java

In this section we will discuss the HelloWorldClient application. We aren't going to dive into the details at this moment – we will defer this discussion until the *Developing SOAP Clients* section. However, we touch on some key points within the application. The source-code for the entire application is listed overleaf:

```java
import org.apache.soap.Constants;
import java.net.URL;
import org.apache.soap.Fault;
import org.apache.soap.rpc.Call;
import org.apache.soap.rpc.Response;
import org.apache.soap.rpc.Parameter;

public class HelloWorldClient {

  static String DEFAULT_ENDPOINT = "http://localhost:8080/soap/servlet/rpcrouter";

  public static void main (String args[]) throws Exception {

    String endPoint = DEFAULT_ENDPOINT;

    //Process Arguments
    if (args.length == 1) {
      endPoint = args[0];
    } else if (args.length > 1) {
      System.out.println("java HelloWorldClient [endpoint]");
    }

    // Build the SOAP RPC request message using the Call object
    Call call = new Call ();
    call.setTargetObjectURI ("urn:HelloWorldService");
    call.setMethodName ("getMessage");
    call.setEncodingStyleURI(Constants.NS_URI_SOAP_ENC);

    // Create a URL object, which represents the endpoint
    URL url = new URL(endPoint);

    // Send the SOAP RPC request message using invoke() method
    Response resp = call.invoke (url, "");

    // Check the response.
    if (resp.generatedFault ()) {                    // Error Occured
      Fault fault = resp.getFault ();
      System.out.println ("The Following Error Occured: ");
      System.out.println ("  Fault Code   = " + fault.getFaultCode ());
      System.out.println ("  Fault String = " + fault.getFaultString ());
    } else {                                         // Completed Successfully
      Parameter result = resp.getReturnValue ();
      System.out.println (result.getValue ());
    }
  }
}
```

Let's look at two Apache SOAP API's that are used in the application: `Call` and `Response`. The `Call` object is responsible for setting up the details of the request:

```
// Build the SOAP RPC request message using the Call object
Call call = new Call();
call.setTargetObjectURI("urn:HelloWorldService");
call.setMethodName("getMessage");
call.setEncodingStyleURI(Constants.NS_URI_SOAP_ENC);
```

The above code snippet builds a SOAP request message that specifies that the RPC method call request should be routed to the "`HelloWorld`" service and that the `getMessage()` method should be invoked.

The `Call.invoke()` method sends the request to the SOAP server. The following code snippet depicts this:

```
// Create a URL object, which represents the endpoint
URL url = new URL(endPoint);

// Send the SOAP RPC request message using invoke() method
Response resp = call.invoke(url, "");
```

In the above code snippet a `java.net.URL` object is constructed from the string representation of the endpoint for the Apache SOAP runtime. If the user doesn't provide a different endpoint as a parameter then the endpoint will be `http://localhost:8080/soap/servlet/rpcrouter`. The return value is a `Response` object, which contains the response from the server.

The following code snippet checks the response received back from the server and displays a SOAP Fault message if an error occurred. Otherwise, it displays the value returned by the `getMessage()` method:

```
// Check the response.
if (resp.generatedFault ()) { // Error Occured
  Fault fault = resp.getFault ();
  System.out.println ("The Following Error Occured: ");
  System.out.println ("  Fault Code   = " + fault.getFaultCode ());
  System.out.println ("  Fault String = " + fault.getFaultString ());
} else {                      // Completed Successfully
  Parameter result = resp.getReturnValue ();
  System.out.println (result.getValue ());
}
```

The SOAP request message generated by the `HelloWorldClient` application is below:

```
POST /soap/servlet/rpcrouter HTTP/1.0
Host: localhost
Content-Type: text/xml; charset=utf-8
Content-Length: 414
SOAPAction: ""

<?xml version='1.0' encoding='UTF-8'?>
<SOAP-ENV:Envelope xmlns:SOAP-ENV="http://schemas.xmlsoap.org/soap/envelope/"
```

```
                    xmlns:xsi=http://www.w3.org/1999/XMLSchema-instance
                    xmlns:xsd="http://www.w3.org/1999/XMLSchema">
    <SOAP-ENV:Body>
      <ns1:getMessage xmlns:ns1="urn:HelloWorldService"
          SOAP-ENV:encodingStyle="http://schemas.xmlsoap.org/soap/encoding/">
      </ns1:getMessage>
    </SOAP-ENV:Body>
  </SOAP-ENV:Envelope>
```

The SOAP response message sent back to the application is below:

```
HTTP/1.1 200 OK
Content-Type: text/xml; charset=utf-8
Content-Length: 485
Date: Wed, 19 Dec 2001 04:10:28 GMT
Server: Apache Tomcat/4.0.1 (HTTP/1.1 Connector)
Set-Cookie: JSESSIONID=D712520676C524504110A4C5D6E672E9;Path=/soap

<?xml version='1.0' encoding='UTF-8'?>
<SOAP-ENV:Envelope xmlns:SOAP-ENV="http://schemas.xmlsoap.org/soap/envelope/"
                   xmlns:xsi="http://www.w3.org/1999/XMLSchema-instance"
                   xmlns:xsd="http://www.w3.org/1999/XMLSchema">
  <SOAP-ENV:Body>
    <ns1:getMessageResponse xmlns:ns1="urn:HelloWorldService"
        SOAP-ENV:encodingStyle="http://schemas.xmlsoap.org/soap/encoding/">
    <return xsi:type="xsd:string">Hello World!</return>
  </ns1:getMessageResponse>
  </SOAP-ENV:Body>
</SOAP-ENV:Envelope>
```

Job Resumé Repository Service

In the previous section we discussed how to deploy and run a "Hello World" service. In upcoming sections we will dive into the details of how to develop a SOAP service and SOAP client using the Apache SOAP toolkit. We are going to use a more complex example to do this. The example will be based on a fictional staffing company that desired to create a "Job Resumé Repository Service" that allows resumés to be submitted (for the purpose of storing) and retrieved. In this section we will discuss:

❑   The motivation for developing this application

❑   How different components of the application interact by discussing the sequence diagrams for submitting and retrieving a resumé

❑   Assumptions made when this service was developed

❑   Configuring the environment so that service can be run

The Motivation

The motivation behind the development of this service was that the company currently had numerous applications that had the ability of submitting resumés to and retrieving resumés from its their database. Some applications were client-server and others were web-based. The majority of the web-based applications were accessible via their intranet and others were being accessed via the Internet. The goal of the staffing company was to remove the redundant functionality from all of its applications and only use the "Job Resumé Repository Service" to handle the submitting and retrieving of resumes. It also wanted the service to be utilized by other staffing companies across the Internet, which is easily achievable since SOAP can be transported using HTTP.

Sequence Diagrams

Instead of using a command-line SOAP client to access the service like the one we used in the "Hello World" service we developed a web-based SOAP client. A high-level sequence diagram for submitting a resumé and retrieving a resume is shown below:

Submit Resumé Sequence Diagram

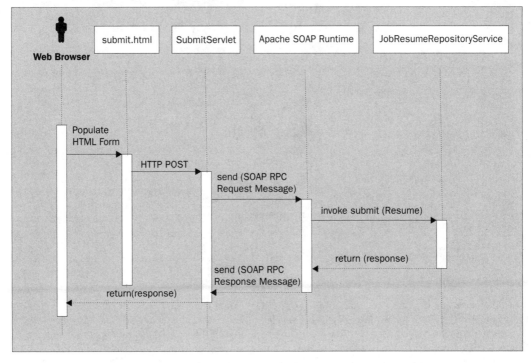

In the above sequence diagram an end user populates an HTML form with the contents of a resumé. Once the resumé is submitted, it is sent to a servlet called SubmitServlet. First, the SubmitServlet takes the form variables and creates a Resume object to represent the contents that were entered on the form. Secondly, the Apache SOAP client API is used to create and send a SOAP RPC request message that specifies that the submit method of the Job Resumé Repository Service should be invoked with the Resume object as the parameter. When this message is received by the Apache SOAP runtime the RPC request is forward to the JobResumeRepositoryService class, which actually implements the method. After the request is processed the response is sent back to the Apache SOAP runtime. The return value is then packaged in a SOAP RPC response message and sent back to the SubmitServlet. The SubmitServlet generates some HTML based on the return value and sends it back to the web browser.

Retrieve Resumé Sequence Diagram

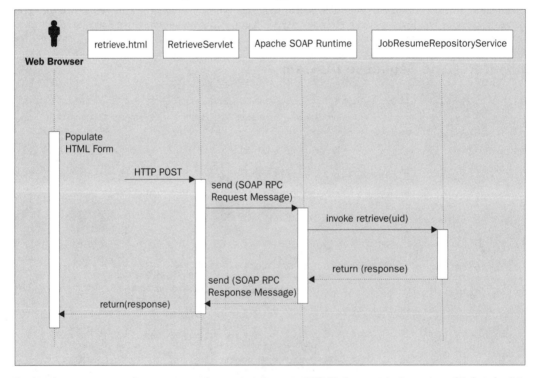

In the above sequence diagram an end user populates an HTML form with the unique ID (uid) of the resumé to retrieve. The request is sent to a servlet called RetrieveServlet. The RetreiveServlet uses the Apache SOAP client API to create and send a SOAP RPC request message that specifies that the retrieve method of the Job Resumé Repository Service should be invoked with the uid as the parameter. When this message is received by the Apache SOAP runtime the RPC request is forwarded to the JobResumeRepositoryService class, which actually implements the retrieve() method. After the request is processed the response is sent back to the Apache SOAP runtime. The return value is a Resume object if the uid was valid, otherwise the value is null. The Resume object is packaged in a SOAP RPC response message and sent back to the RetreiveServlet. If the return value is not null then the RetrieveServlet generates an HTML page that represents the resumé and sends it back to the web browser.

Assumptions

In order to concentrate on aspects of Apache SOAP there is minimal error checking. Likewise, security mechanisms that would normally be needed for such a service will not be considered. Furthermore, resumés are stored in memory instead of a relational or object-oriented database.

Configuring the Service and Client

In this section we will discuss how to configure the environment so that we can run the Job Resumé Repository Service. This discussion is based on the assumption that the steps in the *Installing Apache SOAP* section were followed.

The Service

The class that implements the Job Resumé Repository Service is located in `jobresumerepositoryservice.jar`. The contents of the JAR is below:

```
META-INF/MANIFEST.MF
com/wrox/jobresume/service/JobResumeRepositoryService.class
```

In order to make the service available to the Apache SOAP runtime we need to copy the `jobresumerepositoryservice.jar` to `%TOMCAT_HOME%\ \WEB-INF\lib\`.

The Web-Based Client

The files for the web-based client are located in `jobresumerepositoryclient.war`. The contents of the WAR file is below:

```
META-INF/MANIFEST.MF
WEB-INF/web.xml
WEB-INF/classes/com/wrox/jobresume/client/submit/SubmitServlet.class
                                         /retrieve/RetrieveServlet.class

index.html
wroxlogo.gif
retrieve.html
submit.html
```

In order to execute the client we have to copy the `jobresumerepositoryclient.war` to `%TOMCAT_HOME%\webapps\`.

The Resumé Class

The `Resume` class is used by both the service and the client, so it is packaged in its own JAR called `jobresumerepositorycommon.jar`. The contents of the JAR file is below:

```
META-INF/MANIFEST.MF
com/wrox/jobresume/common/Resume.class
```

In order for the service and client to use the `Resume.class` we have to copy the `jobresumerepositorycommon.jar` to `%TOMCAT_HOME%\\lib`.

Registering the Service

In this section we will discuss how to register the Job Resumé Repository Service using the command-line tool or the web-based tool.

Command Line

In order to register the service via the command line we need to have a deployment descriptor. The name of the file that has the deployment descriptor for this service is `JobResumeRepositoryDD.xml`. It is listed below:

```xml
<?xml version="1.0"?>
<isd:service xmlns:isd="http://xml.apache.org/xml-soap/deployment"
                  id="urn:JobResumeRepositoryService">
  <isd:provider type="java"
                scope="Application"
                methods="retrieve submit">
    <isd:java class="com.wrox.jobresume.service.JobResumeRepositoryService"
        static="false"/>
  </isd:provider>

  <isd:faultListener>org.apache.soap.server.DOMFaultListener</isd:faultListener>

  <isd:mappings>
    <isd:map encodingStyle="http://schemas.xmlsoap.org/soap/encoding/"
             xmlns:x="urn:jobresume" qname="x:resume"
             javaType="com.wrox.jobresume.common.Resume"
             java2XMLClassName="org.apache.soap.encoding.soapenc.BeanSerializer"
             xml2JavaClassName="org.apache.soap.encoding.soapenc.BeanSerializer"/>
  </isd:mappings>

</isd:service>
```

The command to register the service is:

```
> java org.apache.soap.server.ServiceManagerClient
http://localhost:8080/soap/servlet/rpcrouter deploy JobResuméRepositoryDD.xml
```

If successful, nothing should be output to the screen.

Web-Based Tool

To access the administration tool point a browser to http://localhost:8080/soap/admin/. Click the Deploy button and populate the form using the values in the following table then click Deploy at the bottom of the page.

ID	`urn:JobResumeRepositoryService`
Scope	Application
Methods	retrieve submit
Provider Type	Java
Provider Class	`com.wrox.jobresume.service.JobResumeRepositoryService`
Type Mapping	Encoding Style=SOAP, Namespace URI=`urn:jobresume`, Local Part=`resume`, Java Type=`com.wrox.jobresume.common.Resume`, Java to XML Serializer= `org.apache.soap.encoding.soapenc.BeanSerializer`, XML to Java Serializer= `org.apache.soap.encoding.soapenc.BeanSerializer`
Default Mapping Registry Class	`org.apache.soap.server.DOMFaultListener`

Running the Service

Let's run service to ensure that we set up the service and client correctly. This can be done by restarting the Tomcat engine if it was already running or starting the Tomcat engine if it wasn't started. Point a browser to http://localhost:8080/jobresumérepository, click Retrieve resumé, enter 1000 and click Retreive. If your screen looks like this:

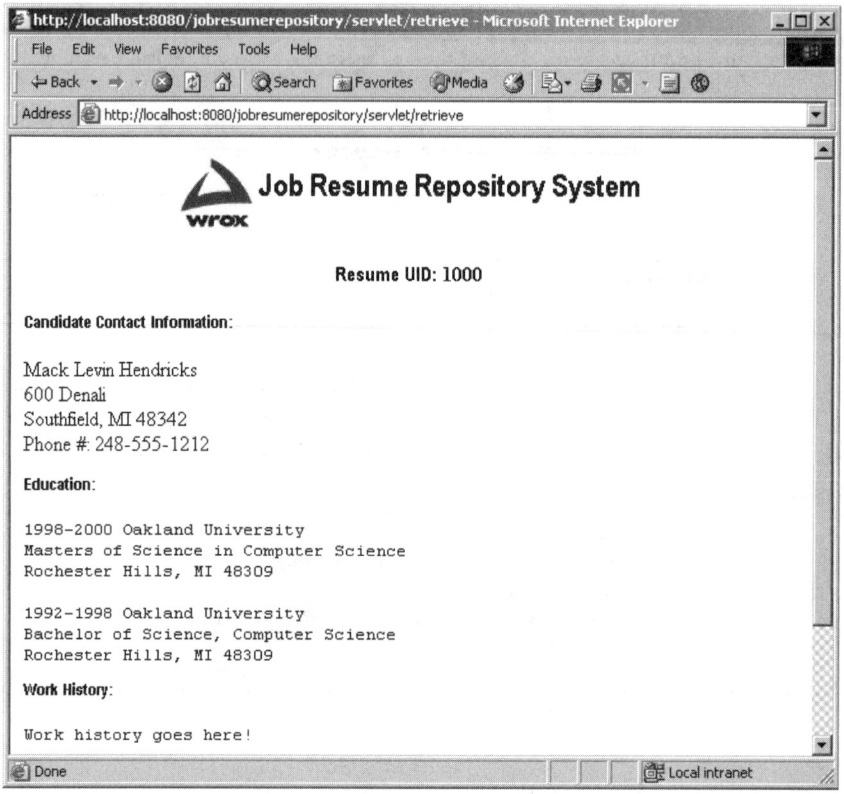

Then you are configured properly. The resumé shown above is the default resumé.

Developing SOAP Services

In this section we will dive into the details of creating a SOAP service. In this section we will discuss:

- Apache SOAP Architecture
- Pluggable Provider Architecture
- Service Implementation Class
- Type Mapping (including serialization)

In order to illustrate some of topics discussed in the chapter we will look at parts of the Job Resumé Repository System that was introduced in the previous section.

Apache SOAP Architecture

The Apache SOAP server-side facilities allow code artifacts to be accessible from SOAP clients without the code artifacts having to be SOAP-aware. This means that no code has to be added to code artifacts to make them work with Apache SOAP. So in essence, the server-side facilities of Apache SOAP act as a bridge between SOAP clients and code artifacts. The following diagram illustrates this:

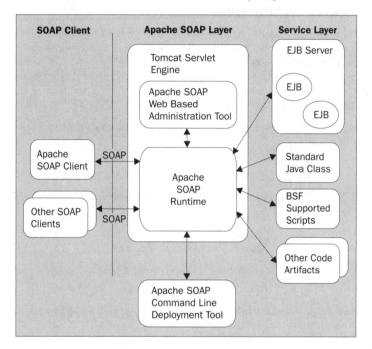

To help explain how this works let's go through the process of accessing a standard Java code artifact:

1. The Apache SOAP run-time environment has to be configured to route requests to a particular code artifact. This is known as service registration or deployment. This is done using the command-line tool or the web-based administration tool that's provided with Apache SOAP. We discussed both methods in the *Deploying and Running a "Hello World" Service* section.

2. An Apache SOAP client or another SOAP 1.1-compliant SOAP client sends an RPC-based SOAP request message to the Apache SOAP runtime. This request contains the name of the service and the name of methods to invoke.

3. The Apache SOAP runtime validates that the service is registered and that the requested methods are marked for exposure to SOAP clients. If either validation fails, a SOAP Fault message is sent back to the SOAP client.

4. The Apache SOAP runtime dispatches the RPC method request to the code artifact.

5. The code artifact processes the method call and sends back a return value to the Apache SOAP run-time environment.

6. The Apache SOAP runtime packages the return value in a SOAP response message and sends it back to the client.

Pluggable Provider Architecture

Code artifacts are supported within Apache SOAP through the Pluggable Provider architecture. This is a layer of abstraction between the Apache SOAP runtime and the components that know how to interact with the code artifacts, which are called Providers. A Provider is a Java class that is responsible for locating, loading, and invoking a code artifact. It also is responsible for packaging the return value into a SOAP Envelope when necessary. Apache SOAP provides Providers for each one of the default code artifacts. Below is a diagram of the architecture:

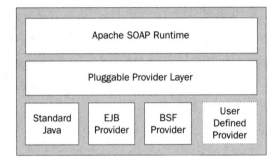

The architecture also provides support for User-Defined Providers; these are Providers that can be developed to handle other code artifacts. This would be useful if we had some code artifacts that we developed in a non-Java language that we wanted to make available as a service and we didn't want to invest the time or money in converting them to Java. For example, we might have some C++ classes that contain functionality that we want to make available as a service. Instead of rewriting the classes we could develop a Provider that knows how to handle C++ code artifacts. Likewise, we could write a Java Messaging Server (JMS) provider.

Service Implementation Class

A standard Java class that implements a service is sometimes known as the service implementation class. The Standard Java Provider invokes this class when the Apache SOAP runtime receives a request for the service from a SOAP client.

Let's look at the service implementation class for the Job Resumé Repository Service. It contains functionality for storing and retrieving resumés using the `submit()` and `retrieve()` methods, respectively. The service is implemented by the `com.wrox.jobresume.service` `JobResumeRepositoryService` class. It's located in `JobResumeRepositoryService.java`, which is listed below:

```
package com.wrox.jobresume.service;

import java.util.Hashtable;
```

```java
import com.wrox.jobresume.Resume;

public class JobResumeRepositoryService extends Object {
  private Hashtable resumeList = null;
  private int resumeUID;

  public JobResumeRepositoryService() {

    // Initiate the resumeList
    resumeList = new Hashtable();

    // Initiate the resumeCounter to 1000
    resumeUID = 1000;

    // Create a default resume
    Resume resume = createDefaultResume();
    submit(resume);
  }

  public String submit(Resume resume) throws IllegalArgumentException {
    if (resume == null) {
      throw new IllegalArgumentException("The resume argument must not be null");
    }
    try {
      // Generate a uid for the resume
      String uid = new Integer(resumeUID).toString();
      System.out.println("UID=" + uid);
      resumeUID+=1;

      // Store the uid with the resume object
      resume.setUid(uid);

      // Store the resume object in the hashtable
      resumeList.put(resume.getUid(),resume);
      return uid ;                              // return the generated uid
    } catch (NullPointerException e) {
      // completed unsuccesfully - the resumé was not stored
      return null;
    }
  }

  public Resume retrieve(String uid) throws IllegalArgumentException {
    if (uid == null) {
      throw new IllegalArgumentException("The uid argument must not be null");
    }
    return (Resume)resumeList.get(uid);
  }

  public Resume createDefaultResume() {
    String fName = "Mack";
    String mName = "Levin";
    String lName = "Hendricks";
    String address = "600 Denali";
    String city = "Southfield";
```

```
    String state = "MI";
        String zip = "48342";
      · String pNumber = "248-555-1212";
        String education = "1998-2000 Oakland University\n" +
                           "Masters of Science in Computer Science\n" +
                           "Rochester Hills, MI 48309\n\n" +
                           "1992-1998 Oakland University\n" +
                           "Bachelor of Science, Computer Science\n" +
                           "Rochester Hills, MI 48309";
        String wHistory = "Work history goes here!";
        String references = "Available upon Request";

        Resume resume = new Resume(fName, mName, lName, address,city, state,
                                zip, pNumber, education, wHistory, references);

        return resume;
    }
}
```

The submit() method takes a Resume object as a parameter. The Resume object contains attributes that represent a physical resumé. We will discuss the details of the Resume object in a later section. The submit() method also generates a unique ID(uid) to uniquely identify the Resume object, stores the uid as part of the Resume object, and stores the Resume object in a Hashtable with the uid as the key. Also, if the Resume object was stored successfully then the uid is returned to the calling application, which in our case is a SOAP client. The retrieve() method retrieves a Resume object from the Hashtable using the uid. Notice that a default resume is created and stored in the HashTable with a uid value of 1000.

Type Mappings

According to the SOAP specification, information can only be transmitted between a sender and receiver via XML. This means that Java types cannot be exchanged without being serialized to/deserialized from XML.

Apache SOAP uses type mappings to determine how Java types should be serialized to/deserialized from XML. Type mappings are implemented using a Java class, with the default type mapping class being org.apache.soap.encoding.SOAPMappingRegistry. This class contains type mappings for primitive Java types, wrapper classes for primitive Java types, and some other useful types that we will discuss in the next section. If we want to transmit user-defined types from an Apache SOAP server we have to override the SOAPMappingRegistry class so that the new type is included. We will discuss how to register user defined types from an Apache SOAP client in the *Developing SOAP Clients* section. Type mapping can also be defined using a deployment descriptor, which will be discussed in an upcoming section.

Each type mapping contains the following information:

❑   URI describing the encoding style

❑   Qualified name (QName) for the XML element

❑   Java class that implements the type

❑   Java classes responsible for serializing to/deserializing from the type

Apache SOAP provides support for three encoding styles: SOAP, Literal XML, and XMI.

As discussed in Chapter 2, the SOAP specification recommends that SOAP encoding be used, but other encoding styles may be defined and used. Apache SOAP provides support for the SOAP encoding style, which is identified by the http://schemas.xmlsoap.org/soap/encoding/ Uniform Resource Identifier (URI), which defines the schema for the encoding style. This encoding style defines a type system that is very similar to programming languages.

Apache SOAP also provides support for the literal XML encoding style. The literal XML encoding style allows DOM XML elements to be included as parameters and returned from an RPC method call. This encoding style is useful if wanting to send and receive XML documents.

XML Metadata Interchange (XMI) provides a way to interchange object-oriented models and data using XML. XMI is a standard from the OMG (Object Management Group). A number of companies are in the process of supporting the XMI specification or already provide support in one or more of their products such as TogetherSoft and Rational Rose. To illustrate how XMI might be useful let's look at a scenario that consist of two software development firms that are collaborating on developing a large-scale enterprise product. Let's refer to the companies as Company A and Company B. Company A uses TogetherSoft to model part of the project, whereas Company B uses Rational Rose to model another part of the project. This, makes it very difficult to collaborate since the models are stored in a proprietary fashion. However, if TogetherSoft and Rational Rose both support XMI then the model could be exchanged with out having to worry about incompatibility issues. More information about XMI can be found at http://www.omg.org/technology/documents/formal/xmi.htm.

The QName is the fully qualified name for the XML element that represents the Java type. In other words, each user-defined type must have a namespace associated with it. For example, a user-defined Java type `Myint` would look this:

```
<x:Myint xmlns:x="urn:MyNamespace">2</Myint>
```

The name of the fully qualified (`package.classname`) Java class that implements the type should be specified. For the `Myint` type the class would be specified as something like this: `com.wrox.example.Myint`.

In order for a type to be transmitted it must capable of being serialized to/deserialized from XML. Apache SOAP handles serialization through the use of Java classes that know how to handle the serialization needs of a type. A class that handles the serialization must implement the `org.apache.soap.util.xml.Serializer`. A class that handles deserialization must implement `org.apache.soap.util.xml.Deserializer`. A single class may implement both to provide both serialization and deserialization for the data class. As to whether to provide one or two classes, it really doesn't matter if one or two classes are used. It only matters that the methods defined by the interface are implemented. The `Serializer` interface requires that a `marshall()` method be implemented. Likewise the `Deserializer` interface requires an `unmarshall()` method to be implemented. So, a class that handles both serialization and deserialization must define both the `marshall()` and `unmarshall()` methods.

Below is the Apache SOAP deserializer class for the int type:

```
package org.apache.soap.encoding.soapenc;

import java.io.*;
import org.w3c.dom.*;
import org.apache.soap.util.xml.*;
import org.apache.soap.*;
import org.apache.soap.util.*;
import org.apache.soap.rpc.*;

public class IntDeserializer implements Deserializer {
   public Bean unmarshall(String inScopeEncStyle, QName elementType,
                          Node src, XMLJavaMappingRegistry xjmr,
                          SOAPContext ctx)
                 throws IllegalArgumentException {

      Element root = (Element)src;
      String value = DOMUtils.getChildCharacterData(root);

      return new Bean(int.class, new Integer(value));
   }
}
```

The src argument contains a XML element with a type of int that needs to be unmarshaled back into an int primitive type. The src variable is type cast upward to an Element object, the DomUtils.getChildCharacterData() method is used to obtain the value of the XML element and the value is returned via a class called Bean. The purpose of the Bean class is to simply represent the type and value of an unmarshaled element.

Default Type Mappings

In efforts to speed up the development of SOAP applications and for convenience purposes, Apache SOAP predefines and registers type mappings in the org.apache.soap.encoding.SOAPMappingRegistry class for primitive types (that is, int, float, and so on), wrapper classes (that is, java.lang.Integer, java.lang.Float), and other types. Below is a list of the other types:

❑   Java arrays

❑   java.lang.String

❑   java.util.Date

❑   java.util.GregorianCalendar

❑   ava.util.Vector

❑   java.util.Hashtable

❑   java.util.Map (available when using JDK 1.2 and above)

❑   java.math.BigDecimal

❑   javax.mail.internet.MimeBodyPart

❏ `java.io.InputStream`

❏ `javax.activation.DataSource`

❏ `javax.activation.DataHandler`

❏ `org.apache.soap.util.xml.QName`

❏ `org.apache.soap.rpc.Parameter`

User-Defined Types

If Apache SOAP clients need to exchange user-defined types with Apache SOAP services, we need to register the new type mapping with the Apache SOAP runtime. In this section we will discuss two ways to register user-defined type mappings:

❏ Register via the Deployment Descriptor

❏ Override the `SOAPMappingRegistry` class

Register via the Deployment Descriptor

The first method consists of registering the type using the deployment descriptor, which we discussed in the *Deploying and Running a "Hello World" Service* section. This method is the easiest method, but the major drawback is that the type would have to be registered each time it was used with a different service. In other words, services that want to utilize the type would have to add the type mapping information to its deployment descriptor. This is appropriate for data types that are application-specific and rarely reused.

Type mappings are specified through the use of the `mappings` element, which is an optional child element of the `<service>` element. To illustrate this, let's look at the deployment descriptor for the Job Resumé Repository Service (`JobResumeRepositoryDD.xml`):

```
<isd:service xmlns:isd="http://xml.apache.org/xml-soap/deployment"
             id="urn:JobResuméRepositoryService">
  <isd:provider type="java"
                scope="Application"
                methods="retrieve submit">
    <isd:java class="com.wrox.jobresumé.service.JobResuméRepositoryService"
    static="false"/>
  </isd:provider>

  <isd:faultListener>org.apache.soap.server.DOMFaultListener</isd:faultListener>

  <isd:mappings>
    <isd:map encodingStyle="http://schemas.xmlsoap.org/soap/encoding/"
          xmlns:x="urn:jobresume" qname="x:resume"
          javaType="com.wrox.jobresume.common.Resume"
          java2XMLClassName="org.apache.soap.encoding.soapenc.BeanSerializer"
          xml2JavaClassName="org.apache.soap.encoding.soapenc.BeanSerializer"/>
  </isd:mappings>

</isd:service>
```

The deployment descriptor for the Job Resumé Repository Service is similar to the one for the Hello World service except that a mapping element now has to be used since the `Resume` type has to be exchanged between Apache SOAP clients and Apache SOAP servers. The mapping element contains one or more <map> elements, which define an actual type mapping. The `encodingStyle` attribute is used to specify the encoding schema that the mapping should use. We are using the preferred encoding method, which is http://schemas.xmlsoap.org/soap/encoding/. The `xmlns` and `qname` attributes are used to specify the namespace and element name of the type that's being defined. So, the fully qualified name for the `Resume` type will be `urn:jobresume:resume`. The `javaType` attribute is used to specify the fully qualified class name of the class that implements the type. So, the fully qualified class for the `Resume` type is `com.wrox.jobresume.common.Resume`. The `java2XMLClassName` and the `xml2JavaClassName` attributes are used to specify the serializier and deserializer for the type. Since the `Resume` class conforms to the JavaBean specification we are able to use the `BeanSerializer` class that comes with Apache SOAP, which is capable of handling both the serialization and deserialization.

Override the SOAPMappingRegistry Class

An alternative to registering a user-defined type using a deployment descriptor is to override the `SOAPMappingRegistry` class with another class that has the new type defined. This method would allow the type mapping to be centralized in one place. This would alleviate the need to register the type for each service that needs it. This is appropriate for types that are used for multiple services, rather than a type that's only used by one service.

Serialization

Apache SOAP provides serializers for all the default types discussed earlier. We can also provide our own serializers. However, Apache SOAP provides a serializer for JavaBeans. It can be used to serialize and deserialize classes that conform to the JavaBean specification. The serializer is realized in the `org.apache.soap.encoding.soapenc.BeanSerializer` class.

The `BeanSerializer` class can handle serialization as long as the class that implements the type complies with a subset of the rules defined by the JavaBean specification. Not all the rules for JavaBeans apply here as the specification covers all types of JavaBeans including GUI beans, which our data type classes are not. Below is list of those rules that apply taken from the Apache SOAP web site:

❑ It MUST have a no-argument constructor

❑ It MUST expose all interesting state through properties

❑ It MUST not matter what order the accessors for the properties (that is, the `setXXX`/`getXXX` methods) are [called] in

The `Resume` type used in the Job Resumé Repository Service conforms to the JavaBean specification, with all of the attributes being serializable. So, we don't have to worry about serializaton, the `BeanSerializer` will handle it. Let's look at the `Resume` class to illustrate how it conforms to the JavaBean specification, which is located in `Resume.java`:

```
package com.wrox.jobresume.common;

public class Resume extends Object {

  private String firstName;
  private String middleName;
```

```
    private String lastName;
    private String uid; //Unique identifier
    private String address;
    private String city;
    private String state;
    private String zipcode;
    private String phoneNumber;
    private String education;
    private String workHistory;
    private String references;

    public Resume() { }

    public Resume(String firstName, String middleName, String lastName,
                  String address, String city, String state,
                  String zipcode, String phoneNumber, String education,
                  String workHistory, String references) {
      this.firstName = firstName;
      this.middleName = middleName;
      this.lastName = lastName;
      this.address = address;
      this.city = city;
      this.state = state;
      this.zipcode = zipcode;
      this.phoneNumber = phoneNumber;
      this.education = education;
      this.workHistory = workHistory;
      this.references = references;
    }

    // accessor/mutators removed for brevity's sake
    public String toString() {
      return "UID: " + uid + "\n" +
             "First Name: " + firstName + "\n" +
             "Middle Name: " + middleName + "\n" +
             "Last Name: " + lastName + "\n" +
             "Address: " + address + "\n" +
             "City:" + city + "\n" +
             "State:" + state + "\n" +
             "Zipcode:" + zipcode + "\n" +
             "Phone Number:" + phoneNumber + "\n" +
             "Education:" + education + "\n" +
             "Work History" + workHistory + "\n" +
             "References" + references + "\n";
    }
}
```

Note that the Resume class contains a no-argument constructor:

```
public Resumé() { }
```

Also note that the state is exposed through properties:

```
public class Resume extends Object {

    private String firstName;
    private String middleName;
    private String lastName;
    private String uid;                      //Unique identifier
    private String address;
    private String city;
    private String state;
    private String zipcode;
    private String phoneNumber;
    private String education;
    private String workHistory;
    private String references;
    ...
}
```

Lastly, each one of the above properties is accessible via accessor/mutator methods. The accessor and mutator methods for uid is below:

```
public String getUid() {
    return uid
}

public void setUid(String uid) {
    this.ssn = uid
}
```

The uid property is how each Resume is uniquely identified.

Developing SOAP Clients

In the previous section we discussed how to develop services using the Apache SOAP server-side API. In this section we focus on how to develop a SOAP client using the Apache SOAP client-side API. The Apache SOAP client-side API can be used to build a thick or thin client (that is, for a web browser, mobile phone, and so on). The SOAP client that we built for the Hello World service is an example of a thick client. We will focus on discussing web-based SOAP clients in this section. To illustrate the concepts, we will discuss the web-based SOAP client for the Job Resumé Repository Service that allows a user to submit and retrieve a resumé.

A user enters a resumé by using an HTML form that contains fields for entering resumé information. The name of the HTML file that contains the form is submit.html. It is shown below:

```html
<html>
<head><title>Wrox Job Resume System - Submit Resume</title></head>
<body>
  <p align='center'><img align='middle' src='wroxlogo.gif'</img> <font
face='Arial Narrow' size='5'><b>Job Resume Repository System</b></font></p>
  <p align="center"><font face="Arial Narrow" size="-1"><b>Submit
Resume</b></font></p>

<form method="POST" action="servlet/submit">
<table border="0" width="44%">
    <tr>
      <td width="34%"><font face="Arial Narrow" size="2">First Name: </font></td>
      <td width="72%"><input type="text" name="firstName" size="20">
        <font face="Arial Narrow" size="2">   </font></td>
    </tr>
    <tr>
      <td width="34%"><font face="Arial Narrow" size="2">Middle Name: </font></td>
      <td width="72%"><input type="text" name="middleName" size="20"></td>
    </tr>
    <tr>
      <td width="34%"><font size="2" face="Arial Narrow">Last
        Name:        </font></td>
      <td width="72%"><input type="text" name="lastName" size="20"></td>
    </tr>
  </table>
  <p><font face="Arial Narrow" size="2"> Street Address:</font>
    <input type="text" name="address" size="30"></p>
  <p><font size="2" face="Arial Narrow">City:</font>
    <input type="text" name="city" size="22"><font face="Arial Narrow"
size="2">   
  State</font>:<input type="text" name="state"
size="4">       
    <font size="2" face="Arial Narrow"> Zip Code:</font><input type="text"
name="zipcode" size="11">
  </p>
  <p><font face="Arial Narrow" size="2">Telephone Number:</font><input type="text"
name="phoneNumber" size="20"></p>
  <p><font size="2" face="Arial Narrow">Education:</font></p>
  <p><textarea rows="5" name="education" cols="57"></textarea></p>
  <p> </p>
  <p><font size="2" face="Arial Narrow">Work History:</font></p>
  <p><textarea rows="5" name="workHistory" cols="57"></textarea></p>
  <p> </p>
  <p><font face="Arial Narrow" size="2">References:</font></p>
  <p><textarea rows="5" name="references" cols="57"></textarea></p>
  <p> </p>
  <p align="left">
    <input type="submit" value="Submit" name="B1"><input type="reset"
value="Reset" name="B2">
     <font face="Arial Narrow" size="2">[<a
href='index.html'>Home</a>]</font>
  </p>
</form>
</body>
</html>
```

Once the form is populated and submitted, the form is processed using a servlet called
`SubmitServlet`. The output sent back to browser after successfully processing the resumé is below:

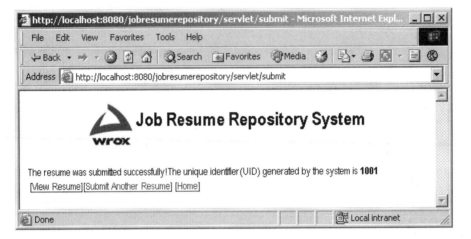

Note that a unique identifier (UID) is generated for the resumé. This isn't being generated by the
`SubmitServlet`, but is being created by the Job Resumé Repository Service. The uid is used to
retrieve the resumé. If we click the **View Resumé** link on the above screenshot then the resumé will be
retrieved from the service. This is done using another servlet called `RetrieveServlet`. If the retrieve
resumé button is clicked the following page will be displayed:

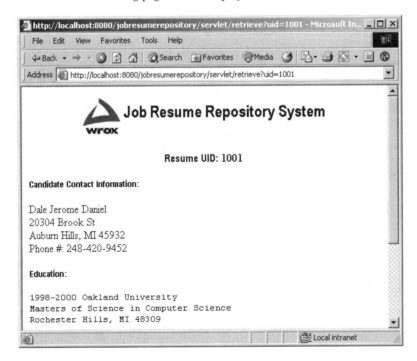

In upcoming sections we will discuss the SubmitServlet and RetrieveServlet to see how the Apache SOAP client API is used to access the Job Resumé Repository Service.

SubmitServlet

The SubmitServlet class is located in SubmitServlet.java. The class is listed below:

```java
package com.wrox.jobresume.client.submit;

// Imports needed for the Servlet API
import javax.servlet.http.HttpServlet;
import javax.servlet.http.HttpServletRequest;
import javax.servlet.http.HttpServletResponse;
import javax.servlet.ServletException;
import javax.servlet.ServletConfig;
import java.io.PrintWriter;

// Imports needed for the Apache SOAP API
import org.apache.soap.encoding.SOAPMappingRegistry;
import org.apache.soap.encoding.soapenc.BeanSerializer;
import org.apache.soap.Constants;
import org.apache.soap.SOAPException;
import org.apache.soap.Fault;
import org.apache.soap.util.xml.QName;
import org.apache.soap.rpc.Call;
import org.apache.soap.rpc.Parameter;
import org.apache.soap.rpc.Response;
import java.net.URL;

// Other Imports
import java.util.Vector;
import com.wrox.jobresume.Resume;

public class SubmitServlet extends HttpServlet {

  /** The URL where the rpcrouter servlet is located.  It's the interface
    * into the Apache SOAP engine that is responsible for routing web service
    * requests to the corresponding service implementation.
    */
  static String RPCROUTER = "http://localhost:8080/soap/servlet/rpcrouter";

  // Initializes the servlet
  public void init(ServletConfig config) throws ServletException {
    super.init(config);
  }

  // Destroys the servlet
  public void destroy() { }

  protected void processRequest(HttpServletRequest request,
                                HttpServletResponse response)
              throws ServletException, java.io.IOException {
```

```
     response.setContentType("text/html");
     java.io.PrintWriter out = response.getWriter();

     out.println("<html>");
     out.println("<body>");
     out.println("<p align='center'><img align='middle'
src='../wroxlogo.gif'</img> <font face='Arial Narrow' size='5'><b>Job Resumé
Repository System</b></font></p>");

     /** Create a Resumé object and populate it with the resumé information
      *  provided on the form
      */

     Resume resume = new Resume();
     resume.setFirstName(request.getParameter("firstName"));
     resume.setMiddleName(request.getParameter("middleName"));
     resume.setLastName(request.getParameter("lastName"));
     resume.setAddress(request.getParameter("address"));
     resume.setCity(request.getParameter("city"));
     resume.setState(request.getParameter("state"));
     resume.setZipcode(request.getParameter("zipcode"));
     resume.setPhoneNumber(request.getParameter("phoneNumber"));
     resume.setEducation(request.getParameter("education"));
     resume.setWorkHistory(request.getParameter("workHistory"));
     resume.setReferences(request.getParameter("references"));

     SOAPMappingRegistry smr = new SOAPMappingRegistry();
     BeanSerializer beanSer = new BeanSerializer();

     // Map the types
     smr.mapTypes(Constants.NS_URI_SOAP_ENC,
                  new QName("urn:jobresume", "resume"),
                  Resume.class, beanSer, beanSer);

     // Setup the Call
     Call call = new Call();

     call.setSOAPMappingRegistry(smr);
     call.setTargetObjectURI("urn:JobResumeRepositoryService");
     call.setMethodName("submit");
     call.setEncodingStyleURI(Constants.NS_URI_SOAP_ENC);

     // Add the parameters
     Vector params = new Vector();

     params.addElement(new Parameter("resume", Resume.class, resume, null));

     call.setParams(params);

     // Invoke the call
     Response resp = null;

     try {
       URL url = new URL(RPCROUTER);
```

```
      resp = call.invoke(url, "");
    } catch (SOAPException e) {
      out.println("Caught SOAPException (" +
                  e.getFaultCode() + "): " +
                  e.getMessage());
    }


    // Check the response
    if (!resp.generatedFault()) {                 //Successful response
      Parameter ret = resp.getReturnValue();
      String value = (String) ret.getValue();

      if (value != null) {
        out.println(
"<font face='Arial Narrow' size='2'>The resumé was submitted successfully!" +
"The unique identifier(UID) generated by the system is <b>" + value +
"</b></font><br>");
      } else {
        out.println(
"<font face='Arial Narrow' size='2'>The resumé was not submitted successfully
:-(</font><br>");

        out.println(
"<font face='Arial Narrow' size='2'> [<a href='../servlet/retrieve?uid="
+ value + "'>View Resume</a>]" +
"[<a href='../submit.html'>Submit Another Resumé</a>] [
  <a href='../index.html'>Home</a>]</font>");
      }
    } else {                         //Unsuccessful response
      Fault fault = resp.getFault();

      out.println("Generated fault: ");
      out.println("  Fault Code   = " + fault.getFaultCode());
      out.println("  Fault String = " + fault.getFaultString());
    }

  out.println("</body>");
  out.println("</html>");
  out.close();
}

/** Handles the HTTP <code>GET</code> method.
 * @param request servlet request
 * @param response servlet response
 */
protected void doGet(HttpServletRequest request, HttpServletResponse response)
                throws ServletException, java.io.IOException {
  processRequest(request, response);
}

/** Handles the HTTP <code>POST</code> method
 * @param request servlet request
 * @param response servlet response
 */
```

```
protected void doPost(HttpServletRequest request, HttpServletResponse response)
            throws ServletException, java.io.IOException {
  processRequest(request, response);
}


// Returns a short description of the servlet
public String getServletInfo() {
  return "Job Resumé Repository System SubmitServlet";
}
}
```

All of the magic happens in the processRequest() method, which is called if the request is either a GET or POST.

Obtaining the Interface

In order to write a SOAP client we first have to obtain the interface description of the service. The interface of a service is the methods that are exposed. We can obtain the interface by either looking at WSDL file for the service or looking at the implementation (code artifact) of the service. For the Job Resume Repository Service example we have the implementation, so we can look at that to obtain the signature of exposed methods. The signatures of the methods are below:

❑   String Submit(Resume resume)

❑   Resume Retrieve(String uid)

Registering User-Defined Types

Now that we know the interface for the service we must ensure that we have the class file for each user-defined type in the Java classpath. We also have to make sure any custom serializers and deserializiers are registered for parameters we are sending and receiving, respectively. We also have to make sure that their class files are part of the Java classpath. In regard to the Job Resumé Repository Service example, we handled this in the *Job Resumé Repository* section, but we have to register a serializer/deserializer for the Resume.class. Since the Resume.class conforms to the JavaBean standard we are able to use the BeanSerializer class that comes with Apache SOAP to handle the serialization. The code snippet below shows how this is done:

```
SOAPMappingRegistry smr = new SOAPMappingRegistry();
BeanSerializer beanSer = new BeanSerializer();

// Map the types
smr.mapTypes(Constants.NS_URI_SOAP_ENC,
        new QName("urn:jobresumé", "resumé"),
            Resumé.class, beanSer, beanSer);
```

In the above snippet, the mapTypes() method of the SOAPMappingRegistry class is used to the register the "resume" type. The syntax for the mapTypes() method is below:

```
public void mapTypes(java.lang.String encodingStyleURI,
            QName elementType, java.lang.Class javaType,
            Serializer s, Deserializer ds)
```

The encodingStyleURI is used to specify the encoding style that should be used to encode the type. We are using the SOAP encoding style, which is defined by the Constants.NS_URI_SOAP_ENC() static method. The elementType argument takes a variable of type QName, which contains the fully qualified element name (namespace.element) of the type. The javaType element contains the class that implements the type. The "s" and "ds" arguments should contain objects that handle serialization and deserialization, respectively. In our case, the Resume type is JavaBean, which can be serialized and deserialized by the BeanSerializier class.

Setting Up the Request

We are now ready to set up the SOAP request. This is done through the use of the org.apache.soap.rpc.RPCMessage.Call object. The Call object is responsible for setting up the details of the request:

```
// Setup the Call
Call call = new Call();

call.setSOAPMappingRegistry(smr);
call.setTargetObjectURI("urn:JobResuméRepositoryService");
call.setMethodName("submit");
call.setEncodingStyleURI(Constants.NS_URI_SOAP_ENC);
```

The setSOAPMappingRegistry() method is used to set up a reference to a SOAPMappingRegistry object so that the CALL object is aware of types that will be sent and received. It's worth noting that we wouldn't call this method if we were only using the predefined types because Apache SOAP has the majority of the types defined by default. However, we are using a user-defined type so the method must be called.

The setTargetObjectURI() method is used to specify the name of the service to which the request should be routed. In our case, the name of the service is urn:JobResumeRepositoryService.

The setMethodName() method is used to specify the name of the method that we want to execute. In our case, the method is called submit.

The setEncodingStyleURI() method is used to specify the encoding style that should be used in encoding the SOAP message. In the above code snippet, the value provided to the method specifies that SOAP encoding should be used. Note that the Constants class has many useful constants defined for SOAP.

Specifying Parameters

Since the submit() method requires a parameter, parameters have to be added to the Call object:

```
// Add the parameters
Vector params = new Vector();

params.addElement(new Parameter("resumé", Resumé.class, resumé, null));
call.setParams(params);
```

Parameters are added to the Call object by using the setParams() method. The setParams() method takes a Vector of Parameter objects as an argument. In our case there will be only one Parameter object in the array since the submit() method only takes one parameter. The Parameter object represents an argument or return value to a method call. The syntax of the parameter constructor is shown overleaf:

```
Parameter(java.lang.String name, java.lang.Class type,
           java.lang.Object value, java.lang.String encodingStyleURI)
```

The name parameter is used to specify the name of the argument, which in our case is resume. The type parameter should contain the Java class that implements the argument (that is, String.class, Integer.class, and so on), which in our case is Resume.class. The value parameter should contain the value of the argument, which in our case is resume (an instance of the Resume class that we created). The encodingStyleURI parameter could optionally be used to specify the encoding style that should be used for encoding the type.

Invoking the Call

Now that the SOAP request is properly set up we can now the call:

```
// Invoke the call
Response resp = null;

try {
  URL url = new URL(RPCROUTER);
  resp = call.invoke(url, "");
} catch (SOAPException e)  {
  out.println("Caught SOAPException (" +
              e.getFaultCode() + "): " + e.getMessage());
}
```

The invoke() method is used to send the SOAP request to the SOAP service. The method signature of the invoke() method is below:

```
public response invoke(java.net.URL url, java.lang.String SOAPActionURI)
```

The url parameter is used to specify the endpoint for the Apache SOAP runtime. The SOAPActionURI is used to specify the action to be called at the specified URL.

The invoke() method has to be within a try...catch clause because it throws a SOAPException. A SOAPException will be thrown if the Call object is set up incorrectly, or if there are network problems, and so on. The invoke() method returns a Response object, which represents the response to the call.

Interpreting the Response

In this section we will discuss how the response from a SOAP server should be handled.

Successful Response

If the response doesn't contain a fault, then the return value can be obtained by first calling the getReturnValue() method, which puts the return value into a Parameter object. The getValue() method of the Parameter object can then be used to obtain the actual value and manipulate the value as needed. The value returned is the UID of the resumé that was submitted. If the value is not null then the value is printed.

```
      // Check the response
      if (!resp.generatedFault()) {              //Successful response
        Parameter ret = resp.getReturnValue();
        String value = (String) ret.getValue();

        if (value != null) {
          out.println(
        "<font face='Arial Narrow' size='2'>The resumé was submitted successfully!" +
        "The unique identifier(UID) generated by the system is <b>" + value +
        "</b></font><br>");
        } else {
          out.println(
        "<font face='Arial Narrow' size='2'>The resumé was not submitted successfully
        :-(</font><br>");

          out.println(
        "<font face='Arial Narrow' size='2'> [<a href='../servlet/retrieve?uid="
        + value + "'>View Resumé</a>]" + "[<a href='../submit.html'>Submit Another
Resumé</a>] [<a href='../index.html'>Home</a>]</font>");
        }
      }
```

Unsuccessful Response

If the response does contain a fault, we can obtain the fault from the Response object by using the
getFault() method, which returns a Fault object. The Fault object contains a getFaultCode()
and getFaultString() method, which can be used to obtain the fault code and the fault
string, respectively.

```
      else {                              //Unsuccessful response
        Fault fault = resp.getFault();

        out.println("Generated fault: ");
        out.println ("  Fault Code   = " + fault.getFaultCode());
        out.println ("  Fault String = " + fault.getFaultString());
      }
```

RetrieveServlet

The RetrieveServlet class is located in RetrieveServlet.java. The class is listed below:

```
package com.wrox.jobresume.client.retrieve;

// Imports needed for the Servlet API
import javax.servlet.http.HttpServlet;
import javax.servlet.http.HttpServletRequest;
import javax.servlet.http.HttpServletResponse;
import javax.servlet.ServletException;
import javax.servlet.ServletConfig;
import java.io.PrintWriter;

// Imports needed for the Apache SOAP API
```

```java
import org.apache.soap.encoding.SOAPMappingRegistry;
import org.apache.soap.encoding.soapenc.BeanSerializer;
import org.apache.soap.Constants;
import org.apache.soap.SOAPException;
import org.apache.soap.Fault;
import org.apache.soap.util.xml.QName;
import org.apache.soap.rpc.Call;
import org.apache.soap.rpc.Parameter;
import org.apache.soap.rpc.Response;
import java.net.URL;

// Other Imports
import java.util.Vector;
import com.wrox.jobresume.common.Resume;

public class RetrieveServlet extends HttpServlet {

  static String RPCROUTER = "http://localhost:8080/soap/servlet/rpcrouter";

  // Initializes the servlet
  public void init(ServletConfig config) throws ServletException {
    super.init(config);
  }

  // Destroys the servlet
  public void destroy() { }

  protected void processRequest(HttpServletRequest request,
                                HttpServletResponse response)
              throws ServletException, java.io.IOException {

    response.setContentType("text/html");
    java.io.PrintWriter out = response.getWriter();

    out.println("<html>");
    out.println("<body>");
    out.println("<p align='center'><img align='middle'
src='../wroxlogo.gif'</img> <font face='Arial Narrow' size='5'><b>Job Resumé
Repository System</b></font></p>");

    // Get the Unique ID (UID) of the resumé from the form
    String uid = request.getParameter("uid");

    SOAPMappingRegistry smr = new SOAPMappingRegistry();
    BeanSerializer beanSer = new BeanSerializer();

    // Map the types
    smr.mapTypes(Constants.NS_URI_SOAP_ENC,
                 new QName("urn:jobresume", "resume"),
                 Resume.class, beanSer, beanSer);

    // Setup the Call
    Call call = new Call();
```

```
      call.setSOAPMappingRegistry(smr);
      call.setTargetObjectURI("urn:JobResumeRepositoryService");
      call.setMethodName("retrieve");
      call.setEncodingStyleURI(Constants.NS_URI_SOAP_ENC);

      // Add the parameters
      Vector params = new Vector();
      params.addElement(new Parameter("uid", String.class, uid, null));

      call.setParams(params);

      // Invoke the call.
      Response resp = null;

      try {
        URL url = new URL(RPCROUTER);
        resp = call.invoke(url, "");
      } catch (SOAPException e) {
        out.println("Caught SOAPException (" +
                    e.getFaultCode() + "): " +
                    e.getMessage());
      }

      // Check the response
      if (!resp.generatedFault()) //Successful response {
        Parameter ret = resp.getReturnValue();
        Resume value = (Resume) ret.getValue();

        if (value != null)
          displayResume(out,value);

        else
          out.println("<font face='Arial Narrow' size='2'>The resumé for uid " + uid
+ " could not be found.</font><br><br>");

        out.println("<font face='Arial Narrow' size='2'>[<a
href='../retrieve.html'>Retrieve A Resumé</a>] [<a
href='../submit.html'>Submit A Resumé</a>]" +
                          " [<a href='../index.html'>Home</a>]</font>");
      } else {        //Unsuccessful response
        Fault fault = resp.getFault();

        out.println("Generated fault: ");
        out.println("  Fault Code   = " + fault.getFaultCode());
        out.println("  Fault String = " + fault.getFaultString());
      }

    out.println("</body>");
    out.println("</html>");
    out.close();
  }

  /** Handles the HTTP <code>GET</code> method.
```

```
 * @param request servlet request
 * @param response servlet response
 */
protected void doGet(HttpServletRequest request, HttpServletResponse response)
            throws ServletException, java.io.IOException {
  processRequest(request, response);
}

/** Handles the HTTP <code>POST</code> method.
 * @param request servlet request
 * @param response servlet response
 */
protected void doPost(HttpServletRequest request, HttpServletResponse response)
            throws ServletException, java.io.IOException {
  processRequest(request, response);
}

// Returns a short description of the servlet
public String getServletInfo() {
  return "Job Resumé Repository System SubmitServlet";
}

public void displayResume(PrintWriter out, Resume resume) {
  out.println("<center><b><font face='Arial Narrow' size='3'>Resume UID:
</font>" + resume.getUid() + "<br></b></center><br>");
  out.println("<b><font face='Arial Narrow' size='2'>Candidate Contact
Information: </font></b><br><br>");
  out.println(resume.getFirstName() + " " + resume.getMiddleName() + " " +
resume.getLastName() + "<br>\n");
  out.println(resume.getAddress() + "<br>\n");
  out.println(resume.getCity() + ", " + resume.getState() + " " +
resume.getZipcode() + "<br>\n");
  out.println("Phone #: " + resume.getPhoneNumber() + "\n
</center></font><br>");
  out.println("<b><font face='Arial Narrow' size='2'>Education:
</font></b><br><pre>" + resume.getEducation() + "</pre><br>");
  out.println("<b><font face='Arial Narrow' size='2'>Work History:
</font></b><br><pre>" + resume.getWorkHistory() + "</pre><br>");
  out.println("<b><font face='Arial Narrow' size='2'>References:
</font></b><br><pre>" + resume.getReferences() + "</pre><br>");
  }
}
```

This servlet is very similar to the SubmitServlet. The main difference between the servlets is that it invokes the retrieve() method instead of the submit(). So the Call object would be set up like this:

```
Call call = new Call();

call.setSOAPMappingRegistry(smr);
call.setTargetObjectURI("urn:JobResuméRepositoryService");

call.setMethodName("retrieve");

call.setEncodingStyleURI(Constants.NS_URI_SOAP_ENC);
```

Debugging SOAP Clients and Services

When debugging Apache SOAP clients and services it's useful to look at the SOAP messages that are being exchanged between the client and the Apache SOAP server. Also, by looking at the SOAP messages one can gain a better understanding of how SOAP works. TCP tunnel/monitor tool packaged with Apache SOAP provides this capability. The tool acts as a proxy – requests from a SOAP client are retrieved, displayed, and forwarded to a SOAP server. Likewise, a response from a SOAP server is received, displayed, and forwarded back to the SOAP client. To start the tool, use the following syntax:

```
>java org.apache.soap.util.net.TcpTunnelGui listenport tunnelhost tunnelport
```

Where `listenport` is the port that SOAP clients will use to send SOAP requests, the `tunnelhost` and `tunnelport` are the hostname/IP address and port number of where the SOAP server is running. The following command could be used to start the tool listening on port 9090 with request being forwarded to `localhost` on port `8080` (where the SOAP server is running):

```
>java org.apache.soap.util.net.TcpTunnelGui 9090 localhost 8080
```

The following window will appear:

We can peek at the SOAP message that was generated by `submitResume` servlet by simply changing the `RPCROUTER` global variable so that it points to the port that the TCP tunnel/monitor tool is listening on. So, now the `RPCROUTER` variable would look like the following:

```
static String RPCROUTER = "http://localhost:9090/rpcrouter";
```

After recompiling the servlet try to submit a resumé. The end result should look something like this:

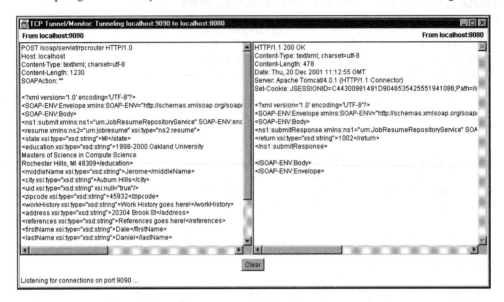

The textbox on the left contains the SOAP message sent by the SOAP client. The textbox on the right contains the SOAP message received from the SOAP server.

Summary

In this chapter we discussed Apache SOAP 1.1, an opensource implementation of SOAP 1.1 and SOAP with Attachments. We covered the following topics:

❑   History of Apache SOAP; specifically, we discussed the fact that IBM originally developed Apache SOAP, which was called IBM-SOAP

❑   Axis, the next generation of Apache SOAP was discussed.

❑   Installing Apache SOAP

❑   Deploying and running a service

❑   Developing an Apache SOAP service

❑   Developing an Apache SOAP client

❑   Type mapping

❑   Serialization

❑   Pluggable Provider architecture

❑   Debugging SOAP clients and services

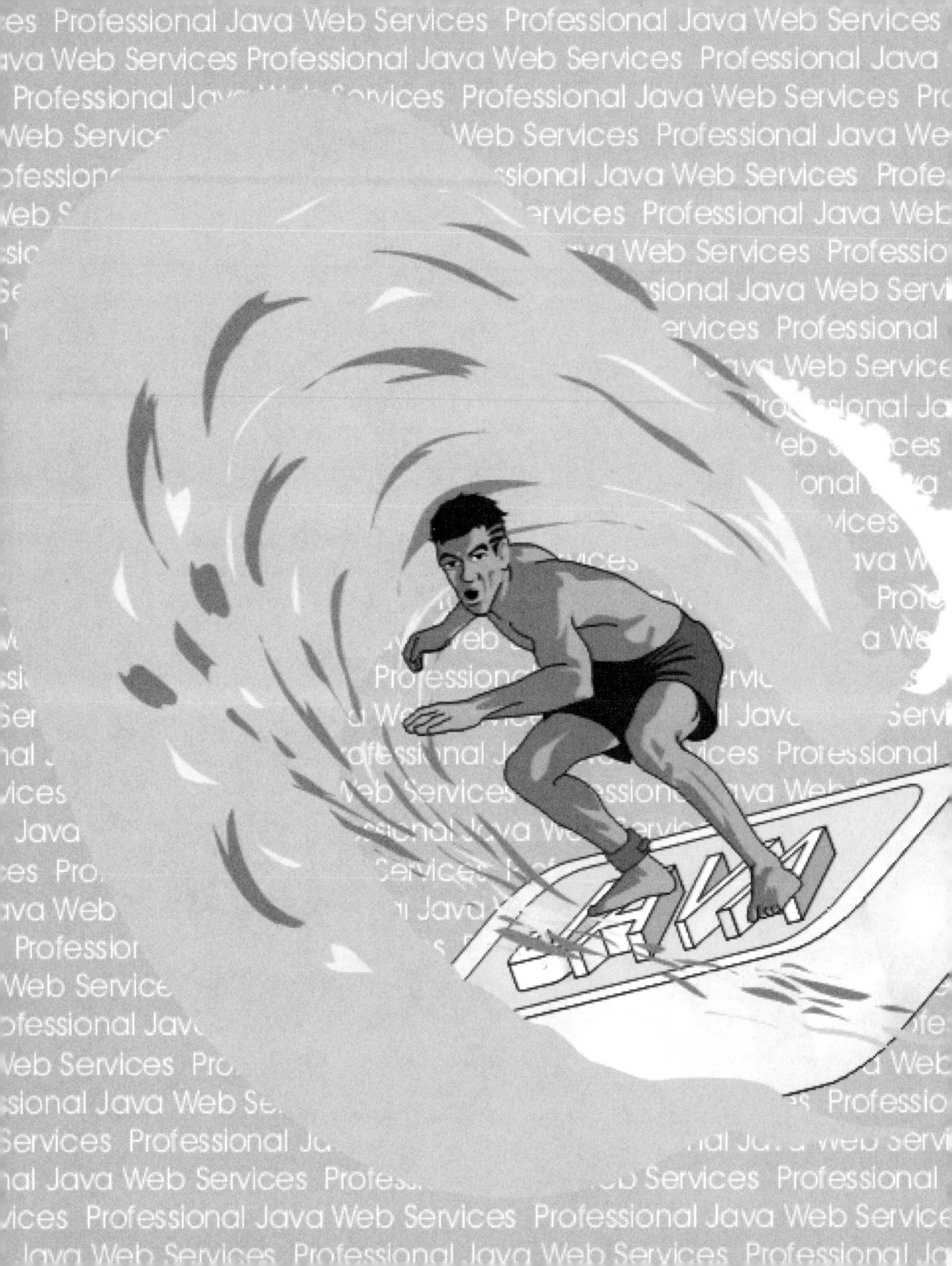
Professional Java Web Services

WSDL

In the introductory chapters of this book, we discussed the architectural background of Web Service technologies. One of the key arguments for taking advantage of these technologies is that they allow applications to communicate with each other over any network, usually the Internet. More importantly, these applications do not necessarily have to share the same language.

We need a way to describe the external services, or **interfaces**, that an application offers so that an application can dynamically bind to a service. This must be done independently of any platform or programming language. The **Web Services Definition Language (WSDL)** sets out to define a system for describing services. The language specification contains an XML Schema that describes the XML structure that each WSDL document must follow (http://www.w3.org/XML/Schema/).

In this chapter, you will learn what this specification consists of and how to access a WSDL document from Java. The language specification describes the individual elements that each WSDL document contains. Thus, to understand WSDL, we need to look at what these elements are and what kind of information they carry.

We will then focus on WSDL4J, an API for Java that provides access to all of the WSDL constructs. This API allows us to develop Java applications that either build a new WSDL document, or retrieve an existing one and parse its content, without the need to use lower level XML.

Finally, we will learn how to create a simple client that reads a WSDL document and generates a dynamic request to the service described in that document. While there are many ways to do this, we will look at one example, using the GLUE platform; a framework for distributed networking using Web Services standards.

WSDL Document Structure

WSDL was defined in a joint effort by IBM, Microsoft, and Ariba and has been submitted to the W3C organization for standardization. The current version is WSDL 1.1, and you can find the specification at http://www.w3.org/TR/wsdl/.

A WSDL document represents the external interface to a Web Service. In other words, it is to Web Services what **Interface Definition Language (IDL)** is to the CORBA world. However, besides describing the offered interface, a WSDL document also contains the location (or 'endpoint' as the specification refers to it) of the service. The service registry is available on a predictable and well-known location on the network, allowing the client to contact it in a reliable way. This ultimately means an additional benefit – that of location independence. Services may be moved according to business or deployment considerations in a way that eliminates the need to inform clients of the changes made.

> *Endpoint programming can also be compared to socket programming: an application that binds to a socket requires knowledge of the address to bind to, and the application protocol that operates at the socket – that is, the list of accepted input messages and expected output message formats.*

The combination of both the interface and the endpoint make a service accessible to a client.

In order to be as flexible as possible, WSDL defines the various components of a service that can then be reused to define different services. The components that make up a service include:

❑   Data types: (`String`, `int`, `Object`, amongst others.) Data types in WSDL are known as **types**.

❑   Input and output parameters of a service: A parameter of a service invocation is called a **message**.

❑   Relationship between input and output parameters: The method signature, also known as **operations**.

❑   Logical grouping of operations: This can be equated with a given object, which is a logical grouping of methods (we ignore the data view of an object for the purpose of this discussion). This logical grouping is known as a **Port Type**.

❑   Protocol to be used for accessing an object's methods: The only options currently defined in the WSDL specification are SOAP, HTTP, and MIME to describe MIME-encoded message formats – this is known as a **binding**.

❑   Address of the service: The address of a service in addition to the components above defines the **service**.

The first four of these should be familiar to us as Java developers; it is usual to need to know the object you are accessing, the method, and its input and output parameters. Usually, knowledge of all the methods an object exposes is not mandatory, but is desirable. The last two items in the list above are required for distributed applications. Although SOAP and HTTP are currently the only protocols supported, it does not necessarily follow that they will not be replaced or complemented by others before too long. The address of the service is required and merely describes the network location of the service.

The structure of a WSDL document maps this in the following way:

❑   The `<types>` element defines the data types used.

❑   The `<message>` elements define the messages that are used by the service.

❑ The `<operation>` elements define request-response messages that are used by the individual functions offered by a service.

❑ A `<portType>` element wraps a collection of operations.

❑ The `<binding>` element describes how a port type is mapped to a network invocation protocol such as SOAP.

❑ The `<service>` element and its contained `<port>` element contain the location of a service implementation on the network.

The following diagram summarizes the main elements of WSDL that can occur in a document:

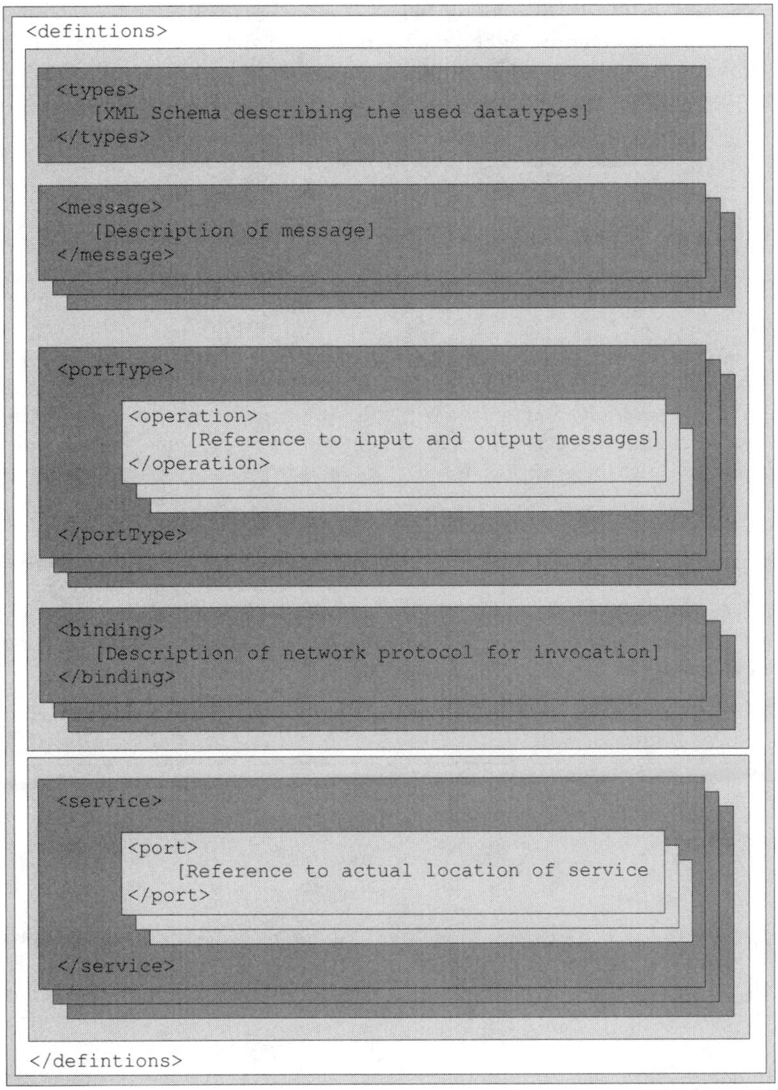

```
<defintions>

    <types>
        [XML Schema describing the used datatypes]
    </types>

    <message>
        [Description of message]
    </message>

    <portType>

            <operation>
                [Reference to input and output messages]
            </operation>

    </portType>

    <binding>
        [Description of network protocol for invocation]
    </binding>

    <service>

            <port>
                [Reference to actual location of service
            </port>

    </service>

</defintions>
```

We will look at each of these elements in more detail, but first, let us clarify the role of namespaces in a WSDL document.

A Note on Namespaces

Since every WSDL document is an XML document, namespaces are defined within . In order to maximize the reusability of the components of a WSDL document, many of the elements in WSDL contain attributes to reference other elements, either within or outside of the document. For example, the <binding> element defines an attribute that points to a <portType> element.

We will discuss these in more detail below, but here you should note that all of these references should be fully namespace-qualified. For example, let us assume that the target namespace of a WSDL document is http://www.addressbook.com/definitions/AddressBookRemoteInterface. Moreover, this namespace has a prefix of tns defined with it. In this case, the binding element would resemble the following:

```
<binding name="AddressBookBinding" type="tns:AddressBook">
    ...
</binding>
```

The type attribute refers to the <portType> element called AddressBook and is fully namespace-qualified.

This is something to consider with many of the attributes that are defined for WSDL elements. Many of them are references to other parts of the document. It is important to note which of these references must be fully namespace-qualified and we will point those out as we go along. The rule of thumb should be that all references to other parts of the document should be fully qualified, including the namespace of the element they refer to.

Besides this, the default namespace that each WSDL document should be using is http://schemas.xmlsoap.org/wsdl/. Again, this is what we will be using in the following samples.

Here is a list of namespaces that you will frequently see in WSDL documents, together with their recommended prefixes:

Prefix	Namespace URI	Description
wsdl	http://schemas.xmlsoap.org/wsdl/	WSDL namespace for WSDL framework
soap	http://schemas.xmlsoap.org/wsdl/soap/	WSDL namespace for WSDL SOAP binding
http	http://schemas.xmlsoap.org/wsdl/http/	WSDL namespace for WSDL HTTP GET & POST binding

Prefix	Namespace URI	Description
mime	`http://schemas.xmlsoap.org/wsdl/mime/`	WSDL namespace for WSDL MIME binding.
soapenc	`http://schemas.xmlsoap.org/soap/encoding/`	Encoding namespace as defined by SOAP 1.1
soapenv	`http://schemas.xmlsoap.org/soap/envelope/`	Envelope namespace as defined by SOAP 1.1
xsi	`http://www.w3.org/2001/XMLSchema-instance`	Instance namespace as defined by XML Schema
xsd	`http://www.w3.org/2001/XMLSchema`	Schema namespace as defined by XML Schema

The <definitions> Element

The root element of each WSDL document is the `<definitions>` element. Typically, it will contain attributes defining the namespaces used in the WSDL document. Here is an example for what this will typically look like:

```
<?xml version="1.0" encoding="UTF-8"?>
<!-- File: AddressBookService.wsdl -->

<definitions name="AddressBookService"
    targetNamespace="http://localhost:8080/Wrox/wsdl/AddressBook-service.wsdl"
    xmlns="http://schemas.xmlsoap.org/wsdl/"
    xmlns:tns="http://localhost:8080/wrox/wsdl/AddressBook-service.wsdl"
    xmlns:binding=
            "http://www.addressbook.com/definitions/AddressBookRemoteInterface"
    xmlns:soap="http://schemas.xmlsoap.org/wsdl/soap/">

  <!-- Contents of file here -->

</definitions>
```

The <import> Element

A WSDL document is not necessarily contained in one physical file. It can be split up into multiple files. For example, interface or data type information can be kept separate from concrete endpoint definitions. This allows reuse of the potentially standardized interface definitions from actual implementations in a running server. Moreover, schema definitions, as contained in the `<types>` element, could be imported from separate locations. Most tools and platforms should support some kind of separation between the various parts of a WSDL definition.

WSDL contains an element called `<import>` that supports this separation. It contains two attributes, one defining the location of the imported document, and one defining its namespace.

The following example shows a WSDL document that contains only one `<service>` element. The actual interface definition is contained in a separate file, `AddressBook-interface.wsdl`, that is included using the `<import>` element. We assume here that all files are located on the local machine, at port 8080:

```
<?xml version="1.0" encoding="UTF-8"?>
<!-- File: AddressBookService.wsdl -->

<definitions name="AddressBookService"
    targetNamespace="http://localhost:8080/Wrox/wsdl/AddressBook-service.wsdl"
    xmlns="http://schemas.xmlsoap.org/wsdl/"
    xmlns:tns="http://localhost:8080/wrox/wsdl/AddressBook-service.wsdl"
    xmlns:binding=
            "http://www.addressbook.com/definitions/AddressBookRemoteInterface"
    xmlns:soap="http://schemas.xmlsoap.org/wsdl/soap/">

    <import namespace=
            "http://www.addressbook.com/definitions/AddressBookRemoteInterface"
            location="http://localhost:8080/test/wsdl/AddressBook-interface.wsdl"/>

    <service name="AddressBookService">
      <port name="AddressBookPort" binding="binding:AddressBookBinding">
        <soap:address location="http://localhost:8080/Wrox/servlet/rpcrouter"/>
      </port>
    </service>

</definitions>
```

You can see that the interface definitions are expected to exist in a file called `AddressBook-interface.wsdl`. We will now assume that the interface definition file includes an XML Schema, `AddressBook-schema.xsd`, again via the `<import>` element. The following example shows this file (for now don't worry about the other elements, we will get to them shortly):

```
<?xml version="1.0" encoding="UTF-8"?>
<!-- File: AddressBook-interface.wsdl -->

<definitions name="AddressBookRemoteInterface"
    targetNamespace=
        "http://www.addressbook.com/definitions/AddressBookRemoteInterface"
    xmlns="http://schemas.xmlsoap.org/wsdl/"
    xmlns:tns="http://www.addressbook.com/definitions/AddressBookRemoteInterface"
    xmlns:xsd="http://www.w3.org/2001/XMLSchema"
    xmlns:xsd1="http://www.addressbook.com/schemas/AddressBookRemoteInterface"
    xmlns:soap="http://schemas.xmlsoap.org/wsdl/soap/">

  <import
      namespace="http://www.addressbook.com/schemas/AddressBookRemoteInterface"
      location="http://localhost:8080/test/wsdl/AddressBook-schema.xsd"/>

  <message name="getAddressRequest">
    <part name="person" type="xsd:string"/>
  </message>
```

```
    <message name="getAddressResponse">
     <part name="result" type="xsd1:Address"/>
    </message>

    <portType name="AddressBook">
      <operation name="getAddress">
        <input name="getAddressRequest" message="tns:getAddressRequest"/>
        <output name="getAddressResponse" message="tns:getAddressResponse"/>
      </operation>
    </portType>

    <binding name="AddressBookBinding" type="tns:AddressBook">
      <soap:binding style="rpc" transport="http://schemas.xmlsoap.org/soap/http"/>
      <operation name="getAddress">
        <soap:operation soapAction="urn:AddressBook" style="rpc"/>
        <input>
          <soap:body use="encoded"
              encodingStyle="http://schemas.xmlsoap.org/soap/encoding/"/>
        </input>
        <output>
          <soap:body use="encoded"
              encodingStyle="http://schemas.xmlsoap.org/soap/encoding/"/>
        </output>
      </operation>
    </binding>

</definitions>
```

Note that there is no <types> element here. If an XML Schema is included using the <import> element, as is the case here with AddressBook-schema.xsd, there need not be a <types> element wrapping the definitions. Here is the XML Schema that defines the Address type:

```
<?xml version="1.0"?>
<!-- File: AddressBook-schema.xsd -->
<schema
  xmlns="http://www.w3.org/2001/XMLSchema"
  targetNamespace="http://www.addressbook.com/schemas/AddressBookRemoteInterface"
  xmlns:xsd1="http://www.addressbook.com/schemas/AddressBookRemoteInterface">

  <complexType name="Address">
    <all>
      <element name="zipcode" type="string"/>
      <element name="city" type="string"/>
      <element name="street" type="string"/>
    </all>
  </complexType>

</schema>
```

Note that whenever you use this style of importing several WSDL files, you must make sure that the location attribute of the <import> element points to the right file – in other words, you must maintain the original content if you move files between servers.

The <types> Element

Any meaningful Web Service will deal with data. Data must be passed to the service, returned from the service, or both. As Java developers, we use Java objects and primitive types for the exchange of data between different parts of our applications. In distributed applications, these objects are typically passed over a network in binary format. In other words, they are **marshaled** or **serialized**. Both sides of the communication path know how to serialize and deserialize the data into objects.

In the Web Services world, the principle is the same, except that the serialization of objects is into and out of XML, in order to reap the benefit of using platform-neutral data. If you are offering a service, you must tell your clients what kind of data you expect and what kind of data they can expect you to return. The simplest example here is the stock quote example: the input parameter is a String symbol name. The return value is a Float stock value. In many cases, more complex data structures are exchanged.

This is what is defined in the <types> element in a WSDL document. Again, the use of XML Schema is not mandated by the specification, but you can safely assume that most Web Services will use it. In cases where data types are used that are defined by the XML Schema Datatypes definition (http://www.w3.org/TR/xmlschema-2), the Web Service may simply contain references to the XML Schema Type definition.

Let us continue the theme of an address book service. One of the data types that it deals with is a representation of an address. In our case, let us assume an address has three fields, namely the street, the city, and the zip code, all of which are strings. The XML Schema defining this data type could be wrapped by a <types> element looking like this simple example:

```
<types>
  <xsd:schema xmlns:xsd="http://www.w3.org/2001/XMLSchema">
    <xsd:element name="Address">
      <xsd:complexType>
        <xsd:sequence>
          <xsd:element name="street" type="xsd:string"/>
          <xsd:element name="city" type="xsd:string"/>
         <xsd:element name="zipcode" type="xsd:string"/>
        </xsd:sequence>
      </xsd:complexType>
    </xsd:element>
  </xsd:schema>
</types>
```

To summarize, the <types> element contains the definition of the data types that a service deals with. In almost all cases, this is an XML Schema definition. If it is missing, this means that a service is only using basic data types like strings, integers, and so on.

Note that several ways of defining an XML schema can currently be found on the Internet. The standard for XML schemas has evolved over the past two years. You should make sure that you always use the latest available standard. Which version is used can typically be identified by looking at the namespace declaration at the top of the schema. The current namespace is "http://www.w3.org/2001/XMLSchema".

The <message> Element

A message is a conceptual unit of data that may be exchanged. A message may be made up of a number of arguments – in the case of a method call all of the parameters to the method would be represented by a single message. For this purpose, each <message> element contains one or more <part> elements that form the actual pieces of the message. Each <part> element refers to a type defined in the <types> element on the document.

For example, in our address book example, let us assume that two messages exist. The first is called personMessage and contains the name of a person in the form of a string. The second contains an address and the name of the person living at that address. The definition of these messages in a WSDL document would look like this:

```
<definitions
    ...
    xmlns:tns="http://www.addressbook.com/definitions/AddressBookRemoteInterface"
    xmlns:xsd="http://www.w3.org/2001/XMLSchema"
    ... >

  <message name="personMessage">
    <part name="person" type="xsd:string"/>
  </message>

  <message name="addressMessage">
    <part name="personPart" type="xsd:string"/>
    <part name="addressPart" type="tns:Address"/>
  </message>

</definitions>
```

The references to the types of the individual parts are namespace-qualified. For example, the Address type that was declared in the <types> element is referred to as tns:Address. The namespace prefix tns: will need to be defined in the header of the WSDL document.

By now we have defined the messages that a Web Service deals with and the data types that these messages contain. Now we are ready to put these messages to work.

The <operation> and <portType> Elements

The next step in defining a Web Service is to bring the messages as declared by the <message> elements into a useful sequence. The WSDL specification calls this an **operation**. An operation is represented by one or more messages. There are four different types of operations:

- ❑ **One Way**: This kind of operation defines a message that is sent from a client to a service without any response from that service.

- ❑ **Request-Response**: This is the most common kind of operation. A client sends a request to a service and receives a response message as a result of that request.

- ❑ **Solicit-Response**: A solicit-response operation defines a message sent from the service to the client that results in a message from the client back to that service. This is not a very common use of Web Services.

❑   **Notification**: The service sends a message to the client, perhaps one that the client has subscribed to.

The kind of operation that we are most interested in is the request-response. You can just think of it as a **remote procedure call (RPC)**. A remote procedure call is a call to a function across process boundaries that takes some parameters and returns a result. A request-response operation is similar. A request to a service results in a response being returned. This operation consists of an input message and an output message. The messages that are used by this kind of operation must be defined by <message> elements in the WSDL document.

The following extract shows an <operation> definition for our address book demo. It takes the name of the person that we look for as the input message and returns the entire address of this person using the messages that we created in the previous section. Note that an <operation> element is always contained in a <portType> element.

```
<portType name="AddressBook">
  <operation name="getAddress">
    <input message="personMessage"/>
    <output message="addressMessage"/>
  </operation>
</portType>
```

In Java terms, an operation maps to a method in a class. Each method has one or more input parameters (represented by the 'input' message) and a return value (represented by the 'output' message). For example, a Java method implementing the operation described above would have the following signature:

```
public Address getAddress(String personMessage);
```

One-way operations can be mapped to either methods that have no return value, or messages to an asynchronous message-driven service (for example, a service that responds to a JMS message queue). For the remainder of this chapter, we will only focus on request-response operations, since they are currently the most common ones.

In WSDL, one or more operations can be bundled into a <portType> element. Again, coming from a Java background, you can map a port type to a class. A Java class has any number of methods that can be called on its instances. Similarly, a Web Service port type defines any number of operations. However, you should note that a <portType> is only a conceptual bundling of operations. You may bundle all operations in one WSDL document in one or multiple <portType> elements – this is a design decision you make (or if you use a tool to create WSDL, the tool may make that decision for you). Mapping all methods of one class into one port type is such a design decision.

At this point, we can map parameters and return values to messages, and we can use those messages in operations that are contained in port types. This fully describes the functional interface of the service, but does not give any information about the exact details of invoking that service. So now it is time to specify how these port types can actually be invoked, which is what the <binding> element does.

The <binding> Element

The <binding> element describes the mechanism that is used by a service to communicate with a client. This element is more complex than the previous elements. The reason for this is that it is quite open as to what you can put into it. WSDL was written so that it is independent from the actual mechanism that is used to access a service. You know by now that SOAP is the dominant choice for this access, as discussed in Chapter 2, however, other mechanisms are also possible. The WSDL specification mentions two other mechanisms, namely HTTP and MIME. Later in this section, we will also have a look at what a possible Java binding might look like. In addition to SOAP and HTTP, the specification describes a MIME binding. This can be used to describe how a certain message is encoded with respect to its MIME type.

SOAP Binding

In general, any binding information will repeat the elements of a given port type (the operations and their respective input and output messages) and add information to it that is specific for the particular protocol. For example, the SOAP binding for our AddressBook port type may look as follows:

```
<binding name="AddressBookBinding" type="AddressBook">
  <soap:binding style="rpc" transport="http://schemas.xmlsoap.org/soap/http"/>
  <operation name="getAddress">
    <soap:operation soapAction="urn:addressbook"/>
    <input>
      <soap:body encodingStyle="http://schemas.xmlsoap.org/soap/encoding/"
                 namespace="urn:addressbook"
                 use="encoded"/>
    </input>
    <output>
      <soap:body encodingStyle="http://schemas.xmlsoap.org/soap/encoding/"
                 namespace="urn:addressbook"
                 use="encoded"/>
    </output>
    <fault>
      <soap:fault encodingStyle="http://schemas.xmlsoap.org/soap/encoding/"
                  namespace="urn:addressbook"
                  use="encoded"/>
    </fault>
  </operation>
</binding>
```

This <binding> element is always followed by another element, which is specific to the protocol that is used – in this case it is SOAP. In other words, every Web Service that is accessible via SOAP will have a <binding> element followed by a <soap:binding> element in its WSDL definition.

The style attribute of the <soap:binding> element is set to rpc. The other choice for this attribute, which is also the default if none is defined, is document. The difference between the two is important, because it has an impact on how you communicate with the service. If set to rpc, all parameters that are sent to the service are wrapped in an XML element that is named after the operation as defined in the <operation> element. If the style is document, all messages are directly copied into the envelope without the wrapper. Thus, if you are developing a client application that communicates with a service via SOAP, the style attribute defines how the individual SOAP messages are constructed.

So why would you use one style or the other? This really depends on the kind of service. The values that you can set the `style` attribute to, rpc and document, are actually very accurate names. If your service consists of a function that takes a set of parameters and then returns a value, then rpc style is what you would use. If your service is more message-based and deals directly with XML documents, you will want to use document style. Typically, a document style Web Service will use literal encoding. While this is discussed in detail in the SOAP chapter of this book, let us simply state here that no mapping between Java objects and XML is done in that case. A client of such a Web Service directly adds an XML document to the SOAP envelope, and the server will pass this document to the service unchanged.

The `transport` attribute defines HTTP as the network protocol over which the messages will be sent by using the appropriate namespace.

The `<soap:operation>` element defines an attribute called soapAction that contains the SOAP action header for the service. The SOAP action header is mandatory for SOAP requests that are sent via HTTP. The receiver of the HTTP SOAP request envelope can use this field to identify which exact service is invoked. It could be some kind of unique identifier that the server uses to route the request to the right service implementation. However, you should note that there are also other ways of doing this. For example, the Apache SOAP implementation uses the `<Body>` element's namespace attribute as this identifier and ignores the SOAP action header. Even if the SOAP action header is not used, it must still be present. It can contain an empty string. If you implement and deploy a service that is accessible through SOAP over HTTP, you should always define this attribute. Leaving it empty should be considered a bad practice.

Both the `<input>` and the `<output>` elements contain a `<soap:body>` element. This basically defines how the request and response envelopes are encoded. You read earlier that the data structures that a service deals with are sent across the network in XML format. The encodingStyle attribute specifies which actual format was used to do this. In the services that exist today, you will mostly find two encoding schemes: SOAP encoding and literal XML. SOAP encoding (which is what is used in the example above) is a way of encoding data as described in the SOAP specification. Literal XML means that data is simply sent back and forth as XML documents, without any encoding at all.

The `<soap:body>` element also contains a namespace attribute. If defined, this will be used as the namespace of the first element within the `<Body>` element of the SOAP envelope. This is important to note here, because the Apache SOAP implementation uses the value of this attribute to identify the target URI of the invoked service. In the example above, the service would have to be deployed in Apache SOAP with the id urn:AddressBook.

The `<fault>` element can also contain a `<soap:fault>` element that is used to convey error information.

HTTP Binding

HTTP binding is another binding mechanism that is mentioned by the WSDL specification. It is intended mainly for invoking a Web Service from within a web browser in one of three ways:

- ❑ HTTP GET with URL encoding
- ❑ HTTP GET with URL replacement
- ❑ HTTP POST

These methods allow a service to be used by any standard HTTP browser. This means that service will be available to a wide range of clients from desktop web browsers to WAP-based cellular phones.

Let us use our address book example again and define the three different kinds of HTTP bindings for it. The first example shows the use of the HTTP GET verb, together with a URL-encoded input message:

```
<binding name="AddressBookHTTPBinding" type="tns:AddressBook">
  <http:binding verb="GET"/>
  <operation name="getAddress">
    <http:operation location="addressbook"/>
    <input>
      <http:urlEncoded/>
    </input>
    <output>
      <mime:content type="text/html"/>
    </output>
  </operation>
</binding>
```

The <http:binding> element lets you define which HTTP verb is supported by the service. Typically, this will be either GET or POST. The <http:operation> element defines the location of the service, relative to a base URI that is defined in the WSDL <port> element. We will get to that later. Let us just assume for this sample that the base URI of the service is http://www.abc.com.

The <http:urlEncoded> element defines that standard URL encoding is used for this request. In the example, the input message consists of one part, namely "person", which is of type string. If there were multiple parts, they would be separated in the URL by a semi-colon.

The binding example above could lead to the following HTTP request:

```
GET, URL="http://www.abc.com/addressbook?person=Joe"
```

Here is the second example, which uses HTTP GET with URL replacement binding:

```
<binding name="AddressBookHTTPBinding" type="tns:AddressBook">
  <http:binding verb="GET"/>
  <operation name="getAddress">
    <http:operation location="addressbook/(person)"/>
    <input>
      <http:urlreplacement/>
    </input>
    <output>
      <mime:content type="text/html"/>
    </output>
  </operation>
</binding>
```

This binding is similar to the first one, but it handles the input parameter differently. It also uses the GET verb, but does not use standard URL encoding for the parameter. Instead, the parameter is built into the location string of the <http:operation> element. The string (person) will be replaced with the value of the message part with the same name. Here is the resulting request:

```
GET, URL=http://www.abc.com/addressbook/Joe
```

The third example uses a POST verb and looks like this:

```
<binding name="AddressBookHTTPBinding" type="tns:AddressBook">
  <http:binding verb="POST"/>
  <operation name="getAddress">
    <http:operation location="addressbook"/>
    <input>
      <mime:content type="application/x-www-form-urlencoded"/>
    </input>
    <output>
      <mime:content type="text/html"/>
    </output>
  </operation>
</binding>
```

This binding will work with a web page that contains a form in which the input parameters can be entered. Instead of using the <http:urlEncoded> or <http:urlReplacement> element, it defines a MIME type for form encoding. The <mime:content> element is actually defined in the MIME binding, which we will cover in the following section. The resulting request looks like this:

```
POST, URL=http://www.abc.com/addressbook, PAYLOAD="person=Joe"
```

Note that in our address book example, the returned response is still an XML document containing the address information. It is assumed here that the client issuing the request would be able to process this return

MIME Binding

This binding can be used together with the SOAP or the HTTP binding to add MIME encoding capabilities to a service. It supports the following MIME types:

❑ multipartRelated - This type defines a message that consists of more than one part, all encoded in possibly different MIME types.

❑ text/XML - This type defines a message that is formatted in XML. This can be either a SOAP message (in other words, an XML document within a SOAP envelope) or a simple XML document.

❑ Others - All other MIME types are supported, as long as no information other than the MIME type string is required.

For example, let us assume that together with an address of a person, we want to retrieve their picture. Here is the binding for this:

```
<binding name="AddressBookBinding" type="AddressBook">
  <soap:binding style="rpc" transport="http://schemas.xmlsoap.org/soap/http"/>
  <operation name="getAddress">
    <soap:operation soapAction="urn:addressbook"/>
    <input>
      <soap:body encodingStyle="http://schemas.xmlsoap.org/soap/encoding/"
```

```
                        namespace="urn:addressbook"
                        use="encoded"/>
        </input>
        <output>
          <mime:multipartRelated>
            <mime:part>
              <soap:body parts="personPart addressPart"
                         encodingStyle="http://schemas.xmlsoap.org/soap/encoding/"
                         namespace="urn:addressbook"
                         use="encoded"/>
            </mime:part>
            <mime:part>
              <mime:content part="picturePart" type="image/jpeg"/>
            </mime:part>
          </mime:multipartRelated>
        </output>
      </operation>
    </binding>
```

The definition of the output message contains the <mime:multipartRelated> element, which indicates that multiple differently encoded parts are returned. All of these parts are contained in separate <mime:part> elements. The first part contains a <soap:body> element. This means that a regular SOAP envelope is returned, and it contains the personPart and addressPart pieces of the output message. The second part contains the binary image (in other words, the person's picture). MIME types like this one can be described by the <mime:content> element. In this example, we assume that an additional part called picturePart has been defined for the output message.

You can find additional information about sending MIME encoded messages over SOAP in the SOAP chapter of this book. For the remainder of this chapter, we will only work with the SOAP binding.

Java Binding?

To make it clear right away, the WSDL specification does not currently define any Java binding, though it may add one in the future. It would provide a way to optimize the use of a Web Service considerably, if certain conditions were met. If a Web Service is invoked across a network, significant work must be done: all data must be converted into XML format before making the call. It must then be converted back into whatever local format the service implementation supports upon arrival at the server. The same happens on the way back. However, in cases where both the client and the server use Java, and if the service implementation can be embedded into the client process, a simple local call would do the job! Or, if a local call is not possible, RMI may be used as the communication protocol. This is simply to say that the concept of the binding allows specifying all kinds of protocol details that a client can use to communicate with a Web Service. If both client and service implementation use Java, it makes sense to use communication means that are defined for the Java language.

Remember that multiple bindings can be specified for a Web Service in one WSDL document. Providing a Java binding on top of the more common SOAP binding would allow you to skip many of the encoding steps that are needed in a distributed, programming language-neutral environment, thus providing for much better performance!

In any case, the WSDL specification allows the usage of any type of binding; the ones mentioned are just examples. To make sure that any client can access your Web Service, you should always at least define either SOAP or HTTP bindings.

The <service> and <port> Elements

This is the last piece of the puzzle – the <service> element. Until now, we have seen elements that describe which exact interface is offered by a service and how to invoke. So the only remaining information we need is where to send the actual request. This is what the <service> element contains. To be exact, the <port> element within the <service> element contains this information. Several ports can be specified. Each port is specific for the type of binding that was described in the <binding> element. In other words, the port definition for a SOAP binding is different from that for other bindings. This also allows one Web Service to be accessible through multiple ports at the same time.

Here is what the port definition for the address book sample might look like. This example points to an Apache SOAP server and a separate port for the HTTP binding we described earlier:

```
<service name="AddressBookService">
  <port name="SOAPPort" binding="tns:AddressBookSOAPBinding">
    <soap:address location="http://www.abc.com/soap/servlet/rpcrouter"/>
  </port>
  <port name="HTTPPort" binding="tns:AddressBookHTTPBinding">
    <soap:address location="http://www.abc.com"/>
  </port>
</service>
```

WSDL and Java

So far, we have talked a lot about XML and the content of a WSDL document, all in a programming language-neutral fashion. Now it is time to look at all this from a Java programmer's perspective.

Top-down versus Bottom-up

In the Web Services world, you can be the provider of a service, a requestor, or both. Your usage of WSDL will differ, depending on which role you play, so we will look at each of them separately.

Let us assume that you are a provider and want to implement your service in Java. There are two approaches that you can take; you can follow a top-down or a bottom-up approach.

With the top-down approach, you already have an existing WSDL definition of a service. For example, a standardized WSDL definition may exist for the retrieval of an entry in an address book. If you want to provide a service implementation for an address book and follow the standard, you have to translate the data type definitions that exist in the WSDL document into Java classes. You also have to provide a Java class that offers a method for each defined operation.

Using the bottom-up approach means that you have existing Java code that you want to offer as a Web Service. In this case, you need to create a WSDL document that maps your Java code. Again, a mapping between the Java types and the XML-based <types> element in the WSDL document is needed.

If you are a service requestor, you follow a process that is similar to the top-down approach. You have the definition of a service in WSDL. In order to access this service, you need to create the appropriate data structures and interpret the returned data properly. The two main issues here are the type mapping in the provider case and the usage of the provided binding information.

For example, if a SOAP binding exists in the WSDL document, you need to create Java client code that sends the correct SOAP envelope to the service. The Apache SOAP implementation is a package that supports this.

No standard way of doing this exists today. However, efforts are underway to define the exact mapping of an XML document into a Java object and vice versa, so that this will be resolved in the future. The initiatives within the Java Community Process (JCP) that address this are the Java Architecture for XML Binding (JAXB – http://java.sun.com/xml/jaxb/index.html) and the Java API for XML-based RPC (JAX-RPC – http://java.sun.com/jaxrpc/index.html). In most simple cases, this mapping is a pretty straightforward process. Moreover, tools exist already that support both the top-down and bottom-up approach, making it relatively easy for you as a Java developer to choose the most suitable approach.

Mapping WSDL Terms into Java Terms

A WSDL document describes the interface of a Web Service. Since we are focusing on Java usage here, we can try to map the terms that are used in WSDL into the Java world. Please note that this mapping is by no means standardized in any way and is only meant as a guideline.

WSDL term	Java term
<types>	class
<message>	method parameters or return value
<operation>	method
<portType>	class

The WSDL for Java (WSDL4J) API

The first part of this chapter explained the elements of WSDL and how the language can be used to describe a Web Service. In the second part of the chapter, we will look at how a WSDL document can be created and/or interpreted from within a Java program.

The WSDL4J API provides complete access to WSDL documents through Java. It is currently developed as an open source project and can be found at http://oss.software.ibm.com/developerworks/projects/wsdl4j/. At the same time, a WSDL API has been proposed to the Java Community Process, in order to try to standardize a Java API for it. The proposal was submitted as JSR 110. You can find out its latest status and more details at http://jcp.org/jsr/detail/110.jsp.

The WSDL4J API exists in a package called javax.wsdl and contains mainly interfaces and a few classes. To use it, you need access not only to this package, but also to an implementation of the defined interfaces. The one that we will use here is contained in the IBM Web Services Toolkit, which can be found at http://www.alphaworks.ibm.com/tech/webservicestoolkit/.

In the future, there will probably be more implementations of the API that you can choose from. Moreover, it may change slightly, so please keep that in mind as you work with some of the code samples that are listed below. These samples were created using the IBM Web Services Toolkit version 2.4.

But before we dive into the details of *how* to access a WSDL document via WSDL4J, let us briefly discuss *why* we would want to do this. We will consider creation and access separately, because they imply different usage scenarios.

WSDL Document Creation

Only service providers need to create WSDL documents. A service requestor will never do that. Obviously, you can create a WSDL document manually, using any text editor or XML editor. But hopefully you will have a tool available that generates the document for you, based on existing code that you have already developed. For example, the IBM Web Services Toolkit, which you can download for free, comes with a tool that generates WSDL documents from existing Java code. The GLUE platform, which is covered in more detail later in the chapter, has a similar tool. This leaves us with two reasons why you would want to create a WSDL document via a Java program; either you are a tool vendor yourself and want to integrate WSDL document creation into your tool environment, or you have a tool, but for some reason, the tool does not support the specific kind of WSDL document that you need. Well, of course, a third reason may be that you are just curious and want to figure out how it works.

In all of those cases, the document creation will probably include some kind of introspection of existing Java classes, which are turned into WSDL definitions. Moreover, you may have to deal with already existing XML Schemas that describe the data structures of your service. These may be copied into the WSDL document or imported into it by using an <import> element.

WSDL Document Access

Service requestors need to access WSDL documents in order to find out what services they offer and how they can be invoked. Again, you should have a tool environment that parses an existing WSDL document for you and creates some client code that you can integrate into your application. The IBM Web Services Toolkit and GLUE, again, offer such functionality. Or you may manually create client code that matches the definitions given in an existing document.

This leaves us with the following usage scenarios: you may, again, be a tools vendor who wants to add WSDL handling to a tooling product. This could include client code generation for a specific service, or the conversion of WSDL data into some internal format.

The other usage scenario for programmatic access to WSDL is the creation of dynamic calls to a service at runtime. Here, you do not generate code that can later be used to invoke the Web Service; rather you create these calls dynamically at runtime. A complete example for this will follow in a later section of this chapter.

Even if you do not play any of the roles described here, you may still want to play around with the API we describe here. Accessing WSDL with this API will help you a great deal in understanding the different artifacts of the language, especially if you are not too familiar with XML.

WSDL4J Interfaces

For the most part, the WSDL4J API consists of Java interfaces that do not provide any implementation. Thus, if you want to use this API, you also need to obtain a package that implements this API. The examples that are provided in this section are based on the WSDL4J implementation that is currently shipped with the IBM Web Services Toolkit. In the future, slight changes to the API may occur, and other implementations may be available for you to use. In the first part of this section, we will focus on the interfaces that are defined in the core WSDL4J, which are independent of any implementation details.

The javax.wsdl.Definition class

Some of the design of WSDL4J is modeled after the Java API of XML Parsing (JAXP), http://java.sun.com/xml/jaxp/index.html, and the W3C DOM API. Like JAXP, this API provides an entry point (that is, factory) to a core element from which other elements can be built. For example, the JAXP API provides the notion of a `DocumentBuilderFactory`, which lets you create a `DocumentBuilder` object. This object, in turn, lets you create an instance that implements the `org.w3c.dom.Document` interface. This interface provides creation methods for all kinds of other elements that are used in the XML DOM space, like `Node`, `Element`, and so forth. This allows an application to work with standardized interfaces only, and be independent from the actual implementation.

The concept in WSDL4J is similar. The core interface in this package is called `javax.wsdl.Definition`. Once you have obtained an object that implements this interface, you can use it to create other more down-level instances for things like messages, port types, and so forth. Thus, the `javax.wsdl.Definition` class provides `createXXX()` methods like `createBinding()`, `createMessage()`, or `createOperation()`. These methods return instances that implement the respective interfaces defined in WSDL4J.

Thus, if used properly, the WSDL4J API makes it possible to write applications that use only the standard interfaces, working with any implementation.

Document Creation and Document Access

We mentioned above that in order to work with Java representations of the WSDL language elements, an application can use instances of `javax.wsdl.Definition`. But how do you obtain such an instance? There are two ways; either you create an entirely new instance using the `javax.wsdl.factory.DefinitionFactory` class, or you create an instance from an existing WSDL document. Let us look at both cases.

We have looked at usage scenarios for programmatic access to WSDL before. If, for one of the reasons that we mentioned above, you want to create a new WSDL document from scratch, you start with creating a new `javax.wsdl.Definition` instance via the `javax.wsdl.factory.DefinitionFactory.newDefinition()` method. Before you can use that method, use the static `newInstance()` method in the same class to get a factory instance. The following code sample shows how you can create a new `javax.wsdl.Definition` instance using this mechanism. Admittedly, this example is not a very useful application, but you get the idea. We'll add more content to this application as we go along. You can download all of the code shown here, including setup instructions, from the download section for this book at the Wrox web site:

```
import com.ibm.wsdl.xml.*;
import javax.wsdl.*;
import javax.wsdl.factory.*;

public class WSDL4JCreateSample {
  public static void main(String[] args) {
    try {
      Definition def = DefinitionFactory.newInstance().newDefinition();
    } catch (WSDLException ex) {
      System.out.println("Exception - fault code : "+ex.getFaultCode());
    }
  }
}
```

If you are accessing an existing WSDL document and want to parse it into a
`javax.wsdl.Definition` instance, you need to write different code. Here you need to read and parse
the document first and then initialize the `Definition` instance with its content. The WSDL4J API
provides no abstract factory class or any method in the existing factory classes to do this. You can
expect that this will be added at a later time.

For now, we have to use a concrete class in the `com.ibm.wsdl.xml` package that is shipped with the
IBM Web Services Toolkit, called `WSDLReader` (there is also a class called `WSDLWriter` in that
package and we will talk about it a little bit later). This class contains a number of static `readWSDL()`
methods that all read in existing WSDL documents from different sources. They all return an instance
of `javax.wsdl.Definition`. Moreover, this class has a method called `setImportDocuments()`
(and the respective `getImportDocuments()`). If you set this flag to true, `<import>` elements in the
parsed document will be resolved.

The following example shows how you can parse the `AddressBook-service.wsdl` document from
the previous section and create a `javax.wsdl.Definition` instance from it. Again, this example does
not really do anything meaningful, but we will add more useful code to it later:

```
import com.ibm.wsdl.xml.*;
import javax.wsdl.*;
import org.xml.sax.*;

public class WSDL4JReadSample {
  public static void main(String[] args) {
    try {
      Definition def = WSDLReader.readWSDL(null,
              new InputSource(
                  "http://localhost:8080/wrox/wsdl/AddressBook-service.wsdl"));
    } catch (WSDLException ex) {
      System.out.println("Exception - fault code : "+ex.getFaultCode());
    }
  }
}
```

Imports

Besides the `javax.wsdl.Definition` interface, the WSDL4J API defines Java wrapper interfaces for
all of the WSDL elements. These provide methods that allow you to get and set their content, and thus
allow us to build a complete WSDL document or parse an existing one. Let us look at some of the
contained interfaces in more detail, beginning with the `javax.wsdl.Import` interface.

Once you have obtained an instance of `javax.wsdl.Definition`, you can retrieve its contained
`<import>` elements via the `getImports()` method. If you know that one or more `<import>` elements
for a specific namespace exist, you can retrieve them using a call to `getImports()` that lets you pass
the name of the namespace URI as a parameter.

The actual Java wrapper class for `<import>` elements is `javax.wsdl.Import`. The `getImports()`
methods return a `java.util.Map` object. This Map contains a `Vector` of `javax.wsdl.Import`
objects, keyed by the namespace URI that they use.

The following example, `WSDL4JImportSample.java`, shows how you can obtain a list of imports contained in a WSDL document. It retrieves a `javax.wsdl.Definition` object from a `WSDLReader`, and then uses that to iterate over the list of contained `javax.wsdl.Import` objects. For the input, we will use the address book example again. It contains one import for the XML schema:

```java
import com.ibm.wsdl.xml.*;
import javax.wsdl.*;
import org.xml.sax.*;
import java.util.*;

public class WSDL4JImportSample {
  public static void main(String[] args) {
    try {
      Definition def = WSDLReader.readWSDL(null,
              new InputSource(
                "http://localhost:8080/wrox/wsdl/AddressBook.wsdl"));
      Map importsMap = def.getImports();
      System.out.println("Number of imports found : "+importsMap.size());

      Iterator iterator = importsMap.keySet().iterator();
      while (iterator.hasNext()) {
        String key = (String)iterator.next();
        Enumeration enum = ((Vector)importsMap.get(key)).elements();
        while (enum.hasMoreElements()) {
          Import importObject = (Import)enum.nextElement();
          System.out.println("Found import.");
          System.out.println("\tNamespace URI is : "+
                                    importObject.getNamespaceURI());
          System.out.println("\tLocation URI is : "+
                                    importObject.getLocationURI());
        }
      }
    } catch (WSDLException ex) {
      System.out.println("Exception - fault code : "+ex.getFaultCode());
    }
  }
}
```

When you run this program, it will produce the following output:

```
Number of imports found : 1
Found import.
  Namespace URI is : http://www.addressbook.com/schemas/AddressBookRemoteInterface
  Location URI is : http://localhost:8080/wrox/wsdl/AddressBook-schema.xsd
```

To play around with different WSDL documents, you may want to pass their URL as a parameter to the program, rather than hard-coding it, as in the example above.

Messages and Parts

Next, we want to find out which messages are contained in a WSDL document and which parts are contained in a message. You will see that this is a relatively easy task when you use the WSDL4J API. The `javax.wsdl.Definition` interface provides a method named `getMessages()`, which returns all of the messages in a `java.util.Map` object. You can also retrieve an individual message if you know its fully qualified name. We'll create an example of that later. But first, let us look at an example that iterates over all messages contained in the WSDL document and their parts:

```
import com.ibm.wsdl.xml.*;
import javax.wsdl.*;
import org.xml.sax.*;
import java.util.*;

public class WSDL4JMessageSample {
  public static void main(String[] args) {
    try {
      Definition def = WSDLReader.readWSDL(null,
              new InputSource(
                "http://localhost:8080/wrox/wsdl/AddressBook.wsdl"));
      Map messagesMap = def.getMessages();
      System.out.println("Number of messages found : "+messagesMap.size());
      Iterator iterator = messagesMap.keySet().iterator();
      while (iterator.hasNext()) {
        QName key = (QName)iterator.next();
        Message messageObject = (Message)messagesMap.get(key);
        System.out.println("Found Message.");
        System.out.println("\tMessage local name is : "+
                        messageObject.getQName().getLocalPart());
        System.out.println("\tMessage namespace URI is : "+
                        messageObject.getQName().getNamespaceURI());
        Map partsMap = messageObject.getParts();
        Iterator pIterator = partsMap.keySet().iterator();
        while (pIterator.hasNext()) {
          String pKey = (String)pIterator.next();
          Part partObject = (Part)partsMap.get(pKey);
          System.out.println("\tFound part.");
          System.out.println("\t\tPart name is "+ partObject.getName());
          System.out.println("\t\tPart type is "+ partObject.getTypeName());
          System.out.println("\t\tPart element name is "+
                        partObject.getElementName());
        }
      }
    } catch (WSDLException ex) {
      System.out.println("Exception - fault code : "+ex.getFaultCode());
    }
  }
}
```

This program, when run with the address book sample WSDL file that is listed in the previous section, produces the following output:

```
Number of messages found : 2
Found Message.
   Message local name is : getAddressResponse
   Message namespace URI is :
http://www.addressbook.com/definitions/AddressBookRemoteInterface
   Found part.
      Part name is result
      Part type is http://www.addressbook.com/schemas/AddressBookRemoteInterface:Address
      Part element name is null
Found Message.
   Message local name is : getAddressRequest
   Message namespace URI is :
http://www.addressbook.com/definitions/AddressBookRemoteInterface
   Found part.
      Part name is person
      Part type is http://www.w3.org/2001/XMLSchema:string
      Part element name is null
```

Now that we have parsed the WSDL document down to message part level, what can we do with it? The `javax.wsdl.Part` interface provides information about the name of an element and, more importantly, about its type. This information is given in the form of `javax.wsdl.QName` objects. We have not discussed this class yet. It represents a fully qualified name of an element in an XML document. 'Fully qualified' means that both the name of an element and the namespace URI for which this name is defined are specified. This uniquely identifies a name within an XML document.

Unfortunately, the WSDL4J API does not give any further support when it comes to type handling. For example, in the program above, we found out that the WSDL definition contains a message called `getAddressResponse`, which contains a part called `result` of type `http://www.addressbook.com/schemas/AddressBookRemoteInterface:Address`. Let us assume you want to generate some code that interacts with this Web Service. To do this, you might have to know what exactly this type consists of, or, in other words, you would have to work with the `<types>` element in the WSDL document that describes it. The WSDL4J API provides no classes or methods that would let you parse an XML Schema in the `<types>` element. You can retrieve the content of the `<types>` element as an XML DOM element (in other words, an instance of `org.w3c.dom.Element`). After that, you're on your own. This means, for example, that you have write to XML parsing logic to find out that the type `Address` consists of three fields of type string, namely `zipcode`, `city`, and `street`.

Operations and Port Types

So far, we have looked at the messages and their contained parts. Now we can take the next step, namely turning messages into operations and port types. You have learned earlier that there are four kinds of operations, namely one-way, request-response, solicit-response, and notification. For most Web Services, the defined operations are of type request-response, meaning that the `<operation>` element contains exactly one input and one output message.

In the following sample, we will see how a new WSDL document can be created that contains the correct operations and port type definitions for our address book Web Service. Let us assume that we have some existing Java code that implements the address book function. There is a class called `Address` that look like this:

```java
public class Address {
  protected String street;
  protected String city;
  protected String zipcode;

  public String getStreet() {
    return street;
  }

  public void setStreet(String street) {
    this.street = street;
  }

  public String getCity() {
    return city;
  }

  public void setCity(String city) {
    this.city = city;
  }

  public String getZipcode() {
    return zipcode;
  }

  public void setZipcode(String zipcode) {
    this.zipcode = zipcode;
  }
}
```

We have created an XML Schema definition that maps this class. It defines a complex type named `Address` that has three elements of type string. You have already seen this schema in a previous section of this chapter, but here it is again:

```xml
<?xml version="1.0"?>
<!-- File: AddressBook-schema.xsd -->
<schema
  xmlns="http://www.w3.org/2001/XMLSchema"
  targetNamespace="http://www.addressbook.com/schemas/AddressBookRemoteInterface"
  xmlns:xsd1="http://www.addressbook.com/schemas/AddressBookRemoteInterface">

  <complexType name="Address">
    <all>
      <element name="zipcode" type="string"/>
      <element name="city" type="string"/>
      <element name="street" type="string"/>
    </all>
  </complexType>

</schema>
```

134

We also have a class called `AddressBook` that has one method in it, called `getAddress()`. It takes a `String` as a parameter and returns an `Address` object. Here is its source code – the code that shows the retrieval of the actual `Address` object is left out here:

```
public class AddressBook {
  public Address getAddress(String person) {
    // implementation left out...
  }
}
```

This is the method that we want to map into a request-response operation. To build a complete, working WSDL document, there are a number of things we need to do.

Create the Definition Object

First, we need to create an instance of `javax.wsdl.Definition`. This is done through a factory method, as we mentioned earlier. Moreover, we need to define a number of namespaces that are later used in the content of the WSDL document. The code is shown below (the complete sample can be downloaded from the Wrox web site for this book in a file called `WSDL4JCreateSample.java`):

```
Definition def = DefinitionFactory.newInstance().newDefinition();
def.addNamespace("tns",
        "http://www.addressbook.com/definitions/AddressBookRemoteInterface");
def.addNamespace("xsd1",
        "http://www.addressbook.com/schemas/AddressBookRemoteInterface");
def.addNamespace("xsd", "http://www.w3.org/2001/XMLSchema");
def.addNamespace("soap", "http://schemas.xmlsoap.org/wsdl/soap/");
def.setTargetNamespace(
        "http://www.addressbook.com/definitions/AddressBookRemoteInterface");
```

We will use the `Definition` object to create all other objects that we need.

You can now write the resulting WSDL document to an actual file using the `com.ibm.wsdl.xml.WSDLWriter` class (note that you may want to change the target location of the file):

```
try {
  WSDLWriter.writeWSDL(def, new FileWriter(
          "c:\\jakarta-tomcat-3.2.1\\webapps\\wrox\\wsdl\\AddressBook.wsdl"));
} catch (IOException io) {
  System.out.println("IO Exception : "+io);
}
```

If you simply run the code listed above, it will produce the following output:

```
<?xml version="1.0" encoding="UTF-8"?>
<definitions
    targetNamespace=
      "http://www.addressbook.com/definitions/AddressBookRemoteInterface"
    xmlns:xsd="http://www.w3.org/2001/XMLSchema"
    xmlns:xsd1="http://www.addressbook.com/schemas/AddressBookRemoteInterface"
```

135

```
        xmlns:tns="http://www.addressbook.com/definitions/AddressBookRemoteInterface"
        xmlns:soap="http://schemas.xmlsoap.org/wsdl/soap/"
        xmlns="http://schemas.xmlsoap.org/wsdl/">
    </definitions>
```

Create the Import Object

The method that we want to expose as a Web Service returns an `Address` object. As we mentioned above, this class was mapped to a schema. This schema is imported into the WSDL document via the `<import>` element:

```
Import importObject = def.createImport();
importObject.setLocationURI(
        "http://localhost:8080/test/wsdl/AddressBook-schema.xsd");
importObject.setNamespaceURI(
        "http://www.addressbook.com/schemas/AddressBookRemoteInterface");
def.addImport(importObject);
```

Note that using the `Definition` object to create the `Import` object does not automatically add this object to the `Definition`. You can also see again here that this code is completely independent from any implementation of the WSDL4J API; it is only using the interfaces defined in the `javax.wsdl` package.

This code adds the following element to the `<definitions>` element:

```
<import
    namespace="http://www.addressbook.com/schemas/AddressBookRemoteInterface"
    location="http://localhost:8080/test/wsdl/AddressBook-schema.xsd"/>
```

Create the Message and Part Objects

Now we are ready to create the Java wrappers for the `<part>` and `<message>` elements. The `getAddress()` method takes a `String` as its input parameter and returns an object of type `Address`, so we need to define a message for each. Both messages contain one part, namely the input `String` and the returned `Address`, respectively:

```
Part addressPart = def.createPart();
addressPart.setName("result");
addressPart.setTypeName(
  new QName("http://www.addressbook.com/definitions/AddressBookRemoteInterface",
            "Address"));

Part personPart = def.createPart();
personPart.setName("person");
personPart.setTypeName(
  new QName("http://www.w3.org/2001/XMLSchema", "string"));

Message iMessage = def.createMessage();
iMessage.setUndefined(false);
iMessage.setQName(
  new QName("http://www.addressbook.com/definitions/AddressBookRemoteInterface",
            "getAddressRequest"));
```

```
iMessage.addPart(personPart);
def.addMessage(iMessage);

Message oMessage = def.createMessage();
oMessage.setUndefined(false);
oMessage.setQName(
  new QName("http://www.addressbook.com/schemas/AddressBookRemoteInterface",
            "getAddressResponse"));
oMessage.addPart(addressPart);
def.addMessage(oMessage);
```

All of the namespace qualifiers that you use must have been declared on the Definition object via the
addNamespace() method. In this example, we use
"http://www.addressbook.com/definitions/AddressBookRemoteInterface" as the
namespace URI, but you can basically pick any URI of your choice here.

You also have to set the undefined flag of each new Message object to false, otherwise it will be
ignored later on when we write the actual WSDL file.

The sample code above adds the following to our WSDL document:

```
<message name="getAddressResponse">
  <part name="result" type="xsd1:Address"/>
</message>
<message name="getAddressRequest">
  <part name="person" type="xsd:string"/>
</message>
```

Creating the Operation and PortType Objects

We can now create the operation that represents the getAddress() method and add it to a
<portType>. The operation is a request-response operation, which means that it has one input and one
output message:

```
Input input = def.createInput();
input.setMessage(iMessage);

Output output = def.createOutput();
output.setMessage(oMessage);

Operation operation = def.createOperation();
operation.setUndefined(false);
operation.setName("getAddress");
operation.setStyle(OperationType.REQUEST_RESPONSE);
operation.setInput(input);
operation.setOutput(output);

PortType portType = def.createPortType();
portType.setUndefined(false);
portType.addOperation(operation);
portType.setQName(
  new QName("http://www.addressbook.com/definitions/AddressBookRemoteInterface",
            "AddressBook"));
def.addPortType(portType);
```

The `Operation` and `PortType` objects both contain a flag named `undefined` that must be set to `false`. Here is the output that these lines of code add to the WSDL document:

```
<portType name="AddressBook">
  <operation name="getAddress">
    <input message="tns:getAddressRequest"/>
    <output message="tns:getAddressResponse"/>
  </operation>
</portType>
```

Bindings

In the previous sections, we created a WSDL document that is only missing two things to be usable: the `<binding>` element and the `<port>` element. In this section, you will learn how to create a `Binding` object.

This is slightly different from the previous code. WSDL does not restrict the kinds of bindings you can add. The specification defines two types of bindings as examples, namely one for SOAP and one for HTTP. Within the `<binding>` element, you have a mix of elements defined by WSDL and elements that are specific to the type of binding.

Here is what this looks like. Note that the elements are not complete; this example just shows the structure of the `<binding>` element and where the so-called **extensibility elements** are placed.

```
<binding>
<!-- add specific binding extensibility element here -->
<!-- for SOAP, this is 'soap:binding' -->
  <operation>
    <!-- add specific operation extensibility element here -->
    <!-- for SOAP, this is 'soap:operation' -->
    <input>
      <!-- add specific operation extensibility element here -->
      <!-- for SOAP, this is 'soap:body' -->
    </input>
    <output>
      <!-- add specific operation extensibility element here -->
      <!-- for SOAP, this is 'soap:body' -->
    </output>
  </operation>
</binding>
```

Let us reiterate this: extensibility elements are elements that are specific for a certain type of binding and are contained within other elements in the `<binding>` element. Currently WSDL4J does not define specific Java classes for the SOAP and HTTP extensibility elements. The only interface contained in the API is the `javax.wsdl.ExtensibilityElement` interface. This could change over time. However, currently you have to look at your particular WSDL4J implementation package for implementations of the interface. For example, the implementation contained in the IBM Web Services Toolkit 2.4 has extensibility element implementations for SOAP in the `com.ibm.wsdl.extensions.soap` package. Similarly, implementations for HTTP exist in a package called `com.ibm.wsdl.extensions.http`.

The following example shows how you can build SOAP bindings for the address book sample. Note that classes beginning with the word SOAP are not created via the javax.wsdl.Definition object. They are all imported from the com.ibm.wsdl.extensions.soap package. The elements that are not extensibility elements (for example, BindingOperation) are still created through the javax.wsdl.Definition object:

```
Binding binding = def.createBinding();
binding.setUndefined(false);
binding.setQName(new
QName("http://www.addressbook.com/definitions/AddressBookRemoteInterface",
    "AddressBookBinding"));
binding.setPortType(portType);

SOAPBinding soapBinding = new SOAPBinding();
soapBinding.setStyle("rpc");
soapBinding.setTransportURI("http://schemas.xmlsoap.org/soap/http");
binding.addExtensibilityElement(soapBinding);

BindingOperation bindingOperation = def.createBindingOperation();
bindingOperation.setName("getAddress");

SOAPOperation soapOperation = new SOAPOperation();
soapOperation.setStyle("rpc");
soapOperation.setSoapActionURI("urn:AddressBook");
bindingOperation.addExtensibilityElement(soapOperation);

BindingInput bindingInput = def.createBindingInput();
SOAPBody soapBody = new SOAPBody();
soapBody.setUse("encoded");
soapBody.setNamespaceURI("urn:AddressBook");
Vector stylesVector = new Vector();
stylesVector.addElement("http://schemas.xmlsoap.org/soap/encoding/");
soapBody.setEncodingStyles(stylesVector);
bindingInput.addExtensibilityElement(soapBody);
bindingOperation.setBindingInput(bindingInput);

BindingOutput bindingOutput = def.createBindingOutput();
bindingOutput.addExtensibilityElement(soapBody);
bindingOperation.setBindingOutput(bindingOutput);

binding.addBindingOperation(bindingOperation);
def.addBinding(binding);
```

Other bindings, for example for HTTP, are created in a similar way. The code above creates the following XML elements:

```
<binding name="AddressBookBinding" type="tns:AddressBook">
    <soap:binding style="rpc" transport="http://schemas.xmlsoap.org/soap/http"/>
    <operation name="getAddress">
        <soap:operation soapAction="urn:AddressBook" style="rpc"/>
        <input>
            <soap:body
                use="encoded"
```

```
                    namespace="urn:AddressBook"
                    encodingStyle="http://schemas.xmlsoap.org/soap/encoding/"/>
             </input>
             <output>
                <soap:body
                   use="encoded"
                   namespace="urn:AddressBook"
                   encodingStyle="http://schemas.xmlsoap.org/soap/encoding/"/>
             </output>
         </operation>
      </binding>
```

Service and Port

The last missing piece is the `<service>` element with its contained `<port>` element. This will point to the actual location of the service. In our example, we assume that the service has been installed on the `localhost` at port 8080:

```
Port port = def.createPort();
port.setName("AddressBookPort");
port.setBinding(binding);

SOAPAddress soapAddress = new SOAPAddress();
soapAddress.setLocationURI("http://localhost:8080/wrox/servlet/rpcrouter");
port.addExtensibilityElement(soapAddress);

Service service = def.createService();
service.setQName(new QName(
    "http://www.addressbook.com/definitions/AddressBookRemoteInterface",
    "AddressBookService"));
service.addPort(port);
def.addService(service);
```

here is the `<service>` element that is created by the code above:

```
<service name="AddressBookService">
    <port name="AddressBookPort" binding="tns:AddressBookBinding">
        <soap:address location="http://localhost:8080/Wrox/servlet/rpcrouter"/>
    </port>
</service>
```

This completes the definition of the service.

Dynamic Service Invocation from WSDL

So far in this chapter, you have learned what elements are contained in a WSDL document and how you can describe existing functions using this language. We then looked at how the WSDL4J API lets you access existing WSDL documents or create new ones from Java. In this section, we will look at how an existing WSDL document can be used to create a call to a Web Service dynamically. That is, we will not generate code that can invoke a particular service; rather we will try to create a Web Service client that can call *any* service based on its WSDL definition.

Invoking a Web Service dynamically will most likely be useful in test or evaluation scenarios where you try to find out how a particular service functions. As soon as you are ready to integrate a service into production level code, you will most likely generate some client proxy code that accesses this service. This avoids the overhead of retrieving, parsing, and interpreting the WSDL definition. Moreover, it lets you add specific code that a certain service may require.

We will look at two examples that show how a service can be invoked dynamically. We will begin with the Web Services Invocation Framework and then take a closer look at the GLUE platform.

The Web Services Invocation Framework

The **Web Services Invocation Framework (WSIF)** allows the dynamic invocation of a Web Service, based solely on the WSDL definition for that service. It is available for download from the IBM AlphaWorks website at http://www.alphaworks.ibm.com/tech/wsif. At the time of writing, version 1.0 of the framework was available. Future versions will most likely provide bug fixes and additional functionality that is currently not supported.

The WSIF is based on the WSDL4J API that was discussed in the previous section. It provides additional classes that allow you to parse a WSDL document and also to use its defined binding and port information to create an actual call to that service. Here is how this works in a few sentences:

1. The WSDL document is read into a `javax.wsdl.Definition` object.

2. Using this object, a `com.ibm.wsif.WSIFDynamicPortFactory` object is created. All type mapping between the XML types declared in the WSDL and the Java classes that are used in the client are defined on this factory.

3. A `com.ibm.wsif.WSIFPort` object is obtained from the factory.

4. All messages (both input and output) and parts from the WSDL document are wrapped in WSIF objects: `com.ibm.wsif.WSIFMessage` and `com.ibm.wsif.WSIFPart`.

5. `executeRequestResponseOperation()` on the `com.ibm.wsif.WSIFPort` object is used to invoke the service. The result of the call can be retrieved from the passed output message (`com.ibm.wsif.WSIFMessage`).

That is everything you need to do. We will now walk through a code sample that shows you how these steps look in Java code. You can also find the complete example, called `WSIFSample.java`, in the download section for this book at the Wrox web site.

Step 1 was to read in the WSDL document and store it in a `javax.wsdl.Definition` object. We will assume here that a file named `AddressBook.wsdl` exists. Note that the package declarations are omitted to make the code more readable:

```
import javax.wsdl.*;
import org.xml.sax.*;
import java.io.*;
import com.ibm.wsdl.xml.*;
import com.ibm.wsif.*;
```

```
public class WSIFSample {
  public static void main(String[] args) throws Exception {
    Definition def = WSDLReader.readWSDL(null,
      new InputSource("http://localhost:8080/wrox/wsdl/AddressBook.wsdl"));
```

Next, create the dynamic port factory and define the type mapping:

```
WSIFDynamicPortFactory dpf = new WSIFDynamicPortFactory(def);
dpf.mapType(
    new QName("http://www.addressbook.com/schemas/AddressBookRemoteInterface",
              "Address"),
    Address.class);
```

Note that in order to make a dynamic call, Java classes must already exist for the types that are declared in the <types> element of the WSDL document (or in the schema that is included via an <import> element). In our case, this is the Address class.

Now we can retrieve the com.ibm.wsif.WSIFPort object and wrap the messages and parts:

```
WSIFPort port = dpf.getPort();

WSIFMessage input = port.createInputMessage();
WSIFMessage output = port.createOutputMessage();
WSIFMessage fault = port.createFaultMessage();

WSIFPart inputPart = new WSIFJavaPart(java.lang.String.class, "Joe Smith");
input.setPart("person", inputPart);
```

If you wanted to write a client that is completely generic and can read and interpret any WSDL document, you would have to add code here that reads the part definitions and fills in appropriate values. For example, in our address book case, the input message contains one part of type string. We can map this into the code above. To make this dynamic, you would have to read the part definition from the WSDL document. You would then detect for this case that the input message contains one part that is of type string. Given this information, you could build the com.ibm.wsif.WSIFPart object.

We are now ready to invoke the service:

```
port.executeRequestResponseOperation("getAddress", input, output, fault);
```

This is the only place where the <operation> is referenced by its name. The result of the call can now be retrieved from the output message:

```
WSIFPart outputPart = output.getPart("result");
Address address = (Address)outputPart.getJavaValue();
System.out.println("Resulting address is:");
System.out.println("\tStreet  : "+address.getStreet());
System.out.println("\tCity    : "+address.getCity());
System.out.println("\tZipcode : "+address.getZipcode());
  }
}
```

An important thing that this code shows is that the service is invoked independent from the actual protocol that is used. In other words, this code will work for a SOAP binding as well as for an HTTP binding of the service, and no additional client package is required. The WSIF uses something called a **dynamic provider** for this. Based on the specification in the WSDL document, a provider is used that implements the right protocol. For example, if `<soap:binding>` is specified, a class called `WSIFDynamicProvider_ApacheSOAP` is used to make the call. However, this never shows up in the client code.

This example shows how we can deal with a Web Service on a WSDL level, without requiring any knowledge about the protocol it supports and how the service was implemented. The use of an abstract API like WSDL4J, together with additional support for dynamic invocation as provided by the WSIF, makes this possible.

The GLUE platform also supports the dynamic invocation of Web Services via a WSDL document definition. However, this platform offers a lot more, so it is worth a more detailed look.

GLUE

GLUE is a complete environment for Web Services. Its homepage is located at http://www.themindelectric.com/products/glue/glue.html. At the time of this writing, the most current version is GLUE 2.0. The Standard Edition was used for all of the samples shown below.

GLUE provides support for all of the relevant Web Services technologies, like WSDL, UDDI, and SOAP. It comes with an embedded web server, a SOAP engine, a UDDI server and client, and a console that allows the administration of deployed and registered services. All XML processing is done using Electric XML, which comes with GLUE, but is also available separately. The API supported by Electric XML is similar to the JDOM API. Services can be hosted by the contained HTTP server environment, application servers such as BEA WebLogic, or on other servlet containers like Apache Tomcat.

GLUE is implemented completely in Java and supports both Java clients to invoke Web Services and Java objects to be exposed as Web Services. The complete runtime is contained in a jar file that is less than 500 Kbytes in size.

Publishing a Service

The GLUE documentation uses the term "publishing" a service. Here, this means that a service is available on a server and accepts client requests. It does not mean that the service is published in a UDDI registry (see the next chapter for more on UDDI). This is different from what other packages call it. For example, in the Apache SOAP implementation, a service is 'deployed'.

To publish a new Web Service, GLUE needs a WSDL document that describes it. You can create a WSDL document from existing Java code using a command line GLUE tool called `java2wsdl`. Let us use the address book example from above to see how the WSDL file can be built from existing Java code. Here is the code for the `AddressBook` again, showing one method that returns an `Address` object. In this example, we will simply return a hard-coded address:

```
public class AddressBook {
  public Address getAddress(String person) {
    Address address = new Address();
    address.setStreet("4210 1st Street NW");
```

```
      address.setCity("Rochester, MN");
      address.setZipcode("55901");
      return address;
   }
}
```

Again we use the `Address` class that was listed earlier.

To create the WSDL document from this, you enter the following on the command line:

> **java2wsdl AddressBook -s -e http://localhost:8004/glue/urn:AddressBook**

The `-s` option directs the tool to generate SOAP bindings. HTTP bindings can be generated by specifying `-g`. The parameter `-e` lets you define the endpoint URL under which a client can invoke the service can be reached by a client. In our case, this is `http://localhost:8004/glue/urn:AddressBook`. For more available options on this command, please consult the GLUE documentation.

This will create the following WSDL document:

```
<?xml version='1.0' encoding='UTF-8'?>
<!--generated by GLUE on Thu Dec 13 17:59:14 CST 2001-->
<definitions name='AddressBook'
        targetNamespace='http://www.themindelectric.com/wsdl/AddressBook/'
        xmlns:tns='http://www.themindelectric.com/wsdl/AddressBook/'
        xmlns:electric='http://www.themindelectric.com/'
        xmlns:soap='http://schemas.xmlsoap.org/wsdl/soap/'
        xmlns:http='http://schemas.xmlsoap.org/wsdl/http/'
        xmlns:mime='http://schemas.xmlsoap.org/wsdl/mime/'
        xmlns:xsd='http://www.w3.org/2001/XMLSchema'
        xmlns:soapenc='http://schemas.xmlsoap.org/soap/encoding/'
        xmlns:wsdl='http://schemas.xmlsoap.org/wsdl/'
        xmlns='http://schemas.xmlsoap.org/wsdl/'>
  <types>
    <schema xmlns='http://www.w3.org/2001/XMLSchema'
            xmlns:tns='http://www.themindelectric.com/package/'
            targetNamespace='http://www.themindelectric.com/package/'>
      <complexType name='Address'>
        <sequence>
          <element name='street' nillable='true' type='string'/>
          <element name='city' nillable='true' type='string'/>
          <element name='zipcode' nillable='true' type='string'/>
        </sequence>
      </complexType>
    </schema>
  </types>
  <message name='getAddress0SoapIn'>
    <part name='arg0' type='xsd:string'/>
  </message>
  <message name='getAddress0SoapOut'>
    <part name='Result'
        xmlns:ns1='http://www.themindelectric.com/package/'
```

```
            type='ns1:Address'/>
    </message>
    <portType name='AddressBookSoap'>
      <operation name='getAddress' parameterOrder='arg0'>
        <input name='getAddress0SoapIn' message='tns:getAddress0SoapIn'/>
        <output name='getAddress0SoapOut' message='tns:getAddress0SoapOut'/>
      </operation>
    </portType>
    <binding name='AddressBookSoap' type='tns:AddressBookSoap'>
      <soap:binding style='rpc'
                    transport='http://schemas.xmlsoap.org/soap/http'/>
      <operation name='getAddress'>
        <soap:operation soapAction='getAddress' style='rpc'/>
        <input name='getAddress0SoapIn'>
          <soap:body use='encoded'
                    namespace='http://tempuri.org/AddressBook'
                    encodingStyle='http://schemas.xmlsoap.org/soap/encoding/'/>
        </input>
        <output name='getAddress0SoapOut'>
          <soap:body use='encoded'
                    namespace='http://tempuri.org/AddressBook'
                    encodingStyle='http://schemas.xmlsoap.org/soap/encoding/'/>
        </output>
      </operation>
    </binding>
    <service name='AddressBook'>
      <port name='AddressBookSoap' binding='tns:AddressBookSoap'>
        <soap:address location='http://127.0.0.1:8004/glue'/>
      </port>
    </service>
</definitions>
```

As you can see, it turned the endpoint definition address into an IP address, which is not portable. You may have to change it in case you offer your Web Service on another address.

This WSDL file can also be generated implicitly by GLUE if you publish the service directly. This publishing is done via the `electric.registry.Registry` class, which provides a number of static methods for it. Publishing the `AddressBook` example to the web server that is packaged with GLUE and automatically generating WSDL for it can be coded in two lines of Java!

You can find this sample as `GLUEPublishAddressBook.java` in the download section for this book at the Wrox web site, together with instructions on how to set up your environment to compile and run it:

```
import electric.registry.*;
import electric.server.http.*;

public class GLUEPublishAddressBook {
  public static void main(String[] args) {
    try {
      HTTP.startup("http://localhost:8004/glue");
      Registry.publish("urn:AddressBook", AddressBook.class);
    } catch (Exception e) {
      System.out.println("Exception is publish : "+e);
    }
  }
}
```

Running this program will start up the web server on the specified port (8004 in this case) and make the `AddressBook` class available as a Web Service on it. The listed source code is derived from one of the samples that ship with GLUE. For more detailed information and more examples, we suggest that you download GLUE and work through its documentation. You can look at the WSDL that is generated dynamically by opening the following URL in a browser window: http://localhost:8004/glue/urn:AddressBook.wsdl. It will show the same WSDL document that we created above with the `java2wsdl` tool.

If you want to deal with WSDL from within your Java application, GLUE offers an alternative API to the WSDL4J API described above. It offers similar functionality, providing Java wrapper classes for the elements of WSDL.

Invoking a Service

To make a call (that is, send a SOAP request) to a service, a local representation of that service is needed. This is a local proxy object that you can make calls to, which will then forward the request to the actual service. To use a service from a client program requires two steps; you generate a local Java interface that provides the service interface in Java using the `wsdl2java` tool, which we will describe in a minute. At runtime, you bind to the service and GLUE will create an instance of the local Java interface for you that you can then use to make calls to the service as if they were local calls.

Alternatively, you can directly invoke the service on the Registry and omit the creation of the local proxy altogether. We will look at an example for both cases here, which will also show what the differences between the two are and why you would want to use one or the other.

Let us assume that we want to invoke the address book service that was published above. We will pretend that we don't know how the service was implemented; all we have is the WSDL document. We will use this to create the Java interface through the `wsdl2java` tool. Invoke this tool on the command line with the following command:

```
> wsdl2java http://localhost:8004/glue/urn:AddressBook.wsdl
```

Note how we specify the location of the WSDL document. The definition points directly to the GLUE server and takes advantage of the WSDL document that is created implicitly when a service is published.

The tool creates four new files:

❑   `Address.java` is created from the complex type definition in the WSDL document. It contains only three public `String` attributes, namely `street`, `city`, and `zipcode`:

```
public class Address {
  public String street;
  public String city;
  public String zipcode;
}
```

❑   `IAddressBook.java` is an interface that represents the service on the client. An instance that implements this interface will be returned when you bind to the service:

```
public interface IAddressBook {
  Address getAddress( String person );
}
```

❑   AddressBookHelper.java contains some code that lets you avoid downcasting the result of
     the bind() call to the IAddressBook interface:

```
import electric.registry.Registry;
import electric.registry.RegistryException;

public class AddressBookHelper {
  public static IAddressBook bind() throws RegistryException {
    return bind("http://localhost:8004/glue/urn:AddressBook.wsdl");
  }

  public static IAddressBook bind(String url) throws RegistryException {
    return(IAddressBook) Registry.bind(url, IAddressBook.class);
  }
}
```

❑   AddressBook.map contains the mapping definition between the fields in the complex type
     definition of the WSDL document and the attributes of the generated Address class. This file
     can be used to change the default mapping that GLUE uses when making a call to the service.
     In our case, we will use the defaults and thus won't use this file.

We are now ready to create a client program that will invoke the service. This is as easy as publishing
the service, since it requires only a few lines of code:

```
import electric.registry.*;

public class GLUEBindAddressBook {
  public static void main(String args[]) throws Throwable {
    IAddressBook addressBook = AddressBookHelper.bind();
    Address address = addressBook.getAddress("someone");
    System.out.println("Resulting address is:");
    System.out.println("\tStreet  : "+address.street);
    System.out.println("\tCity    : "+address.city);
    System.out.println("\tZipcode : "+address.zipcode);
  }
}
```

The call to the bind() method returns a local proxy that you can use to invoke the Web Service. All
the details of building the SOAP request envelope and interpreting the response envelope are handled
under the covers. This way of invoking a service via its local proxy will be the most common way of
using Web Services. You can find the complete source for this example as
GLUEBindAddressBook.java in the download section for this book at the Wrox web site.

As we had mentioned above, you can also make a call directly to the service without generating the
proxy. In that case, you use the invoke() method on the Registry. You pass the address of the
WSDL document to it, plus the name of the method that you want to invoke and any parameters. The
returned value can be downcast to the right type. The following listing, available for download as
GLUEInvokeAddressBook.java, shows this code:

```
import electric.registry.*;

public class GLUEInvokeAddressBook {
  public static void main(String args[]) throws Throwable {
    Address address = (Address)Registry.invoke(
                      "http://localhost:8004/glue/urn:AddressBook.wsdl",
                      "getAddress", new Object[] { "someone" } );
    System.out.println("Resulting address is:");
    System.out.println("\tStreet  : "+address.street);
    System.out.println("\tCity    : "+address.city);
    System.out.println("\tZipcode : "+address.zipcode);
  }
}
```

Which of the two options you use depends on what service you call and how often you call it. In most cases, it will be more convenient to generate the proxy and obtain an instance of it through the `bind()` method of the generated helper class.

These samples show that GLUE provides a very simple and lightweight alternative to other Java-based Web Services solutions. It uses the WSDL language for both server and client side processing. It does not require creating any kind of proxy or helper, even though it supports the generation of them.

In this chapter, we have not covered the UDDI capabilities of GLUE. Please refer to the product documentation for more information on this topic.

Summary

The Web Service Definition Language (WSDL) is a language that allows you to describe the external interface that is provided by a Web Service. Moreover, it lets you add specific information about the protocol that you can use to invoke the service, including its address on the network. In this chapter, you have learned which XML elements are provided by the language specification to build a complete Web Service definition.

To create a new WSDL document, or read an existing one, from a Java program, the WSDL for Java (WSDL4J) API can be used. It provides full programmatic access to all of the elements defined in the specification.

The GLUE product provides an alternative Java implementation for all relevant Web Service standards, namely WSDL, SOAP, and UDDI. The samples in this chapter have shown how you can easily provide a Web Service to a client, or how to create a client that invokes an existing Web Service, based on the WSDL description of that service.

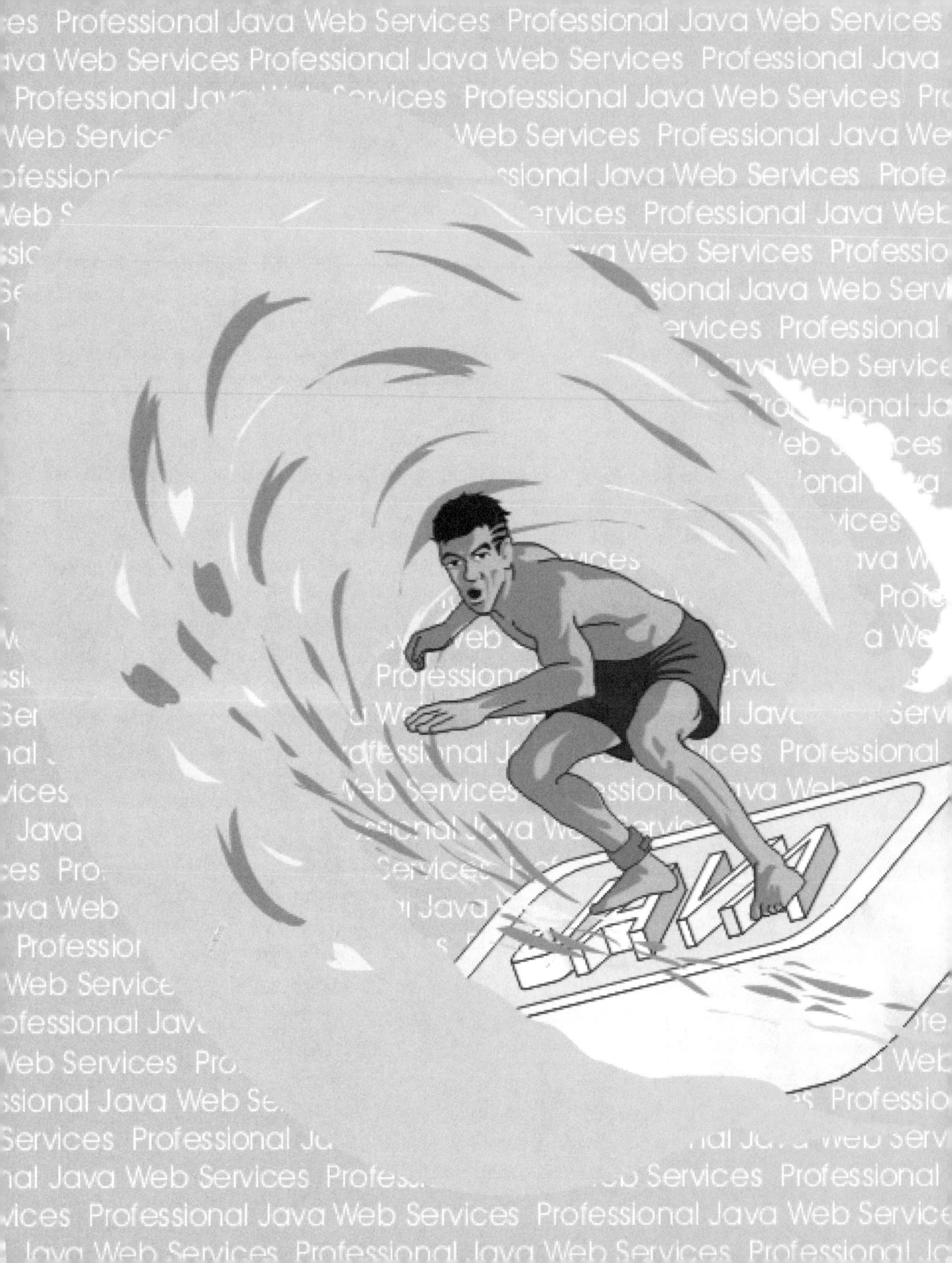
Professional Java Web Services

UDDI

One of the key success factors of Web Services technology is that a mechanism is provided for developers of Web Services to offer them to potential clients. Moreover, clients need a way to find out about services offered by potential suppliers or customers. **Universal Description, Discovery, and Integration (UDDI)** addresses these issues.

In this chapter, you will learn how a UDDI registry is structured and how to publish and retrieve information to and from such a registry. We will then look at a Java API that will allow us to do these things from within a Java application. The UDDI4J API from IBM provides Java wrappers for all of the UDDI artefacts. It is an open source project, so that we can work with its actual sourcecode. Other APIs exists, and more may be created over time, but we will only cover the UDDI4J API as an example.

Finally, we will describe some of the existing registries, including one that you can download and install on your own computer.

Introduction

Web Services technology is all about allowing applications to communicate with each other over the Internet, without requiring a great deal of human intervention. This includes both user-to-program and program-to-program communication. Everyone should be able to use any service, independent of the platform that the service is running on and the programming language that is used.

The basic concept behind this is that of a **service oriented architecture (SOA)**, in which three roles are defined:

- ❑ Service requestor
- ❑ Service provider
- ❑ Service broker

What we will focus on in this chapter is the service broker, which allows a requestor to find the appropriate provider of a service. The broker part is typically represented by a registry that contains references to available services. The registry can be queried via a well-defined interface.

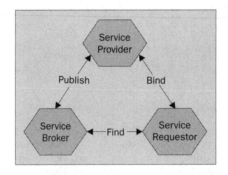

This web services registry, typically called an UDDI registry, contains information about existing services and the companies that offer them.

Several public UDDI registries exist today, hosted by Hewlett-Packard (https://uddi.hp.com/uddi/index.jsp), IBM (http://www-3.ibm.com/services/uddi/), and Microsoft (http://uddi.microsoft.com/default.aspx).

> *At the time of this writing, the available public registries support UDDI version 1.0. Registries supporting version 2.0 are in beta. The samples given in this chapter use the current 2.0 beta registries.*

Eventually, there should be a number of registries existing that will form some kind of hierarchical tree, thus reducing the load of the existing registries. The registries replicate all of their information between each other, so that each registry always contains all available information.

UDDI contains of a number of specifications that describe how a registry stores data and how it can be accessed. It was initially created by three companies, namely by Ariba, IBM, and Microsoft. However, since it can only be successful if it has widespread support, a community was created that takes the specifications forward and turns them into a standard. This community, called **uddi.org**, is open for companies that want to participate in the evolution of the technology. You can find its homepage at http://uddi.org. It now has several hundred members, including every major software company.

UDDI consists of four main specifications:

❑ The data structure specification describes what kind of data is stored in UDDI. Like other web services technologies, the UDDI data structure is based on XML. In other words, platform- and programming language-neutrality is achieved by describing all of the relevant structures as XML documents. This data structure can be described through an XML Schema. This schema is actually published as a separate document available from the UDDI web site.

❑ The programmer's API specification contains how a UDDI registry can be accessed. There are two types of API, namely **publishing functions** and **inquiry functions**. The publishing functions are used to create and update existing entries in the registry. The inquiry functions are all read-only and allow the existing entries to be queried programmatically. We will look at these in more detail later.

The API is programming language-independent. This is accomplished by describing the request and return data in terms of an XML document. These request and return structures map the actual content of the registry quite closely. The existing registries offer access via SOAP over HTTP. This means that the request and return XML documents are wrapped into SOAP envelopes. The inquiry functions are available over HTTP, whereas the publishing functions are accessible via HTTPS and require a user ID and password to be passed along with each request. Each UDDI registry provides ways for a user to obtain a valid user ID and password.

❑ The **replication specification** contains descriptions of how registries replicate information among themselves. This information is only needed for those who want to implement their own registry and integrate it with other existing registries.

❑ Finally, there is the **Operator's specification**, which again targets only those who are implementing or running a UDDI registry. It defines policies for security (for example, that a user ID is required and that all changes to the registry must be audited) and for data management (for example, how many entities can be created by an account; and how are whitespaces handled, among other things). While the spec does not mandate that an operator follow a certain policy, it requires that each operator publish what policies are enabled and enforced.

The current version for all of these specifications is 2.0. However, at the time of this writing, the public registries only support the 1.0 level. Support for the latest version is in beta. All of the coding samples that are listed further below have been created with the 2.0-compliant beta UDDI registries.

UDDI Registries

In this section, we want to focus on the registries themselves, prior to looking at the way their data is structured. There are three public UDDI registries in production right now, and you are going to create a personal user account for the IBM registry for yourself, in order to run the later examples.

The IBM Registry

The IBM UDDI registry is located at http://www.ibm.com/services/uddi/.

It provides a test area and a production area. The test area is open for everyone as a testing environment before adding any information to the public registry. Additionally, it also contains a beta version of the UDDI version 2-compliant registry. Eventually, the beta registry will be merged into production mode and these URLs may change, so that it is a good idea to check on the registry homepage for the latest valid URLs.

- ❑ The production registry inquiry API access point is http://www-3. ibm.com/services/uddi/inquiryapi/

- ❑ The access point for the publish API is https://www-3.ibm.com/services/uddi/protect/publishapi/

- ❑ The access points for the test area are http://www-3.ibm.com.services/uddi/testregistry/inquiryapi/ and https://www-3.ibm.com/services/uddi/testregistry/protect/publishapi/, respectively

- ❑ The access points for the UDDI version 2 compliant-registry are http://www-3.ibm.com.services/uddi/v2beta/inquiryapi/ and https://www-3.ibm.com/services/uddi/v2beta/protect/publishapi/, respectively

Note that these access points are used when sending requests to the registry via SOAP. In other words, entering these URLs in a browser window does not make much sense.

Creating a User Account on the UDDI v2Beta Test Registry

To operate the examples in this chapter, we will need a user ID and password. Navigate to http://www-3.ibm.com/services/uddi/ and click on the UDDI Business Registry V2 Beta link on the right-hand side of the page. You will be informed that you are about to view pages over a secure connection.

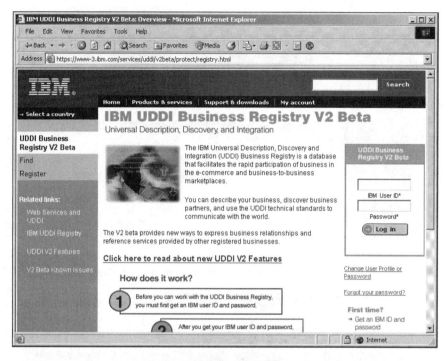

Click on the First time? link under the log-on box and follow the simple registry instructions. Within 15 minutes you should be e-mailed your activation key, which you enter when prompted the first time you log on to the site with your user ID and password. Once your account is activated (you should see a screen telling you this), you can use your ID and password as parameters in the code that we will look at later on.

The web site itself contains an integrated administration environment for the registry, which allows us to find, create, and update entries. Overleaf is a screenshot showing how you can create a new Locator (that is, <categoryBag>) for a <businessEntity> element. We will look at these elements in the next section.

Once you log on, the web site will show you all of the entries that you own. You can then edit each entry, adding new information as shown below. The exact look of the screen may change with newer versions of the registry over time. There is also a Help function available, in case you need to have more detailed information.

The inquiry API is supported by simple and advanced search pages, which let you enter information about the entries that you are looking for. For example, let us assume you have created the business entry for "Bill's Office Services" by using the example code listed below. This code added a <categoryBag> to this entry, pointing to NAICS key 541611, which we can now use as search criteria here:

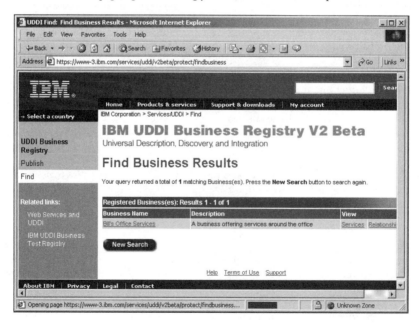

The % sign in the Starting with entry field indicates that we want a list of all businesses in that category, regardless of their name. Here is the result page, again, assuming you have run the code sample that created this entry:

The Microsoft Registry

The Microsoft registry is at http://uddi.microsoft.com/ and also provides a production and a test environment. Its handling is similar to the IBM registry. The access points for the production registry are at http://uddi.microsoft.com/inquire/ and https://uddi.microsoft.com/publish/. The access points for the test registry are http://test.uddi.microsoft.com/inquire and https://test.uddi.microsoft.com/publish. Note that in order to register with the Microsoft registry, you need to obtain a .NET Passport account.

By the way, unlike with the IBM registry, you can enter the access point URLs mentioned above in your browser window, and you will automatically be redirected to a readable web page.

Here is an example again, showing how you find a business entry by its NAICS code:

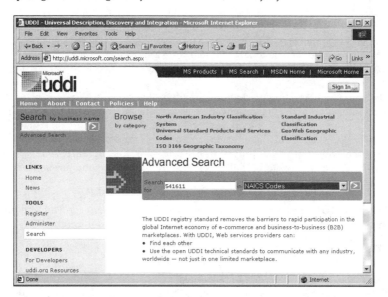

Something interesting to note about the Microsoft registry is that it is very compatible with Internet Explorer. If you have Internet Explorer 5 installed on your system, enter the word uddi followed by a blank and then the string you are looking for in UDDI. When you hit enter, Internet Explorer will automatically forward your request to the Microsoft UDDI registry.

Other Registries

At this time, two more companies have announced that they will provide publicly accessible UDDI registries. These companies are Hewlett-Packard and SAP.

At the time of this writing, the HP registry was not fully operational and in beta. You can expect that it will provide similar find and publish features to the other existing registries. Remember that the content of each registry is replicated once a day, so regardless of which one you use, you will find the same information. The homepage for the HP registry is http://uddi.hp.com/.

SAP has not yet started to make its registry available. You can find the press release about the SAP UDDI Registry at http://sap.com/solutions/technology/news.asp?pressID=629.

Other registries may follow in the future. It is always a good idea to check on the news web site of uddi.org for latest news. The URL for this page is http://uddi.org/.

Private UDDI Registries

So far we have only talked about the publicly available registries. They can be accessed over the Internet and contain all of the information about all web services on the planet. So, why would you ever want to run your own UDDI registry? Well, there are several reasons. First of all, you can operate your own registry on your own machine for testing purposes. It is more convenient to handle and it may be faster than to use than one of the remote test registries.

Secondly, and also more importantly, it allows you to establish your own registry of services, possibly only for your organization. We have talked about software reuse for many years – here is a standardized way of storing that information and making it available to other people in the organization.

Another issue you may have wondered about already is that of trust. When using web services, I make someone else's software a part of my application. What tells me that I can trust the service to be accurate, scalable, and reliable? Some manual evaluation would probably take place before any web service is used by a mission-critical application. You can use the private UDDI registry as a place where you store all of the evaluated and approved web services for your organization. Note, however, that a private UDDI registry may not support all of the features offered by the public registries, for example its auditing and replication functionality.

Having your own UDDI registry makes sense in a lot of cases. Where can you find one? Over time, many products will come out offering UDDI services in some form or another.

There are already several options:

❑ Private IBM UDDI Registry (free download at http://www.alphaworks.ibm.com/tech/UDDIreg/). This registry runs on either IBM WebSphere Application Server or on Apache Tomcat. It uses a DB2 database to store its content.

❑ pUDDIng: Find it at http://www.opensorcerer.org/.

❑ Microsoft also offers a UDDI registry as part of its .NET offering. It is part of the Microsoft .NET Server Application Environment, which is currently in beta. You can find more information about it at http://www.microsoft.com/windows.NETserver/developers/default.asp.

UDDI Data Structure

Generally speaking, a UDDI registry contains information about businesses and the services these businesses offer. These services are not necessarily web services, or even computer related at all. In fact, UDDI was designed so that it can hold arbitrary information about a business. It serves not only as an access point for information about services, but also about the businesses themselves.

Data in UDDI is structured similarly to a telephone book, in the way that phone numbers are stored and catalogued. Or, in other words, consider the data in a UDDI registry to be structured in 'white pages', 'yellow pages', and 'green pages':

❑ **White pages:**
UDDI contains information about businesses' names, addresses, phone numbers, and so on.

❑ **Yellow pages:**
These contain business listings based on the types of these businesses. Similarly, UDDI lets you find entries sorted by a business type or by the industry it operates in.

❑ **Green pages:**
These are used to indicate the services each business offers, including all of the technical information involved in interacting with or using the service, such as parameters, endpoint values, and so on.

This kind of structuring can be applied to both the publishing and retrieving of data in UDDI. If you publish information about your company or business, you should add information such as that mentioned above – address and phone numbers, some type of categorization of your business, and finally the services it offers. Similarly, you can also find businesses in the registry based on search criteria such as name or location, the product produced, or on the type of Web Service offered.

The following picture shows an overview of the main elements contained in UDDI. We will look at all of those elements in detail next.

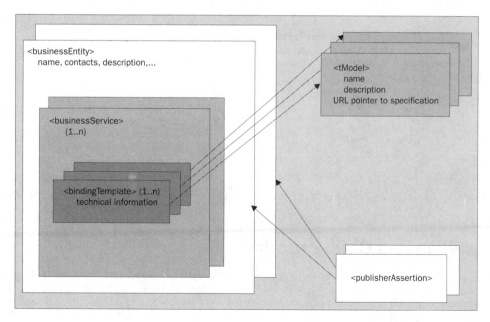

tModel

We will begin with information that can be shared among various entries in the registry, or data that is not associated with just one particular business.

One of the key elements in UDDI is the **tModel**. A `tModel` represents a technical specification in a UDDI registry. This technical specification can describe all kinds of things – for example, a standard for exchanging data between businesses, or the definition of a certain web service's interface. Thus, if you create a new web service and describe it in WSDL, this WSDL definition will eventually be stored as a `tModel` in UDDI. We will come back to this later.

For now, just remember that a `tModel` has a unique identifier and contains a pointer to a specification. A service requestor can use this to find services that offer functionality complying with certain standards.

By the way, many of the entries in a UDDI registry require a unique identifier. The registry always generates this identifier when a new entry is created. The identifier is a DCE UUID (Unique Universal Identifier), and there are various ways of implementing an algorithm that creates a UUID – which one is used is up to the registry. Here is an example for a UUID:

```
UUID:C0B9FE13-179F-413D-8A5B-5004DB8E5BB2
```

Here is an example `tModel`, referring to an existing WSDL specification:

```
<tModel authorizedName="wstkDemo"
    operator="ATOST/services/uddi"
    tModelKey="UUID:7C91BE10-EA7F-11D5-A6D4-9EAB24E10238">

  <name>Addressbook tModel</name>

  <overviewDoc>
    <overviewURL>
      http://localhost:8080/Wrox/wsdl/Addressbook-service.wsdl
    </overviewURL>
  </overviewDoc>
</tModel>
```

A `tModel` typically also contains `<identifierBag>` and `<categoryBag>` elements, which we will look at next.

Identifiers and Categorization

A wide variety of information can be disseminated in UDDI. This can be both technical and non-technical information, covering industries and businesses and all the data that they deal with. To find information in such a registry requires this information to be well categorized for ease of use. A user (and this can be a human or a program querying the registry) must be able to define search criteria that minimize the number of returned entries, simply because the number of entries in UDDI will eventually become very large.

The UDDI elements **identifier** and **category** are an attempt to address this problem. Actually, identifier and category are not really elements in UDDI. In other words, they are conceptual elements rather than actual XML elements in the schema. The specification defines XML elements called <identifierBag> and <categoryBag>, which always contain one or more elements. This allows us to collect a number of identifiers and/or categories into one collection that can be handled as a single element. In other words, they serve as a collection type, just as you would use a Bag in the Java language.

Let us start with <identifierBag>. An identifier in UDDI allows tagging an entry in the registry with additional information. Identifiers are **qualified key-value pairs**. What does this mean? Well, each identifier has a key and value for that key. But this information alone may not be good enough, because we also need to know what kind if key this is. For example, almost every large company in the US has what is called a DUNS number, (For more information on DUNS numbers, go to http://www.dnb.com/english/duns/default.asp.) This number identifies the business in any kind of transaction, and in fact, it is required when doing business with the federal government in the US. It makes sense to add the DUNS number to a business' entry in the UDDI registry, in case someone wants to find a company based on this information. So, you can create an identifier and change the key's value to the correct DUNS number. But what would be the key?

This is where an additional piece of information comes in: the tModel reference. In addition to the key-value pair, each identifier contains a reference to a tModel. We heard earlier that a tModel represents a technical fingerprint or specification. This includes cases where a tModel is built to represent a namespace. In the DUNS number example, a tModel was created to represent the DUNS number namespace. This tModel is referred to in the identifier. This way, we can detect that the identifier is meant to show the DUNS number of our company. Again, this is why you can think of the identifier as a key-value pair, because the pair has a reference to a namespace with it that indicates what kind of pair it is.

As we mentioned above, there is no such thing as an identifier element defined in UDDI. The name of the actual element containing the information is <keyedReference>. One or more <keyedReference> elements can be grouped in an <identifierBag>. <identifierBag> elements can occur in several places in the UDDI registry, wherever additional classification of data is helpful.

A category is very similar to an identifier. In fact, a category is an identifier with a predefined namespace. In other words, the creators of UDDI thought it would be a good idea to have some predefined taxonomies that make categorization of UDDI entries easier. They defined four namespaces, each one represented by a tModel, which we can use to classify our data:

- **UNSPSC – Universal Standard and Products Classification**
  This standard contains definitions for different products

- **NAICS – North American Industry Classification System**
  This standard defines a classification system for businesses based on the industry that they operate in

- **ISO 3166 – Geographic Classification System**
  This is a standard that describes different regions and locations around the world

- **Other** – This taxonomy is for general type keywords

Just like the case of identifiers, categories are represented in UDDI by a <keyedReference> element. Multiple categories are contained in a <categoryBag>.

So how are categories and identifiers used? Let us assume that you want to create an entry in UDDI for your company, and that this company is in the computer manufacturing business. Moreover, we will assume that the company is located in Bavaria in Germany. This can be expressed by creating three <keyedReference> elements:

❑ One represents the product code for computers in the UNSPSC standard

❑ The next one contains the industry code for computer manufacturers as defined in NAICS

❑ The third category shows the geographical code for Bavaria-Germany as defined in ISO 3166

All three <keyedReference> elements are added to a <categoryBag>.

Since a <keyedReference> contains a key-value pair and a reference to a tModel, what does this look like for the example above? Well, the <keyedReference> for the NAICS code for your company will have a key named Electronic Computer Manufacturing with a value of 334111. The referenced tModel will have the ID UUID:C0B9FE13-179F-413D-8A5B-5004DB8E5BB2, which represents the NAICS standard.

As you can see, you need some level of tooling to set these values properly – doing these things manually does not make a lot of sense, unless you are a tool vendor providing UDDI access. For example, the IBM Web Services Toolkit comes with a class called com.ibm.wstk.uddi.TModelKeyTable, which contains static String attributes for all of the commonly used tModelKeys. The NAICS tModel identifier mentioned above, for example, is provided as com.ibm.wstk.uddi.TModelKeyTable.NAICS_TMODEL_KEY.

The following picture shows a conceptual view of what <categoryBag> and <identifierBag> look like:

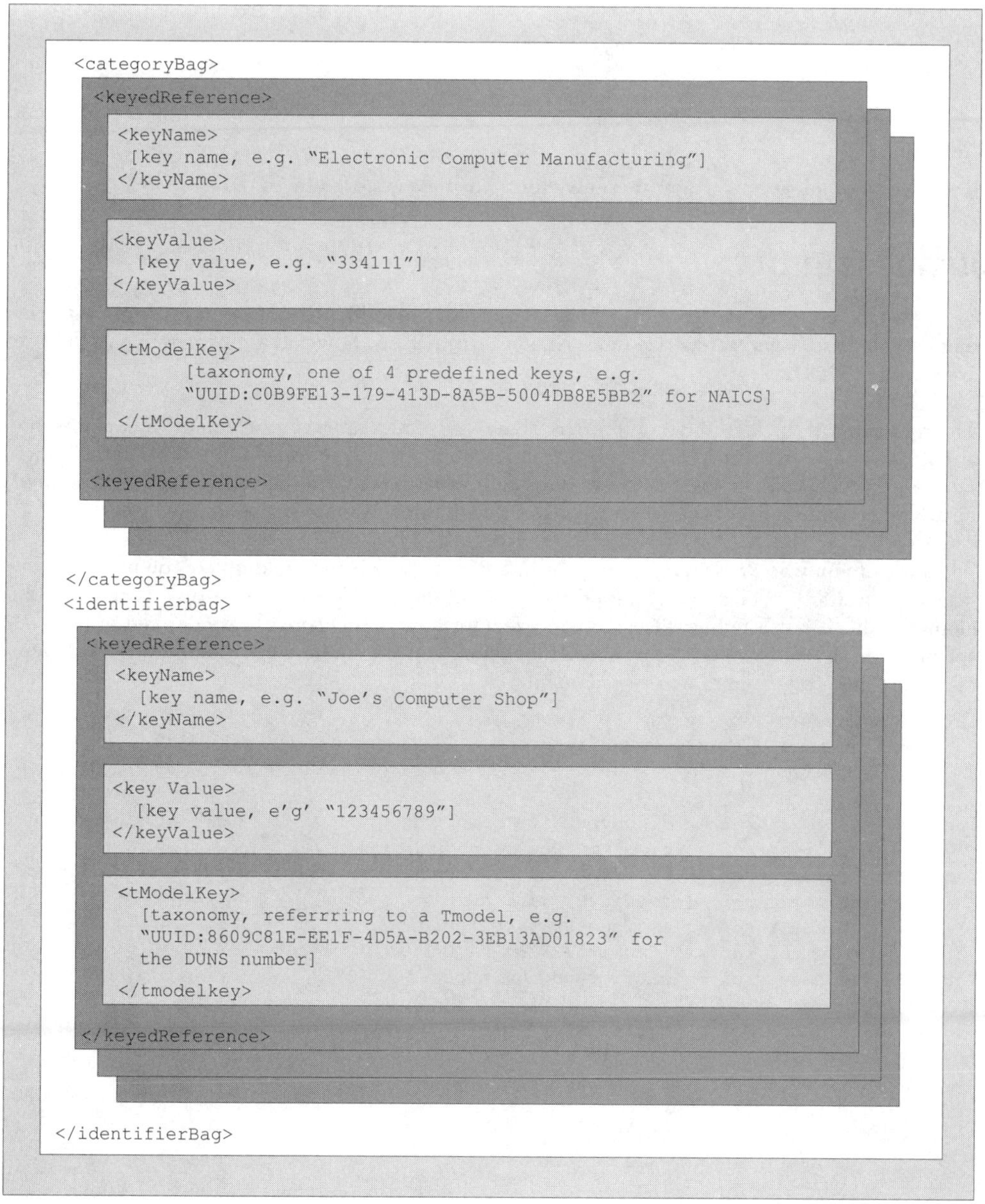

```
<categoryBag>
    <keyedReference>
        <keyName>
        [key name, e.g. "Electronic Computer Manufacturing"]
        </keyName>

        <keyValue>
        [key value, e.g. "334111"]
        </keyValue>

        <tModelKey>
            [taxonomy, one of 4 predefined keys, e.g.
            "UUID:C0B9FE13-179-413D-8A5B-5004DB8E5BB2" for NAICS]
        </tModelKey>

    <keyedReference>

</categoryBag>
<identifierbag>
    <keyedReference>
        <keyName>
        [key name, e.g. "Joe's Computer Shop"]
        </keyName>

        <key Value>
        [key value, e'g' "123456789"]
        </keyValue>

        <tModelKey>
        [taxonomy, referrring to a Tmodel, e.g.
        "UUID:8609C81E-EE1F-4D5A-B202-3EB13AD01823" for
        the DUNS number]
        </tmodelkey>

    </keyedReference>

</identifierBag>
```

Here is an example `<categoryBag>` containing one entry for the business type mentioned above:

```
<categoryBag>
  <keyedReference
    keyName="Electronic Computer Manufacturing"
    keyValue="334111"
    tModelKey="UUID:C0B9FE13-179F-413D-8A5B-5004DB8E5BB2"/>
</categoryBag>
```

Next, we will look at how exactly an entry for a business is stored in UDDI.

`<businessEntity>`

So far, we have looked at tModels, which let you store identifiers and categories, and other elements that let you classify and categorize data. Now it is time to see how actual businesses and their services are stored in UDDI.

The root entry of the UDDI data hierarchy is the `<businessEntity>` element. It contains information about a business – its name, its address, its phone number, and so forth. On top of that, it contains a `<categoryBag>` and an `<identifierBag>`, allowing the entry to be categorized as described above. Finally, it contains a list of service entries, but we will look at those in the following section.

For those of you who know how to read XML Schema, here is the (incomplete) definition of the `<businessEntity>` element, copied directly out of the specification. We won't do this for all of the elements; this is just listed here to give you a feel for how these elements are defined in the specification. Even if you don't know XML Schema, you should be able to figure out what elements are contained in a `<businessEntity>` element.

```
<element name = "businessEntity">
  <complexType>
    <sequence>
      <element ref = "discoveryURLs" minOccurs = "0"/>
      <element ref = "name" maxOccurs = "unbounded"/>
      <element ref = "description" minOccurs = "0" maxOccurs ="unbounded"/>
      <element ref = "contacts" minOccurs = "0"/>
      <element ref = "businessServices" minOccurs = "0"/>
      <element ref = "identifierBag" minOccurs = "0"/>
      <element ref = "categoryBag" minOccurs = "0"/>
    </sequence>
    <attribute ref = "businessKey" use = "required"/>
    <attribute ref = "operator"/>
    <attribute ref = "authorizedName">
  </complexType>
</element>
```

The following picture shows the content of the <businessEntity> element in a graphical form. Note that it is showing the concept only; for a definition of the exact structure you need to consult the specification.

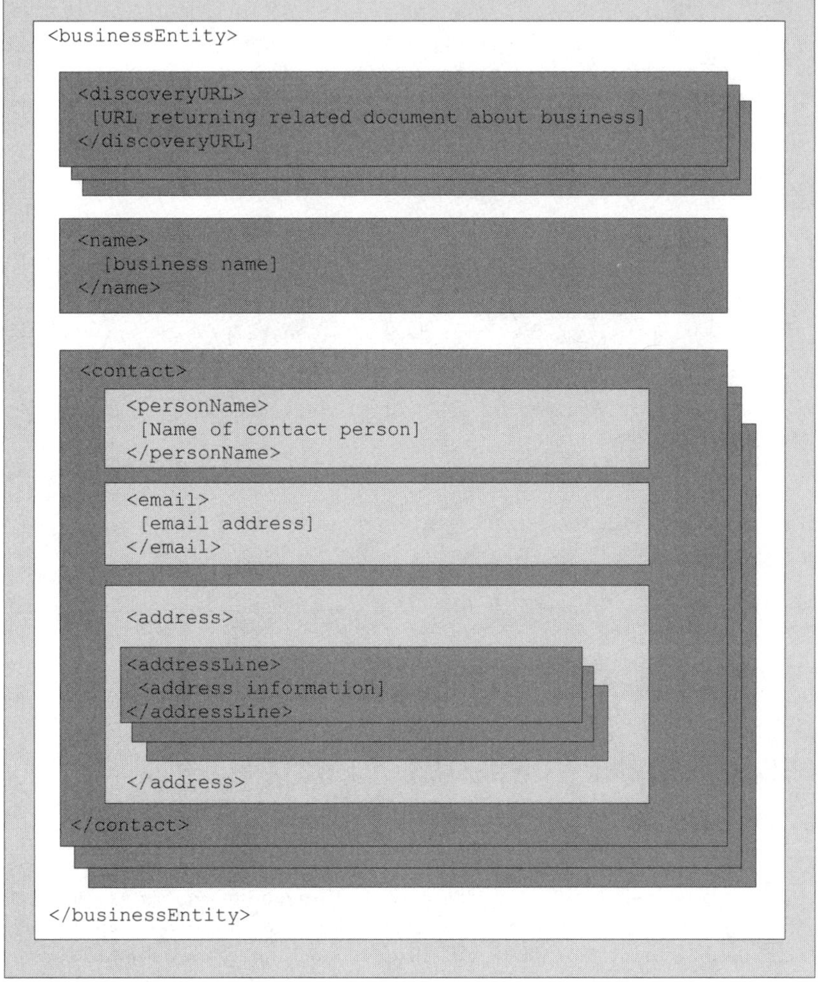

```
<businessEntity>

    <discoveryURL>
    [URL returning related document about business]
    </discoveryURL]

    <name>
      [business name]
    </name>

    <contact>

        <personName>
        [Name of contact person]
        </personName>

        <email>
        [email address]
        </email>

        <address>

        <addressLine>
         <address information]
        </addressLine>


        </address>
    </contact>

</businessEntity>
```

To keep things simple, this picture does not show the <categoryBag> or <identifierBag> entries.

Here is an example of what a concrete <businessEntity> entry might look like. This is basically an instance of the schema listed above. The business entry listed has one category that identifies the type of business in the NAICS taxonomy.

```
<businessEntity businessKey="4C890B30-EB6D-11D5-A947-97BA25522F30">
  <discoveryURLs>
    <discoveryURL useType="businessEntity">
        http://www.ibm.com/services/uddi/uddiget?businessKey=318C6450-EB6B-11D5-
        A947-97BA25522F30 </discoveryURL>
```

```
        </discoveryURLs>
        <name>Bill's Office Services</name>
        <description>A business offering services around the office</description>
        <contacts>
          <contact>
            <personName>Joe Smith</personName>
            <email>joes@officeservices.com</email>
            <address>
              <addressLine>1234 1st Ave SW</addressLine>
              <addressLine>Rochester, MN 55902</addressLine>
              <addressLine>USA</addressLine>
            </address>
          </contact>
        </contacts>
        <categoryBag>
        <keyedReference
            keyName="Administrative Management and General Management Consulting
            Services"
            keyValue="541611"
            tModelKey="UUID:C0B9FE13-179F-413D-8A5B-5004DB8E5BB2"/>
        </categoryBag>
      </businessEntity>
```

Note that the <discoveryURL> element is generated by the UDDI registry when the entry is created. This URL shows how a copy of the entry could be obtained using a simple HTTP GET request. For example, you can use this URL in a browser window. You can add additional URLs that return other documents about this entry. What exactly these URLs would return is not defined.

As we will see, we can create these structures either through an administration application for a UDDI registry, or programmatically through UDDI for Java, which we will explore in detail later.

<businessService>, <bindingTemplate>, and <tModelInstanceDetails> elements

Once you have a business registered in UDDI using the <businessEntity> element, you can start describing the services the business offers. This is done through the <businessService> element. Although we expect those services to be web services, or at least computer-related, they don't have to be. The <businessService> element contains the name of a service, an optional description, a <categoryBag> (note that these occur in all kinds of elements in the UDDI hierarchy) and a list of <bindingTemplate> elements.

Here is an example for a <businessService> element. The example represents an address book service, which is also categorized by a <categoryBag>:

```
<businessService
      businessKey="4C890B30-EB6D-11D5-A947-97BA25522F30"
      serviceKey="47FC56D0-ECD0-11D5-8EA6-926A0B6F3A63">
  <name>Addressbook Service</name>
  <description>A service offering address book capabilities</description>
  <bindingTemplates/>
```

```
<categoryBag>
  <keyedReference
      keyName="Office administration or secretarial services"
      keyValue="80161501"
      tModelKey="UUID:DB77450D-9FA8-45D4-A7BC-04411D14E384"/>
</categoryBag>
</businessService>
```

The serviceKey attribute contains the unique identifier of the entry in the registry. It is automatically generated when the entry is created. The businessKey attribute indicates which <businessEntity> entry this service belongs to. The example above shows an entry that has no <bindingTemplate>; (this is indicated by an empty <bindingTemplates> element). We will add one next.

The <bindingTemplate> element contains specific information about a service. However, the <businessService> element is not required to contain any <bindingTemplate>, their use is optional, so that a <businessService> structure with just a name and a description is perfectly valid.

```
<businessService>

    <name>
    [service name, e.g. "Addressbook Service"]
    </name>

    <description>
    [description, e.g. "A service offering addressbook capabilities"]
    </description>

    <bindingTemplate>

        <description>
        [description, e.g. "Binding Template for Addressbook Service"]
        </description>

        <accessPoint>
        [access point, e.g. "http://www.acme.com/addressbook"]
        </accessPoint>

        <tModelInstanceDetails>
        [details about the tModels that this service is associated with]
        </tModelInstanceDetails>

    </bindingTemplate>


    <categoryBag>
        <keyedReference>
        [qualified key-value pair]
        </keyedReference>

    </categoryBag>

</businessService>
```

A `<bindingTemplate>` contains two things: a so-called access point and a `<tModelInstanceDetails>` element. We will get to those in a second. But first, let us look at the access point, or `<accessPoint>`, which is what the actual element is called. This element is defined as a string, meaning that it could contain all kinds of information – it could be a URL, or an e-mail address, or even a telephone number.

Assume in the case of the following example that the company Rent-A-Sitter offers babysitting services. It has a `<businessEntity>` entry in a public UDDI registry, which contains a `<categoryBag>` with one category, namely 91111902 – Nanny or babysitting services in the UNSPSC taxonomy. The `<businessEntity>` element also contains two `<businessService>` entries, one called Preschool babysitting, the other one called Infant babysitting. There is a `<bindingTemplate>` in each, containing different phone numbers for each type of service. This shows that companies that have nothing to do with computers can use UDDI registries!

Now let us look at the `<tModelInstanceDetails>` element. As the name suggests, it contains references to tModel entries in the registry. The combination of tModels that are referenced here forms the technical fingerprint for the offered service. By the way, the `<tModelInstanceDetails>` does not directly contain pointers to tModels, it holds `<tModelInstanceInfo>` elements, which have the actual key (that is, the unique identifier) of the tModel in them, together with more detailed information about that tModel. One of the elements contained in the instance details is called `<overviewDoc>`, and contains yet another element called `<overviewURL>`, which is a pointer to additional documentation about the tModel. We mention this here, because this element will become important when we discuss the relationship between UDDI and WSDL, so bear with us.

```
<tModelInstanceDetails>
  <tModelInstanceInfo>

    <tModelKey>
     tkey, e.g. "UUID:4795F3E0-ECD0-11D5-8EA6-926A0B6F3A63"]
    </tModelKey>

    <description>
     [description, e.g. "Instance info for addressbook service"]
    </description>

    <tModelInstanceDetails>
      <description>
       [description, e.g. "instance detail"]
      </description>

      <overviewDoc>
       [reference to a document with more details, for example a
       WSDL implementation file]
      </overviewDoc>

      <instanceParms>
       [string containing additional parameters]
      </instanceParms>

    </tModelInstanceDetails>

  </tModelInstanceInfo>

</tModelInstanceDetails>
```

Before we move on, let us revisit the structure that allows the binding of a <businessService> entry to a tModel entry once more: the <businessService> element contains a <bindingTemplate> element, which contains a <tModelInstanceDetails> element, which contains a <tModelInstanceInfo> element, which contains a <tModelKey> element, which references the unique identifier of a tModel.

Here is an example <bindingTemplate> element in XML. Note that the serviceKey attribute points to the <businessService> element in which this <bindingTemplate> is contained.

```
<bindingTemplate
    bindingKey="48A91190-ECD0-11D5-8EA6-926A0B6F3A63"
    serviceKey="47FC56D0-ECD0-11D5-8EA6-926A0B6F3A63">
  <accessPoint URLType="http">
      http://localhost:8080/soap/servlet/rpcrouter
  </accessPoint>
  <tModelInstanceDetails>
    <tModelInstanceInfo
        tModelKey="UUID:4795F3E0-ECD0-11D5-8EA6-926A0B6F3A63">
      <instanceDetails>
        <overviewDoc>
          <overviewURL>
              http://localhost:8080/Wrox/wsdl/AddressbookService.wsdl
          </overviewURL>
        </overviewDoc>
      </instanceDetails>
    </tModelInstanceInfo>
  </tModelInstanceDetails>
</bindingTemplate>
```

We have now seen all of the elements that form a unique description of a business and its services. The last remaining element we need to look at is the <publisherAssertion> element.

publisherAssertion

The <publisherAssertion> element was added in version 2.0 of UDDI. It provides support for linking two <businessEntity> elements together. Many of today's businesses are very large and do a variety of things – just take IBM as an example. It offers many different products and services, in many different countries. While it is theoretically possible to create one large <businessEntity> for all of IBM, it isn't practical. But even if multiple <businessEntity> entries are created for different organizations within IBM, it is still desirable to link them together – after all, they all represent the same company. This is where the <publisherAssertion> element comes in. A <publisherAssertion> element contains links to two <businessEntity> elements, thus indicating an association between the two.

At the time of this writing, none of the public UDDI registries support version 2.0 of the specifications; however, this should change soon. The UDDI for Java API supporting version 2.0 is currently in beta and may be finalized by the time you read this.

UDDI and WSDL

Both UDDI and WSDL are often mentioned when we talk about Web Services. Indeed, WSDL is the way to describe a web service and UDDI is where you store information about it. So this may lead you to believe that there is a dedicated place for WSDL documents in UDDI. The truth is, however, that WSDL is not mentioned in the UDDI data structure specification at all! So where do you store your WSDL document?

First of all, the WSDL document is not physically copied into the UDDI registry, it must exist somewhere on the Web where it is accessible via a URL, and this URL is what it stored in the registry. The complete set of rules describing how to refer to a WSDL-described web service from within UDDI is given in a document called "*Using WSDL in a UDDI Registry*" that you can download from the uddi.org web site (See http://uddi.org/pubs/wsdlbestpractices-V1.05-Open-20010625.pdf). While the content of this document is not part of the official UDDI specification, it is assumed that everyone will follow the rules laid out in it. Let us briefly walk through these rules.

According to this document, information about a web service is stored in various places. It takes into consideration that a WSDL document may be split up into several parts, for example, one for the "interface" and one for the "implementation" definition. Since the interface definition of a web service (that is, port types and bindings) can be considered a technical specification, it may be stored as a tModel in UDDI. In this case, the <overviewDoc> element in a tModel will contain the URL of the actual WSDL document. Note that this can also be a URL that points into a document (using a "fragment identifier"). For example, if you have a WSDL document containing more than one binding, but you want to refer to a specific binding in your tModel, you can point to that binding within the document.

On top of that, the tModel must contain a <categoryBag> with a category that points to the WSDL specification itself. This is done by giving the <keyedReference> element in the <categoryBag> the key "uddi-org:types", the value "wsdlSpec", and using the "Other" taxonomy. This shows another good use of the categorization features of UDDI: if you want to look only for tModels that contain WSDL definitions, you can specify a <categoryBag> similar to the one described above as the search criteria when querying for a <tModel>. This allows you to filter out any tModel that does not fit the category you are looking for.

Here is an example for a <tModel> that describes a WSDL interface definition. Note how the entry contains two <keyedReference> elements, one indicating that this tModel describes a WSDL definition, and one indicating the type of service that is offered.

```
<tModel
    tModelKey="UUID:4795F3E0-ECD0-11D5-8EA6-926A0B6F3A63"
    operator="ATOST/services/uddi"
    authorizedName="wstkDemo">
  <name>
      Addressbook tModel
  </name>
  <overviewDoc>
    <overviewURL>
        http://localhost:8080/Wrox/wsdl/Addressbook-service.wsdl
    </overviewURL>
  </overviewDoc>
  <categoryBag>
    <keyedReference
```

```
        tModelKey="UUID:C1ACF26D-9672-4404-9D70-39B756E62AB4"
        keyName="uddi-org:types"
        keyValue="wsdlSpec">
    </keyedReference>
    <keyedReference
        tModelKey="UUID:DB77450D-9FA8-45D4-A7BC-04411D14E384"
        keyName="Office administration or secretarial services"
        keyValue="80161501">
    </keyedReference>
  </categoryBag>
</tModel>
```

Once you have created or found a WSDL interface definition as a tModel, let us assume you want to offer a service that implements this interface. You will create a <businessService> element with a <bindingTemplate> that references the interface's tModel. This reference is contained in the <tModelInstanceInfo> element within the <bindingTemplate>. But the <bindingTemplate> not only contains information about the supported interface, it also provides the required data about the implementation. The <accessPoint> element in the <bindingTemplate> points to the network access point of the offered service. If SOAP is the protocol supported by the service, this is the SOAP endpoint URL (or, if you use Apache SOAP, the address of the rpcrouter servlet).

The actual implementation WSDL document is referenced in the <overviewURL> element in the <overviewDoc> element. This is contained in the <tModelInstanceInfo> element in the <bindingTemplate>. The <bindingTemplate> example given in the previous chapter shows what this looks like.

A number of fields need to be set up properly to make all this work. Let's just look at one example: the URL of the interface WSDL document is stored in the tModel, but it is also contained in the <import> element of the implementation WSDL document. Moreover, the <accessPoint> element in the <bindingTemplate> must contain the same address as the <port> definition in the implementation WSDL document.

Since it is fairly easy to make mistakes when doing this, you should be using a higher-level API or tool to publish WSDL documents in UDDI. One example is the IBM Web Services Toolkit Client API, which provides methods that make it easy to store WSDL documents in UDDI, without requiring any knowledge about the details discussed above. However, the convention described is just that: a convention. Storing WSDL in UDDI is not described in any specification, so it relies on everyone doing the 'right thing' to make finding WSDL in UDDI a simple task.

UDDI API

Now that we have learned how UDDI data is structured, the next question is how do we access it? The UDDI API specification describes this. The things that are covered in this specification are:

❑ What protocol is used to access a UDDI registry

❑ What data is sent back and forth

Let us look at both aspects separately.

Protocol

The UDDI API is programming language-neutral. In fact, all of the technologies that form the Web Services architecture are programming language-neutral. It is the only way to ensure widespread use by developers. This is why all of the Web Services specifications make such extended use of XML to describe their data formats. XML allows the tagging of data, thus making it easier to interpret.

The UDDI API specification is no different. All interfaces are described as request and response data structures formatted in XML. Thus, accessing a UDDI registry means sending and receiving XML data. The protocol that was chosen to provide this is SOAP. SOAP is the obvious choice, because it defines the invocation of a function via XML, and it is a Web Service specification. In fact, this leads to an interesting side effect. Since the UDDI API is described in XML, and since it is invoked over SOAP, this automatically means that a UDDI registry is itself a web service! It also means that we can create a WSDL document that defines the UDDI API interfaces and the SOAP binding for it, as well as the endpoint definition for a particular registry.

Other chapters of this book describe how SOAP can be run over multiple network protocols. In the case of UDDI registries, however, SOAP over HTTP is used. To be even more specific, the publishing API functions (that is, the ones actually making changes to data stored in the registry) always run over an HTTPS connection. This is mandated by the UDDI Operator specification.

Another requirement defined in the specification is the use of a user ID and password combination. All publishing functions require credentials to be passed with every request, whereas the inquiry functions are open for everyone. This is accomplished by providing two access URLs to which requests can be sent – one for publishing that uses HTTPS and enforces the sending of user ID and password credentials, and one that uses HTTP and does not require any kind of login. We saw this earlier when we created our account on the UDDI Test Registry v2 beta.

Interfaces

There are two types of API for UDDI, namely one for querying the UDDI repository, and one for publishing to it.

For the most part, both work with data structures as defined by the UDDI data structure specification. For example, if you want to retrieve a <businessEntity> element with a particular business name, the get_businessDetail() function returns a vector of <businessEntity> elements. In other words, you will find many of the elements that were defined in the data structures specification to be reused as response values for the inquiry APIs. Similarly, many of those elements are used as parameters for the publishing APIs.

The inquiry functions can be separated into find_xxx() functions and get_xxx() functions. The find_xxx() functions allow broader queries and return only overview information. For example, the find_business() function returns a list of <businessInfo> elements, rather than the <businessEntity> elements directly. The get_xxx() functions, in turn, return a complete data structure. Thus, it is recommended that you start locating entries in the registry by using the find_xxx() functions and then use the get_xxx() methods on the results to retrieve the full data record for the desired entry. This reduces the amount of data that is sent back and forth and it not only improves performance, but it makes viewing queried information easier as it only returns overview data.

The publish functions allow you to create, change, and delete entries in the registry. Creation and update are both done by functions called save_xxx().

The following table shows the types of elements that exist in the registry together with the API functions that are defined for them. Note, however, that this is not a complete list of all functions, it only shows the most important ones. For more details, please refer to the UDDI Programmer's API specification.

Element type	Find Method	Get Method	Save Method	Delete Method
`<tModel>`	`find_tModel()`	`get_tModelDetail()`	`save_tModel()`	`delete_tModel()`
`<businessEntity>`	`find_business()`	`get_businessDetail()`	`save_business()`	`delete_business()`
`<businessService>`	`find_service()`	`get_serviceDetail()`	`save_service()`	`delete_service()`
`<bindingTemplate>`	`find_binding()`	`get_bindingDetail()`	`save_binding()`	`delete_binding()`

We mentioned above that the UDDI API is defined in a programming language-neutral way, namely in XML. This means that you communicate with the registry by sending and receiving XML documents. The following example shows an XML document for a save_business() function call, which creates a new <businessEntity> entry in the registry.

```
<save_business generic="2.0" xmlns="urn:uddi-org:api_v2">
  <authInfo>wstkDemo:wstkPwd</authInfo>
  <businessEntity>
    <name>Bill's Office Services</name>
    <description>
        A business offering services around the office
    </description>
    <contacts>
      <contact>
        <personName>Joe Smith</personName>
        <email>joes@officeservices.com</email>
        <address>
          <addressLine>1234 1st Ave SW</addressLine>
          <addressLine>Rochester, MN 55902</addressLine>
          <addressLine>USA</addressLine>
        </address>
      </contact>
    </contacts>
    <categoryBag>
      <keyedReference
          keyName="Administrative Management and General Management Consulting
          Services"
          keyValue="541611"
          tModelKey="UUID:C0B9FE13-179F-413D-8A5B-5004DB8E5BB2" />
    </categoryBag>
  </businessEntity>
</save_business>
```

This API has two parameters, each represented by an element within the `<save_business>` element. The first is the authentication information containing the user ID and password identifying who creates the entry. The second one is the `<businessEntity>` element itself that will be created.

You will see that the UDDI for Java API provides the complete set of APIs (as defined in the UDDI API specification) as Java objects. It also wraps the SOAP protocol layer that lets you send requests to an UDDI registry and receive responses from it. Thus, we will focus on the Java API from here on in.

You should also note that an effort is currently under way to define a Java API for XML registries in general within the Java Community Process. It is called the **Java API for XML Registries**, or **JAXR**. This API, which is not finalized at the time of this writing, will cover not only UDDI registries, but also other XML-based business registries, such as the ebXML registry. Thus, the API is more generic and abstract than the UDDI4J, which is defined directly on top of the UDDI specifications. You can find the description of the API at http://jcp.org/jsr/detail/93.jsp.

UDDI for Java (UDDI4J)

Now that we know what the UDDI data structure and its API look like, there is nothing to stop us from writing applications that read and write data from and to a UDDI registry. However, all of the data that we have looked at so far has been described in XML, and the UDDI API is implemented using the SOAP protocol. So how can I use this with Java? The answer is the UDDI for Java (UDDI4J) API. UDDI4J is an open source project, and you can find it at http://www-124.ibm.com/developerworks/projects/uddi4j/. The actual version that we used for this chapter is the version 2 (beta).

The UDDI4J API serves several purposes:

❑ It wraps the UDDI data structures in Java objects

❑ It wraps the request and return structures of the UDDI API

❑ It provides a simple client proxy that wraps the SOAP invocation layer

Data Structure Wrapper Classes

For each element type that is defined in the UDDI Data Structure specification, there is a Java wrapper class in UDDI4J. Let us start by looking at the package structure for these wrappers.

The package `org.uddi4j` contains only two classes. The `UDDIElement` class is the parent class for all wrappers. It covers some of the XML-related handling, and is never used directly in an application. The `UDDIException` class is a general-purpose exception class that is used throughout the API.

This table shows the UDDI4J packages and what they contain:

Package name	Description
`org.uddi4j`	The `UDDIElement` class, which all element wrapper classes inherit from, and the `VectorNodeList` class

Package name	Description
`org.uddi4j.client`	The `UDDIProxy` class
`org.uddi4j.datatype`	Classes wrapping types that occur in multiple places, for example, `Description` or `Name`
`org.uddi4j.datatype.assertion`	Class wrapping the `<publisherAssertion>` element
`org.uddi4j.datatype.business`	Classes wrapping the `<businessEntity>` element and other related types, such as `Contact`
`org.uddi4j.datatype.binding`	Classes wrapping the `<bindingTemplate>` element and related types, such as `TmodelInstanceDetails`
`org.uddi4j.datatype.service`	Classes wrapping the `<businessService>` element
`org.uddi4j.datatype.tmodel`	Class wrapping the `<tModel>` element
`org.uddi4j.util`	Classes wrapping several other elements that do not fit in any of the packages listed above, for example, `<categoryBag>` and `<identifierBag>`
`org.uddi4j.request`	Classes wrapping the Request API element types, such as `FindTModel` or `SaveBusiness` (see *Request and Response Wrapper Classes* section below)
`org.uddi4j.response`	Classes wrapping the Response API element types, such as `BusinessInfo` or `ServiceDetail` (see *Request and Response Wrapper Classes* section below)
`org.uddi4j.transport`	Classes for the various transport protocols that are supported, for example ApacheSOAP or HPSOAP

Naturally, the wrapper classes themselves closely match the element type that they wrap. For example, let us look at the `<businessEntity>` element. Here is the schema definition for this element again:

```
<element name = "businessEntity">
  <complexType>
    <sequence>
      <element ref = "discoveryURLs" minOccurs = "0"/>
      <element ref = "name" maxOccurs = "unbounded"/>
      <element ref = "description" minOccurs = "0" maxOccurs ="unbounded"/>
      <element ref = "contacts" minOccurs = "0"/>
      <element ref = "businessServices" minOccurs = "0"/>
      <element ref = "identifierBag" minOccurs = "0"/>
      <element ref = "categoryBag" minOccurs = "0"/>
    </sequence>
    <attribute ref = "businessKey" use = "required"/>
    <attribute ref = "operator"/>
    <attribute ref = "authorizedName">
  </complexType>
</element>
```

And here is how this type is mapped to the `org.uddi4j.datatype.business.BusinessEntity` class. This is far from being a complete listing; it just shows how the elements contained in the schema are mapped to attributes of the class in Java:

```java
public class BusinessEntity extends UDDIElement {
    public static final String UDDI_TAG = "businessEntity";

    protected Element base = null;

    String businessKey = null;
    String operator = null;
    String authorizedName = null;
    DiscoveryURLs discoveryURLs = null;
    Contacts contacts = null;
    BusinessServices businessServices = null;
    IdentifierBag identifierBag = null;
    CategoryBag categoryBag = null;

    // Vector of Description objects
    Vector description = new Vector();
    Vector nameVector = new Vector();

    public BusinessEntity() {

    public BusinessEntity(String businessKey, String name) {
        this.businessKey = businessKey;
        nameVector.addElement(new Name(name));
    }

    // Lots of code left out…
}
```

The code that is not listed here then contains all of the getters and setters for the attributes. There are a few interesting things here that you should note. All elements that are contained in <businessEntity> are mapped to either basic Java types or to other UDDI4J wrapper types. For example, the <categoryBag> element is mapped to an attribute of type `org.uddi4j.util.CategoryBag`.

Elements that can occur more than once are mapped to helper types that wrap multiple UDDI types. For example, the <businessEntity> element can contain zero or more <businessService> elements. This is mapped to Java by introducing a class called `org.uddi4j.datatype.service.BusinessServices`. It contains a Vector with objects of type `org.uddi4j.datatype.service.BusinessService`. Thus, to retrieve the list of services registered for a business, you obtain the `BusinessServices` object (using the `getBusinessServices()` method), and then use its `getBusinessServiceVector()` method to retrieve the list of `BusinessService` objects.

This principle is implemented throughout the API. If the contained element can be mapped directly to a base Java type, but occurs more than once, there will be a `java.util.Vector` object. For example, the <businessEntity> element contains an element called <description>. It is of type `String` and can occur zero or more times. This is mapped in the `BusinessEntity` class to a `java.util.Vector` containing `java.lang.String` objects.

Again, the <businessEntity> element is just one example where this applies – you will find the same concept used in all of the wrapper classes. Since these classes are used only as holders of data, they all contain get and set methods for their contained attributes and not much more. Converting to and from XML is done through the methods inherited from the org.uddi4j.UDDIElement class.

The following example shows how to extract information about the services a business offers from a given BusinessEntity instance. This code, together with a description of how to set it up, can be found at the download section for this book at the Wrox web site.

```
import org.uddi4j.*;
import org.uddi4j.response.*;
import org.uddi4j.client.*;
import org.uddi4j.datatype.*;
import org.uddi4j.datatype.business.*;
import org.uddi4j.datatype.service.*;
import org.uddi4j.datatype.tmodel.*;
import org.uddi4j.util.*;
import org.uddi4j.transport.*;

import java.util.*;
import java.net.*;

public class UDDI4JBusinessSample {
```

This sample retrieves an existing <businessEntity> entry from a UDDI registry. It is assumed that this entry exists, with a business name of "Bill's Office Services". You can create this entry using the UDDI4JPublishSample class, which we will look at next.

```
public static final String inquiryURL =
   "http://www-3.ibm.com/services/uddi/v2beta/inquiryapi";

protected UDDIProxy proxy = null;
protected BusinessEntity businessEntity = null;

public static void main(String args[]) throws Exception {
  UDDI4JBusinessSample sample = new UDDI4JBusinessSample();
  try {
    sample.init();
    sample.findBusiness();
    sample.displayBusinessInfo();
  } catch (Exception e) {
    System.out.println("Exception : " + e);
    e.printStackTrace();
  }
}

// Creates a new proxy instance for the specified access URLs
protected void init() throws MalformedURLException,
                            UDDIException,
                            TransportException {
  proxy = new UDDIProxy(new URL(inquiryURL), null);
}
```

```
// Finds a specific business entry by its name
protected void findBusiness() throws UDDIException, TransportException {

  // Creates a Vector of Name objects, which is used for the inquiry
  Vector names = new Vector();
  names.addElement(new Name("Bill's Office Services"));

  // Makes the call on the proxy
  BusinessList list = proxy.find_business(names, null, null,
                                        null, null, null, 0);
  BusinessInfos infos = list.getBusinessInfos();

  // If the returned vector is empty, no business could be found
  if (infos.getBusinessInfoVector().size() == 0) {
    throw new RuntimeException("No business found!");
  }
  // Obtains the unique identifier for this entry in the registry
  BusinessInfo info =
    (BusinessInfo) infos.getBusinessInfoVector().elementAt(0);
  String businessKey = info.getBusinessKey();

  // Uses the unique identifier to obtain the full record
  businessEntity =
    (BusinessEntity) proxy.get_businessDetail(businessKey)
      .getBusinessEntityVector().elementAt(0);
}
// Displays detailed information about a specific businessEntity entry
// in the registry

protected void displayBusinessInfo() {

  // print out some information about the entry
  System.out.println("Business Key : " + businessEntity.getBusinessKey());
  System.out.println("Business Name : "
                    + businessEntity.getDefaultNameString());

  // Sees if it contains a categoryBag
  CategoryBag cb = businessEntity.getCategoryBag();
  if (cb != null) {

    // A categoryBag contains a vector of keyedReference elements
    // Loop over each one
    Vector keyedReferences = cb.getKeyedReferenceVector();
    Enumeration enum = keyedReferences.elements();
    while (enum.hasMoreElements()) {
      KeyedReference kr = (KeyedReference) enum.nextElement();

      // Each keyed Reference element contains three values,
      // namely the key name and value, plus the tModel key
      System.out.println("\tKey name : " + kr.getKeyName());
      System.out.println("\tKey Value : " + kr.getKeyValue());
      System.out.println("\tTModel Ref ID : " + kr.getTModelKey());
    }
  }
}
```

```
System.out.println();

// Finds out about the contained service entries
// again, all service entries are contained in a vector
BusinessServices bs = businessEntity.getBusinessServices();
if (bs != null) {
  Vector services = bs.getBusinessServiceVector();
  Enumeration enum = services.elements();
  while (enum.hasMoreElements()) {

    // Prints out each service's name and key
    BusinessService service = (BusinessService) enum.nextElement();
    System.out.println("\tService Name : "
                       + service.getDefaultNameString());
    System.out.println("\tService Key : " + service.getServiceKey());
  }
}
}
}
```

Note that many elements that can occur inside another entry one or more times are wrapped in a Vector instance. For example, a <CategoryBag> element can contain several <keyedReference> elements. The CategoryBag class provides a method called getKeyedReferenceVector(). This method returns a Vector that holds all KeyedReference objects for that CategoryBag.

Running the Example – UDDI4JBusinessSample

In order to access a UDDI registry, you need to be registered as a user of the UDDI v2 Beta test registry. All registries provide a mechanism for this, and will give you a user ID-/password pair as part of the registration process, which we looked at above. User ID and password are not needed for read-only access to a registry, so we need not concern ourselves with this just yet.

To compile and run this code, there are several JAR files that need to be in your CLASSPATH variable. Obviously you will adjust this classpath according to the configuration of your own machine:

```
C:\javawebservices\Ch05> set CLASSPATH=.;C:\soap-2_2\lib\xerces.jar;C:\soap-
2_2\lib\soap.jar;C:\soap-2_2\lib\activation.jar;C:\soap-
2_2\lib\mail.jar;C:\uddi4j\lib\uddi4j.jar
```

Now download the above UDDI4JbusinessSample.java file into the C:\javawebservices\Ch05 directory and compile it:

```
C:\javawebservices\Ch05> javac UDDI4JBusinessSample.java
```

Now, run the code:

```
C:\javawebservices\Ch05> java UDDI4JbusinessSample
```

You should see the following output:

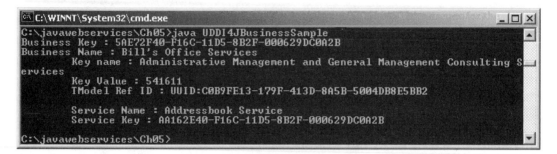

Request and Response Wrapper Classes

We have seen previously mentioned that the UDDI API specification uses the data types defined in the UDDI Data Structure specification. On top of that, some additional structures are defined for the API. For example, most find_xxx() functions let the user specify additional search criteria. For each function, a new request element type is defined that contains all of the parameters for that function. Similarly, if a function returns more than a simple UDDI element, a new type definition exists for the response type. The UDDI4J contains wrapper classes for these additional elements in the org.uddi4j.request and org.uddi4j.response packages.

For example, the save_business() API function defines a request structure that allows sending multiple <businessEntity> elements to be sent to the registry for creation or update. Moreover, it requires authentication information to be sent along with the request, in other words a valid user ID and password. The UDDI4J API defines a class called SaveBusiness that contains both a vector of BusinessEntity objects and an AuthInfo object.

To mention another example, let us look at the find_service() function. This function returns a list of <businessService> entries in the registry. Its parameters are a business key, a vector of Name objects, a <categoryBag>, a <tmodelBag> (this element, which we have not mentioned so far, allows addition multiple tModelKeys to a vector), <findQualifier> elements (we will look at <findQualifier> in more detail a little later), and the maximum number of returned results. UDDI4J wraps the parameters for the find_service() function into a new type called org.uddi4j.request.FindService. This class contains attributes matching the parameters as defined by the API. It is also a simple Java wrapper, just this time it does not wrap a UDDI data type, it wraps a request message for a particular API.

The find_service() function returns a list of <businessService> elements. However, since this list could possibly be very long, the function does not return the complete structure. It only returns a list of information objects that can then be used to retrieve the full data. This has to do with the intended usage pattern we had mentioned before, namely to use the find_xxx() methods to locate entries and use the get_xxx() functions to fully retrieve them. Thus, the find_service() function returns a list of <serviceInfo> elements. These contain the name of the service and its unique key, which can then be used with the get_service() function to retrieve the actual <businessService> entry. The <serviceInfo> element is not defined in the UDDI Data Structures specification. It is specific for the find_service() function and is only defined for this function. UDDI4J wraps; this in a class named org.uddi4j.response.ServiceInfo.

Client Proxy

So far we have discussed the UDDI4J classes that wrap the UDDI Data Structures, and classes that wrap the request and response structures as defined by the UDDI API. The only missing pieces are the API functions themselves. UDDI4J provides all of the inquiry and publish API functions in one class, which is called org.uddi4j.client.UDDIProxy. This class also includes the actual invocation of a request on a UDDI registry via SOAP. A client program using it need not be concerned with the details of the SOAP protocol to access UDDI, as it can do this by defining a constructor that takes two URLs as arguments: one for the inquiry API access point and one for the publish API access point. These are kept separate, because the publish API will be accessed over a secure HTTPS connection, while for the inquiry API there is no need to do this. The following sample shows how you can create a proxy object that connects to the IBM UDDI Version 2 Beta registry:

```
UDDIProxy up = new UDDIProxy(
    new URL("http://www-3.ibm.com/services/uddi/v2beta/inquiryapi"),
    new URL("https://www-3.ibm.com/services/uddi/v2beta/protect/publishapi"));
```

Note that in order to create a URL that uses HTTPS, you need to do add some special classes to your classpath. We will look at this in the following code sample section.

The request wrapper classes that we discussed in the previous section are not used by the methods offered in the UDDIProxy class. Instead, the methods take individual parameters without requiring them to be wrapped into a single object. The method implementation then builds the appropriate request structure from it.

For example, look at the implementation of the UDDIProxy.find_service() method listed below (this code is copied from the current version 2 beta sourcecode):

```
public ServiceList find_service(String businessKey, Vector names,
                                CategoryBag categoryBag, TModelBag tModelBag,
                                FindQualifiers findQualifiers, int maxRows)
                  throws UDDIException, TransportException {
    FindService request = new FindService();
    request.setBusinessKey(businessKey);
    request.setNameVector(names);
    request.setCategoryBag(categoryBag);
    request.setTModelBag(tModelBag);
    request.setFindQualifiers(findQualifiers);

    if (maxRows>0) {
        request.setMaxRows(maxRows);
    }
    return new ServiceList(send(request, true));
}
```

As you can see, the code creates a new request object and stores the passed arguments in it. However, the returned value wraps the response element as defined in the UDDI API specification.

Here you can see another example that shows how to create a new <businessEntity> entry. The entry also contains a <categoryBag>, identifying the kind of industry this business operates (the code is in UDDI4JPublishSample.java).

```java
import java.net.*;
import java.util.*;

import org.uddi4j.*;
import org.uddi4j.client.*;
import org.uddi4j.response.*;
import org.uddi4j.datatype.business.*;
import org.uddi4j.datatype.*;
import org.uddi4j.util.*;
import org.uddi4j.transport.*;

public class UDDI4JPublishSample {
```

This example creates a new <businessEntity> entry with a <categoryBag>, which is then stored in the registry.

```java
  public static final String inquiryURL =
    "http://www.ibm.com/services/uddi/v2beta/inquiryapi";
  public static final String publishURL =
    "https://www-3.ibm.com/services/uddi/v2beta/protect/publishapi";
  public static final String userid = "[insert UDDI v2Beta Test Registry ID]";
  public static final String password = "[insert UDDI v2Beta Test Registry
      password]";

  protected UDDIProxy proxy = null;
  protected String authInfo = null;

  public static void main(String args[]) throws Exception {

    System.setProperty("java.protocol.handler.pkgs",
                       "com.sun.net.ssl.internal.www.protocol");
    java.security.Security
      .addProvider(new com.sun.net.ssl.internal.ssl.Provider());

    UDDI4JPublishSample sample = new UDDI4JPublishSample();
    try {
      sample.init();
      sample.publishBusiness();
    } catch (Exception e) {
      System.out.println("Exception : " + e);
    }
  }

  // Creates a new proxy instance for the specified access URLs

  protected void init() throws MalformedURLException,
                               TransportException,
                               UDDIException {
    proxy = new UDDIProxy(new URL(inquiryURL), new URL(publishURL));
```

```
    // Gets an authentication token
    // Passes in userID and password registered at the UDDI site
    authInfo = proxy.get_authToken(userid, password).getAuthInfoString();
}

// Creates a new businessEntity entry in the registry , including a categoryBag

protected void publishBusiness()
        throws UDDIException, TransportException {

    // Creates a new keyedReference for the categoryBag. The name and
    // value come from the NAICS standard. The tModelKey points to the
    // NAICS taxonomy tModel. This is a hardcoded value.
    KeyedReference kr =
      new KeyedReference("Administrative Management and General Management
          Consulting Services","541611");
    kr.setTModelKey("UUID:C0B9FE13-179F-413D-8A5B-5004DB8E5BB2");

    Vector krVector = new Vector();
    krVector.addElement(kr);

    // The categoryBag contains a vector of keyedReference objects
    CategoryBag cb = new CategoryBag();
    cb.setKeyedReferenceVector(krVector);

    // Creates an Address object - each object contains a vector of
    // addressStrings that describe the address
    org.uddi4j.datatype.business.Address address =
      new org.uddi4j.datatype.business.Address();
    Vector addressStrings = new Vector();
    addressStrings.add("1234 1st Ave SW");
    addressStrings.add("Rochester, MN 55902");
    addressStrings.add("USA");
    address.setAddressLineStrings(addressStrings);

    // A Contact contains a name, a vector of Address objects and a
    // vector with email addresses
    Contact contact = new Contact();
    contact.setPersonName("Joe Smith");

    Vector addresses = new Vector();
    addresses.add(address);
    contact.setAddressVector(addresses);

    Vector emails = new Vector();
    emails.add(new Email("joes@officeservices.com"));
    contact.setEmailVector(emails);

    // Several Contact objects are contained in a Contacts object, which
    // can be added to the businessEntity entry
    Contacts contacts = new Contacts();
    Vector contactVector = new Vector();
    contactVector.add(contact);
    contacts.setContactVector(contactVector);
```

```
        BusinessEntity be = new BusinessEntity();
        be.setDefaultNameString("Bill's Office Services", "en");
        be.setDefaultDescriptionString("A business offering services around the
            office");
        be.setBusinessKey("");
        be.setContacts(contacts);


        be.setCategoryBag(cb);
```

The save_business() function expects a vector of businessEntity objects, so we'll create one here with one element in it – then we can save the entry, which will cause it to be created in the registry.

```
        Vector beVector = new Vector();
        beVector.addElement(be);

        proxy.save_business(authInfo, beVector);
        System.out.println("Business saved.");
    }
}
```

Again, you can find the complete, commented listing in the download section for this book at the Wrox web site.

Running the Example – UDDI4JBusinessSample

This is example is slightly more complex than the previous one, as the Publish API must be accessed through an HTTPS connection and requires that a user ID and password be verified.

Authentication and SSL

Before you can run the previous example, we should explain two things that we have not yet discussed. The listed code stores a new entry in the registry. This requires that a user ID and password be submitted. Every method on the UDDIProxy instance that will result in an update takes an AuthInfo object as one of its parameters. Each UDDI registry provides a way to register as a new user and obtain a valid user ID and password. Typically, you will use a user ID and password combination once, in order to obtain an AuthInfo object, and cache this object for all future uses.

Secondly, the existing production registries offer publishing only through an HTTPS connection. If you are using the JDK 1.4, this is not a problem and is supported by the JDK. However, if you are using an earlier version of the JDK, a regular Java client cannot create a URL object that uses this protocol, as this will result in a MalformedURLException. To fix this, and to run the code above, you need to install an implementation of the **Java Secure Sockets Extension (JSSE)** – while there are other ways to provide support for HTTPS, we find this one to be the simplest. You can get more information and download the package at http://java.sun.com/products/jsse. The package contains the jsse.jar, jcert.jar, and jnet.jar files, which must be added to the classpath for the client. Moreover, you need to add the following two lines to the beginning of your code:

```
System.setProperty("java.protocol.handler.pkgs",
                    "com.sun.net.ssl.internal.www.protocol");
java.security.Security.addProvider(new com.sun.net.ssl.internal.ssl.Provider());
```

So the `CLASSPATH` variable should be set like this:

```
C:\javawebservices\Ch05> set CLASSPATH=.;C:\soap-2_2\lib\xerces.jar;C:\soap-
2_2\lib\soap.jar;C:\soap-2_2\lib\activation.jar;C:\soap-
2_2\lib\mail.jar;C:\uddi4j\lib\uddi4j.jar;C:\jsse1.0.2\lib\jsse.jar;C:\jsse1.0.2
\lib\jcert.jar;C:\jsse1.0.2\lib\jnet.jar
```

Compile the code and run it with the following prompt:

```
C:\javawebservices\Ch05> java UDDI4JPublishSample
```

The output should resemble the following:

```
Business saved.
```

<FindQualifier>

Many of the inquiry APIs in UDDI accept an additional parameter called `<findQualifier>`. This parameter contains data that indicates additional filter criteria and how the returned results should be sorted. For that purpose, the `org.uddi4j.util.FindQualifier` class provides a number of static variables that indicate how the server should handle the request.

Assume, for example, that you are looking for a list of `<businessEntity>` elements in UDDI, whose name attributes all start with a given string. Moreover, you want to make sure that only entries that match the exact case of the string are returned, and you want them returned in ascending order. Here is what a request like that would resemble (you can find this example in the `UDDI4JFindSample.java` file in the download section for this book at the Wrox web site):

```java
import org.uddi4j.*;
import org.uddi4j.response.*;
import org.uddi4j.client.*;
import org.uddi4j.datatype.*;
import org.uddi4j.datatype.business.*;
import org.uddi4j.datatype.service.*;
import org.uddi4j.datatype.tmodel.*;
import org.uddi4j.util.*;
import org.uddi4j.transport.*;

import java.util.*;
import java.net.*;

public class UDDI4JFindSample {
```

This sample retrieves a list of `<businessEntity>` entries based on a given set of `<FindQualifier>` elements. It will return all entries whose names start with an "I".

```java
    public static final String inquiryURL =
      "http://www-3.ibm.com/services/uddi/v2beta/inquiryapi";

    protected UDDIProxy proxy = null;
```

```
    protected BusinessEntity businessEntity = null;

    public static void main(String args[]) throws Exception {
      UDDI4JFindSample sample = new UDDI4JFindSample();
      try {
        sample.init();
        sample.list("I", sample.proxy);
      } catch (MalformedURLException urle) {
        System.out.println("Bad URL Exception! " + urle);
      } catch (Exception e) {
        System.out.println("Exception : " + e);
        e.printStackTrace();
      }
    }

    // Creates a new proxy instance for the specified access URLs

    protected void init()
          throws MalformedURLException, UDDIException, TransportException {
      proxy = new UDDIProxy(new URL(inquiryURL), null);
    }

    // Retrieves a list of businessEntity elements based on a FindQualifier entry

    public BusinessList list(String businessName, UDDIProxy proxy)
          throws UDDIException, TransportException {

      Vector v = new Vector();
      v.addElement(new FindQualifier(FindQualifier.caseSensitiveMatch));
      v.addElement(new FindQualifier(FindQualifier.sortByNameAsc));

      FindQualifiers findQualifiers = new FindQualifiers();
      findQualifiers.setFindQualifierVector(v);

      Vector names = new Vector();
      names.addElement(new Name(businessName));
      BusinessList list = proxy.find_business(names, null, null, null, null,
                                       findQualifiers, 0);
      return list;
    }
  }
```

This code may be run in a similar manner to the other example programs.

Example: Creating <tModel> and <businessService> elements

In this section, we will try to build a more or less complete example that shows how you can use UDDI4J to access any UDDI registry. The name of the file with the complete listing is `UDDI4JCompleteSample.java`. We will create a sample program that creates a new `tModel`. It will then find a particular `<businessEntity>`, create a new `<businessService>` element for it, and associate it with the new `tModel` created earlier. We will also assume that the service is represented by a WSDL document, so that we get to use the conventions of adding WSDL to UDDI with some real code.

```java
import org.uddi4j.*;
import org.uddi4j.response.*;
import org.uddi4j.client.*;
import org.uddi4j.datatype.*;
import org.uddi4j.datatype.service.*;
import org.uddi4j.datatype.binding.*;
import org.uddi4j.datatype.tmodel.*;
import org.uddi4j.util.*;
import org.uddi4j.transport.*;

import java.util.*;
import java.net.*;

public class UDDI4JCompleteSample {
```

This example shows how you can add information about a service described by a WSDL document to an existing `<businessEntity>` entry in a UDDI registry. It creates a new `tModel`, then creates a new `<businessService>` and `<bindingTemplate>`.

The example expects an existing `<businessEntity>` element, with the name of the business being "Bill's Office Services". You can use the `UDDI4JPublishSample` class to create such an entry.

```java
// The following Strings point to the current IBM version 2 beta registry
// the URLs may change over time as the version 2 registry is rolled into
// production

public static final String inquiryURL =
   "http://www-3.ibm.com/services/uddi/v2beta/inquiryapi";
public static final String publishURL =
   "https://www-3.ibm.com/services/uddi/v2beta/protect/publishapi";
public static final String userid = "[insert your UDDI Test Registry ID here]";
public static final String password = "[insert your UDDI Test Registry password
   here]";

protected UDDIProxy proxy = null;
protected String authInfo = null;
protected String tModelKey = null;
protected String businessKey = null;
protected String serviceKey = null;
protected String bindingKey = null;

public static void main(String args[]) throws Exception {
```

The following code enables the client to create an HTTPS connection URL. This is not necessary if you run this code on a JDK version 1.4

```
System.setProperty("java.protocol.handler.pkgs",
                   "com.sun.net.ssl.internal.www.protocol");
java.security.Security
  .addProvider(new com.sun.net.ssl.internal.ssl.Provider());

UDDI4JCompleteSample sample = new UDDI4JCompleteSample();
try {
  sample.init();
  sample.saveTModel();
  sample.findBusiness();
  sample.addService();
  sample.addBindingTemplate();
} catch (Exception e) {
  System.out.println("Exception : " + e);
}
}
```

The class declares some static final `Strings` with some constant settings, that is, the URLs of the UDDI registry, and the user ID and password. In this example, the URL points to the Version 2 Beta of the IBM Public UDDI registry. When trying to run this code, it may be a good idea to check if this URL has changed.

The remainder of the code consists mainly of five methods that do the actual work. We will look at each one of them separately.

First, we need to create an instance of `UDDIProxy` that we can use to send requests to the registry. We also need to establish an `AuthInfo` object, which is later needed for the publishing calls. The `init()` method handles this.

```
// Creates a new proxy instance for the specified access URLs

protected void init()
        throws MalformedURLException, UDDIException, TransportException {

  proxy = new UDDIProxy(new URL(inquiryURL), new URL(publishURL));

  // Gets an authorization token
  // Passes in userid and password registered at the UDDI site
  authInfo = proxy.get_authToken(userid, password).getAuthInfoString();
}
```

After setting up the `UDDIProxy` and `AuthInfo` objects, we will create a new `tModel` instance that represents the WSDL interface definition of our service. This means that the `<overviewURL>` of the `<overviewDoc>` element in the `tModel` points to the location of the WSDL interface. Moreover, the new `tModel` will contain a `<categoryBag>` with two entries: one pointing to the WSDL specification, which indicates that this `tModel` represents a WSDL definition. The other one indicates the kind of service we are defining by using the appropriate UNSPSC code.

```
// Creates a new tModel, representing a web service WSDL document, and saves it
// in the registry

protected void saveTModel() throws UDDIException, TransportException {

    TModel tm = new TModel();
    tm.setName("Addressbook tModel");

    // Need to set empty key, this indicates to the
    // registry that we are creating a new entry
    tm.setTModelKey("");

    // The URL of the WSDL interface definition goes into the
    // overviewDoc / overviewURL element of the tModel
    OverviewDoc od = new OverviewDoc();
    od.setOverviewURL("http://localhost:8080/Wrox/wsdl/Addressbook-service.wsdl");
    tm.setOverviewDoc(od);

    // The first keyedReference points to the WSDL spec to indicate
    // that this tModel refers to a WSDL document
    KeyedReference kr1 = new KeyedReference("uddi-org:types", "wsdlSpec");
    kr1.setTModelKey("UUID:C1ACF26D-9672-4404-9D70-39B756E62AB4");

    // The second keyedReference indicates the type of service that
    // is offered, by UNSPSC code
    KeyedReference kr2 =
        new KeyedReference("Office administration or secretarial services",
                           "80161501");
    kr2.setTModelKey("UUID:DB77450D-9FA8-45D4-A7BC-04411D14E384");

    Vector krv = new Vector();
    krv.addElement(kr1);
    krv.addElement(kr2);

    CategoryBag cb = new CategoryBag();
    cb.setKeyedReferenceVector(krv);

    tm.setCategoryBag(cb);

    // Save tModel
    Vector entities = new Vector();
    entities.addElement(tm);
    TModelDetail r = proxy.save_tModel(authInfo, entities);

    tModelKey = ((TModel) r.getTModelVector().elementAt(0)).getTModelKey();
    System.out.println("Created tModel with key " + tModelKey);
    System.out.println("tmodel is " + tm.toString());
}
```

An interesting thing here is the fact that the save() method on the proxy object takes a Vector as the second parameter. This means it can save several tModel instances in one call. You will note that most save() methods on the proxy are set up this way, requiring you to pass a Vector even if it contains only one element.

The next method will find the <businessEntity> entry that we will add the new service entry to. It is assumed here that this entry already exists. You can create it manually, or you can run the publish example (in UDDI4JPublishSample.java) mentioned above.

```java
// Retrieves the key of a particular businessEntity element - the name of this
// business must be "Bill's Office Services". The samples assumes that this
// entry already exists. You can use the UDDI4JPublishSample class to create
// this entry.

protected void findBusiness() throws UDDIException, TransportException {
  Vector names = new Vector();
  names.addElement(new Name("Bill's Office Services"));
  BusinessList bl = proxy.find_business(names, null, null,
                                        null, null, null, 0);
  Vector biVector = bl.getBusinessInfos().getBusinessInfoVector();
  if (biVector.size() == 0) {
    throw new RuntimeException("Could not find business!!");
  }

  // Assume that only one entry with that name exists
  businessKey = ((BusinessInfo) biVector.elementAt(0)).getBusinessKey();
  System.out.println("Found business with key " + businessKey);
}
```

The following method will create a new <businessService> entry and associate it with the <businessEntity>. It, too, has a <categoryBag> in it that defines the type of business service offered here.

```java
// Creates a new businessService element and associates it with the
// businessEntity element retrieved earlier. Also adds a categoryBag to the new
// entry

protected void addService() throws UDDIException, TransportException {

  BusinessService bs = new BusinessService();
  bs.setDefaultNameString("Addressbook Service", "en");

  // The business key was retrieved earlier
  bs.setBusinessKey(businessKey);

  // Must be set to empty to indicate new entry
  bs.setServiceKey("");

  // Must add vector with bindingTemplates, even though it
  // is empty here
  Vector btv = new Vector();
  BindingTemplates bts = new BindingTemplates();
  bts.setBindingTemplateVector(btv);
  bs.setBindingTemplates(bts);

  KeyedReference kr =
    new KeyedReference("Office administration or secretarial services",
                       "80161501");
```

```
        kr.setTModelKey("UUID:DB77450D-9FA8-45D4-A7BC-04411D14E384");

        Vector krv = new Vector();
        krv.addElement(kr);

        CategoryBag cb = new CategoryBag();
        cb.setKeyedReferenceVector(krv);

        bs.setCategoryBag(cb);

        // Save service
        Vector entities = new Vector();
        entities.addElement(bs);
        ServiceDetail r = proxy.save_service(authInfo, entities);

        serviceKey =
           ((BusinessService) r.getBusinessServiceVector().elementAt(0))
             .getServiceKey();
        System.out.println("Create service with key " + serviceKey);
    }
```

Note that even though the new <businessService> entry contains no <bindingTemplate> yet, an empty one must be added here.

Finally, we can add the <bindingTemplate> to the new <businessService> entry.

```
    // Creates a new bindingTemplate element its instanceDetails point to the WSDL
    // tModel created earlier access point is the SOAP rpcrouter servlet

    protected void addBindingTemplate() throws UDDIException,
                                               TransportException {

      BindingTemplate bt = new BindingTemplate();

      // Associates with businessService entry created earlier
      bt.setServiceKey(serviceKey);

      // Must set to empty to indicate new entry
      bt.setBindingKey("");
```

The AccessPoint indicates where this service can be accessed. In this case, since we have a web service hosted by an Apache SOAP environment, the access point refers to an installed Apache SOAP environment.

```
    AccessPoint ap = new AccessPoint();
    ap.setURLType("http");
    ap.setText("http://localhost:8080/soap/servlet/rpcrouter");

    bt.setAccessPoint(ap);

    // This overviewDoc points to the implementation part of
    // the WSDL document - is then added to the instance details
```

```
OverviewDoc tmod = new OverviewDoc();
tmod
  .setOverviewURL("http://localhost:8080/Wrox/wsdl/AddressbookService.wsdl");

InstanceDetails instanceDetails = new InstanceDetails();
instanceDetails.setOverviewDoc(tmod);
```

The tModelInstanceInfo contains the instance details and is associated with the tModel that we created above through its key.

```
TModelInstanceInfo tmii = new TModelInstanceInfo(tModelKey);
tmii.setInstanceDetails(instanceDetails);

Vector tmiiv = new Vector();
tmiiv.addElement(tmii);

TModelInstanceDetails tmid = new TModelInstanceDetails();
tmid.setTModelInstanceInfoVector(tmiiv);

bt.setTModelInstanceDetails(tmid);

Vector entities = new Vector();
entities.addElement(bt);
BindingDetail r = proxy.save_binding(authInfo, entities);

bindingKey =
  ((BindingTemplate) r.getBindingTemplateVector().elementAt(0))
    .getBindingKey();
System.out.println("Created bindingTemplate with key " + bindingKey);
  }
}
```

There are three interesting parts here that we would like to point out: there is another <overviewDoc> element with an <overviewURL> element in it. This URL points to the implementation part of the WSDL document. Then, there is the <accessPoint> element that contains the target address for each SOAP request. In cases where the server is using the Apache SOAP implementation, this address might refer to the rpcrouter servlet. Finally, the <tModelInstance> element indirectly contains a reference to the tModel that we created in the beginning of the example in the saveTModel() method.

You can compile and run this code in the same way as the other programs, setting the classpath to include the security JARs and inserting your own user ID and password into the code before compilation. To run it, enter:

```
C:\javawebservices\Ch05> java UDDI4JcompleteSample
```

You should get the following output:

```
C:\WINNT\System32\cmd.exe                                    _□x
C:\javawebservices\Ch05>java UDDI4JCompleteSample
Created tModel with key UUID:B6E29E60-F18F-11D5-8B2F-000629DC0A2B
tmodel is org.uddi4j.datatype.tmodel.TModel@231e1b
Found business with key 85D81A80-F18E-11D5-8B2F-000629DC0A2B
Create service with key BA753B00-F18F-11D5-8B2F-000629DC0A2B
Created bindingTemplate with key BC9FBC20-F18F-11D5-8B2F-000629DC0A2B

C:\javawebservices\Ch05>_
```

Summary

In this chapter, you learned how the UDDI specifications describe the content of a registry and how to access it. A UDDI registry is mainly a business registry that allows the registered businesses to store more information about the services they offer and what specifications they support. These specifications are represented by the notion of a so-called tModel, which acts as a container for any kind of unique technical information. Certain conventions must be followed when storing WSDL documents in UDDI.

Access to UDDI from within a Java program is possible through the use of the UDDI for Java (UDDI4J) API. It provides Java wrappers for all of the data types and APIs defined in UDDI.

Besides using one of the public UDDI registries that exist today, you can run your own private UDDI registry. This can be useful in cases where you do not want to take advantages of publicly listed services, but instead want to use the registry for internal use only, or make sure that only approved services are listed.

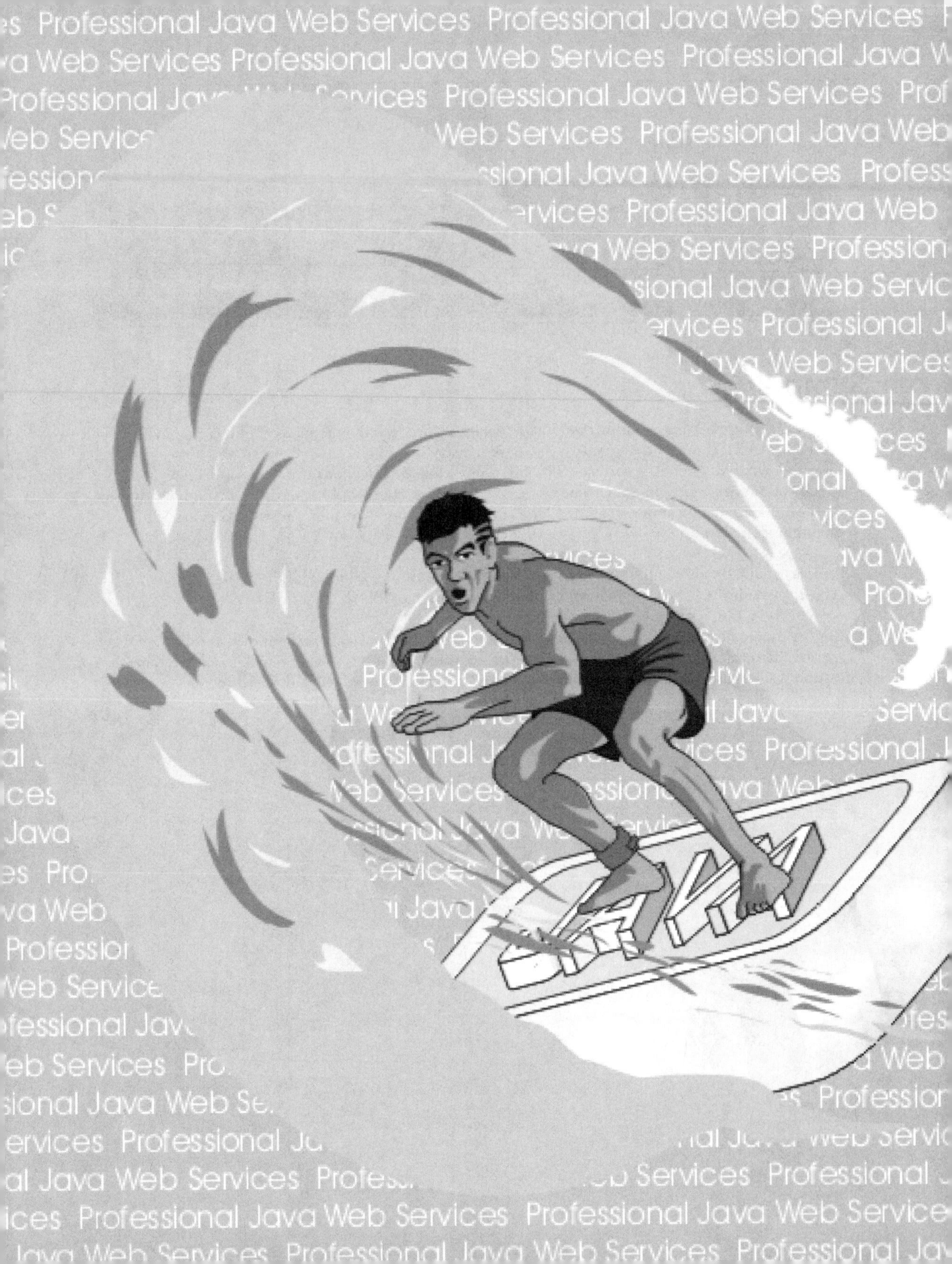
Professional Java Web Services

Java Web Services Security

This chapter will focus on Java Web Services Security. The chapter will cover three main areas: Security Services, Security Techniques and Technologies, and XML Security.

We will begin by looking at the various services a secure application should provide – this will give us some general background on security. Next, we will see that security can be implemented on two general levels: the transport level and the application level. This will highlight the difference between Web Services and more traditional web applications.

From here we will move on to discussing the standards bodies and organizations in existence charged with securing Web Services with existing and new technologies. So as to avoid turning the chapter into a general discussion about general Internet security, we will also look at the Java APIs, Toolkits, and SDKs available.

Security is a big subject. This is not surprising when its scope, complexity, not to mention cost, is considered. Business is increasingly relying on the Internet as *the* transport of its critical communications and transactions, where corporate assets need protecting from misappropriation.

The World Wide Web Consortium (W3C, http://www.w3.org/) has outlined the security risks as falling into three groups, as follows:

1. Bugs or misconfiguration problems in the web server that allow unauthorized remote users to:

- ❑ Steal confidential documents not intended for their eyes
- ❑ Execute commands on the server host machine, allowing them to modify the system
- ❑ Gain information about the web server's host machine that will allow them to break into the system
- ❑ Launch denial-of-service attacks, rendering the machine temporarily unusable

2. Browser-side risks, including:

- ❑ Active content that crashes the browser, damages the user's system, breaches the user's privacy, or merely creates an annoyance
- ❑ The misuse of personal information knowingly or unknowingly provided by the end user

3. Interception of network data sent from browser to server or vice versa via network eavesdropping. Eavesdroppers can operate from any point on the pathway between browser and server including:

- ❑ The network on the browser's side of the connection
- ❑ The network on the server's side of the connection (including intranets)
- ❑ The end-user's Internet service provider (ISP)
- ❑ The server's ISP
- ❑ Either ISP's regional access provider (see http://www.w3.org/Security/faq/wwwsf1.html#GEN-Q1)

There are a number of ways that these risks may be mitigated. The next section talks about the security services we could expect to find to do just that.

Security Services

Here we go into more detail about what we mean by security, and some of the main security services a secure application should provide. A secure application will implement some, if not all, of the following security services:

- ❑ **Identification and Authentication**
  Who are you, and how do we know your identity is genuine?

- ❑ **Authorization**
  Are we allowed to access this data/perform this transaction?

- ❑ **Integrity**
  Is the data you sent me the same as the data I received?

❑ **Privacy**
Are we sure that nobody read the data you sent me?

❑ **Non-repudiation**
How can it prove to a third party that you sent the data to it?

We will look at each service in turn, and point to technologies and techniques underpinning each; the technologies and techniques themselves will be covered in a later section.

Identification and Authentication

Identification and Authentication answers, *who are you, and how do I know your identity is genuine?* There are clearly two steps to such a service.

First, we must obtain the user or application credentials, which might be a username or ID along with a password or PIN. This is usually achieved on the Internet by allowing the user to enter such details in an HTML form and submit these details to the web server for processing. As we shall see, in the context of web services, this might not be possible, especially when the agent to be identified is an application.

Next, we compare this collected information against a store of identities. These identities will be allowed to access the system in some way. If there is a match, we move to the next step, authorization, and eventually access is granted. Otherwise, the process stops here, with the application or user being informed. Sometimes the system trying to be accessed will record an unsuccessful attempt for future reference. As we shall see, deciding whether somebody's identity is genuine is a well-known problem, and involves a network of trust.

Attempts to resolve the issues raised by identification and authentication services are being made. We will not go into technologies such a Lightweight Directory Access Protocol (LDAP), which has become the de facto standard of hosting and accessing user identification and authentication information. Instead, we focus in later sections on the trust services built upon Digital Certificates and first generation Public Key Infrastructure (PKI), showing how they go some way to resolving these issues. Together with the second generation XML Key Management Specification (XKMS, http://www.w3.org/TR/xkms/), we are well on the way to finding a solution.

Authorization

An Authorization service should answer the question, *are you allowed to access this data/perform this transaction?* In other words, once a user or application has been identified and authenticated, the *access privileges* of that user or application are brought into consideration, as applied to the *assets* of that system.

How this is actually implemented depends largely on the system in question. Usually, users of a system are classified into roles and groups, with the assets they are attempting to access falling into these same roles and groups. Simply, whenever a user or application attempts to access an asset on the system, these attributes are compared, and if there is a match, the asset can be accessed.

A standard implementation of an authorization service at the operating-system level is the access control list (ACL) – a set of data associated with an asset that defines the permissions that users and/or groups have for accessing that asset. Most popular operating systems have ACL-based file permissions, for example recent version of Windows and Solaris.

The Java Authentication and Authorization Service (JAAS) is a popular example of such a service at the application level. You can find out more about JAAS at http://java.sun.com/products/jaas/.

Finally, the granularity of this service, that is, to what level should assets be protected, is a key distinguishing factor behind these types of system. Do we need only need to protect our data store in our web service, or should we also be thinking about protecting XML files as well as our Java objects?

In terms of the techniques and technologies designed to answer the web service side of these questions, there is Extensible Access Control Markup Language (XACML) or, as it is also known, Extensible Access Control Language (XACL) (http://www.oasis-open.org/committees/xacml/), and Security Assertion Markup Language (SAML) (http://www.oasis-open.org/committees/security/). We will be looking at both of these later.

Integrity

An integrity service answers the question, *is the data you sent me the same as the data I received?* In other words, this service should ensure that data remains uncorrupted or unchanged from its original intended form while in transit or in storage. As we shall see, the Internet is an insecure network, so preventing this from happening is a key concern.

However, an integrity service differs from the previous two, in that it is relatively focused in its objective, and in consequence, the problem it is trying to solve is well defined.

There are strong solutions in place today, with a combination of digital signatures and strong encryption showing the way forward. However, in the context of web services, we have the added complexity of using these functions on parts of documents, to encrypt and authenticate in arbitrary sequences, and to involve different users or originators. These concerns are in part addressed by the developing specifications in the area of XML-related security: XML encryption (http://www.w3.org/Encryption/2001/) and XML signatures (http://www.w3.org/Signature/).

Privacy

Closely related to Integrity as a service is Privacy. Simply put, we need to worry about keeping data private. There are two common situations in which data should be kept confidential.

First, when invoking an online transaction, important details such as a credit card number or authorization code, should be kept secret, for obvious reasons. The privacy of very sensitive data such as this is largely handled with encryption. This is *privacy of personal communications.*

A second situation might arise when a user is asked to register at a site, completing details that are not necessarily sensitive, as in the case of credit card details, but should nevertheless be treated with privacy in mind. This is *privacy of personal data.*

The use and storage of personal data is receiving more and more attention, especially with European Commission Directive 95/46/EC, effected in United Kingdom law as the Data Protection Act 1998 (http://www.dataprotection.gov.uk/). Anyone processing personal data must comply with the eight enforceable principles of good practice. They say that data must be:

❑ Fairly and lawfully processed

❑ Processed for limited purposes

❑ Adequate, relevant and not excessive

❑ Accurate

❑ Not kept longer than necessary

❑ Processed in accordance with the data subject's rights

❑ Secure

❑ Not transferred to countries without adequate protection

The W3C's Platform for Privacy Preferences (P3P) (see http://www.w3.org/P3P/) is being advocated as a possible way forward to dealing with some of these privacy concerns. We look at P3P briefly later.

Non-repudiation

A non-repudiation service should be able to answer the question, *how can we prove to a third party that I sent, and you received, the identical data?* It refers to the generation and secure storage of evidence to support the resolution of disagreements as to the outcome of electronic transactions. Ultimately, the evidence must be able to prove convincing to a third-party arbitrator, who can resolve a dispute without needing to rely entirely on the words of the disputing parties.

Non-repudiation depends on the use of digital signatures, created by parties who keep their private keys secure. In addition, non-repudiation depends upon the issuance of digital certificates by a trusted and independently audited Certificate Authority (CA) system, and the maintenance of secure records of certificate issuance and life-cycle management, including all steps occurring in the revocation of such certificates in the event of private key compromise or other circumstances leading to certificate revocation. First generation Public Key Infrastructure (PKI), and latterly XML Key Management Specification (XKMS), are the supporting structures for this need.

Security Technologies and Techniques

Here we cover the techniques and technologies underlying many of the services we have already discussed. Encryption, the encoding of the message in such a way that hides its contents from outsiders, is one of the main techniques used in Internet security, and is in fact central to Public Key Infrastructure, and the use of Digital Certificates. To understand these terms, and how they fit together in the puzzle, it is necessary to first introduce Cryptography, the art or science of keeping messages secret. As the branch of mathematics that studies the mathematical foundations of cryptographic methods, Cryptography underlies all aspects of secure messaging, authentication, and digital signatures.

Introduction to Cryptography

Since the TCP/IP transport protocol of the Internet moves data between computers in its original form, it is possible for this data to be read if it is intercepted, as described by the W3C above. A basic need, then, of Internet security is to ensure that if the data is intercepted en route, it cannot be read. Data, whether it be a message or procedure call, should only be read by the intended recipient(s).

Cryptography is the science of keeping data private. In cryptographic terminology, this data is called **plaintext** or **cleartext**. Encoding the data so that the data is unintelligible to those doing the intercepting is called **encryption**. This encrypted data is called the **ciphertext**. The process of converting the ciphertext back into plaintext is called **decryption**. Encryption and decryption usually make use of a **key**, and the coding method is such that only by knowing the proper key can you perform decryption.

Cryptographic Algorithms

All modern cryptographic algorithms use a **key** to control encryption and decryption; a message can be decrypted only if the key matches the encryption key. This doesn't necessarily mean that we use the same key for encryption that we use for decryption, but rather that they are a matched pair.

There are two classes of key-based encryption algorithms:

❑ **Symmetric** (or secret key). Symmetric algorithms use the same key for encryption and decryption (or the decryption key is easily derived from the encryption key).

❑ **Asymmetric** (or public key). Asymmetric algorithms use a different key for encryption and decryption. Also important is that the decryption key cannot be *derived* from the encryption key.

Asymmetric ciphers (also known as **public key algorithms** or generally **public key cryptography**) permit the encryption key to be public, allowing anyone to encrypt with the key, whereas only the intended recipient (who knows the decryption key) can decrypt the message. The encryption key is also called the **public key** and the decryption key the **private key** or **secret key**.

Symmetric Encryption Algorithm

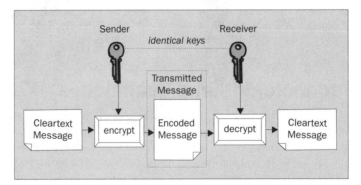

Generally, symmetric algorithms are much faster to execute on a computer than asymmetric ones. A reason for this is that asymmetric public key encryption requires a much longer key than is required with symmetric encryption. In practice they are often used together, so that a public key algorithm is used to encrypt a randomly generated encryption key, and the random key is used to encrypt the actual message using a symmetric algorithm. This is sometimes called hybrid encryption. Hybrid encryption is used in Transport Layer Security (TLS) and its forerunner, Secure Sockets Layer (SSL). Both will be discussed later.

The most popular example of a symmetric cipher is Data Encryption Standard (DES), while RSA is probably the best-known asymmetric encryption algorithm. It will help here to go into a bit of history of the transition between the two.

Asymmetric Encryption Algorithm

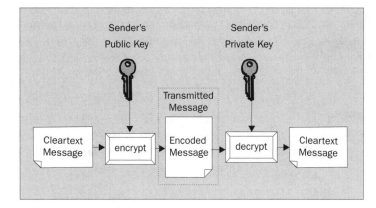

Symmetric or Asymmetric?

There are problems inherent in using a symmetric system, summed up as unwieldy secure key exchange, unsupported trust requirements, and a lack of authentication and non-repudiation.

Data protection using a symmetric algorithm, such as that within DES, is relatively easy in small networks, requiring the exchange of secret encryption keys between each party. But as a network increases in size, so too does the difficulty of securely exchanging secret keys. As a result, the symmetric algorithm solution alone is impractical for even moderately large networks, never the mind the Internet!

There is also a key management issue associated with DES. Each participant must have a different secret key for every person they wish to communicate with. Consequently, each person must trust each and every person using this solution with one of their secret keys. This requires a special understanding between parties, and therefore secure communication cannot take place between parties without some sort of prior business relationship.

DES does not address authentication and non-repudiation. The fact that two parties hold the same key means that either could surreptitiously modify data and it would be impossible to determine who had done it. Another limitation to DES is that it uses a 56-bit key – not considered strong enough for some applications. However, a stronger version of DES, called Triple-DES, can be used to circumvent this concern.

Addressing the problems of authentication and large network privacy protection was Whitfield Diffie and Martin Hellman's theory of secret message exchange without secret keys exchange. This theory was implemented just a year later in 1977 with the invention of the RSA Public Key Cryptosystem by Ronald Rivest, Adi Shamir, and Len Adleman. See http://www.ssh.com/tech/crypto/algorithms.html#rsa for information on RSA.

Rather than using the same key to both encrypt and decrypt the data, the RSA system uses a matched pair of encryption and decryption keys. Each key performs a one-way transformation upon the data. Each key is the inverse function of the other; what one does, only the other can undo.

The RSA Public Key is made publicly available by its owner, while the RSA Private Key is kept secret. To send a private message, an author scrambles the message with the intended recipient's Public Key. Once so encrypted, the message can only be decoded with the recipient's Private Key.

Inversely, the user can also scramble data using their Private Key; in other words, RSA keys work in either direction. This provides the basis for the digital signature, for if the user can unscramble a message with someone's Public Key, the other user must have used their Private Key to scramble it in the first place. Since only the owner can utilize their own private key, the scrambled message becomes a kind of electronic signature – a document that nobody else can produce. Next we will talk about digital signatures.

Digital Signatures

As has already been suggested, Digital Signatures help solve one of the problems of systems such as DES – authentication. Digital Signatures are in actual fact used to serve two purposes:

❑ Confirm data integrity

❑ Ensure the identity of the sender

According to the Internet Engineering Task Force's (IETF) Internet Security Glossary (http://www.ietf.org/rfc/rfc2828.txt), a digital signature is:

> "A value computed with a cryptographic algorithm and appended to a data object in such a way that any recipient of the data can use the signature to verify the data's origin and integrity."

> "Data appended to, or a cryptographic transformation of, a data unit that allows a recipient of the data unit to prove the source and integrity of the data unit and protect against forgery, for example, by the recipient."

A **digital signature** is typically created by computing a **message digest** from a document, and concatenating it with information about the signer, a timestamp, and any other useful information. A **one-way hash function** is used to generate the message digest, similar to a checksum, a fixed length string of numbers from a variable length text message. The "one-way" means that is extremely difficult to turn the fixed string back into the text message. The resulting string is then encrypted using the private key of the signer using a suitable algorithm. The resulting encrypted block of bits is the signature. It is often distributed together with information about the public key that was used to sign it. To verify a signature, the recipient first determines whether it trusts that the key belongs to the person it is supposed to belong to (using the web of trust or a priori knowledge), and then decrypts the signature using the public key of the person. If the signature decrypts properly and the information matches that of the message (proper message digest, and so on), the signature is accepted as valid.

To illustrate, let's say Party A wants to send a message to Party B. Using a digital signature, the following sequence of events will take place:

1. Party A uses a one-way hash function to compute a digest of their text message.

2. Party A then encrypts the digest using their Private Key. This turns it into a digital signature.

3. Next Party A encrypts this digital signature, along with the original message, using the Public Key of Party B.

The encrypted package is transmitted by Party A and received by Party B.

4. Party B uses their Private Key to decrypt the encrypted package, obtaining the message and the digital signature.

5. Party B then uses the Public Key of Party A to decrypt the signature back into the digest created by Party A.

6. Using the same one-way hash algorithm, Party B creates a new digest from the text message. This is then compared with the original hash. This last step both (a) confirms the integrity of the data, and (b) ensures the identity of sender.

Digital Signatures are an important part of Internet Security, and in fact underpin another important security technique: Digital Certificates.

Digital Certificates

A **Digital Certificate** is an electronic document that can be used to identify:

❑ An Individual

❑ A Server

❑ A Company

❑ Some other entity

Just like everyday personal IDs such as a passport, an important part of certificates is that it provides *recognized proof* of a person's identity. Obtaining this proof in the real world will almost certainly involve a third party confirming your are who you say you are – in the case of a passport, a government agency will attest to your name, nationality, date of birth, place of residency, and so on. The checks involved in obtaining the personal ID will depend on the type of ID requested and the entities that are responsible for issuing that ID. In the case of certificates, **certificate authorities (CAs)** are the entities that validate identities and issue certificates.

CAs can be either independent third parties, such as Thawte (http://www.thawte.com/), Entrust (http://www.entrust.com/), and VeriSign (http://www.verisign.com), or organizations running their own certificate-issuing server software (such as Netscape Certificate Server).

A certificate issued by a CA has the following characteristics:

❑ Binds a particular public key to the name of the entity the certificate identifies (such as the name of an individual or a server). This helps prevent the using fake public keys for impersonation – only the public key certified by the certificate will work with the corresponding private key possessed by the entity identified by the certificate.

❑ Always includes the name of the entity it identifies, an expiration date, the name of the CA that issued the certificate, a serial number, and other information.

❑ Most importantly, always includes the digital signature of the issuing CA, which allows the certificate to function as a "letter of introduction" for users who know and trust the CA but don't know the entity identified by the certificate.

Public Key Infrastructure (PKI)

Finally for this section, it is worth saying a few words about Public Key Infrastructure (PKI). PKI is the collection of services required to generate and manage public/private key pairs, as well as issuing and managing digital certificates, collectively termed digital certificate and key lifecycle management. PKI attempts to answer the following fundamental, real-world questions:

❑ How do I generate my private/public key pair?

❑ After I generate this key pair, how do I let the world know what my public key is?

❑ After I publish my public key, how does the world know it is actually mine and not someone else's?

❑ How do I protect the confidentiality of my private key?

❑ What happens if I lose my private key – how do I get a new one and how do I read old encrypted messages that can only be unlocked with the lost key?

❑ If someone keeps a copy of my private key against the day I lose it, what keeps them from using this key to forge my digital signature on documents?

❑ How do applications become "digital certificate aware" so that I can use public key cryptography with them?

❑ Will I need a different digital certificate and key pair for each application, a rather unwieldy and impractical proposition, or will one digital certificate work against all applications that need to present this credential?

We will now talk about Web Services security, and how frameworks such as PKI are being adapted into second-generation security architectures.

Web Application Security

> "One great thing about SOAP is that by using HTTP port 80 you can send requests right through the firewall! However, a bad thing about SOAP is that by using HTTP port 80 you can send requests right through the firewall!"

This amusing – but nevertheless accurate – statement sums up the idea that the web services model has changed the security landscape: in one way web services have simplified communication, but in so doing have circumvented some of the security measures already in place.

This section will talk about security and specifically how it is related to Web Services. Security in this area can be addressed at different layers, from the low-level network layer, up to the transport, and finally the application layer itself. First we will take a brief look at some of the various standards bodies/organizations responsible for developing many of the existing security standards as well as some of the new XML security standards.

Standards Bodies and Organizations

There are several bodies involved in examining the issues and in developing standards for XML Security and Web Services. It is useful to give a brief overview of three of these before we continue with a discussion of the technologies involved.

IETF

The Internet Engineering Task Force (IETF) is a large open international community of network designers, operators, vendors, and researchers concerned with the evolution of the Internet architecture and the smooth operation of the Internet. Within this organization, formal collaborative bodies called Working Groups (WGs) define standards and specifications for different data formats and communications protocols. There are many dozens of these groups, covering everything from the HTML language to HTTP to new versions of the TCP/IP Internet protocols. These WGs may create many documents, two of which are of interest here.

Request for Comments (RFCs)

One formal document prepared and published by a WG is the *Requests for Comments (RFC) document.* RFCs that define specific standards are known as Standards RFCs. Examples of these are available for download at ftp://ds.internic.net/rfc/.

The IETF also publishes RFCs that do not define standards, but instead define generic information about the Internet, or that define experimental protocols that are not finalized "official" standards. These experimental RFCs often evolve before becoming standard RFCs.

Internet Drafts

Before defining an RFC, a working group works through various drafts of the proposed document, with each member of the group providing input, commentary, suggestions, and criticisms. *Internet drafts* are very much works in progress, and can change substantially from version to version. Each draft is assigned a six month expiry date, after which the draft is deleted from the IETF archive sites. Internet drafts are available for download at http://www.ietf.org/ID.html.

More information about IETF can be found at http://www.ietf.org/.

W3C

The World Wide Web Consortium (W3C) was created in October 1994 to lead the World Wide Web to its full potential by developing common protocols that promote its evolution and ensure its interoperability. W3C has more than 500 Member organizations from around the world and has earned international recognition for its contributions to the growth of the Web.

As with the IETF, most of the this work goes on in Working Groups (WGs). WGs typically produce software, test suites, reviews of the deliverables of other groups, and technical reports. (The technical reports are as follows: Note, Working Draft, Last Call Working Draft, Candidate Recommendation, Proposed Recommendation, and finally Recommendation.) These reports range from stating the work in progress and charter of the WG, called Working Drafts, to varying levels of Recommendations, which meet the requirements of the WG to varying degrees. A W3C Recommendation is the final report and end result of extensive consensus building inside and outside of W3C about a particular technology or policy.

More information about the W3C can be found at http://www.w3.org/.

OASIS

The Organization for Structured Information Standards (OASIS) is a non-profit, international consortium dedicated to accelerating the adoption of product-independent formats based on public standards. These standards include SGML, XML, and HTML, as well as others that are related to structured information processing. It is important to note that OASIS *does not compete with*, but rather *builds upon and supplements* the work done by standards bodies such as W3C. In so doing, OASIS focuses on making these standards easy to adopt, and the products practical to use in real-world, open system applications. Where appropriate, OASIS recommends specific application strategies over others as ways in which various products can better provide interoperability for users. Put simply, OASIS helps to apply structured information standards, not create more.

Similarly to the IETF and W3C, Oasis has its own processes. The Technical Committee Process is used to govern technical work, producing various documents along the way.

You can find more information about OASIS at http://www.oasis-open.org/.

Transport Layer Security

As already mentioned, security in the context of web services, and for that matter, security in general, can be addressed at a number of different levels or layers. At the network layer, for example, is Internet Protocol Security (IPSec). As we saw, the Internet is an inherently insecure communication channel, and techniques such as encryption attempt to make data running along this channel secure. By contrast to encryption, IPSec attempts to make the Internet channel itself secure, and it does this by securing the network itself. Network-layer security is beyond the scope of this chapter, but more information concerning IPSec – a list of RFC's and a full-scale implementation – can be found at http://www.ssh.com/products/ipsec/standards.html.

So what is transport layer security? Security can be achieved using a number of various built-in security mechanisms of the Internet transport protocols themselves. Hypertext Transfer Protocol (HTTP) and Simple Mail Transfer Protocol (SMTP) are examples, and each comes with its own set of built-in security measures. However, there are limitations to this approach, particularly when it comes to securing web services. This is what we will cover next.

HTTP/1.0 Basic Authentication Scheme

The HTTP/1.0 basic authentication scheme is based on the model that the user agent, or browser, must authenticate itself with a username and a password for each realm, or area on the server. In terms of a standard web application, the browser would receive the 401 (unauthorized) response message sent by an origin server to challenge the authorization of a user, as specified by the HTTP specification, displaying a challenge dialog. This dialog would request username and password information from the user, and when submitted with correct details, access to the resource would be given.

Much of the processing using basic authentication scheme is hidden from even the developer, as the interaction is handled transparently by HTTP. Likewise, the data we collect is limited to that required by HTTP, that is, the username and password. Another, more popular, and programmatically exposed, method of authentication is that offered by HTML Forms.

Before we leave basic authentication, though, it is interesting to note that in terms of the security services we explored earlier, this scheme is really only a weak identification/authentication service, and does not include any of our other important security services. More information about the HTTP/1.0 basic authentication scheme can be found at http://www.w3.org/Protocols/HTTP/1.0/spec.html#AA.

HTML Forms-based Authentication

The HTML Form approach takes place on a layer above HTTP – HTML. As a result, it is more flexible, meaning that we not only have more programmatic access to the interaction, but also can decide what data we can collect, as we aren't restricted to the username and password fields.

One thing to bear in mind, especially when working with web services, is whether this particular method of authentication is supported. In the case of HTTP/1.0 basic authentication, it should be, and an alternative to the standard dialog is a SOAP client that could also pass this information back to the origin server in order to be authenticated. HTML forms, however, are unlikely to be supported by web service interfacing tools.

Another thing to bear in mind, and something that is associated with both the HTTP/1.0 basic authentication scheme and HTML Forms, is the way in which the username/password combination is transported to the origin server. In the case of HTTP/1.0 basic authentication scheme, data is encoded in base64 format, a format that is very easy to decode. With respect to HTML Forms, it isn't even encoded, and is instead sent using HTTP as cleartext!

A way around this is to combine them with Secure Socket Layer protocol.

Secure Sockets Layer (SSL)

Secure Sockets Layer (SSL) protocol was originally developed by Netscape as an open protocol standard, and these original efforts have been continued with http://www.openssl.org, an open source implementation. (The IETF's Transport Layer Security (TLS) – not to be confused with the title of this section! – standard is based on SSL.) It is available under Request for Comments (RFC) 2246, http://www.ietf.org/rfc/rfc2246.txt?number=2246). SSL is one of the two protocols used to secure web connections – the other is Secure Hypertext Transfer Protocol (SHTTP), which although in many ways more flexible than SSL, suffered from Netscape's original dominance in the marketplace. (Read more at ftp://ftp.uni-siegen.de/pub/rfc/rfc2660.txt.)

SSL in fact provides identification/authentication, integrity, and privacy security services, as we show below. The reader may wish to consult Netscape's Introduction to SSL at http://developer.netscape.com/docs/manuals/security/sslin/index.htm, which was used extensively for this section.

SSL includes two sub-protocols: the SSL record protocol and the SSL handshake protocol. The SSL record protocol defines the format used to transmit data, and the SSL handshake protocol uses the SSL record protocol to exchange a series of messages between an SSL-enabled server and an SSL-enabled client when they first establish an SSL connection.

SSL is a sophisticated protocol that is being used extensively on the Internet today. It provides most of the security services outlined above, but, along with other transport-level services, is not without its problems when it comes to web services.

SOAP/Application Layer Security

When thinking about SOAP security, one of the most straightforward ways to achieve security is by looking at the transmission channels used to exchange SOAP messages. SOAP travels via HTTP inside and outside of corporate networks. Two of the most popular ways to protect HTTP are by using SSL or using Virtual Private Networks(VPNs).

Using SSL is fairly simple and does not require any major change in the code. However, you must keep in mind the overhead added to your web server performance. Using SSL makes the web server work harder to encrypt and decrypt the information being sent via HTTP. If the online application is used by thousands of users SSL must be used very carefully in order not to impact on the user experience with slow page responses.

To implement SSL you, or your system administrator, can register for an SSL certificate and configure a web server, such as IIS or Apache, to communicate via a secure channel.

In the case of VPNs, an encrypted tunnel is set up between two machines or networks allowing the transmission to be secure between the two VPN end points. VPN allows data to be transferred over the public Internet in a secure manner that, to the end user, appears as though it originates from a member of that user's private network. Once the communication arrives at the other end it can be seen in the internal network. The security is in the channel used to transmit the message.

Companies like CISCO, http://www.cisco.com, and Checkpoint, http://www.checkpoint.com, are providers of VPN solutions. VPNs use data security technology to securely connect remote users or sites via the Internet. There are remote access VPNs widely used to connect employees to companies and there are also permanent VPN connections created to maintain two networks connected at all times.

VPN solutions are usually based on IPSec, Internet Protocol Security, a framework of open standards developed by the IETF, Internet Engineering Task Force, to ensure data privacy, data authentication, and user authentication on public networks. One of the main advantages of IPSec is that it operates in the network layer and allows applications to operate transparently between networks.

VPNs uses 56-bit DES or 168-bit 3DES encryption for data privacy. It uses MD5 and SHA-1 for data authentication. DES, an acronym for the Data Encryption Standard, is the name of the Federal Information Processing Standard (FIPS) 46-3, which describes the data encryption algorithm (DEA). The DEA is also defined in the ANSI standard X9.32. DEA is an improvement of the algorithm Lucifer developed by IBM in the early 1970s. MD5 is a message-digest algorithm developed by Rivest. They are meant for digital signature applications where a large message has to be compressed in a secure manner before being signed with the private key. The algorithm takes a message of arbitrary length and produces a 128-bit message digest. The Secure Hash Algorithm (SHA), is specified in the Secure Hash Standard. The algorithm takes a message of less than 264 bits in length and produces a 160-bit message digest.

If your security requirements are very high and your application is going to operate with a small number of sites and clients, a VPN option may be more appropriate. If your project requires exchanges with hundreds of distributed clients over public networks, SSL may be the better option.

As with many aspects of web services, security is made up of emerging standards. This section attempts to paint a picture of these emerging technologies as they appear today.

A lot of standardization effort is going on in XML for a common representation of security information such as signatures, authentication, authorization, key management, and so on. This section will summarize the key elements of each of these efforts, and show how they relate to first-generation security services.

Application-layer security requires more work than channel security. You must change your code to provide security on both the sender and the receiver side of the application. It can offer a higher degree of protection if used in conjunction with channel security options like SSL or a VPN. Security is usually achieved in applications by applying an encryption technology to the data being sent and received. Both the sender and the receiver must share knowledge on how the encryption is done so they can encrypt and decrypt a message. By applying encryption we are addressing the confidentiality requirements to create a secure exchange. In addition since the code must run under the proper service or username we also address some of the authorization requirements as well.

This section will cover the next layer of security, and the one of particular importance to web services: the SOAP or Application Layer of Security. But first we find out why this layer is required.

SOAP Anatomy

When thinking about security, we need to understand the anatomy of the SOAP standards first. The five main areas to keep in mind are:

- The message format
- The encoding
- The RPC conventions used
- The transport bindings – in our case HTTP
- The nature of messages with attachments

The message format is how the SOAP message is packaged before being sent on the network. The message contains the Primary MIME Part and attachments. The Primary MIME part comprises the SOAP Envelope, which in turn contains the SOAP Header and SOAP Body. Overleaf there is a simple image illustrating the basics of how a SOAP message is packaged before being sent on the network:

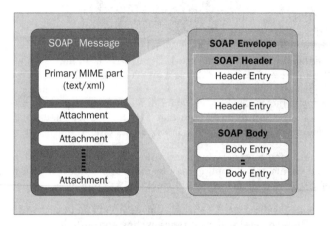

There are some general principles around SOAP messages that we need to consider. The envelope is an XML document. The SOAP body is intended for the recipient. Header entries may target intermediaries and can allow for added features in the future. Any encoding can be specified by element. A sample SOAP Envelope could looks like:

```
<?xml version="1.0" ?>
<SOAP-ENV:Envelope xmlns:SOAP-ENV="SoapEnvelopeURI"
    SOAP-ENV:encodingStyle="SoapEncodingURI">
  <SOAP-ENV:Header>
    <t:Transaction xmlns:t="TxURI" SOAP-ENV:mustUnderstand="1">
      <tid>123456</tid>
    </t:Transaction>
  </SOAP-ENV:Header>
  <SOAP-ENV:Body>
    <m:GetLastTradePrice xmlns:m="ServiceURI">
      <tickerSymbol>BEAS</tickerSymbol>
    </m:GetLastTradePrice>
  </SOAP-ENV:Body>
</SOAP-ENV:Envelope>
```

The SOAP encoding is based on XML schema. It uses simple values, built in types from XML schema, simple data types, enumerations, and arrays of bytes. It can also use compound values like structs, arrays, and complex types. Below are typical request and response SOAP messages:

Request Message

```
<?xml version="1.0" ?>
<SOAP-ENV:Envelope xmlns:SOAP-ENV="SoapEnvelopeURI"
    SOAP-ENV:encodingStyle="SoapEncodingURI">
  <SOAP-ENV:Header>
    <t:Transaction xmlns:t="TxURI" SOAP-ENV:mustUnderstand="1">
      <tid>123456</tid>
    </t:Transaction>
  </SOAP-ENV:Header>
  <SOAP-ENV:Body>
    <m:GetLastTradePrice xmlns:m="ServiceURI">
      <tickerSymbol>BEAS</tickerSymbol>
    </m:GetLastTradePrice>
  </SOAP-ENV:Body>
</SOAP-ENV:Envelope>
```

Response Message

```
<?xml version="1.0" ?>
<SOAP-ENV:Envelope xmlns:SOAP-ENV="SoapEnvelopeURI"
    SOAP-ENV:encodingStyle="SoapEncodingURI">
  <SOAP-ENV:Header>
    <t:Transaction xmlns:t="TxURI" SOAP-ENV:mustUnderstand="1">
      <tid>123456</tid>
    </t:Transaction>
  </SOAP-ENV:Header>
  <SOAP-ENV:Body>
    <m:GetLastTradePriceResponse xmlns:m="ServiceURI">
      <Price>18.53</Price>
    </m:GetLastTradePriceResponse>
  </SOAP-ENV:Body>
</SOAP-ENV:Envelope>
```

Next we are going to explore different ways to apply security to a SOAP-based message exchange. We will examine security considerations, channel security, application level security, digital signatures, and XML encryption.

SOAP Intermediaries

The concept of intermediaries is an important part of the SOAP model for exchanging messages. An intermediary is basically an endpoint, a receiver of a SOAP message, that can also send the same message on to another endpoint. Intermediaries and the message chain concept they introduce allow the development of sophisticated SOAP-based systems. An example of an intermediary might be an Aggregation Service, that is, an information portal that brings together content from several sources, some of which could be Web Services.

But what does this mean for security? Secure transport protocols such as SSL, TLS, and IPSec can provide the integrity and privacy of the message during transmission. However, because messages are received and processed by intermediaries, secure end-to-end communication is not possible if there is no trust association among all the intermediaries even though the communication links between them are trusted. End-to-end security is also compromised if one of the communication links is not secured.

A client of this Aggregation Service might like to know which intermediaries their data is going to go through – can the client trust these intermediaries?

The involvement of intermediaries and the need for end-to-end security increases the importance of the application layer in delivering security services. This is where SOAP/Application Layer Security is required: to guarantee the privacy, integrity, and validity of data, in the context of SOAP Intermediaries.

One important thing to note here is that with network and transport layer security, the SOAP message element does not need to be altered in order to take advantage of the security service. However, with SOAP/Application layer security, we need to modify the SOAP messages themselves – the application endpoint(s) of a SOAP message need to be able to understand the type of security used, along with how and when to apply it. Defining and providing for these message requirements is a key part of the various XML security initiatives described below.

More information concerning web service intermediaries can be found at
http://www.webservicesarchitect.com/content/articles/irani07.asp. Also, the article, *'Delving into SOAP security'*, located at http://www6.software.ibm.com/devtools/news0701/art10.htm argues for the additional SOAP layer of security.

SOAP Security Extensions

The extension modules offered by SOAP 1.1 offer a mechanism whereby security features may be placed into the SOAP message itself. This is achieved by combining the SOAP Header element with security extensions.

SOAP Security Extensions: Digital Signature

Published 6 February 2001, the *SOAP Security Extensions: Digital Signature* W3C Note (see http://www.w3.org/TR/SOAP-dsig/) specifies the syntax and processing rules of a SOAP header entry to carry digital signature information within a SOAP 1.1 Envelope. It proposes that other security features, such as XML Encryption be incorporated as they become available.

Here is an example cited in the document:

```
<SOAP-ENV:Envelope
  xmlns:SOAP-ENV="http://schemas.xmlsoap.org/soap/envelope/">
  <SOAP-ENV:Header>
    <SOAP-SEC:Signature
      xmlns:SOAP-SEC="http://schemas.xmlsoap.org/soap/security/2000-12"
      SOAP-ENV:actor="some-URI"
      SOAP-ENV:mustUnderstand="1">
      <ds:Signature xmlns:ds="http://www.w3.org/2000/09/xmldsig#">
        <ds:SignedInfo>
          <ds:CanonicalizationMethod
            Algorithm="http://www.w3.org/TR/2000/CR-xml-c14n-20001026">
          </ds:CanonicalizationMethod>
          <ds:SignatureMethod Algorithm="http://www.w3.org/2000/09/xmldsig#dsa-
sha1"/>
          <ds:Reference URI="#Body">
            <ds:Transforms>
              <ds:Transform Algorithm="http://www.w3.org/TR/2000/CR-xml-c14n-
20001026"/>
            </ds:Transforms>
            <ds:DigestMethod Algorithm="http://www.w3.org/2000/09/xmldsig#sha1"/>
            <ds:DigestValue>j61wx3rvEPO0vKtMup4NbeVu8nk=</ds:DigestValue>
          </ds:Reference>
        </ds:SignedInfo>
        <ds:SignatureValue>MC0CFFrVLtRlk=...</ds:SignatureValue>
      </ds:Signature>
    </SOAP-SEC:Signature>
  </SOAP-ENV:Header>

  <SOAP-ENV:Body
    xmlns:SOAP-SEC="http://schemas.xmlsoap.org/soap/security/2000-12"
    SOAP-SEC:id="Body">
    <m:GetLastTradePrice xmlns:m="some-URI">
      <m:symbol>IBM</m:symbol>
    </m:GetLastTradePrice>
  </SOAP-ENV:Body>
</SOAP-ENV:Envelope>
```

We can see in the code above a signature header entry, where the SOAP Body is signed and the resulting signature <ds:Signature> is added to the <SOAP-SEC:Signature> header entry. The SOAP-ENV:mustUnderstand="1" entry specifies that the end point intercepting this message must understand this header entry if it is to process the enclosed entries. We can also see that the canonicalization and signature methods are specified.

- ❑ The <SignedInfo> element is the information that is actually signed. Core validation of <SignedInfo> elements comprises of two mandatory processes: validation of the signature over <SignedInfo> and the validation of each Reference digest within <SignedInfo>.

- ❑ The CanonicalizationMethod is the algorithm that is used to canonicalize the <SignedInfo> element before it is digested as part of the signature operation. The SignatureMethod is the algorithm that is used to convert the canonicalized <SignedInfo> into the SignatureValue. It is a combination of a digest algorithm and a key-dependent algorithm and possibly other algorithms such as padding, for example RSA-SHA1.

- ❑ Each <Reference> element includes the digest method and resulting digest value calculated over the identified data object. It also may include transformations that produced the input to the digest operation. The signature is later checked via reference and signature validation.

- ❑ KeyInfo indicates the key to be used to validate the signature. Possible forms for identification include certificates, key names, and key agreement algorithms and information. KeyInfo is optional for two reasons. First, the signer may not wish to reveal key information to all document processing parties. Second, the information may be known within the application's context and need not be represented explicitly. Since KeyInfo is outside of SignedInfo, if the signer wishes to bind the keying information to the signature, a Reference can easily identify and include the KeyInfo as part of the signature.

Signatures over a transformed document do not secure any information discarded by transforms: only those signed are secure. Note that the use of Canonical XML ensures that all internal entities and XML namespaces are expanded within the content being signed. All entities are replaced with their definitions and the canonical form explicitly represents the namespace that an element would otherwise inherit.

Applications that do not canonicalize XML content (especially the SignedInfo element) should not use internal entities and should represent the namespace explicitly within the content being signed, since they cannot rely upon canonicalization to do this for them. Also, users concerned with the integrity of the element type definitions associated with the XML instance being signed may wish to sign those definitions as well (that is, the schema, DTD, or natural language description associated with the namespace/identifier).

You should be very careful of the creation of potential weaknesses between the original and transformed data with applications that operate over the original or intermediary data. An application needs to be cautious when making a trust decision about the character and meaning of transforms. Consider a canonicalization algorithm that normalizes character case (lower to upper) or character composition ('e and accent' to 'accented-e'). A competitor could introduce changes that are normalized and as a result inconsequential to signature validity but matter to a DOM processor. For instance, by changing the case of a character you might influence the result of an XPath selection. A serious risk is introduced if that change is normalized for signature validation but the processor operates over the original data and returns a different result than intended.

More information on canonicalization can be found at http://www.w3.org/TR/xml-c14n/.

We also have the digest, which as you remember, guarantees data integrity, plus the signature itself. Next we look at XML Signature itself, one of the two schemes this extension is designed to wrap around.

The *SOAP Security Extensions: Digital Signature* W3C Note itself is available at http://www.w3.org/TR/SOAP-dsig/.

XML Signature

From the W3C's point of view, more progress has been made on XML Signatures than the Signature Extensions, above, as indicated by the fact that a W3C Working Group (WG) has been formed around it.

The mission of the XML Signature WG is to develop an XML-compliant syntax used for representing the signature of web resources and portions of protocol messages and procedures for computing and verifying such signatures. Interestingly, it is a joint WG of the IETF and W3C. They are quite clear that they do not address broader XML security issues including XML encryption and authorization. We will see both of these below.

XML Signature Examples

XML signatures applied to data within the same XML document as the signature are termed enveloping or enveloped signatures. XML signatures applied to data that is external to the signature element are termed detached signatures. The following extract from the recommendation document is an instance of a simple detached signature:

```
<Signature Id="MyFirstSignature"
              xmlns="http://www.w3.org/2000/09/xmldsig#">
  <SignedInfo>
    <CanonicalizationMethod Algorithm="http://www.w3.org/TR/2001/
              REC-xml-c14n-20010315"/>
    <SignatureMethod Algorithm="http://www.w3.org/2000/09/
              xmldsig#dsa-sha1"/>
    <Reference URI="http://www.w3.org/TR/2000/REC-xhtml1-20000126/">
      <Transforms>
        <Transform Algorithm="http://www.w3.org/TR/2001/REC-xml-c14n-
              20010315"/>
      </Transforms>
      <DigestMethod Algorithm="http://www.w3.org/2000/09/
              xmldsig#sha1"/>
      <DigestValue>j6lwx3rvEPO0vKtMup4NbeVu8nk=</DigestValue>
    </Reference>
  </SignedInfo>
  <SignatureValue>MC0CFFrVLtRlk=...</SignatureValue>
  <KeyInfo>
    <KeyValue>
      <DSAKeyValue>
        <p>...</p><Q>...</Q><G>...</G><Y>...</Y>
      </DSAKeyValue>
    </KeyValue>
  </KeyInfo>
</Signature>
```

The signed information appears within the `<SignedInfo>` element. The algorithms used in calculating the `<SignatureValue>` element are referenced within the signed section. The `<SignatureMethod>` element specifies the algorithm used to convert the canonicalized `SignedInfo` into the `SignatureValue`. It's a combination of a key-dependent algorithm and a digest algorithm, here DSA and SHA-1. The `<KeyInfo>` element indicates the key that is used to validate the signature.

The range of possibilities as to the order in which encryption, signing, modifying, and perhaps more signing may take place, are enormous. Taking the idea of SOAP intermediaries discussed earlier, it is conceivable that applications will be required to pick up from where another intermediary left off and either potentially decrypt data, re-encrypt data decrypted by the current endpoint, or both. This will need to be done in such a manner as not to prevent other intermediaries, or indeed the recipient itself, from decrypting the data. The W3C has published a working draft on decryption transform for XML signature that addresses this situation. This can be found at http://www.w3.org/TR/xmlenc-decrypt. This documents cites the example below as an illustration.

Let's say that the following XML document is to be signed by me. However, part of this document is already encrypted prior to my signing it (`<EncryptedData>...</EncryptedData>`). In addition, I think that the `<cardinfo>` element will be encrypted *after* signing.

```
<order Id="order">
  <item>
    <title>XML and Java</title>
    <price>100.0</price>
    <quantity>1</quantity>
  </item>
  <cardinfo>
    <name>Your Name</name>
    <expiration>04/2002</expiration>
    <number>5283 8304 6232 0010</number>
  </cardinfo>
  <EncryptedData Id="enc1" xmlns="http://www.w3.org/2001/04/xmlenc#">
    ...
  </EncryptedData>
</order>
```

In order to let the recipient of this document know the proper order of decryption and signature verification, we can include the decryption transform (`<Transform>...</Transform>`) in the signature. Assuming that an additional encryption is done on the `<cardinfo>` element above, the recipient would see the following encrypt-sign-encrypt document:

```
<Signature xmlns="http://www.w3.org/2000/09/xmldsig#">
  <SignedInfo>
    ...
    <Reference URI="#order">
      <Transforms>
        <Transform Algorithm="http://www.w3.org/2001/04/decrypt#">
          <Except URI="#enc1" xmlns="http://www.w3.org/2001/04/decrypt#"/>
        </Transform>
        <Transform Algorithm="http://www.w3.org/TR/2000/CR-xml-c14n-20001026"/>
      </Transforms>
      ...
    </Reference>
```

```
    </SignedInfo>
    <SignatureValue>...</SignatureValue>
    <Object>
      <order Id="order">
        <item>
          <title>XML and Java</title>
          <price>100.0</price>
          <quantity>1</quantity>
        </item>
        <EncryptedData Id="enc2" xmlns="http://www.w3.org/2001/04/xmlenc#">
          ...
        </EncryptedData>
        <EncryptedData Id="enc1" xmlns="http://www.w3.org/2001/04/xmlenc#">
          ...
        </EncryptedData>
      </order>
    </Object>
</Signature>
```

The <cardinfo> element has been replaced with <EncryptedData
Id="enc2">...</EncryptedData>. The recipient should first look at the <Signature> element for
verification. It refers to the <order> element by using <Reference URI="#order">, with two
transforms: decryption and canonicalization. The decryption transform instructs the signature verifier to
decrypt all the encrypted data except for that specified in the <Except> element. After decrypting the
<EncryptedData>, the order element is canonicalized and signature-verified.

The progress of this WG can be seen at http://www.w3.org/Signature/, while http://www-
106.ibm.com/developerworks/xml/library/s-xmlsec.html/index.html presents a good introduction to
XML encryption and XML signature from IBM.

XML Encryption

The mission of this WG is to develop the following:

❑ A process for encrypting/decrypting digital content – including XML fragments/documents

❑ An XML syntax used to represent (1) the encrypted content and (2) information that enables
an intended recipient to decrypt it

The following documents are currently accessible from this WG:

❑ *XML Encryption Requirements Working Draft* at http://www.w3.org/TR/xml-encryption-req/

❑ *XML Encryption Syntax and Processing Working Draft* at http://www.w3.org/TR/xmlenc-core/

❑ *Decryption Transform for XML Signature Working Draft* at http://www.w3.org/TR/xmlenc-decrypt/

All three of these are Working Drafts, which, as you will remember, are an early stage in the W3C's
technical document track, both in terms of their stability and community consensus around them.

The XML Encryption Requirements document outlines the design principles, scope, and requirements for XML Encryption. It includes requirements as they relate to the encryption syntax, data model, format, cryptographic processing, and external requirements and coordination. The second and third documents specify a process for encrypting and decrypting XML-based data and representing the result in XML. We will show you some examples of the syntax for the encryption of XML here.

Expressed in shorthand form, the `<EncryptedData>` element has the following structure:

```
<EncryptedData Id? Type?>
  <EncryptionMethod/>?
  <ds:KeyInfo>
    <EncryptedKey>?
    <AgreementMethod>?
    <ds:KeyName>?
    <ds:RetrivalMethod>?
    <ds:*>?
  </ds:KeyInfo>?
  <CipherData>
    <CipherValue>?
    <CipherReference URI?>?
  </CipherData>
</EncryptedData>
```

The question marks in the code are place holders for actual entries.

The `<EncryptedData>` element is at the heart of XML encryption syntax that, with the `<EncryptedKey>` element, is used to transport encryption keys from the originator to a known recipient, and derives from the `<EncryptedType>` abstract type. Data to be encrypted can be any of the following, resulting in an XML encryption element that contains or references the cipher data:

❑ Arbitrary data: `<EncryptedData>` element may become the root of a new XML document or it may become a child element

❑ XML document: `<EncryptedData>` element may become the root of a new document

❑ XML element: `<EncryptedData>` element replaces the element or content in the encrypted version of the XML document

❑ XML element content: `<EncryptedData>` element replaces the element or content in the encrypted version of the XML document

`<EncryptedData>` cannot be the parent or child of another `<EncryptedData>` element, but the actual data encrypted can be anything including existing `<EncryptedData>` or `<EncryptedKey>` elements.

How the granularity of encryption may differ according to different requirements and what the consequences might be, is illustrated in the *XML Encryption Syntax and Processing Working Draft*. The markup below shows an unencrypted XML document with credit card and other personal information:

```
<?xml version='1.0'?>
<PaymentInfo xmlns='http://example.org/paymentv2'>
  <Name>John Smith<Name/>
  <CreditCard Limit='5,000' Currency='USD'>
    <Number>4019 2445 0277 5567</Number>
    <Issuer>Bank of the Internet</Issuer>
    <Expiration>04/02</Expiration>
  </CreditCard>
</PaymentInfo>
```

Mr Smith's credit card number is sensitive information. If the application wishes to keep that information confidential, it can encrypt the <CreditCard> element:

```
<?xml version='1.0'?>
<PaymentInfo xmlns='http://example.org/paymentv2'>
  <Name>John Smith<Name/>
  <EncryptedData Type='http://www.w3.org/2001/04/xmlenc#Element'
              xmlns='http://www.w3.org/2001/04/xmlenc#'>
    <CipherData>
      <CipherValue>A23B45C56</CipherValue>
    </CipherData>
  </EncryptedData>
</PaymentInfo>
```

By encrypting the entire <CreditCard> element from its start to end tags, the identity of the element itself is hidden. Therefore, an electronic eavesdropper will not know whether he used a credit card or money transfer. The <CipherData> element contains the encrypted serialization of the <CreditCard> element.

Consider the scenario in which all the information except the actual credit card number can be in the clear, including the fact that the <Number> element exists:

```
<?xml version='1.0'?>
  <PaymentInfo xmlns='http://example.org/paymentv2'>
    <Name>John Smith<Name/>
    <CreditCard Limit='5,000' Currency='USD'>
      <Number>
        <EncryptedData xmlns='http://www.w3.org/2001/04/xmlenc#'
         Type='http://www.w3.org/2001/04/xmlenc#Content'>
            <CipherData><CipherValue>A23B45C56</CipherValue>
            </CipherData>
        </EncryptedData>
      </Number>
      <Issuer>Bank of the Internet</Issuer>
      <Expiration>04/02</Expiration>
    </CreditCard>
  </PaymentInfo>
```

Both <CreditCard> and <Number> are in the clear, but the character data content of <Number> is encrypted.

If the application scenario requires all of the information to be encrypted, the whole document is encrypted. This applies to arbitrary data including XML documents.

```
<?xml version='1.0'?>
<EncryptedData xmlns='http://www.w3.org/2001/04/xmlenc#'
            Type='http://www.someurl.com/assignments/media-types/text/xml'>
  <CipherData>
    <CipherValue>A23B45C56</CipherValue>
  </CipherData>
</EncryptedData>
```

The `<CipherData>` element can either envelop or reference the raw encrypted data. In the first case, that raw data is shown by the contents of the `<CipherValue>` element, while in the second a `<CipherReference>` element is used, and this encloses a URI that points to the location of the encrypted data.

The progress of this Working Group can be seen at http://www.w3.org/Encryption/2001/, while http://www-106.ibm.com/developerworks/xml/library/s-xmlsec.html/index.html presents a good introduction to XML encryption and XML signature from IBM.

XKMS

The XML Key Management Specification (XKMS, http://www.w3.org/TR/xkms/) was submitted to the W3C in March 2001. It specifies protocols for distributing and registering public keys, suitable for use in conjunction with the proposed standard for XML Signature and an anticipated companion standard for XML encryption. It also defines protocols for the resolution/retrieval of public keys, and association and retrieval of attributes in the form of 'trust assertions' with public keys.

In the specification, a signer may or may not include information about their public signing key ("`<ds:KeyInfo>`") inside the signature block. This key information is designed to allow the signer to communicate "suggestions" to a verifier about which public key to select. Another important property of `<ds:KeyInfo>` is that it may or may not be cryptographically connected to the signature itself. This allows the `<ds:KeyInfo>` to be substituted or supplemented without "breaking" with the digital signature.

For example, Mankee signs a document and sends it to Rob with a `<ds:KeyInfo>` element that specifies only the signing Key Data. On receiving the message, Rob retrieves additional information required to perform the validation of the signature and adds this information into the `<ds:KeyInfo>` element when he passes the document on to Helen.

A `<ds:KeyInfo>` element may include a `<ds:RetrievalMethod>` element, which is a means to communicate information available from a remote location. The `<ds:RetrievalMethod>` element is a feature of and is defined by the XML Signature Specification.

For example, the signer of a document may wish to refer verifiers to a chain of X.509 certificates without having to attach them. `<ds:RetrievalMethod>` consists of a location that, in this case, would refer to a location on the Web from which the certificate chain may be retrieved, a method, and a type.

The objective is to provide a higher-level, more flexible, interface into trust services than currently provided with first-generation public key infrastructures, as described above.

XKMS essentially comprises three services and associated specifications: Key Information Service Specification X-KISS, Key Registration Service X-KRSS, and Trust Assertion Service X-TASS. We will briefly look at each.

Key Information Service Specification X-KISS

X-KISS provides a public key resolution/retrieval and verification service. Low-level X-KISS services allow applications to retrieve a user's certificate. High-level services provide an interface into a range of information linked to the owner of an identified public key, information being provided with supporting trust details.

Key Registration Service Specification X-KRSS

This defines a protocol for the registration of public key information. A user registering for a service may request that additional information is bound to the public key; this may be a name, an identifier, or extended attributes defined by the implementation.

The protocol offers authentication for the applicant and if the key pair is generated by the client a Proof of Possession (POP) of the private key.

Trust Assertion Service X-TASS

The trust assertion specification defines an architecture and protocol for the retrieval statements, known as trust assertions, which are bound to the public key.

With SAML, XACML/XACL, and other initiatives, XKMS is an important element in the large jigsaw that makes up security as applied to XML documents. Its immediate effect is to simplify greatly the management of authentication and signature keys; it does this by separating the function of digital certificate processing, revocation status checking, and certification path location and validation from the application involved – for example, by delegating key management to an Internet Web service.

Other XML Security initiatives

Here we briefly summarize other XML Security initiatives.

SAML

The work undertaken by the OASIS XML-Based Security Services Technical Committee (SSTC) combines two prior, formerly competing, efforts, S2ML and AuthXML. The specification resulting from this process, Security Assertion Markup Language (SAML), allows organizations to exchange authentication, authorization, and profile information securely with their partners. For more information on SAML, see the OASIS SSTC site http://www.oasis-open.org/committees/security/.

XACML/XACL

Extensible Access Control Markup Language is a specification that enables organizations to limit access to services to authenticated, authorized users. It is closely related to SAML, but focuses more on a subject-privilege-object orientated security model in the context of a particular XML document. By writing rules in XACML/XACL, a policy author can define who can exercise what access privileges for a particular XML document, something relevant in the situations cited earlier.

More information on XACML can be found at http://www.oasis-open.org/committees/xacml/.

Platform for Privacy Preferences Project (P3P)

The Platform for Privacy Preferences Project (P3P) enables web sites to express their privacy practices in a standard format that can be retrieved automatically and interpreted easily by user agents. P3P user agents will allow users to be informed of site practices (in both machine- and human-readable formats) and to automate decision-making based on these practices when appropriate. Thus users need not read the privacy policies at every site they visit.

More information on the W3C's P3P can be found at http://www.w3.org/TR/P3P/#Introduction.

Java Security APIs, Toolkits, and SDKs

If it seems the conversation has been more general than focusing on Java Web Services Security, then that is because of the nature of Web Services – the outwardly-exposed elements should be predictably similar, using the same standards, some of which we have covered above. This is a reason behind Web Services being so loosely coupled and interoperable.

However, there are more publicly available code, tool kits, and SDKs for Java than for any other platform, designed to get these technologies into the hands of developers and consultants. These can be roughly divided into two types: those used within the web service boundary, and those used in web service communication.

Java Security APIs

The Java Security APIs from Sun fall into the first group. It is worth mentioning these APIs, as some of them are used in the XML Security toolkits mentioned below.

The current Standard Edition Development Kit is version 1.3. For this version, the following security APIs are available as optional packages for separate download:

❑ Java Authentication and Authorization Service (JAAS)
The Java Authentication and Authorization Service (JAAS) is a set of packages that enable services to authenticate and enforce access controls upon users. It implements a Java version of the standard Pluggable Authentication Module framework, and provides support for user-based, group-based, or role-based access controls. See http://java.sun.com/products/jaas/ for more information.

❑ Java Cryptography Extension (JCE)
The Java Cryptography Extension (JCE) is a set of packages that provide a framework and implementations for encryption, key generation and key agreement, and Message Authentication Code (MAC) algorithms. Support for encryption includes symmetric, asymmetric, block, and stream ciphers. The software also supports secure streams and sealed objects. See http://java.sun.com/products/jce for more information.

❑ Java Secure Socket Extension (JSSE)
The Java Secure Socket Extension (JSSE) is a set of packages that enable secure Internet communications. It implements a Java version of SSL (Secure Sockets Layer) and TLS (Transport Layer Security) protocols and includes functionality for data encryption, server authentication, message integrity, and optional client authentication. Using JSSE, developers can provide for the secure passage of data between a client and a server running any application protocol (such as HTTP, Telnet, NNTP, and FTP) over TCP/IP. See more information at http://java.sun.com/products/jsse.

Each of these APIs is integrated into J2SE, version 1.4 (http://java.sun.com/products/jce/index-14.html), which at time of writing is at beta 3.

Java API for XML Messaging (JAXM)

JAXM, the Java API for XML Messaging, provides a standard way to send messages over the Internet from the Java platform. It is based on the SOAP 1.1 and SOAP with Attachments specifications. Though it is not required JAXM messaging usually takes place within a container, generally a servlet or a J2EE container, like an Application Server. We can combine JAXM for the exchange of SOAP messages with an encryption technology of your preference to deploy secure SOAP messages. For more comprehensive JAXM information you should visit http://java.sun.com/xml/jaxm/.

One of the advantages of using a J2EE container is that you can have a listener that makes it possible to receive messages asynchronously. The listener receives the message as one operation, and the recipient sends a reply as a subsequent operation, making the message asynchronous. A JAXM message is made up of two parts, a required SOAP part and an optional attachment part.

Below is code to create an initial connection to send a SOAP message using JAXM:

```
Context ctx = getInitialContext();
ConnectionFactory cf = (ConnectionFactory)ctx.lookup("SomeConnectionProvider");
Connection con = cf.getConnection()
```

Once the connection object is available, we can move on to create a `MessageFactory` object that is used to create a `Message` object:

```
MessageFactory messageFactory = con.getMessageFactory();
Message m = messageFactory.createMessage();
```

Part of the flexibility of the JAXM API is that it allows the specific usage of a SOAP header. The `Message` object m created in the preceding line of code will support a basic SOAP message. The next step is to populate the message.

There are two ways to add content to a message. Firstly, we can pass a `javax.xml.transform.Source` object to a `SOAPEnvelope` object. The `Source` object can be a `SAXSource` object, a `DOMSource` object, or a `StreamSource` object. The `Source` object contains the content of the message and also the information needed for it to act as source input. A `StreamSource` object will contain the content as an XML document, and the `SAXSource` or `DOMSource` object will contain the content and instructions for transforming it into an XML document. The second option is by creating separate elements containing the content and adding them individually. In this case, you build an XML document using `String`, `Comment`, and `CDATA` objects as required.

The following code fragment illustrates the first step to encrypt the XML data and add content as a `DOMSource` object. The first step is always to get the `SOAPPart` object and use it to get the `SOAPEnvelop` object:

```
//Use encryption libraries to encode the XML field data
EncryptXMLFields("file:///somedir/soap.xml");

SOAPPart soapPart = m.getSOAPPart();
SOAPEnvelope soapEnvelope = soapPart.getSOAPEnvelope();

DocumentBuilderFactory dbf = DocumentBuilderFactory.newInstance();
```

```
DocumentBuilder db = dbf.newDocumentBuilder();
Document doc = db.parse("file:///somedir/soap.xml");

DOMSource domSource = new DOMSource(doc)
SoapEnvelope.setContent(domSource)

//Below is the code to add attachments:
URL url = new URL("http:///img.jpg");
DataHandler dh = new DataHandler(url)
AttachmentPart attachPart = m.createAttachmentPart(dh)
m.addAttachmentPart(attachPart)
```

In this particular approach the XML data was encrypted first. All the fields in the XML document were processed using the encryption technology that is available to the application. The "javax.crypto" package, which is part of the Java Cryptography Extension, JCE, distributed by Sun, comes with several classes for various cryptographic operations.

There other encryption libraries available on the Net you can use. We would recommend looking at the RSA libraries, http://www.rsa.com/, RSA BSAFE Crypto J for example provides state-of-the-art implementation of the most important privacy, authentication, and data integrity routines in Java including source code.

Application-level security addresses most of the basic requirements for secure transfer. It addresses confidentiality by keeping the information secure from individuals, entities, and processes. It is true that a developer could post the source code on the net and everybody would know what was going on, but we assume this is not the case here. To run your application requires the right amount of authorization. The application context must be running with sufficient privileges to access and manipulate the data that will become part of the SOAP exchange. Data integrity is maintained as long as your application does not cause any data to be altered or corrupted during the creation of the SOAP message.

Toolkits and SDKs

Here are a few of the publicly available code fragments, toolkits, and SDKs that tend to fit into the second group – those used in web service communication. A similarly useful list is available at the W3C's XML-Signature Working Group (http://www.w3.org/Signature/):

❑   VeriSign. The VeriSign-sponsored XML Trust Center (http://www.xmltrustcenter.org/) is a vendor-neutral source for information relating to web services security standards work.http://www.xmltrustcenter.org/xmlsig/developer/verisign/index.htm.

❑   IBM XML Security Suite. XML Security Suite is a tool that provides security features such as digital signature, encryption, and access control for XML documents. These features are beyond the capability of transport-level security protocols such as Secure Sockets Layer (SSL). The goals in creating this technology were to contribute to standards development by providing sample implementations and to supply advanced technologies to partners and developers and to gather their input. http://www.alphaworks.ibm.com/tech/xmlsecuritysuite/.

❑   Entrust/Toolkit; for Java http://www.entrust.com/developer/java/index.htm.

❑   IAIK XML Signature Library (IXSIL) http://jcewww.iaik.at/products/ixsil/index.php.

- ❏ NEC XMLDSIG http://www.sw.nec.co.jp/soft/xml_s/appform_e.html.
- ❏ Infomosaic https://www.infomosaic.net/.
- ❏ RSA BSAFE Cert-J http://www.rsasecurity.com/products/bsafe/certj.html.

Summary

This chapter has provided an introduction to security for Java Web Services. We began by identifying some key security risks. This was followed by a breakdown of the security services an application might provide to help circumvent these risks. Next, we looked at some cryptographic techniques already used in Internet security, and discussed what security services they were designed to fit into.

This theoretical first part was followed by a more technically focused discussion of the two different level of web services security – Transport- and Application-level. We concluded that, although transport-level required the least intervention by the web services developer, it suffered from a lack of programmatic access and flexibility; also in the context of SOAP Intermediaries, we had to look for other solutions, offering end-to-end security.

Application-level security in the context of Web Services is a fast-evolving moving domain. One thing we did note was the drive towards standards and interoperability, and here we tried to give an overview of those emerging standards of most interest. We also gave an overview of some of the several toolkits, APIs, and SDKs on offer that implement these standards.

Resources

[1] http://www-106.ibm.com/developerworks/xml/library/s-xmlsec.html/index.html
Good introduction to XML encryption and XML signature from IBM.

[2] http://www6.software.ibm.com/developerworks/education/ws-dsst/ws-dsst-6-1.html
A tutorial outlining the way digital signatures can be incorporated in SOAP messages (requires user registration).

[3] http://www.nue.et-inf.uni-siegen.de/~geuer-pollmann/xml_security.html
Called the XML Security Page, this is an excellent source of information, ranging from standardization/public discussion, to white papers, XML Security in general, commercial products and applications of XML Security. Got [1] from here.

[4] http://www.w3.org/Signature/
W3C's XML-Signature Working Group site. Got [3] from here. One very useful thing it's got is a list of "Publicly Available Code, Tool Kits & SDKs".

[5] http://developer.java.sun.com/developer/technicalArticles/Security/xkms/
An article from Sun that attempts to show how Java can interface with VeriSign's XKMS implementation. The VeriSign SDK is mentioned under Publicly Available Code, Tool Kits & SDKs in above link.

[6] Two good sources for security:
http://digitalid.verisign.com/client/help/technical.htm#2
http://digitalid.verisign.com/client/help/introID.htm

[7] http://www.ssh.com/tech/crypto/
Cryptographic Algorithms. This page lists commonly used cryptographic algorithms and methods and explains the basic underlying concepts. It also tries to give references to implementations and textbooks. Where available, comments are also made about the usefulness or other aspects of the algorithms.

[8] http://digitalid.verisign.com/client/help/introCrypto.htm
VeriSign's Introduction to Cryptography.

[9] http://www-105.ibm.com/developerworks/papers.nsf/dw/security-papers-bynewest?OpenDocument&Count=500
Good resource of IBM Security articles.

[10] http://www-106.ibm.com/developerworks/security/library/s-pki.html?dwzone=security
Another IBM article – PKI: A primer.

[11] http://www-106.ibm.com/developerworks/security/library/s-crypt07.html?dwzone=security
Introduction to cryptography, Part 7: Contents and resource list.

[12] http://www.webservicesarchitect.com/content/articles/irani07.asp
Article about Web Services Intermediaries.

[13] http://www.research.ibm.com/journal/sj/403/benantar.html
The Internet public key infrastructure.

[14] http://www6.software.ibm.com/devtools/news0701/art10.htm
This article describes why the SOAP layer security architecture is necessary by giving a general overview, several scenarios and topologies, and general security requirements.

[15] Bruce Schneier: *Applied Cryptography*, second edition, John Wiley & Sons, 1996. Good, practical introduction to cryptographic algorithms, protocols, and methods. A table of contents, errata, and other information can be found at http://www.counterpane.com/applied.html.

[16] http://www.w3.org/TR/2001/WD-xmlenc-core-20011018/Overview.html. Reference for XML.

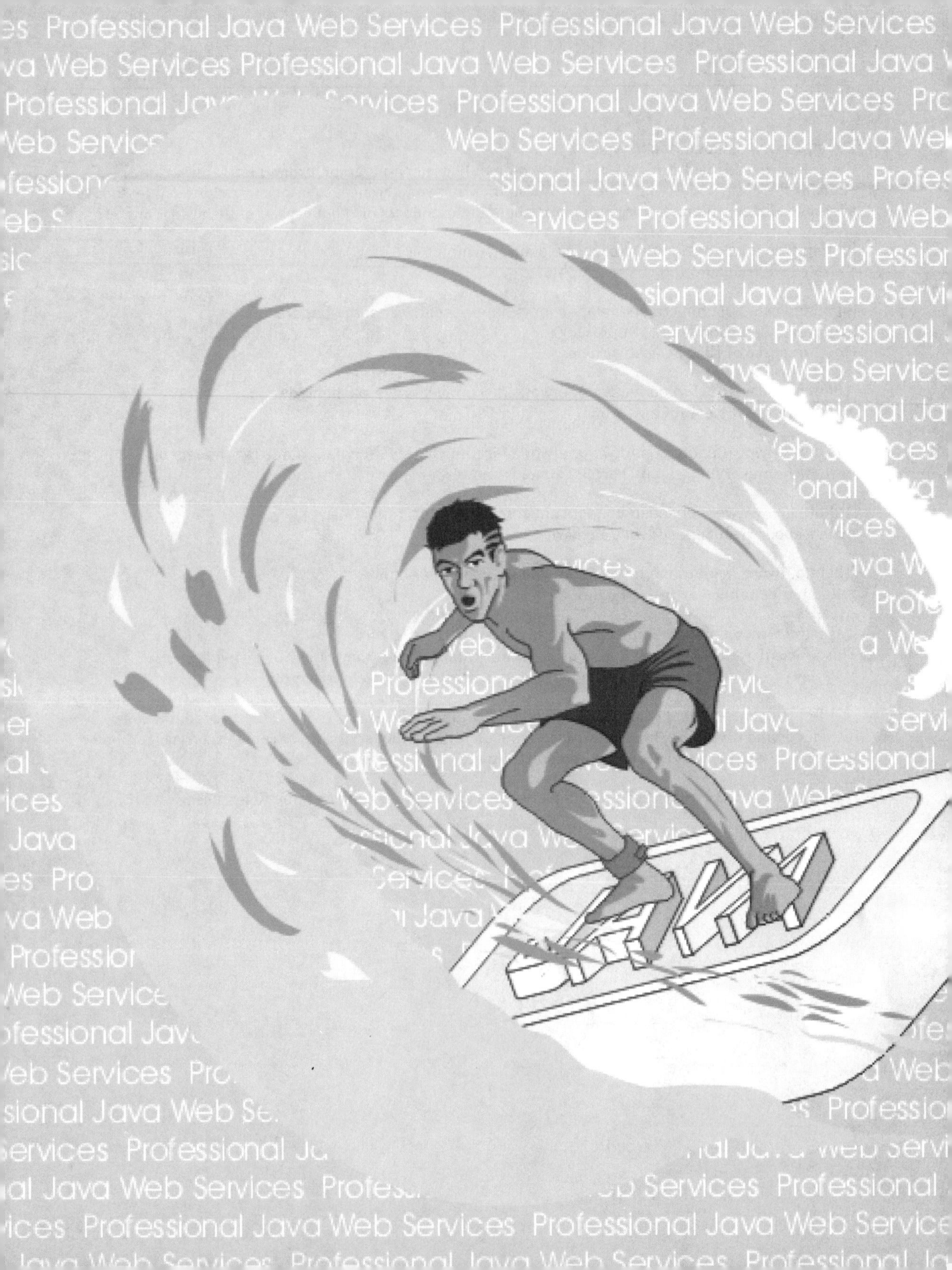
Professional Java Web Services

Health Care Case Study

This chapter is a comprehensive case study that combines all the technologies for Web Services (SOAP, WSDL, and UDDI) into an integrated system. The case study demonstrates how a fictitious health insurance company, Wrox Insurance, uses Web Services to achieve a rapid and low-cost integration project that provides online medical appointments as a Web Service.

We will take a step-by-step approach to the project rather than demonstrating an entire solution in one go. This incremental approach will greatly help to ensure that the application works and will be well understood.

In particular we will cover the following:

- ❑ Describe the Wrox Insurance organization and how it functions with its provider organizations in the context of medical appointments

- ❑ Discuss a Web Services solution to help automate the appointment process across all its providers

- ❑ Develop Web Services using WSDL and SOAP and deploy them using Apache-SOAP as the runtime environment

- ❑ Develop a web site for Wrox Insurance that integrates the different Web Services into a unified interface to the end-user

- ❑ Discuss the role of UDDI in the context of the above system

- ❑ Discuss further improvements that can be made to the system

Wrox Insurance

In this section, we will first describe how Wrox Insurance operates. This will give an idea about the inefficiency present in the system, particularly the system for making an appointment with the doctor. Then we will discuss how we can improve the efficiency of this system using Web Services as an integration tool to achieve better results.

Technology for the sake of technology is rarely a component of real and sustained growth in business environments, and we will try to show the improvements in process, cost, and customer experience possible with Web Services.

Current System

Wrox Insurance is a health insurance company. We will not go into too many details about the entire capabilities of a Health Insurance company. However, it would be good to mention a few things about them.

A Health Insurance company is the one with whom a customer signs up for medical coverage. Normally they provide consumers with several health plans, varying in premiums, insurance coverage, and so on, and the consumer signs up for one of those plans. A plan will usually cover the customer for a period of a year.

A Health Insurance company is thus more of a broker. Hospitals, physician offices, and private medical clinics join as health care providers to this broker. By a care provider, we mean the actual places where the customer will go if they have a medical issue that needs to be addressed.

For example, let's say that I had signed up for "Plan A" at Wrox Insurance which insures me to around $2000/yr of medical expenses. Now, let's say that I had to visit the doctor for my regular mental (oops… medical) checkup. Since Wrox Insurance is just a broker, I obviously cannot go to them for a medical checkup. I have to select a provider: a hospital or physician office. which accepts my health plan from Wrox Insurance.

So, let us see how this medical appointment is done today via Wrox Insurance.

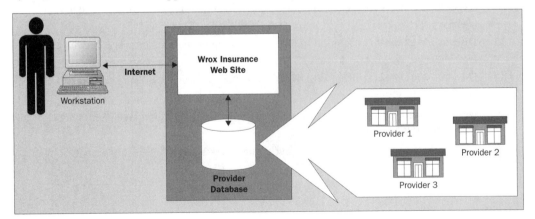

1. The first step is to login to the Wrox Insurance site and determine the list of care providers (from here on referred to as a **Provider**) to Wrox Insurance.

2. Select a Provider depending upon the customer's preferences. For example, distance from home, city, specialisms, and so on

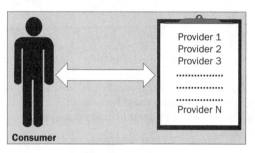

Once the customer has the list of providers, they will have the provider's contact information. They then need to contact the particular provider and ask them if they have an appointment available.

3. Contact the Provider via phone to make an appointment

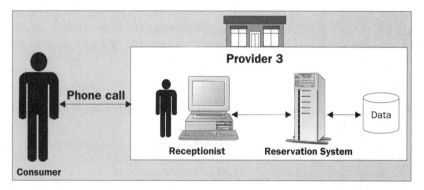

In this step, the customer will mainly interact via the phone with the receptionist or the person responsible for reserving an appointment for them. This will involve the receptionist using an internal reservation system to determine which slots are free. If a particular slot suits the customer's schedules, the receptionist will then book it.

Current System – Inefficiency

From the above description, it should be obvious that the entire process of making an appointment with a provider is a long-drawn and manual one. It involves several disjoint interactions: the customer must first visit the web site to retrieve information about the providers. Once they have that information they need to call and arrange for an appointment. Of course, make a note that what is presented here is a very simple reservation system. In the real world, we will often find that the reservation systems are much more complex due to the nature of the business of the health care insurance company. For example, there are usually several restrictions on changing the providers and the number of visits that can be made to the provider in a year, and so on. We will avoid most of those complications in the system that we develop here to keep the discussion focused on the matter in hand.

Thus, there is inefficiency in all aspects. The time it takes to book an appointment can be a relatively long and painful process for the individual. Wrox Insurance as a company may also be affected since this affects the customer's estimation of the company.

What Wrox Insurance really needs to achieve process efficiency here is to connect all the systems in a seamless manner such that the user can use a single uniform interface to do all the functions.

Wrox Insurance, being a forward thinking organization, wants a system that would serve a dual purpose, that is, it would make their task of integrating different provider systems easier and it would also help the subscriber to easily make a reservation with a particular provider.

In order to prove the concept of an open and standards-based way of developing their system, we will develop a prototype that will not take into consideration all the complex rules that went into developing a reservation system but mainly serves to demonstrate the fact that Web Services could form the basis for a full-featured reservation system.

Enter Web Services

We will begin by identifying the basic functionality that will demonstrate the prototype for a Web Services based reservation system. The goal is also to exercise Web Services technologies like SOAP, WSDL, and UDDI and get familiar with them.

The first task in any such project is to identify what that basic functionality would be. Keep in mind that one of the goals of developing this prototype is also to demonstrate that the subscriber can easily make a reservation. To achieve that it is necessary to identify a particular flow for how the subscriber can make reservations. For that, we can come up with the following sequence of operations:

❑ The subscriber will visit the Wrox Insurance web site and navigate to their reservation section.

❑ The subscriber can then search for the providers that are present depending on several search criteria like city, appointment date, and so on.

❑ Once the subscriber selects a particular provider, they should be presented with a list of appointment slots to choose from. This means that the Wrox Insurance site should have a mechanism to communicate with the providers' back-end reservation systems.

❑ From the list of appointment slots available, the subscriber selects a particular slot and sends the request for making the reservation. The Wrox Insurance site should then send off that request to the provider's back-end reservation system and confirm the reservation back to the subscriber.

This entire flow and the high-level overview of this system is shown below:

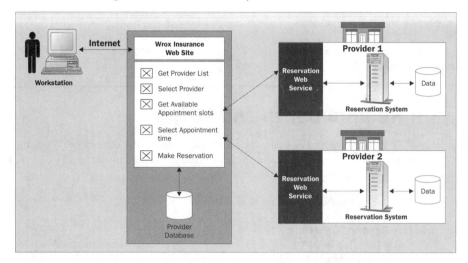

The key features of this system include:

❑ All the (care) providers now expose their reservation system as a Web Service. Thus Wrox Insurance has an open and interoperable mechanism for dealing with all the provider systems irrespective of the back-end reservation systems they are using.

❑ The Wrox Insurance web site will provide a web interface to the consumer. This web interface provides the consumer with information about the different providers but also allows the customer to select a provider, retrieve a list of available appointments for that provider, and send the appointment request seamlessly to the provider reservation system.

There a several benefits that such a Web Services approach would bring to Wrox Insurance:

❑ **Standard Interoperable Access Mechanism**
By using standard Web Services technologies like SOAP, each provider system can now be accessed in an interoperable fashion. This takes the complexity out of the integration project. It definitely makes the job of the Wrox Insurance technology team that of concentrating on improving the functionality rather than getting bogged down in specific integration scenarios with provider systems. Wrox Insurance system now does not have to even worry about the kind of back-end reservation systems used by the providers. As long as they provide a standard SOAP interface that Wrox Insurance expects, there will be no integration issues.

❑ **Expansion is made seamless**
Any new provider that wishes to be part of the Wrox Insurance network must expose their systems as a Web Service. If the Web Service conforms to the interface set by Wrox Insurance, the addition of a new provider system will be almost seamless.

❑ **Cost Savings**
It is widely accepted that project costs escalate dramatically when the project includes integration between disparate systems. By using open and interoperable Web Services technologies, Wrox Insurance diminishes the time needed to develop and maintain such a system. This results in huge cost savings.

In addition to the above benefits, by seamlessly integrating back-end functionality and disparate processes, Wrox Insurance is able to provide to the consumer much more value than was previously possible in a short period of time.

Now that we have an idea about aims that Wrox Insurance wants to achieve, let us go about developing such a system.

Software Requirements and Setup

In this section, we will identify the system software that we need in the case study. We will do the initial setup such that we get all three organizations in the case study, Wrox Insurance, Provider 1, and Provider 2, up and running with their system software.

The following software is needed to run the case study:

❑ **Java Development Kit (JDK 1.3.1)**:
The JDK is installed in `c:\jdk131` and the `JAVA_HOME` environment variable points to `c:\jdk131`. You should be able to configure your system easily even if your `jdk` values are somewhat different.

❑ **Apache Tomcat version 3.2**:
We will discuss the directory structure for this a little later on.

❑ **Apache SOAP toolkit version 2.2**:
Apache SOAP toolkit is installed in `c:\soap-2_2`. The `soap.jar` file, however, is used from the IBM Web Services toolkit below. We basically need the SOAP toolkit for the admin utility and the SOAP router servlet.

❑ **IBM Web Services Toolkit (WSTK) version 2.3 or later**:
This is installed in `c:\ibm-wstk`. The `WSTK_HOME` environment variable points to `c:\ibm-wstk`.

❑ **Xerces XML parser version 1.2**:
The `xerces.jar` file is used from the `c:\ibm-wstk\lib` directory.

❑ **Java Beans Activation Framework (version 1.0.1 or later)**:
The `activation.jar` file is used from the `c:\ibm-wstk\lib` directory.

❑ **JavaMail (version 1.2 or later)**:
The `mail.jar` file is used from the `c:\ibm-wstk\lib` directory.

❑ **JDOM XML parser Beta-7**:
JDOM XML parser is available from **www.jdom.org**. The package is installed in `c:\jdom-b7` and the `jdom.jar` file is in `c:\jdom-b7\build\jdom.jar`.

The software list is a little overwhelming but we will cover configuration specifics as we move along in the chapter.

Initial Setup

Before we move on to discuss the code, it is very important that we discuss the setup of the application and get it running. We will also discuss setting up the directory structures for the application.

High Level Overview

Essentially, we are going to simulate three organizations: Wrox Insurance Company, Provider 1, and Provider 2. This means that we are going to have three instances of Tomcat Server running on the local machine. This is done so that you can run the entire application on the same machine yet simulate three processes running independently of each other, as illustrated below:

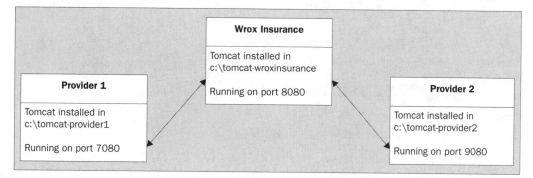

So, let us proceed with setting up Tomcat and SOAP for each of the organizations and also discuss the directory structures for the development.

Wrox Insurance

Wrox Insurance, as we discussed before, is the main organization that will be interacting with the two provider organizations: Provider 1 and Provider 2. The configuration details are given below:

Wrox Insurance Tomcat Server

1. Install the Tomcat Server in `c:\tomcat-wroxinsurance`.

2. In `c:\tomcat-wroxinsurance\conf\config.bat` replace the line:

```
set CP=%CP%;%CLASSPATH%
```

with the following line:

```
set CP=%CLASSPATH%;%CP%
```

This ensures that `xerces.jar`, which will appear in our classpath, will be used for XML parsing by Tomcat instead of the XML classes in Tomcat. This can be done most easily with a search and replace on the statements above.

3. Assuming that the SOAP distribution was unzipped to the `c:\soap-2_2\` directory, copy the entire contents of `c:\soap-2_2\` to `c:\tomcat-wroxinsurance\`. This step will simplify configuration.

4. Make sure that the HTTP Connection handler is listening on port 8080 in the `c:\tomcat-wroxinsurance\conf\server.xml` file. This is the default for Tomcat, and so should happen automatically – it will only be different if you have a previously installed instance of Tomcat with a modified configuration.

Wrox Insurance Development and Runtime Environment

1. Create a directory named `c:\javawebservices\wroxinsurance`. This will contain all the Java code developed for the Wrox Insurance Web Service application.

2. Create a file named `config.bat` in `c:\javawebservices\wroxinsurance` as shown below:

```
set TOMCAT_HOME=c:\tomcat-wroxinsurance
set JWS_HOME=c:\javawebservices
set classpath=%classpath%;%JWS_HOME%\lib\xerces.jar
set classpath=%classpath%;%JWS_HOME%\lib\soap.jar
set classpath=%classpath%;%JWS_HOME%\lib\mail.jar
set classpath=%classpath%;%JWS_HOME%\lib\uddi4j.jar
set classpath=%classpath%;%JWS_HOME%\lib\activation.jar
set classpath=%classpath%;%JWS_HOME%\lib\jmxc.jar
set classpath=%classpath%;%JWS_HOME%\lib\jmxx.jar
set classpath=%classpath%;%JWS_HOME%\lib\log.jar
set classpath=%classpath%;%JWS_HOME%\lib\jdom.jar

set classpath=%classpath%;%JWS_HOME%\wroxinsurance
set classpath=%classpath%;%JWS_HOME%\provider1
set classpath=%classpath%;%JWS_HOME%\provider2

set path=%TOMCAT_HOME%\bin;%PATH%
set path=%path%;c:\wstk-2.4\bin
```

The `config.bat` file shown above is used to set the CLASSPATH correctly to ensure that both the development environment and the runtime environment are set-up correctly.

Provider 1

Provider 1 is one of the providers where consumers can book appointments. The Provider 1 organization hosts its own appointment service. What this means is that we have to simulate another Tomcat environment and development setup on the local machine in order to simulate the actual activities of the Provider 1 organization. The configuration details for Provider 1 are given below but are very similar to the previous instructions for `wroxinsurance`:

Provider 1 Tomcat Server

1. Install the Tomcat Server in `c:\tomcat-provider1`.

2. Change the `tomcat.bat` file as before.

3. Copy the SOAP distribution into the `tomcat\webapps\` directory once more.

4. Since we need to ensure that the Tomcat ports for Provider 1 don't clash with the ones for Wrox Insurance, we will change all the ports to start with 7XXX to 8XXX. Make sure that the HTTP Connection handler is listening on port 7080 in the `c:\tomcat-provider1\conf\server.xml` file. Similarly there are a couple of other ports too in this file which start with "8", used for stopping the server and for SSL support. Change these values to start with "7"

Provider 1 Development and Runtime Environment

5. Create a directory named `c:\javawebservices\provider1`. This will contain all the Java code developed for the Provider1 Web Service application.

6. Create a file named `config.bat` in `c:\javawebservices\provider1` as before but with tomcat home set to `c:\tomcat-provider1` in the first line:

```
set TOMCAT_HOME=c:\tomcat-provider1
set JWS_HOME=c:\javawebservices
#... rest of file as before
```

Provider 2

Provider 2 is another provider that provides the Appointment Web Service. The steps for setting up the Provider 2 environment are identical to those given for Provider 1 above. Of course, the directories and the port numbers are different as shown below:

Provider 2 Tomcat Server

1. Install the Tomcat Server in `c:\tomcat-provider2`.

2. Amend the `tomcat.bat` file.

3. Copy the contents of the SOAP directory to the Tomcat installation.

4. Change the values for all ports in `server.xml` to begin with 9XXX.

Provider 2 Development and Runtime Environment

Create the `c:\javawebservices\provider2` directory and copy the `config.bat` file created for provider 1, changing the TOMCAT_HOME to `c:\tomcat-provider2`.

This completes the setup for making sure that each of the different organizations that we have in our case study, that is, Wrox Insurance, Provider 1, and Provider 2, have their own correctly configured environments. It would be a good idea at this moment to make sure that the configuration is OK, by running each of the three servers as given above. Make sure that the Tomcat Server for each of the organizations is up and running.

In every case, the way that we will start up the Tomcat Server is as follows the illustration below is for the `wroxinsurance` environment:

❑ Open a command window.

❑ Go to the `c:\projavawebservices\wroxinsurance` directory.

❑ Run `config.bat`. This will set the `TOMCAT_HOME` environment variable correctly. It will setup the JAR files correctly for running of the application.

❑ Finally, enter the command **tomcat start** in the command window. This will start up the tomcat server for Wrox Insurance on port 8080.

Repeat for the two providers.

You can check that the three are installed correctly by navigating to the following URLs:

http://localhost:7080/soap
http://localhost:8080/soap
http://localhost:9080/soap

In each case, the resultant output should be the following:

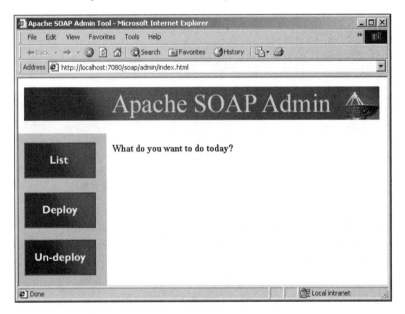

Wrox Insurance Web Services Approach

It is important that we first identify the requirements of the Reservation Web Service and decide upon the kind of interfaces and data exchange that will take place between the Wrox Insurance system and the Reservation Web Service.

Web Service Requirements

We definitely need a common interface for the Reservation Web Service that will reside at each provider. At the same time we also need to decide on the parameters of each method present in the interface.

Web Service Interface

The Web Service interface basically identifies the methods present in the interface. This interface will be implemented by each provider in the form of a Web Service. There are three methods that will currently be supported in this interface:

❑ **Get Provider Information**:
   This method will provide provider information like provider name, provider contact address, and so on.

❑ **Get Appointment Slots**:
   This method will provide a list of appointment slots that are currently available. A consumer can therefore look at these available slots and make a decision if a particular appointment fits their schedule.

❑ **Reserve Appointment**:
   Once a consumer decides to book a particular appointment slot, then this method will be used to book the appointment for the consumer.

Note that the above functionality is fairly basic in order to demonstrate the basic working prototype. It obviously does not have several features that would be present in a real-life reservation system. However it would be worth mentioning some of those points here to give an idea of how this prototype could be further extended:

❑ A consumer would be able to select the choice of providers and reservation slots based on several criteria like distance from home, provider type, that is, general practice, specialists, and so on.

❑ In spite of the fact that we are demonstrating full automation in reserving an appointment, it might still be necessary for the reservation to be done manually in-case of emergencies. So, whether we like it or not, the manual phone reservation system might continue to survive. The Wrox Insurance web site would probably continue to provide a link to this service, so the service may continue to thrive.

❑ There will have to be a mechanism via which the consumer can reschedule or even cancel the appointment.

Many more possibilities exists we will not consider them further. Let us now look at the Java interface that is provided by Wrox Insurance for the above methods. Each provider will have to support this interface in their Reservation Web Service.

Appointment.java

```
package com.wroxinsurance;

public interface Appointment {
```

The `getProviderDetails()` method returns an XML formatted string containing provider information like provider name, provider contact address, provider contact information, and so on.

```
String getProviderDetails();
```

The `getAppointmentSlots()` method takes as input an XML formatted string that contains preferences of the consumer for selecting the appointment slots, that is, day, time, and so on. Since we are keeping the example simple, we shall pass an empty string and return all the providers. But keep in mind that this can be used as a basis to filter the appointment slots based on consumer preferences. It returns an XML string that contains a list of appointment slots available from a particular provider.

```
String getAppointmentSlots(String inputReq);
```

The `reserveAppointment()` method takes as input an XML formatted string that contains the consumer information and the appointment slot that was selected. It returns an XML string that contains the status of the reservation request, that is, whether the reservation was made successfully or not.

```
String reserveAppointment(String inputReq);
}
```

To compile the above file, refer to the following steps (note that these steps will be repeated often across the whole case study):

1. Open a command window.

2. Go to `c:\javawebservices\wroxinsurance`.

3. Create the directory `com\wroxinsurance` inside `c:\javawebservices\wroxinsurance` and copy the above file `Appointment.java` in to this directory.

4. Go to the `c:\javawebservices\wroxinsurance` directory.

5. Run the `config.bat` file. This will set up the `CLASSPATH` correctly as we saw in the setup above.

6. Give the following command at the prompt:

```
javac com/wroxinsurance/Appointment.java
```

Your directory structure should be as follows:

```
C:\javawebservices\wroxinsurance\config.bat
                       com\
                           wroxinsurance\
                                         Appointment.java
                                         Appointment.class
```

XML Data Formats

We will essentially be using XML for passing in requests. At the same time, the response from each of these methods will be available as XML output. Let us now discuss the XML data formats for each of the methods in the interface

The getProviderDetails() Method

The `getProviderDetails()` method does not take any input parameters. It returns an XML string as output that has information about the provider: provider name, provider contact address, contact information, and so on.

Input:
None

Output:

```
<?xml version="1.0" encoding="UTF-8"?>
<PROVIDER-DETAILS PROVIDERID="1">
  <NAME>PROVIDER 1</NAME>
  <ADDR1>123 Street</ADDR1>
  <ADDR2>Suite 100</ADDR2>
  <CITY>San Jose</CITY>
  <STATE>CA</STATE>
  <ZIPCODE>95000</ZIPCODE>
  <PHONE>408-123-4567</PHONE>
  <FAX>408-456-7890</FAX>
  <EMAIL>info@provider1.com</EMAIL>
</PROVIDER-DETAILS>
```

The addresses within are not intended to represent real addresses

The getAppointmentSlots() Method

The `getAppointmentSlots()` method takes as input an XML string that contains the search criteria from the user; preferred date and preferred time. We will not be implementing this functionality in order to keep the case study simple. So the input XML string passed from now on will be an empty string. What the method will return is a list of available appointment slots as an XML string. Since we are not going to be presenting any criteria in the input, as stated, what we will receive are all the available slots from the provider.

Input:
Empty String ""

Output:

```
<?xml version="1.0" encoding="UTF-8"?>
<PROVIDER-APPOINTMENTS PROVIDERID="1">

  <APPOINTMENT ID="A-1000">
    <DATE>1 NOV 2001</DATE>
    <TIME>11:00 AM</TIME>
  </APPOINTMENT>
```

```
    <APPOINTMENT ID="A-1001">
      <DATE>1 NOV 2001</DATE>
      <TIME>2:00 PM</TIME>
    </APPOINTMENT>

    <APPOINTMENT ID="A-1002">
      <DATE>3 NOV 2001</DATE>
      <TIME>8:00 AM</TIME>
    </APPOINTMENT>

  </PROVIDER-APPOINTMENTS>
```

The reserveAppointment() Method

The `reserveAppointment()` method is used to book the appointment selected by the consumer. It takes as input an XML string that identifies the consumer and the appointment that they have selected. It returns an XML string indicating whether the appointment was booked successfully or not. Again, we will keep the example simple by always returning a `<STATUS>` of `OK`.

Input:

```
<?xml version="1.0" encoding="UTF-8"?>
<PROVIDER-APPOINTMENTREQUEST PROVIDERID="1">
  <PATIENTID>CERTIFICATE-123</PATIENTID>
  <APPOINTMENT-ID>A-1002</APPOINTMENT-ID>
</PROVIDER-APPOINTMENTREQUEST>
```

Output:

```
<?xml version="1.0" encoding="UTF-8"?>
<PROVIDER-APPOINTMENTRESPONSE PROVIDERID="1">
  <PATIENTID>CERTIFICATE-123</PATIENTID>
  <APPOINTMENT-ID>A-1002</APPOINTMENT-ID>
  <STATUS>OK</STATUS>
</PROVIDER-APPOINTMENTRESPONSE>
```

Provider Web Services

In this section, we will develop the Appointment Web Service for both Provider 1 and Provider 2. We will also deploy the Web Service in each of the provider environments.

Provider 1

We covered the Appointment Service interface in a previous section. So, what each provider has to do is to provide a service implementation for that interface.

Note that in a real scenario, the Web Service will in all probability integrate with a back-end system that will provide the actual functionality. Since we want to keep it simple here, we will just create stubs for these methods that will return hard-coded data.

Let us now look at the implementation of the Provider1 Appointment Service.

Provider1Appointment.java

```
package com.provider1;

import com.wroxinsurance.Appointment;

import java.io.StringReader;

//JDOM objects required for XML parsing and XML Document creation
import org.jdom.Document;
import org.jdom.Element;
import org.jdom.input.SAXBuilder;
import org.jdom.output.XMLOutputter;

public class Provider1Appointment implements Appointment {

    /** Creates new Provider1Appointment */
    public Provider1Appointment() {
    }
```

The getProviderDetails() method below constructs an XML document that represents the provider details:

```
public String getProviderDetails() {
```

It first creates the root element of the response, that is, PROVIDER_DETAILS, and adds an attribute, PROVIDERID, that uniquely identifies the provider.

```
Element ProviderDetailsRoot = new Element("PROVIDER-DETAILS");
ProviderDetailsRoot.setAttribute("PROVIDERID","1");
```

It then proceeds to add the child elements to the PROVIDER_DETAILS element, that is, ProviderDetailsRoot. The child elements added are NAME, ADDR1, ADDR2, CITY, STATE, ZIPCODE, PHONE, FAX, and EMAIL. Note the use of the setText() method to set the contents for the elements.

```
ProviderDetailsRoot.addContent(new Element("NAME").setText("PROVIDER 1"));
ProviderDetailsRoot.addContent(
                    new Element("ADDR1").setText("123 Street"));
ProviderDetailsRoot.addContent(new Element("ADDR2").setText("Suite 100"));
ProviderDetailsRoot.addContent(
                    new Element("CITY").setText("San Jose"));
ProviderDetailsRoot.addContent(new Element("STATE").setText("CA"));
ProviderDetailsRoot.addContent(new Element("ZIPCODE").setText("95000"));
ProviderDetailsRoot.addContent(
                    new Element("PHONE").setText("408-123-4567"));
ProviderDetailsRoot.addContent(
                    new Element("FAX").setText("408-456-7890"));
ProviderDetailsRoot.addContent(
                    new Element("EMAIL").setText("info@provider1.com"));
```

Once we have constructed our response, we convert the `ProviderDetailsRoot` element to a `Document` object.

```
Document ProviderDetails = new Document(ProviderDetailsRoot);
```

And finally we convert this `Document` into an XML formatted string using the `org.jdom.output.XMLOutputter` class. The constructor for `XMLOutputter` takes two parameters. The first one identifies the indentation of the XML string and the second parameter, which is a `boolean`, inserts line-feeds to format the XML string neatly.

```
XMLOutputter outputter = new XMLOutputter("  ",true);
return outputter.outputString(ProviderDetails);
}
```

The XML response returned is shown below:

```
<?xml version="1.0" encoding="UTF-8"?>
<PROVIDER-DETAILS PROVIDERID="1">
  <NAME>PROVIDER 1</NAME>
  <ADDR1>123 Street</ADDR1>
  <ADDR2>Suite 100</ADDR2>
  <CITY>San Jose</CITY>
  <STATE>CA</STATE>
  <ZIPCODE>95000</ZIPCODE>
  <PHONE>408-123-4567</PHONE>
  <FAX>408-456-7890</FAX>
  <EMAIL>info@provider1.com</EMAIL>
</PROVIDER-DETAILS>
```

The `getAppointmentSlots()` method constructs three sample appointments that are available and can be booked by the consumer. Each appointment has an `id`, `time`, and `date`:

```
public String getAppointmentSlots(String inputReq) {
  Element AppointmentsRoot = new Element("PROVIDER-APPOINTMENTS");
  AppointmentsRoot.setAttribute("PROVIDERID","1");

  //Appointment 1
  Element Appointment1 = new Element("APPOINTMENT");
  Appointment1.setAttribute("ID","A-1000");
  Appointment1.addContent(new Element("DATE").setText("1 NOV 2001"));
  Appointment1.addContent(new Element("TIME").setText("11:00 AM"));

  //Appointment 2
  Element Appointment2 = new Element("APPOINTMENT");
  Appointment2.setAttribute("ID","A-1001");
  Appointment2.addContent(new Element("DATE").setText("1 NOV 2001"));
  Appointment2.addContent(new Element("TIME").setText("2:00 PM"));

  //Appointment 3
  Element Appointment3 = new Element("APPOINTMENT");
  Appointment3.setAttribute("ID","A-1002");
  Appointment3.addContent(new Element("DATE").setText("3 NOV 2001"));
  Appointment3.addContent(new Element("TIME").setText("8:00 AM"));
```

```
      AppointmentsRoot.addContent(Appointment1);
   AppointmentsRoot.addContent(Appointment2);
   AppointmentsRoot.addContent(Appointment3);

   Document AppointmentSlots = new Document(AppointmentsRoot);
   XMLOutputter outputter = new XMLOutputter("  ",true);
   return outputter.outputString(AppointmentSlots);
}
```

For example, the method shown below would return the following appointment slots:

```
<?xml version="1.0" encoding="UTF-8"?>
<PROVIDER-APPOINTMENTS PROVIDERID="1">

  <APPOINTMENT ID="A-1000">
    <DATE>1 NOV 2001</DATE>
    <TIME>11:00 AM</TIME>
  </APPOINTMENT>

  <APPOINTMENT ID="A-1001">
    <DATE>1 NOV 2001</DATE>
    <TIME>2:00 PM</TIME>
  </APPOINTMENT>

  <APPOINTMENT ID="A-1002">
    <DATE>3 NOV 2001</DATE>
    <TIME>8:00 AM</TIME>
  </APPOINTMENT>

</PROVIDER-APPOINTMENTS>
```

The reserveAppointment() method shown below takes as input the appointment request as discussed in the XML formats section, that is, it provides the client information and the appointment ID that the customer is interested in booking. It basically parses the XML information and by default returns an XML structure indicating a status of the request. To keep things simple, it hard codes back a status of OK, but in reality it could integrate with a back-end system.

```
public String reserveAppointment() (String inputReq) {
   System.out.println("Received Appointment");
   System.out.println("--------------------");

   //Parse the Appointment Request
   try {
```

The first step is to parse the XML document, inputReq, received. Refer to the sample XML input document that is shown after the code. To do that we use the org.jdom.input.SAXBuilder class that builds an org.jdom.Document element from the XML string as shown below:

```
SAXBuilder builder = new SAXBuilder();
Document AppointmentReq = builder.build(new StringReader(inputReq));
```

Once we have the `Document` object, `AppointmentReq`, we can then parse it accordingly. We first get the root element `AppointmentReqRoot`.

```
Element AppointmentReqRoot = AppointmentReq.getRootElement();
String providerId = AppointmentReqRoot.getAttribute("PROVIDERID").getValue();
```

Here we get the `PATIENTID` element that identifies the patient or consumer.

```
String patientId = AppointmentReqRoot.getChild("PATIENTID").getText();
```

Here we get the `APPOINTMENT ID` that was selected by the consumer.

```
String apptId = AppointmentReqRoot.getChild("APPOINTMENT-ID").getText();
```

Finally, we create an XML string that represents the response to the reservation request. Note that ideally over here, the provider would have integrated the request into their back-end reservation system. But for the purposes of this prototype, we are always going to return that a successful appointment was made.

```
        //Prepare Response
        Element AppointmentRespRoot = new Element("PROVIDER-APPOINTMENTRESPONSE");
        AppointmentRespRoot.setAttribute("PROVIDERID","1");
        AppointmentRespRoot.addContent(new Element("PATIENTID")
                        .setText(patientId));
        AppointmentRespRoot.addContent(new Element("APPOINTMENT-ID")
                        .setText(apptId));
        AppointmentRespRoot.addContent(new Element("STATUS")
                        .setText("OK"));
        Document AppointmentResponse = new Document(AppointmentRespRoot);
        XMLOutputter outputter = new XMLOutputter("  ",true);
        return outputter.outputString(AppointmentResponse);

    } catch (Exception e) {
        System.out.println("ERROR");
        return "ERROR";
    }
  }
}
```

A sample input to this method could be:

```
<?xml version="1.0" encoding="UTF-8"?>
<PROVIDER-APPOINTMENTREQUEST PROVIDERID="1">
  <PATIENTID>CERTIFICATE-123</PATIENTID>
  <APPOINTMENT-ID>A-1002</APPOINTMENT-ID>
</PROVIDER-APPOINTMENTREQUEST>
```

And the output returned by the method would be:

```
<?xml version="1.0" encoding="UTF-8"?>
<PROVIDER-APPOINTMENTRESPONSE PROVIDERID="1">
  <PATIENTID>CERTIFICATE-123</PATIENTID>
  <APPOINTMENT-ID>A-1002</APPOINTMENT-ID>
  <STATUS>OK</STATUS>
</PROVIDER-APPOINTMENTRESPONSE>
```

To compile the above file, refer to the previously illustrated steps, creating the relevant folder structure for the package and compiling with the following command:

```
> javac com/provider1/Provider1Appointment.java
```

Provider 1 SOAP Service Configuration

Now that the Provider 1 Appointment Web Service is ready, we need to deploy it within the Apache SOAP environment for Provider 1. We will assume that you have some familiarity by now with the Apache SOAP toolkit and how to deploy a SOAP Web Service within it. For more information refer to Chapter 3 on Apache SOAP.

If the Tomcat for `provider1` is not started, make sure it is using the instructions given earlier. Remember that `provider1` is set on port 7080.

Launch a web browser and navigate to http://localhost:7080/soap. The SOAP Admin utility should come up. We will use this service for deploying the applications.

Select `Deploy` and enter the following details for the Provider 1 Service as shown below. Note that the ID is `urn:Provider`. The class name and the method names are the ones that we developed for `Provider1Appointment.java` above.

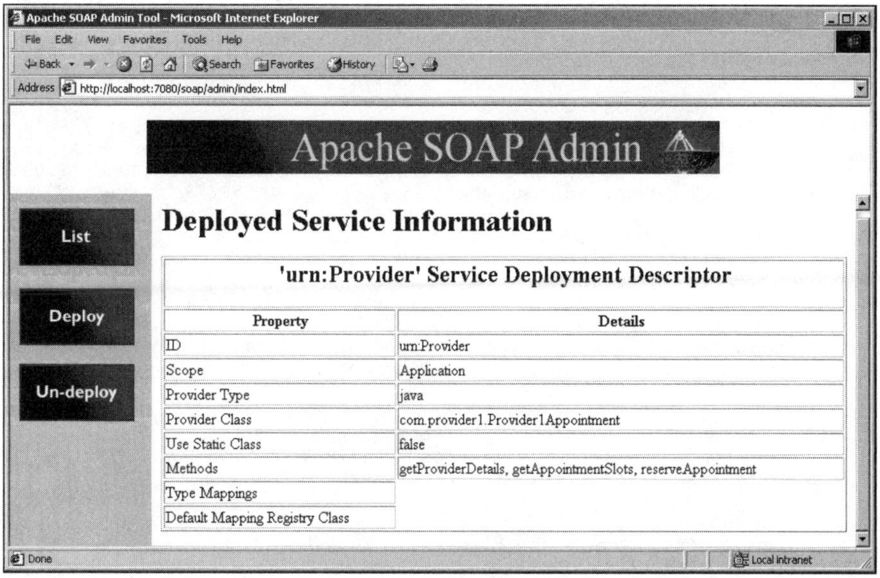

*Note that it is important to give the list of methods in a **whitespace delimited** format. The commas shown above are inserted by the SOAP admin service – doing otherwise will stop the service from working correctly.*

Now, we will take a look at the Provider 2 Appointment Web Service. We will follow the same steps that we did for Provider 1.

Provider 2

The Provider 2 Appointment Web Service code is shown below. It also implements the `Appointment` interface. However it returns different values to help us distinguish between the two different providers.

Provider2Appointment.java

```
package com.provider2;

import com.wroxinsurance.Appointment;

import java.io.StringReader;

//JDOM packages
import org.jdom.input.*;
import org.jdom.output.*;
import org.jdom.*;

public class Provider2Appointment implements Appointment {

  /** Creates new Provider2Appointment */
  public Provider2Appointment() {
  }

  public String getProviderDetails() {

    Element ProviderDetailsRoot = new Element("PROVIDER-DETAILS");
    ProviderDetailsRoot.setAttribute("PROVIDERID","2");
    ProviderDetailsRoot.addContent(new Element("NAME").setText("PROVIDER 2"));
    ProviderDetailsRoot.addContent(
                  new Element("ADDR1").setText("Main Street"));
    ProviderDetailsRoot.addContent(
                  new Element("ADDR2").setText("Suite 200"));
    ProviderDetailsRoot.addContent(
                  new Element("CITY").setText("Cupertino"));
    ProviderDetailsRoot.addContent(new Element("STATE").setText("CA"));
    ProviderDetailsRoot.addContent(new Element("ZIPCODE").setText("94000"));
    ProviderDetailsRoot.addContent(
                  new Element("PHONE").setText("408-111-2222"));
    ProviderDetailsRoot.addContent(
                  new Element("FAX").setText("408-333-4444"));
    ProviderDetailsRoot.addContent(
                  new Element("EMAIL").setText("info@provider2.com"));
    Document ProviderDetails = new Document(ProviderDetailsRoot);
    XMLOutputter outputter = new XMLOutputter("  ",true);
    return outputter.outputString(ProviderDetails);
  }

  public String getAppointmentSlots(String inputReq) {
    Element AppointmentsRoot = new Element("PROVIDER-APPOINTMENTS");
    AppointmentsRoot.setAttribute("PROVIDERID","2");

    //Appointment 1
    Element Appointment1 = new Element("APPOINTMENT");
    Appointment1.setAttribute("ID","B-1000");
```

```
Appointment1.addContent(new Element("DATE").setText("5 NOV 2001"));
    Appointment1.addContent(new Element("TIME").setText("8:00 AM"));

    //Appointment 2
    Element Appointment2 = new Element("APPOINTMENT");
    Appointment2.setAttribute("ID","B-1001");
    Appointment2.addContent(new Element("DATE").setText("6 NOV 2001"));
    Appointment2.addContent(new Element("TIME").setText("5:00 PM"));

    //Appointment 3
    Element Appointment3 = new Element("APPOINTMENT");
    Appointment3.setAttribute("ID","B-1002");
    Appointment3.addContent(new Element("DATE").setText("7 NOV 2001"));
    Appointment3.addContent(new Element("TIME").setText("9:00 AM"));

    AppointmentsRoot.addContent(Appointment1);
    AppointmentsRoot.addContent(Appointment2);
    AppointmentsRoot.addContent(Appointment3);

    Document AppointmentSlots = new Document(AppointmentsRoot);
XMLOutputter outputter = new XMLOutputter("  ",true);
    return outputter.outputString(AppointmentSlots);
  }

  public String reserveAppointment(String inputReq) {
    System.out.println("Received Appointment");
    System.out.println("--------------------");

    //Parse the Appointment Request
    try {
      SAXBuilder builder = new SAXBuilder();
      Document AppointmentReq = builder.build(new StringReader(inputReq));
      Element AppointmentReqRoot = AppointmentReq.getRootElement();
      String providerId = AppointmentReqRoot.getAttribute("PROVIDERID")
                                       .getValue();
      String patientId  = AppointmentReqRoot.getChild("PATIENTID")
                                       .getText();
      String apptId = AppointmentReqRoot.getChild("APPOINTMENT-ID")
                                   .getText();

      //Prepare Response
      Element AppointmentRespRoot = new Element("PROVIDER-APPOINTMENTRESPONSE");
      AppointmentRespRoot.setAttribute("PROVIDERID","2");
      AppointmentRespRoot.addContent(new Element("PATIENTID").setText(patientId));
      AppointmentRespRoot.addContent(
                              new Element("APPOINTMENT-ID").setText(apptId));
      AppointmentRespRoot.addContent(new Element("STATUS").setText("OK"));
      Document AppointmentResponse = new Document(AppointmentRespRoot);
      XMLOutputter outputter = new XMLOutputter("  ",true);
      return outputter.outputString(AppointmentResponse);
    } catch (Exception e) {
      System.out.println("ERROR");
      return "ERROR";
    }
  }
}
```

To compile the above file, refer to the following steps:

1. Open a command window.

2. Go to c:\javawebservices\Ch07\tomcat-provider2.

3. Create the directory `com\provider2` inside `c:\javawebservices\Ch07\tomcat-provider2` and copy the above file `Provider2Appointment.java` into this directory.

4. Go to the `c:\javawebservices\Ch07\tomcat-provider2` directory.

5. Run the `config.bat` file. This will set up the `CLASSPATH` correctly.

6. Give the following command at the prompt:

```
>javac com/provider2/Provider2Appointment.java
```

Provider 2 SOAP Service Configuration

To deploy the Provider 2 Web Service within the Apache SOAP environment, follow the steps as for Provider 1 amending specific details as necessary. Remember that the port for the SOAP Admin utility is 9080. The details for deployment are shown below:

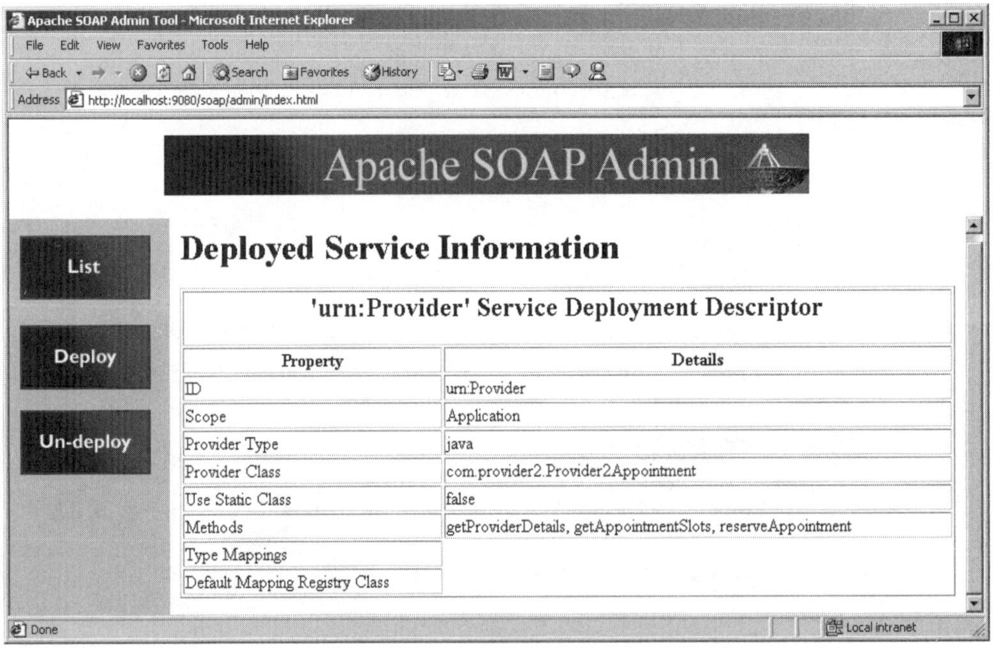

Wrox Insurance – ProviderProxy

So what we have developed so far are the very simple Web Services for the two providers: Provider 1 and Provider 2. We have also deployed the Web Services within the Apache SOAP environment. The diagram shown below demonstrates where we are at right now:

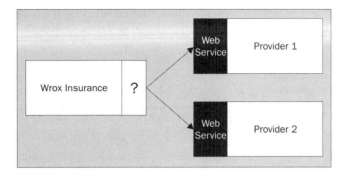

So, what we need now is a mechanism for Wrox Insurance to communicate with the provider web services. In order to reduce the integration effort for every new provider, it is important that we develop a standard way of describing the provider Web Service interface. In Web Services terminology, this is going to be the WSDL (Web Services Definition Language) file for an Appointment Web Service. So the first step would be to generate the WSDL file for the Appointment Web Service.

The WSDL file for the Appointment Web Service will not only define the interface of the Web Service, that is, the methods in it like getProviderDetails(), getAppointmentSlots(), and reserveAppointment(), but at the same time, it will provide the implementation endpoint for each provider, that is, where the provider Web Service is located. Thus a WSDL file will provide Wrox Insurance with the information needed to connect to the provider's Appointment Web Service.

So, once the WSDL file is generated, how will Wrox invoke the provider Web Service? It needs to have some boiler plate code, which we will call the Web Service proxy. This proxy will take as input the endpoint of the provider Web Service and invoke the appropriate method on it.

Thus we need to achieve the following:

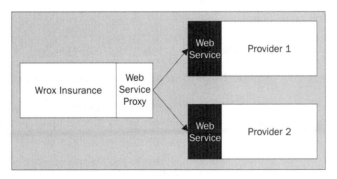

Generating a Web Service Proxy

Let us discuss for a moment how we will be going about doing this. What we have with us now is the fact that both our providers have implemented a standard interface that Wrox Insurance asked to be adhered to. So, from Wrox Insurance's side, as long as the interface is the same, its mechanism to access the Web Service would be the same irrespective of whether it is Provider 1 or Provider 2.

What we are going to do now is to develop a proxy class for accessing the provider Appointment Web Services. We will be generating the proxy class for the Web Service in two steps:

1. Generate the WSDL file for the Web Service

2. Generate a Java proxy class from the WSDL file obtained from step 1

For each of the above steps we will use the IBM Web Services Toolkit (WSTK) version 2.3 or later. As mentioned before, we assume that the IBM WSTK is installed in `C:\wstk-2.4`.

Using wsdlgen

We will look in more depth at **wsdlgen** in Chapter 11; here we will only cover how it is used for this specific example.

> **A the time of writing we have found during testing that wsdlgen does not work with JDK 1.4, if you have any problems please check this is not the cause.**

wsdlgen generates a WSDL file from a Java class file. What it will essentially do is map the Java class and its methods to equivalent WSDL elements.

Since the wsdlgen utility requires a concrete implementation we cannot use the `Appointment` interface that is present in the `c:\javawebservices\Ch07\tomcat-wroxinsurance` directory. So, we will use one of the implementations that we have already developed, the `Provider1Appointment.java` class and the `Provider2Appointment.java` service for Provider 2.

To generate the WSDL file for the Appointment Service, follow these steps:

1. Open a command window.

2. Go to `c:\javawebservices\Ch07\tomcat-wroxinsurance`.

3. Run the `config.bat` file. This will set up the `CLASSPATH` correctly.

4. Start the Tomcat Server for Wrox Insurance by giving the command **tomcat start** at the prompt. Recall that we had configured this server to start up on port 8080.

5. Type the following command:

   ```
   > wsdlgen
   ```

6. This will bring up the following window:

WSDL Generation Tool
Please select the service creation type
Java Class
EJB Jar File
COM Dispatch Interface
Help
< Back
Next >
Cancel

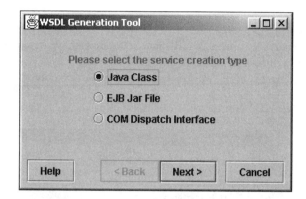

The default, Java Class, is sufficient for our need. Click on Next.

That brings up another window for which you should enter the class name, `com.provider1.Provider1Appointment`, as shown below:

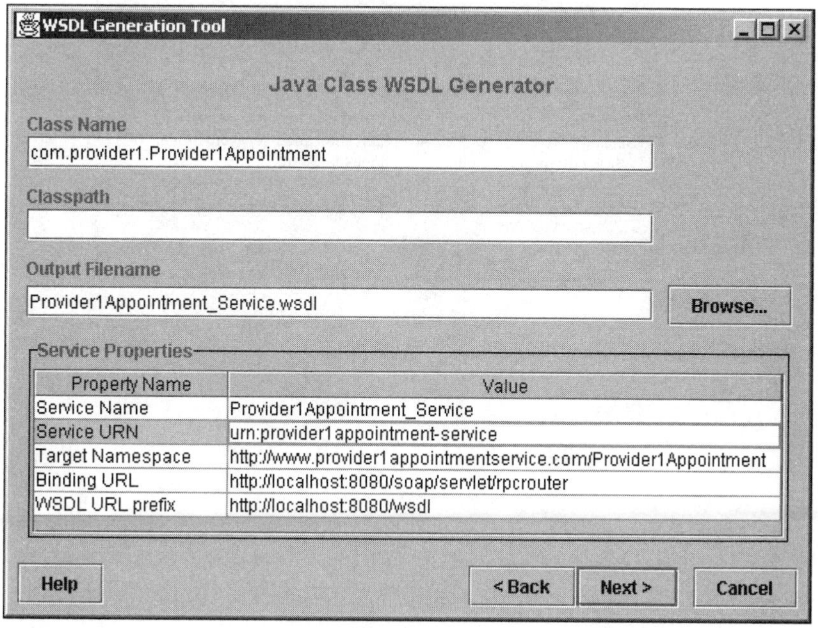

WSDL Generation Tool
Java Class WSDL Generator
Class Name
com.provider1.Provider1Appointment
Classpath
Output Filename
Provider1Appointment_Service.wsdl
Browse...
Service Properties
Property Name
Value
Service Name
Provider1Appointment_Service
Service URN
urn:provider1appointment-service
Target Namespace
http://www.provider1appointmentservice.com/Provider1Appointment
Binding URL
http://localhost:8080/soap/servlet/rpcrouter
WSDL URL prefix
http://localhost:8080/wsdl
Help
< Back
Next >
Cancel

The other details in the diagram are entered as defaults by the WSDL generator. We want to amend some of these. Enter the following values:

Service URN: urn:Provider
(Note that this is the same as the ID that we used when we deployed it in Apache SOAP)
Service Name: Provider1Appointment_Service
Target Namespace: http://provider1.appointmentservice.com

You should also make sure that the remainder of the values are as shown in the screenshot below.

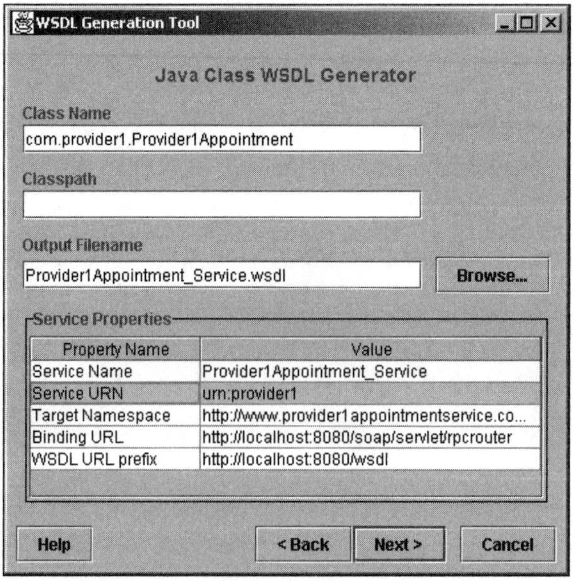

Click on Next.

7. This brings up the dialog shown below; select the methods shown:

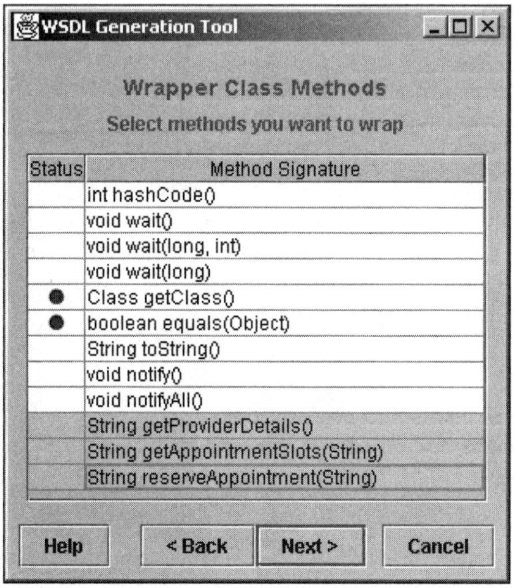

Click on **Next** and confirm your choices.

8. This will generate two WSDL files in the `c:\javawebservices\Ch07\tomcat-wroxinsurance` directory: `Provider1Appointment_Service-interface.wsdl` (the reusable part of the Service definition) and `Provider1Appointment_Service.wsdl` (the implementation/binding specific part of the Service definition)

Let us take a look at the two files (which have been formatted for readability).

Provider1Appointment_Service-interface.wsdl

This is the reusable part of the Web Service definition. It contains the message types and the operations supported by the Web Service. Those operations are highlighted in bold to identify them more easily:

```xml
<?xml version="1.0" encoding="UTF-8"?>
<definitions name="Provider1Appointment_Service"
  targetNamespace="http://provider1.appointmentservice.com-interface"
  xmlns="http://schemas.xmlsoap.org/wsdl/"
  xmlns:soap="http://schemas.xmlsoap.org/wsdl/soap/"
  xmlns:tns="http://provider1.appointmentservice.com-interface"
  xmlns:types="http://provider1.appointmentservice.com-interface/types/"
  xmlns:xsd="http://www.w3.org/2001/XMLSchema">

  <message name="InreserveAppointmentRequest">
    <part name="meth1_inType1" type="xsd:string"/>
  </message>

  <message name="OutreserveAppointmentResponse">
    <part name="meth1_outType" type="xsd:string"/>
```

```
    </message>

  <message name="IngetProviderDetailsRequest"/>

  <message name="OutgetProviderDetailsResponse">
    <part name="meth2_outType" type="xsd:string"/>
  </message>

  <message name="IngetAppointmentSlotsRequest">
    <part name="meth3_inType1" type="xsd:string"/>
  </message>

  <message name="OutgetAppointmentSlotsResponse">
    <part name="meth3_outType" type="xsd:string"/>
  </message>


        <portType name="Provider1Appointment_Service">
          <operation name="reserveAppointment">
            <input message="tns:InreserveAppointmentRequest"/>
            <output message="tns:OutreserveAppointmentResponse"/>
          </operation>

          <operation name="getProviderDetails">
            <input message="tns:IngetProviderDetailsRequest"/>
            <output message="tns:OutgetProviderDetailsResponse"/>
          </operation>

          <operation name="getAppointmentSlots">
            <input message="tns:IngetAppointmentSlotsRequest"/>
            <output message="tns:OutgetAppointmentSlotsResponse"/>
          </operation>
</portType>

  <binding name="Provider1Appointment_ServiceBinding"
           type="tns:Provider1Appointment_Service">
    <soap:binding style="rpc"
                  transport="http://schemas.xmlsoap.org/soap/http"/>

    <operation name="reserveAppointment">
      <soap:operation soapAction="urn:Provider"/>
      <input>
        <soap:body
            encodingStyle="http://schemas.xmlsoap.org/soap/encoding/"
            namespace="urn:Provider"
            use="encoded"/>
      </input>
      <output>
        <soap:body
            encodingStyle="http://schemas.xmlsoap.org/soap/encoding/"
            namespace="urn:Provider"
          use="encoded"/>
      </output>
    </operation>
```

```
      <operation name="getProviderDetails">
        <soap:operation soapAction="urn:Provider"/>
        <input>
          <soap:body
             encodingStyle="http://schemas.xmlsoap.org/soap/encoding/"
             namespace="urn:Provider"
             use="encoded"/>
        </input>
        <output>
          <soap:body
             encodingStyle="http://schemas.xmlsoap.org/soap/encoding/"
             namespace="urn:Provider"
             use="encoded"/>
        </output>
      </operation>

      <operation name="getAppointmentSlots">
        <soap:operation soapAction="urn:Provider"/>
        <input>
          <soap:body
             encodingStyle="http://schemas.xmlsoap.org/soap/encoding/"
             namespace="urn:Provider"
             use="encoded"/>
        </input>
        <output>
          <soap:body
             encodingStyle="http://schemas.xmlsoap.org/soap/encoding/"
             namespace="urn:Provider" use="encoded"/>
        </output>
      </operation>
    </binding>
  </definitions>
```

Wrox Insurance will actually host this part of the service definition at a publicly accessible URL. This will therefore provide access to the WSDL file for any other provider who is interested in implementing the Web Service. So, all the provider has to do now is to download the WSDL file and implement the operations appropriately.

To deploy this WSDL in the Wrox Insurance site, do the following:

1. Create a directory named wsdl in the c:\javawebservices\Ch07\tomcat-wroxinsurance\webapps\ROOT directory.

2. Copy the file generated above, Provider1Appointment_Service-interface.wsdl, to the /wsdl directory.

3. The WSDL file can now be accessed from the following URL:

http://localhost:8080/wsdl/ Provider1Appointment_Service-interface.wsdl

Provider1Appointment_Service.wsdl

```
<?xml version="1.0" encoding="UTF-8"?>
<definitions name="Provider1Appointment_Service"
  targetNamespace="http://provider1.appointmentservice.com"
  xmlns="http://schemas.xmlsoap.org/wsdl/"
  xmlns:interface="http://provider1.appointmentservice.com-interface"
  xmlns:soap="http://schemas.xmlsoap.org/wsdl/soap/"
  xmlns:types="http://provider1.appointmentservice.com"
    xmlns:xsd="http://www.w3.org/2001/XMLSchema">

<import location=
    "http://localhost:8080/wsdl/Provider1Appointment_Service-interface.wsdl"
        namespace="http://provider1.appointmentservice.com-interface">
</import>

<service name="Provider1Appointment_Service">
  <documentation>
    IBM WSTK V2.4 generated service definition file
  </documentation>
  <port binding="interface:Provider1Appointment_ServiceBinding"
        name="Provider1Appointment_ServicePort">
    <soap:address location="http://localhost:8080/soap/servlet/rpcrouter"/>
  </port>
</service>
</definitions>
```

This is really the implementation specific or the binding of the Web Service. Notice the following element:

```
<soap:address location="http://localhost:8080/soap/servlet/rpcrouter"/>
```

This identifies the endpoint at which the Web Service will be listening for requests. Since we have already implemented the Appointment Web Services for Provider 1 and Provider 2, it is appropriate that we deploy this file in their respective server environments such that they are accessible from a URL.

Note the import statement above, which shows that the reusable part of the WSDL definition is still being accessed from the Wrox Insurance URL:

```
http://localhost:8080/wsdl/Provider1Appointment_Service-interface.wsdl
```

Let's now look at the steps for modifying the `Provider1Appointment_Service.wsdl` file for each of the providers.

Modifying Provider1Appointment_Service.wsdl

These steps must be carried out for each provider:

1. Create a directory named `wsdl` in the `c:\tomcat-providerX\webapps\ROOT` directory for each provider, where `X` is the number of the provider.

2. Copy `Provider1Appointment_Service.wsdl` to the above directory. For Provider 2 you should rename the file to `Provider2Appointment_Service.wsdl`

3. For Provider 2, modify the `service` name element in the file as shown below:

```
<service name="Provider2Appointment_Service">
```

4. Change the SOAP address location to relevant for the provider; for Provider 1 this will be 7080, for Provider 2 it will be 9080. The example below shows Provider 1's modification:

```
<soap:address location="http://localhost:7080/soap/servlet/rpcrouter"/>
```

This is the endpoint at which the Provider 1 Appointment Service will be invoked.

5. Make sure that the Tomcat Server is running for each provider. We can now access this WSDL file from the following URL:

http://localhost:port/wsdl/ ProviderXAppointment_Service.wsdl

where port is the port for the specific provider and X is the number of the provider.

This makes sure that we are able to interrogate each of the providers for the service that they offer. Of course, in this example, they offer identical services, with the only differences being the provider name and port number for the Tomcat instance. In a production environment, it is not inconceivable that different providers would offer different services, different levels of support for the various services offered by Wrox Insurance, and so on.

It may also be that through software releases, each provider would make available a different subset of the final system. All this means that in a real system, the WSDL file is important for providing dynamically discovered information about the provider.

Using proxygen

Now that we have deployed the WSDL files correctly, we shift our focus back to the Wrox Insurance site. We can now use the **proxygen** utility from the IBM Web Services Toolkit to generate a Java proxy for the WSDL interface.

Rather than interfacing with the WSDL files programmatically, and therefore painfully slowly (in development terms), this tool provides us with a system for automatically generating Java files that are able to talk to the deployed service. In most current situations, the discovery of services is done at design time. In this case, Wrox Insurance makes development time binding to the services offered by each provider. This is done by the development of the Java proxies, which are then used from the Wrox Insurance online ticketing system for appointments. As long as future providers adhere to the interface defined above, then they can dynamically join this (otherwise static) collaboration of services.

You can see why it is important, as ever, to define the system well before hand. Defining a proxy per client will soon become unmanageable without proper abstraction, even with automation tools being available.

To generate the Java proxy, follow these steps:

1. Make sure that `tomcat-wroxinsurance` is running on port 8080.

2. Go to `c:\javawebservices\Ch07\tomcat-wroxinsurance`.

3. Run the following command: `proxygen Provider1Appointment_Service.wsdl`.

4. This will generate two files; a `Provider1Appointment_ServiceBinding.java` and its compiled version `Provider1Appointment_ServiceBinding.class` in the following directory:

    c:\javawebservices\Ch07\tomcat-
    wroxinsurance\com_interface\provider1appointmentservice\www

5. The java file created is a proxy to the Web Services. The client must invoke this class in order to talk to the Web Service. Note that the directory structure formed above follows the Target Namespace that we specified when we generated the WSDL file.

If we take a look at the `ProviderAppointment_ServiceBinding` class, we will find the following methods:

```
public Provider1Appointment_ServiceBinding(java.net.URL endPointURL)
```

This is the constructor, which takes as input an endpoint URL. So for example, if the Wrox Insurance site wants to invoke the `Provider1Appointment` Web Service, it would pass the following value for the endpoint URL:

    http://localhost:7080/soap/servlet/rpcrouter

Once the constructor has been invoked with the correct endpoint URL, all we have to do then is to invoke the appropriate methods, as previously discussed:

```
public synchronized
java.lang.String getProviderDetails() ()
    throws org.apache.soap.SOAPException

public synchronized
java.lang.String getAppointmentSlots(java.lang.String meth3_inType1)
    throws org.apache.soap.SOAPException

public synchronized
java.lang.String reserveAppointment() (java.lang.String meth1_inType1)
    throws org.apache.soap.SOAPException
```

Testing the Proxy

Now that we have generated the Web Service proxy, we can write a simple console program that will verify that it is working correctly.

Take a look at the `TestProxy.java` file, stored in `c:\javawebservices\Ch07\tomcat-wroxinsurance\com\wroxinsurance` shown below.

TestProxy.java

```
package com.wroxinsurance;

import java.io.StringReader;
import java.io.URL;

import com_interface.provider1appointmentservice.www.*;

public class TestProxy {

  //Provider Web Service Endpoint
  static String provider1URL =
                  "http://localhost:7080/soap/servlet/rpcrouter";
  static String provider2URL =
                  "http://localhost:9080/soap/servlet/rpcrouter";
```

Since we know the endpoints of the two providers' services, we define two strings that hold values to their respective endpoints. Note that in a real system, these values could be present in, for example a configuration file or database.

```
  public static void main(String[] args) {

    try {
      //Provider1 Web Service
      Provider1Appointment_ServiceBinding service =
          new Provider1Appointment_ServiceBinding(new URL(provider1URL));
```

Now, we will use the Web Service proxy generated. Notice that as we mentioned before, the constructor for the `ProviderAppointment_ServiceBinding` class takes in a URL that points to the endpoint for the Web Service, in this case `Provider1`.

```
      String providerDetails = service.getProviderDetails();
```

Next we invoke the `getProviderDetails()` method on this proxy. This will make a SOAP request across to the Web Service for Provider 1 and call the `getProviderDetails()` method on the `com.provider1.Provider1Appointment` class.

```
      //Print out Provider1 Details
      System.out.println(providerDetails);
```

We print out the details obtained from the invocation. We do exactly the same thing for the Provider 2 Appointment Web Service, the only change is that we provide a different endpoint.

```
          //Provider2 Web Service
          service = new Provider1Appointment_ServiceBinding (new URL(provider2URL));
          providerDetails = service.getProviderDetails();

          //Print out Provider2 Details
          System.out.println(providerDetails);
      } catch (Exception e) {
          System.out.println(e.getMessage());
      }
    }
}
```

To compile and run the above program, follow these steps:

1. Go to `c:\javawebservices\Ch07\tomcat-wroxinsurance`.

2. Create the above file `TestProxy.java` inside `com\wroxinsurance` in the `c:\javawebservices\Ch07\tomcat-wroxinsurance` directory.

3. Run the `config.bat` file. This will set the `CLASSPATH` correctly.

4. Compile the file using the following command:

```
javac com/wroxinsurance/TestProxy.java
```

5. Make sure that the Tomcat Servers for both Provider 1 and Provider 2 are running. Recollect that we will need to open up separate command windows for each of them and run Tomcat.

6. Finally run the program by giving the following command:

```
java com.wroxinsurance.TestProxy
```

7. We get the following output:

```
C:\javawebservices\Ch07\tomcat-wroxinsurance>java com.wroxinsurance.TestProxy
<?xml version="1.0" encoding="UTF-8"?>
<PROVIDER-DETAILS PROVIDERID="1">
  <NAME>PROVIDER 1</NAME>
  <ADDR1>123 Street</ADDR1>
  <ADDR2>Suite 100</ADDR2>
  <CITY>San Jose</CITY>
  <STATE>CA</STATE>
  <ZIPCODE>95000</ZIPCODE>
  <PHONE>408-123-4567</PHONE>
  <FAX>408-456-7890</FAX>
  <EMAIL>info@provider1.com</EMAIL>
</PROVIDER-DETAILS>
```

```
<?xml version="1.0" encoding="UTF-8"?>
<PROVIDER-DETAILS PROVIDERID="2">
 <NAME>PROVIDER 2</NAME>
 <ADDR1>Main Street</ADDR1>
 <ADDR2>Suite 200</ADDR2>
 <CITY>Cupertino</CITY>
 <STATE>CA</STATE>
 <ZIPCODE>94000</ZIPCODE>
 <PHONE>408-111-2222</PHONE>
 <FAX>408-333-4444</FAX>
 <EMAIL>info@provider2.com</EMAIL>
</PROVIDER-DETAILS>
```

Let us now start developing all these Web Services to provide them in an integrated fashion by developing the Wrox Insurance web site.

Wrox Insurance – Web Site

We will now start developing the Wrox Insurance web site. In the web site, we will provide an appointment service to the consumer in an integrated fashion. By an integrated fashion, we mean the user can do the following from the web browser:

❑   Browse to the Wrox Insurance web site.

❑   Locate the different providers currently in the web site.

❑   Select a particular provider and retrieve the available appointments.

❑   Select a particular appointment and make the reservation. The system contacts the provider Appointment Service and comes back with a status confirming whether the reservation was made or not.

This would provide tremendous value to the consumer now, who prior to this system had to actually call the provider office and fix the appointment. The savings in time are an added bonus, as is the fact that further levels of integration can provide automated processing of customer related interactions between the two companies.

We will be developing a simple JSP application for the Wrox Insurance web site. Before we jump into the JSP pages, let us first develop utility classes that map the XML responses received from the Appointment Web Service into convenient JavaBeans that we can use from the JSP pages.

Supporting Classes

The two classes that we will develop map the XML response received from the `getProviderDetail()` and `getAppointmentSlots()` methods into `ProviderDetail` and `ApppointmentDetail` classes respectively.

Finally, we will also develop a `ProviderProxy` class, which is the main JavaBean that we will use from the JSP pages. The `ProviderProxy` class will perform the following functions:

❑ It will interact with the Web Service proxy class that we generated in the previous section, `ProviderAppointment_ServiceBinding`.

❑ It will map the parse XML response received from the Appointment Web Service into the appropriate Java classes that can be used from the JSP page.

Let us take a look at the classes now:

ProviderDetail.java

The `ProviderDetail` class is a data class, a JavaBean that provides simple accessor/mutator methods for the attributes of a provider such as `providerid`, `providername`, `provideraddress`, and so on.

```
package com.wroxinsurance;

public class ProviderDetail {

    String providerId;
    String providerName;
    String addr1;
    String addr2;
    String city;
    String state;
    String zipcode;
    String phone;
    String fax;
    String email;

    public ProviderDetail() {}

    // accessors and mutators cut for the sake of brevity. See the source
    // if in doubt
}
```

AppointmentDetail.java

The `AppointmentDetail` is a data class, a JavaBean that contains simple accessor/mutator methods for `appointment` details like appointment ID, appointment date, and appointment time.

```
package com.wroxinsurance;

public class AppointmentDetail {

    String appointmentId;
    String appointmentDate;
    String appointmentTime;

    // accessors and mutators cut for the sake of brevity.
    // see the source code if in doubt
    public AppointmentDetail() {}
}
```

ProviderProxy.java

The `ProviderProxy` class, as we described above, is going to be the main class that we will use in the JSP pages to interact with the Web Services. This means that it will be responsible for communicating with the proxy that will talk to the Web Services. It will also be responsible for parsing the XML responses back into the appropriate classes: `ProviderDetail` and `AppointmentDetail`. This will make it easier for us when we develop the JSP pages.

The `ProviderProxy` class has the following methods:

❑ **ArrayList getProviders()**
This method returns an `ArrayList` of providers that were initialized in the constructor.

❑ **String getProviderURL(String providerId)**
This method returns the provider URL for the particular `providerId`. For example, for `Provider1`, `getProviderURL()` would return a value of `http://localhost:7080/soap/servlet/rpcrouter`.

❑ **ProviderDetail getProviderDetail(String providerId)**
This method takes in a `providerId` and provides the details about the provider as an instance of the `ProviderDetail` bean that we just saw above. The method uses the `getProviderURL()` method to retrieve the `endPoint` of the Appointment Web Service. Once it has the endpoint, it uses `ProviderAppointment_ServiceBinding` to bind to that endpoint to invoke the `getProviderDetails()` method on the service. The XML result from the service is then package into an instance of `ProviderDetail`.

❑ **ArrayList getAvailableAppointments(String providerId)**
This method works in the same manner as above, except that it invokes the `getAppointmentSlots()` method of the Appointment Web Service. It returns an `ArrayList`, which contains a collection of `AppointmentDetail` instances.

❑ **String makeReservation(String clientId, String providerId, String ApptId)**
This method is responsible for making the reservation for a particular appointment slot. It takes in as input the `clientId` (a unique number that identifies the consumer that is provided by the insurance company), the `providerId`, and the `ApptId` (appointment 10) that was selected from the list of appointments that were returned from the `getAvailableAppointments()` method above.

It functions in the same manner as the above two methods, retrieving the endpoint of the Web Service first and then invoking the `reserveAppointment()` method on the Appointment Web Service. It returns the status string `"OK"` indicating that the reservation was made successfully.

It should now be easy to understand the `ProviderProxy` utility class shown below:

```
package com.wroxinsurance;

import java.net.URL;

import com_interface.provider1appointmentservice.www.*;

import java.util.ArrayList;
```

```
import java.util.List;
import java.util.Iterator;
import java.util.Hashtable;

import java.io.StringReader;

//JDOM packages
import org.jdom.input.SAXBuilder;
import org.jdom.output.XMLOutputter;
import org.jdom.Document;
import org.jdom.Element;

public class ProviderProxy {

   Hashtable providerUrl;  //Stores the providerURLs hashed by providerId
   ArrayList providerList; // The list of current providers
```

The constructor below initializes the two providers that we have been using throughout the system. It also sets up the endpoint for the provider web services. Note that we have used this approach to keep the example simple. In a real scenario this could be read from a database or configuration file, and so on.

```
public ProviderProxy() {
   providerUrl = new Hashtable(2);
   providerUrl.put("Provider 1",
               "http://localhost:7080/soap/servlet/rpcrouter");
   providerUrl.put("Provider 2",
               "http://localhost:9080/soap/servlet/rpcrouter");

   providerList = new ArrayList(2);
   providerList.add("Provider 1");
   providerList.add("Provider 2");
}

public ArrayList getProviders() throws Exception {
   return providerList;
}

public String getProviderURL(String providerId) throws Exception {
   return (String) providerUrl.get(providerId);
}
```

The getProviderDetails() method takes as input a providerId and returns back an XML string containing the provider information.

```
public ProviderDetail getProviderDetails(String providerId) throws Exception {
```

The proxy code that we generated is used here. We initialize the `Provider1Appointment_ServiceBinding` constructor with the `endPoint` URL for the provider.

```
Provider1Appointment_ServiceBinding service =
        new Provider1Appointment_ServiceBinding(
            new URL(getProviderURL(providerId)));
```

Once we have done that, we can invoke the method (`getProviderDetails()`) on the proxy. The proxy will then forward it as a SOAP request to the provider Web Service. It receives a SOAP response from the provider Web Service. It packages this back as an XML string, `providerDetails`.

```
String providerDetails = service.getProviderDetails();
```

We then use the JDOM API as we have seen before to parse the information into local variables.

```
//Parse the ProviderDetail Information
try {
    SAXBuilder builder = new SAXBuilder();
    Document provDetailDoc = builder.build(new StringReader(providerDetails));
    Element provDetailRoot = provDetailDoc.getRootElement();
    String providerName = provDetailRoot.getChild("NAME").getText();
    String addr1 = provDetailRoot.getChild("ADDR1").getText();
    String addr2 = provDetailRoot.getChild("ADDR2").getText();
    String city  = provDetailRoot.getChild("CITY").getText();
    String state = provDetailRoot.getChild("STATE").getText();
    String zipcode = provDetailRoot.getChild("ZIPCODE").getText();
    String phone = provDetailRoot.getChild("PHONE").getText();
    String fax = provDetailRoot.getChild("FAX").getText();
    String email = provDetailRoot.getChild("EMAIL").getText();
```

Once we have the information stored into local variables, we populate the `providerDetail` JavaBean by invoking the appropriate setter methods on it.

```
    ProviderDetail providerDetail = new ProviderDetail();
    providerDetail.setProviderId(providerId);
    providerDetail.setProviderName(providerName);
    providerDetail.setAddr1(addr1);
    providerDetail.setAddr2(addr2);
    providerDetail.setCity(city);
    providerDetail.setState(state);
    providerDetail.setZipcode(zipcode);
    providerDetail.setPhone(phone);
    providerDetail.setFax(fax);
    providerDetail.setEmail(email);

    return providerDetail;

} catch (Exception e) {
    throw e;
}
}
```

The `getAvailableAppointments` method takes as input a `providerId` and returns an `ArrayList` of `AppointmentDetail` objects.

```
public ArrayList getAvailableAppointments(String providerId) throws Exception {

    ArrayList AvailableAppointmentsList = new ArrayList();
```

Once again we initialize the `Provider1Appointment_ServiceBinding` constructor with the provider's URL and invoke the `getAppointmentSlots()` method on this proxy. Note that we had mentioned that we are not going to develop complex search functionality; instead we are going to return all the appointments for the provider. So, we are passing an empty string as a parameter to the `getAppointmentSlots()` method.

```
Provider1Appointment_ServiceBinding service =
            new Provider1Appointment_ServiceBinding(
                new URL(getProviderURL(providerId)));
String ApptList = service.getAppointmentSlots("");
```

Once we get the XML result back, we might get more than one appointment. So, we need to parse the information out individually and construct a collection of `AppointmentDetail` objects.

```
//Parse the Appointment Detail Information
try {
    SAXBuilder builder = new SAXBuilder ();
    Document ApptListDoc  = builder.build(new StringReader(ApptList));
    Element  ApptListRoot = ApptListDoc.getRootElement();
```

We retrieve here a `java.util.Iterator` which will have the number of the appointments.

```
List list = ApptListRoot.getChildren("APPOINTMENT");
Iterator iterator = list.iterator();
```

For each `Appointment` element, we construct the `AppointmentDetail` object and add it to the `AvailableAppointmentsList` object, which is an `ArrayList`.

```
while (iterator.hasNext()) {
    Element Appointment = (Element)iterator.next();
    String ApptId = Appointment.getAttribute("ID").getValue();
    String ApptDate = Appointment.getChild("DATE").getText();
    String ApptTime = Appointment.getChild("TIME").getText();

    AppointmentDetail ApptDetail = new AppointmentDetail();
    ApptDetail.setAppointmentId(ApptId);
    ApptDetail.setAppointmentDate(ApptDate);
    ApptDetail.setAppointmentTime(ApptTime);

    AvailableAppointmentsList.add(ApptDetail);
    }
    return AvailableAppointmentsList;

} catch (Exception e) {
    throw e;
}
}
```

The `makeReservation()` method takes as input the `clientId` (a unique identifier for the consumer given by Wrox Insurance), the `providerId` at which the appointment is being made, and the `ApptId`, which identifies the appointment. It returns an XML string that indicates whether the reservation was made successfully or not. For the purposes of our example, remember that the provider Web Service always returns a successful result.

```
public String makeReservation(String clientId,
                              String providerId,
                              String ApptId) throws Exception {
```

We first construct the reservation request:

```
//Make the XML Request
Element rootElement = new Element("PROVIDER-APPOINTMENTREQUEST");
rootElement.setAttribute("PROVIDERID",providerId);
rootElement.addContent(new Element("PATIENTID").setText(clientId));
rootElement.addContent(new Element("APPOINTMENT-ID").setText(ApptId));
Document AppointmentDetails = new Document(rootElement);
XMLOutputter outputter = new XMLOutputter("  ",true);
String AppointmentRequest = outputter.outputString(AppointmentDetails);
```

We initialize the `Provider1Appointment_ServiceBinding` constructor with the provider's URL and invoke the `reserveAppointment()` method on this proxy.

```
Provider1Appointment_ServiceBinding service =
            new Provider1Appointment_ServiceBinding(
               new URL(getProviderURL(providerId)));
String result = service.reserveAppointment(AppointmentRequest);
```

It returns the XML result, which we parse using the `org.jdom.input.SAXBuilder` class. We parse out the STATUS element and return that.

```
//Parse the MakeReservation Result
try {
  SAXBuilder builder = new SAXBuilder();
  Document ReservationResult = builder.build(new StringReader(result));
  Element  ReservationResultRoot = ReservationResult.getRootElement();
  String   status = ReservationResultRoot.getChild("STATUS").getText();

  return status;

} catch (Exception e) {
  throw e;
  }
 }
}
```

Wrox Insurance Web Site Setup

Before we start developing the pages, let us first make sure that everything is set up as far as the Tomcat configuration and the database configuration is concerned.

Tomcat Settings

1. Go to `c:\javawebservices\Ch07\tomcat-wroxinsurance\webapps` and create a directory named `wroxinsurance` inside it.

2. Create another folder within this called `WEB-INF` with the `wroxinsurance` directory you have just created. This will create a web application in Tomcat.

3. Create the web deployment descriptor file `web.xml` in the `WEB-INF` subdirectory in `%TOMCAT_HOME%\webapps\wroxinsurance`. The contents of the `web.xml` file are shown below:

```xml
<?xml version="1.0" encoding="ISO-8859-1"?>

<!DOCTYPE web-app PUBLIC
    "-//Sun Microsystems, Inc.//DTD Web Application 2.2//EN"
    "http://java.sun.com/j2ee/dtds/web-app_2_2.dtd">

<web-app>
  <display-name>Wrox Insurance</display-name>
  <description>
    Wrox Pro Java Web Services - Wrox Insurance Case Study
  </description>
</web-app>
```

Now we can place all our JSP files in the `%TOMCAT_HOME%\webapps\wroxinsurance` directory. And assuming that the Tomcat Server is running for Wrox Insurance, we can access the web site from the following url:

http://localhost:8080/wroxinsurance

The JSP pages

Let us now get going on the JSP page development. Note that all these pages should be saved to the `%TOMCAT_HOME%\webapps\wroxinsurance` directory.

Take a look at the `index.jsp` page as seen in the browser. It displays a simple page with a few links in a navigation bar like **Home**, **News**, and **Online Appointments**.

Online Appointments is the link that we will click to lead us into the appointment process.

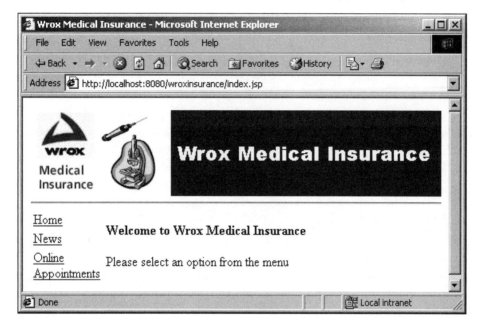

The index.jsp page is shown below:

index.jsp

Note that in each of the pages, we will be following a convention where the main JSP page is a composite page that consists of a header, a left navigation menu (Home, News, and Online Appointments) and a details page that displays the main content.

```
<%@page contentType="text/html"%>
<html>

<head>
  <title>Wrox Medical Insurance</title>
</head>

<body>
  <table border="0" cellpadding="0" cellspacing="0" width="100%">
    <tr><td width="100%"><%@include file="banner.jsp"%></td></tr>
    <tr><td width="100%">
      <table border="0" cellpadding="0" cellspacing="0" width="100%">
        <tr><td width="100%"><hr/></td></tr>
        <tr>
          <td width="100%">
            <table border="0" cellpadding="0" cellspacing="0" width="100%">
              <tr>
                <td width="18%">
                  <jsp:include page="menu.jsp" flush="true"/>
    </td>
                <td width="82%">
                  <jsp:include page="index-details.jsp" flush="true"/>
                </td>
              </tr>
```

```
                </table>
              </td>
            </tr>
          </table>
        </td>
      </tr>
    </table>
  </body>

</html>
```

So basically the meat of the JSP code will be present in each of the included page as shown above. We will follow the same pattern for each of the JSP's. Let us take a look at the `index-details.jsp` page, this will give a good understanding of how the detail page is included. Henceforth as we go through all the pages in the site, we will cover the detail page only for simplicity.

index-details.jsp

```
<b>Welcome to Wrox Medical Insurance</b>
<br/>
<br/>
<p> Please select an option from the menu
```

The above contents are thus visible in the `index.jsp` page.

Now, once we click on the **Online Appointments** link in the `index.jsp` page menu, we are led to the `appointment.jsp` page, which shows the list of providers present in the system. Take a look at the output below.

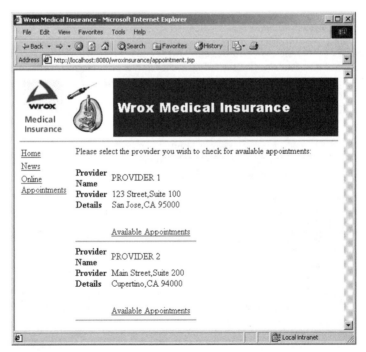

Let's take a look at the `appointment-details.jsp`, which is really the content that we are seeing above.

appointment-details.jsp

```
<%@page language="java" errorPage="ErrorHandler.jsp"%>

<%@page import="java.util.ArrayList"%>
<%@page import="com.wroxinsurance.ProviderProxy"%>
<%@page import="com.wroxinsurance.ProviderDetail"%>
```

We import the necessary classes, `ProviderProxy` and `ProviderDetail`.

```
<p>Please select the provider you wish to check for available appointments:</p>
<table border="0" cellpadding="0" cellspacing="0" width="46%">
<%
    ProviderProxy client = new ProviderProxy();
    ArrayList providerList = client.getProviders();
```

We first create an instance of the `ProviderProxy` client class and invoke the `getProviders()` method on this class. The `getProviders()` method will query the database to retrieve a list of provider IDs.

Then for each provider ID, we invoke the `getProviderDetails()` method on the `ProviderProxy` class instance. This method will query the database first to retrieve the `providerURL`, and it will then invoke the `getProviderDetails()` method on Web Service proxy class that we generated. The result obtained is then returned as an instance of the `ProviderDetail` bean, from which the accessor methods are used to display the details in the browser.

```
    for (int i=0;i<providerList.size();i++) {
        String providerId = (String) providerList.get(i);
        ProviderDetail detail = client.getProviderDetails(providerId);
%>
    <tr>
        <td width="20%" valign="top"><b>Provider Name</b></td>
        <td width="46%"><%=detail.getProviderName()%></td>
    </tr>
    <tr>
        <td width="20%" valign="top"><b>Provider Details</b></td>
        <td width="46%"><%=detail.getAddr1()%>,
            <%=detail.getAddr2()%><br/>
            <%=detail.getCity()%>,
            <%=detail.getState()%> 
            <%=detail.getZipcode()%>
            <br/>
            <br/>
            <br/>
        </td>
    </tr>
    <tr>
        <td width="20%" valign="top"></td>
        <td width="46%">
```

```
<a href="provider-appointments.jsp?providerid=<%=detail.getProviderId()%>">
    Available Appointments
</a>
    </td>
  </tr>
  <tr>
    <td width="66%" colspan="2" valign="top"><hr/></td>
  </tr>
<%
  }
%>
</table>
```

A customer having got this far would now click on the **Available Appointments** link, which leads to the `provider-appointments.jsp` page that retrieves the appointments that are available for booking. Note that we pass the `providerId` as a query parameter to this page to help the JSP page retrieve the appointment list for that particular provider.

The list of available appointments is shown below:

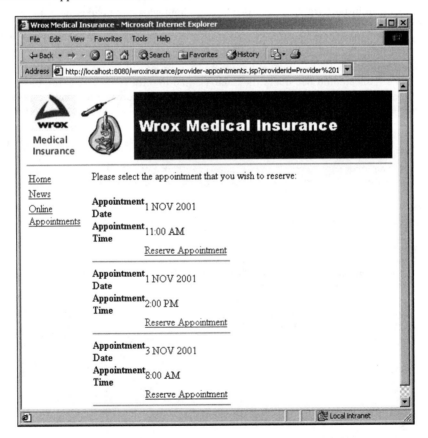

Let us look at the `provider-appointments-details.jsp` page, which renders the above output:

provider-appointments-details.jsp

```
<%@page language="java" errorPage="ErrorHandler.jsp"%>

<%@page import="java.util.ArrayList"%>
<%@page import="com.wroxinsurance.ProviderProxy"%>
<%@page import="com.wroxinsurance.AppointmentDetail"%>

<p>Please select the appointment that you wish to reserve:</p>
<table border="0" cellpadding="0" cellspacing="0" width="46%">
<%
    // Retrieve the providerId from the Request
    String providerId = request.getParameter("providerid");
    ProviderProxy client = new ProviderProxy();
    ArrayList aptlist = client.getAvailableAppointments(providerId);
```

As seen above, this page uses the same mechanism of creating an instance of the `ProviderProxy` class and invoking the `getAvailableAppointments()` method on the proxy instance. The result is a collection of `AppointmentDetail` instances that are iterated through to show the appointments available.

```
    for (int j=0;j<aptlist.size();j++) {
      AppointmentDetail apt = (AppointmentDetail) aptlist.get(j);
%>
      <tr>
        <td width="20%" valign="top"><b>Appointment Date</b></td>
        <td width="46%"><%=apt.getAppointmentDate()%></td>
      </tr>
      <tr>
        <td width="20%" valign="top"><b>Appointment Time</b></td>
        <td width="46%"><%=apt.getAppointmentTime()%><br/></td>
      </tr>
      <tr>
        <td width="20%" valign="top"></td>
    <%
        StringBuffer apptReservationURL = new StringBuffer();
        apptReservationURL.append("reserve-appointmentform.jsp?");
        apptReservationURL.append("providerId=" + providerId + "&");
        apptReservationURL.append("apptId=" + apt.getAppointmentId() + "&");
        apptReservationURL.append("apptdate=" + apt.getAppointmentDate() + "&");
        apptReservationURL.append("appttime=" + apt.getAppointmentTime());
    %>
        <td>
          <a href="<%=apptReservationURL.toString()%>">Appointment</a></td>
      </tr>
      <tr>
        <td width="66%" colspan="2" valign="top"><hr/></td>
      </tr>
    <%
    }
    %>
</table>
```

We can now select a particular appointment and click on the **Reserve Appointment** link. This will lead us to the `reserve-appointmentform.jsp`, which is shown below. It accepts a `clientId`, a unique identification for the client. Note that the provider ID, appointment ID, appointment date, and appointment time were passed as query parameters to this page.

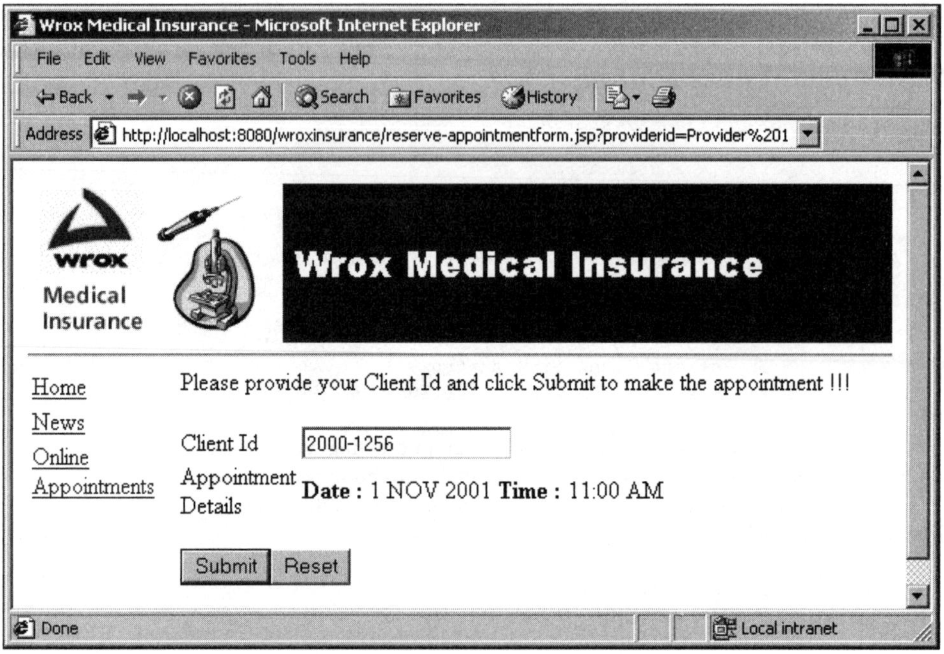

The `reserve-appointmentform-details.jsp` page is shown below:

reserve-appointmentform-details.jsp

```
<%@page language="java" errorPage="ErrorHandler.jsp"%>

<%@page import="java.util.ArrayList"%>
<%@page import="com.wroxinsurance.ProviderProxy"%>
<%@page import="com.wroxinsurance.AppointmentDetail"%>

<%
  // Retrieve the providerId from the Request
  String providerId = request.getParameter("providerid");
  String apptId      = request.getParameter("apptid");
  String apptDate    = request.getParameter("apptdate");
  String apptTime    = request.getParameter("appttime");
%>

Please provide your Client Id and click Submit to make the appointment !!! <br/>

<form method="POST" action="reserve-appointment.jsp" name="SubmitFrm">
  <table border="0" cellpadding="0" cellspacing="0" width="100%">
    <tr>
      <td width="17%">Client Id</td>
      <td width="83%"><input type="text" name="clientid" size="20"></td>
    </tr>
    <tr>
      <td width="17%">Appointment Details</td>
```

```
      <td width="83%"><b>Date :</b> <%=apptDate%> <b>Time :</b><%=apptTime%>
      </td>
    </tr>
  </table>
  <p><input type="submit" value="Submit" name="SubmitBtn">
     <input type="reset" value="Reset" name="ResetBtn"></p>
     <input type="hidden" name="appointmentid" value="<%=apptId%>">
     <input type="hidden" name="providerid" value="<%=providerId%>">
</form>
```

As highlighted above, the `FORM` will post the data to the `reserve-appointment.jsp` page, which will make the reservation for the particular appointment. The page is shown below.

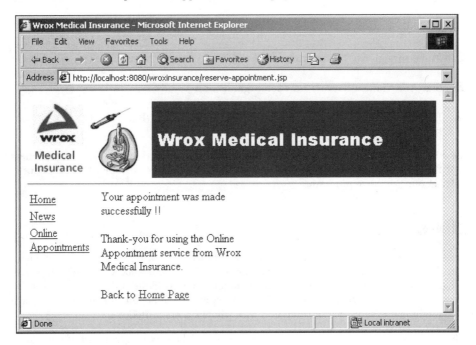

The `reserve-appointment-details.jsp` page is shown below:

reserve-appointment-details.jsp

```
<%@page language="java" errorPage="ErrorHandler.jsp"%>

<%@page import="java.util.ArrayList"%>
<%@page import="com.wroxinsurance.ProviderProxy"%>

<table border="0" cellpadding="0" cellspacing="0" width="46%">
<%
  String providerId    = request.getParameter("providerid");
  String appointmentId = request.getParameter("appointmentid");
  String clientId      = request.getParameter("clientid");
ProviderProxy client = new ProviderProxy();
  String result = client.makeReservation(clientId,providerId,appointmentId);
```

Notice that this is the `makeReservation()` method on the `ProviderProxy` that will book the appointment for the consumer.

```
    if (result.equalsIgnoreCase("OK")) {
      out.println("Your appointment was made successfully !!");
    } else {
      out.println("FAILURE. Could not make the appointment !!!");
    }
  %>

  <br/><br/>
  Thank-you for using the Online Appointment service from
  Wrox Medical Insurance.
  <br/><br/>Back to <a href="index.jsp">Home Page</A>
</table>
```

This completes the development of our Wrox Insurance web site. To run the web site correctly, do the following:

1. Make sure all the JSP pages are present in `c:\tomcat\webapps\wroxinsurance`

2. Start the Tomcat Servers for each organization

3. Launch a browser instance and point to the following URL:
http://localhost:8080/wroxinsurance

We now have a working integrated distributed system for making reservations. The providers can manage their resources, while we provide a point of contact for the customer to arrange for care with a provider in our insurance program.

To Close

You can see how this can be extended for the entire process, allowing us to make improvements across the board. In addition, the service oriented nature of these systems makes it possible to segment systems in such a way that small grained processes may be integrated without unduly affecting other systems still in place. This also means that the benefits from this systems will be felt sooner, and it is much more satisfying, and manageable, when compared with whole system switchovers.

Finally, it allows for fine-grained, low risk maintenance of the services, that part of the system can be brought down without disabling the entire system. Now, while it is certainly possible to design current software systems so that minimum disruption of the overall system is caused through the maintenance and consequent downtime of one potion of it, it is no easy task, and it is made less so when two or more companies, with differing systems for software development, and often non-complimentary business drivers, attempt to collaborate on inter-enterprise integration efforts.

In Web Services, as you can see, supplier details are abstracted to core services, which can be managed by the supplier. The process, however, is opaque to the customer, who merely sees a single point of access facility for their insurance related services. The decision-making process is streamlined for the customer, and can be further assisted through automated optimization made according to geographical location using customer details or relevant specialist knowledge at the care provider, to mention only a few possibilities. In addition, initial commitment to projects can be quite small but have a significant effect on the enterprise systems. Further integration efforts, once the first few projects have been done, can be achieved quickly as the two companies gain experience in working together, and in having a single lightweight protocol and architecture for integration.

In the area of security, we saw in Chapter 6, that there is room for maturity. Specifically, a single universally accepted stack for authentication, authorization, non-repudiation, and so on is not available. In scenarios such as the one given here, it may very well be possible to justify (in cost and performance) permanently connected SSL links between the providers and Wrox Insurance that will provide this support. Where ad hoc connections are made, as has been postulated in Web Services vision statements, this is not practical or even possible, however in ongoing long standing business relationships that are more typically in need of the integration possibilities offered by Web Services, this is much more imaginable.

Early performance indications are quite encouraging though. Simple tests show that with the addition of caching (for example the provider details could easily be cached), and with properly optimized data flow, Web Services systems perform comparably well. More complex tests are sure to follow. However, you should be aware that trade offs are always made, and in this case, ease of integration and the promise of dynamic binding for future business partners are very attractive. In particular, the benefits of provider maintenance of their own processes, the smooth and speedy integration of future providers, and access to incremental integration efforts are very compelling.

Both of the above may be solved, at least partially, through the use of dedicated networks, although one of the enduring attractions of Web Services is the ubiquity of Internet connectivity and IP networks that make such systems possible.

Summary

In this chapter, we covered a comprehensive case study where we developed an integrated medical appointment system using Java Web Services.

Note that the case study covered here was kept simple in order to demonstrate the entire system. However, in a real system, there would be several features that would need to be built in to make it appropriate.

In this case study, we covered the following areas:

- ❑ Discussed the design and the common Web Service interface for the Appointment Web Service
- ❑ Provided simple implementations of the Appointment Web Service for two sample Providers
- ❑ Generated the WSDL files and proxy code using IBM WSTK tools so that Wrox Insurance could integrate the calls easily into their web site
- ❑ Developed the Wrox Insurance JSP-based web site that used the Web Service proxy to integrate web services from each provider

While there are some further levels of discussion possible, including security, performance, and projected ROI for integration projects, Web Services are currently too young for a meaningful discussion of these points. We have covered in brief some of these point to end the chapter.

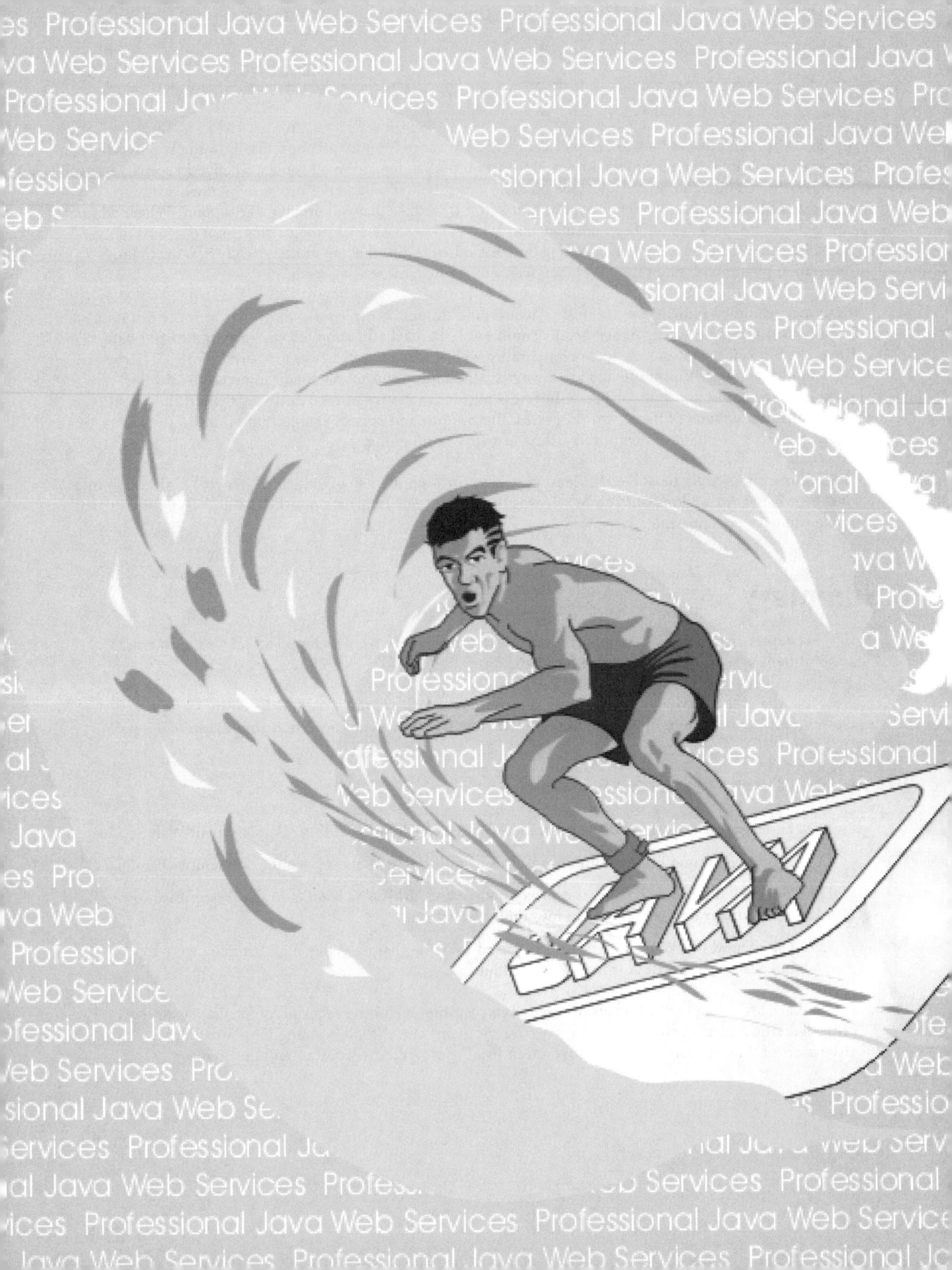
Professional Java Web Services

Web Service Enabling J2EE Applications

The Java 2 Enterprise Edition (J2EE) standard from Sun Microsystems can be used to build large-scale distributed, component-based, multi-tier applications. Since its introduction, it is the standard for developing and deploying large-scale enterprise systems based on Java.

A large number of organizations have already deployed applications based on the J2EE platform. These organizations have understood the importance of exposing certain existing functionality in their applications as a web service. Since web services technologies are built on open standards such as **Web Services Definition Language (WSDL)** and **Simple Object Access Protocol (SOAP)**, exposing the functionality as a web service would provide these organizations with several benefits. It will allow them to integrate more easily with the partner applications, and by publishing their WSDL definitions to a global registry like **Universal Description, Discovery, and Integration (UDDI)**, they would expose their web service to a larger audience.

In this chapter, we will take an example organization and explain how they will expose pieces of their current functionality as a web service using some of the existing tools that are available today. The chapter will not get into too many design discussions on J2EE, neither will it attempt to create a detailed J2EE application. Instead it will try to focus on taking an existing J2EE application and expose it as a web service.

During the course of this chapter, we will cover the following:

❑ Developing a simple J2EE application including deployment of the application on WebLogic 6.1. The application WroxCuisine is a site that provides recipes for cuisine from all around the world

❑ The use of CapeClear's CapeConnect (http://www.capeclear.com) product to expose the EJB functionality in the J2EE application as a web service

❑ How to write clients using a variety of tools, such as Apache SOAP and CapeClear's CapeStudio, to access the web service

The J2EE Application – WroxCuisine

In the next few sections, we will build a very simple J2EE application. The application is not meant to be a tutorial on how to build J2EE applications, rather it is intended to set the course for the later sections of this chapter where we will expose some of the functionality that we build here as a web service.

In the next few sections, we will cover the following:

❑ Design of the WroxCuisine application

❑ Development of Enterprise Java Bean (EJB) components

❑ Development of the front-end of the application via **Java Server Pages**

❑ Deployment of the application in WebLogic 6.1

To set up and run the J2EE WroxCuisine application, and the web services section of this chapter, you will need the following:

❑ Java Development Kit version 1.3.1 from Sun Microsystems

❑ WebLogic 6.1 application server from BEA

❑ CapeConnect Three Web Services Platform from CapeClear Software

❑ CapeStudio 1.1 – Web Services Development Tool from CapeClear Software

❑ Apache SOAP version 2.2 (which contains the `soap.jar`, `xerces.jar` and `xalan.jar` files) from Apache

Design of the WroxCuisine Application

The J2EE application is called WroxCuisine. It is an online site that provides recipes for world cuisine. The application has in its database recipes for countries like the UK, India, Thailand, and so on. A visitor to the site can select a particular country whose cuisine they are interested in and the site will display the recipes for that country in the database. The user can then drill down into the details of any specific recipe.

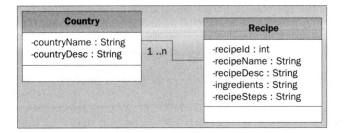

From the above description, you can see that we will have two main types of objects in the system:

❑ Country
  This object will hold information about each country for which we have recipes in the
  database. For the sake of simplicity, we will capture the countryId (uniquely identifies a
  country in the database), country name and country description.

❑ Recipe
  This object will hold information about each recipe in the system. It will contain information
  on the recipe ID, recipe name, recipe description, the country the recipe belongs to, recipe
  ingredients and recipe steps. To keep our database design simple, we will be using a comma-
  delimited list to store the recipe ingredients and the recipe steps.

Architecture of the WroxCuisine J2EE Application

Let's look now at the architecture of the application, and how we will structure our application into the
different components according to the J2EE specification.

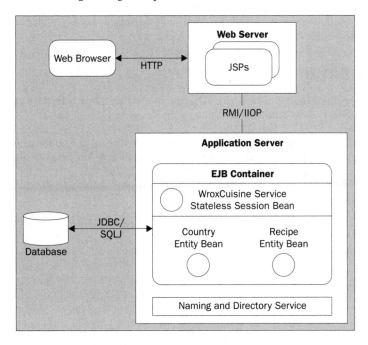

The `Country` and `Recipe` objects that we talked about in the previous section will be implemented as simple JavaBeans. We will assume that the tables and the information for the same will already be present in the database – that is, we will not develop any functionality to create, edit or modify country or recipe information in the database, though that would not be a difficult task.

We will then create a WroxCuisine service bean as shown in the diagram. This is a stateless session bean and it will act as a service bean. It will retrieve country and recipe information from the database. The WroxCuisine service bean will have methods for retrieving information from the system such as country information (`countryname`, `countrydesc`), list of recipes for a country, recipe details, and so on. Since we are not dealing with the functionality to create or modify information in the database, we will not have any functions for the same in the WroxCuisine service bean. One of the features that we will build into this bean is that all information retrieved from the database will be converted into XML format. This will greatly help us later when we expose the functionality as a web service.

The web tier to the application will be written using **Java Server Pages (JSP)**. The JSP will primarily interact with the WroxCuisine service bean to retrieve the necessary information that needs to be shown on the standard web-browser interface. They will retrieve references to the WroxCuisine service bean via the **Java Naming and Directory Interface (JNDI)**. Since the information retrieved from the WroxCuisine service bean will be presented in XML format, we will use XSL transformations to format our data for presentation in the JSP pages.

In the next few sections, we will start building this application, piece by piece. First we will discuss setting up the database (we will be using the Cloudscape Database, an evaluation version of which is shipped with WebLogic 6.1). Then we will develop the service bean (the WroxCuisine stateless session bean). Finally, we will build the front-end to the application using JSP, utilizing XML and XSL in the process.

After we have built the above, we will then describe the steps necessary to deploy the J2EE application in WebLogic Server 6.1.

Database Setup

We will be using the evaluation version of Cloudscape RDBMS that is installed as a part of the standard WebLogic 6.1 Server installation.

We shall first take a look at the database schema for the WroxCuisine application and then go through the Cloudscape SQL utility to create the schema and populate it will sample data. We will also set up the database pool and data source settings for WebLogic Server 6.1.

Database Schema

The database `WroxCuisineDB` will use the following schema shown below:

```
CREATE TABLE COUNTRY (
  COUNTRYID INTEGER PRIMARY KEY,
  COUNTRYNAME VARCHAR(50),
  COUNTRYDESC VARCHAR(500));


CREATE TABLE RECIPE (
  RECIPEID INTEGER PRIMARY KEY,
```

```
COUNTRYID INTEGER,
RECIPENAME VARCHAR(100),
RECIPEDESC VARCHAR(500),
RECIPEINGREDIENTS VARCHAR(1000),
RECIPESTEPS VARCHAR(1000));
```

The COUNTRY table is shown below:

Column Name	Column Description
COUNTRYID	A unique ID for the country. This is the primary key.
COUNTRYNAME	The country name
COUNTRYDESC	A description for the country

The RECIPE table is shown below:

Column Name	Column Description
RECIPEID	A unique ID for the recipe
RECIPENAME	The recipe name
COUNTRYID	The country that this recipe belongs to
RECIPEDESC	A brief description of what the recipe is about
INGREDIENTS	A semi-colon separated list of ingredients. For example, "1 tbsp. sugar; 2 cups water; ½ lb potatoes; ..."
RECIPESTEPS	A semi-colon-separated list of steps required in making this recipe. For example, "1. Bring water to a boil; 2. Add sugar to it; ..."

Database Creation

Let us now use the Interactive SQL utility provided by Cloudscape to create the schema and populate it with some sample data.

We will assume that an environment variable called WL_HOME has been set which points to the directory where WebLogic 6.1 has been installed.

Let us assume that WL_HOME points to C:\bea\wlserver6.1. The Cloudscape RDBMS is present in WL_HOME\samples\eval\cloudscape.

Make sure that the WebLogic 6.1 Server instance is not running.

Open a command window and go to the WL_HOME\samples\eval\cloudscape\data directory. Start the Interactive SQL utility called **IJ** by giving the following command:

```
C:\bea\wlserver6.1\samples\eval\cloudscape\data> java -classpath
%WL_HOME%\lib\weblogic.jar;..\lib\cloudscape.jar;..\lib\tools.jar
COM.cloudscape.tools.ij
```

You should see the following at the prompt:

```
ij version 3.5 (c) 1997-2000 Informix Software, Inc.
ij>
```

To create the database give the following command at the `ij>` prompt:

ij>CONNECT 'jdbc:cloudscape:WroxCuisineDB;create=true';

This creates a database named `WroxCuisineDB`. At this time, there are no tables created in the `WroxCuisineDB`. To create the `COUNTRY` and `RECIPE` tables, give the following command at the `ij>` prompt:

ij> CREATE TABLE COUNTRY (COUNTRYID INTEGER PRIMARY KEY, COUNTRYNAME VARCHAR(50), COUNTRYDESC VARCHAR(500));

To create the `RECIPE` table, give the following command:

ij> CREATE TABLE RECIPE (RECIPEID INTEGER PRIMARY KEY, COUNTRYID INTEGER, RECIPENAME VARCHAR(100), RECIPEDESC VARCHAR(500), RECIPEINGREDIENTS VARCHAR(1000), RECIPESTEPS VARCHAR(1000));

The above DDL is provided in the `\javawebservices\Ch08\wroxcuisine\sql\ddl.sql` file, in the code download for this chapter.

Finally, we can populate the above tables with the sample data provided in the `data.sql` file by giving the appropriate SQL `INSERT` statements. An example is shown below:

```
ij> INSERT INTO COUNTRY VALUES (1, 'UK','UK');
1 rows inserted/updated/deleted
ij> INSERT INTO COUNTRY VALUES (2, 'INDIA','INDIA')
1 rows inserted/updated/deleted
ij> INSERT INTO COUNTRY VALUES (3, 'THAILAND','THAILAND')
1 rows inserted/updated/deleted
ij> INSERT INTO RECIPE VALUES (1,1,'Chocolate Almond Cake','A Secret Recipe from
England','4 oz plain chocolate;2 tbs water;4 oz butter - cubed;4 oz icing sugar -
sieved;4 oz ground almonds;4 oz Rich Tea - broken up','1. Bring an inch of water
to the boil in a saucepan. ;2. Place a pyrex bowl inside the saucepan. ;3. Melt
chocolate and water in the bowl. ;4. Add butter a bit at a time. ;5. Stir in icing
sugar and almonds. ;6. Break biscuits and fold into mixture. ;7. Put in 1 pint
loaf tin. ;8. Cover and leave to cool. Freeze.;9. Use within 2 months. ;10. Thaw
at room temperature.')
1 rows inserted/updated/deleted
ij> INSERT INTO RECIPE VALUES (2,1,'Cauliflower and Stilton Soup','A Delicious
Soup','1 tbs. oil;1 onion, chopped;3/4 pt. chicken stock;1 lb cauliflower broken
into florets;6 tbs. creme fraiche;6 oz stilton, crumbled;Salt and pepper','1. Heat
oil in a heavy based saucepan, add onions and sweat down.;2. Add stock and
cauliflower and cook until tender.;3. Add creme fraiche and stilton and liquidize
until very smooth.;4. Strain soup into a clean saucepan and reheat gently, DO NOT
```

```
BOIL.;5. Season with salt and pepper. Serves four.')
1 rows inserted/updated/deleted
ij> INSERT INTO RECIPE VALUES (3,2,'Naan','Indian Bread','Flour (maida) 500 gms.
;Baking powder 1 tsp. ;Soda-bi-carb ½ tsp.;Sugar 2 tsps. ;Egg 1 no. ;Milk 1 cup
;Onion seeds 2 tsps. ;Oil 3 tsps. ;Salt To taste','1. Sieve flour with baking
powder, soda bicarb and salt. Mix sugar, egg, milk and water. Knead it well into a
medium  soft dough. ;2. Apply oil and cover it with cloth for 1 hour ;3. Make 10
equal sized balls;4. Roll it into a round shape;5. Now put it on a cloth pad and
cook in a preheated oven (250 º C) by placing it on a greased tray.;6. Remove when
it is crisp and golden brown on both sides.;7. Serve hot topped with butter.')
```

The above DDL is provided in the
\javawebservices\Ch08\wroxcuisine\sql\data.sql file, in the code download for
this chapter.

WebLogic Database Setup

In the WroxCuisine J2EE application that will be developed in the next few sections, we need to make sure that we configure JDBC correctly for use through WebLogic Server 6.1. To do that, we need to set up two things as shown below:

1. **Set up WebLogic Server 6.1 to use Cloudscape**

Add the `cloudscape.jar` file present in `%WL_HOME%\samples\eval\cloudscape\lib` directory to the `CLASSPATH` variable in the `startWebLogic.cmd` file present in `%WL_HOME%\config\mydomain` directory.

To allow WebLogic to use the database we need to add an environment property: `cloudscape.system.home` to the `startWebLogic.cmd` file.

Shown below is the standard Java command to start the WebLogic server in the `startWebLogic.cmd` file. Be sure to add the environment entry in bold.

```
...
echo on
"%JAVA_HOME%\bin\java" -hotspot -ms64m -mx64m -classpath "%CLASSPATH%"
-Dweblogic.Domain=mydomain
-Dcloudscape.system.home=./samples/eval/cloudscape/data
-Dweblogic.Name=myserver "-Dbea.home=d:\bea"
-Dweblogic.management.password=%WLS_PW%
-Dweblogic.ProductionModeEnabled=%STARTMODE%
"-Djava.security.policy==c:\bea\wlserver6.1/lib/weblogic.policy"
weblogic.Servergoto finish
...
```

All the database files will then be assumed to be under `cloudscape.system.home\data` directory.

2. Database Connection Pool

Make sure that your WebLogic server is running and go to the WebLogic console URL (http://localhost:7001/console) to set up the JDBCConnectionPool as shown below. Click Create:

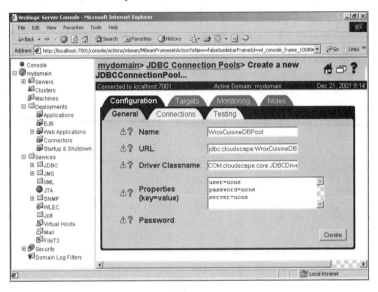

3. Data Source

Once we have set up the database connection pool: WroxCuisineDBPool, we can then set up the data source in WebLogic as shown below. Navigate to this screen through the use of the tree on the left of your screen, clicking on Data Sources, and then Configure a New JDBC Data Source...:

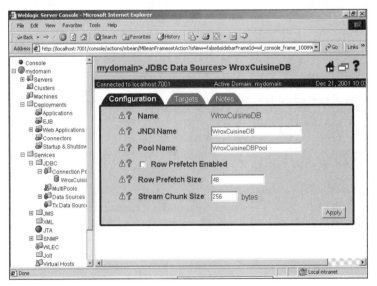

Thus, to get a JDBC Connection object, we can now use code that looks like this:

```
InitialContext ctx = new InitialContext();
javax.sql.DataSource ds = (javax.sql.DataSource)ctx.lookup("WroxCuisineDB");

Connection conn = ds.getConnection();
```

Now that we have the database setup complete, let us move on to developing our WroxCuisineService session bean.

Development of WroxCuisineService Session Bean

In this section we shall develop the WroxCuisineService session bean. This session bean will provide methods that will allow you to retrieve the country and recipe information from the database. It will use JDBC to communicate with the database and retrieve the appropriate information. The information returned by the WroxCuisineService session bean will be in XML format. The use of XML as the data format helps us in targetting this information to a variety of clients. Also, it will blend in quite well when we expose our session bean as a web service later on in this chapter.

In this section we will:

❑ Develop JavaBeans (Recipe.java and Country.java) for the recipe and country objects in the database

❑ Develop the WroxCuisineService session bean

❑ Develop a helper class called XMLGenerator.java, which will convert the information received about countries and recipes into XML formats

❑ Develop a DirectoryService.java helper class that will help us in doing JNDI lookups

Before we move into the code for the above, let us define the directory structure that will be used:

```
%BOOK_HOME%\Ch08\wroxcuisine\
                    src\
                        com\
                            wroxcuisine\
                                        ejb\ (WroxCuisineService EJB sources)
                                        META-INF (Deployment Descriptors)
                                        xml\ (XMLGenerator.java class)
                                        helpers\ (Recipe and Country JavaBeans
                                                    and DirectoryService.java)
                            xml-jars\ (This contains the xerces.jar, xalan.jar and
                                        jdom.jar files)
```

We will go into the details of the build script a little later in the chapter. For now, we'll focus on the source code.

Country and Recipe JavaBeans

The Recipe and Country JavaBeans provide setter and getter methods as shown below. Both these files will be present in the
C:\javawebservices\Ch08\wroxcuisine\src\com\wroxcuisines\helpers directory.

Country.java

```
package com.wroxcuisine.helpers;

public class Country {
```

Below we define the three attributes (countryId, countryName and countryDesc) that we defined for the COUNTRY object in the database schema:

```
int countryId;
String countryName;
String countryDesc;

public Country() {}
```

Shown below are get/set methods for the countryId, countryName and countryDesc attributes:

```
public java.lang.String getCountryDesc() {
  return countryDesc;
}
public void setCountryDesc(java.lang.String countryDesc) {
  this.countryDesc = countryDesc;
}

public java.lang.String getCountryName() {
  return countryName;
}
public void setCountryName(java.lang.String countryName) {
  this.countryName = countryName;
}

public int getCountryId() {
  return countryId;
}
public void setCountryId(int countryId) {
  this.countryId = countryId;
}
}
```

Recipe.java

Below we define the six attributes (recipeId, countryId, recipeName, recipeDesc, recipeIngredients and recipeSteps) that we defined for the RECIPE object in the Database Schema section. Note that recipeIngredients and recipeSteps are in the form of a comma-separated list of elements.

```
package com.wroxcuisine.helpers;

public class Recipe {

  int recipeId;
  int countryId;
  String recipeName;
  String recipeDesc;
  String recipeIngredients;
  String recipeSteps;


  public Recipe() {}
```

Shown below are get/set methods for the recipeId, countryId, recipeName, recipeDesc, recipeIngredients and recipeSteps attributes.

```
public int getCountryId() {
  return countryId;
}

public void setCountryId(int countryId) {
  this.countryId = countryId;
}

public int getRecipeId() {
  return recipeId;
}

public void setRecipeId(int recipeId) {
  this.recipeId = recipeId;
}

public java.lang.String getRecipeIngredients() {
  return recipeIngredients;
}

public void setRecipeIngredients(java.lang.String recipeIngredients) {
  this.recipeIngredients = recipeIngredients;
}

public java.lang.String getRecipeName() {
  return recipeName;
}

public void setRecipeName(java.lang.String recipeName) {
  this.recipeName = recipeName;
}

public java.lang.String getRecipeSteps() {
  return recipeSteps;
}

public void setRecipeSteps(java.lang.String recipeSteps) {
```

```
    this.recipeSteps = recipeSteps;
  }

  public java.lang.String getRecipeDesc() {
    return recipeDesc;
  }

  public void setRecipeDesc(java.lang.String recipeDesc) {
    this.recipeDesc = recipeDesc;
  }
}
```

WroxCuisineService Session Bean

Our session bean will be the main interface presented to the web tier. The web tier will invoke service methods in the bean, which will in turn use JDBC to retrieve the information from the database and create the `Recipe` and `Country` objects. Since we are primarily concerned with accessing this information, we will provide the following service methods in the `WroxCuisineService` Session bean.

❏   `String GetAllCountries() throws RemoteException, EJBException;`

This method returns a XML formatted string that retrieves a collection of all countries and their information in the database. It utilizes the `Country` JavaBean that we developed earlier. The XML representation shown below is returned by the `XMLGenerator` class, which we shall cover later.

```xml
<?xml version="1.0" encoding="UTF-8"?>
<COUNTRYLIST>
  <COUNTRY>
    <COUNTRYID>1</COUNTRYID>
    <COUNTRYNAME>UK</COUNTRYNAME>
    <COUNTRYDESC>UK</COUNTRYDESC>
  </COUNTRY>
  <COUNTRY>
    <COUNTRYID>2</COUNTRYID>
    <COUNTRYNAME>INDIA</COUNTRYNAME>
    <COUNTRYDESC>INDIA</COUNTRYDESC>
  </COUNTRY>
  <COUNTRY>
    <COUNTRYID>3</COUNTRYID>
    <COUNTRYNAME>THAILAND</COUNTRYNAME>
    <COUNTRYDESC>THAILAND</COUNTRYDESC>
  </COUNTRY>
</COUNTRYLIST>
```

❏   `String GetRecipeDetails(int recipeId)`

This method will return an XML-formatted `String` that returns the recipe details given a particular `RecipeId`. An XML result is shown below, using recipe ID `2` as an example. We had seen in the database schema section that the recipe ingredients, and recipe steps, were packed as a comma-separated list into single columns called `RECIPEINGREDIENTS` and `RECIPESTEPS` respectively. The `XMLGenerator.java` class will parse this comma-separated list of ingredients into individual XML elements `<INGREDIENTS>` and `<STEPS>` as shown below.

```
<?xml version="1.0" encoding="UTF-8"?>
<RECIPE RECIPEID="2" COUNTRYID="1">
  <RECIPENAME>Cauliflower and Stilton Soup</RECIPENAME>
  <RECIPEDESC>A Delicious Soup</RECIPEDESC>
  <RECIPEINGREDIENTS>
    <INGREDIENT INGREDIENTNUM="1">1 tbs. oil</INGREDIENT>
    <INGREDIENT INGREDIENTNUM="2">1 onion, chopped</INGREDIENT>
    <INGREDIENT INGREDIENTNUM="3">3/4 pt. chicken stock</INGREDIENT>
    <INGREDIENT INGREDIENTNUM="4">1 lb cauliflower broken into
        florets</INGREDIENT>
    <INGREDIENT INGREDIENTNUM="5">6 tbs. creme fraiche</INGREDIENT>
    <INGREDIENT INGREDIENTNUM="6">6 oz stilton, crumbled</INGREDIENT>
    <INGREDIENT INGREDIENTNUM="7">Salt and pepper</INGREDIENT>
  </RECIPEINGREDIENTS>
  <RECIPESTEPS>
    <STEP STEPNUM="1">1. Heat oil in a heavy based saucepan, add onions and sweat
        down.
    </STEP>
    <STEP STEPNUM="2">2. Add stock and cauliflower and cook until tender.</STEP>
    <STEP STEPNUM="3">3. Add creme fraiche and stilton and liquidize until very
        smooth.</STEP>
    <STEP STEPNUM="4">4. Strain soup into a clean saucepan and reheat gently, DO
        NOT BOIL.</STEP>
    <STEP STEPNUM="5">5. Season with salt and pepper. Serves four.</STEP>
  </RECIPESTEPS>
</RECIPE>
```

❑   String GetRecipesByCountry(int CountryId)

This method returns all recipes present in the database for a particular country. The XML result is shown below, using India (countryId = 2) as an example:

```
<?xml version="1.0" encoding="UTF-8"?>
<RECIPELIST>
  <RECIPE RECIPEID="3" COUNTRYID="2">
    <RECIPENAME>Naan</RECIPENAME>
    <RECIPEDESC>Indian Bread</RECIPEDESC>
    <RECIPEINGREDIENTS>
      <INGREDIENT INGREDIENTNUM="1">Flour (maida) 500 gms. </INGREDIENT>
      <INGREDIENT INGREDIENTNUM="2">Baking powder 1 tsp. </INGREDIENT>
      <INGREDIENT INGREDIENTNUM="3">Soda-bi-carb ½ tsp.</INGREDIENT>
      <INGREDIENT INGREDIENTNUM="4">Sugar 2 tsps. </INGREDIENT>
      <INGREDIENT INGREDIENTNUM="5">Egg 1 no. </INGREDIENT>
      <INGREDIENT INGREDIENTNUM="6">Milk 1 cup </INGREDIENT>
      <INGREDIENT INGREDIENTNUM="7">Onion seeds 2 tsps. </INGREDIENT>
      <INGREDIENT INGREDIENTNUM="8">Oil 3 tsps. </INGREDIENT>
      <INGREDIENT INGREDIENTNUM="9">Salt To taste</INGREDIENT>
    </RECIPEINGREDIENTS>
    <RECIPESTEPS>
      <STEP STEPNUM="1">1. Sieve flour with baking powder, soda bicarb and salt.
          Mix sugar, egg, milk and water. Knead it well into a medium soft dough.
      </STEP>
      <STEP STEPNUM="2">2. Apply oil and cover it with cloth for 1 hour </STEP>
      <STEP STEPNUM="3">3. Make 10 equal sized balls</STEP>
```

```
      <STEP STEPNUM="4">4. Roll it into a round shape</STEP>
      <STEP STEPNUM="5">5. Now put it on a cloth pad and cook in a preheated oven
          (250 º C) by placing it on a greased tray.</STEP>
      <STEP STEPNUM="6">6. Remove when it is crisp and golden brown on both
          sides.</STEP>
      <STEP STEPNUM="7">7. Serve hot topped with butter.</STEP>
    </RECIPESTEPS>
  </RECIPE>
</RECIPELIST>
```

❑   `String GetAllRecipes() throws RemoteException, EJBException;`

This method returns all recipes present in the database. It categorizes the XML result by country. The output XML format is shown below:

```
<?xml version="1.0" encoding="UTF-8"?>
<RECIPELIST>
  <RECIPE RECIPEID="1" COUNTRYID="1">
    -------
  </RECIPE>
  <RECIPE RECIPEID="2" COUNTRYID="1">
    -------
  </RECIPE>
    -----
    -----
</RECIPELIST>
```

❑   `String GetRandomRecipe() throws RemoteException, EJBException;`

This method returns a random recipe from the database. The XML result is the same as that for the `GetRecipeDetails()` method.

Let us now look at the code for the `WroxCuisineService` session bean. Note that the EJB source files for the `WroxCuisineService` EJB discussed below are present in the `C:\javawebservices\Ch08\wroxcuisine\src\com\wroxcuisine\ejb` directory.

WroxCuisineServiceHome.java

The home interface for the `WroxCuisineService` bean contains a single `create()` method as shown below. This is in line with the default `create()` method that all stateless session beans need to have, as per the EJB specification.

```java
package com.wroxcuisine.ejb;

import javax.ejb.EJBHome;
import javax.ejb.CreateException;
import javax.ejb.EJBException;
import java.rmi.RemoteException;

public interface WroxCuisineServiceHome extends EJBHome {
  WroxCuisineService create()
      throws CreateException, EJBException, RemoteException;
}
```

WroxCuisineService.java

The `WroxCuisineService.java` is the interface that defines the business methods of the bean. These are the methods that will be invoked by our web tier and later on in the chapter when we expose our `WroxCuisineService` EJB as a web service. The methods shown below are the ones that will be available for invocation.

```
package com.wroxcuisine.ejb;

import javax.ejb.EJBObject;
import java.rmi.RemoteException;
import javax.ejb.EJBException;


public interface WroxCuisineService extends EJBObject {
```

The method signatures that are shown below have been discussed earlier. Just to recap, each of these methods will return an XML representation of the result.

```
String GetAllCountries() throws RemoteException, EJBException;

String GetRecipesByCountry(int CountryId)
    throws RemoteException, EJBException;

String GetAllRecipes() throws RemoteException, EJBException;

String GetRecipeDetails(int recipeId)
    throws RemoteException, EJBException;

String GetRandomRecipe() throws RemoteException, EJBException;
}
```

WroxCuisineServiceEJB.java

Here is the implementation class for the `WroxCuisineService` session bean:

```
package com.wroxcuisine.ejb;

import javax.ejb.SessionBean;
import javax.ejb.SessionContext;
import java.rmi.RemoteException;
import javax.ejb.EJBException;
import javax.ejb.CreateException;

import javax.naming.*;
import java.util.*;
import java.sql.*;
import javax.sql.*;

// JDOM Packages
import org.jdom.input.*;
import org.jdom.output.*;
import org.jdom.*;
```

```
// XML Helpers
import com.wroxcuisine.xml.XMLGenerator;
import com.wroxcuisine.helpers.Recipe;
import com.wroxcuisine.helpers.Country;
import com.wroxcuisine.helpers.DirectoryService;

public class WroxCuisineServiceEJB implements SessionBean {
  private SessionContext ctx;
```

The methods shown below are standard ones on a session EJB. We are going to restrict ourselves to the defaults as shown below:

```
public void setSessionContext(SessionContext context)
    throws RemoteException, EJBException {
  ctx = context;
}

public void ejbActivate() throws RemoteException, EJBException {}

public void ejbPassivate() throws RemoteException, EJBException {}

public void ejbRemove() throws RemoteException, EJBException {}

public void ejbCreate()
    throws CreateException, EJBException, RemoteException {}
```

The `GetAllCountries()` method gets the `DataSource` object for the `WroxCuisineDB` data source that we set up in WebLogic previously. It uses a SQL SELECT statement to retrieve all the countries present in the database:

```
public String GetAllCountries() {
  try {
    ArrayList countries = new ArrayList();

    InitialContext ctx = DirectoryService.getInitContext();
    DataSource ds = (DataSource) ctx.lookup("WroxCuisineDB");
    Connection conn = ds.getConnection();
    Statement st = conn.createStatement();
    ResultSet rs = st.executeQuery("SELECT * FROM COUNTRY");
```

Once it retrieves the `ResultSet`, it wraps each `Country` object into the `Country` JavaBean we covered before. It populates an `ArrayList` that maintains the collection of `Country` objects present in the database.

```
    while (rs.next()) {
      Country c = new Country();
      c.setCountryId(rs.getInt("COUNTRYID"));
      c.setCountryName(rs.getString("COUNTRYNAME"));
      c.setCountryDesc(rs.getString("COUNTRYDESC"));
      countries.add(c);
    }
    st.close();
    conn.close();
```

Finally, it invokes the `getAllCountriesXML()` static method on the `XMLGenerator` class, which returns the XML representation for the `Country` list.

```
    return XMLGenerator.getAllCountriesXML(countries, true);

  } catch (Exception e) {
    throw new EJBException(e);
  }
}
```

The GetRecipesByCountry() method takes a countryId as a parameter and retrieves all the recipes for that country from the database.

```
public String GetRecipesByCountry(int countryId) {
  try {
    ArrayList recipes = new ArrayList();

    InitialContext ctx = DirectoryService.getInitContext();
    DataSource ds = (DataSource) ctx.lookup("WroxCuisineDB");
    Connection conn = ds.getConnection();
    Statement st = conn.createStatement();
    ResultSet rs =
      st.executeQuery("SELECT * FROM RECIPE WHERE COUNTRYID = "
                        + countryId);
```

Once it retrieves the ResultSet, it wraps each Recipe data object into the Recipe JavaBean that we covered before. It adds the entire collection of recipes to an ArrayList called recipes.

```
    while (rs.next()) {
      Recipe r = new Recipe();
      r.setRecipeId(rs.getInt("RECIPEID"));
      r.setCountryId(rs.getInt("COUNTRYID"));
      r.setRecipeName(rs.getString("RECIPENAME"));
      r.setRecipeDesc(rs.getString("RECIPEDESC"));
      r.setRecipeIngredients(rs.getString("RECIPEINGREDIENTS"));
      r.setRecipeSteps(rs.getString("RECIPESTEPS"));
      recipes.add(r);
    }
    st.close();
    conn.close();
```

Finally, it invokes the getAllRecipesXML() static method on the XMLGenerator class which gives back an XML representation of the Recipe list.

```
    return XMLGenerator.getAllRecipesXML(recipes, true);
  } catch (Exception e) {
    throw new EJBException(e);
  }
}
```

The GetAllRecipes() method is similar to the one above, except that it returns back the entire list of recipes in the database for all of the countries in the database.

```
public String GetAllRecipes() {
  try {
    ArrayList recipes = new ArrayList();

    InitialContext ctx = DirectoryService.getInitContext();
    DataSource ds = (DataSource) ctx.lookup("WroxCuisineDB");
    Connection conn = ds.getConnection();
    Statement st = conn.createStatement();
    ResultSet rs = st.executeQuery("SELECT * FROM RECIPE");

    while (rs.next()) {
      Recipe r = new Recipe();
      r.setRecipeId(rs.getInt("RECIPEID"));
      r.setCountryId(rs.getInt("COUNTRYID"));
      r.setRecipeName(rs.getString("RECIPENAME"));
      r.setRecipeDesc(rs.getString("RECIPEDESC"));
      r.setRecipeIngredients(rs.getString("RECIPEINGREDIENTS"));
      r.setRecipeSteps(rs.getString("RECIPESTEPS"));
      recipes.add(r);
    }
    st.close();
    conn.close();

    return XMLGenerator.getAllRecipesXML(recipes, true);

  } catch (Exception e) {
    throw new EJBException(e);
  }
}
```

The GetRecipeDetails() method takes in a recipeId parameter that identifies a unique recipe and gives back an XML representation for the recipe.

```
public String GetRecipeDetails(int recipeId) {
  try {

    Recipe r = new Recipe();

    InitialContext ctx = DirectoryService.getInitContext();
    DataSource ds = (DataSource) ctx.lookup("WroxCuisineDB");
    Connection conn = ds.getConnection();
    Statement st = conn.createStatement();
    ResultSet rs =
      st.executeQuery("SELECT * FROM RECIPE WHERE RECIPEID = "
                      + recipeId);

    while (rs.next()) {
      r.setRecipeId(rs.getInt("RECIPEID"));
      r.setCountryId(rs.getInt("COUNTRYID"));
      r.setRecipeName(rs.getString("RECIPENAME"));
```

```
        r.setRecipeDesc(rs.getString("RECIPEDESC"));
        r.setRecipeIngredients(rs.getString("RECIPEINGREDIENTS"));
        r.setRecipeSteps(rs.getString("RECIPESTEPS"));
      }
      st.close();
      conn.close();
```

Once it builds the `recipe` object `r`, it invokes the `getRecipeXML()` static method of the `XMLGenerator` class to get the XML representation for the recipe.

```
        return XMLGenerator.getRecipeXML(r, true);
      } catch (Exception e) {
        throw new EJBException(e);
      }
    }
```

The `GetRandomRecipe()` method retrieves a random recipe from the database. It can be used by the web site to display a "Recipe of the Day". It first retrieves the count of the number of recipes that are present in the database and seeds the `Random` class with that count. It then retrieves the next random integer that really is a `recipeId` and retrieves the recipe information from the database.

```
public String GetRandomRecipe() {
  try {

    int recipeCount = 0;
    InitialContext ctx = DirectoryService.getInitContext();
    DataSource ds = (DataSource) ctx.lookup("WroxCuisineDB");
    Connection conn = ds.getConnection();
    Statement st = conn.createStatement();
    ResultSet rs =
      st.executeQuery("SELECT COUNT(*) AS RECIPECOUNT FROM RECIPE");

    if (rs.next()) {
      recipeCount = rs.getInt("RECIPECOUNT");
    }
    st.close();
    conn.close();

    // Now we have the count
    Random rand = new Random();
    int recipeId = rand.nextInt(recipeCount);
    return this.GetRecipeDetails(recipeId);

  } catch (Exception e) {
    throw new EJBException(e);
  }
 }
}
```

Deployment Descriptor

Let us now take a look at the deployment descriptor for our WroxCuisineService session bean. It will have ejb-jar.xml and the accompanying weblogic-ejb-jar.xml deployment descriptor file that is necessary for deployment into WebLogic Server 6.1.

The deployment descriptor describes the bean and at the same time can be used to declaratively specify the services that it needs from the EJB container, for example, transaction handling, security, and so on.

Note that both the ejb-jar.xml and weblogic-ejb-jar.xml will be present in the C:\wroxcuisine\src\ejb\com\wroxcuisine\META-INF directories.

ejb-jar.xml

```
<?xml version="1.0"?>

<!DOCTYPE ejb-jar PUBLIC
    '-//Sun Microsystems, Inc.//DTD Enterprise JavaBeans 2.0//EN'
    'http://java.sun.com/dtd/ejb-jar_2_0.dtd'>

<ejb-jar>
  <enterprise-beans>
```

We are declaring the WroxCuisineService session bean below with the respective class names for the home and remote interfaces, and the EJB class.

```
    <session>
      <ejb-name>WroxCuisineService</ejb-name>
      <home>com.wroxcuisine.ejb.WroxCuisineServiceHome</home>
      <remote>com.wroxcuisine.ejb.WroxCuisineService</remote>
      <ejb-class>com.wroxcuisine.ejb.WroxCuisineServiceEJB</ejb-class>
```

Our session bean is a stateless session bean and leaves the transaction management to the WebLogic Server 6.1 container – in other words, it is container-managed.

```
      <session-type>Stateless</session-type>
      <transaction-type>Container</transaction-type>
    </session>
  </enterprise-beans>
  <assembly-descriptor>
    <container-transaction>
      <method>
        <ejb-name>WroxCuisineService</ejb-name>
      <method-name>*</method-name>
      </method>
      <trans-attribute>Required</trans-attribute>
    </container-transaction>
  </assembly-descriptor>
</ejb-jar>
```

weblogic-ejb-jar.xml

To deploy the `WroxCuisineService` session bean in Weblogic Server 6.1 we need an additional descriptor file that is specific to WebLogic, `weblogic-ejb-jar.xml` file. The important thing to note in this descriptor is the `<jndi-name>` element, the value of which will be used to look up the home interface of the `WroxCuisineService` session EJB.

```
<?xml version="1.0"?>
<!DOCTYPE weblogic-ejb-jar PUBLIC
'-//BEA Systems, Inc.//DTD WebLogic 6.0.0 EJB//EN'
'http://www.bea.com/servers/wls600/dtd/weblogic-ejb-jar.dtd'>
<weblogic-ejb-jar>
  <weblogic-enterprise-bean>
    <ejb-name>WroxCuisineService</ejb-name>
    <jndi-name>WroxCuisineService</jndi-name>
  </weblogic-enterprise-bean>
</weblogic-ejb-jar>
```

Now that we have seen the `WroxCuisineService` session bean, let us take a look at the `XMLGenerator` class.

XMLGeneration

We will write a helper class called `XMLGenerator.java`, which will help in creating the XML documents as described in the previous section. The `WroxCuisineService` bean will use JDBC to retrieve the information from the database and it will pass this data to the `XMLGenerator` class, which has methods to provide the XML result for the same. This process is depicted below for a sample method:

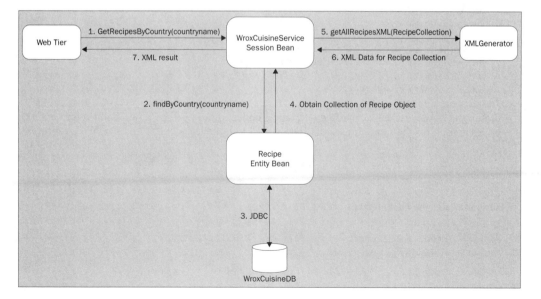

The above diagram demonstrates how a particular call from the web tier to the `WroxCuisineService` is translated by the `WroxCuisineService` bean into appropriate JDBC invocations on the `WroxCuisineDB` database. Also note, that once the results are obtained from the `WroxCuisineDB` database, the result is then sent to the `XMLGenerator` class which will create the appropriate XML format for the request. This XML format is then finally sent back to the web tier.

Shown below is the code for the `XMLGenerator` class. It basically has methods for generating the XML response from the equivalent Java objects. These XML formats are the same ones discussed in the previous section. Note that we are using JDOM (version b7) at http://www.jdom.org/downloads/index.html to create the XML result. You could use any XML parser available out there to do the same, for instance Xerces from the Apache Software Foundation (http://xml.apache.org/xerces2-j/index.html).

XMLGenerator.java

The `XMLGenerator.java` source is shown below. Note that it will be present in the `C:\wroxcuisine\src\com\wroxcuisine\xml` directory.

```
package com.wroxcuisine.xml;

import java.util.*;
import java.io.*;

// WroxCuisine EJB Packages
import com.wroxcuisine.ejb.*;

// JDOM Packages
import org.jdom.*;
import org.jdom.input.*;
import org.jdom.output.*;

import com.wroxcuisine.helpers.Recipe;
import com.wroxcuisine.helpers.Country;

public class XMLGenerator {
```

The `getAllRecipesXML()` method will take a collection of `Recipe` objects and return an XML representation for the same. It uses the JDOM API to build the `<RECIPELIST>` XML representation.

```
public static String getAllRecipesXML(Collection recipes,
                                      boolean xmlHeader) throws Exception {
```

Here it creates the **root element**: `<RECIPELIST>`.

```
Element rootElement = new Element("RECIPELIST");
```

For each `Recipe` object, it invokes the `getRecipeXML()` method in this class which returns back an XML representation for the recipe. It adds each such element to the `<RECIPELIST>` root element.

```
Iterator iterator = recipes.iterator();
while (iterator.hasNext()) {
  Recipe recipe = (Recipe) iterator.next();
  Document doc = getRecipeXML(recipe);
  rootElement.addContent((Element) doc.getRootElement().clone());
}
```

Finally it creates a `String` XML representation from the `rootElement` object and returns that string to the calling object.

```
XMLOutputter output = new XMLOutputter("  ", true);
if (xmlHeader) {
  Document doc = new Document(rootElement);
  return output.outputString(doc);
} else {
  return output.outputString(rootElement);
}
}
```

The `getRecipeXML()` object returns back the XML representation of the recipe i.e. `<RECIPE ….>`. It basically takes in a `Recipe` object and simply creates a `rootElement <RECIPE>` and child elements for it, containing the `<RECIPEID>`, `<COUNTRYID>`, and so on.

Note that this method is also responsible for parsing the comma-separated columns for `recipeIngredients` and `recipeSteps` into the appropriate `<STEP>` and `<INGREDIENT>` collections respectively.

```
public static Document getRecipeXML(Recipe recipe) throws Exception {
  try {

    // ROOT ELEMENT
    Element rootElement = new Element("RECIPE");

    rootElement.setAttribute("RECIPEID",
                          String.valueOf(recipe.getRecipeId()));
    rootElement.setAttribute("COUNTRYID",
                          String.valueOf(recipe.getCountryId()));

    // RECIPENAME
    Element recipeName = new Element("RECIPENAME");
    recipeName.setText(recipe.getRecipeName());

    // RECIPEDESC
    Element recipeDesc = new Element("RECIPEDESC");
    recipeDesc.setText(recipe.getRecipeDesc());

    // RECIPESTEPS
    Element recipeSteps = new Element("RECIPESTEPS");
```

```
// String Tokenize over here
String RecipeSteps = recipe.getRecipeSteps();
StringTokenizer steps = new StringTokenizer(RecipeSteps, ";");
int stepnum = 1;
while (steps.hasMoreElements()) {
  Element recipeStep = new Element("STEP");
  recipeStep.setAttribute("STEPNUM", String.valueOf(stepnum));
  recipeStep.setText((String) steps.nextElement());
  recipeSteps.addContent(recipeStep);
  stepnum++;
}

// INGREDIENTS
Element recipeIngredients = new Element("RECIPEINGREDIENTS");

// String Tokenize over here
String strIngredients = recipe.getRecipeIngredients();
StringTokenizer ingredients = new StringTokenizer(strIngredients,
        ";");
int ingredientnum = 1;
while (ingredients.hasMoreElements()) {
  Element recipeIngredient = new Element("INGREDIENT");
  recipeIngredient.setAttribute("INGREDIENTNUM",
                          String.valueOf(ingredientnum));
  recipeIngredient.setText((String) ingredients.nextElement());
  recipeIngredients.addContent(recipeIngredient);
  ingredientnum++;
}

// Create the Structure
rootElement.addContent(recipeName);
rootElement.addContent(recipeDesc);
rootElement.addContent(recipeIngredients);
rootElement.addContent(recipeSteps);

XMLOutputter output = new XMLOutputter("  ", true);
Document doc = new Document(rootElement);
return doc;
} catch (Exception e) {
throw new Exception(e.getMessage());
}
}
```

This method is similar to the one above, except that it takes an additional boolean parameter xmlHeader, which if set to true, will create the XML preamble `<?xml version="1.0" encoding="UTF-8"?>`. The getRecipeXML() method above does not return this XML preamble.

```
public static String getRecipeXML(Recipe recipe,
                          boolean xmlHeader) throws Exception {

    try {

        // ROOT ELEMENT
```

```
Element rootElement = new Element("RECIPE");

rootElement.setAttribute("RECIPEID",
                         String.valueOf(recipe.getRecipeId()));
rootElement.setAttribute("COUNTRYID",
                         String.valueOf(recipe.getCountryId()));

// RECIPENAME
Element recipeName = new Element("RECIPENAME");
recipeName.setText(recipe.getRecipeName());

// RECIPEDESC
Element recipeDesc = new Element("RECIPEDESC");
recipeDesc.setText(recipe.getRecipeDesc());

// RECIPESTEPS
Element recipeSteps = new Element("RECIPESTEPS");

// String Tokenize over here
String RecipeSteps = recipe.getRecipeSteps();
StringTokenizer steps = new StringTokenizer(RecipeSteps, ";");
int stepnum = 1;
while (steps.hasMoreElements()) {
  Element recipeStep = new Element("STEP");
  recipeStep.setAttribute("STEPNUM", String.valueOf(stepnum));
  recipeStep.setText((String) steps.nextElement());
  recipeSteps.addContent(recipeStep);
  stepnum++;
}


// INGREDIENTS
Element recipeIngredients = new Element("RECIPEINGREDIENTS");

// String Tokenize over here
String strIngredients = recipe.getRecipeIngredients();
StringTokenizer ingredients = new StringTokenizer(strIngredients,
        ";");
int ingredientnum = 1;
while (ingredients.hasMoreElements()) {
  Element recipeIngredient = new Element("INGREDIENT");
  recipeIngredient.setAttribute("INGREDIENTNUM",
                                String.valueOf(ingredientnum));
  recipeIngredient.setText((String) ingredients.nextElement());
  recipeIngredients.addContent(recipeIngredient);
  ingredientnum++;
}

// Create the Structure
rootElement.addContent(recipeName);
rootElement.addContent(recipeDesc);
rootElement.addContent(recipeIngredients);
rootElement.addContent(recipeSteps);

XMLOutputter output = new XMLOutputter("   ", true);
```

```
      if (xmlHeader) {
        Document doc = new Document(rootElement);
        return output.outputString(doc);
      } else {
        return output.outputString(rootElement);
      }
    } catch (Exception e) {
      throw new Exception(e.getMessage());
    }
  }
```

The getAllCountries() method takes in a collection of Country objects and returns the appropriate XML representation for it.

```
  public static String getAllCountriesXML(Collection countries,
                              boolean xmlHeader) throws Exception {

    try {
      SAXBuilder builder = new SAXBuilder();

      // ROOT ELEMENT
      Element rootElement = new Element("COUNTRYLIST");

      Iterator iterator = countries.iterator();
      while (iterator.hasNext()) {
        Country country = (Country) iterator.next();
        Element countryElement = new Element("COUNTRY");
        countryElement
          .addContent(new Element("COUNTRYID")
          .setText(String.valueOf(country.getCountryId())));
        countryElement
          .addContent(new Element("COUNTRYNAME")
          .setText(country.getCountryName()));
        countryElement
          .addContent(new Element("COUNTRYDESC")
          .setText(country.getCountryDesc()));
        rootElement.addContent(countryElement);
      }

      XMLOutputter output = new XMLOutputter("  ", true);
      if (xmlHeader) {
        Document doc = new Document(rootElement);
        return output.outputString(doc);
      } else {
        return output.outputString(rootElement);
      }
    } catch (Exception e) {
      throw new Exception(e.getMessage());
    }
  }
}
```

DirectoryService.java

The `DirectoryService.java` file performs JNDI lookups. It has a single method called `getInitContext()` which is used to retrieve the `InitialContext` object for WebLogic Server 6.1. The `DirectoryService.java` file is present in the `C:\javawebservices\Ch08\wroxcuisine\src\com\wroxcuisine\helpers` directory.

```
package com.wroxcuisine.helpers;

import javax.naming.*;
import java.util.*;

public class DirectoryService {

  public DirectoryService() {}

  public static InitialContext getInitContext() {
    InitialContext ctx = null;
    Hashtable env = new Hashtable();
    env.put(Context.INITIAL_CONTEXT_FACTORY,
            "weblogic.jndi.WLInitialContextFactory");
    env.put(Context.PROVIDER_URL, "t3://localhost:7001");
    try {
      ctx = new InitialContext(env);
    } catch (Exception e) {
      System.out.println(e.getMessage());
    }
    finally {
      return ctx;
    }
  }
}
```

Deploying the EJB

We will deploy the `WroxCuisineService` EJB now, and we will also write a simple console program to verify that it is working. As stated before, we will be using WebLogic Server 6.1 (http://www.bea.com/products/weblogic/server/index.shtml). If using WebLogic 6.1, the default directory will be `C:\bea\wlserver6.1`.

Let us refer to this directory as `WL_HOME` from now on.

Shown below is the build file that is used to package the EJB files for deployment into Weblogic Server 6.1.

Before you run the build file, ensure that your `CLASSPATH` contains the following files:

```
Set CLASSPATH=.;%WL_HOME%\lib\weblogic.jar;C:\javawebservices\Ch08\wroxcuisine\
xml-jars\jdom.jar;C:\javawebservices\Ch08\wroxcuisine\xml-jars\xerces.jar;C:\
javawebservices\Ch08\wroxcuisine\xml-jars\xalan.jar
```

build.bat

The build.bat file will need to be present in the C:\javawebservices\Ch08\wroxcuisine\src directory. You can run the file from there.

```
SET WL_HOME=C:\bea\wlserver6.1

@REM Create the build directory, and copy the deployment descriptors into it
mkdir build build\META-INF
copy com\wroxcuisine\ejb\META-INF\*.xml build\META-INF
```

This compiles all the EJB files and the supporting files, such as the XMLGenerator.java, Recipe.java, Country.java and DirectoryService.java files:

```
@REM Compile EJB classes into the build directory (jar preparation)
javac -d build com\wroxcuisine\ejb\*.java com\wroxcuisine\helpers\*.java
com\wroxcuisine\xml\*.java
```

This creates the JAR file for the EJB:

```
@REM Make a EJB jar file, including XML deployment descriptors
cd build
jar cv0f CuisineEJB.jar META-INF com
cd ..
```

Finally to make the EJB ready for deployment in WebLogic, we need to generate the WebLogic-specific EJB JAR file by running the ejbc utility provided within WebLogic:

```
@REM EJBC
java -classpath %WL_HOME%/lib/weblogic.jar weblogic.ejbc -compiler javac
build\CuisineEJB.jar build\CuisineEJB_WL.jar
```

Deploying the CuisineEJB_WL.jar file in WebLogic 6.1

After you run the above build.bat file, you will have a CuisineEJB_WL.jar file in C:\javawebservices\Ch08\wroxcuisine\src\build directory. To deploy this EJB in WebLogic 6.1, do the following:

Add the C:\javawebservices\Ch08\wroxcuisine\xml-jars\xalan.jar, C:\javawebservices\Ch08\wroxcuisine\xml-jars\xerces.jar and C:\javawebservices\Ch08\wroxcuisine\xml-jars\jdom.jar files to the CLASSPATH variable in the startWebLogic.cmd file. This is present in the %WL_HOME%\config\mydomain directory.

Ensure that your WebLogic 6.1 Server instance is running. Open your browser and navigate to the WebLogic Console utility (http://localhost:7001/console). Click on the **EJB/Install a new EJB...** option, and you will be presented with a screen as shown below:

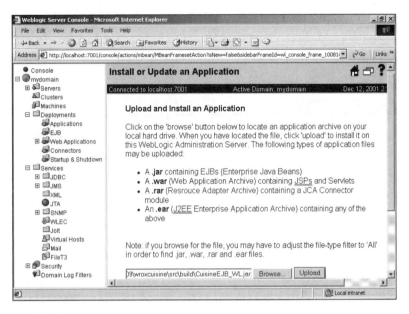

Select the `CuisineEJB_WL.jar` file as shown and click on Upload. You should be able to see the EJB listed in the installed EJBs list.

Testing the WroxCuisineService EJB

Now that we have installed the `WroxCuisineService` EJB, let us write a simple console program to verify the installation. Here is the `TestWroxCuisineService.java` file.

TestWroxCuisineService.java

The `TestWroxCuisineService` program tests the `GetAllCountries()` method of the `WroxCuisineService` EJB. It does a lookup on the JNDI name of the EJB, such as `WroxCuisineService`, to retrieve the home object. It then uses the `create()` method to create the remote interface – `WroxCuisineService`.

Once it has that, it invokes the `GetAllCountries()` method on the remote interface, which returns the XML representation for the same.

```
package com.wroxcuisine.client;

import com.wroxcuisine.ejb.*;
import com.wroxcuisine.helpers.*;

import java.util.*;
import javax.naming.*;

import java.sql.*;
import javax.sql.*;

public class TestWroxCuisineService {
```

```
    public TestWroxCuisineService() {}

    public static void main(String args[]) {

      try {
        InitialContext ctx = DirectoryService.getInitContext();
        Object objService = ctx.lookup("WroxCuisineService");
        WroxCuisineServiceHome servicehome =
          (WroxCuisineServiceHome) javax.rmi.PortableRemoteObject
            .narrow(objService, WroxCuisineServiceHome.class);
        WroxCuisineService service = servicehome.create();
        String xmlOutput = service.GetAllCountries();

        System.out.println(xmlOutput);
      } catch (Exception e) {
        e.printStackTrace();
        System.out.println(e.getMessage());
      }
    }
  }
```

To run this program, create the above file in the
C:\javawebservices\Ch08\wroxcuisine\src\com\wroxcuisine\client directory.

Ensure that the classpath is the same as before:

```
set CLASSPATH=.;%WL_HOME%\lib\weblogic.jar;C:\javawebservices\Ch08\
wroxcuisine\xml-jars\jdom.jar;C:\javawebservices\Ch08\wroxcuisine\xml-
jars\xerces.jar;C:\javawebservices\Ch08\wroxcuisine\xml-jars\xalan.jar
```

Go to the C:\javawebservices\Ch08\wroxcuisine\src directory and compile the
TestWroxCuisineService.java file by giving the following command:

```
C:\javawebservices\Ch08\wroxcuisine\src> javac
com/wroxcuisine/client/TestWroxCuisineService.java
```

Run the program with the following command:

```
C:\javawebservices\Ch08\wroxcuisine\src> java
com.wroxcuisine.client.TestWroxCuisine
```

You should see the following output:

```
C:\WINNT\System32\cmd.exe                                              _ □ ×
C:\javawebservices\Chap08\wroxcuisine\src>java com.wroxcuisine.client.TestWroxCu
isineService
<?xml version="1.0" encoding="UTF-8"?>
<COUNTRYLIST>
   <COUNTRY>
      <COUNTRYID>1</COUNTRYID>
      <COUNTRYNAME>UK</COUNTRYNAME>
      <COUNTRYDESC>UK</COUNTRYDESC>
   </COUNTRY>
   <COUNTRY>
      <COUNTRYID>2</COUNTRYID>
      <COUNTRYNAME>INDIA</COUNTRYNAME>
      <COUNTRYDESC>INDIA</COUNTRYDESC>
   </COUNTRY>
   <COUNTRY>
      <COUNTRYID>3</COUNTRYID>
      <COUNTRYNAME>THAILAND</COUNTRYNAME>
      <COUNTRYDESC>THAILAND</COUNTRYDESC>
   </COUNTRY>
</COUNTRYLIST>

C:\javawebservices\Chap08\wroxcuisine\src>_
```

Development of the Web Tier

The web tier for the application will be developed using JSPs. The architecture that will be used will be JSP Model 1 Architecture, which completely employs JSP. We are not focusing on the web tier development and architecture. Rather we just want a set of pages up and running quickly to verify the development of the EJBs we created in the previous section.

We will have three basic JSP pages for the application as shown below:

The flow of the application is as follows:

1. The user is first shown the home page: index.jsp. This page is a composite page that dynamically includes another page called getallcountrydetails.jsp, which displays all the countries in the database.

2. You can click on any one of the countries displayed in the index.jsp page. This will send the request to another page – getcountryrecipes.jsp, which is another composite page that displays the recipes for that country.

3. Finally, you can select a particular recipe displayed in the getcountryrecipes.jsp page. This will display the getrecipe.jsp page, which displays the details of the recipe.

Each of these pages communicates to the WroxCuisineService session bean and calls the appropriate method on them. As we discussed before, the output from the WroxCuisineService bean is in XML format, and we will employ XSLT technology that will translate the XML format into equivalent HTML output. This can then be displayed inside the browser.

We will not go into the details of each page. Instead we will discuss how the first page, index.jsp, is rendered. We will provide all the JSP files along with their respective XSL files in the code accompanying this chapter, so when you deploy the entire application, you will be able to view all the JSP files.

Each of the JSP files uses a class called XSLTransform.java, which performs the XSLT Transformation. The XSLTransform.java utilizes jdom.jar and the associated XSL Transformation API. The XSLTransform.java file is available in the code download for this chapter. The purpose of the JSP application here is just to give you a flavor of creating an end-to-end J2EE application.

The index.jsp file when viewed in the browser is shown below:

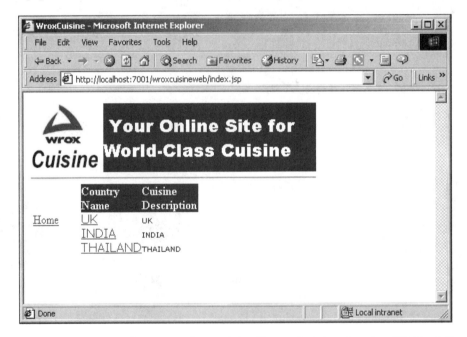

Let's take a look at index.jsp. Once we understand this file, we find that the other JSP files follow the same mechanism.

index.jsp

```
<%@page contentType="text/html"%>
<html>
<head>
<title>WroxCuisine</title>
</head>
<body>
```

```
<table border="0" cellpadding="0" cellspacing="0" width="72%">
  <tr>
    <td width="100%"><%@include file="banner.jsp"%></td>
  </tr>
  <tr>
    <td width="100%">
      <table border="0" cellpadding="0" cellspacing="0" width="100%">
        <tr>
          <td width="100%">
            <hr>
          </td>
        </tr>
        <tr>
          <td width="100%">
            <table border="0" cellpadding="0" cellspacing="0" width="100%">
              <tr>
                <td width="18%"><jsp:include page="menu.jsp"
flush="true"></jsp:include></td>
                <td width="82%"><jsp:include page="getallcountriesdetails.jsp"
flush="true"></jsp:include></td>
              </tr>
            </table>
          </td>
        </tr>
      </table>
    </td>
  </tr>
</table>
</body>
</html>
```

From the above JSP code, notice that the `<jsp:include>` tag is highlighted. This tag dynamically inserts the contents of the getallcountriesdetails.jsp at run time. Now, we will look at the getallcountriesdetails.jsp file.

getallcountriesdetails.jsp

```
<%@page import="javax.naming.*"%>
<%@page import="com.wroxcuisine.ejb.*" errorPage="ErrorHandler.jsp"%>
<%@page import="com.wroxcuisine.xml.*"%>
<%@page import="com.wroxcuisine.helpers.*"%>
<%@page import="java.util.*"%>

<%
  InitialContext ctx = DirectoryService.getInitContext();
  Object objService = ctx.lookup("WroxCuisineService");
  WroxCuisineServiceHome servicehome = (WroxCuisineServiceHome)
    javax.rmi.PortableRemoteObject.narrow(objService,WroxCuisineServiceHome.class);
  WroxCuisineService service = servicehome.create();
  String xmlOutput = service.GetAllCountries();
```

We first obtain a reference to the `WroxCuisineServiceHome` by using JNDI. Once we have a reference to the home interface of the `WroxCuisineService` bean, we call the `create()` method on it, to retrieve the remote reference. We can then invoke the `GetAllCountries()` method which will return us the XML-formatted data, as we saw in the previous section.

Since we are targeting HTML-based clients, we need to transform the XML data into the appropriate HTML data. We make use of a utility class calls `XSLTransform` that has setter methods for the XML data and the XSL file that we wish to use to perform the translation. The XSL files are currently present in the directory shown in the code below. It is not an elegant solution, but nonetheless serves the purpose of the example. Finally we call the `getTransformedData()` on the `XSLTransform` class, and it will return us the appropriately transformed data, which, in our case, is HTML that can be directly displayed in the browser.

```
//Transform the Data using the appropriate XSL
XSLTransform transformer = new XSLTransform();
transformer.setXmlData(xmlOutput);

transformer.setXslFileURL("C:/javawebservices/Ch08/wroxcuisine/web/xsl/
    GetAllCountriesResponse.xsl");
out.println(transformer.getTransformedData());
%>
```

Deploying the Web Application

First, let us take a look at our development directory structure as shown below:

```
%BOOK_HOME%\Ch08\wroxcuisine\
                        web\
                            build-webapp.bat
                            banner.jsp
                            ErrorHandler.jsp
                            getcountrydetails.jsp
                            getcountryrecipes.jsp
                            getcountryrecipesdetails.jsp
                            getrecipe.jsp
                            getrecipedetails.jsp
                            index.jsp
                            menu.jsp
                        images\
                            wroxcook.jpg
                        WEB-INF\
                            web.xml
                        classes\
                            com\
                                wroxcuisine\
                                ejb\
                                    WroxCuisineServiceHome.class
                                    WroxCuisineService.class
                                xml\
                                    XSLTransform.class
```

```
                                        helpers\
                                                DirectoryService.class
                        xsl\
                            GetAllRecipes.xsl
                            GetRecipeDetails.xsl
                            GetAllCountriesResponse.xsl
                            GetRecipesByCountryResponse.xsl
```

The `WroxCuisineServiceHome.class` and `WroxCuisineService.class` are the home interface and remote interface of the `WroxCuisineSession` EJB that we developed. Similarly the `DirectoryService.class` is the JNDI helper class that we developed before.

To build this web application, there is a `build-webapp.bat` file, present in the `C:\javawebservices\Ch08\wroxcuisine\web` directory. This file is responsible for compiling the Java classes and generating the web application archive (WAR) file.

The build file is shown below:

build-webapp.bat

```
SET WEBAPP_CLASSESDIR=C:\javawebservices\Ch08\wroxcuisine\web\WEB-INF\classes
set DEPLOY_DIR=%WL_HOME%\config\mydomain\applications

REM Delete the existing Web application
del %DEPLOY_DIR%\wroxcuisineweb.war

@REM This ensures that the WroxCuisine Web Application has the EJB interfaces and
the XML helper files
javac -d %WEBAPP_CLASSESDIR%
..\src\com\wroxcuisine\ejb\WroxCuisineServiceHome.java
..\src\com\wroxcuisine\ejb\WroxCuisineService.java
javac -d %WEBAPP_CLASSESDIR%  ..\src\com\wroxcuisine\xml\XSLTransform.java
javac -d %WEBAPP_CLASSESDIR%  ..\src\com\wroxcuisine\helpers\DirectoryService.java

REM Package into JAR
jar cvf wroxcuisineweb.war *
```

After you run this build file, you will have a `wroxcuisineweb.war` file that is ready for deployment into WebLogic 6.1. The steps for deploying the web application are shown below:

1. Ensure that your WebLogic 6.1 Server instance is running

2. Open your browser and navigate to the WebLogic console utility (http://localhost:7001/console)

3. Select the Web Applications/Install a New Web Application ... option. Select the `wroxcuisineweb.war` file as shown below and click on Upload.

313

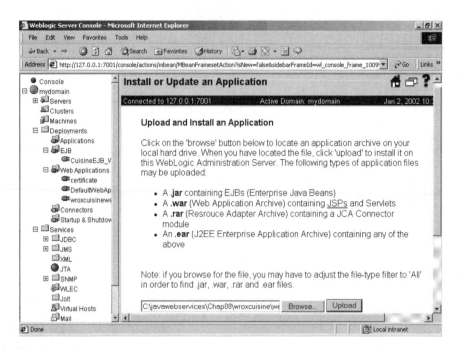

From your browser point to http://localhost:7001/wroxcuisineweb to run your JSP application.

Enabling Web Services

In the next few sections until the end of the chapter, we will:

❑   Take a conceptual look at the programming model for web services

❑   Describe, via working examples, a popular web services platform from CapeClear (http://www.capeclear.com). We will use their platform to expose the functionality that we developed in our EJBs as a web service.

❑   Implement web services clients using a variety of APIs, such as SOAPDirect from CapeClear and Apache SOAP

❑   Cover CapeStudio, a RAD-tool for web services development. We will demonstrate how to rapidly develop clients using CapeStudio by accessing web services from 3rd party brokerages like www.xmethods.net or www.salcentral.com.

Web Services – An Introduction

We have already covered the basics of web services in earlier chapters. We will briefly take you through the web services programming model from the point of view of what we have accomplished so far in this chapter. This will also help set the tone for the remainder of the chapter, when we will actually use the tools to write the web services.

WroxCuisine is the **service provider**. As the service provider, WroxCuisine creates a WSDL document for others to analyze and determine how to invoke their service. Since WroxCuisine is interested that its service reaches a wide audience, it is important that they publish it in a global registry. This is where the **service registry/brokerage** comes into play. The organization that is interested in using some of the external web services completes the picture. They are known as the **service consumer**, who scans brokerages/registries for web services that they may be interested in. Once they are interested in a particular web service, they retrieve the WSDL document for that web service. The WSDL provides them enough information in terms of endpoint URLs, operations, messages, and such that they can invoke the web service over the Internet using an open protocol, like SOAP.

Let's start learning about the web services tools that we can use today to enable existing applications in organizations as web services.

CapeConnect Web Services Platform

CapeConnect from www.capeclear.com is a web services platform that enables web service providers to convert existing EJB, CORBA, and standard Java applications in web services without any additional programming. CapeConnect is available under a 21-day trial basis, and you may get promotional emails once you have downloaded the software.

In the next few sections, we will cover the following:

- ❑ CapeConnect Architecture
- ❑ Configuring CapeConnect with WebLogic, since we are interested in exposing the WroxCuisine EJBs that we developed as a web service
- ❑ Setting up the WroxCuisine service as a web service in CapeConnect

Architecture

The CapeConnect architecture is shown below:

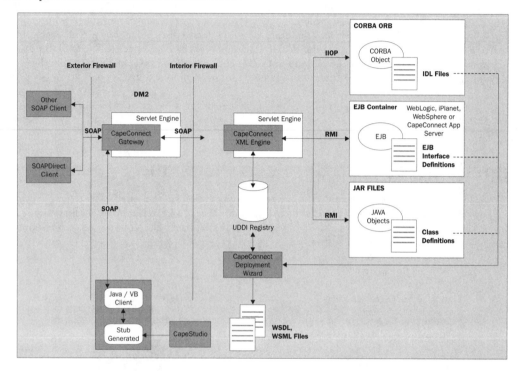

It consists of the following parts:

❑ **CapeConnect Gateway**
This is a servlet that receives the incoming SOAP calls from clients. CapeConnect provides a SOAPDirect API, which makes writing SOAP clients extremely easy. At the same time, you can use any standard SOAP implementation like Apache SOAP to write your clients. We will cover the writing of both SOAPDirect and Apache clients later on in the chapter.

❑ **CapeConnect XML Engine**
The CapeConnect XML engine receives the SOAP requests from the CapeConnect gateway. The XML engine that translates these SOAP requests into appropriate invocations on the EJBs, Java classes, and CORBA classes.

❑ **CapeConnect EJB Server**
One of the major advantages of the CapeConnect platform is that it provides a full-fledged J2EE application server also. This means that you can deploy your EJBs within the CapeConnect J2EE container itself.

❑ **Integration with other J2EE application servers**
CapeConnect provides full connectivity to popular J2EE application Servers like BEA WebLogic, IBM Websphere, Netscape iPlanet Server, and so on. This means that you can continue to deploy your EJBs in the application server of your choice, and by using CapeConnect as your web services platform you can expose those EJBs as web services.

❑ **CapeConnect Deployment Wizard**
CapeConnect also provides a deployment wizard that can generate WSDL files out of EJB interface definitions. This will help in creating WSDL descriptions for your EJBs, which can then be used by service consumers wishing to learn about the capabilities of your web service.

❑ **CapeStudio**
CapeStudio is RAD tool that takes a WSDL definition and generates a VB or Java stub, that can be then used by the containing client application to invoke web services. This would enable an organization to rapidly develop clients that consume web services.

Now that we have looked at the different parts of the CapeConnect architecture, let us move on to enabling our WroxCuisineService session EJB as a web service. Please follow the instructions in Appendix A for installation of CapeConnect Three platform. Make sure that you have configured a WebLogic Server in CapeConnect as specified in the *Identifying WebLogic Server to CapeConnect Three* section.

We know that CapeConnect, along with its web services platform, also provides a full-fledged J2EE application server. But for the purposes of understanding the flexibility of CapeConnect, we will utilize the EJBs that are already deployed in WebLogic. We will then use CapeConnect to configure the EJB component as a web service. It is important to understand that organizations such as WroxCuisine have invested time and money in developing applications before the advent of web services. It is practical to protect this investment in the existing application server and expose that via a tool like CapeConnect.

Configuring the WroxCuisine Web Service in CapeConnect

Before we start to configure our WroxCuisine EJB as a web service, it is important that we refresh what we have seen in the first part of this chapter.

We developed the WroxCuisine application, which provided a list of recipes for cuisine from all around the world. The application, at its business/data layer, consisted of a WroxCuisineService session bean that provided a façade to the datastore information that was represented by the entity beans Country and Recipe.

We exposed the following methods in the WroxCuisineService session EJB:

❑ GetAllCountries()

❑ GetAllRecipes()

❑ GetRecipesByCountry()

❑ GetRecipeDetails()

❑ GetRandomRecipe()

Each of the methods above provided an XML-formatted response. Now, that WroxCuisine has decided to expose this functionality as a web service, we need to take a look at a conceptual diagram of web services again with respect to WroxCuisine:

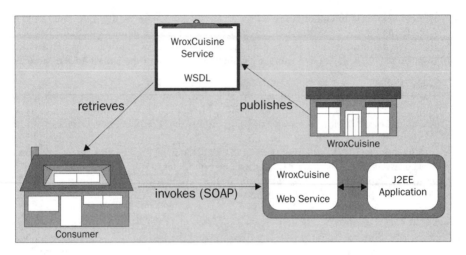

As we can see from the diagram, WroxCuisine would write a web service that could publish its functionality in a WSDL document. This WSDL document will be retrieved by interested consumers, who can then invoke the web service via SOAP.

The CapeConnect architecture allows for web services to be hosted inside its engine. Once it receives a SOAP request, it invokes the WroxCuisineService session bean that is deployed in the WebLogic application server.

In summary, we will expose the WroxCuisineService Session EJB as a web service via the CapeConnect architecture. We will use the CapeConnect deployment wizard to install the web service in CapeConnect and to generate the WSDL files. Additionally, we will develop SOAP clients using SOAPDirect from CapeConnect, and Apache SOAP.

Assuming that you have already started CapeConnect Console, click on the Tools | CapeConnect Deployment Wizard... option from the console window.

This will bring up a window where you need to specify the EJB jar file for the WroxCuisineService EJB that we have developed previously. Select the name of the service as WroxCuisineService. Click on Add and navigate to C:\javawebservices\Ch08\wroxcuisine\src\build\WroxCuisineEJB.jar file as shown below. Select the directory C:\wroxcuisine\wsdl which is where the deployment wizard will create the WSDL file for the same. Click on Next.

This will bring up an additional component information page. We can enter any additional JAR files that our EJB might need here. Since we don't need that, we can leave the entries as they are. Make sure that the JNDI Name is WroxCuisineService. Remember, we deployed the WroxCuisineService EJB in WebLogic with this JNDI name. Click on Next.

This will bring up the WSDL generation options. Since we are not going to be using Microsoft SOAP Clients, we can deselect the WSML generation option. Note the default SOAP endpoint, through which we will be accessing the web service. This is the default SOAP endpoint for CapeConnect Three, so do not modify that for our example. Click on Next.

This will bring us to a very important page. Make sure that the web service name is WroxCuisineService, as the object name is also WroxCuisineService, and make sure that the server is selected correctly – it should be **weblogic_1**, which we configured during the CapeConnect Three installation. Click on Next.

This is where we can publish the web service to the UDDI registry implementation available in CapeConnect Three. Since we are not using the UDDI feature here, uncheck the Publish the Web service in the UDDI Registry box. Click on Next.

This will start generating your WSDL file and the web service setting will be created in CapeConnect Three (it actually adds an entry for your web service in the `webservicemap.xml` file found in `C:\CapeClear\CapeConnectThree\xmlengine\conf` directory). Click on Deploy.

We have now deployed our web service in CapeConnect Three.

To verify that the Web service is deployed in CapeConnect Three, do the following:

❏   In the CapeConnect Console program, click on Edit | Web Service Settings... as shown
below. This will bring up a list of web services deployed currently in CapeConnect.

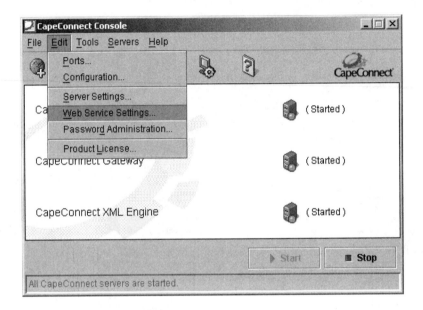

❑ You should be able to find the WroxCuisineService web service listed, as shown below:

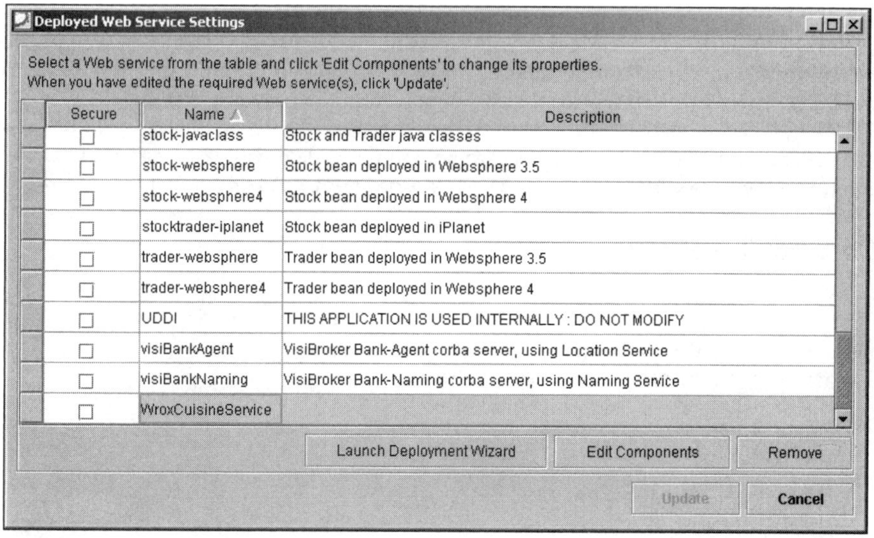

Web Services Clients

Now that we have set up our web service in CapeConnect, it is time to write clients that can use this web service.

Keeping in line with the web services standards, the clients will need to communicate using the SOAP protocol. They will also send SOAP requests over to the CapeConnect gateway, which would then pass the SOAP request to the CapeConnect XML engine. The CapeConnect XML engine will look up the servermap.xml file that retrieves the mapping component name (JNDI) and the server name. It will then delegate the call to the component inside the application server via RMI/IIOP, receive the response, package it as a SOAP response and return it back to the CapeConnect gateway, which gives will then send a SOAP response to the client.

There are different SOAP toolkits that are available in the market that allow you to write client programs that can send and receive SOAP messages. In this chapter we will use the SOAPDirect API, which is a part of the CapeConnect platform itself. Later on we will also take a look at the Apache SOAP toolkit, which is an Open Source SOAP API (see Chapter 3 for more details).

Using SOAPDirect from CapeConnect

The SOAPDirect API is packaged in the form of a JAR file: soapdirect.jar found in the C:\CapeClear\CapeConnectThree\client directory. Basically there are two kinds of objects that encapsulate the SOAP request/reply mechanism:

❑ SDRequest
This object allows us to create and send requests. Each request is a call to a single method in our component – the EJB that we have exposed as a web service

❑ SDReply
This object allows us to receive the result from the method call on the EJB

Let's have a look at the client code that will access our WroxCuisineService web service. The CapeConnectClient.java program uses the SOAPDirect API from CapeClear to invoke the WroxCuisineService web service that we deployed in the previous section.

The CapeConnectClient.java file is available in the code download – copy this to your C:javawebservices\Ch08\wroxcuisine\soapdirect-client directory.

CapeConnectClient.java

```
// Java Program to access Web Service hosted in CapeConnect

import com.capeclear.soapdirect.SDRequest;
import com.capeclear.soapdirect.SDReply;
import com.capeclear.soapdirect.SDFault;
import com.capeclear.soapdirect.SDUtils;
import com.capeclear.soapdirect.SDUri;

import java.io.File;

public class CapeConnectClient {
  public static void main(String[] args) throws Exception {
```

Note that the SOAP endpoint that we had mentioned in the previous section was http://localhost:8080/ccgw/GWXmlServlet, so the code below is just formatting the gatewayURL string to point to that. Also note that the CapeClear gateway runs on port 8080. The gatewayURL is the CapeConnect gateway that will receive the SOAP request from the client program.

```
        String gatewayURL;
        String hostname = "localhost";
        String port = "8080";
        gatewayURL = "http://" + hostname + ":" + port + "/ccgw/GWXmlServlet";
```

These strings define the web service name, the bean name (JNDI) and the method name that we wish to invoke on the bean (EJB).

```
        String appName = "WroxCuisineService";
        String beanName = "WroxCuisineService";
        String opName = "GetAllRecipes";   // Get All Recipes
```

Here we are building the URI of the target object. SDUri is one of the utility classes in the SOAPDirect API that helps in building the target URI. It takes as input the web service name that is, the application name, the bean name, and the method name of the EJB that we wish to invoke.

The URI format in CapeConnect is shown below:

```
capeconnect:applicationName:beanName#methodname
```

The SDRequest object is then initialized with the target URI. In this scenario, we are going to be invoking the GetAllRecipes() method on the bean.

```
SDUri targetURI = SDUtils.toTargetURI(appName, beanName, opName);
SDRequest sdRequest = new SDRequest(targetURI);
```

The method below finally sends the request over to the gatewayURL. Notice that you did not have to code to the SOAP format at all. The invoke() method will make sure internally that your Java code request is translated into the equivalent SOAP request.

```
SDReply reply = sdRequest.invoke(gatewayURL);
if (reply.isFault()) {
  SDFault fault = reply.getFault();
  System.out.println("SOAP Fault Occured");
  System.out.println("Fault Actor: " + fault.getFaultActor());
  System.out.println("Fault Code: " + fault.getFaultCode());
  System.out.println("Fault String: " + fault.getFaultString());
  System.out.println("Fault Detail: " + fault.getFaultDetail());
} else {
  System.out.println("Message returned from server: "
                     + reply.getString());
  }
 }
}
```

Running the CapeConnectClient program

To run the above program, create a directory named
C:\javawebservices\Ch08\wroxcuisine\soapdirect-client. Copy the above file,
CapeConnectClient.java, into this directory, making sure that the following JAR file is in your
system CLASSPATH:

```
C:\CapeClear\CapeConnectThree\client\soapdirect.jar
```

Go to C:\javawebservices\Ch08\wroxcuisine\soapdirect-client and compile the file
as follows:

```
C:\javawebservices\Ch08\wroxcuisine\soapdirect-client>javac CapeConnectClient.java
```

Start the WebLogic server, and then the CapeConnect server. Run the CapeConnectClient.class
file in the directory, as follows:

```
C:\javawebservices\Ch08\wroxcuisine\soapdirect-client>java CapeConnectClient
```

The output of the program is shown below. Notice that the output is the same XML-formatted response for recipes that we described several sections earlier.

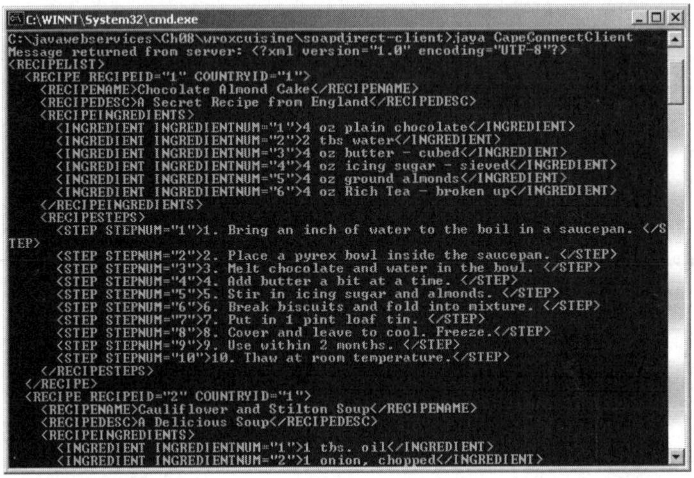

```
C:\javawebservices\Ch08\wroxcuisine\soapdirect-client>java CapeConnectClient
Message returned from server: <?xml version="1.0" encoding="UTF-8"?>
<RECIPELIST>
  <RECIPE RECIPEID="1" COUNTRYID="1">
    <RECIPENAME>Chocolate Almond Cake</RECIPENAME>
    <RECIPEDESC>A Secret Recipe from England</RECIPEDESC>
    <RECIPEINGREDIENTS>
      <INGREDIENT INGREDIENTNUM="1">4 oz plain chocolate</INGREDIENT>
      <INGREDIENT INGREDIENTNUM="2">2 tbs water</INGREDIENT>
      <INGREDIENT INGREDIENTNUM="3">4 oz butter - cubed</INGREDIENT>
      <INGREDIENT INGREDIENTNUM="4">4 oz icing sugar - sieved</INGREDIENT>
      <INGREDIENT INGREDIENTNUM="5">4 oz ground almonds</INGREDIENT>
      <INGREDIENT INGREDIENTNUM="6">4 oz Rich Tea - broken up</INGREDIENT>
    </RECIPEINGREDIENTS>
    <RECIPESTEPS>
      <STEP STEPNUM="1">1. Bring an inch of water to the boil in a saucepan. </S
TEP>
      <STEP STEPNUM="2">2. Place a pyrex bowl inside the saucepan. </STEP>
      <STEP STEPNUM="3">3. Melt chocolate and water in the bowl. </STEP>
      <STEP STEPNUM="4">4. Add butter a bit at a time. </STEP>
      <STEP STEPNUM="5">5. Stir in icing sugar and almonds. </STEP>
      <STEP STEPNUM="6">6. Break biscuits and fold into mixture. </STEP>
      <STEP STEPNUM="7">7. Put in 1 pint loaf tin. </STEP>
      <STEP STEPNUM="8">8. Cover and leave to cool. Freeze.</STEP>
      <STEP STEPNUM="9">9. Use within 2 months. </STEP>
      <STEP STEPNUM="10">10. Thaw at room temperature.</STEP>
    </RECIPESTEPS>
  </RECIPE>
  <RECIPE RECIPEID="2" COUNTRYID="1">
    <RECIPENAME>Cauliflower and Stilton Soup</RECIPENAME>
    <RECIPEDESC>A Delicious Soup</RECIPEDESC>
    <RECIPEINGREDIENTS>
      <INGREDIENT INGREDIENTNUM="1">1 tbs. oil</INGREDIENT>
      <INGREDIENT INGREDIENTNUM="2">1 onion, chopped</INGREDIENT>
```

Using Apache SOAP

Apache SOAP is an Open Source implementation of the SOAP API. It allows us to create SOAP clients that produce, send, and receive SOAP messages. For a detailed look at Apache Soap see Chapter 3.

To use the Apache SOAP API, download the SOAP distribution from http://xml.apache.org/. Unzip the distribution; the main file of importantance to us is the `soap.jar` file. In our setup, the `soap.jar` file is present in the `C:\soap-2_2\lib\` directory.

Add the `soap.jar` file to your system `CLASSPATH`.

Let's take a look at the Java client program written using the Apache SOAP API. Copy the `ApacheSOAPClient.java` file to the `C:\javawebservices\Ch08\wroxcuisine\Apache-client` directory.

ApacheSOAPClient.java

```
import java.net.*;
import java.util.*;

import org.apache.soap.Constants;
import org.apache.soap.Fault;
import org.apache.soap.SOAPException;
import org.apache.soap.rpc.Call;
import org.apache.soap.rpc.Parameter;
import org.apache.soap.rpc.Response;

public class ApacheSOAPClient {
  public static void main(String[] args) throws Exception {

    String endPoint = "http://localhost:8080/ccgw/GWXmlServlet";
```

The `String endPoint` is used to define the CapeConnect gateway endpoint where the SOAP request will be sent.

```
Call call = new Call();
call
  .setTargetObjectURI("capeconnect:WroxCuisineService:WroxCuisineService");
call.setMethodName("GetRecipesByCountry");
call.setEncodingStyleURI(Constants.NS_URI_SOAP_ENC);
Vector params = new Vector();
params.addElement(new Parameter("countryId", String.class, "2", null));
call.setParams(params);
```

We saw in the SOAPDirect API there was the `SDRequest` object, which was used to build the request that had to be sent to the CapeConnect gateway. In the case of Apache SOAP, that class is `Call`. Similar in approach to the SOAPDirect API, the `Call` object is initialized with the target URI that will be interpreted by the CapeConnect XML engine to invoke the method on the appropriate bean.

We provide a parameter to the `GetRecipesByCountry()` method by building a new `Parameter` object. Note that the `GetRecipesByCountry()` method needs a `countyId` that identifies a country. In this case, the `countryId = 2` is passed.

Finally, we send the request over to the `endPoint` using the `invoke()` method as shown below:

```
// Invoke
Response response =
  call
    .invoke(new URL(endPoint),
    "capeconnect:WroxCuisineService:WroxCuisineService#GetRecipesByCountry");

if (!response.generatedFault()) {
  System.out.println("SUCCESS");
  Parameter result = response.getReturnValue();
  System.out.println(result.getValue());
} else {
  System.out.println(response.getFault().getFaultString());
}
  }
}
```

Running the ApacheSOAPClient Program

Create a directory named `C:\javawebservices\Ch08\wroxcuisine\Apache-client`. Copy the above file `ApacheSOAPClient.java` into this directory from the code download, making sure that the following JAR files are in your system `CLASSPATH`:

```
C:\soap-2_2\lib\soap.jar;C:\xerces-1_4_3\xerces.jar
```

(Any XML parser should do, depending on your preference, but it should be namespace-aware.)

Go to `C:\javawebservices\Ch08\wroxcuisine\Apache-client` and compile the file as follows:

```
C:\javawebservices\Ch08\wroxcuisine\Apache-client> javac ApacheSOAPClient.java
```

Start the WebLogic server, and then the CapeConnect server, and then run the
ApacheSOAPClient.class file as follows:

```
C:\javawebservices\Ch08\wroxcuisine\apache-client> java ApacheSOAPClient
```

Using CapeStudio to Generate Client Code for our WroxCuisine Service

We now know how to write SOAP clients to our service using two SOAP libraries: the SOAPDirect
toolkit from CapeConnect and the Apache SOAP toolkit from Apache.

You must have noticed that you had to write the SOAP code for accessing the web service. Wouldn't it
be appropriate to have a tool that can generate the SOAP code for you as a Java stub? Then all you
would need to do is to invoke this Java stub without getting into the specifics of SOAP programming.
Most of these tools need a WSDL definition for a web service, so that they can generate the appropriate
Java code to invoke that web service.

We shall take a look at a tool available from CapeClear itself called **CapeStudio**, which takes WSDL
files and generates Java stubs that we can use to invoke the web service. One thing to note is that
CapeStudio is much more than a simple WSDL-to-Java converter, and also provides a sophisticated
mapping tool to map XML to WSDL, amongst others. For now, we shall only be looking at generating
the web service invocation code from within CapeStudio for the WroxCuisineService web service,
which we have already deployed in CapeConnect Three.

CapeStudio is a **Rapid Application Development (RAD)** tool that is a standalone web services development environment. One of its great features is the ability to take a WSDL file and generate either Java stubs or Visual Basic stubs, which can then be invoked from a Java client program or a VB client program.

This tool therefore presents an extremely productive way of taking WSDL definitions of services and rapidly developing client applications that use these services. Remember that when we deployed the `WroxCuisineService` web service in CapeConnect earlier, we had already generated the WSDL file for the service – `C:\javawebservices\Ch08\wroxcuisine\WroxCuisineService.wsdl`. We shall provide this file to CapeStudio.

> *Please refer to Appendix A where we have provided detailed installation instructions on setting up CapeStudio.*

Start the CapeStudio program. Once the program has started, click on the WSDL Assistant icon shown in the diagram below:

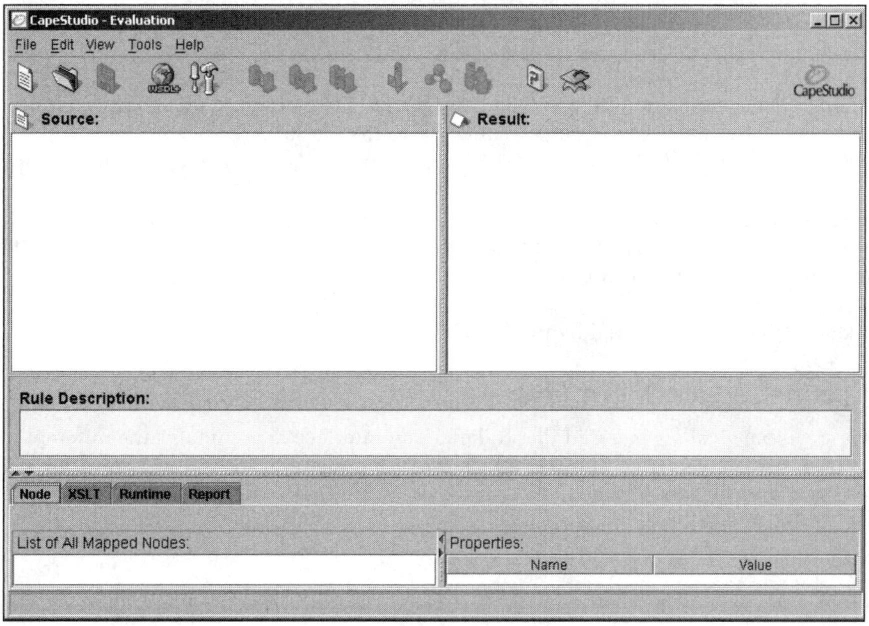

This brings up the WSDL Assistant window as shown below:

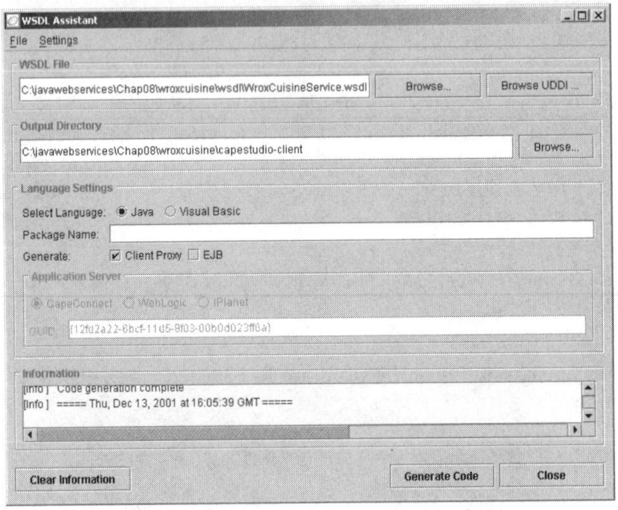

Open **Edit | Web Services Settings**. Select the WSDL file that we generated through the CapeConnect Console. Select the **Target Language** as Java. Give the output directory as `C:\javawebservices\Ch08\wroxcuisineClient` and leave the package name empty.

Click on the **Generate Code** button – this will start generating the Java source code, or in other words, the stubs. We will see the current status shown in the **Information** window. Finally, when the code generation is complete, we can now integrate this stub into our Java code.

Let's look at the code generated by the CapeStudio tool.

WroxCuisineServiceClient.java

This is an automatically generated file. It defines an interface that contains the different methods of the `WroxCuisineWebService`. You will notice that it has methods for `GetAllCountries()`, `GetAllRecipes()`, amongst others.

```
/**
 * WroxCuisineServiceClient
 *
 * Generated by Cape Studio WSDL Assistant : DO NOT MODIFY
 *
 * WSDL Assistant (c) 2001 Cape Clear Software Ltd.
 *
 * Date Generated: ===== Sat, Dec 1, 2001 at 07:23:17 PST =====
 */

/**
 * WroxCuisineServiceClient
 */
public interface WroxCuisineServiceClient {
```

```
/**
 * GetAllCountries
 */
public java.lang.String GetAllCountries ( ) throws java.rmi.RemoteException;

/**
 * GetRecipesByCountry
 */
public java.lang.String GetRecipesByCountry ( int arg0 ) throws
    java.rmi.RemoteException;

/**
 * GetAllRecipes
 */
public java.lang.String GetAllRecipes ( ) throws java.rmi.RemoteException;

/**
 * GetRecipeDetails
 */
public java.lang.String GetRecipeDetails ( int arg0 ) throws
    java.rmi.RemoteException;

/**
 * GetRandomRecipe
 */
public java.lang.String GetRandomRecipe ( ) throws java.rmi.RemoteException;
}
```

WroxCuisineServiceClientImpl.java

Since the above file, `WroxCuisineServiceClient.java`, was an interface, CapeStudio also generates this Java file, which is basically an implementation of the interface. Appropriate SOAPDirect API code is also written to invoke the web service.

```
/**
 * WroxCuisineServiceClientImpl
 *
 * Generated by Cape Studio WSDL Assistant : DO NOT MODIFY
 *
 * WSDL Assistant (c) 2001 Cape Clear Software Ltd.
 *
 * Date Generated: ===== Sat, Dec 1, 2001 at 07:23:17 PST =====
 */

/**
 * WroxCuisineServiceClient Implementation
 */
public class WroxCuisineServiceClientImpl
    extends com.capeclear.capeconnect.soap.proxy.BaseSoapProxy
    implements WroxCuisineServiceClient {
/**
 * Constructor
 *
```

```
 * @param endpointURI the URI of the SOAP Message Router
 */
public WroxCuisineServiceClientImpl ( java.lang.String endpointURI )
    throws java.net.MalformedURLException {
      super(endpointURI);
}
```

This is the SOAPDirect-generated stub for invoking the `GetAllCountries()` method. Notice that the return type is a `String`, that will be our XML-generated response for all the countries in the database. You will notice that it also sets up the SOAP parameters such as calling style.

```
/**
 * GetAllCountries
 */
public java.lang.String GetAllCountries (  ) throws java.rmi.RemoteException{
  java.util.HashMap options = new java.util.HashMap();
  options.put(com.capeclear.capeconnect.soap.proxy.SoapProxy.KEY_CALL_STYLE,
      "rpc");
  options.put(com.capeclear.capeconnect.soap.proxy.SoapProxy.KEY_CALL_USE,
      "encoded");
  options.put(com.capeclear.capeconnect.soap.proxy.SoapProxy.KEY_SCHEMA_VERSION,
      "http://www.w3.org/2001/XMLSchema");
  $_setProxyOptions(options);
```

Finally, it uses the `invokeRequest()` method in the SOAPDirect API to invoke the `GetAllCountries()` method on our web service.

```
java.lang.Object $__result = $_invokeRequest(
    "capeconnect:WroxCuisineService:WroxCuisineService#GetAllCountries",
    "capeconnect:WroxCuisineService:WroxCuisineService",
    "GetAllCountries", new java.lang.String[] {
}, new java.lang.Object[] {
}, java.lang.String.class);
    return (java.lang.String) $__result;
}
```

The remaining stubs below follow a similar pattern, and should be easy to comprehend.

```
/**
 * GetRecipesByCountry
 */
public java.lang.String GetRecipesByCountry ( int arg0 ) throws
    java.rmi.RemoteException{
  java.util.HashMap options = new java.util.HashMap();
  options.put(com.capeclear.capeconnect.soap.proxy.SoapProxy.KEY_CALL_STYLE,
      "rpc");
  options.put(com.capeclear.capeconnect.soap.proxy.SoapProxy.KEY_CALL_USE,
      "encoded");
  options.put(com.capeclear.capeconnect.soap.proxy.SoapProxy
      .KEY_SCHEMA_VERSION, "http://www.w3.org/2001/XMLSchema");
```

```
    $_setProxyOptions(options);

java.lang.Object $__result = $_invokeRequest(
    "capeconnect:WroxCuisineService:WroxCuisineService#GetRecipesByCountry",
    "capeconnect:WroxCuisineService:WroxCuisineService","GetRecipesByCountry",
    new java.lang.String[] {
  "arg0"},

new java.lang.Object[] {
  new java.lang.Integer(arg0)}, java.lang.String.class);
  return (java.lang.String) $__result;
}

/**
 * GetAllRecipes
 */
public java.lang.String GetAllRecipes (  ) throws java.rmi.RemoteException{
  java.util.HashMap options = new java.util.HashMap();
    options.put(com.capeclear.capeconnect.soap.proxy.SoapProxy.KEY_CALL_STYLE,
        "rpc");
    options.put(com.capeclear.capeconnect.soap.proxy.SoapProxy.KEY_CALL_USE,
        "encoded");
    options.put(com.capeclear.capeconnect.soap.proxy.SoapProxy
        .KEY_SCHEMA_VERSION, "http://www.w3.org/2001/XMLSchema");

    $_setProxyOptions(options);

    java.lang.Object $__result = $_invokeRequest(
        "capeconnect:WroxCuisineService:WroxCuisineService#GetAllRecipes",
        "capeconnect:WroxCuisineService:WroxCuisineService",
        "GetAllRecipes", new java.lang.String[] {

    }, new java.lang.Object[] {

    }, java.lang.String.class);
  return (java.lang.String) $__result;
  }

/**
 * GetRecipeDetails
 */
public java.lang.String GetRecipeDetails ( int arg0 )
    throws java.rmi.RemoteException{
  java.util.HashMap options = new java.util.HashMap();
  options.put(com.capeclear.capeconnect.soap.proxy.SoapProxy.KEY_CALL_STYLE,
      "rpc");
  options.put(com.capeclear.capeconnect.soap.proxy.SoapProxy.KEY_CALL_USE,
      "encoded");
  options.put(com.capeclear.capeconnect.soap.proxy.SoapProxy
      .KEY_SCHEMA_VERSION, "http://www.w3.org/2001/XMLSchema");

  $_setProxyOptions(options);

  java.lang.Object $__result = $_invokeRequest(
```

```
          "capeconnect:WroxCuisineService:WroxCuisineService#GetRecipeDetails",
          "capeconnect:WroxCuisineService:WroxCuisineService",
          "GetRecipeDetails", new java.lang.String[] {
        "arg0"
        }, new java.lang.Object[] {
        new java.lang.Integer(arg0)
      },
      java.lang.String.class
    );
    return (java.lang.String) $__result;
  }


  /**
   * GetRandomRecipe
   */
  public java.lang.String GetRandomRecipe (  ) throws java.rmi.RemoteException{
    java.util.HashMap options = new java.util.HashMap();
    options.put(com.capeclear.capeconnect.soap.proxy.SoapProxy.KEY_CALL_STYLE,
        "rpc");
    options.put(com.capeclear.capeconnect.soap.proxy.SoapProxy.KEY_CALL_USE,
        "encoded");
    options.put(com.capeclear.capeconnect.soap.proxy.SoapProxy
        .KEY_SCHEMA_VERSION, "http://www.w3.org/2001/XMLSchema");

    $_setProxyOptions(options);

    java.lang.Object $__result = $_invokeRequest(
        "capeconnect:WroxCuisineService:WroxCuisineService#GetRandomRecipe",
        "capeconnect:WroxCuisineService:WroxCuisineService",
        "GetRandomRecipe", new java.lang.String[] {
      }, new java.lang.Object[] {
    }, java.lang.String.class);
    return (java.lang.String) $__result;
  }
}
```

WroxCuisineServiceClientFactory.java

This is the factory class that we will use in our Java program. Notice that the create() method requires the endPoint URL. The create() method will return an instance of the WroxCuisineServiceClient. Given the instance of this class, one can easily invoke the methods on the service, such as GetRecipesByCountry(), and so on.

```
/**
 * WroxCuisineServiceClientFactory.java
 *
 * Generated by Cape Studio WSDL Assistant : DO NOT MODIFY
 *
 * WSDL Assistant (c) 2001 Cape Clear Software Ltd.
 *
 * Date Generated: ===== Sat, Dec 1, 2001 at 07:23:17 PST =====
 */
```

```java
/**
 * Client Factory
 */
public class WroxCuisineServiceClientFactory {

  private static java.util.HashMap options = new java.util.HashMap();
  static {
    options.put(com.capeclear.capeconnect.soap.proxy.SoapProxy.KEY_CALL_STYLE,
        "rpc");
    options.put(com.capeclear.capeconnect.soap.proxy.SoapProxy.KEY_CALL_USE,
        "encoded");
    options.put(com.capeclear.capeconnect.soap.proxy.SoapProxy.KEY_SCHEMA_VERSION,
        "http://www.w3.org/2001/XMLSchema");
  }

  static {com.capeclear.xml.schema.types.SchemaTypeRegistry registry =
    com.capeclear.xml.schema.types.SchemaTypeRegistry.getInstance();
  }

  private static java.lang.String ENDPOINT =
      "http://localhost:8080/ccgw/GWXmlServlet";

  /**
   * create
   */
  public static WroxCuisineServiceClient create( )
      throws java.net.MalformedURLException {
    WroxCuisineServiceClientImpl impl = new WroxCuisineServiceClientImpl(
        ENDPOINT);
    impl.$_setProxyOptions((java.util.Map)options.clone());
    return impl;
  }

  /**
   * create
   *
   * @param username the services user name
   * @param password the users password
   */
  public static WroxCuisineServiceClient create( java.lang.String username, char[]
      password ) throws java.net.MalformedURLException {
    WroxCuisineServiceClientImpl impl = new WroxCuisineServiceClientImpl(
        ENDPOINT );
    impl.$_setCallerCredentials(username, password);
    impl.$_setProxyOptions((java.util.Map)options.clone());
    return impl;
  }

  /**
   * create
   *
   * @param endpoint the URI to the SOAP message router
   */
  public static WroxCuisineServiceClient create( java.lang.String endpoint )
```

```
        throws java.net.MalformedURLException {
    WroxCuisineServiceClientImpl impl = new WroxCuisineServiceClientImpl(
        endpoint );
    impl.$_setProxyOptions((java.util.Map)options.clone());
    return impl;
}


/**
 * create
 *
 * @param endpoint the URI of the SOAP message router
 * @param username the services user name
 * @param password the users password
 */
public static WroxCuisineServiceClient create( java.lang.String endpoint,
        java.lang.String username, char[] password )
    throws java.net.MalformedURLException {
    WroxCuisineServiceClientImpl impl = new WroxCuisineServiceClientImpl(
        endpoint );
    impl.$_setCallerCredentials(username, password);
    impl.$_setProxyOptions((java.util.Map)options.clone());
    return impl;
    }
}
```

Now, that we have seen the generated code, let's take a look at the client program to access the same service method: GetRecipesByCountry().

TestCuisineService.java

```
public class TestCuisineService {
  public static void main(String[] args) {
    try {
```

We first invoke the static method on the factory class, WroxCuisineServiceClientFactory, which will return us a WroxCuisineServiceClient instance. Since the return type is an interface, we typecast it with an appropriate implementation, WroxCuisineSericeClientImpl, that has been generated for us by CapeStudio.

```
        WroxCuisineServiceClientImpl client =
            (WroxCuisineServiceClientImpl) WroxCuisineServiceClientFactory.create();
```

Now we can invoke methods on the implementation class, as shown below for GetAllRecipes().

```
        System.out.println(client.GetAllRecipes());
    } catch (Exception e) {
        System.out.println(e);
    }
  }
}
```

You should be impressed by the fact that all we need to do now is just invoke the method. We don't even need to know about the SOAPDirect calls.

Note that by using CapeStudio, we can eliminate the errors that might creep in if we attempted to write all the invocation code ourselves. Another benefit that this approach provides is that we alienate ourselves from knowing the SOAP API. We can simply use these stubs to invoke the web services without getting into the specifics of any particular SOAP API.

Running the TestCuisineService Program

Go to the `C:\javawebservices\Ch08\wroxcuisine\capestudio-client` directory. Copy the above file `TestCuisineService.java` into this directory, making sure that the following JAR files are in your system `CLASSPATH`:

```
C:\CapeClear\CapeStudio\lib\soapdirect.jar
C:\CapeClear\CapeStudio\lib\studiosoap.jar
```

Go to `C:\javawebservices\Ch08\wroxcuisine\capestudio-client` and compile all the above files as follows:

```
C:\javawebservices\Ch08\wroxcuisine\capestudio-client>javac *.java
```

Make sure that WebLogic Server and CapeConnect have been started, and run the `WorldCuisineClient.class` file as follows:

```
C:\ javawebservices\Ch08\wroxcuisine\capestudio-client>java TestCuisineService
```

Notice that the output (shown below) is the same XML-formatted response for recipes that we have observed in the previous programs.

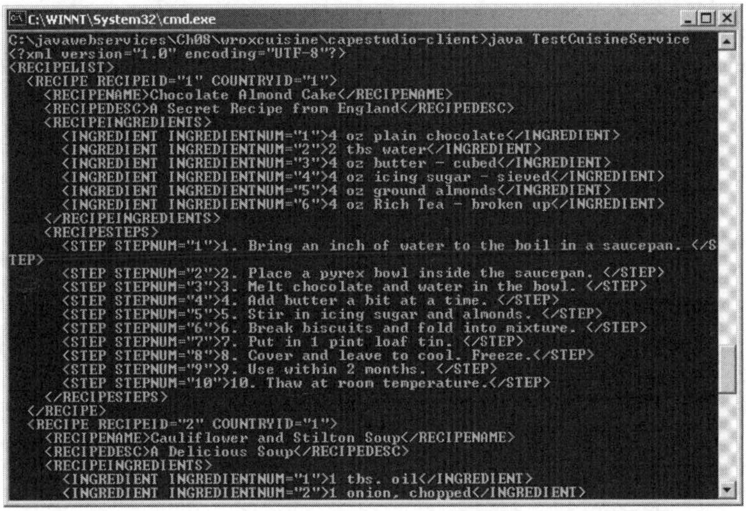

Using CapeStudio to Access Third Party Web Services

In this section, we will look at how WroxCuisine can publicize its cuisine web service. We will take a look at a growing number of organizations that are calling themselves **web services brokerages**. We will then see how we can access a third-party web service hosted at one of these brokerage houses.

Web Service Brokerage/Registry

What is a web service brokerage? In simple terms, it is a repository of web services from different clients. This repository is then searched by prospective client organizations that are interested in looking for a particular web service to augment their current existing application. Take a look at the diagram shown below:

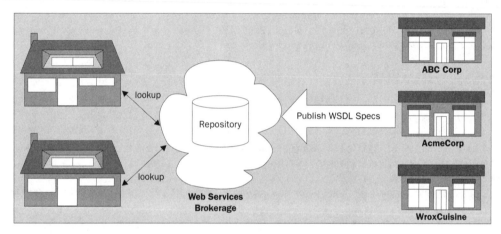

Organizations like WroxCuisine, AcmeCorp (and so on) are interested in ensuring that the web services that they provide are publicized to a large number of organizations. This method acts as a very effective marketing tool. As we learnt before, publishing their WSDL specification details would provide enough information to a consumer organization to check out the different operations exposed by the web service, and since the WSDL contains endpoint information, that would be sufficient for them to invoke the web service.

Consumer organizations on the other hand visit these web services brokerage houses to look up the directory of published web services. If they find a particular web service interesting, and they are interested in trying it out, they can obtain the WSDL for that service and understand the different methods, their parameters, endpoint URL, and so on.

So, web services brokerages in short are bringing together a very large audience that is interested in renting components rather than building them from scratch. At the same time, it would not be fair to say that web services brokerages host just a collection of web services. They provide a host of other features too, such as watching a web service for any change in WSDL definitions, and so on.

It should now be easy for you to understand how we can use the CapeConnect platform to generate our WSDL file and send the details to a web services brokerage like SalCentral or X-Methods (www.xmethods.net).

X-Methods Directory

In this section, we will take a look at X-Methods, which provides a registry of hundreds of web services. These are web services that we can use in our applications today.

Let's assume that we are a fictitious company called WroxSoft, that is interested in setting up a portal for all technical books. WroxSoft wants to retrieve prices from a popular online bookstore, such as Barnes and Noble (www.bn.com). So, given an ISBN number for the book, WroxSoft wants to retrieve the price for the same at Barnes and Noble. We are lucky that there is exactly such a web service hosted at www.xmethods.net, the particular url (http://www.xmethods.net/detail.html?id=7) for which is shown below:

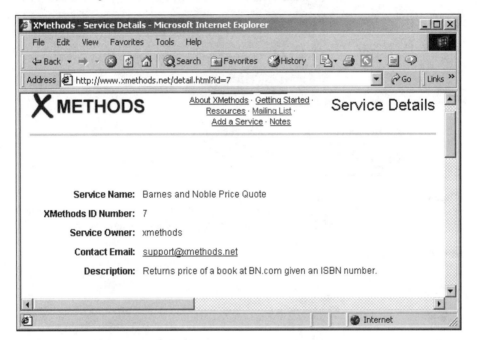

The steps to actually invoke the service would be as follows:

❑ Download the WSDL file for the service. If you notice in the screenshot above, there is a WSDL URL. Just click on the file and save the `BNQuoteService.wsdl` file to the `C:\javawebservices\Ch08\wroxcuisine\xmethods` directory.

❑ Generate the Java stubs for the WSDL file using CapeStudio WSDL Assistant. Shown below is the WSDL Assistant for generating the stubs:

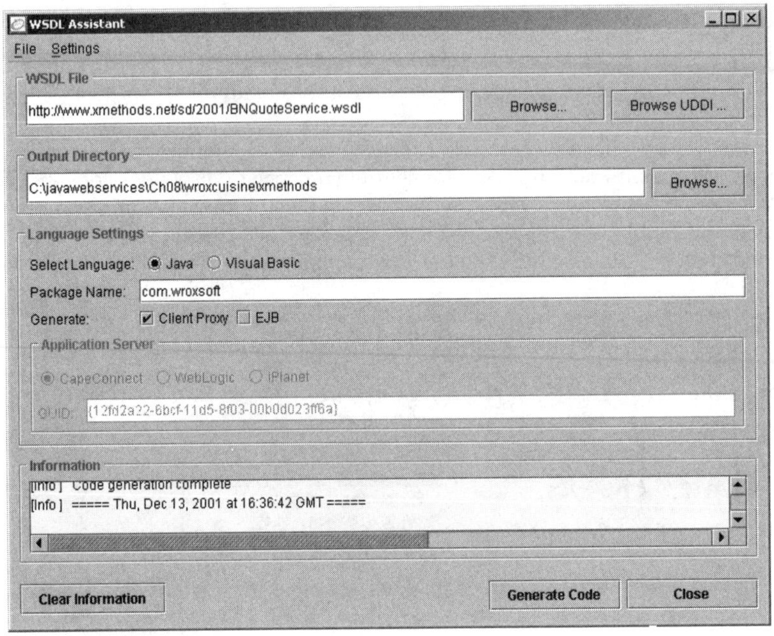

The CapeStudio WSDL Assistant generates the Java stubs in the same fashion as our `WroxCuisineWebService`. Look at the stubs shown below. Do not worry about the generated code, it is quite simple to understand, and follows a similar pattern to the code generated previously.

BNQuotePortTypeClient.java

```java
/**
 * BNQuotePortTypeClient
 *
 * Generated by Cape Studio WSDL Assistant : DO NOT MODIFY
 *
 * WSDL Assistant (c) 2001 Cape Clear Software Ltd.
 *
 * Date Generated: ===== Thu, Nov 29, 2001 at 05:59:13 PST =====
 */
        package com.wroxsoft;

/**
 * BNQuotePortTypeClient
 */
public interface BNQuotePortTypeClient {

  /**
   * getPrice
   */
  public float getPrice ( java.lang.String isbn ) throws java.rmi.RemoteException;
}
```

BNQuotePortTypeClientImpl.java

```java
/**
 * BNQuotePortTypeClientImpl
 *
 * Generated by Cape Studio WSDL Assistant : DO NOT MODIFY
 *
 * WSDL Assistant (c) 2001 Cape Clear Software Ltd.
 *
 * Date Generated: ===== Thu, Nov 29, 2001 at 05:59:13 PST =====
 */
package com.wroxsoft;

/**
 * BNQuotePortTypeClient Implementation
 */
public class BNQuotePortTypeClientImpl
    extends com.capeclear.capeconnect.soap.proxy.BaseSoapProxy
    implements BNQuotePortTypeClient {

    /**
     * Constructor
     *
     * @param endpointURI the URI of the SOAP Message Router
     */
    public BNQuotePortTypeClientImpl ( java.lang.String endpointURI )
        throws java.net.MalformedURLException {
      super(endpointURI);
    }

    /**
     * getPrice
     */
    public float getPrice ( java.lang.String isbn )
        throws java.rmi.RemoteException {
      java.util.HashMap options = new java.util.HashMap();
      options.put(com.capeclear.capeconnect.soap.proxy.SoapProxy.KEY_CALL_STYLE,
          "rpc");
      options.put(com.capeclear.capeconnect.soap.proxy.SoapProxy.KEY_CALL_USE,
          "encoded");

      $_setProxyOptions(options);

      java.lang.Object $__result = $_invokeRequest("", "urn:xmethods-
          BNPriceCheck", "getPrice", new java.lang.String[] {"isbn"},
          new java.lang.Object[] {isbn }, java.lang.Float.class);
      return ((java.lang.Float)$__result).floatValue();
    }
  }
```

BNQuotePortTypeClientFactory.java

```java
/**
 * BNQuotePortTypeClientFactory.java
 *
 * Generated by Cape Studio WSDL Assistant : DO NOT MODIFY
 *
 * WSDL Assistant (c) 2001 Cape Clear Software Ltd.
 *
 * Date Generated: ===== Thu, Nov 29, 2001 at 05:59:13 PST =====
 */
package com.wroxsoft;

/**
 * Client Factory
 */
public class BNQuotePortTypeClientFactory {

  private static java.util.HashMap options = new java.util.HashMap();

  static {
    options.put(com.capeclear.capeconnect.soap.proxy.SoapProxy.KEY_CALL_STYLE,
        "rpc");
    options.put(com.capeclear.capeconnect.soap.proxy.SoapProxy.KEY_CALL_USE,
        "encoded");
  }

  static {
    com.capeclear.xml.schema.types.SchemaTypeRegistry registry =
        com.capeclear.xml.schema.types.SchemaTypeRegistry.getInstance();
  }

  private static java.lang.String ENDPOINT =
      "http://services.xmethods.net:80/soap/servlet/rpcrouter";

  /**
   * create
   */
  public static BNQuotePortTypeClient create( )
      throws java.net.MalformedURLException {
    BNQuotePortTypeClientImpl impl = new BNQuotePortTypeClientImpl( ENDPOINT );
    impl.$_setProxyOptions((java.util.Map)options.clone());
    return impl;
  }

  /**
   * create
   *
   * @param username the services user name
   * @param password the users password
   */
  public static BNQuotePortTypeClient create( java.lang.String username, char[]
      password ) throws java.net.MalformedURLException {
    BNQuotePortTypeClientImpl impl = new BNQuotePortTypeClientImpl( ENDPOINT );
    impl.$_setCallerCredentials(username, password);
```

```
    impl.$_setProxyOptions((java.util.Map)options.clone());
    return impl;
  }

  /**
   * create
   *
   * @param endpoint the URI to the SOAP message router
   */
  public static BNQuotePortTypeClient create( java.lang.String endpoint )
      throws java.net.MalformedURLException {
    BNQuotePortTypeClientImpl impl = new BNQuotePortTypeClientImpl( endpoint );
    impl.$_setProxyOptions((java.util.Map)options.clone());
    return impl;
  }

  /**
   * create
   *
   * @param endpoint the URI of the SOAP message router
   * @param username the services user name
   * @param password the users password
   */
  public static BNQuotePortTypeClient create( java.lang.String endpoint,
      java.lang.String username, char[] password ) throws
      java.net.MalformedURLException {
    BNQuotePortTypeClientImpl impl = new BNQuotePortTypeClientImpl( endpoint );
    impl.$_setCallerCredentials(username, password);
    impl.$_setProxyOptions((java.util.Map)options.clone());
    return impl;
  }
}
```

Now, let's look at a simple Java client program to test the stub. Of course `WroxSoft` would implement a call to this stub in a more integrated fashion, within the context of a larger application, but for the purposes of our understanding, it should be sufficient to see it work via a Java client program.

BNQuoteClient.java

```
package com.wroxsoft;

public class BNQuoteClient {
  public static void main(String[] args) {
    try {
      String endPoint =
        "http://services.xmethods.net:80/soap/servlet/rpcrouter";
      BNQuotePortTypeClient client =
        BNQuotePortTypeClientFactory.create(endPoint);
      float pricequote =
        client.getPrice("1861005083");   // Wrox - Professional EJB
      System.out.println("Price at BN is : $" + pricequote);
    } catch (Exception e) {
      System.out.println(e.getMessage());
    }
  }
}
```

Notice that from the X-Methods URL for the Barnes and Noble Quote Service, we obtain the endpoint URL, where the service call will be intercepted. We pass that in the client program shown above. The rest of the code is a simple invocation of the `getPrice()` method exposed by the web service.

Running the BNQuoteClient Program

In order to run this program, go to the
`C:\javawebservices\Ch08\wroxcuisine\xmethods\com\wroxsoft` directory and copy the
`BNQuoteClient.java` file into this directory, making sure that the following JAR files are in your
system CLASSPATH:

```
C:\CapeClear\CapeStudio\lib\soapdirect.jar
C:\CapeClear\CapeStudio\lib\studiosoap.jar
```

Go to `C:\javawebservices\Ch08\wroxcuisine\xmethods` directory and compile all the files as
follows:

```
C:\javawebservices\Ch08\wroxcuisine\xmethods>javac com/wroxsoft/*.java
```

Run the `BNQuoteClient.class` file as follows:

```
C:\javawebservices\Ch08\wroxcuisine\xmethods>java com.wroxsoft.BNQuoteClient
```

The output is shown below:

```
C:\WINNT\System32\cmd.exe

C:\javawebservices\Ch08\wroxcuisine\xmethods>javac com/wroxsoft/*.java

C:\javawebservices\Ch08\wroxcuisine\xmethods>java com.wroxsoft.BNQuoteClient
Price at BN is : $59.99

C:\javawebservices\Ch08\wroxcuisine\xmethods>
```

Summary

Web services are here to stay. It is evident that in the near future, organizations will be interested in
taking existing applications that they already have in-house, and exposing certain parts of that
functionality as web services. Organizations will be able to broadcast their services to a larger audience,
and since web services are built on open-interoperable standards, organizations stand to gain immensely
in terms of integration costs, interoperability across different platforms, and so on. At the same time, just
as we have learnt from software experience that it is a good practice to use existing reusable code, it is
recommended to look at the web services that already exist and utilize the services that they offer.

During the course of this chapter, we covered the following:

❑ Implementation and deployment of a J2EE application: WroxCuisine on WebLogic Server 6.1

❑ Exploration of the CapeConnect web services platform, exposing existing EJBs as web services

❑ Creation of a variety of web service clients, using CapeClear's SOAPDirect and Apache SOAP

❑ Examination of CapeStudio, which is a RAD-tool for web services development, and its ability
to generate stubs from WSDL definitions of existing web services

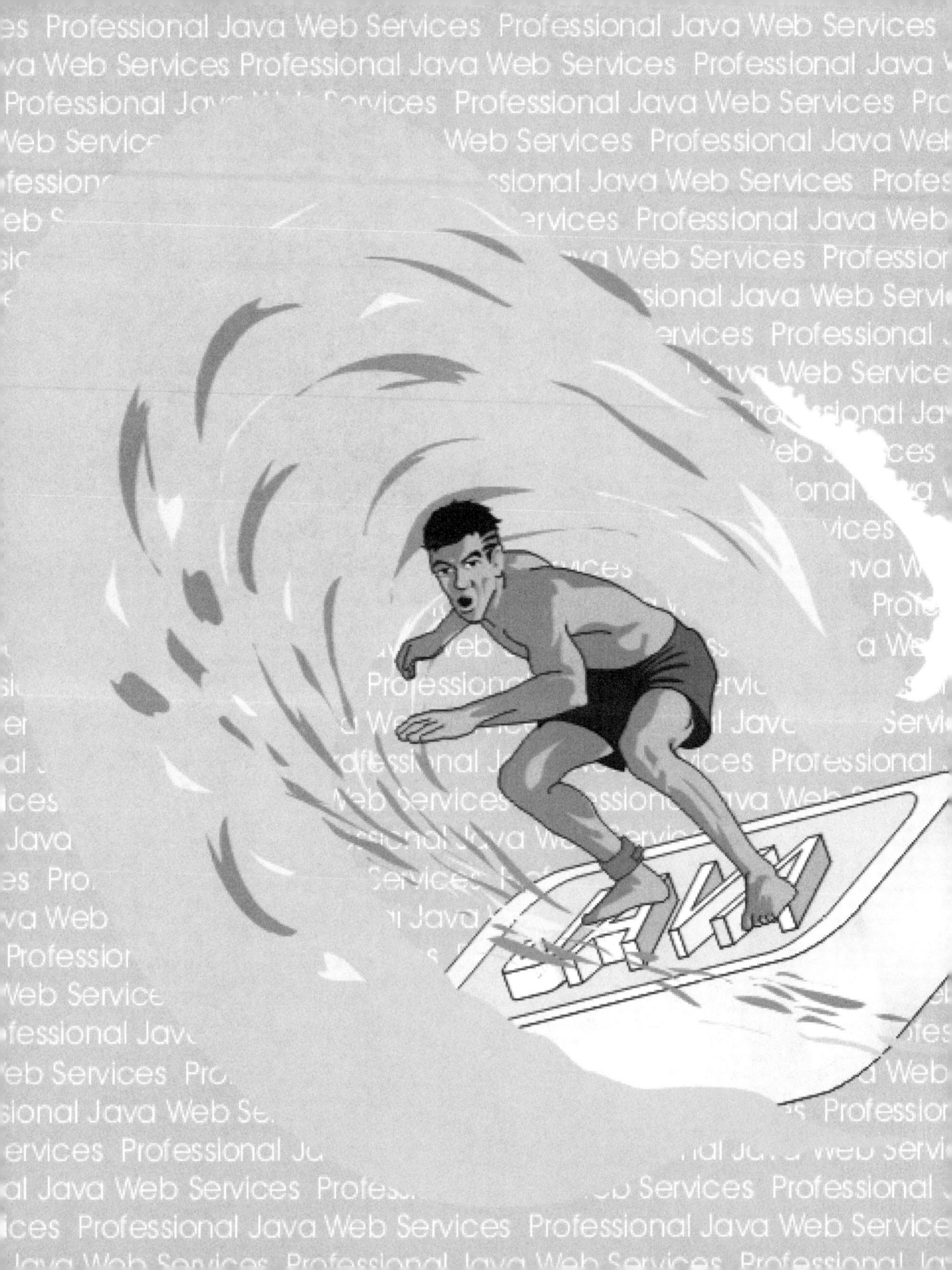
Professional Java Web Services

SAP and Web Services

One of the primary goals of the various Web Services initiatives is to tie together disparate systems in a loosely coupled manner. Buyers want to be able to submit data to suppliers in an on-line electronic format without the need for formal application-to-application integration. Many such organizations are looking to connect their own homegrown business systems to their business partners' proprietary systems.

However, the vast majority of large organizations rely on commercial Enterprise Resource Planning (ERP) applications and Customer Relationship Management (CRM) applications for their enterprise business needs. SAP is considered by many to be the world's leading provider of collaborative e-business solutions – which include both the ERP and CRM spectrums (among others).

Analysts estimate that SAP has over 36,000 installations serving 10 million users at 13,500 organizations in 120 countries across the globe. Founded in 1972 by five former IBM systems engineers, SAP has been in the enterprise software business for over 29 years. Organizations that rely on SAP's R/3 product for their enterprise e-business needs will want to provide a Web Services layer on top of their R/3.

Customers can then access these systems directly, and make the external R/3 software part and parcel of their own business processes. In this chapter we'll take a look at SAP's product and investigate some strategies for using Web Services with SAP.

> **Throughout the remainder of this chapter we will use the term "SAP" to refer generically to both the R/3 and mySAP products.**

Topics covered in this chapter include:

❑   An Introduction to mySAP and R/3

❑   SAP's Programming Interfaces

❑   SAP Internet Business Framework

❑   SAP's Middleware Architecture

❑   Using Java to Connect to SAP as a Web Service with bTalk

❑   SAP's Future Technology Direction

Introduction to mySAP and R/3

SAP released a client-server version of its Enterprise Resource Planning application under the name "**R/3**" back in 1992. The SAP R/3 product was delivered as a three-tier client-server architecture that consisted of a database layer, a business layer (of sorts), and a presentation layer. SAP built the R/3 product using its own proprietary fourth-generation language called **Advanced Business Application Programming (ABAP)**.

The R/3 software has undergone a number of revisions since its original release in 1992. The most recent, Internet-enabled version of SAP's product line is marketed under the name "mySAP". Through mySAP (http://www.mysap.com/) the R/3 product is morphing from a single, tightly integrated product into a more open, component-based system. The mySAP product allows customers to build highly customized, loosely coupled systems based upon the underlying R/3 framework.

SAP offers a very comprehensive set of enterprise application products:

❑   mySAP Enterprise Portals

❑   mySAP Supply Chain Management

❑   mySAP Customer Relationship Management

❑   mySAP E-Procurement

❑   mySAP Product Lifecycle Management

❑   mySAP Business Intelligence

❑   mySAP Financials

❑   mySAP Human Resources

❑   mySAP Mobile Business

❑   mySAP Marketplace by SAPMarkets

❑   mySAP Hosted Solutions

❑   mySAP Technology

Each of these large solution offerings features a number of sub-modules, for example Supply Chain Management would include modules such as Materials Management, Quality Management, and Plant Maintenance. Customers are free to implement only those modules that are specific to their needs. SAP supplies a default mySAP system and the customer is free to modify the functionality of the individual SAP modules through SAP's programming interfaces.

SAP's Programming Interfaces

SAP insulates the developer from the complexities of the underlying SAP system through the concept of **Business Objects**. Real-world objects (for example a purchase or an employee time card) are modeled as business objects in the R/3 System. The SAP Business Objects are essentially black boxes that contain the data and the business rules for the individual business object. Essentially, the SAP Business Objects form the traditional Business Tier – data and processing rules.

An application program that accesses a SAP Business Object and its data only needs certain "required" information to execute the object's methods. Therefore, a developer can work with the SAP Business Objects and invoke their methods without understanding the object's underlying implementation details. For example, the programmer need not care about the complexity of the employee time card, provided that they can retrieve, update, insert, and delete time card records through a simple programming interface.

To achieve this encapsulation, the SAP Business Objects are constructed as entities with multiple layers as shown in the following figure. There are four layers that together create the SAP Business Objects – the Kernel, the data Integrity layer, the Interfaces, and the Access layer:

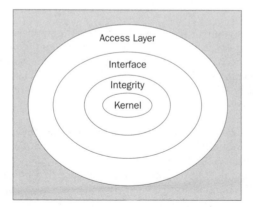

The core of a SAP Business Object is the **Kernel**, which represents the core data for an object. The Kernel of the Employee Time Card object would be the physical database object that stores the time card. The **Integrity layer** holds the business logic of the object – the business rules and constraints that apply to the Business Object. This layer manages aspects such as data integrity rules for the Employee Time Card Object, for example a data integrity rule might limit the number of hours for the time card to less than fifty. It also controls the referential integrity of Business Objects interfaced with other business objects in the SAP system, such as ensuring that the employee ID that you enter for a time card object matches a valid employee record.

The **Interface layer** documents the implementation and structure of the SAP Business Object, and defines the object's interface to the outside world. The Interface layer defines the attributes and methods that the object exposes to the outside world. In the case of the Employee Time Card, this would include attributes such as hours, employee ID, job code, and so on. This would also include any methods that are exposed to the developer, such as the ability to add new time card records, update existing records, or calculate employee pay from a time card record.

The last layer of the Business Object is the **Access layer** and is the most conceptual of the four layers. The tools and technologies that developers use to access the third layer (the Interface) *are* found in the **Access layer**. Thus, both Java and Web Services are representative of the components that might be used in the Access layer.

Each of SAP's Business Objects behaves in a similar fashion to conventional programming objects, such as those in Java. All SAP Business Object types and their methods are identified and described in the **Business Object Repository (BOR)**, which is essentially the "data dictionary" for SAP's objects. The Interface layer shows the Business Objects as they are defined in the BOR. Through the Interface layer, developers can determine how to access SAP Business Objects and access the data contained within the objects. In the simplest form, the Interface Layer is the programmer's "Application Programming Interface" (API) for SAP. There are three main Interface types in the SAP System:

❑   Business APIs (BAPIs)

❑   Remote Function Calls (RFCs)

❑   Intermediate Documents (IDocs)

Business APIs

Business Application Programming Interfaces (BAPIs) are the standard programming interface for SAP. BAPIs are based on an object-oriented concept and are stored in the BOR in the SAP environment. Through the BAPI layer, SAP insulates the developer from the complexities of the underlying objects. The BAPI provides access to high-level methods for objects as well as lower-level services such as database commits and rollbacks. Programmers can use the BAPI directly within other languages such as Microsoft's Visual Basic and IBM's Visual Age for Java.

SAP offers a library of pre-built BAPIs, and customers can create their own BAPI objects and store them in the same BOR. The critical difference between the two is that SAP's built-in BAPIs will be more stable, having a longer history. SAP-supplied BAPIs are not normally affected by changes to the underlying SAP software or data. Programmers can reference BAPI objects within ABAP programs (see the *Remote Function Call* section for details on ABAP).

BAPIs can be used for both synchronous and asynchronous communication to a SAP component. Internally, SAP handles synchronous and asynchronous communications differently. Synchronous operations require the host program to wait for the function to complete, while asynchronous operations work like a message queue. For example, a communication from within SAP to an external application (such as an Electronic Data Interchange message) does not require the host program to wait for the operation to complete before it can continue forward. Synchronous BAPI calls are managed by **Remote Function Calls**.

Remote Function Call

The Remote Function Call (RFC) is the SAP version of the venerable Remote Procedure Call technology. RFCs are very simple and straightforward, and they require minimal overhead. SAP has built the RFC technology into the ABAP language, so it is a core capability of SAP R/3 and mySAP.

As mentioned earlier, SAP's own internal proprietary programming language is ABAP. SAP provides an interactive development environment (ABAP Workbench) that developers can use to write ABAP code. SAP built the R/3 system using ABAP and the latest version, ABAP Objects, is an object-oriented version of ABAP. R/3 will run applications written using ABAP as well as applications using ABAP Objects. ABAP Objects use a single inheritance model and offer support for object features such as encapsulation, polymorphism, and persistence. The original version of ABAP was more like a traditional structured language, much like a cross between Oracle's PL/SQL and COBOL.

RFCs are stored in the RFC Library, but BAPIs can also be accessed by RFCs. Although SAP provides a large library of BAPIs, customers may need to resort to writing custom RFCs for a number of reasons:

❑ Customer-modifications to SAP database tables will cause BAPIs based on those tables to break. While it is not common for SAP developers to modify the core database tables, this does occasionally happen. In such cases, it may be necessary to create a custom RFC to replace a standard BAPI object that no longer works.

❑ When SAP does not provide a BAPI for the required task or business process.

❑ When a custom-built RFC is needed to resolve specific performance issues.

SAP developers can use RFCs to transmit data to external systems. However, SAP provides a specialized set of tools for moving data between systems that simplifies this process.

Intermediate Documents (IDocs)

Intermediate Documents (IDocs) are designed to facilitate the exchange of information between SAP systems and external systems (although they can be used for SAP to SAP transmissions as well). IDocs are nothing more than simple ASCII data streams. These data streams can be stored as formatted disk files.

An IDoc might be used to represent all of the information for a single employee, or all of the data for a complete customer invoice. IDoc data exchanges are called messages, just as Electronic Data Interchange (EDI) data files are called messages. The processing logic for IDoc messages follows the "normal course" of the operation of a SAP system.

First, the SAP Application creates/updates data through normal functions, ABAP programs, and so on. Messages for the IDocs system are stored in a SAP message table (usually NAST). The NAST table serves as a sort of message queue. Messages are stored as records in the table, which are then picked up by other SAP programs via the IDoc "engine".

The IDoc engine reviews messages and calls functions to create the appropriate output file. SAP R/3 systems can exchange messages with external systems through the IDocs subsystem as shown in the following figure:

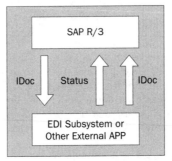

The IDocs mechanism is ideal for transferring data between disparate systems (or multiple SAP systems). SAP can write IDocs messages directly to data ports – which can connect directly to external systems via TCP/IP or HTTP. SAP can also write IDocs messages as ASCII disk files, which can be transmitted via e-mail or FTP. IDocs share some similarity with the SOAP protocol itself. SAP provides several built-in "bindings" for IDocs messages, such as HTTP and FTP. Data is sent to these protocols in a very structured, standardized format.

Each IDoc comprises a control record and a data record (or records). The control record stores the administrative information for the IDoc – including origin/destination and a description of the contents. Programmers are responsible for writing functions to handle each inbound and outbound IDocs message. The control record maps the IDocs message to the appropriate "program" or function.

The control record has a fixed format structure, as defined in the data dictionary. The control record acts like the basic address information for an IDoc message. IDoc data "records" fill the remainder of the IDoc message. Each data record is structured as a fixed length line of 1000 characters in length. Each record contains a segment name, followed by the segment data. Each segment name matches an associated data dictionary structure in the SAP system. IDocs data can contain multiple hierarchies, such as order headers and order details. Thus, a single IDocs message can hold a great deal of information.

By default, SAP manages inbound and outbound IDocs through a series of tables (EDID4 and EDIDC). However, the SAP programmer can create custom ABAP routines to manage IDoc messages and bypass SAP's own internal mechanisms. SAP implements EDI through the IDocs mechanism. R/3 uses preformatted RFC servers for inbound and outbound EDI messages.

Summarizing External Access Strategies

BAPI, RFC, and IDocs form the core of SAP's external access strategy. These technologies can be used individually or together to access data within the SAP environment. The BAPIs provide the most stable access to core SAP functions, and SAP offers an enormous array of BAPI objects with mySAP and R/3. RFCs provide a lower-level access to SAP. Programmers can attain improved performance and have a finer grain of control over SAP through RFC routines. IDocs offer the simplest mechanism for moving data between disparate SAP systems (and third-party systems). Message-transfer applications, such as EDI, are best implemented by using IDocs. In the next section, we'll concentrate on the middleware technology that allows external code, such as Java, to gain access to BAPIs and RFCs within SAP.

SAP Internet-Business Framework

SAP's mySAP software is built on an architecture that supports a collaborative, web-based approach to enterprise computing. SAP calls its architecture the **Internet-Business Framework**, and it is composed of a number of technologies including the SAP portal technology, Exchange infrastructure, and the SAP Web Application server.

SAP comes equipped with hundreds of different interface objects – namely the BAPIs and RFCs that were described in the preceding sections. The combination of SAP's middleware technology and APIs forms the core of the Internet-Business Framework. In order to make these objects as accessible as possible, SAP offers the **Interface Repository** (IFR). IFR is an XML-based web repository and its aim is to publish all **standard** SAP interfaces centrally.

The IFR contains XML-based implementations of all of the BAPI, RFC, and IDocs interfaces. Developers can access the IFR through a public web site that is managed by SAP: http://ifr.sap.com/. At the highest level of the hierarchy the IFR organizes the interfaces by SAP version (46C, 46B, and so on.) and major subsystems as shown in the following figure:

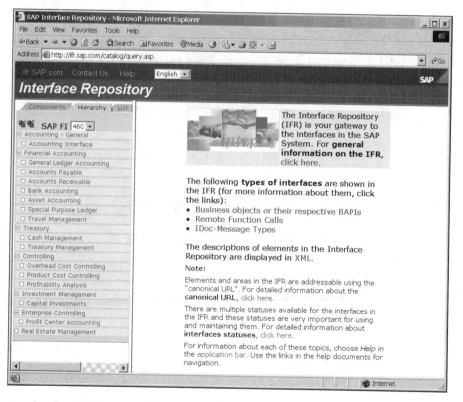

Application developers who are working on local SAP systems have access to the complete list of BAPIs, RFCs, and IDocs through the ABAP workbench. The IFR is available for those developers who need remote access to SAP. SAP populates the IFR with the imports, exports, and methods for all of the standard BAPI, RFC, and IDocs interfaces.

Thus, the IFR would not contain any interfaces for any custom-built procedures for a specific company or installation of SAP. However, the IFR is a great starting point for understanding the ins-and-outs of SAP's native interfaces. Through the IFR, developers can search for interfaces across the various releases of mySAP. At the highest level, the IFR is organized by the category of the component. Since SAP encompasses a very broad range of functionality, the list of component areas is quite substantial:

- SAP BASIS (Basis Technology)
- SAP FI (Financials)
- SAP LO (Logistics)
- SAP HR (Human Resources)
- SAP APO (Advanced Planner & Optimizer)
- SAP CRM (Customer Relationship Management)
- SAP BW (Business Information Warehouse)
- SAP CFM (Corporate Finance Management)
- SAP SEM (Strategic Enterprise Management)
- SAP CA-JVA (Joint Venture Accounting)
- SAP IS-AD (Aerospace & Defense/Engineering & Construction)
- SAP IS-AFS (Apparel and Footwear)
- SAP BANKING (Banking)
- SAP IS-H (Healthcare)
- SAP INSURANCE (Insurance)
- SAP IS-M (Media)
- SAP IS-OIL (Oil & Gas)
- SAP IS-T (Telecommunications)
- SAP IS-U/CCS (Utilities – Customer Care & Service)
- SAP DI (Discrete Industries)

The IFR is further organized within component areas by the release number of the SAP software. The following figure displays the detailed business components for the General Ledger Business Object within the SAP FI (Financials) component for SAP 46C:

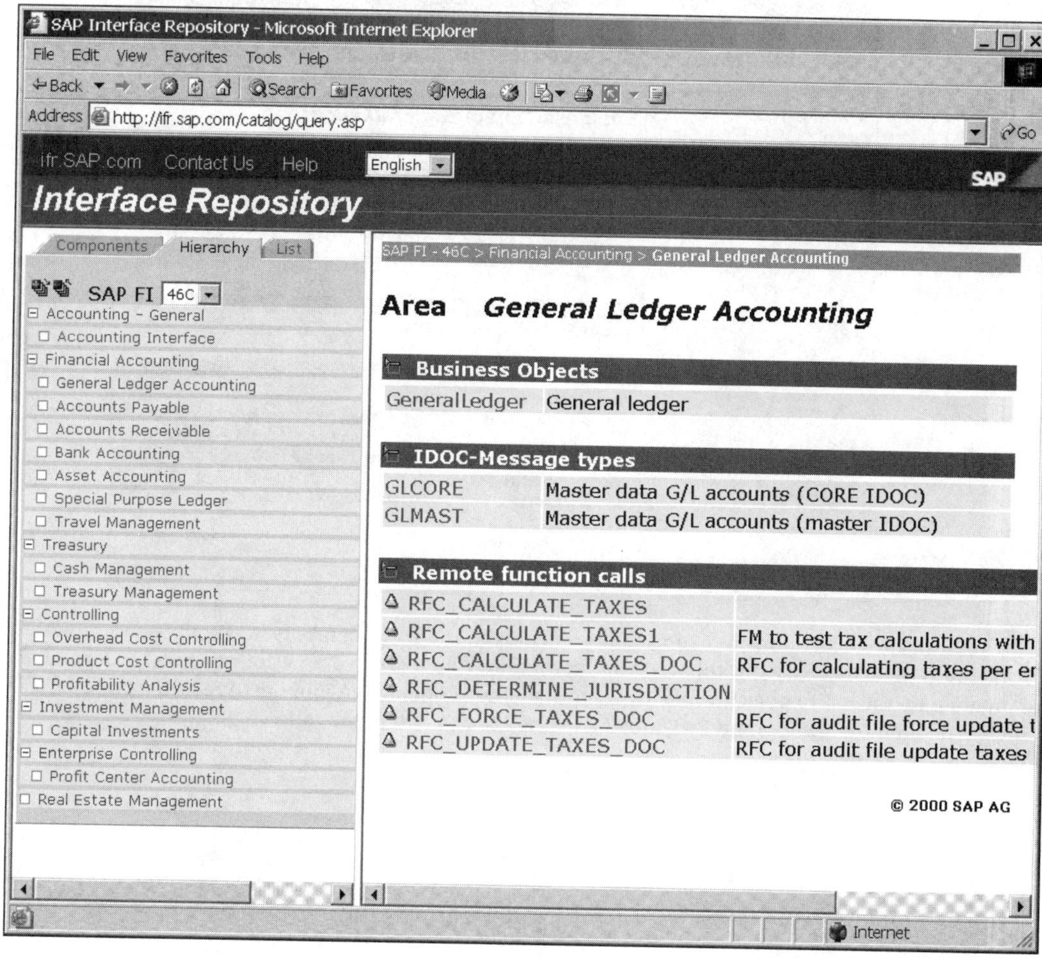

The left-hand side of the panel lists the hierarchy of available interfaces, which are further sub-divided into major categories. The General Ledger Accounting entry is highlighted in the preceding figure. It contains three different types of sub-components, Business Objects, IDOC-Message types, and Remote function calls. The Business Object GeneralLedger is detailed in the following figure:

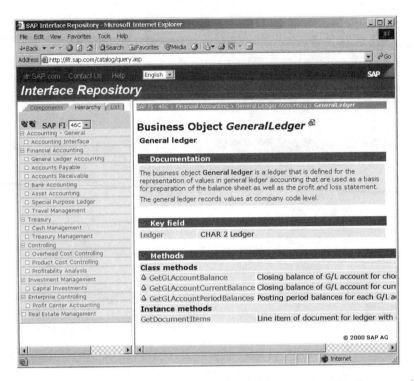

The Business Object `GeneralLedger` is an example of a BAPI component. It offers a number of methods that can be used within an ABAP program. There are two types of methods; `Class` methods operate on the entire object, while `Instance` methods operate on individual records. For example, the class method `GetGLAccountBalance()` method is detailed in the following figure:

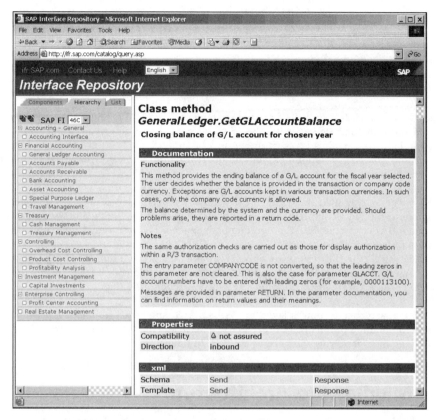

Programs pass data to BAPI methods via `Import` parameters and receive data back from methods via `Export` parameters. `Import` parameters supply the values that the BAPI method needs in order to complete the requested operation. The `GeneralLedger.GetGLAccountBalance()` method accepts four parameters; `Companycode`, `Currencytype`, `Fiscalyear`, and `Glacct`. SAP stores information for multiple companies within a single instance of mySAP. The `Companycode` parameter causes the method call to select data for a specific business entity within the installation.

The `Currencytype` field determines the currency output of the method call, and the `Fiscalyear` determines the financial reporting period for the account balance calculation. Developers can even select specific general ledger accounts by using the `Glacct` field. All SAP BAPIs work in a similar fashion – each will require a number of `Import` parameters into order to work properly.

The `Import` parameters are generally simple, scalar values. BAPI `Export` values can either be simple scalar values or complex data structures. In the case of the `GeneralLedger.GetGLAccountBalance()` method, the `Export` data is a table structure and a return code. The table structure is much like the record structure of a database table, as shown in the following code from the `GetGLAccountBalance()` method:

```
COMP_CODE     CHAR 4    Company Code
GL_ACCOUNT    CHAR 10   G/L account number
FISC_YEAR     NUMC 4    Fiscal year
BALANCE       DEC 23.4  Account Balance
CURRENCY      CUKY      Currency Key
CURRENCY_ISO  CHAR 3    ISO currency code
```

Each of the return fields within the structure contains the data that is returned by the method call. Of course, methods that update data within the SAP system may not return any values. In any case, the `Export` will always contain a `Return` structure. SAP supplies the `Return` structure to mark the status of the method call. As a programmer, you can interrogate the `Return` structure for `success/failure` codes and error text.

The IFR documents the BAPIs, RFCs, and IDocs that are available within the SAP system. A SAP programmer can build a complete, functional business process by coding a new BAPI or RFC using the documented BAPIs and the ABAP programming language. The resulting ABAP program acts and behaves in a similar fashion to any other program. It can be executed as a server-side program or batch process. Currently, the IFR repository only serves as a documented interface for SAP-supplied interfaces. In the future, the IFR will undoubtedly be compatible with UDDI. Indeed, the IFR may ultimately become a UDDI directory for SAP business functions.

While the IFR acts as a document layer for BAPIs, RFCs, and IDocs, it does not provide remote access to these programming protocols. In order to use external technology to access SAP through SAP's programming interfaces, you will need to use SAP Middleware technology.

SAP's Middleware Architecture

The critical elements of SAP's business framework are the RFCs and BAPIs. Developers can use the SAP Graphical User Interface tools to gain direct access to BAPIs and RFCs and build programs using the ABAP language. SAP makes these same APIs available through "external languages" by means of other, layered technologies. To assist programmers and developers, each ERP vendor supplies middleware architecture to support third-party connectivity. Historically, ERP vendors did not supply a direct route to web-enabling ERP systems, although this is starting to change. SAP has announced plans to support both Java and ABAP within its application server engine.

In the past, however, SAP provided the "Automation Kit", which allowed third-party programming languages to access SAP's APIs.

This kit includes a server process called the JRFC Server that accepts RFC messages from an external source. It also includes the Orbix Daemon and a set of RFC C++ class libraries (`librfc32.dll`). Alternatively, you could use almost any Java Native Interface (JNI) implementation to connect Java programs to the SAP C++ libraries. The use of C++ is linked to the legacy of client-server. Most ERP vendors offered a Windows-based user interface for client-server computing, and C++ was the logical choice for providing an API on the Windows platform. The following figure shows SAP's traditional middleware technology stack (from a Java perspective):

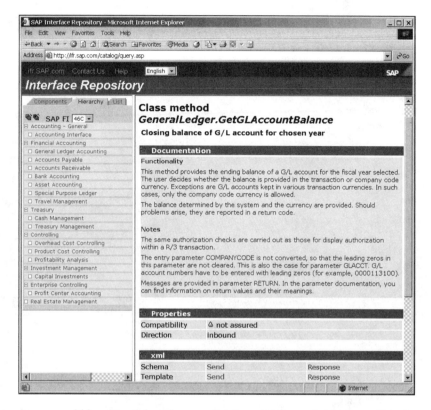

The client program could be a standalone Java application, or Java code running within the control of an application server. Although this approach worked, there were issues with performance, reliability, and complexity. Each program call had to pass through many layers of software. As a result, it was slow and it was easy to run into configuration problems with all of the various pieces of software. To simplify access to SAP from Java, SAP now provides the **SAP Java Connector (JCo)**. JCo enables two-way communication between mySAP components via APIs. JCo will also support the **Java Connector Architecture (JCA) 1.0 standard** acting as a resource adapter, which provides instant integration of SAP solutions in any J2EE environment supporting this specification. SAP's JCo is not the same thing as JCA, as JCo is SAP-specific technology. SAP's longer term vision is to support Java natively within its proprietary application server, through technology that is based upon JCo. In order to get access to detailed SAP JCo information, you need to be a registered SAP customer.

SAP Java Connector

The **SAP Java Connector** (JCo) is a middleware library that permits Java-based applications to access SAP functions through Remote Function Calls (and SOAP). Physically, JCo is nothing more than a Java library of connector classes. JCo supports BAPI, RFCs, and IDocs interfaces.

This design allows JCo to operate much more closely with client programs and application servers. SAP, IBM, and HAHT Commerce collaborated on the original Java interface for SAP with a product that was called **Common RFC Interface for Java (CRI4J)**.

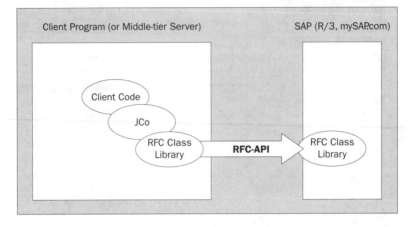

SAP's JCo library provides a wealth of features that simplify the process of connecting to mySAP and R/3 from Java. In particular, there are three key features that JCo offers developers (as compared to CRI4J):

❑ Streamlined connection process to SAP

❑ Pooled Server-side connections

❑ Load Balancing

The common interface (CRI4J) required the programmer to select a specific middleware interface as part of the connection process. SAP JCo offers integrated middleware and therefore a simplified connection process. JCo library can also pool connections to SAP, with the addClientPool() method giving the developer control over the number of simultaneous connections. This allows a larger number of "user" applications to share a more limited number of connections to SAP.

In order to interact with SAP data structures, the programmer must make use of a **repository** object. JCo connection pools can share a single repository across different user sessions. This results in faster performance and lower resource utilization. The server layer of JCo can even be spread across servers to further improve performance. Traffic can be load-balanced across a cluster of servers as required.

Working with JCo

Experienced Java Developers will find that working with JCo is a straightforward process. The challenge is in the understanding of the underlying BAPIs and RFCs. Java developers can download the documentation for SAP JCo kit directly from SAP using a public FTP site, ftp://ftp.sap.com/pub/sapjco/. The documentation includes HTML-based documentation, sample Java sourcecode, and a tutorial in Adobe PDF format.

Unfortunately, JCo only provides the "connection architecture" to a SAP system – it does not provide a running R/3 or mySAP environment. Furthermore, you cannot download JCo runtime software without a valid SAP customer license.

> You can get access to a working SAP system through a number of third-party tools that use JCo. We'll be using Backsoft's bTalk (http://www.backsoft.com) for just this purpose in the next section.

The easiest way to understand JCo is to take a look at a fragment of Java/JCo code:

```
import com.sap.mw.jco.*;

...

        myJcoclient = JCO.createClient("777",    // SAP client
                "jmilbery",                       // userid
                "*******",                        // password
                "EN",                             // language
                "meat.backsoft.com",              // host name
                "00");                            // system number
        myJcoclient.connect();
        JCO.Attributes attributes = myJcoclient.getAttributes();
        System.out.println("Connection attributes:\n" +
                            "---------------------\n" + attributes);
    ...
}
```

In order to work with JCo, you must import the required JCo libraries (as shown in the first line of the preceding code fragment). The foundation of a JCo session is the connection client. In order to connect to a remote SAP instance, you must supply at least six pieces of information as shown in the preceding code fragment (in the first line after the import statement). The createClient() method requires additional parameters in order to use Single Sign-on and to support load balancing. End users have been overwhelmed by the number of usernames and passwords that they need to access all of the required applications within the enterprise. Single Sign-on is a strategy in which applications can transfer responsibility for authentication to a single, centralized server. End users need only keep track of a single username and password, and the single sign-on server handles the interaction with all of the individual applications. In all, there are over 30 additional parameters for the createClient() method in order to deal with single sign-on requirements. The first element is the SAP client, here 777, which specifies a unique client number for the SAP installation. The next two elements are the SAP userid and password that the program will use to connect to the SAP system. These must be valid SAP credentials. The functions that the JCo program will be able to "run" within SAP are controlled by the userid and password.

Although JCo permits you to call any BAPI function, the user credentials control the specific BAPIs and RFCs that the session has permission to execute. SAP supports a wide variety of language codes and the language parameter allows you to set the specific language code for the current session (English, in our example case). SAP supports literally dozens of different languages, including double-byte characters such as Japanese Kanji. JCo makes use of a server layer that is responsible for connecting to the SAP subsystem.

The host name parameter is the DNS name of the host that JCo will use to locate the server. The last parameter is the SAP system number, which defaults to 00 for servers that have a single installation of SAP R/3 or mySAP. After you supply the required connection parameters, you can connect to SAP through the connect() method.

The client connection stores more information than the list of parameters that you supply to it. For example, once the user connects to SAP, the software assigns the system id (SYSID) to the user session. Our sample code cycles through all of the various properties of the connection object. Some of these will be familiar to us already (since we input them ourselves into the createClient() method). The reference to the JCO Attributes object in the preceding fragment of code displays all of the connection information for our connection object. The next fragment of code is the "heart" of our sample program:

```
JCO.ParameterList input = JCO.createParameterList();
input.appendValue("REQUTEXT", JCO.TYPE_CHAR, 255, "Simple JCO Test");
JCO.ParameterList output = JCO.createParameterList();
output.addInfo("ECHOTEXT", JCO.TYPE_CHAR, 255);
output.addInfo("RESPTEXT", JCO.TYPE_CHAR, 255);
myJcoclient.execute("STFC_CONNECTION", input, output);
System.out.println("The RFC function 'STFC_CONNECTION'" +
                   "returned the following EXPORTS:\n" );

for (int i = 0; i < output.getFieldCount(); i++) {
   System.out.println("Name: " + output.getName(i) +
                      " Value: " + output.getString(i));
}

myJcoclient.disconnect();
```

Once we have successfully connected to SAP, we are ready to work with BAPIs and RFCs. In order to get the data that we are looking for, we need to be familiar with the individual BAPIs and RFCs within each SAP subsystem. The IFR can assist you with this familiarization process. Our example case is very simple, since we are using the STFC_CONNECTION RFC, which simply echoes our connection information from the SAP session. All BAPIs and RFCs receive parameter values by use of IMPORTS.

As a developer you will create one ParameterList object for IMPORTS and one ParameterList object for EXPORTS. The IMPORT process is relatively simple, since all that you need to do is to use the appendValue() method to add IMPORT parameters. The STFC_CONNECTION RFC accepts a single input string, which is simply echoed back to the calling session. EXPORTS are more complicated to process, since they are not necessarily scalar values.

In fact, EXPORTS can return multiple **records** as well as multiple **fields**. The STFC_CONNECTION RFC returns a single record with multiple field values and the getName()/getString() methods will extract the name-value pairs for the fields that are returned by the RFC.

A complete discussion of programming with JCo is outside the scope of this chapter. Suffice it to say that there are specialized methods for cycling through complicated EXPORTS with JCo. You can find additional information on working with JCo in the documentation kit that is available from SAP's web site (ftp.sap.com/pubs/sapjco).

The final step in the process is to disconnect from the SAP session once your processing is complete. A complete program, TryJco.java, which implements this simple JCo call, is shown below:

```java
import com.sap.mw.jco.*;

public class TryJco {
  JCO.Client myJcoclient = null;

  public int doJco() {
    try {
      // Create a client connection to SAP
      myJcoclient = JCO.createClient(
              "777",                    // SAP client
              "jmilbery",               // userid
              "*******",                // password
              "EN",                     // language
              "meat.backsoft.com",      // host name
              "00");                    // system number

      // Open the connection
      myJcoclient.connect();

      // Print the Connection Attributes
      JCO.Attributes attributes = myJcoclient.getAttributes();
      System.out.println("Connection attributes:\n" +
              "---------------------\n" + attributes);
      // Create the input parameter list
      JCO.ParameterList input = JCO.createParameterList();

      // Set the import parameter
      input.appendValue("REQUTEXT", JCO.TYPE_CHAR, 255, "Simple JCO Test");

      // Create the out parameter list
      JCO.ParameterList output = JCO.createParameterList();

      // Specify the parameters types the function will be returning
      output.addInfo("ECHOTEXT", JCO.TYPE_CHAR, 255);
      output.addInfo("RESPTEXT", JCO.TYPE_CHAR, 255);

      // Call the RFC function
      myJcoclient.execute("STFC_CONNECTION", input, output);

      // Print the result
      System.out.println(
          "The RFC function 'STFC_CONNECTION' returned the following EXPORTS:\n" +
              "--------------------------------------------------------------");
      for (int i = 0; i < output.getFieldCount(); i++) {
        System.out.println("Name: " + output.getName(i) +
                        " Value: " + output.getString(i));
      }

      // Close the connection
      myJcoclient.disconnect();
```

```
        return 1;

    } catch (Exception ex) {
        System.out.println("Caught an exception: \n" + ex);
        if (myJcoclient != null) {
            myJcoclient.disconnect();
        }
        return -1;
    }
}

public static void main (String[] argv) {
    int retstat;
    TryJco myTryJco = new TryJco();
    retstat = myTryJco.doJco();
}
}
```

The output from running this simple Java program is shown in the following figure.

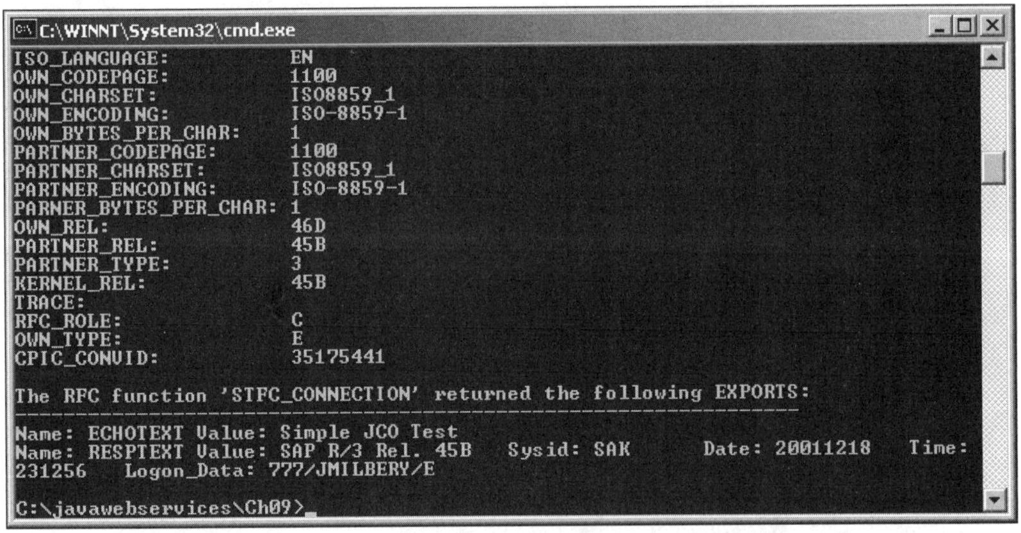

The top portion of the output lists the attributes that are derived from the connection object. The remainder of the output comes from the EXPORT section of the STFC_CONNECTION RFC object. This sample program follows the same logic that is outlined in the code fragments that we discussed in detail in the sections that precede the complete code listing. This is probably the simplest middleware test that you could run with SAP. The program simply connects to SAP and echoes a text string that the program passes into SAP.

Most organizations will want to control the power of the underlying SAP system by using a combination of BAPIs and RFCs within a single program (or as part of a larger Web Service). While you could build these programs by hand using ABAP, JCo, and Java there are some powerful third-party alternatives available. These third-party solutions handle much of the complexity in working with SAP middleware. In the next section, we'll look a Backsoft's bTalk, a powerful suite of Java objects that interact with JCo.

Using Java to Connect to R/3 with bTalk

One of the fundamental principles of the Internet in general, and Web Services in particular, is the ability to assemble your applications using "best of breed" technology. SAP offers a number of different middleware connectivity options for mySAP and R/3. Several SAP partners have built advanced technology on top of SAP's middleware and you can use this technology to add a Web Services layer to your SAP systems.

One example of this type of technology is Backsoft's bTalk (http://www.btalk.com/) software. bTalk for SAP R/3 is software designed to work with SAP's middleware technologies to extend SAP to the Internet. bTalk works directly with Java and is compatible with any application server that supports Java, including the SAP Web Application Server, Apache/Tomcat, Macromedia JRUN, BEA WebLogic, and IBM WebSphere.

The primary objective of bTalk is to take full advantage of the application server. Through the application server layer, bTalk can also access Web Services standards, such as XML and SOAP.

bTalk's Architecture

bTalk is built upon a component architecture. These components are constructed using a combination of Java and C++ and they encapsulate the logic, data, and integration for SAP's R/3. As a developer, you can use pure Java to talk to SAP via bTalk, but bTalk uses some C++ code to handle the interaction between Java and SAP's C++ libraries. Over the longer term, we would expect this to change as SAP adds support for native Java middleware. At the developer level, each bTalk component maps to a corresponding SAP BAPI object (or custom-built RFC).

These core components are delivered as Java Beans, which hide the complexity of the underlying SAP APIs from the application developer. bTalk's Java Beans provide the necessary method calls and offer error handling and validation. bTalk's Java Beans simplify the integration process through the following features:

- ❑ Attribute Checking
- ❑ Maintaining SAP field lists for all BAPIs and RFCs
- ❑ Dynamically generating empty objects
- ❑ Validating import parameters
- ❑ Returning BAPI/RFC data in Java Structures
- ❑ Working with Java Server Pages

Although we can manage most of these services ourselves by using plain Java code and SAP's JCo, bTalk can radically simplify the process. It allows you to use Java and XML to develop Internet-based applications that work with SAP R/3 and mySAP. bTalk generates Java Components and Web Pages for BAPIs and RFCs.

Through bTalk we can gain access to the sophisticated features of JCo without having to write the low-level code. bTalk matches its components to each individual BAPI within the SAP system. This allows developers to interact with SAP in a very granular way using the Java language.

Installing and Configuring bTalk

You can download a copy of bTalk through the Backsoft web site at the following address: http://www.btalk.com/content_bTalkdownload.cfm. The installation process is outlined in a short installation document that accompanies the software and you should not have any trouble following the installation instructions for the client interface.

bTalk provides a developer interface for building and testing Java code and it also includes the run-time components that connect bTalk to an application server. bTalk is not "middleware" in the traditional sense of the word. As a developer, you will always host bTalk within an application server environment.

> *One of the more powerful aspects of the bTalk environment is its ability to generate "ready to run" web pages based on Java Server Pages. In the previous chapter we concentrated on generating WSDL for Java programs with IBM's Web Services ToolKit (WSTK). However, IBM has announced plans to support the generation of WSDL from Java Servlets and JavaServer Pages. Through bTalk, developers will be able to generate JSP pages for SAP transactions and then use a tool such as IBM's Web Services Development Environment to generate WSDL for these pages.*

Once you have installed the software, you will need to configure bTalk to work with your application server. Most of the configuration options are available within the bTalk environment (under the Options menu). You should be able to accept the defaults for many of these parameters. The exceptions are the output paths. bTalk generates components, HTML pages, and Java Server Pages. You must instruct bTalk to output these generated objects into the proper path for your application server.

We are using the same Tomcat server as in the previous IBM chapter. The default path for JSP applications with Tomcat is the %TOMCAT_HOME%\webapps\ROOT\WEB-INF path. We've mapped the output for bTalk to the appropriate Tomcat directories for our example code.

There are some specific installation instructions for configuring Tomcat to work with bTalk. You will want to check bTalk's web site for the most current information on working with Tomcat at http://www.btalk.com/content_bTalkSupport.cfm?Note=3.

bTalk will automatically generate Java component code (Beans) into the "Bean Path" directory. You will need to be sure that your classpath setting includes this directory tree (%TOMCAT_HOME%\webapps\ROOT\WEB-INF). Otherwise, the Tomcat server will not be able to find the bTalk JavaBean files at run time.

Working with bTalk

bTalk is a native Java application that runs as a standalone program. Backsoft makes it easy to work with bTalk and SAP by providing remote access to R/3 for you. When you download the installation kit, Backsoft will supply logon credentials for SAP that you can use to connect to R/3. You can create a new R/3 session by using the Logon menu button as shown in the following figure:

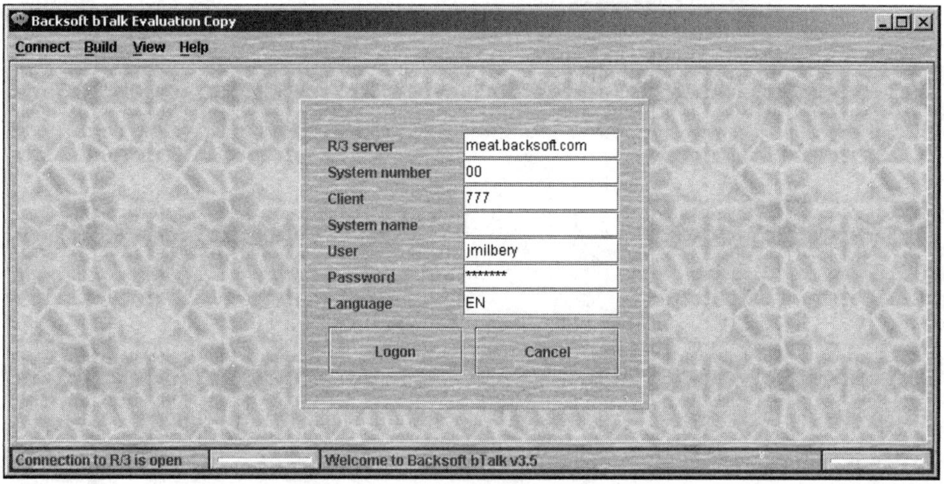

One of the first things that you will notice is that the connection dialog window displays all of the same parameters that the JCo createClient() method uses. That is because bTalk uses JCo under the covers.

Once you have verified that your connection to the remote R/3 system works, you could edit the TryJco.java code to use your bTalk logon credentials. After you compile the TryJco.java program with these changes it will run directly against Backsoft's R/3 installation.

bTalk maintains a connection to the SAP Business Objects Library as shown in the following figure:

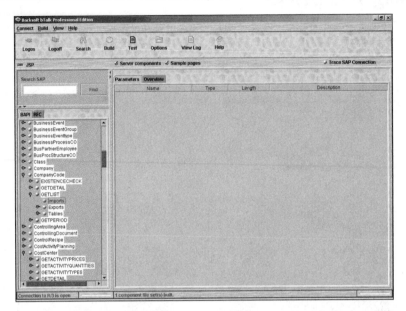

The bTalk BAPI/RFC display panel on the left-hand side of the screen essentially replaces SAP's IFR. In fact, the bTalk BAPI/RFC panel is specific to each individual installation of SAP R/3 and mySAP. Thus, it will include custom-coded BAPIs and RFCs that you will not find in the public IFR. You can scroll down through the list of BAPIs and RFCs to find the function that you wish to access. The panel as shown in the preceding figure is highlighting the GETLIST method from the CompanyCode BAPI. You can build and execute a JavaBean and JSP by highlighting the CompanyCode BAPI in the left-hand panel and using the **Build/Test** buttons.

bTalk automatically generates an HTML page that accepts parameters and chains to a JSP page. The following figure shows the generated HTML page for the GETLIST method for the CompanyCode BAPI:

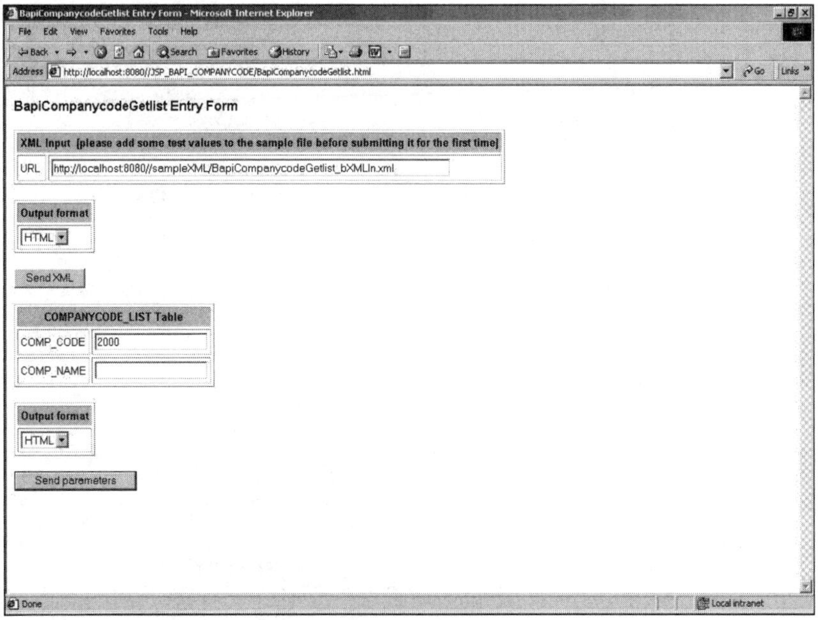

The generated HTML page includes form fields for all of the IMPORTS that the BAPI/RFC transaction requires. In the case of the CostCenter GetList method, the IMPORTS are nothing more than a text string for the COMP_CODE (Company code) or COMP_NAME (Company name). These import parameters effectively allow the user to search for Cost Center information by the company's internal SAP company code value, or the actual company name. Underneath the covers, bTalk provides a JSP page to process the transaction, and a suite of JavaBeans that work with JCo. The generated JSP page for CostCenterGetList is shown in the following block of code:

```
<%-- Name          : BapiCostcenterGetlist.jsp --%>
<%-- Description    : This sample JavaServer Page accesses R/3 using the function
BAPI_COSTCENTER_GETLIST --%>
<%-- SAP Version    : 45B --%>
<%-- Copyright      : 2000 by Backsoft Corporation, http://www.backsoft.com, All
Rights Reserved. --%>
<%-- Generated by : Backsoft Corporation --%>
<%-- Generated      : Dec 18, 2001 --%>

<%@ page info="This JSP servlet calls the SAP R/3 function
BAPI_COSTCENTER_GETLIST" %>
<%@ page errorPage="exception.jsp" isThreadSafe="false" import="com.sap.mw.jco.*"
%>
<%@ page import="java.net.*, java.util.*, org.w3c.dom.*, org.xml.sax.*,
javax.xml.parsers.*" %>
```

```jsp
<%-- instantiate a global SapJCOConnectionBean, then connect to R/3 --%>
<jsp:useBean id="connection" scope="session"
class="com.backsoft.btalk.sap.SapJCOConnectionBean">

  <jsp:setProperty name="connection" property="host" value="meat.backsoft.com"/>
  <jsp:setProperty name="connection" property="systemNumber" value="00"/>
  <jsp:setProperty name="connection" property="client" value="777"/>
  <jsp:setProperty name="connection" property="user" value="jmilbery"/>
  <jsp:setProperty name="connection" property="password" value="*****"/>
  <jsp:setProperty name="connection" property="language" value="EN"/>

  <% if (!connection.connect(true)) throw new Exception("R/3 connection failed");
%>

</jsp:useBean>

<%-- instantiate a JCOBapiCostcenterGetlistBean, then bind the connection to it --
%>
<jsp:useBean id="proxy" scope="request"
class="com.backsoft.btalk.sap.JCOBapiCostcenterGetlistBean">

  <% proxy.setConnection(connection); %>

  <% if (request.getParameter("command").equals("Send parameters")) { %>
    <jsp:setProperty name="proxy" property="companycode"/>
    <jsp:setProperty name="proxy" property="companycodeto"/>
    <jsp:setProperty name="proxy" property="controllingarea"/>
    <jsp:setProperty name="proxy" property="controllingareato"/>
    <jsp:setProperty name="proxy" property="costcenter"/>
    <jsp:setProperty name="proxy" property="costcentergroup"/>
    <jsp:setProperty name="proxy" property="costcenterto"/>
    <jsp:setProperty name="proxy" property="date"/>
    <jsp:setProperty name="proxy" property="personincharge"/>
    <jsp:setProperty name="proxy" property="personinchargeto"/>

    <% int rowNum = 0; %>
    <% rowNum = proxy.addEmptyCostcenterlistTableRow(); %>
    <% proxy.setCostcenterlistTableCellByString(rowNum, "CO_AREA",
request.getParameter("costcenterlist_coarea")); %>
    <% proxy.setCostcenterlistTableCellByString(rowNum, "COSTCENTER",
request.getParameter("costcenterlist_costcenter")); %>
    <% proxy.setCostcenterlistTableCellByString(rowNum, "COCNTR_TXT",
request.getParameter("costcenterlist_cocntrtxt")); %>

  <% } %>

</jsp:useBean>

<%-- if necessary, parse input XML to get import parameters --%>
<% if (request.getParameter("command").equals("Send XML")) { %>

  <%-- instantiate a BapiCostcenterGetlist parser, and pass it a reference to the
proxy bean --%>
  <jsp:useBean id="parser" scope="request"
```

```
class="com.backsoft.btalk.sap.JCOBapiCostcenterGetlistParser">

    <jsp:setProperty name="parser" property="validation" value="true"/>
    <jsp:setProperty name="parser" property="verbosity" value="0"/>

    <% parser.setURL(request.getParameter("url")); %>
    <% parser.setProxyBean(proxy); %>

  </jsp:useBean>

  <%-- run the input XML through the bXML parser bean --%>
  <% parser.parseXML(); %>

<% } %>

<%-- instantiate a global BapiTransactionCommitBean, binding the connection to it
--%>
<jsp:useBean id="commit" scope="application"
class="com.backsoft.btalk.sap.JCOBapiTransactionCommitBean">
</jsp:useBean>
<% commit.setConnection(connection); %>

<%-- make sure the R/3 connection is still good --%>
<% if (!connection.isConnected()) {connection.reconnect();} %>
<%-- call BAPI_COSTCENTER_GETLIST via the JCOBapiCostcenterGetlistBean, then
commit the transaction --%>
<% proxy.run(); %>
<% commit.run(); %>

<%-- branch according to the chosen output format --%>
<% switch (Integer.parseInt(request.getParameter("output")))
{
  case (1): %> <%@ include file="BapiCostcenterGetlistHTML.jsp" %> <% break;
  case (2): %> <%@ include file="BapiCostcenterGetlistbXML.jsp" %> <% break;
  default : throw new IllegalArgumentException("Support for this format is not
available yet");
}
 %>
```

The JSP page is very straightforward. You will notice that it includes the necessary parameters to the JCo `createClient()` method, albeit through a bTalk generated Java Bean – `com.backsoft.btalk.sap.SapJCOConnectionBean`. As a developer, you are free to modify the calling HTML page or the JSP to suit your own specific processing needs. The output of calling the JSP page is shown in the following figure:

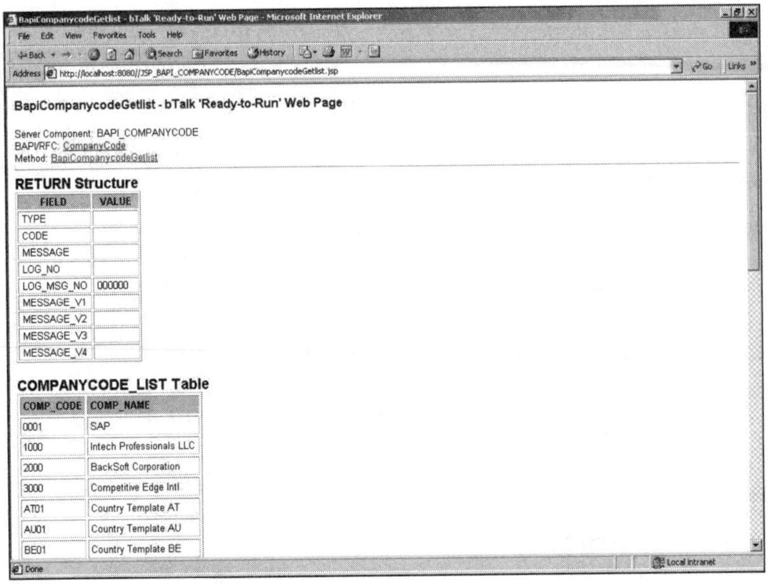

The output of the JSP page is a list of Cost Center codes that is shown within a table. This is a very common type of operation. The calling program supplies a parameter for a SAP BAPI, and the server program returns the resulting data.

Developers who are very familiar with the BAPIs and RFCs within a standard SAP system can interact with the bTalk Java objects immediately. If you are not familiar with your particular SAP installation, you may not have access to valid IMPORT parameter values that are required to run specific BAPIs or RFCs. In most cases, the SAP BAPIs require specific parameter values in order to fetch data from the SAP system.

The following figure shows the chart of General Ledger accounts within SAP with the company code "2000" for the Backsoft trial SAP system. As a developer, you would need to know what the values are for the company code (or use another BAPI transaction to get them) before you could run the transaction. This function is closely related to the CompanyCode GetList BAPI. You can generate this page by choosing Build/Test for the GeneralLedgerAccount GetList() method calling from within bTalk.

bTalk, Java, and WSDL

As a developer, you can use bTalk (and by extension, SAP's JCo) to create JSPs and Java programs that interact with SAP's BAPIs. bTalk sends the output of a BAPI as an HTML page or as an XML document. You could choose to link several BAPIs together into a more complex business process by combining multiple bTalk Java Beans into a complex set of JSPs or Servlets.

This does raise the question of whether or not one would choose to use an accounting system that is assembled from a set of services over the Web. More than likely, companies will choose to make use of what you might call buyer/supplier services as a start. For example, it is probably more likely that a developer would use a service to submit an order from an internal system over the Web to SAP. Of course, one can already do this today by using the web-enabled version of SAP. However, the use of Java and Web Services allows the developer to access the order entry component from within internal applications rather than a web page. Thus, company "A" could choose to enhance its internal purchase order system to automatically enter approved purchase orders into a remote SAP system at company "B".

The resulting JSPs can then be wrapped in WSDL and published in a UDDI directory. The following two blocks of code are the generated WSDL Service and Service Interface definitions for the `TryJco.java` program. These WSDL documents were generated using IBM's WSTK toolkit (as described in Chapter 4).

First, the WSDL Service Interface – `TryJco_Service-interface.wsdl`:

```
<?xml version="1.0" encoding="UTF-8"?>
<definitions name="TryJco_Service"
  targetNamespace="http://www.TryJcoservice.com/TryJco-interface"
  xmlns="http://schemas.xmlsoap.org/wsdl/"
  xmlns:soap="http://schemas.xmlsoap.org/wsdl/soap/"
  xmlns:tns="http://www.TryJcoservice.com/TryJco-interface"
  xmlns:types="http://www.TryJcoservice.com/TryJco-interface/types/"
```

```
        xmlns:xsd="http://www.w3.org/2001/XMLSchema">

        <message name="IndoJcoRequest"/>

        <message name="OutdoJcoResponse">
          <part name="meth1_outType" type="xsd:int"/>
        </message>

        <portType name="TryJco_Service">
          <operation name="doJco">
            <input message="tns:IndoJcoRequest"/>
            <output message="tns:OutdoJcoResponse"/>
          </operation>
        </portType>

        <binding name="TryJco_ServiceBinding" type="tns:TryJco_Service">
          <soap:binding style="rpc" transport="http://schemas.xmlsoap.org/soap/http"/>
          <operation name="doJco">
            <soap:operation soapAction="urn:TryJco-service"/>
            <input>
              <soap:body encodingStyle="http://schemas.xmlsoap.org/soap/encoding/"
                         namespace="urn:TryJco-service"
                         use="encoded"/>
            </input>
            <output>
              <soap:body encodingStyle="http://schemas.xmlsoap.org/soap/encoding/"
                         namespace="urn:TryJco-service"
                         use="encoded"/>
            </output>
          </operation>
        </binding>

    </definitions>
```

The following code is the service definition file – `TryJco_Service.wsdl`:

```
<?xml version="1.0" encoding="UTF-8"?>
<definitions name="TryJco_Service"
  targetNamespace="http://www.TryJcoservice.com/TryJco"
  xmlns="http://schemas.xmlsoap.org/wsdl/"
  xmlns:interface="http://www.TryJcoservice.com/TryJco-interface"
  xmlns:soap="http://schemas.xmlsoap.org/wsdl/soap/"
  xmlns:types="http://www.TryJcoservice.com/TryJco"
  xmlns:xsd="http://www.w3.org/2001/XMLSchema">

  <import location="http://localhost:8080/wsdl/TryJco_Service-interface.wsdl"
          namespace="http://www.TryJcoservice.com/TryJco-interface">
  </import>

  <service name="TryJco_Service">
    <documentation>IBM WSTK V2.4 generated service definition file</documentation>
    <port binding="interface:TryJco_ServiceBinding" name="TryJco_ServicePort">
      <soap:address location="http://localhost:8080/soap/servlet/rpcrouter"/>
```

```
        </port>
    </service>

</definitions>
```

SAP's Future Directions

SAP recently announced an updated architecture for mySAP and R/3 that will carry them forward into J2EE and Web Services arenas. It has divided its technology stack into three core components:

❑ SAP Web Application Server

❑ SAP Exchange Infrastructure

❑ SAP Portal Infrastructure

SAP Web Application Server

SAP considers the SAP Web Application Server to be a two-personality application server with support for J2EE standards and ABAP (the two "personalities" are Java and ABAP code). SAP's ABAP is much like Java in that they are both considered to be "platforms" as well as languages. Many of the core transactional aspects of the SAP system rely on critical features within the ABAP platform. As it currently stands, the SAP Web Application Server can support Java access to BAPIs and RFCs through JCo. By the middle of 2002, SAP plans to support in-memory access from Java to ABAP and ABAP to Java. This promises to be a high-performance solution for programming with SAP. The architecture of this new solution is shown in the following figure:

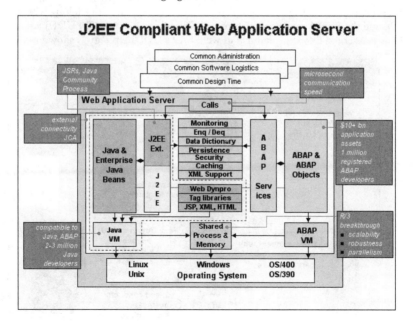

SAP has also announced plans to use Java to re-write the entire user interface of mySAP (and R/3). The first modules that make use of this new user interface are expected to roll out to the market in the first half of 2002. The new user interface will be based on open standards, namely JavaServer Pages, HTML, and XML. This is a monumental undertaking, since the SAP user-interface is composed of over 150,000 screens, reports, and dialog boxes.

This modified UI will allow developers to have an unprecedented level of control over the user experience. The client layer (JSP, HTML, and XML) will be extremely customizable. The application layer can be constructed with both Java and ABAP. SAP does not plan to re-write any of the core ABAP functions in Java, but developers will be able to access them natively from Java code in the middle tier.

The updated application server includes support for J2EE, HTTP, HTTPS, XML, and SOAP. From the SAP perspective, the SAP Web Application Server becomes the platform for delivering Web Services. Any J2EE program can be "run" on the SAP Web Application Server. Thus, a bTalk "application" based on the `CompanyCode GetList` method that we developed in the preceding section could be deployed on the SAP Web Application Server.

Even IBM's WSTK toolkit can work with the forthcoming release of the server, which makes your existing investments in Web Services upwardly compatible with SAP's future technology.

SAP Exchange Infrastructure

SAP's Exchange Infrastructure is the second pillar of the SAP technology stack. SAPMarkets Inc, CommerceOne Inc, and SAP jointly developed the Exchange Infrastructure technology. It is designed to allow process-centric collaboration across internal and external systems, with the twin goals of reducing cost and improving business innovation.

The Exchange Infrastructure includes business process design tools, workflow tools, and a directory of products and services. SAP has announced plans to host a UDDI directory (along with Microsoft, IBM, Sun, and HP), and the Exchange Infrastructure will play a key role in SAP's UDDI strategy. In fact, the IFR is likely to be merged into this platform as well. SAP's UDDI strategy is shown in the following figure:

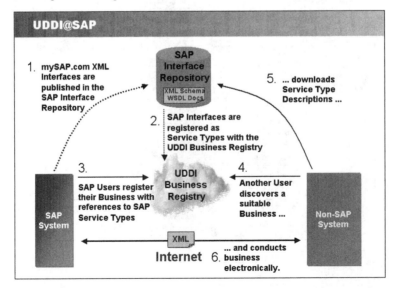

Customers can use the public installation of the Exchange Infrastructure and IFR to offer "public" services. They will also be able to host their own internal version of the Exchange Infrastructure for "private" services. Once this initiative is complete, SAP plans to generate default Web Services for all of its standard BAPI modules. This will give customers a head start with Web Services on the SAP platform, but it is still just a starting point. Most SAP customers have large investments in customized BAPIs and RFCs that will have to be "Web Service-enabled".

SAP's Portal Infrastructure

The third pillar in SAP's technology stack is the SAP Portal Infrastructure, which is based on the TopTier Portal Server that SAP acquired in 2001. The current generation of SAP's Portal Infrastructure is a unified product from SAP, SAP Portals (formerly TopTier), and Yahoo!, Inc.

The SAP Portal product provides users with a single browser-based desktop from which to work. Core SAP content (screens, reports, BAPIs, RFCs, and IDocs) are accessible as "mini-applications" within the portal framework. External applications, such as news feeds, stock quotes, and weather are available within the same portal environment.

Partner applications can also be integrated into the portal as "mini-applications". End users can gain access to all of their internal and external applications through a single user ID and password via SAP's single sign-on integration. SAP views the Portal Infrastructure as the logical desktop for the user. Over the longer term, SAP expects that users will gain access to registered Web Services through the portal interface, as shown in the following figure:

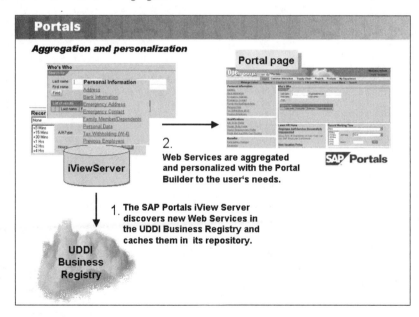

The SAP portal maintains a "repository" of the available mini-applications. In the future, it will be able to discover new services using UDDI (through the Exchange Infrastructure). The Portal Server will load Web Services into the repository and make them available to end users (and the services themselves will be run on the SAP Web Application Server).

Summary

In this chapter we have introduced you to the fundamentals of SAP's mySAP and R/3. These products form the business foundation for many of the world's largest corporations. As these businesses embrace Web Services you will find that much of the underlying content for these services will come from ERP, CRM, and HR applications such as mySAP and R/3.

We have also looked at SAP's BAPIs, RFCs, and IDocs, which are the primary programming interfaces for modifying and adapting a SAP system. SAP documents these interfaces in the Internet Business Framework Repository. As Web Service developers, you will need to access this repository to understand the internal business procedures that form the core of SAP. SAP's Middleware Architecture allows third-party programming languages, such as Java, to interact with a SAP system.

We successfully built a standalone Java program using SAP's Java Connector and also generated Java Server Pages that interact with SAP BAPIs. We took at look at using the bTalk tool set to generate Java Server Pages for SAP BAPIs and RFCs. In the last part of this chapter we had a glimpse of SAP's future technology direction – one that embraces the various Web Services standards, Java, WSDL, XML, UDDI, and SOAP.

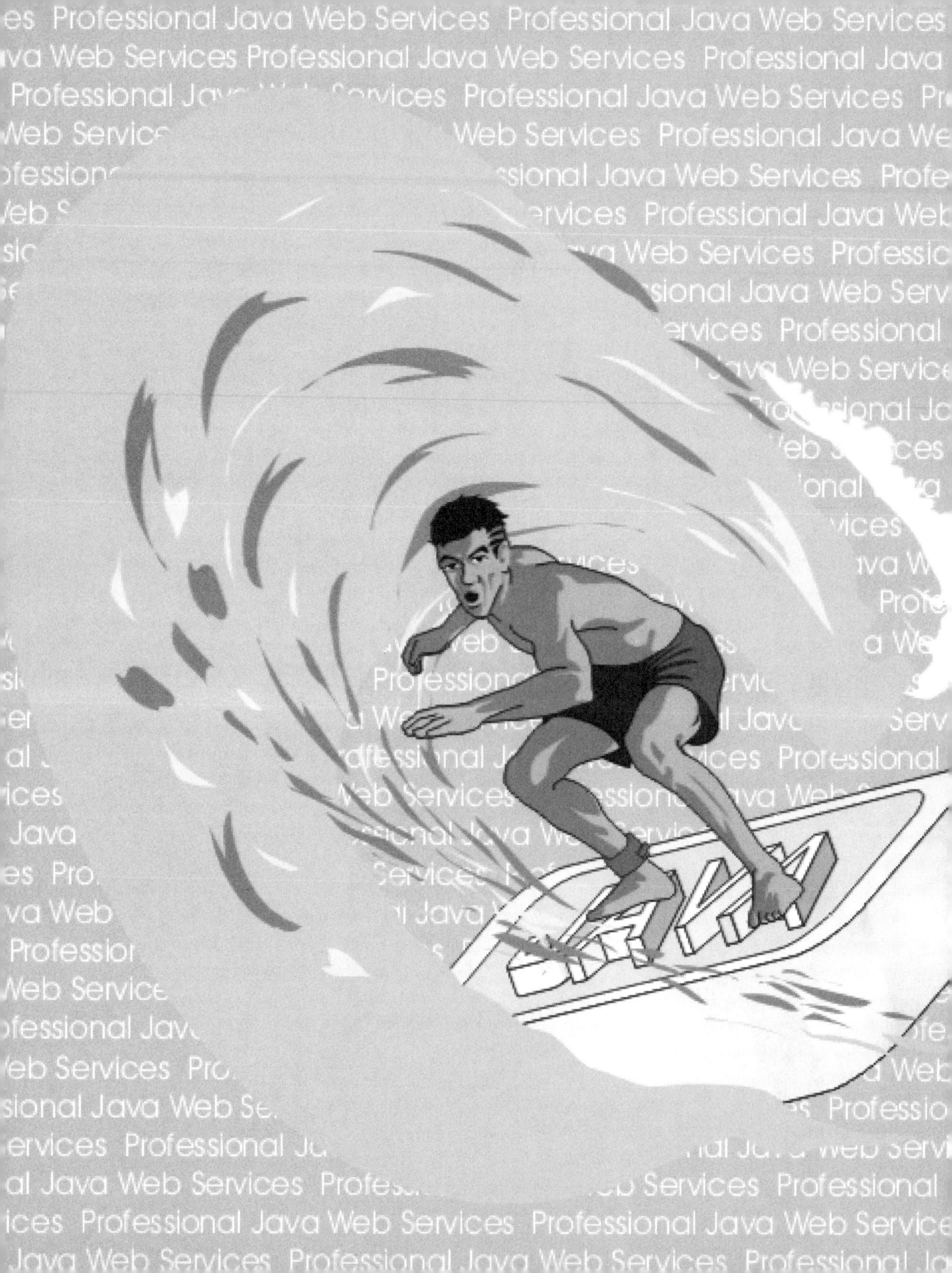
Professional Java Web Services

IBM and Web Services

IBM has always been at the forefront of many cutting edge technologies. IBM's WebSphere application server is one of the market leaders (along with BEA's WebLogic) amongst application developers and enterprise customers, and the team at IBM continues to enhance WebSphere with new functionality. SOAP, XML, and web services are all part of IBM's technology roadmap for the future of computing.

These technologies are finding their way into all layers of the IBM server technology stack – DB2, Visual Age for Java and WebSphere. Part of IBM's technical strategy is to preview new technologies through their DeveloperWorks program and the AlphaWorks research center. For example, WebSphere's wireless processing capabilities were originally offered through AlphaWorks as part of their "transcoding" technology. IBM eventually rolled the transcoding research into a number of commercial products under the WebSphere brand. Likewise, IBM has been previewing some Web Services technology through AlphaWorks. In particular, they have offered a number of WSDL tools and technologies, which will ultimately become part of the IBM technology stack. In this chapter, we'll take a look at some of these tools and how you can leverage them within your existing infrastructure.

Topics covered in this chapter include:

- ❑   A brief introduction to IBM's Server Technology Stack
- ❑   Working with IBM's UDDI Registry
- ❑   Implementing a simple web service with Tomcat/Apache
- ❑   Working with IBM's Web Services ToolKit (WSTK)
- ❑   Deploying and publishing with IBM UDDI4J

If you are familiar with IBM's family of products, then you might want to skip over the next section and move straight into *Working with IBM's UDDI Registry*.

The IBM Server Technology Platform

IBM manufactures and sells hundreds of different software products and related technologies, but there are four core server technologies that allow you to build dynamic e-business applications on the IBM platform. In effect, these four products form the software foundation that IBM offers for building Internet-base, e-commerce applications. These four product families include:

❑ WebSphere

❑ MQSeries

❑ DB2

❑ Tivoli

These four product stacks are meant to provide a complete **enterprise** solution, but you are not **required** to use them all as a complete set. Each product is designed to handle certain aspects of your dynamic e-business (web service) problem – as shown in the following figure.

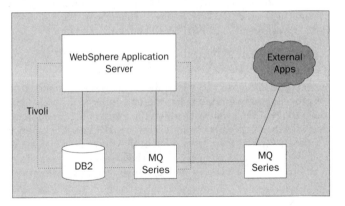

In the following section we will take a look at each product family in a little more detail.

IBM WebSphere

IBM's WebSphere brand encompasses several classes of product. At the very core, WebSphere is IBM's entry in the application server marketplace. There are two major editions of the WebSphere application server – Advanced Edition and Enterprise Edition. WebSphere Advanced Edition is itself written in Java, and it is probably the most popular edition in the WebSphere product family. WebSphere Advanced Edition 4.0 provides built-in support for all of the required web services capabilities – SOAP, UDDI, WSDL, XML, and J2EE 1.2 (JSP, Servlets, EJBs, JMS, and so on.). WebSphere Enterprise Edition is based on IBM's Component Broker technology and includes support for Microsoft COM objects, C++ code, and CORBA assets (within the same J2EE application server environment). WebSphere Advanced Edition and Enterprise Edition are considered to be the **foundation products** on which the WebSphere platform is built.

10

IBM offers two types of extension products for WebSphere – **foundation extensions** and **application accelerators**. **Foundation extensions** are additional pieces of technology that can be applied to the WebSphere foundation platform. For example, IBM has built a layer of portal technology (WebSphere Portal Server) that works hand-in-hand with WebSphere. There are foundation extensions to address all sorts of application requirements, including:

❑   Caching and Performance (WebSphere Edge Server)

❑   Voice Recognition (WebSphere Voice Server)

❑   Wireless Applications (WebSphere Transcoding Publisher and WebSphere Everyplace Suite)

❑   Personalization (WebSphere Personalization Server)

❑   Mainframe Access (WebSphere Host Integration Server)

In simple terms, the WebSphere foundation extensions are pieces of add-on functionality that enhance the WebSphere platform. **Application accelerators**, on the other hand, provide pre-built solutions that run on top of the WebSphere foundation platform. In effect, they are pre-built blocks of code that can be installed into the WebSphere server. Each provides a specific business function. For example, WebSphere Payment Manager provides code and tools that allow applications to process payments (credit cards, checks and so on.) via the Web. WebSphere Commerce Suite, WebSphere Payment Manager, and WebSphere Business Integrator are all application accelerators.

The advantage of IBM's approach with the WebSphere platform is that the developer has the freedom to pursue a **build-and-buy** approach to development. On the one hand, you are free to develop those components that are unique to your business using standard Java technology. On the other hand, you can also buy pre-prepared blocks of functionality that can be integrated into a single stack of technology – making it easier to manage and maintain.

IBM's web services technology can be used with open-source application server solutions such as the Apache HTTP Server and Tomcat. Although IBM embeds a version of the Apache server into the WebSphere product, developers can use IBM's web services technology with non-embedded versions of the Apache software that are made available through Apache.org. However, WebSphere is an important brand for IBM and you can be sure that all of their web service initiatives will be built to work with WebSphere as the **primary** delivery platform.

IBM offers two sets of development tools that can be used to develop code for the WebSphere platform. WebSphere Studio is a very specialized application development environment that provides Java Servlet and Java Server Pages tools. IBM's Visual Age for Java is a more full-featured interactive development environment (IDE) for building Java applications on the WebSphere platform. Visual Age offers a large array of wizards, code-completion tools, and debugging utilities to assist you in the development of large, complex e-business applications.

MQSeries

IBM's MQSeries product provides application-to-application messaging across a large number of hardware and operating system platforms. MQSeries comes equipped with a framework, tools, server technology, and adapters that connect applications to one another. In some cases, one application can connect directly to a second application without the need for additional software (such as MQSeries). For example, through web services you are free to connect one Java program to another directly using SOAP and RPC calls.

However, there are many instances in which the delivery of a message from one program to another cannot be **guaranteed** (or encounters a substantial time lag). For example, you might have an order processing application that allows your customers to place orders via a web site. In the background, your web application transfers the orders to an older mainframe application via a batch interface. The class of software that would sit in the middle of these two applications and guarantee the delivery of the web order to the mainframe application is called a "message queue". MQSeries is IBM's message queue software. It is the middleware layer of software in the middle that can guarantee the delivery of both synchronous and asynchronous messages. Thus, as a developer, you could connect to a mainframe application using MQSeries, and you could wrap the MQSeries layer with your own Java code and WSDL to build an asynchronous web service for your existing mainframe code.

Consider this simple example. You have an existing mainframe application, written in COBOL, that handles credit authorization for your customers. The credit authorization process is time consuming, and your new Java applications are not permitted to connect to the mainframe directly. MQSeries becomes the middleware that connects your Java program (and by extension your web service) to the mainframe COBOL application. MQSeries handles the verifiable delivery of message traffic between these two applications. This design allows you to preserve your investment in your mainframe application and still take advantage of leading edge web services technology. By supporting asynchronous messaging you can also improve the scalability of your applications. Programs at the edge of your network are not forced to wait for critical resources at the core of your network.

IBM offers a number of enhancements to the MQSeries platform that provide additional application functionality. MQSeries Workflow is a business process management system that enables the definition and execution of business processes that span applications and platforms. Sun provides the **Java Message Service (JMS)** programming interface that allows Java programs to access messaging services. In this model, MQSeries is the technology that sits under the JMS interface. Let's go back to our fictional credit application for a moment: the authorization process might have a complete workflow of its own, including some manual intervention and management approval.

Through MQSeries Workflow you are able to design these workflows directly into the messaging layer – as the rules change, you can quickly reconfigure the workflow to adapt to these changes. Neither the client code nor the web services need to be modified in order to take advantage of these changes in process flow.

IBM DB2

The foundation for persistent applications is the database layer, and the DB2 Universal Database is IBM's foray into the RDBMS market. For many of you, the database will be hidden behind layers of JDBC code, but it is still an important part of the web services equation. IBM DB2 can fully support JDBC, but it also features a number of important extensions that you may take advantage of directly through web services. IBM DB2 Version 7.2 has been extended to support XML, UDDI, and SOAP directly through the DB2 XML Extender.

Through the XML Extender, XML documents can be stored directly within the DB2 database (as individual columns or as a series of rows within a table) – and accessed via a set of functions and XPath instructions. You can invoke DB2 SQL statements and stored procedures directly through web service operations. This allows database-savvy developers to work directly with the database layer without the need for intermediary coding. The following figure outlines this simple strategy for using web services to access enterprise data within DB2.

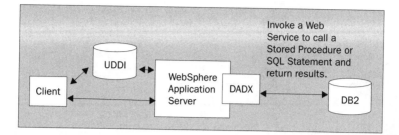

Client programs use WSDL to locate web services within private UDDI directories. The WebSphere application server connects to a DB2 database, and invokes a stored procedure or SQL statement, and returns results in XML format through SOAP to the client application. Through this mechanism, developers can access and update DB2 data without the need for complex programming.

IBM has developed a specialized technology called the **Web Services Object Runtime Framework (WORF)** that makes this process work. As of this writing the software is still in beta format, but you can download it from the IBM DB2 Extenders web site at http://www.ibm.com/software/data/db2/extenders/xmlext/.

There are two key types of query operations that are supported using this technology. You can build XML-based queries that create XML documents from DB2 relational data (XML documents can be stored within DB2 in a similar manner). The alternative is to use standard SQL queries and stored procedures against DB2 and return results using a default XML tagging format. The first technique provides a more fine-grained control over the formatting of the resultant data, while the second method concentrates on quickly getting data in and out of the database.

The key to both of these approaches is a specialized file that is called the **document access definition extension (DADX)**. The DADX is a specialized XML file that describes the operations that the DB2 web service can perform:

```
<?xml version="1.0"?>
<DADX xmlns="http://schemas.ibm.com/db2/dxx/dadx"
    xmlns:xsd="http://www.w3.org/1999/XMLSchema"
    xmlns:dtd1="http://schemas.netu.org/alumni/getdonations.dtd"
    xmlns:wsdl="http://schemas.xmlsoap.org/wsdl/">
  <wsdl:documentation>Queries Alumni Donations at NetU</wsdl:documentation>

  <operation name="listDonors">
    <wsdl:documentation>List the Alumni that have given gifts</wsdl:documentation>
    <query>
      <SQL_query>
        SELECT DISTINCT LASTNAME, FIRSTNAME from ALUMNI where ID in (SELECT ID
        FROM DONATIONS)
      </SQL_query>
    </query>
  </operation>

  <operation name="queryGiftsByAlumni">
    <wsdl:documentation>Finds the gifts for a selected Alumni</wsdl:documentation>
    <query>
```

```
        <SQL_query>
            SELECT AMOUNT, GIFT_DATE FROM DONATIONS WHERE ID = :alumniID
        </SQL_query>
        <XML_result name="GIFTS" element="dtd1:Gift"/>
        <parameter name="alumniID" type="xsd:string"/>
    </query>
  </operation>

  <operation name="queryGiftsByGradYear">
    <wsdl:documentation>
        Finds the gift total for each alumni grad year using a stored procedure
    </wsdl:documentation>
    <query>
      <SQL_call>CALL sqlproc_queryGifts(:classYr)</SQL_call>
    </query>
  </operation>

</DADX>
```

The preceding example DADX describes three simple services for a university alumni database. The first operation, listDonors, fetches the unique list of lastname and firstname of all the alumni that have made donations to the university. The second operation, queryGiftsByAlumni, accepts a parameter value to fetch the amount and gift_date for a selected alumni record – the results are returned according a specialized XML DTD that is embedded in the database.

The last operation, queryGiftsByGradYear, is based a DB2 stored procedure that accepts a single parameter. IBM permits developers to build DADX files using any text editor, but there are plans to offer specialized DADX tools for client-code generation. IBM's DADX technology is geared specifically towards the DB2 database. In one way, it is based on industry standards (since it is XML based). However, the DB2 database is the only product that will process DADX files as they exist today.

Tivoli

Developers will use WebSphere, MQSeries, and DB2 to build and run applications. Tivoli is IBM's application management technology – it manages the IBM middleware that runs web services. The Tivoli framework provides tools and utilities for monitoring the status, performance, and availability of applications. IBM provides specialized managers for all three components – WebSphere, DB2, and MQSeries.

In the near term, most of the Tivoli technology that you would use to monitor your web services applications is based WebSphere, DB2, and MQSeries technology. As of this writing, IBM does not offer any specific Tivoli modules for web services. However, IBM is in the process of manufacturing specialized Tivoli components that will manage web services directly. In fact, IBM is already offering a reference implementation of Tivoli Management Extensions for Java that can be used to manage Java-based web services.

The management layer becomes much more important than ever before with web services. Through web services, your applications will gain new "customers" transparently to your existing applications. New clients will locate services using UDDI and build new applications that use your web service components without necessarily involving your company directly in the process. These "users" of your system may incorporate your public web services modules into their applications on their own.

These users will come to depend on your web services components, and it is vitally important that you ensure that your web service applications are behaving as expected. Tivoli provides the tools to manage this process for the IBM stack of server products.

Working with IBM's UDDI Registry

IBM has a wealth of technology initiatives that are ongoing in the web services space. When you consider the various server technologies (WebSphere, Visual Age, DB2, MQSeries) and standards (XML, UDDI, WSDL, SOAP) that are in play, it's easy to miss the forest for the trees. Fortunately IBM provides a relatively simple solution in the form of the **Web Services ToolKit** (**WSTK**).

IBM's WSTK is a software development kit that includes a run-time environment and examples to aid in designing and executing your first web service application. The toolkit includes some simple examples of web services. More importantly, it offers a demonstration as to how some of the emerging technology standards, such as SOAP, UDDI, and WSDL, work together. IBM offers the WSTK technology through their AlphaWorks web site free of charge. In this chapter we'll demonstrate how to perform the following:

- ❏ Create a UDDI account on the IBM Test Registry
- ❏ Download and deploy a local web services test platform (Tomcat/SOAP)
- ❏ Insulate web services using IBM's Web Services ToolKit
- ❏ Deploy web services WSDL definitions to the IBM Test UDDI Registry

UDDI and WSDL

As developers you will use **Universal Description Discovery and Integration** (UDDI) as a method for publishing and finding services descriptions. Through the registry, you can locate services that meet your needs and include them in your own applications. Using UDDI, a buyer would be able to determine how to send orders to a supplier through a web service. (See Chapter 5 for more information on UDDI).

The Web Services ToolKit is designed to simplify the process of generating Web Services Description Language (WSDL) code. Service description information that is contained within a WSDL document is complementary to the information within a UDDI directory.

Technically speaking, UDDI provides support for many different types of service descriptions, but it does not necessarily offer **direct** support for WSDL. However, the two technologies can work together, and it is possible to map a WSDL service definition into a UDDI registry. WSTK generates WSDL code for your web services, and the UDDI4J API can map these WSDL documents into UDDI registries. When you install WSTK, you will need to select a UDDI registry to use, and IBM's Test Registry is an ideal choice.

Creating a Test UDDI Account

The IBM WSTK technology works with UDDI to register WSDL documents for web services. In its current incarnation, it supports four "public" registries:

- ❑ IBM UDDI Test Registry
- ❑ IBM UDDI Public Registry
- ❑ Microsoft UDDI Test Registry
- ❑ Microsoft UDDI Public Registry

A number of the larger technology corporations (HP, SAP, IBM, Microsoft) have announced that they will be providing public UDDI registries. Developers and consumers of web services will be able to create accounts on these public "directories" and upload their service information into this searchable public forum. These same vendors are offering "test" registries that allow developers the opportunity to work with UDDI without having to release their web services into production. WSTK also supports a local, "private" UDDI registry that uses DB2 as the data store for registry data. Within a single organization there will be many cases in which you will want to support local, non-public UDDI registries for web services that are run within the corporate firewall. In fact, many web services pundits believe that there will be more private directories than public UDDI entries. Fortunately, the technology works the same for both public and private directories.

For our example purposes, however, it makes sense to use IBM's Test Registry, which has been built for the express purpose of being a **test repository** for UDDI/WSDL information. You can access the IBM UDDI Test Registry from IBM's web site at:
https://www-3.ibm.com/services/uddi/testregistry/protect/registry.html.

The following figure shows the main UDDI Test Registry page from the IBM web site.

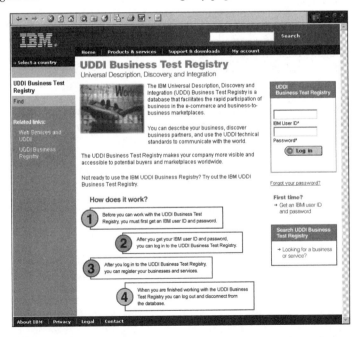

The UDDI Business Test Registry can be accessed free of charge, provided that you have an IBM user ID and password. (IBM customers that have registered with the IBM web site and DeveloperWorks members already have an IBM account.) You can use your existing IBM user ID and password (generated in Chapter 5) to connect to the registry through the logon section of the web page – but you will need to **activate** your registry account before you can use it.

> **The registration process is simple. Once you have entered your IBM user ID and password, use the links to navigate through the remainder of the registration process. After you complete the registration, the UDDI registry will send you an activation code via e-mail. The next time that you log onto the UDDI registry you will be asked to supply the activation code – then your account will be fully enabled. If you have the user ID and password generated from the v2 Beta UDDI Registry in Chapter 5, you will have to activate the Test Registry separately (you will be allowed to use the same user ID and password, but will be sent a different activation key).**

Initially, your account will be blank. Through the browser-based interface you can quickly create new **business entities** and **service definitions** (two of the four required UDDI data types). In the UDDI model, the business entity is the service provider, and each business can contain multiple business services.

It's a simple process to use the browser-based HTML panels to create your first business entity and then provide contact information for that entity. In order to work with the WSTK software you will want to have a registered business entity loaded into the IBM UDDI Test Registry. The browser interface will guide you through the process of registering a new business entity. We've used a fictional university called "NETU" as the business entity for our UDDI entry. When you have added a new entity (and provided all of the required contact information) you should be able to drill down into the entity name and view the business **Key** as shown in the following figure:

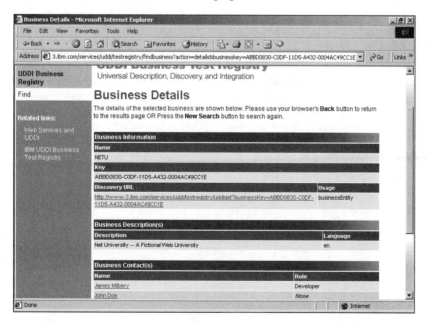

This registry is accessible through a number of additional interfaces, including Java code and a browser plug-in (which is available with the WSDE kit). IBM's WSDE (Web Services Development Environment) is another AlphaWorks project for defining web services that is likely to become part of IBM's WebSphere Studio commercial product. For the moment, all that you need to be concerned with is the business information Name and Key.

Implementing a Simple Web Service

The IBM WSTK kit comes equipped with a pre-configured WebSphere application server (which is part of the reason that the download kit is so large), but you may wish to make use of the standard Tomcat platform to build and deploy a simple web service. There are three pieces of software that you will need in order to build and invoke your first web service:

- ❑   Tomcat 3.2
- ❑   Apache SOAP 2.2
- ❑   Apache Xerces XML Parser 1.4.4
- ❑   Java Activation Framework (JAF) 1.0.1
- ❑   Java Mail 1.2

You probably have already downloaded this software for previous examples in the book. The starting point for your web services implementation is the Tomcat application server.

Tomcat 3.2 is the recommended version to use with Apache SOAP, so download Tomcat 3.2 from the Jakarta web site using the following URL: http://jakarta.apache.org/tomcat/index.html.

Unpack the archive to a root directory on your local machine. Once you have unpacked the Tomcat server and set its TOMCAT_HOME variable to the installation directory, you can download the Apache SOAP installation kit, and the Xerces XML parser and unzip them into directory trees.

For the Xerces XML parser, navigate to the main web site, http://xml.apache.org/xerces-j/, and then use the Download link to get to the Xerces-J-bin-1.4.4 archive. (There may be newer versions of this library available, and you are free to use them. However, they may **not** work with the examples that we've used here. We have tested the examples in this chapter with several different versions of each of the products – Tomcat, Xerces, SOAP, and WSTK. However, if you have problems with a specific release of any component, we suggest that you drop back to the specific versions that are referenced here.)

The Apache SOAP files can be downloaded at the following web site: http://xml.apache.org/soap/index.html. You will need to use the Download button here as well to locate the version 2.2 archive for your selected platform.

The JAF JAR (activation.jar) and Java Mail JAR (mail.jar) are both available from the Sun Microsystems site (www.sun.com). Copy these JARs, and your xerces.jar into the lib directory of your SOAP installation (in our case, C:\soap-2_2\lib), along with your soap.jar file.

Configuring the Tomcat server to use the SOAP libraries and Xerces parser is a relatively simple process. All that you need to do is to add the xerces.jar and soap.jar files to your classpath. On our sample system, including the files for our SOAP application, this results in the following classpath definition (add the following lines of code to your %TOMCAT_HOME%bin\tomcat.bat file:

```
echo.
set CLASSPATH=.;C:\soap-2_2\lib\xerces.jar;C:\soap-2_2\lib\soap.jar; C:\soap-
2_2\lib\mail.jar; C:\soap-2_2\lib\activation.jar;C:\javawebservices\Ch10\alumni
echo Using CLASSPATH: %CP%
set CLASSPATH=%CP%
```

The last step in the process is to add a <content> entry to your Tomcat server configuration file so that it automatically works with the Apache SOAP subsystem. You will need to edit the \conf\server.xml file in the Tomcat directory to include the following text (add the lines that are highlighted):

```
<Context path="/examples"
         docBase="webapps/examples"
         crossContext="false"
         debug="0"
         reloadable="true" >
</Context>

<Context
         path="/soap"
         docBase="C:/soap-2_2/webapps/soap"
         crossContext="true"
         debug="0"
         reloadable="true">
</Context>

<Context
         path="/alumni"
         docBase="C:/javawebservices/Ch10/alumni"
         crossContext="false"
         debug="0"
         reloadable="true">
</Context>
```

This context entry should be placed within the section of the server.xml file that is marked with the "<!-- Tomcat Root Context -->" comment. (Remember to replace the string "C:/soap2_2" with the root directory into which you installed the Apache SOAP 2.2 code.) Alternatively, you can simply copy the SOAP.WAR archive to the WEBAPPS directory for your Tomcat server.

This context entry creates the equivalent of an Apache alias for the Tomcat server. In the preceding block of code, we have used the directory C:\soap-2_2\webapps\soap as the physical directory location. This is the local directory into which we will load the SOAP files for our application. The docBase entry in the server.xml file associates the "/soap" portion of a URL string (such as http://myserver.com/soap/) with the physical directory on your server. You will want to use a directory that is specific to your installation. The root directory (C:/soap-2_2 in our case) is the main directory into which we unloaded the SOAP libraries. At this point in the process, you are ready to run the Tomcat server. By default the server will use port 8080, but you can modify this by editing the port parameter value in the server.xml file.

Start Tomcat and have it running in the background – using the `startup.bat/startup.sh` scripts in the `/bin` subdirectory of your Tomcat installation.

Creating a Simple Web Service

The next step in the process is to create a very simple web service. Theoretically speaking, the core business logic for your web service could be almost anything, a Java class, JavaBean, EJB, Servlet, JSP, or even a COBOL program. (Although you would most likely wrap platform-specific code with Java code for web services.)

Consider the following block of simple Java code:

```java
import java.util.Date;
import java.io.*;
import java.text.*;

public class alumniDonations {
  public float showCash(String paramClassYear) {
    String today = DateFormat.getInstance().format(new Date());
    int classYear = Integer.parseInt(paramClassYear);
    switch (classYear) {
    case 1995:
      System.out.println("As of " + today
                      + " the Class of 1995 has donated $2,779,444");
      return 2779444F;
    case 1996:
      System.out.println("As of " + today
                      + " the Class of 1996 has donated $3,233,242");
      return 3233242F;
    case 1997:
      System.out.println("As of " + today
                      + " the Class of 1997 has donated $3,342,048");
      return 3342048F;
    case 1998:
      System.out.println("As of " + today
                      + " the Class of 1998 has donated $3,196,344");
      return 3196344F;
    case 1999:
      System.out.println("As of " + today
                      + " the Class of 1999 has donated $3,487,049");
      return 3487049F;
    case 2000:
      System.out.println("As of " + today
                      + "the Class of 2000 has donated $3,910,120");
      return 3910120F;
    default:
      System.out.println("No data for class value");
      return 1F;
    }
  }
}
```

This very simple Java program is based on the Net University database schema. The Net University schema is a simple data model that has objects (and data) for a fictional university.

While you do not need to use this data model for the examples in this chapter, you can download it from the Internet at the following address:

(http://www.makingthetechnicalsale.com/kuromaku/Netuniversity50.exe).

The program accepts a single string parameter for the year of graduation. The string is converted into an integer and then the program executes a switch block to output a string of text that shows the total amount of donations to the university for the selected class year – and returns the dollar amount as a floating point value.

In reality, this is about as simple a block of code as you could possibly get. There are no database connections, no URLs to be processed, no resources that have to be marshaled, and the output is a simple text string and a single floating point value. For all practical purposes such a simple program would not be a likely candidate for a web service. However, it is very important that you start simply with web services. There are so many moving parts and so many different software standards that it is very easy to get lost.

First of all, create a local directory for the alumniDonations class at C:\javawebservices\Ch10\alumni, and copy the alumniDonations.java source from the Wrox code download into this directory. Add the alumni directory to your classpath, along with the following JAR files:

```
set CLASSPATH=.;C:\soap-2_2\lib\xerces.jar;C:\soap-2_2\lib\mail.jar;C:\soap-
2_2\lib\soap.jar;C:\soap-2_2\lib\activation.jar
```

Compile the code:

```
C:\javawebservices\Ch10\alumni>javac alumniDonations.java
```

Create a JAR file to hold the compiled Java code:

```
C:\javawebservices\Ch10\alumni>jar -cf alumni.jar alumniDonations.class
```

The next step in the process is to implement the required client code to access the web service. Theoretically, we might want to actually **deploy** the service before we run it, but it is just as easy to create the client code first.

```
import java.net.*;
import java.util.*;
import org.apache.soap.*;
import org.apache.soap.rpc.*;

public class alumniClient {
  public static void main(String argv[]) throws Exception {

    /**
     * argv[0] = Server address ?
```

```
      * http://<servername>:<port>/soap/servlet/rpcrouter
 */

 // argv[1] = Class year - 1995, 1996, 1997, 1998, 1999, 2000

 URL soapURL = new URL(argv[0]);
 String urn = "urn:alumni:alumnidonations";
 Call call = new Call();
 call.setTargetObjectURI(urn);
 call.setMethodName("showCash");
 call.setEncodingStyleURI(Constants.NS_URI_SOAP_ENC);
 Vector callParms = new Vector();
 callParms.addElement(new Parameter("paramClassYear", String.class,
                            argv[1], null));
 call.setParams(callParms);

 try {
   System.out.println("Calling Web Service URL " + soapURL
                      + " with URN = " + urn);
   Response response = call.invoke(soapURL, "");
   Parameter result = response.getReturnValue();
   System.out.println("Web Service Response = " + result.getValue());
 } catch (SOAPException err) {
   System.out.println("SOAP Error " + err.getFaultCode() + ","
                      + err.getMessage());

 }
  }
 }
```

The client code is also quite simple, and it has been implemented using the SOAP **RPC (Remote Procedure Call)** interface. You pass the program the address of the SOAP server (Tomcat) and a string parameter value for the class year. The client program passes a URN "urn:alumni:alumnidonations" as part of the invocation of the service.

At this point in the process, we have not yet defined the URN for our sample application – but we will do so before we run the client code. Parameters to the underlying class and method (alumniDonations) are sent to the web service by the Parameter object. For each parameter you must provide the argument name, the type of the argument, the value of the argument, and the encoding style. The method call is sent to the SOAP endpoint by the invoke() method.

In order to run this SOAP-based client, you must compile the client code and register the web service with the SOAP Server.

Set the classpath again and compile the alumniClient.java code:

```
C:\javawebservices\Ch10\alumni>javac alumniClient.java
```

Access the deployment panels for your web service by navigating to the administration panel:

```
http://localhost:8080/soap/admin/index.html
```

The XML-SOAP administration client provides three basic functions:

- ❏ List
- ❏ Deploy
- ❏ Un-deploy

The List button displays a list of installed web services (of which there are none at this point). Using the Deploy button you can create an entry for this new web service. In order to deploy the alumniDonations web service, you will need to provide five pieces of information to the registration panel.

The first item is the **identifier**, which matches the URN value that was written into the client code. The URN follows a standard format. In our example case it will be the string "urn" followed by the name of the web service that the client code will use to reference the service (alumnidonations). The resulting string for our example is urn:alumni:alumnidonations. (See Chapter 3 for a complete discussion of SOAP and URN naming conventions.)

The **scope** of this service will be a "request" service, since a new instance will be created for each user. While this may not be a scalable solution, it fits the purpose of this simple example.

The **methods** field contains a list of the methods that are exposed within this web service. While the alumniDonations class has only a single method, a more complex web service could support a variety of methods within a class.

The **provider** for our web service is Java. This particular release of Apache/SOAP only supports Java and bean scripts, and this is one of the reasons why we'll be looking at the WSTK software.

The final element of our web service is the **Java provider**. The provider class maps to the name of the underlying class (alumniDonations), which is not a static class. (This is taken literally from the class definition of your SOAP service. If your code uses "static" classes, then you will need to mark the entry with the "static" qualifier.)

Once you enter the appropriate values into the fields on the HTML page and press the Deploy button the deployment data is stored inside a binary file (DeployedServices.ds).

The results of adding the `alumniDonations` web service to the local Tomcat installation are shown in the following figure:

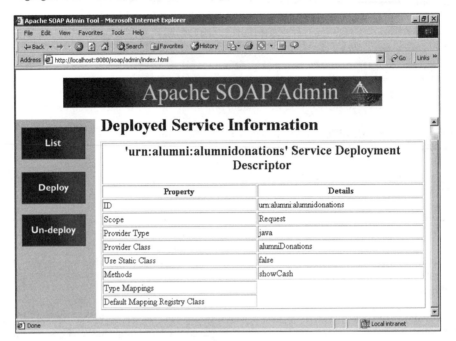

After you have deployed the web service, you can use the `alumniClient` class to run the code and display the output as shown in the following figure:

The basic flow of web services is derived from this very simple example. We've set up the Tomcat server to handle our SOAP requests using RPC over HTTP, but you are free to use any other transport protocol to deliver SOAP messages.

In the following block of code you can see the detailed SOAP message that is sent as an HTTP POST. You will remember that we defined this web service as a POST operation through the browser interface. The top portion of the message is the envelope, which contains namespace information for the envelope itself, XML schema, and the XML schema for the datatypes.

The critical portion of the message is the envelope body. Since we are using a SOAP RPC call, the body of the message is relatively simple. It contains a reference to the name of the method (showCash()), the URN that was defined as the name for the web service, and the various parameter values that are being passed along with the RCP.

```
POST /soap/servlet/rpcrouter HTTP/1.0

Host: localhost:8070
Content-Type: text/xml
Content-Length: 434
SOAPAction: ""

<SOAP-ENV:Envelope xmlns:SOAP-ENV="http://schemas.xmlsoap.org/soap/envelope/"
    xmlns:xsi="http://www.w3.org/1999/XMLSchema-instance"
    xmlns:xsd="http://www.w3.org/1999/XMLSchema">
  <SOAP-ENV:Body>
    <ns1:showCash xmlns:ns1="urn:alumni:alumnidonations" SOAP-
        ENV:encodingStyle="http://schemas.xmlsoap.org/soap/encoding/">
      <paramClassYear xsi:type="xsd:string">1996</paramClassYear>
    </ns1:showCash>
  </SOAP-ENV:Body>
</SOAP-ENV:Envelope>
```

The response message is also returned as an XML message using a standard HTTP reply. The return message includes the XSI/XSD type definitions for the datatype of the return result (which is a floating point value in our simple case.)

```
HTTP/1.0 200 OK

Content-Type: text/xml; charset=UTF-8
Content-Length: 1109
Set-Cookie2: JSESSIONID=fcf3am8rk1;Version=1;Discard;Path="/soap"
Set-Cookie: JSESSIONID=fcf3am8rk1;Path=/soap
Servlet-Engine: Tomcat Web Server/3.2.3 (JSP 1.1; Servlet 2.2; Java 1.3.0_02;
Windows 2000 5.0 x86; java.vendor=Sun Microsystems Inc.)

<SOAP-ENV:Envelope xmlns:SOAP-ENV="http://schemas.xmlsoap.org/soap/envelope/"
    xmlns:xsi="http://www.w3.org/1999/XMLSchema-instance"
    xmlns:xsd="http://www.w3.org/1999/XMLSchema">
  <SOAP-ENV:Body>
    <ns1:showCash xmlns:ns1="urn:alumni:alumnidonations" SOAP-
        ENV:encodingStyle="http://schemas.xmlsoap.org/soap/encoding/">
      <return xsi:type="xsd:float"> 3233242.00</return>
    </ns1:showCash>
  </SOAP-ENV:Body>
</SOAP-ENV:Envelope>
```

For our simple alumniDonations example, you can see how easy it is to send SOAP messages back and forth using RPC-HTTP and XML. This example case is very straightforward, since we are using Java for both ends of the equation and we are not attempting to pass complex objects across the wire.

One of the main issues with this example is that we are essentially hard-coding this SOAP application. Once the web service has been defined to the Tomcat server, the client application has to know where to find the web service. One solution to this problem is to insulate the web service in WSDL code and to store the resulting WSDL in a UDDI registry.

Working with IBM's Web Services ToolKit

IBM maintains two public web sites that allow developers to gain access to new technologies in advance of their deployment into the marketplace. IBM's **DeveloperWorks** web site (http://www.ibm.com/developerworks) is the resource for training materials, tools, and code. You will find lots of interesting code samples and discussion groups on the DeveloperWorks web site.

IBM's **AlphaWorks** web site (http://www.ibm.com/alphaworks/) is the primary destination for emerging technologies. IBM uses the AlphaWorks web site to preview new technology to the market. Sometimes this technology eventually finds its way into commercial IBM products – but this is not always the case.

There are two interesting web services technology kits available on the AlphaWorks web site. IBM's **Web Services Development Environment (WSDE)** is a standalone tool for XML and web services development. IBM has plans to include major components from WSDE in their WebSphere Studio Development tool.

IBM's Web Services ToolKit, on the other hand, is a software development kit for designing and executing web service applications. Through WSTK, web services and clients can automatically find one another (through UDDI) and can collaborate without additional programming or human intervention. WSTK is essentially a development tool kit that is separate from any particular Java IDE or application server. You can use WSTK to create WSDL files from your existing Java code using a simple set of command line utilities. The WSTK can be downloaded from IBM's AlphaWorks web site at the following URL:

> http://www.alphaworks.ibm.com/aw.nsf/download/webservicesToolKit/

Installing WSTK

The WSTK installation is relatively straightforward. IBM packages the WSTK installation kit as a self-installing InstallShield program, for Windows and Linux. (Each new version of the software seems to get larger, as of this writing it was just about 43 MB in size.) You simply download the executable and run it locally on your desktop to install the software. The installation script handles almost all of the installation tasks, but there are some specific choices that you will want to make during the installation process.

In particular, you will want to select the **custom** install. This will allow you to install all of the WSTK demos, as shown in the following figure.

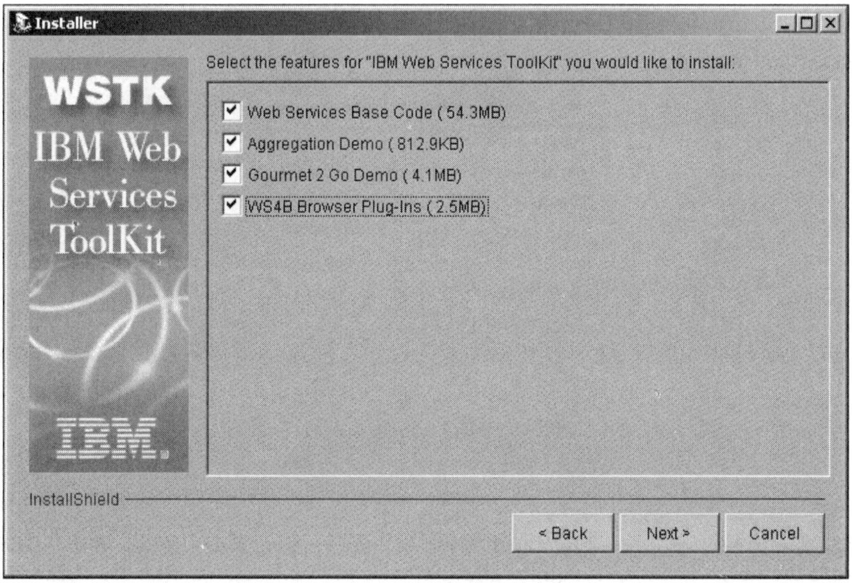

The remainder of the installation is self-explanatory.

Configuring the WSTK

The WSTK installation program will automatically run the WSTK configuration program (`%WSTK_HOME%\bin\wstkconfig.bat`) once the WSTK software has been installed. The configuration program links WSTK with your application server, and configures the software to work with a UDDI directory. The first panel to appear in the Web Services ToolKit Configuration Tool is the Configure WebServers panel as shown in the following figure:

The WSTK software comes equipped with an embedded version of the WebSphere application server, and this is the simplest configuration to follow. However, you will get a lot more out of WSTK by using one of the external application server interfaces, such as Tomcat. By using the Tomcat interface you can work with the configuration files more directly. In order to connect WSTK to your application server, you will need to know the `port number`, `host server` name and the `physical server location`. (The only tricky item is the server location, and the help panels can direct you to the right directory location. In our example case, we've used `c:\jakarta-tomcat-3.2.3` as the physical server location.)

The second panel in the configuration tool handles the UDDI interface, as shown in the following figure:

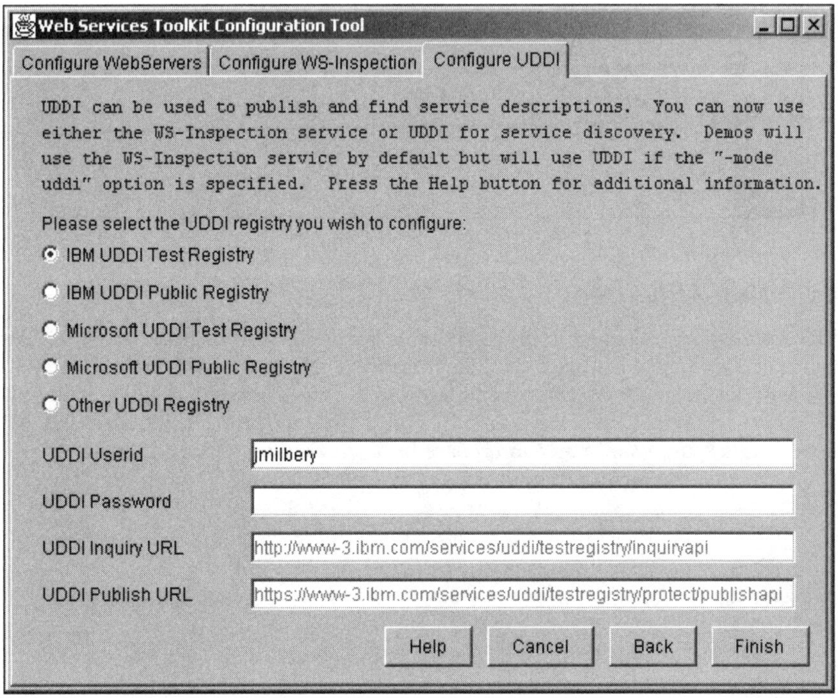

The UDDI registry is the repository for the WSDL files that you create with WSTK. IBM provides a standalone version of the UDDI registry that you can install locally within your environment. This local registry uses DB2 as the registry data store. Organizations will ultimately need to have both types of registries available.

A local, private registry will be used for both intranet web services and extranet web services – and a public registry for Internet web services clients. (You can access all three registries from the IBM web site at http://www-3.ibm.com/services/uddi/). Should you wish to use a private UDDI/DB2 along with WSTK, you can download a UDDI kit from the AlphaWorks web site. The examples in the next section are based on the IBM UDDI Test Registry, but they should work with any of the registries that are listed on the preceding panel.

> If you plan on using your IBM UDDI Test Registry account, make sure that you have
> created your account and activated the account as discussed in the preceding section
> entitled *Creating a Test UDDI Account*. Use your IBM UDDI Test Registry UDDI user
> ID and UDDI password on the **Configure UDDI** panel to configure the registry.
> (Make sure that your Tomcat server is not running during the configuration process.)

Finally, you should see a message box like the one below. Adjust your files accordingly:

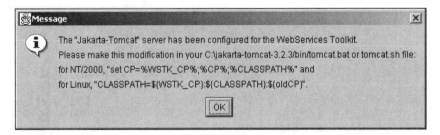

Post-installation Adjustments

The WSTK installation uses specific versions of the Xerces and SOAP libraries, and it also requires a small change to the Tomcat configuration file (`%TOMCAT_HOME%/conf/server.xml`). The IBM WSTK software uses URLs to locate WSDL documents for any web services that you create. In order to locate these documents, the WSTK references an alias within the application server. Ultimately, you will want to make use of this feature, and you can prepare for this eventuality by adding a new context entry to the Tomcat server (in the section of the `server.xml` file in Tomcat's `conf` directory that is marked with the string "`<!-- Tomcat Root Context -->`") as follows:

```
<Context
    reloadable="true"
    path="/wsdl"
    docBase="C:\javawebservices\Ch10\alumni"
    debug="0"/>
</Context>
```

The `docBase` entry should match the physical directory where you will store the WSDL files. For the sake of simplicity, we used the same directory in which the alumni Java source code is stored (`C:\javawebservices\Ch10\alumni`). The resulting context section of the Tomcat `server.xml` file (in the `%TOMCAT_HOME%/conf` directory) will contain the following entries:

```
    <Context reloadable="true" path="/ecounter_services"
docBase="c:\wstk24/demos/entity" debug="0"/>
    <Context reloadable="true" path="/counter_services"
docBase="c:\wstk24/demos/stateful" debug="0"/>
    <Context reloadable="true" path="/combine_services"
docBase="c:\wstk24/demos/stateless" debug="0"/>
    <Context reloadable="true" path="/comadder_services"
docBase="c:\wstk24/demos/comadder" debug="0"/>
    <Context reloadable="true" path="/addressbook_services"
docBase="c:\wstk24/demos/addressbook" debug="0"/>
    <Context reloadable="true" path="/xkms" docBase="c:\wstk24/demos/xkms"
debug="0"/>
    <Context reloadable="true" path="/buy_services"
docBase="c:\wstk24/demos/httpr" debug="0"/>
```

```
    <Context reloadable="true" path="/stockquote_services"
docBase="c:\wstk24/demos/stockquote" debug="0"/>
    <Context reloadable="true" path="/wsdl2java"
docBase="c:\wstk24/demos/wsdl2java" debug="0"/>
    <Context reloadable="true" path="/attachment_services"
docBase="c:\wstk24/demos/attachments" debug="0"/>
    <Context reloadable="true" path="/webservice_services"
docBase="c:\wstk24/demos/webservice" debug="0"/>
    <Context reloadable="true" path="/aggr"
docBase="c:\wstk24/demos/aggregation/webapps/aggregation" debug="0"/>
    <Context reloadable="true" path="/g2g_services"
docBase="c:\wstk24/demos/g2g/services" debug="0"/>
    <Context reloadable="true" path="/httpr"
docBase="c:\wstk24/httpr/webapps/httpr" debug="0"/>
    <Context reloadable="true" path="/axis" docBase="c:\wstk24/axis/webapps/axis"
debug="0"/>
    <Context reloadable="true" path="/soap" docBase="c:\wstk24/soap/webapps/soap"
debug="0"/>
    <Context reloadable="true" path="/soap-admin"
docBase="c:\wstk24/soap/webapps/soap/admin" debug="0"/>
    <Context reloadable="true" path="/g2g"
docBase="c:\wstk24/demos/g2g/webapps/g2g" debug="0"/>
    <Context reloadable="true" path="/wsdl" docBase="c:\alumni" debug="0"/>
```

The changes that the WSTK installation makes to the Tomcat `server.conf` file are mostly path settings for the various demos. The one major change that you need to be aware of is the redirection of the SOAP aliases. Once you have installed WSTK, your local copy of Tomcat will rely on the SOAP libraries that are shipped with WSTK.

Working with WSTK

The primary goal of the Web Services ToolKit is to make it easier to create, publish, and execute web services.

In order to achieve this goal, the software provides a number of built-in services:

❑ Client run-time API that implements service discovery and service proxy functionality for a number of UDDI registries

❑ Server-side deployment of services based on SOAP

❑ A set of tools including a WSDL generator, Java classes for manipulating WSDL documents programmatically, and a proxy client generator

❑ Samples, demos, and code previews

The first tool that you will make use of is the WSDL generator. As discussed in detail in previous chapters, WSDL is essentially a description of the capabilities of a given web service – stored in XML format.

WSTK provides the `wsdlgen.bat` (`wsdlgen.sh` for UNIX) script that starts the WSDL generator, as shown in the following figure:

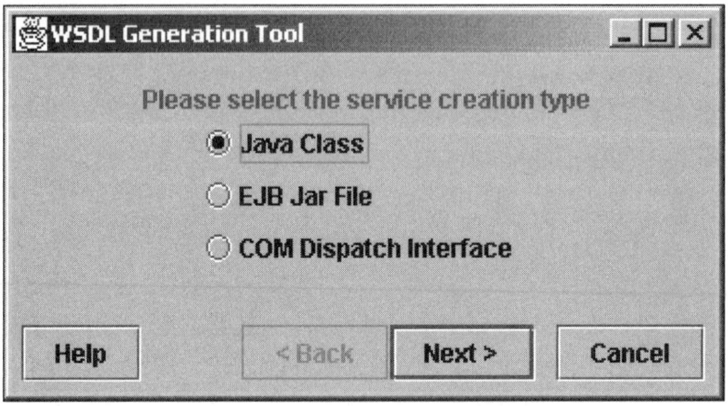

The starting point for the WSDL generation process is the type of service that you want to wrap in WSDL code. WSTK can generate WSDL descriptions from Java class files, EJBs, and COM objects. You will most likely start off by using a simple Java class (such as `alumniDonations`). The second panel in the WSDL generation interface allows you to select a particular Java class to be used for the code generation process, as shown in the following figure:

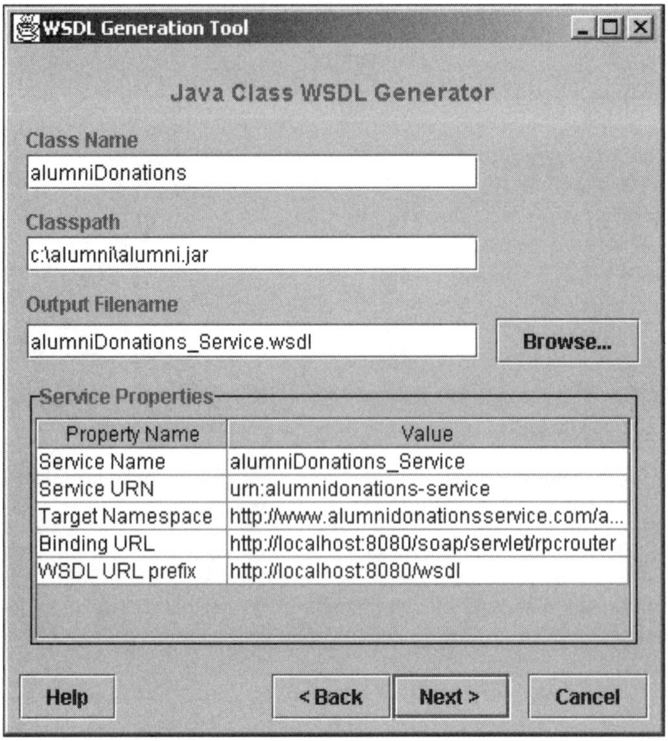

The class name field points to the fully qualified class name (package and class) that you wish to provide access to using a Java wrapper. The class that you select must adhere to the following requirements:

❑ Non-abstract

❑ Not an interface

❑ Have public non-static methods

The `alumniDonations` class is not part of a package (as shown in the preceding figure), so it can be referenced directly. Classes that have package definitions require that you include the package information (for example: `com.ibm.samples.NasdaQuotes`). If the class you specified is not in the environment `classpath` setting, you must add a classpath entry for the class name value. You are free to reference both directory paths and JAR files, but you must be sure to include classpaths for any classes that are required for the construction of the "class name" class (that is, superclasses and utility classes).

The WSDL generator will suggest a file name for you automatically. The full WSDL document is written to the **Output Filename** location. Within the same directory, additional WSDL files for implementation and interface are written for use with the UDDI-based registry and the web service client. The **Service Name** and **Service URN** follow the same conventions discussed in previous sections. A valid URN is a string beginning with `urn:` followed by a unique string for the service. The WSDL generator automatically designates a namespace identifier for the service, but you are permitted to enter your own values by overwriting the text in the **Value** textboxes.

The WSDL generator picks up the server definition from the Tomcat installation and automatically designates a binding URL for the SOAP transport. The final element in the generation process is a URL prefix that the client program can reference to access the generated WSDL. You will need to have this context path defined in the Tomcat `server.xml` file in order to generate the proxy client later on.

The next panel in the generation wizard is shown in the following figure:

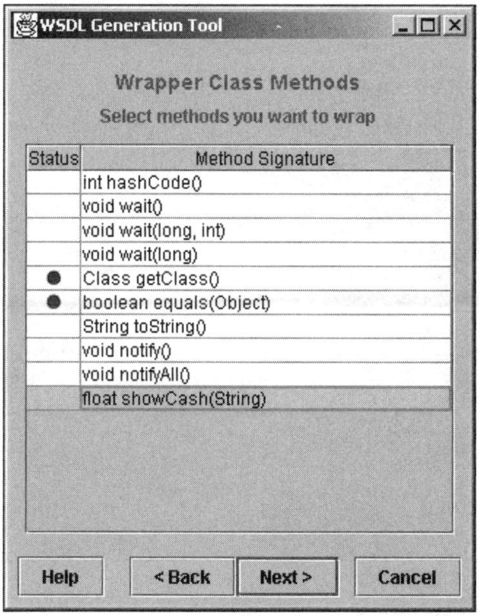

The WSDL generator will automatically present you with a list of public methods for the Java class that you selected on the Class panel. Methods that make use of non-primitive data types will cause problems for the current incarnation of the generator. The interface marks such methods with a red dot so that you will be aware of this issue. The method that we have exposed in the `alumniDonations` class is the `showCash()` method, which returns a simple float value – so there is no red dot next to the `showCash()` method.

The generator automatically displays a mapping panel that can assist you with the process of mapping of non-primitive data types – as shown in the following figure:

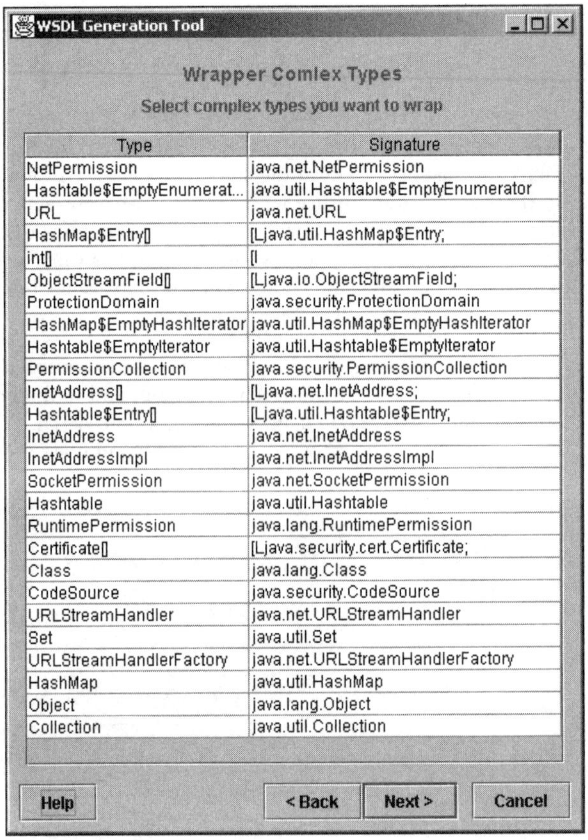

Complex data types are any non-primitive Java data types. WSDL supports the following primitive data types directly:

❑ `int, short`

❑ `double, float`

❑ `long`

❑ `String`

- ❏ `char`
- ❏ `byte`
- ❏ `boolean`

The WSDL generator UI generates a table for all of the complex types that were encountered in any of the selected methods. Complex types that are defined within other complex types are automatically added to this list. (One major omission in this version of the software is support for arrays – you cannot map arrays with the generator).

The WSDL generator creates three files from your selected class:

- ❏ A deployment descriptor – `DeploymentDescriptor.xml`
- ❏ A service file – `<classname>_Service.wsdl`
- ❏ A service interface file – `<classname>_Service-interface.wsdl`

The deployment descriptor file contains the same data elements that you would have used to manually add the web service to the Tomcat server. You will notice that it contains all of the same elements, written in an XML format.

```
<isd:service xmlns:isd="http://xml.apache.org/xml-soap/deployment"
id="urn:alumnidonations-service" checkMustUnderstands="false">
  <isd:provider type="java" scope="Application" methods="showCash">
    <isd:java class="alumniDonations" static="false"/>
  </isd:provider>
</isd:service>
```

In fact, you could load this XML file into the Tomcat server programmatically, by using the following Java code:

```
C:\javawebservices\Ch10\alumni>java org.apache.soap.server.ServiceManagerClient
http://localhost:8080/soap/servlet/rpcrouter deploy DeploymentDescriptor.xml
```

This block of code is executed as a standalone program, but you could reference the same class file dynamically within your own code to load the new web service "on the fly".

The WSDL generator creates a "service" file that describes the new web service. The generated WSDL service code for the `alumniDonations` service appears below:

```
<?xml version="1.0" encoding="UTF-8"?>
<definitions name="alumniDonations_Service"
  targetNamespace="http://www.alumnidonationsservice.com/alumniDonations"
  xmlns="http://schemas.xmlsoap.org/wsdl/"
  xmlns:interface="http://www.alumnidonationsservice.com/alumniDonations-
      interface"
  xmlns:soap="http://schemas.xmlsoap.org/wsdl/soap/"
  xmlns:types="http://www.alumnidonationsservice.com/alumniDonations"
    xmlns:xsd="http://www.w3.org/2001/XMLSchema">
```

```
<import
    location="http://localhost:8080/wsdl/alumniDonations_Service-interface.wsdl"
    namespace="http://www.alumnidonationsservice.com/alumniDonations-interface">
</import>

<service
    name="alumniDonations_Service">
  <documentation>IBM WSTK V2.4 generated service definition file</documentation>
  <port
      binding="interface:alumniDonations_ServiceBinding"
        name="alumniDonations_ServicePort">
    <soap:address location="http://localhost:8080/soap/servlet/rpcrouter"/>
  </port>
</service>

</definitions>
```

The core element of the service file is the `<definitions>` element. Each WSDL service file will generally define a single service, but this is not a hard requirement. The first attribute within the definition element is the `name` attribute, which indicates the purpose of the web service. The WSDL generator uses the name of the Java class with the suffix `Service` for the `name`.

The WSDL generator adds a number of XML namespaces directly after the name. The `targetNamespace` defines a unique name for the logical namespace. The WSDL generator constructs an artificial, unique name from the Java class as well. The interface URI and the types URI are set to match this name namespace. The remainder of the namespace entries refer to the various XML and SOAP namespaces that are required by SOAP.

The `<import>` element maps to a URL-based location where the interface to the web service can be located. Client programs can reference this URL to gain access to the interface definition of the web service. (This element refers to the third file that is generated by the WSDLGEN program – the **public** interface to the service is not the same as the **definition** of the service itself.) The remaining elements in the service definition refer to elements that are defined in the last file – the interface definition file:

```
<?xml version="1.0" encoding="UTF-8"?>
<definitions name="alumniDonations_Service"
  targetNamespace="http://www.alumnidonationsservice.com/alumniDonations-
interface"
  xmlns="http://schemas.xmlsoap.org/wsdl/"
  xmlns:soap="http://schemas.xmlsoap.org/wsdl/soap/"
  xmlns:tns="http://www.alumnidonationsservice.com/alumniDonations-interface"
  xmlns:types="http://www.alumnidonationsservice.com/alumniDonations-
interface/types/"
    xmlns:xsd="http://www.w3.org/2001/XMLSchema">

<message
      name="InshowCashRequest">
  <part name="meth1_inType1"
    type="xsd:string"/>
</message>

<message
name="OutshowCashResponse">
```

```
      <part name="meth1_outType"
        type="xsd:float"/>
  </message>


  <portType
        name="alumniDonations_Service">
    <operation
          name="showCash">
      <input
          message="tns:InshowCashRequest"/>
      <output
      message="tns:OutshowCashResponse"/>
    </operation>
  </portType>


  <binding
      name="alumniDonations_ServiceBinding"
        type="tns:alumniDonations_Service">
    <soap:binding style="rpc"
        transport="http://schemas.xmlsoap.org/soap/http"/>
    <operation
          name="showCash">
      <soap:operation
          soapAction="urn:alumnidonations-service"/>
      <input>
        <soap:body
            encodingStyle="http://schemas.xmlsoap.org/soap/encoding/"
            namespace="urn:alumnidonations-service"
            use="encoded"/>
      </input>
      <output>
        <soap:body
            encodingStyle="http://schemas.xmlsoap.org/soap/encoding/"
            namespace="urn:alumnidonations-service" use="encoded"/>
      </output>
    </operation>
  </binding>

</definitions>
```

The top portion of the service interface definition file matches the definitions in the service file (the name, namespace, and so on). The new elements of the definition appear in the latter part of this last file. The bottom portion of the service file can be divided into three sections: <message>, <binding>, and <service>. Each <message> element corresponds to the inputs and outputs of the various methods of the underlying class. During the WSDL generation process, the developer chooses the methods in the class file. The WSDL generator creates input and output messages for each of these classes. (Void classes do not have output messages.) The WSDL generator defines a unique name for each input and output message and uses the proper XML/SOAP data format for the datatype of the message. The alumniDonations Web Service accepts a single string parameter, for the class year, and outputs a single floating point value in return.

These unique message names are embedded into the <portType> definition for the web service. The <portType> element contains all of the selected methods for a given Java class. Each method maps to an <operation> element within the <portType>. The alumniDonations class has only a single method selected, so the WSDL service interface contains only a single operation. Operation elements are further divided into input and output messages, and these messages map back to the <message> element names that appear in the preceding section of the WSDL document.

The final section of the WSDL service implementation is the <binding> element. The binding element maps a <portType> definition using a specified protocol (SOAP, CORBA, DCOM, and so on.) We have chosen to provide the alumniDonations web service using RPC over HTTP with SOAP encoding, but WSDL supports other alternatives. Theoretically, we could make the alumniDonations service available through other protocols, simply by adding additional bindings. (WSTK supports COM objects in the current version of the WSTK, which would use an alternate binding.)

Within the binding element there is a <service> definition. The <service> element is essentially a collection of ports. The <service> names that are referenced within the <binding> element are defined in the second WSDL file, the service document. In order to use the alumniDonations web service, you will need to have access to both files.

Generating a Proxy Client

The final step in the WSTK process is to generate client code for the web service. One of the potentially powerful features of using a WSDL generator is the ability to generate client code from WSDL documents. This eliminates the need to manually create client programs. WSTK includes a client proxy generator (in the /bin directory within WSTK_HOME) that can create a Java SOAP-based client directly from the WSDL that you generate. The proxy generation utility runs as a Windows batch file (or as a UNIX shell script):

```
C:\javawebservices\Ch10\alumni>%WSTK_HOME%\bin\proxygen
alumniDonations_Service.wsdl
```

The generation program accepts the WSDL (Web Services Description Language) service document as a parameter. However, the proxy generation program (com.ibm.wstk.tools.gen.ui.Main), also expects the service interface file to be available through the application server. For the example case, alumniDonations, this means that the alumniDonations_Service-interface.wsdl file needs to be available at the URL http://localhost:8080/wsdl/alumniDonations_Service-interface.wsdl.

The output of the proxy generator is a Java source and matching class file. WSTK automatically adds a long package name to the generated code (although you can override this by using the -package qualifier).

```
package com.alumnidonationsservice.www.alumniDonations_interface;
/** Proxy object
"com.alumnidonationsservice.www.alumniDonations_interface.alumniDonations_ServiceB
inding"   */

public class alumniDonations_ServiceBinding
{
  public static java.net.URL[] _KnownServiceLocations= null;
  private org.apache.soap.rpc.Call _____call=new org.apache.soap.rpc.Call();
  private java.net.URL _____url= null;
```

```
   private java.lang.String SOAPActionURI = "";
   private org.apache.soap.encoding.SOAPMappingRegistry smr =
_____call.getSOAPMappingRegistry();
   static
   {
     try{
     _KnownServiceLocations= new java.net.URL[]{
       new java.net.URL("http://localhost:8080/soap/servlet/rpcrouter")
     };
     }catch(java.net.MalformedURLException e ){_KnownServiceLocations= new
java.net.URL[0];};
   }
   public alumniDonations_ServiceBinding(java.net.URL endPointURL)
   {
           _____call.setTargetObjectURI("urn:alumnidonations-service");

_____call.setEncodingStyleURI("http://schemas.xmlsoap.org/soap/encoding/");
     this._____url = endPointURL;
     this.SOAPActionURI = "urn:alumnidonations-service";
   }
   public synchronized float showCash (java.lang.String meth1_inType1)   throws
org.apache.soap.SOAPException
   {
     if(_____url == null) throw new
org.apache.soap.SOAPException(org.apache.soap.Constants.FAULT_CODE_CLIENT, "A URL
must be specified \"alumniDonations_ServiceBinding\"." );
     this._____call.setMethodName("showCash");
     java.util.Vector _____parms  = new java.util.Vector(1);
     _____parms.addElement( new org.apache.soap.rpc.Parameter("meth1_inType1",
java.lang.String.class, meth1_inType1, null));
     this._____call.setParams(_____parms);
     org.apache.soap.rpc.Response _____resp =
this._____call.invoke(_____url, SOAPActionURI);
     if(_____resp.generatedFault())
     {
       org.apache.soap.Fault _____fault = _____resp.getFault();
       throw new  org.apache.soap.SOAPException(_____fault.getFaultCode(),
_____fault.getFaultString());
     }
     return
((java.lang.Float)_____resp.getReturnValue().getValue()).floatValue();
   }
}
```

The generated client code is somewhat verbose, but the structure of the code is quite simple. If you compare the generated code with the original, manually-coded client class (alumniClient.java), you will notice some similarities. The main difference is that the generated client insulates you from the specifics of the SOAP implementation. The **generated** class definition declares a number of local attributes, and then verifies the service location (the Tomcat server). This client would be called by another "host" client, which further insulates the host client from the specifics of the underlying SOAP calls. The "host" client first uses the alumniDonations_ServiceBinding() method to bind the service (and find the access point). It then calls the generated showCash method with the required meth1_inType1 parameter. Remember: the WSDL service implementation file determines the particulars of this input parameter.

The proxy generator handles the conversion of the output parameter (meth1_outType1) back into the floating-point value. The web service must be deployed to the Tomcat server (or your particular application server) in order for the client code to work. The WSDL generator creates a unique service name, so the alumniDonations web service must be deployed to the Tomcat server using the new definitions as listed in the service file. You could load the definition programmatically by using the ServiceManagerClient class:

```
C:\javawebservices\Ch10\alumni>java org.apache.soap.server.ServiceManagerClient
http://localhost:8080/soap/servlet/rpcrouter deploy DeploymentDescriptor.xml
```

Alternatively, you could use the HTML-based SOAP manager to manually enter the values for the web service as we did earlier.

All that remains is to compile and run the client code. However, the WSTK software still has more capabilities loaded into its bag of tricks. In the last section, we will use the IBM UDDI Test Registry and WSTK to both deploy the web service and register it with a UDDI registry.

Deploying and Publishing with IBM UDDI4J

IBM's Web Services ToolKit includes the capability to publish your web service through the UDDI4J API. UDDI4J is a Java class library that provides an API to interact with a UDDI registry – such as the IBM UDDI Test Registry. As discussed in previous chapters in this book, UDDI provides three basic functions:

❑ **Publish**:
Register a web service (or business)

❑ **Find**:
Finds a particular Web service (or business)

❑ **Bind**:
Connects to, and interacts with, a web service

The UDDI4J is a very straightforward API. You can find detailed information about using the API on the IBM DeveloperWorks web site, and additionally, it is discussed in depth in Chapter 5. For example, the following snippet of code creates a connection to the IBM UDDI Test Registry:

```
UDDIProxy proxy = new UDDIProxy();

proxy.setInquiryURL("http://www-3.ibm.com/services/uddi/testregistry/inquiryapi");

proxy.setPublishURL("https://www-
3.ibm.com/services/uddi/testregistry/protect/publishapi");
```

WSTK further simplifies UDDI access by offering an additional level of abstraction. When you configure your WSDL environment with the configuration utility, WSTK sets up an additional proxy layer using the UDDI registry that you choose during the configuration process. This means that the deployment code that you write will work with any of the supported registries.

> **In practice, we have encountered some small bugs and ongoing configuration issues with the various UDDI registries. You will want to access the developer forums on the AlphaWorks web site to keep abreast of the latest issues with UDDI and WSTK.**

The WSTK software provides sample Java programs that can deploy a web service through UDDI4J. A simple program to deploy the `alumniDonations` service might look like this:

```java
import com.ibm.wstk.service.registry.ServiceRegistryProxy;
import com.ibm.wstk.service.provider.ServiceProvider;
import com.ibm.wstk.service.definition.soap.SOAPServiceDefinition;
import com.ibm.wstk.service.util.CategoryList;
import com.ibm.wstk.uddi.TModelKeyTable;

public class alumniDonationsDeploy {

  public static void main(String[] argv) throws Exception {

    // ----------------------------------------------------------
    // Collect the input arguments
    // ----------------------------------------------------------
    String serviceDefinitionWSDL = argv[0];
    String serviceDeployment = argv[1];
    String soapRouter = argv[2];

    // ----------------------------------------------------------
    // Use whatever UDDI registry you selected
    // in the WSTK Configuration Tool
    // ----------------------------------------------------------
    ServiceRegistryProxy srp = new ServiceRegistryProxy();

    // ----------------------------------------------------------
    // assuming that you haven't yet registered yourself as
    // a Service Provider, do the following steps. If you
    // have already registered as a service provider, you
    // should use your existing registration
    // ----------------------------------------------------------
    CategoryList spCatList = new CategoryList();
    spCatList.addCategory(TModelKeyTable.UNSPSC, "84121801",
                    TModelKeyTable.UNSPSC_TMODEL_KEY);
    ServiceProvider sp = new ServiceProvider("NETU", "AlumniDonations",
                                    spCatList);
    sp = srp.publish(sp);

    System.out.println();
    System.out.println("Service Provider Published");
    System.out.println("\t" + sp.getName());
    System.out.println("\t" + sp.getBusinessKey());
    System.out.println();

    // ----------------------------------------------------------
    // now we deploy and publish the service itself
    // ----------------------------------------------------------
```

```
        CategoryList sdCatList = new CategoryList();
        sdCatList.addCategory(TModelKeyTable.UNSPSC, "84121801",
                            TModelKeyTable.UNSPSC_TMODEL_KEY);
        SOAPServiceDefinition sd =
          new SOAPServiceDefinition(serviceDefinitionWSDL, sdCatList,
                                serviceDeployment, soapRouter);

        sd.createServiceManagerProxy().deployService(sd);    // - deploy
        srp.publish(sp, sd);                                 // - publish

        System.out.println();
        System.out.println("Service Description Published");
        System.out.println("\t" + sd.getName());
        System.out.println("\t"
                            + sd.getServiceImplementation().getServiceKey());
        System.out.println("\t" + serviceDefinitionWSDL);
        System.out.println("\t" + soapRouter);
        System.out.println();

        System.out.println("Done!");
    }
}
```

This simple block of code connects to the UDDI registry and registers your business. Next, it creates the service entry in the registry and then deploys the service to your designated application server. The program accepts three input parameters:

❑   `http://localhost:8080/wsdl/alumniDonations_Service.wsdl`

❑   `C:\javawebservices\Ch10\alumni\DeployDescriptor.xml`

❑   `http://localhost:8080/soap/servlet/rpcrouter`

The first parameter is a URL to the `alumniDonations_Service` WSDL file, and the second parameter is the deployment descriptor file. The deploy program uses the `DeployDescriptor.xml` file (as discussed in the previous section) to write the service into the local Tomcat application server. The final parameter is the address of the SOAP server that is hosting the deployed service.

IBM provides a very powerful client-based UDDI browser that offers a wealth of tools for working directly with UDDI and WSDL in their web services development environment software. You may wish to download this additional tool set in order to simplify your interaction with the UDDI Test Registry.

The deploy program adds the new service to the UDDI registry, and then deploys the service to the Tomcat server. Other users can access the WSDL descriptor through the URL that is published to the UDDI registry. The software automatically locates the service interface file (`alumniDonations_Service-interface.wsdl`) – so that users can generate their own, local proxy clients for the published web service. If you were to deploy the web service to a publicly available Tomcat server (or WebSphere application server), then clients could generate and run their own clients without any knowledge of how the `alumniDonations` code works. (Of course, they would need a local copy of the WSTK software installed in order to run the proxy generation process.)

Summary

In this chapter we've looked at an end-to-end solution for building and deploying a Java-based web service using IBM's WSTK technology and standard Tomcat/SOAP server technology. Although WSTK is not a commercial product, it does provide a good outline of the services that WSDL-generators are meant to provide.

In the first part of this chapter we introduced you to IBM's stack of server technologies. Each of these products has some role in the deployment of web services. The implementation requirements for your own web services will determine the exact mix of IBM server products that you will need to use.

The second section introduced you to IBM's UDDI Test Registry, where you can register your business and your web services. We then implemented a very simple web service using Tomcat and Apache SOAP. The code for this first web service is relatively simple, but it requires the developer to have specific knowledge about the implementation details of the RPC-based SOAP service. We then introduced the concept of using IBM's WSTK to abstract the developer from the specifics of underlying web services using WSDL. Finally, we fed the generated WSDL documents back into the UDDI registry, where other developers can quickly access the new web service.

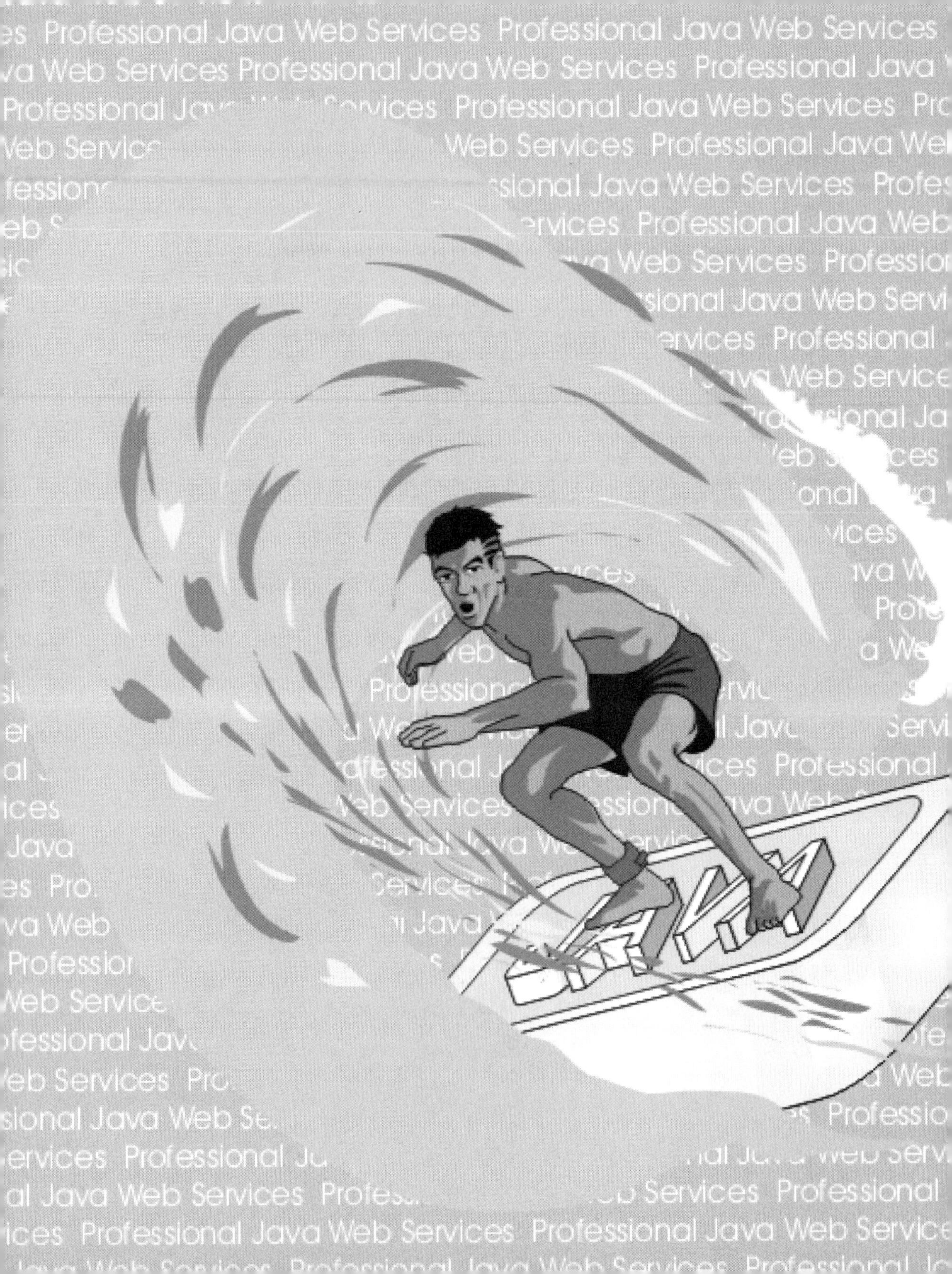
Professional Java Web Services

JAXM and JAX-RPC

In this chapter, we will discuss two Java specifications, Java **A**PI for **X**ML **M**essaging (**JAXM**) and Java API for **X**ML-based **RPC** (**JAX-RPC**). JAXM was designed to enable developers to write business applications that support emerging standards, which are based on Simple Object Access Protocol 1.1 (SOAP 1.1) and SOAP with Attachments specifications such as ebXML. JAXM can be thought of as a generic specification for transmitting XML documents of any type, whereas the JAX-RPC specification is focused on defining the mechanism for doing RPC method calls and responses using an XML-based protocol, such as SOAP 1.1. However, JAX-RPC is not bound to just SOAP 1.1 but is modular enough to work with other XML-based protocols such as the **XML P**rotocol (**XMLP**). More information about XMLP is located at http://www.w3.org/2000/xp/.

JAXM versus JAX-RPC

JAXM and JAX-RPC can be confusing since they both enable developers to write applications that are capable of exchanging XML data via the SOAP 1.1 and SOAP with Attachments protocols. At a macro level, the difference between JAXM and JAX-RPC is that JAXM focuses on allowing developers to build applications using emerging industry messaging standards based on SOAP 1.1 and SOAP with Attachments such as ebXML. JAX-RPC has a focus on enabling developers to create applications that are capable of accessing remote systems through the use of RPC calls embedded within SOAP 1.1 messages. The following chart lists the similarities and differences at the micro level between JAXM and JAXM-RPC. The chart is not meant to be an exhaustive list, but provides some insight into the scope of both APIs:

Feature	JAXM	JAX-RPC
SOAP 1.1 support	✓	✓
SOAP with Attachments support	✓	✓
Capable of using industry messaging standards (that is, ebXML)	✓	
Remote Procedure Calls	✓	✓
WSDL to stub creation		✓
Synchronous messaging	✓	✓
Asynchronous messaging	✓	
Quality of Service (QoS) features (that is, reliable messaging)	✓	

As shown in the table, RPC calls can also be done using JAXM, but JAX-RPC has the capability of taking a WSDL description of a service and creating the necessary stubs that would allow the service to be invoked. They both allow synchronous messaging. Another difference between JAXM and JAX-RPC is in terms of Quality of Service (QoS) features that would be provided by a JAXM and JAX-RPC run-time system. A typical JAXM provider would provide support for reliable messaging with guarantees of delivery and message routing. On the other hand, a JAX-RPC run-time system does not provide these services. Additional information on the differences between the two protocols is located at http://www.theserverside.com/resources/pdf/J2EE-WebServices-DevGuide.pdf.

JAXM

As mentioned above, JAXM enables developers to build applications using emerging industry messaging standards that are based on SOAP 1.1 and SOAP with Attachments. JAXM makes this possible by providing an API that allows the creation of SOAP 1.1 and SOAP with Attachment messages. It also provides developers with the ability to create messages based on higher-level protocols through the use of message profiles. These will be covered later. The need for higher-level protocols stems from the fact that SOAP 1.1 does not contain all the features you might need in a messaging system, such as security and routing. An example of a higher-level protocol is ebXML.

Status of Specification

The JAXM specification was developed following the Java Community Process. The current version is 1.0, which has been designated as a Final Draft. It can be obtained from http://java.sun.com/xml/jaxm/. A reference implementation of JAXM is now available as part of the Java XML Pack (JAX Pack), which we discuss later within this section.

Architecture

An application that utilizes JAXM is known as a **JAXM client** or **application**. Depending upon the scenario, a JAXM application can play the role of a client, a server, or both. To visualize this, let's look at a supply-chain integration example. Let's suppose that we have three companies that are parts suppliers, A, B, and C. Let's also assume that they all use JAXM applications. Supplier A sends an order create request to B, supplier B in turn sends an order create request to supplier C, which supplies supplier B with the parts that are needed to create the parts that were requested by Supplier A. The following diagram depicts this:

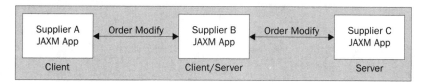

In this scenario, supplier A takes the role of a client when it sends an order create request. Supplier B takes the role of a server when receiving the order create request from supplier A. Supplier B then takes the role of a client when it sends the order create request to supplier C. To simplify, a JAXM application can assume a client role when it needs to request a service, and assumes a server role when it performs a service.

A JAXM application falls into two categories; one that uses a JAXM provider and one that doesn't. A JAXM application that uses a JAXM provider can support asynchronous messaging whereas JAXM applications that don't use a JAXM provider are limited to synchronous messaging.

Standalone JAXM Application

A JAXM application implemented using the J2SE is referred to as a **standalone JAXM application**. A standalone JAXM application is assumed to be a client of a web service that uses a synchronous messaging model such as request-response. Such a client establishes a connection directly with the service (using a URL), sends its request, and is blocked until receiving the response. The following sequence diagram depicts this:

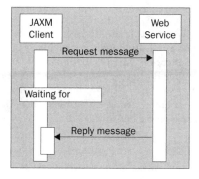

Note that the functionality provided by a standalone JAXM application is analogous to what's provided by current SOAP 1.1 implementations, such as Apache SOAP.

JAXM Application Using a JAXM Provider

Another way to use JAXM is with a **JAXM provider**. In this type of configuration, a JAXM application is deployed into a J2EE web container or a J2EE EJB container. The application maintains a connection to its JAXM provider, and all messages sent and received by the application go through the JAXM provider. The following diagram depicts this configuration:

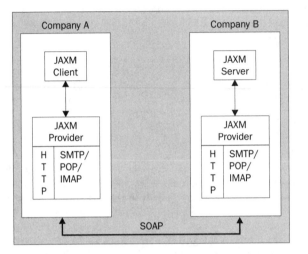

In the above diagram, company A is assuming the client role and company B is assuming the server role, but depending on the scenario, the roles could be swapped. Note that the JAXM client and server do not communicate directly. Instead, all messages are exchanged through their JAXM providers. It is also worth noting that we can think of a JAXM application that has assumed the role of a server as a service provider, providing services to JAXM applications that are assuming the role of a client.

The JAXM specification doesn't define the specific capabilities of a JAXM provider, but leaves this to the discretion of different messaging provider vendors. An example of functionality that could be provided is reliable messaging with a guarantee of delivery and message routing. Putting these types of services into providers alleviates the need to have this type of logic hard-coded within every application. Instead, this functionality is located in a central location that can be leveraged by multiple applications.

Moreover, this configuration gives more flexibility with regards to the style of messaging it can use and the roles it can assume. A JAXM application using a provider can assume the role of a client or server, whereas a standalone JAXM application can only assume a role of client. Looking back at the supply-chain integration example, supplier B can't be a standalone JAXM client because it needs to have the capability of assuming a client or server role depending on whether supplier B is making an order create request or responding to an order create request. However, there are some rules that a JAXM application assuming the role of a server has to follow.

Server Role Requirements

The requirements for a JAXM application to operate in a server role are:

❑ **SOAP 1.1 and SOAP with Attachments compliance** – This allows messages sent by non-JAXM clients (that is, Apache SOAP, Microsoft SOAP) to be processed

❑ **Support for both one-way and request-response styles of messaging**

It is worth noting that the requirement for request-response style messaging is to ensure that a JAXM application in a server role is capable of receiving requests from a standalone JAXM application, which only supports this style of messaging.

JAXM Application to JAXM Provider Communication

A JAXM application is completely abstracted from the implementation details of its JAXM provider. Furthermore, a JAXM application is only aware of its provider when it establishes a connection with it. In addition, the way in which a JAXM application communicates with a JAXM provider is not defined and is considered to be private. In other words, it is up to the JAXM vendor to decide how to implement this. This will allow vendors to differentiate themselves from one another by allowing them to provide different features. For example, a JAXM vendor may provide a failover feature, which would consist of a JAXM application having the ability to use an alternative JAXM provider if the primary one wasn't available for some reason. It is also worth noting that a JAXM application is not required to be located within the same JVM as the provider. Per the JAXM specification, it is expected that the majority of JAXM applications that are web-based (located in a J2EE container) will use a JAXM provider.

Message Profiles

As stated before, a JAXM implementation must support the SOAP 1.1 and SOAP with Attachments specifications. However, these specifications don't define information that is necessary for enterprise-level messaging applications such as:

❏ Guaranteed delivery

❏ Message routing

❏ Message correlation (identifiying the previously sent request for which the current message is a response)

However, other messaging protocols based on SOAP 1.1 and SOAP with Attachments define this type of information. JAXM supports the use of these protocols through **message profiles**. Message profiles allow other messaging protocols to operate on top of SOAP. A JAXM implementation may choose to support a number of industry-standard specifications through message profiles. The reference implementation of JAXM contains support for ebXML and the **Web Services Routing Protocol** (**WS-Routing**), formally known as the **SOAP Routing Protocol** (**SOAPRP**). WS-Routing is a simple, stateless, SOAP-based protocol for routing SOAP messages in an asynchronous manner over a variety of transports like TCP, UDP, and HTTP. With WS-Routing, the entire message path for a SOAP message (as well as its return path) can be described directly within the SOAP envelope. It supports one-way messaging, two-way messaging such as request-response and peer-to-peer conversations, and long running dialogs. For additional information about WS-Routing checkout the specification, located at http://msdn.microsoft.com/library/default.asp?url=/library/en-us/dnsrvspec/html/ws-routing.asp.

Security

Support for security features and capabilities for message transport are implementation-specific. In other words, each JAXM implementation has the flexibility of deciding how to implement the security. Likewise, authentication of JAXM applications to JAXM providers is also considered an implementation detail that should be handled by the JAXM implementation. Note that having security not formally defined like the EJB and servlet specifications may cause huge incompatibility problems. For example, a JAXM application created using an implementation developed by one vendor with a security framework may not be compatible with the security framework of another JAXM vendor. It is worth noting that the reference implementation doesn't handle any security issues.

The Reference Implementation

As mentioned previously, a reference implementation of JAXM is now available as part of the Java API for XML, which is known as the **JAX Pack**. The JAX Pack is an easy way for developers to obtain the APIs that are needed to create XML-enabled applications. The current release of the JAX Pack, Winter 01, includes early access versions of the following APIs:

- ❑ Java API for XML Processing/Parsing (JAXP)
- ❑ Java API for XML Messaging (JAXM)
- ❑ Java API for XML-based RPC (JAX-RPC)
- ❑ Java API for XML Registries (JAXR)

Eventually, it will also contain the Java Architecture for XML Binding (JAXB). More information about the JAX Pack can be obtained from http://java.sun.com/xml/javaxmlpack.html.

The JAXM reference implementation features:

- ❑ A client-side run-time library, which can be used to send messages to remote parties either directly, or using a provider
- ❑ Messages that can be received synchronously (using a request-response model) or asynchronously (using a one-way model)
- ❑ Support for HTTP (no other protocols are supported)
- ❑ More than a half dozen sample applications
- ❑ Support for ebXML and SOAP Routing Protocol (SOAPRP) through messaging profiles

JAXM Examples

In this section, we will see how to use the JAXM reference implementation to develop the following:

- ❑ A standalone JAXM application
- ❑ A JAXM application using a JAXM provider

Before diving into these examples, let's discuss how to obtain and install the JAXM reference implementation

Obtaining and Installing the JAXM Reference Implementation

As mentioned in the *Reference Implementation* section, the JAXM API is bundled as part of the JAX Pack. Do the following to obtain and install the JAXM reference implementation:

1. Download the JAX Pack from http://java.sun.com/xml/downloads/javaxmlpack.html

2. Unzip the JAX Pack to a directory such as C:\dev

Assuming that you unpacked the JAX Pack to C:\dev, you should have a new subdirectory called java_xml_pack-winter01. Note that the name of the subdirectory may be different depending on what release of the JAX Pack is available at the time of reading this chapter. Your directory structure should look something like this:

Standalone JAXM Example

The first example that we are going to discuss consists of using the JAXM API to create a standalone JAXM application that acts as a client to the Job Resume Repository Service defined using the Apache SOAP toolkit in Chapter 3. The application allows a resume to be retrieved using its unique identifier (uid). This application is developed as a J2SE command-line application. The name of the standalone JAXM application is JAXMRetrieveResume. The sequence diagram for this example is below:

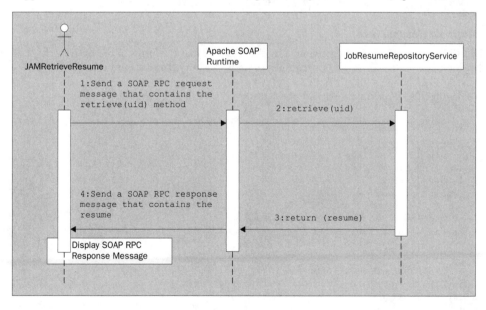

The JAXMRetrieveResume application uses the JAXM API to send a SOAP RPC request message to the Apache SOAP server. This message specifies that the retrieve method should be invoked. Once the SOAP message arrives, the Apache run-time environment forwards the method call request to the JobResumeRepositoryService class, which actually implements the service. The uid parameter is used to retrieve a resume. If successful, a Resume object is returned to the Apache SOAP runtime, which, in turn, forwards the Resume object (as XML) to the JAXMRetrieveResume application as the payload of a SOAP RPC response message. The JAXMRetrieveResume application then prints out the SOAP RPC response message.

Setting the CLASSPATH

In order to run the example, we have to properly set the CLASSPATH. The CLASSPATH variable should be set up to include every JAR file that's in the %JAXM_HOME%\lib directory, and the xerces.jar and xalan.jar files from the %JAXP_HOME% directory, where %JAXM_HOME% and %JAXP_HOME% reflect the directories that contain the JAXM and JAXP APIs. Based on where we have installed the JAX Pack, the values for %JAXM_HOME% and %JAXP_HOME% are:

```
JAXM_HOME=c:\dev\java_xml_pack-winter01-dev\jaxm-1.0.1-ea1
JAXP_HOME=c:\dev\java_xml_pack-winter01-dev\jaxp-1.2-ea1
```

The following code snippet shows a Windows batch file called setJAXM-CP.bat that could be used to properly set the CLASSPATH:

```
set JAXM_HOME=C:\dev\java_xml_pack-winter-01-dev\jaxm-1.0.1-ea1
set JAXP_HOME=C:\dev\java_xml_pack-winter-01-dev\jaxp-1.2-ea1

set CLASSPATH=%JAXM_HOME%\lib\activation.jar;%JAXM_HOME%\lib\dom4j.jar
set CLASSPATH=%CLASSPATH%;%JAXM_HOME%\lib\jaxm.jar;%JAXM_HOME%\lib\jndi.jar
set CLASSPATH=%CLASSPATH%;%JAXM_HOME%\lib\log4j.jar;%JAXM_HOME%\lib\mail.jar
set CLASSPATH=%CLASSPATH%;%JAXM_HOME%\jaxm\jaxm-client.jar;%JAXP_HOME%\xalan.jar
set CLASSPATH=%CLASSPATH%;%JAXP_HOME%\xerces.jar;.3\crimson.jar;
```

JAXMRetrieveResume.java

This file contains the logic to generate a SOAP message that conforms to the SOAP 1.1 specification so that the retrieve() method of the Job Resume Repository Service can be invoked.

We first need to import the required packages:

```
// Imports needed for JAXM
import javax.xml.soap.SOAPEnvelope;
import javax.xml.soap.SOAPConnectionFactory;
import javax.xml.soap.SOAPConnection;
import javax.xml.soap.SOAPMessage;
import javax.xml.soap.SOAPPart;
import javax.xml.soap.SOAPBody;
import javax.xml.soap.MessageFactory;
import javax.xml.soap.SOAPElement;
import javax.xml.messaging.URLEndpoint;

// Imports needed for processing the output
import javax.xml.transform.TransformerFactory;
import javax.xml.transform.Transformer;
import javax.xml.transform.Source;
import javax.xml.transform.stream.StreamResult;
```

The following code snippet defines the RPCROUTER variable, which defines the endpoint for the Apache SOAP RPC server. It is responsible for receiving SOAP requests that contains RPC method calls and routing them to the correct service:

```
/*
 * A Standalone JAXM Application that retrieves a resume from the Job Resume
 * Repository Service (JRRS)
 */

public class JAXMRetrieveResume {

  static final String RPCROUTER =
    "http://localhost:8080/soap/servlet/rpcrouter";
```

The following code snippet handles the processing of the command-line arguments. The application only requires one argument, the `uid`. If not present, the application will display usage information and exit:

```
public static void main(String args[]) {

  try {
    String uid = null;
    boolean argumentsProcessed = false;

    // Obtain the uid of the resume to retrieve from the command line
    if (args.length == 2) {
      if (args[0].equalsIgnoreCase("-UID")
              || args[0].equalsIgnoreCase("/UID")) {
        uid = args[1];
        argumentsProcessed = true;
      }
    }
    if (argumentsProcessed == false) {
      System.out.println(
        "Usage: JAXMRetreiveResume [-uid <uid> | /uid <uid>]");
      return;
    }
```

The following lines of code will create a `SOAPConnectionFactory` object, which can be used to create a `SOAPConnection` object. The `SOAPConnection` object is used by client applications that want to send request-response style SOAP messages directly to the recipient without going through a messaging provider. In this example, we are acting as the SOAP client and the Apache SOAP RPC server is the recipient:

```
SOAPConnectionFactory scf = SOAPConnectionFactory.newInstance();
SOAPConnection connection = scf.createConnection();
```

Next, a new instance of the `MessageFactory` object is created. This class is used to create a `SOAPMessage` object. The `SOAPMessage` class is the root class for all SOAP messages. A `SOAPMessage` object consists of a SOAP part and optionally one or more attachment parts, which comply with the SOAP 1.1 and SOAP with Attachments specifications, respectively:

```
MessageFactory mf = MessageFactory.newInstance();

// Create a SOAP message using the message factory
SOAPMessage msg = mf.createMessage();

// Obtain a reference to the SOAP part of the message
SOAPPart soapPart = msg.getSOAPPart();
```

Use the `SOAPPart` class to obtain a reference to the `SOAPEnvelope` class. The `SOAPEnvelope` class represents the envelope part of a SOAP message:

```
SOAPEnvelope envelope = soapPart.getEnvelope();
```

In this example, we will specify the data types of parameters using the XML Schema specification. In order to do this, we have to set up the proper namespaces using the `SOAPEnvelope.addNamespaceDeclaration()` method:

```
envelope.addNamespaceDeclaration(
    "xsi", "http://www.w3.org/1999/XMLSchema-instance");
envelope.addNamespaceDeclaration(
    "xsd", "http://www.w3.org/1999/XMLSchema");
```

Obtain a reference to the `SOAPBody` object, which models the contents of a SOAP body element within a SOAP message:

```
SOAPBody body = envelope.getBody();
```

The following line of code uses the `SOAPBody.addChildElement()` method to add a fully qualified child element to the body object with a name of `retrieve`. This element represents the RPC method call that should be invoked by the Apache SOAP RPC server. Notice that a reference to the new child element is returned to a variable called `rpcMethodCall` with a type of `SOAPElement`. The `SOAPElement` type is the superclass for all the JAXM classes that model SOAP objects defined by the SOAP 1.1 specification, which include the `SOAPEnvelope` and `SOAPBody`:

```
SOAPElement rpcMethodCall = body.addChildElement(
    "retrieve", "ns1", "urn:JobResumeRepositoryService");
```

The XML created from the above code snippet is below:

```
<soap-env:Envelope
    xmlns:soap-env="http://schemas.xmlsoap.org/soap/envelope/"
    xmlns:xsi="http://www.w3.org/1999/XMLSchema-instance"
    xmlns:xsd="http://www.w3.org/1999/XMLSchema">

  <soap-env:Header/>
  <soap-env:Body>
    <ns1:retrieve xmlns:ns1="urn:JobResumeRepositoryService">
      // ...
    </ns1:retrieve>
  </soap-env:Body>

</soap-env:Envelope>
```

Next, the `uid` parameter of the retrieve RPC method call is specified as a child element:

```
SOAPElement rpcParam = rpcMethodCall.addChildElement("uid");
```

Specify the data type and value of the `uid` parameter as a string by using the following lines of code:

```
rpcParam.addAttribute(envelope.createName("xsi:type"), "xsd:string");
rpcParam.addTextNode(uid);
```

Note that the `SOAPElement.addAttribute()` method used in the above code snippet requires two parameters; the name of the attribute and the value of the attribute. The name of the object is specified using a `Name` type. A `Name` type represents a fully qualified XML name. A `Name` type can be created using the `SOAPEnvelope.createName()` method. The XML created from the above code snippet is below:

```
<soap-env:Envelope
    xmlns:soap-env="http://schemas.xmlsoap.org/soap/envelope/"
    xmlns:xsi="http://www.w3.org/1999/XMLSchema-instance"
    xmlns:xsd="http://www.w3.org/1999/XMLSchema">

  <soap-env:Header/>
  <soap-env:Body>
    <ns1:retrieve xmlns:ns1="urn:JobResumeRepositoryService">
      <uid xsi:type="xsd:string">1000</uid>
    </ns1:retrieve>
  </soap-env:Body>
</soap-env:Envelope>
```

We now have to create an instance of the `URLEndpoint` class, which is simply used to represent the endpoint URL of the Apache SOAP RPC Server:

```
URLEndpoint endpoint = new URLEndpoint(RPCROUTER);
```

The `msg` and `endpoint` objects are then passed as parameters to the `SOAPConnection.call()` method. This method handles the sending of the SOAP message to the endpoint specified by the `endpoint` object. The `call()` method blocks until a `SOAPMessage` object is received back from the remote server. In our case, the `SOAPMessage` object received from the remote server is stored in a variable called `reply`:

```
SOAPMessage reply = connection.call(msg, endpoint);
```

The following code snippet instantiates a `Transformer` class. This class is used to transform the XML stream received from the remote server to a format that can be displayed using `System.out`:

```
TransformerFactory tFact = TransformerFactory.newInstance();
Transformer transformer = tFact.newTransformer();
```

The following code snippet actually obtains the content of the SOAP message and puts it into a `Source` object. A `Source` object represents a XML stream:

```
Source src = reply.getSOAPPart().getContent();
```

427

The following code snippet specifies where the XML stream should be transformed:

```
StreamResult result = new StreamResult(System.out);
```

The following line of code actually handles the transformation by passing the `src` and `result` objects to the `Transformer.transform()` method. Note that this method also handles printing the SOAP message on the console:

```
transformer.transform(src, result);
```

Lastly, we close the connection:

```
connection.close();
```

We will only use basic error handling for the code as shown below:

```
    } catch (Throwable e) {
      e.printStackTrace();
    }
  }
}
```

To compile the code we can use the `setJAXM-CP.bat` file to set the `CLASSPATH` and compile the class using the command:

```
> javac JAXMRetrieveResume.java
```

Running the Standalone JAXM Example

The command line to retrieve the default resume with a `uid` of 1000 would look like this:

```
> java JAXMRetrieveResume -uid 1000
```

The output from the application is a SOAP message that contains the resume. The following screenshot shows the output:

JAXM Using a JAXM Provider

In order to explain how to use JAXM with a JAXM Provider we are going to discuss an example that is provided with the JAXM Reference Implementation (RI) called `jaxm-remote`. This example uses the JAXM provider provided with the RI to send and receive an ebXML message. In this example, the JAXM application acts as both the sender and the receiver. The following diagram depicts the interactions between the JAXM application and the JAXM provider:

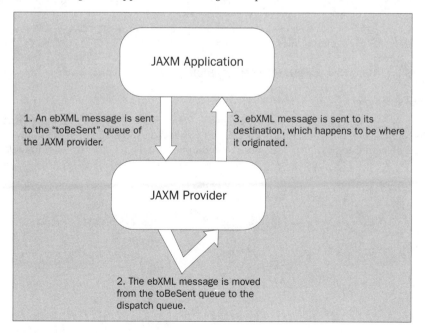

In the above diagram, the JAXM application sends an ebXML message to the JAXM provider. The JAXM provider stores the message in a "toBeSent" queue. During its next processing cycle, the JAXM provider moves the message to the dispatch queue and sends the message back to the JAXM application.

The JAXM application consists of two servlets: SendingServlet and ReceivingServlet. The SendingServlet is responsible for maintaining a connection to the JAXM provider and sending an ebXML message. The ReceivingServlet is responsible for receiving messages that are dispatched from the JAXM provider.

Now that we have a basic understanding of the example let's discuss how to configure our environment so that we can run the example.

Configure Tomcat 3.2.x and Install the JAXM-Remote Application

We must first install Tomcat if its not already installed. If not installed, instructions for downloading Tomcat 3.2.x are located in the "*Download and Unpack Tomcat 3.2.x*" section of Chapter 3. Once installed, we need to do the following steps.

1. Copy all the .jar files from <JAXM-HOME>/lib into <TOMCAT-HOME>/lib

2. Copy xerces.jar and xalan.jar from <JAXP-HOME>/ into <TOMCAT-HOME/lib/WEB-INF/lib

3. Copy the jaxm-client.jar file from <JAXM-HOME>/jaxm into <TOMCAT-HOME>//lib

4. Copy <JAXM-HOME>/jaxm/jaxm-provider.war into <TOMCAT-HOME>/webapps

5. Copy <JAXM-HOME>/samples/jaxm-remote.war into <TOMCAT-HOME>/webapps; note that this file contains the jaxm-remote application

6. Start Tomcat by executing <TOMCAT-HOME>/bin/catalina.bat

Running the Example

Now that we are configured, let's run the example. Point your browser to http://localhost:8080/jaxm-remote/ and click on here to send the ebXML message. You should receive the following message: Message delivered to provider. Also, check the output from Tomcat, which should look like this:

The above screenshot shows the ebXML message that was printed out by the `ReceivingServlet` when it received the message from the JAXM provider. Double-check your Tomcat settings if you receive error when running the example.

Now that we know how to run the application let's look at the sourcecode for the `SendingServlet` and the `ReceivingServlet`.

SendingServlet.java

The `SendingServlet.java` file contains the sourcecode for the `SendingServlet`. It is located within the `jax-remote.war` file at `WEB-INF\src\remote\sender\`. As stated previously, the `SendingServlet` is responsible for sending messages to a JAXM provider.

In order to communicate with a JAXM provider we must first obtain a connection to the provider. This is usually done in the `init()` method so that the connection is created when it's first loaded into memory. A connection is obtained through the `ProviderConnectionFactory` method `newInstance()`, which will create a connection to the default provider implementation. The following code snippet shows the `init()` method:

```
public class SendingServlet extends HttpServlet {
  private static Category logger = Category.getInstance("Samples/Remote");

  private String from ="http://www.wombats.com/remote/sender";
  private String to = "http://www.wombats.com/remote/sender";
  private String data = "http://127.0.0.1:8080/jaxm-remote/index.html";

  private ProviderConnectionFactory pcf;
  private ProviderConnection pc;
  private MessageFactory mf = null;

  private static final String providerURI =
                          "http://java.sun.com/xml/jaxm/provider";

  public void init(ServletConfig servletConfig) throws ServletException {
    super.init(servletConfig);
```

```
    try {
       pcf = ProviderConnectionFactory.newInstance();
       pc = pcf.createConnection();
    } catch(Exception e) {
       logger.error("Unable to open connection to the provider", e);
    }
    // Rest of Init method
  }
  // Rest of SendingServlet.java
}
```

In the above example, the `pc` object contains a connection to the provider. We use the `pc` object to obtain a list of supported message profiles from the JAXM provider. This is done to ensure that the provider supports the type of messages that we want to send. The following code snippet shows this:

```
public void doGet(HttpServletRequest req, HttpServletResponse resp)
    throws ServletException {
  try {
  // Create a message factory.
  if (mf == null) {
     ProviderMetaData metaData = pc.getMetaData();
     String[] supportedProfiles = metaData.getSupportedProfiles();
     String profile = null;

     for(int i=0; i < supportedProfiles.length; i++) {
       if(supportedProfiles[i].equals("ebxml")) {
         profile = supportedProfiles[i];
         break;
       }
     }
```

If the ebXML message profile is supported, then the profile variable will contain a string that represents the ebXML profile. We then create a `MessageFactory` object by using the `ProviderConnecion.createMessageFactory()` method. This method takes a `String` as an argument, which specifies the type of `MessageFactory` object to create. The following code snippet shows this:

```
           mf = pc.createMessageFactory(profile);
```

The above code is not really necessary since we already know that the reference implementation support ebXML and WS-Routing (formally SOAPRP) messages. But, the check should be done in practice to ensure that a messages profile is supported before sending messages. We can now use the `MessageFactory.creatMessage()` method to create an `EbXMLMessageImpl` object called ebXMLMsg. This class currently supports setters and getters for the mandatory parts of the ebXML message header. The following code snippet shows this:

```
    // Create a message from the message factory
    EbXMLMessageImpl ebxmlMsg = (EbXMLMessageImpl)mf.createMessage();
```

We can now use the setters and getters to specify what should be in the message. The following code snippet shows the setters and getters that are used in this example:

```
ebxmlMsg.setSender(new Party(from));
ebxmlMsg.setReceiver(new Party(to));

Service service = new Service("SupplierOrderProcessing");
ebxmlMsg.setRefToMessageId("20001209-133003-28572@example.com");
ebxmlMsg.setCPAId("http://example.com/cpas/ourcpawithyou.xml");
ebxmlMsg.setConversationId("20001209-133003-28572");
ebxmlMsg.setService(service);
ebxmlMsg.setAction("NewOrder");
Manifest manifest = new Manifest("manifest", "1.0");
Reference ref = new Reference("pay01", "cid:pay01",
                              "http://regrep.org/gci/purchaseorder");
Schema schema = new Schema(
                    "http://regrep.org/gci/purchaseorder.xsd", "1.0");
ref.setSchema(schema);

Description desc = new Description("en-us");
desc.setText("PurchaseOrder for widgets");
ref.setDescription(desc);
manifest.addReference(ref);
ebxmlMsg.setManifest(manifest);
```

We won't discuss the getter and setters, but details for each can be found in the Javadocs bundled with the JAXM reference implementation. This example also shows how to add an attachment to an ebXML message. The code snippet is shown below:

```
URL url = new URL(data);

AttachmentPart ap = ebxmlMsg.createAttachmentPart(
                            new DataHandler(url));

ap.setContentType("text/html");

// Add the attachment part to the message.
ebxmlMsg.addAttachmentPart(ap);
```

In the above example, the index.html file that is part of the example is pulled in as an attachment. The next interesting part of the example shows how to write the message to a file:

```
FileOutputStream sentFile = new FileOutputStream("sent.msg");
ebxmlMsg.writeTo(sentFile);
sentFile.close();
```

Lastly, we send the message using the ProviderConnection.send() method. The following code snippet shows this:

```
pc.send(ebxmlMsg);
```

433

The ebXML message sent to the JAXM provider looks like this:

```
--7960257.1009136196143.JavaMail.Administrator.92acb
Content-Type: text/xml

<soap-env:Envelope
        xmlns:soap-env="http://schemas.xmlsoap.org/soap/envelope/">
  <soap-env:Header>
  <eb:MessageHeader
      xmlns:eb="http://www.ebxml.org/namespaces/messageHeader"
      eb:version="1.0" soap-env:mustUnderstand="1">
    <eb:From>
      <eb:PartyId eb:type="URI">
        http://www.wombats.com/remote/sender
      </eb:PartyId>
    </eb:From>
    <eb:To>
      <eb:PartyId eb:type="URI">
        http://www.wombats.com/remote/sender
      </eb:PartyId>
    </eb:To>
    <eb:CPAId>http://example.com/cpas/ourcpawithyou.xml</eb:CPAId>
    <eb:ConversationId>20001209-133003-28572</eb:ConversationId>
    <eb:Service eb:type="">SupplierOrderProcessing</eb:Service>
    <eb:Action>NewOrder</eb:Action>
    <eb:MessageData>
      <eb:MessageId>f14c7928-5481-4ce0-b5ec-b82d51efbf08</eb:MessageId>
        <eb:RefToMessageId>
          20001209-133003-28572@example.com
        </eb:RefToMessageId>
      <eb:Timestamp>1009136196143</eb:Timestamp>
    </eb:MessageData>
  </eb:MessageHeader>
  </soap-env:Header>
  <soap-env:Body>
    <eb:Manifest xmlns:eb="http://www.ebxml.org/namespaces/messageHeader"
                 eb:id="manifest"
                 eb:version="1.0">
      <eb:Reference eb:id="pay01"
              xmlns:xlink="http://www.w3.org/1999/xlink"
              xlink:href=cid:pay01
              xlink:role="http://regrep.org/gci/purchaseorder">
        <eb:Schema eb:version="1.0"
                eb:location="http://regrep.org/gci/purchaseorder.xsd"/>
      </eb:Reference>
    </eb:Manifest>
  </soap-env:Body>
</soap-env:Envelope>
--7960257.1009136196143.JavaMail.Administrator.92acb
Content-Type: text/html

<html>
  <body>
This is an example of a roundtrip JAXM message exchange via the remote
provider..
<p> Click <a href="sender">here</a> to send the message
  </body>
</html>

--7960257.1009136196143.JavaMail.Administrator.92acb--
```

ReceivingServlet.java

The `ReceivingServlet.java` file contains the sourcecode for the `ReceivingServlet`. It is located within the `jax-remote.war` file at `WEB-INF\src\remote\reciever\`.

JAXM promotes a standard way of delivering messages asynchronously to a JAX application. This is done by having the application extend from a servlet called JAXMServlet and implement an interface called the OnewayListener. The JAXMServlet is a superclass for components that live in a servlet container that receives JAXM messages such as the ReceivingServlet. The OnewayListener is a interface for components (such as, servlets) that are intended to be consumers of one-way (asynchronous) JAXM messages. The receiver of a one-way message is sent the message in one operation, and a response may or may not be sent. If sent, it is done in a different operation in a timeframe that could vary between seconds and days. This interface contains one method called OnMessage(), which we discuss in a moment. But, first let's look at the code for the ReceivingServlet, which is listed below:

```
public class ReceivingServlet extends JAXMServlet implements OnewayListener {
  private static Category logger = Category.getInstance("Samples/Remote");

  private ProviderConnectionFactory pcf;
  private ProviderConnection pc;
  private static final String providerURI =
                              "http://java.sun.com/xml/jaxm/provider";

  //private MessageFactory messageFactory;
  public void init(ServletConfig servletConfig) throws ServletException {
    super.init(servletConfig);
    try {
      pcf = ProviderConnectionFactory.newInstance();
      pc = pcf.createConnection();
      setMessageFactory(new EbXMLMessageFactoryImpl());
    } catch (Exception e) {
      e.printStackTrace();
      throw new ServletException(
              "Couldn't initialize Receiving servlet " + e.getMessage());
    }
  }

  public void onMessage(SOAPMessage message) {
    System.out.println("On message called in receiving servlet");
    try {
      System.out.println("Here's the message: ");
      message.saveChanges();
      message.writeTo(System.out);
    } catch(Exception e) {
      logger.error("Error in processing or replying to a message", e);
    }
  }
}
```

Notice that the init() method creates a connection to the JAXM Provider that is similar to the one that is made in the init() method of the SendingServlet, except that a method called JAXMServlet.setMessageFactory is called. This method is used to specify what type of messages will be received. In this example, the method is invoked with an instance of the ebXML implementation class called EbXMLMessageFactoryImpl.

The OnMessage() method has the responsibility of receiving a SOAP message and processing it. In this example, it simply wrote the message to System.out.

JAX-RPC

The JAX-RPC 1.0 specification provides mechanisms for doing RPC method calls and responses using an XML protocol that contains conventions for doing RPC method calls and responses. The specification defines how this can be done using SOAP 1.1 but JAX-RPC has a modular design that enables it to support future XML protocols. JAX-RPC consists of two parts:

❑   An API for invoking services

❑   Requirements for implementing a run-time system to provide services

Applications that utilize the API for invoking services are referred to as **JAX-RPC service clients**. Services provided by the run-time system are referred to as **JAX-RPC services**.

In this section we will:

❑   Examine the status of the specification

❑   Define a JAX-RPC service

❑   Invoke a JAX-PRC service client

To clarify, these topics will be covered without looking at the specifics of the reference implementation or any other implementation.

Status of the Specification

Like JAXM, JAX-RPC 1.0 was also developed under the Java Community Process (JCP). The current version of the specification is 0.6. It is currently at the Public Review stage of the JCP process. This means that it's still subject to change. However, the concepts discussed in the upcoming sections should still be valid even if the API is tweaked and refined. The specification is available from http://java.sun.com/xml/downloads/jaxrpc.html and a reference implementation of JAX-RPC is bundled as part of the JAX Pack, which is available from the same URL.

Defining a JAX-RPC Service

In this section we will discuss the process of defining a JAX-RPC service. The following topics will be covered:

❑   Defining the service definition interface (the remote interface for the service)

❑   Type mapping (the ability to map between Java types and XML types so that they can be transmitted between a service client and a JAX-RPC service)

❑   Implementing the service definition

❑   Packaging the service

❑   Defining the deployment descriptor

❑   Service deployment

Defining the Service Definition Interface

The first step in creating a JAX-RPC service is to define the service interface. This is the responsibility of the service developer. Simply put, a service developer is a person who creates the service. So, we are assuming the role of a service developer. This is the interface that the JAX-RPC service will use to invoke methods on the service. The service interface is defined using a Java interface shown below:

```
package com.wrox.jobresume.jaxrpc;

import com.wrox.jobresume.common.Resume;

public interface JobResumeRepositoryProvider {

  String submit(Resume resume)
          throws java.rmi.RemoteException, IllegalArgumentException;
  Resume retrieve(String uid)
          throws java.rmi.RemoteException, IllegalArgumentException;
}
```

In the example above, the interface for the Job Resume Repository Service is defined. This is the same service that was defined using the Apache SOAP toolkit in Chapter 3. We are now defining it as a JAX-RPC service. JAX-RPC refers to this interface as the service definition interface.

Type Mapping

In order for data types to be transmitted between a service client and a service, both have to know how to map between Java types and XML data types. This is also known as serialization and deserialization. Serialization is the process of transforming a Java type (object) to an XML representation. Likewise, deserialization is the process of transforming an XML representation to a Java type. In our example, we only need to be concerned about the serialization/deserialization of three Java types: int, String, and Resume because these are the only values that will be transmitted between a service client and a service. The int data type is a primitive type. The following table contains a list of the supported Java primitive types and their associated XML data types:

Java Primitive Type	XML Data Type
Boolean	xsd:Boolean
Byte	xsd:short
Int	xsd:int
Long	xsd:long
Float	xsd:float
Double	xsd:double

Based on the above table, the int data type would be encoded as xsd:int. The following code snippet illustrates this:

```
int number = 1;
```

would be encoded as:

```
<number xsi:type="xsd:int">1</number>
```

The String type is a Java standard type. The following table contains a list of the supported Java standard types and their associated XML data types:

Java Class	XML Data Type
java.lang.String	xsd:string
java.math.BigInteger	xsd:integer
java.math.BigDecimal	xsd:decimal
java.util.Calendar	xsd:dateTime
java.util.Date	xsd:dateTime

Based on the above table, the String data type would be encoded as xsd:string. The following variable of type String:

```
String fullname = new String("Eric Hamilton");
```

would be encoded as:

```
<fullname xsi:type="xsd:string">Eric Hamilton</fullname>
```

The Resume type is a user-defined type that was also used in the Apache SOAP version of this service. It is used to represent a resume within the Job Repository System. In order for the Resume type to be serializied/deserializied in the Apache SOAP version of the system, it had to follow the JavaBean design pattern. JAX-RPC can also handle the serialization/deserialization of JavaBeans as long as the types within the JavaBean consist of types defined in the Java primitive and Java standard tables above. The following variable of type Resume:

```
Resume myresume = new Resume();
myresume.setFirstName("Mack");
myresume.setMiddleName("Levin");
myresume.setLastName("Hendricks");
myresume.setUid("100");
// ...
```

would be encoded as:

```
<Resume>
  <firstname>Mack</firstname>
   <middlename>Levin</middlename>
  <lastname>Hendricks</lastname>
  <uid>1000</uid>
  // ...
</Resume>
```

Implementing the Service Definition Class

Now that the service has been defined it must be implemented. A JAX-RPC implementation is required to provide support for developing and deploying a JAX-RPC service on a servlet container. However, a service could optionally be developed and deployed using the EJB programming model or on a J2SE-based JAX-RPC implementation. From this point forward we will focus on developing and deploying a service in a servlet container. The service developer is also responsible for implementing the service. So, we continue to assume the role of a service developer.

JAX-RPC refers to a class that implements a service as a service definition class. The service definition class implements the service definition interface. During deployment, the service definition class will be linked with a servlet provided by the JAX-RPC runtime. We will refer to this servlet as the JAX-RPC servlet from this point forward. The linked servlet will delegate actions to the service definition class. The following sequence diagram of the submit method for the Job Resume Repository service will depict this:

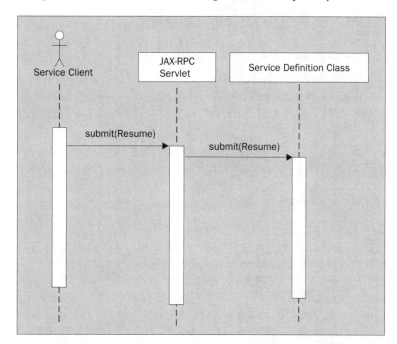

In the above diagram, a service client invokes the submit() method of the Job Resume Repository interface. The JAX-RPC servlet receives the request and delegates it to the service definition class.

JAX-RPC doesn't define how the delegation happens. Those details are left to the discretion of each JAX-RPC implementation to decide how to implement.

The service definition class is required to implement the javax.servlet.Servlet interface. This interface defines the lifecycle methods (init(), service(), destroy()) for a servlet. By implementing the Servlet interface, the service definition class has the same lifecycle model or behavior as the linked servlet. The JAX-RPC servlet manages the lifecycle of the service definition class by delegating the init() and destroy() methods to the service definition class. To clarify, the lifecycle of the service class definition is not managed by the servlet container, but by the linked servlet. The following code snippets shows the service definition class for the Job Resume Repository Service:

```
package com.wrox.jobresume.jaxrpc;

import javax.servlet.Servlet;
import java.util.Hashtable;
import com.wrox.jobresume.common.Resume;

public class JobResumeRepositoryProviderImpl
            implements Servlet, JobResumeRepositoryProvider {

  private Hashtable resumeList;
  private int resumeUID;

  // Initializes the servlet
  public void init(ServletConfig config) throws ServletException {

    // Create an Hashtable to hold the resumes
    resumeList = new Hashtable();

    // Initiate the resumeCounter to 1000
    resumeUID = 1000;

    // Create a default resume
    Resume resume = createDefaultResume();
    submit(resume);
  }

  // Destroys the servlet
  public void destroy() {

    // Releases Memory
    resultList = null;
  }

  // Returns a short description of the service definition class
  public String getServletInfo() {
    return "Job Resume Repository Service Definition Class";
  }

  // Stores a resume in the Hashtable
  public int submit(Resume resume) throws java.rmi.RemoteException,
                                          IllegalArgumentException {

    if (resume == null) {
      throw new IllegalArgumentException(
        "The resume argument must not be null");
    }
    try {

      // Generate a uid for the resume
      String uid = new Integer(resumeUID).toString();
      resumeUID += 1;

      // Store the uid with the resume object
      resume.setUid(uid);
```

```
        // Store the resume object in the hashtable
        resumeList.put(resume.getUid(), resume);
        return uid;    // return the generated uid
    } catch (NullPointerException e) {

        // completed unsuccesfully - the resume was not stored
        return null;
    }
}


// Retrieves a resume from the Hashtable
public Resume retrieve(String uid) throws java.rmi.RemoteException,
                                        IllegalArgumentException {
    if (uid == null) {
        throw new IllegalArgumentException(
            "The resume argument must not be null");
    }
    return (Resume) resumeList.get(uid);
}


// For Brevity, the createDefaultResume() method was omitted
public javax.servlet.ServletConfig getServletConfig() {
    return null;
}

public void service(javax.servlet.ServletRequest servletRequest,
                    javax.servlet.ServletResponse servletResponse)
    throws javax.servlet.ServletException, java.io.IOException {}
}
```

In the above code snippet, the `JobResumeRepositoryProviderImpl` class implements the `Servlet` and `JobResumeRepositoryProvider` interfaces. The `submit()` method takes a `Resume` object as a parameter, generates and assigns a unique identifier to the `uid` field of the `Resume`, and stores it in a `Hashtable` using the `uid` as the key. The `uid` is returned to the calling service client if the operation was successful. Otherwise, the value is `null`. The unique identifier (`uid`) is how each `Resume` object is uniquely identified. The `retrieve()` method takes a `uid` as a parameter and uses it to retrieve the related `Resume` object from the `Hashtable`. The `Resume` object is then returned to the calling service client.

Notice that the code within the `submit()` and `retrieve()` methods is exactly the same as the Apache SOAP implementation of the service. However, the instantiation of the `Hashtable` used to store resumes in memory, an `int` variable that keeps track of UIDs, and the creation of a default resume has moved to the `init()` method. Likewise, the release of memory for these variables has moved to the `destroy()` method. This will allow variables to be instantiated and destroyed when the linked servlet calls the `init()` and `destroy()` method, respectively.

Another noteworthy comment is that a service definition class such as the `JobResumeRepositoryProviderImpl` class is allowed to obtain references to resources (that is, JDBC data sources, LDAP, and so on) and Enterprise JavaBeans. JNDI should be used to look up these resources and Enterprise JavaBeans.

Packaging the Service

The service definition, which includes the service definition interface and service definition class, must be packaged using the Web Application Archive (WAR) format specified in the Servlet specification. The service developer packages the following information in a WAR file:

- One or more service definition interfaces
- One or more service definition classes
- Java classes for serialization/deserialization of data types
- Resources required by the service definition (such as, JPEG images, XML documents)
- A deployment descriptor that ties all of the components of a service definition together
- A WSDL document that describes the defined services (optional)

The contents of the WAR file for the Job Resume Repository Service would look something like this:

```
/WEB-INF/jaxrpc.xml
/WEB-INF/classes/apps/resume/JobResumeRepositoryProvider.class
                         JobResumeRepositoryProviderImpl.class
                         Resume.class
```

The `jaxrpc.xml` file is the standard deployment descriptor for the JAX-RPC service definitions, which we will discuss in the next section. The `/WEB-INF/classes` directory contains service definition classes, `JobResumeRepositoryProvider.class` (interface) and `JobResumeRepositoryProviderImpl.class` (implementation).

The deployer will consume the WAR file and bind the service to an XML protocol and transport such as SOAP and HTTP, respectively. In addition, other information that is necessary for deployment will be added to the WAR file.

Defining the Deployment Descriptor

The service developer must create a deployment descriptor, which specifies deployment information about a service definition. As stated previously, the deployment descriptor is packaged as `jaxrpc.xml` within the WAR file. The JAX-RPC defines additional deployment descriptor elements based on the Servlet specification. These additional elements will be standardized in the J2EE 1.3 and Servlet 2.4 specifications. As mentioned before, a WAR file must contain one or more service definitions. During the writing of this book, the XML schema for the deployment descriptor wasn't defined. However, many of the elements for the schema were defined. Each service definition must be defined using a service-definition element and should contain the following elements:

Element	Description	Required
Display-name	This element specifies a name that is intended to be displayed by the deployment tool.	
Description	This optional element includes any information that the service developer (WAR producer) wants to provide to the deployer. Typically, the deployment tool displays this information.	

Element	Description	Required
service-definition-name	This element specifies the name of a service definition. This name must be unique among all service definitions specified in the same WAR.	✓
service-definition-interface	This element specifies the fully qualified name of the service definition interface.	✓
Service-definition-class	This element specifies the fully qualified name of the service class that implements the service definition interface.	✓
wsdl-document-location	This element specifies the location of the WSDL document that contains the WSDL description of this service definition.	
binding-name	This element specifies the qualified name of the binding that should be used for this service. This element is within the scope of the WSDL document, which is at the location wsdl-document-location.	

Based on the above table, the deployment descriptor for the Job Resume Repository Service might look something like this:

```
<service-definition>
  <service-definition-name>
    JobResumeRepositoryService
  </service-definition-name>
  <service-definition-interface>
    apps.resume.JobResumeRepositoryProvider
  </service-definition-interface>
  <service-definition-class>
    apps.resume.JobResumeRepositoryProviderImpl
  </service-definition-class>
</service-definition>
```

The service developer may specify additional deployment requirements for a service definition by specifying them in a web.xml file, which is the standard web application deployment descriptor. For example, the service developer may use the <ejb-local-ref> element to define a reference to a local EJB from the service definition class.

Service Deployment

Once a JAX-RPC service has been defined, implemented, and packaged into a WAR file, it's consumed by the deployer. The deployer is a person who has the responsibility of doing the following:

❑ Define one or more protocol bindings that bind a service definition to an actual XML-based protocol and transport. An example of a protocol binding is SOAP 1.1 over HTTP.

443

❑ Define one or more service ports that define an endpoint with a specific address and protocol binding.

❑ Export the WSDL server description file that represents the service.

❑ Deploy the service.

These can be done manually or through the use of a deployment tool provided by the JAX-RPC implementation.

Defining a Protocol Binding

A deployer may specify any number of protocol bindings for a single service definition, as long as the protocol bindings are supported by the underlying servlet container-based JAX-RPC implementation. If provided by the service developer, the deployer can use the WSDL description of the service as a hint to identify the protocol binding that should be used. The location of the WSDL file is specified by the <wsdl-document-location> element within the deployment descriptor. Otherwise, the deployer is required to provide the necessary information for defining the protocol binding. Let's define HTTP as the protocol binding for the Job Resume Repository Service.

Defining a Service Port

The deployer is also responsible for defining the service port for a service, which consist of two parts. The first part consists of defining a service port, which consists of assigning a unique endpoint address for a service definition class. The endpoint address must correspond to a transport that was specified by one of the protocol bindings for the service. For example, the endpoint for the Job Resume Repository Service could be defined as http://www.wrox.com/resumerepository, which is consistent with the HTTP transport that's defined for the protocol binding.

The second part consists of the deployer linking a JAX-RPC servlet class with the service definition class. The JAX-RPC implementation is responsible for providing the servlet class and defining how to implement the linking. The JAX-RPC specification doesn't define how to implement either of them, except that the linked servlet must correspond to the configured transport binding for a service port. For example, this means that the linked servlet must inherit from the javax.servlet.http.HttpServlet class if the HTTP transport is used.

Exporting the WSDL Service Description File

It is required that a WSDL-based service description be generated and exported during the deployment process. A JAX-RPC service client can use the WSDL file to generate stubs for invoking the service.

Service client developers can also use the WSDL file to construct the proper SOAP messages to invoke methods using other SOAP 1.1-compliant toolkits such as Apache SOAP.

Deploying the Service

Before deploying the service, the deployer has to add some additional information to the WAR file, which was developed by the service developer. The information consists of the following:

❑ Servlet classes used for the definition of service ports and linked with the service definition classes

❑ web.xml, the standard servlet deployment descriptor that specifies deployment information for servlet classes used for the definition of service ports

❑ A JAR file that packages the classes for the JAX-RPC run-time system (optional)

Based on the above, the WAR file for the Job Resume Repository Service would now look something like this:

```
/WEB-INF/jaxrpc.xml
/WEB-INF/webxml
/WEB-INF/classes/apps/resume/JobResumeRepositoryProvider.class
                         JobResumeRepositoryProviderImpl.class
                         Resume.class
/WEB-INF/com/vendor/xml/rpc/JAXRPCServlet.class
/WEB-INF/lib/runtime.jar
```

The JAXRPCServlet class represents a servlet class that would be generated by a JAX-RPC implementation based on the protocol binding and service port definitions. It would also contain logic that would link the servlet to the JobResumeRepositoryImpl class, which is the service definition class. The web.xml file would contain the deployment descriptor for the JAXRPCServlet class. The runtime.jar file represents the classes that would be needed for the JAX-RPC run-time system to operate. Alternately, the runtime.jar could be configured within the operational environment so that it could be used with multiple services. This would alleviate the need to deploy the runtime each time a new service was deployed.

Invoking a JAX-RPC Service

In this section we will discuss how a JAX-RPC service client can invoke methods of a JAX-RPC service. A JAX-RPC service client can also be used to invoke methods of services that were built using another SOAP 1.1-compliant toolkit such as Apache SOAP. We will focus on discussing how to invoke methods on a JAX-RPC service though. A JAX-RPC service client can be developed using the J2EE or J2SE programming model.

To invoke a JAX-RPC service, the service client can import a WSDL document and generate a Java-based client-side representation of the service based on information within the WSDL document. This client-side representation includes stub classes, service definition interface, and implementation-specific classes. The service client can then be developed using these generated classes. Note that the WSDL file that was generated when we deployed the Job Resume Repository Service could be used.

In order to invoke methods on the Job Resume Repository Service, we must first obtain a reference to the service. This is done by using a component provider. A component provider references an external service using a logical name called a service reference by looking up an instance of the service class using the Java Naming Directory Interface (JNDI). In this example, the service reference name is JobResumeRepositoryService. The following code snippet illustrates this:

```
// Get access to the Job Resume Repository Service
Context ctx = new InitialContext();
JobResumeRepositoryService rps =
  ctx.lookup("java:comp/env/JobResumeRepositoryService");
```

Once a reference to the service is obtained, the component provider can use the service reference (rps in the above example) to get access to an instance of the generated stub, which implements the service definition interface. This is done by using the getResumeRespositoryProviderPort() method. The following code snippet illustrates this:

```
// Obtain a reference to the generated stub for the service
JobResumeRepositoryProvider rrp = rps.getJobResumeRepositoryProviderPort()
```

The generated stub can be used to invoke methods on the service. The following code snippet illustrates calling the submit() method:

```
Resume resume = // create a new resume object and populate with data

// Call the submit method provided by the service
String uid= rrp.submit(resume);
```

In the above code snippet, a Resume object is instantiated, populated with data, and sent to the Job Resume Repository Service as a parameter to the submit() method. The uid for the Resume object is returned if the operation was successful.

The following code snippet illustrates how to call the retrieve() method:

```
String uid = // some uid

// Call the retreive method provided by the service
Resume resume = rrp.retreive(uid);
```

In the above code snippet, a uid is sent as a parameter to the retrieve() method and a Resume object is retrieved if a Resume object matching the uid exists.

Summary

In this chapter, we have looked at two new Java specifications, JAXM and JAX-RPC. They can be confusing since they are both based on SOAP 1.1 and SOAP with Attachments. The main difference between the protocols is that JAXM is focused on providing mechanisms to allow any XML document to be exchanged, whereas JAX-RPC is focused on providing mechanisms that allows developers to access software components on remote systems.

In the JAXM part of the chapter we covered the following:

❑   The status of the JAXM specification

❑   The architecture of JAXM

❑   The ability to transmit different types of XML documents using message profiles such as ebXML and WS-Routing

❑   Security concerns

❑   Downloading and installing the JAX Pack, which contains JAXM

In the JAX-RPC part of the chapter we covered the following:

- ❑ The status of the JAX-RPC specification
- ❑ Type mapping
- ❑ The process of defining a JAX-RPC service, deploying it, and invoking a JAX-RPC service

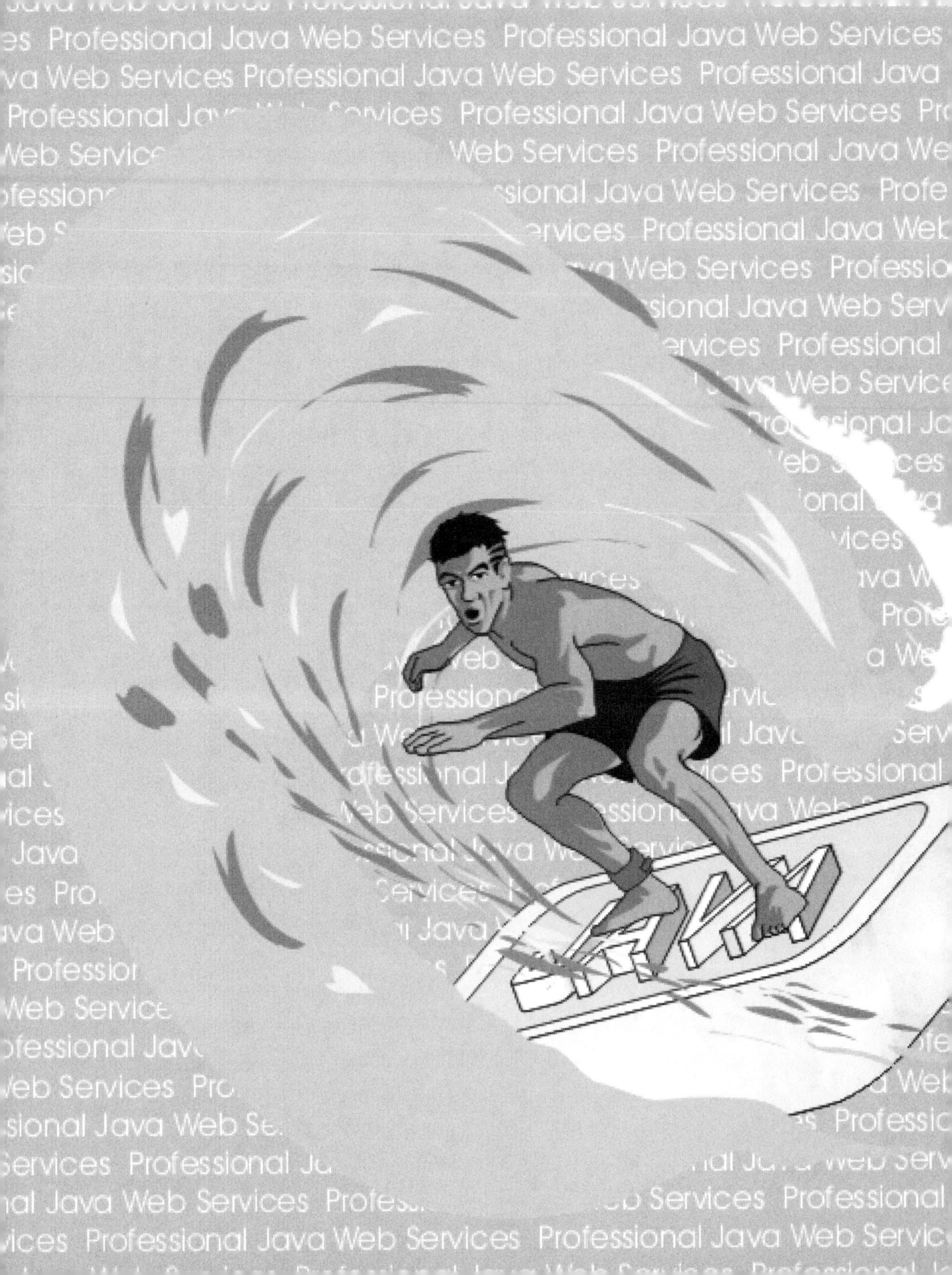
Professional Java Web Services

JAXR

"Someday," say the forward-thinking Web Service architects, "our applications will automatically discover and implement new Web Services dynamically." Well, if that is ever to happen, we must have a programmatic way of discovering and implementing Web Services. The **Java API for XML Registries** (**JAXR**) is Sun's official Java high-level abstraction layer for communicating with an XML registry via some form of XML messaging (like SOAP). This chapter will discuss the JAXR architecture and public API.

However, at the time of writing JAXR is not finished (currently at version 0.7), there is not yet a working full release of the technology. Because of this, future releases of JAXR may contain minor or even major changes. In addition, the JAXR code samples do not compile, as at the time of writing Sun has yet to release a working demo of the API and no vendors have yet implemented the API.

This chapter will tell you how to use JAXR with what information is presently available. We will cover the following:

- ❑ Brief review of the leading XML registries: ebXML and UDDI
- ❑ JAXR architectural overview
- ❑ How to use JAXR

XML Registries

If you are familiar with UDDI and ebXML, you can skip this section. Otherwise, it may be worth referring to Chapters 5 before continuing. For competion's sake we'll summarize them here.

While previous discussions of what constitutes an **XML registry** assume that the data is stored as XML. In addition to the query/response protocol being XML, an XML registry can be more simply defined as providing XML-based messaging protocol access for manipulating the registry. The registry doesn't have to store data as XML; it's free to use whatever data storage mechanism it wishes. Alternative examples include LDAP and even standard relational databases.

XML registries provide centralized repositories for organizations to advertise their existence, describe their business, and provide web services that their partners can access.

Before we get too excited about this data-interoperability solution, we should consider the catch: there are competing XML registry standards. At the last count, there are at least five standards, though only two have garnered much popularity: ebXML and UDDI.

ebXML versus UDDI

The differences between ebXML and UDDI can perhaps best be summarized by understanding the differences in the scope of the two standards. ebXML is a broad initiative whose goal is to define a body of world-wide standards for how e-commerce is done. The ebXML standard for an XML registry is a key of part of that effort. UDDI, however, was initially created by certain parties anxious to implement XML registries but dissatisfied with the pace of the ebXML effort. The scope of UDDI isn't to define all of the global e-commerce protocols; rather, it is simply concerned with XML registries.

ebXML can therefore be considered a functional superset of UDDI. UDDI-based XML registries are designed to store basic information about a business and an index of its Web Services. ebXML registries are designed to store this and additional information relating to the business, legal, and logistical details of an organization. Thus, UDDI aims to expose the Web Services a company offers and how they are used; ebXML wants to describe the big picture: the who, what, where, why, and when of an organization's e-commerce initiatives.

Currently, it appears that both the UDDI and ebXML standards will co-exist for a while. The UDDI participants say that organizations should store information in the central UDDI Business Registry and then reference another entry in an ebXML registry if desired, as this would then allow interoperability between the two standards. Both these standards are subject to constant change however, and UDDI could grow in scope and provide an alternative to all that ebXML provides. Or ebXML could overwhelm the existing support for UDDI and become the dominant standard.

JAXR and XML Registries

Ultimately, no one can be certain what the XML registry marketplace will look like a year from now. Both the ebXML and UDDI standards are constantly evolving. Keeping up with these standards and creating client programs that interface with them would be quite a complex undertaking.

JAXR exists to try and make creating an XML registry client as easy as possible. Its goal is to abstract all of the existing XML registry concepts to an implementation-neutral level, allowing developers to write JAXR code that can communicate with any XML registry.

The JAXR information model uses the ebXML Registry Information Model as its basis rather than the UDDI data structures. The JAXR API is designed to support multiple registries with the ebXML Registry Information Model being more generic and extensible than the UDDI data structures. To quote the JAXR, "Information models take time to develop. It was easier to start with a study of existing registry information models and improve upon it [than start from scratch]" (JAXR Public Review Draft 2, p. 104). Because of this characteristic, it was possible to extend the ebXML Registry Information Model to satisfy the needs of UDDI and other registries.

The JAXR Architecture

Given the current evolving standards of existing and emerging XML registry specifications, the JAXR API has been designed around a **service provider framework** model. That is, the JAXR API specifies a generic API for accessing an XML registry and leaves the lower-level details about how to actually talk to a given XML registry to a **provider**. The providers that JAXR uses to communicate with specific XML registries are called **JAXR providers**.

If you are a bit perplexed about the service provider framework think about the JDBC API. The JDBC API defines a set of general functionality, but you have to load a specific JDBC driver to translate that general functionality into the language of your specific database. This is also true for JAXR, since a specific provider will mediate between the JAXR calls a given application makes, and the registry for which it is acting as proxy:

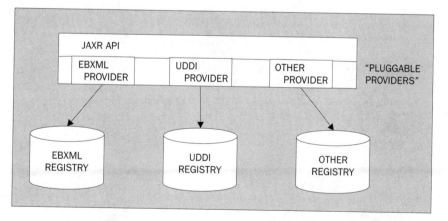

By implementing the service provider architecture (also called a "pluggable provider"), JAXR aims to be compatible with both current and future registry standards – assuming that the high-level JAXR API proves to be durable.

It is assumed that future JAXR provider vendors will leverage the existing and emerging JAXP (XML parsing), JAXB (binding XML to Java objects), JAXRPC, and JAXM standards.

Due to the widely varying capabilities of the diverse XML registry specifications, it is difficult to create a single API for XML registries. The designers of the specification decided that instead of creating an API that accessed the combination of all of the various functionality sets, the least common denominator so to speak, they would introduce a mechanism for allowing some JAXR providers to implement more functionality than others.

Each JAXR provider must have a capability level that defines which interfaces from the JAXR it implements. Capability levels are non-negative integral values. For now, only two capability levels have been defined: 0 and 1. Essentially, JAXR providers with capability level 0 are UDDI providers, and JAXR providers with capability level 1 are ebXML providers.

We will discuss both later in the chapter.

The JAXR API: How do I use it?

The JAXR API is a pretty complex API, and it's still subject to change. We'll review how JAXR works as of the version 0.7 (Public Review Draft 2 – released November 13, 2001). First, we'll provide a high-level summary of how to use the API via two use cases, and then we'll go into greater detail about the objects and methods of the API exposed by the use cases. Finally, we'll provide some additional information about the API that wasn't discussed in the use cases.

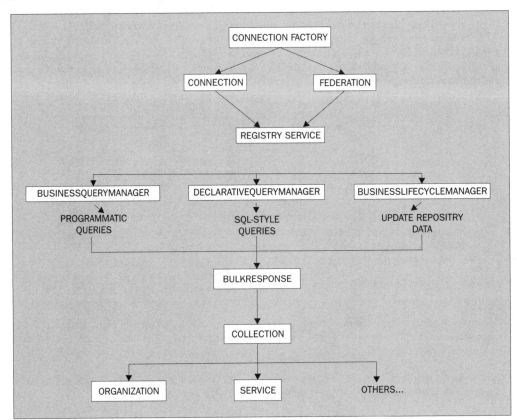

Using JAXR to query information from an XML registry

To illustrate how to use JAXR, let's outline the steps to obtain a list of web services that an organization offers. In this hypothetical use case, let's say we want to find out what web services WROX makes available. Here are the steps (don't worry if you aren't familiar with the objects listed here; this is just a logical overview):

1. Obtain a reference to a `ConnectionFactory` **object**.

2. Using the `ConnectionFactory`, **obtain a** `Connection` **object**. Connections enable either asynchronous or synchronous communication with an XML registry.

3. Using the `Connection`, **obtain a** `RegistryService`. The `RegistryService` interface is the key interface that enables developers to obtain additional interfaces that allow the manipulation of the underlying registry.

4. Using the `RegistryService`, **obtain a** `BusinessQueryManager`. The `BusinessQueryManager` interface contains several methods for searching a registry, it is also known as the focused query interface.

5. Use the `BusinessQueryManager` **to find the entry for WROX in the registry.** `findOrganizations()` accepts SQL-style search parameters and returns all matching results.

6. If successful, the above method will return an `Organization` **representing WROX.**

7. Use the `Organization` **to obtain a collection of all of the web services that WROX offers.**

Again, the above list is just an overview. The subsequent text of this chapter will go into detail about how each of these objects works. The code for the above example is very readable, and I'll list it here:

Code for JAXR Use Case Example

```
import javax.xml.registry.*;
import javax.xml.registry.infomodel.*;

/**
 * A simple demonstration of how to use the JAXR API to query an XML registry.
 * Looks up an entry for the WROX Press organization and obtains a list of
 * all the web services that pertain to said organization. Note that
 * basic error checking isn't present to handle what would happen if
 * there wasn't an entry for WROX in the registry.
 */
public class JAXRExample {

  // Returns a Collection of Services that WROX provides
  public Collection getWROXServices() {

    // Instantiate a ConnectionFactory from the JAXR provider
    // NOTE - because no JAXR providers presently exist, I reference a
```

```
        // hypothetical class: ProviderConnectionFactory.
        ConnectionFactory connectionFactory = ProviderConnectionFactory.newInstance();

        // Set required configuration properties before obtaining a Connection
        Properties properties = new Properties();
        properties.put("javax.xml.registry.queryManagerURL",
                    "http://a.registry.com/query");
        properties.put("javax.xml.registry.lifeCycleManagerURL",
                    "http://a.registry.com/modify");
        properties.put("javax.xml.registry.factoryClass",
                    "com.vendor.jaxr.ProviderConnectionFactory");
        connectionFactory.setProperties(properties);

        // Now that the ConnectionFactory is configured, obtain a Connection
        Connection connection = connectionFactory.createConnection();

        // Make the Connection synchronous to ensure that the transactions
        // are complete before control is returned to our class
        connection.setSynchronous(true);

        // Obtain the RegistryService
        RegistryService registryService = connection.getRegistryService();

        // Obtain the BusinessQueryManager
        BusinessQueryManager businessQueryManager =
                registryService.getBusinessQueryManager();

        // Build the objects necessary to make a query
        Collection names = new LinkedList();
        names.add("WROX Press");

        // Execute the query
        BulkResponse bulkResponse = businessQueryManager.findOrganizations(
                                    null, names, null, null, null, null);

        // Get the results of the query
        Collection organizations = bulkResponse.getCollection();
        Organization wrox = (Organization) organizations.iterator().next();

        // Get the services that WROX offers
        Collection services = wrox.getServices();

        connection.close();

        return services;
    }
}
```

Using JAXR to Update Information in an XML Registry

Another useful example would be to show how to use JAXR to update information in an XML registry. We'll give a use case for adding a new web service to WROX offerings. Many of the steps for this use case are the same as the previous example. We'll include the previous steps here and add new ones in bold text:

1. Obtain a reference to a `ConnectionFactory` object.

2. Using the `ConnectionFactory`, obtain a `Connection` object.

3. **Use the** `Connection` **method to authenticate with the registry**. Because the previous example was read-only, no authentication was necessary.

4. Using the Connection, obtain a `RegistryService`.

5. Using the `RegistryService`, obtain a `BusinessQueryManager`.

6. Use the `BusinessQueryManager` to find the entry for WROX in the registry.

7. If successful, the above method will return an `Organization` representing WROX.

8. **Using the** `RegistryService`, **obtain a** `BusinessLifeCycleManager`. `BusinessLifeCycleManager` is used to make changes to the registry.

9. **Use the** `BusinessLifeCycleManager` **to create a new** `Service`. Service is the JAXR object representing a web service.

10. **Use the** `BusinessLifeCycleManager` **to create a new** `ServiceBinding`. `ServiceBinding` provides detailed information about a web service, such as the access URL and specifications for the service. The `Service` object is a container for `ServiceBinding` objects.

11. **Add the** `ServiceBinding` **to** `Service`.

12. **Add the** `Service` **to** `Organization`. `Organization` represents WROX.

13. **Use the** `BusinessLifeCycleManager` **to save the modified** `Organization`.

Code for JAXR use case example

Once again, we'll provide sample code that illustrates the use case. This is based on the previous code example introduced in the first use case.

```
import javax.xml.registry.*;
import javax.xml.registry.infomodel.*;
import java.net.PasswordAuthentication;

/**
 * A simple demonstration of how to use the JAXR API to update an XML registry.
```

```
 * Looks up an entry for the WROX press organization and adds a new web service
 * to it.
 */
public class JAXRExample {

  // Adds a new service to WROX

  public boolean addWROXService(String serviceName, String serviceURL) {

      // Instantiate a ConnectionFactory from the JAXR provider
      // NOTE - because no JAXR providers presently exist, I reference a
      // hypothetical class: ProviderConnectionFactory.
      ConnectionFactory connectionFactory = ProviderConnectionFactory.newInstance();

      // Set required configuration properties before obtaining a Connection
      Properties properties = new Properties();
      properties.put("javax.xml.registry.queryManagerURL",
                  "http://a.registry.com/query");
      properties.put("javax.xml.registry.lifeCycleManagerURL",
                  "http://a.registry.com/modify");
      properties.put("javax.xml.registry.factoryClass",
                  "com.vendor.jaxr.ProviderConnectionFactory");
      connectionFactory.setProperties(properties);

      // Now that the ConnectionFactory is configured, obtain a Connection
      Connection connection = connectionFactory.createConnection();

      // Because we're updating information, we must authenticate with the registry
      PasswordAuthentication passwordAuthentication =
              new PasswordAuthentication("username", "password".toCharArray());
      Set credentials = new HashSet();
      credentials.add(passwordAuthentication);
      connection.setCredentials(credentials);

      // Make the Connection synchronous to ensure that the transactions
      // are complete before control is return to our class
      connection.setSynchronous(true);

      // Obtain the RegistryService
      RegistryService registryService = connection.getRegistryService();

      // Obtain the BusinessQueryManager
      BusinessQueryManager businessQueryManager =
              registryService.getBusinessQueryManager();

      // Build the objects necessary to make a query
      Collection names = new LinkedList();
      names.add("WROX Press");

      // Execute the query
      BulkResponse bulkResponse = businessQueryManager.findOrganizations(
                                  null, names, null, null, null, null);

      // Get the results of the query
```

```
Collection organizations = bulkResponse.getCollection();
Organization wrox = (Organization) organizations.iterator().next();

    // Obtain the BusinessLifeCycleManager
    BusinessLifeCycleManager businessLCM =
            registryService.getBusinessLifeCycleManager();

    // Create a new service
    Service service = businessLCM.createService(serviceName);

    // Create a new servicebinding and add it to the service
    ServiceBinding serviceBinding = businessLCM.createServiceBinding();
    serviceBinding.setAccessURI(serviceURL);
    service.addServiceBinding(serviceBinding);

    // Add the service to the organization
    wrox.addService(service);

    // Save the organization
    Organizations orgs = new LinkedList();
    orgs.add(wrox);
    bulkResponse = businessLCM.saveOrganizations(orgs);

    // saveOrganizations() returns a Collection containing the Key of each
    // Organization that was saved correctly, check if one Key is present
    // to indicate that WROX was update
    try {
      Collection keys = bulkResponse.getCollection();
      if (keys.size() > 0) {
        return true;
      } else {
        return false;
      }
    } finally {
      connection.close();
    }
  }
}
```

The Major JAXR Objects

Now that we've examined the use cases and seen how the code looks, let's talk further about the JAXR objects exposed in the use cases.

ConnectionFactory

```
public abstract class ConnectionFactory {
  public ConnectionFactory newInstance() throws JAXRException {}
  public abstract Connection createConnection() throws JAXRException {}
  public abstract Federation createFederation(java.util.Collection connections)
                         throws JAXRException {}
```

```
    public abstract java.util.Properties getProperties() throws JAXRException {}
    public abstract void setProperties(java.util.Properties properties)
                        throws JAXRException {}
}
```

The first step to using JAXR is obtaining a reference to a `ConnectionFactory` object. `ConnectionFactory` is a abstract base class, used by factory classes to make a connection; working implementations of `ConnectionFactory` are yet to be created by JAXR providers. A `ConnectionFactory` should preferably be obtained using JNDI. However, in the absence of a JNDI data store, the following factory method is provided:

```
public ConnectionFactory newInstance() throws JAXRException
```

In the event that multiple `ConnectionFactory` implementations are available, you can set a system property called `"javax.xml.registry.ConnectionFactoryClass"` with the value of the `ConnectionFactory` class to instantiate. The property can be set in the following ways:

1. When executing the JVM, use the `-D` option to set a system property. Under Windows, the syntax is:

```
java -Djavax.xml.registry.ConnectionFactoryClass=
        com.jaxr.provider.ProviderConnectionFactory
```

2. From within your code, use the System object:

```
System.setProperty("javax.xml.registry.ConnectionFactoryClass",
                    "com.jaxr.provider.ProviderConnectionFactory");
```

After obtaining a `ConnectionFactory`, various properties must be set that are used when creating a connection. Once the `ConnectionFactory` is populated with the properties it will subsequently create as many `Connection` objects as desired reusing the same properties (or new ones, set again). Properties are set with the following method:

```
public abstract void setProperties(java.util.Properties properties)
                        throws JAXRException {}
```

The `Properties` object should be populated with the following values:

Property Name	Data Type	Description
javax.xml.registry.queryManagerURL	String	URL to the query manager service within the target registry provider
javax.xml.registry.lifeCycleManagerURL	String	URL to the life cycle manager service within the target registry provider

Property Name	Data Type	Description
javax.xml.registry.factoryClass	String	Fully qualified class name of the ConnectionFactory that is in use

Note that JAXR providers may require that additional properties be passed into the createConnection() method. We cannot provide more information about these properties because at press time no JAXR providers exist.

The main use of ConnectionFactory is, intuitively enough, to obtain Connection objects, which in turn represent physical connections to an XML registry.

JAXR also supports distributed queries across multiple XML registries. A special interface, Federation, exists to facilitate such queries. The Federation interface can be obtained by putting all Connections in the distributed query into a Collection and calling the following method:

```
public abstract Federation createFederation(java.util.Collection connections)
                            throws JAXRException {}
```

Because Federation extends Connection, it can be used in place of a Connection in JAXR code.

Connection

```
public interface Connection {
   void close() throws JAXRException;
   public Set getCredentials() throws JAXRException;
   public RegistryService getRegistryService() throws JAXRException;
   boolean isClosed() throws JAXRException;
   public boolean isSynchronous() throws JAXRException;
   public void setCredentials(Set credentials) throws JAXRException;
   public void setSynchronous(boolean sync) throws JAXRException;
}
```

Connection represents our network connection to the XML registry. Connection's primary purpose in life is to provide an accessor method for a RegistryService. RegistryService as previously mentioned is a container for key objects used to manipulate the XML registry. The accessor method is:

```
public RegistryService getRegistryService() throws JAXRException;
```

If authentication is required to perform certain operations against an XML registry, Connection provides accessor and mutator methods for authentication:

```
public Set getCredentials() throws JAXRException;
public void setCredentials(Set credentials) throws JAXRException;
```

Credentials consist of either a digital certificate and private key or a username/password. If a digital certificate is to be used, the credentials parameter should contain a instance of javax.security.auth.x500. Otherwise, credentials should contain an instance of java.net.PasswordAuthentication.

Interestingly enough, a `Connection` can be either synchronous or asynchronous. That is, when performing queries against an XML registry, `Connection` can either (a) wait for the transaction to complete before control is returned to the executing thread (synchronous), or (b) return control to the thread immediately and have the results returned whenever they are available (asynchronous).

Synchronous behavior is typical for most Java APIs; we call a method and get a response before moving on. Asynchronous behavior, however, is handled in a custom manner, and will be defined when we look at `BulkResponse`. You can check and modify the synchronicity of `Connection` via:

```
public boolean isSynchronous() throws JAXRException;
public void setSynchronous(boolean sync) throws JAXRException;
```

Finally, once we have finished with a `Connection` we should close it. We can also check if a `Connection` has already been closed using the methods `close()` and `isClosed()`.

RegistryService

```
public interface RegistryService {
    BulkResponse getBulkResponse(String requestId) throws InvalidRequestException,
                                                          JAXRException;
    BusinessLifeCycleManager getBusinessLifeCycleManager() throws JAXRException;
    BusinessQueryManager getBusinessQueryManager() throws JAXRException;
    CapabilityProfile getCapabilityProfile() throws JAXRException;
    DeclarativeQueryManager getDeclarativeQueryManager()
                        throws JAXRException, UnsupportedCapabilityException;
    ClassificationScheme getDefaultPostalScheme() throws JAXRException;
    LifeCycleManager getLifeCycleManager() throws JAXRException;
    String makeRegistrySpecificRequest(String request) throws JAXRException;
}
```

As mentioned earlier, JAXR providers have a capability level, either 0 or 1, which defines how much functionality they implement. This method:

```
CapabilityProfile getCapabilityProfile() throws JAXRException;
```

returns a `CapabilityProfile` interface, which in turn has a method, `getCapabilityLevel()` that returns an `int` value defining the capability level of the `RegistryService`'s underlying JAXR provider. The standard way to discover the capability level of the service is given below:

```
int level = registryService.getCapabilityProfile().getCapabilityLevel();
```

In JAXR, modifications to a registry are made using `LifeCycleManager` and `BusinessLifeCycleManager`. These objects can be obtained using:

```
BusinessLifeCycleManager getBusinessLifeCycleManager() throws JAXRException;
LifeCycleManager getLifeCycleManager() throws JAXRException;
```

`BusinessLifeCycleManager` extends `LifeCycleManager`, but `BusinessLifeCycleManager` has no methods beyond capability level 0. It's not clear why methods to obtain both `LifeCycleManager` and `BusinessLifeCycleManager` have been provided. It may be for authentication reasons.

The `BusinessQueryManager` and `DeclarativeQueryManager` interfaces are used for making read-only queries against a registry. They are obtained using:

```
BusinessQueryManager getBusinessQueryManager() throws JAXRException;
DeclarativeQueryManager getDeclarativeQueryManager()
                    throws JAXRException, UnsupportedCapabilityException;
```

In the event that JAXR doesn't provide the required functionality, a "backdoor" method is provided:

```
String makeRegistrySpecificRequest(String request) throws JAXRException;
```

This method takes a string XML request in a registry specific format, sends the request to the registry and returns a string that is the registry specific XML response. Use this method if JAXR doesn't explicitly support functionality in the XML registry that you need to access.

The final two methods in this object will be defined at a later point in this chapter, when the objects they involve are defined:

```
BulkResponse getBulkResponse(String requestId) throws InvalidRequestException,
                                                    JAXRException;
ClassificationScheme getDefaultPostalScheme() throws JAXRException;
```

BulkResponse and JAXRResponse

```
public interface BulkResponse extends JAXRResponse {
  Collection getCollection() throws JAXRException;
  Collection getException() throws JAXRException;
  boolean isPartialResponse() throws JAXRException;
}

public interface JAXRResponse {
  String getRequestId() throws JAXRException;
  int getStatus() throws JAXRException;
  boolean isAvailable() throws JAXRException;
}
```

Results from JAXR transactions are returned in the form of `BulkResponse` objects, which are in turn built on `JAXRResponse` objects. To obtain the results of the transaction, use this method:

```
Collection getCollection() throws JAXRException;
```

You should probably also check if your transaction was completed successfully with:

```
boolean isPartialResponse() throws JAXRException;
```

If the above method returns `true`, then you might also want to use:

```
Collection getException() throws JAXRException;
```

to determine why the transaction failed.

Recall that transactions against an XML registry can be either synchronous or asynchronous. If the `Connection` object has been set to asynchronous mode, a `BulkReponse` object is returned before it is completely populated with the results of the transaction. To ensure that a `BulkResponse` has been populated, use:

```
boolean isAvailable() throws JAXRException;
```

which is inherited from `JAXRResponse`. If the method returns true, start accessing the `BulkResponse`. If not, try again after a short period.

BusinessQueryManager

```
public interface BusinessQueryManager extends QueryManager {
  BulkResponse findAssociations(
    Collection findQualifiers,
    Collection associationTypes,
    boolean sourceObjectConfirmed,
    boolean targetObjectConfirmed
  ) throws JAXRException;

  BulkResponse findOrganizations(
    Collection findQualifiers,
    Collection namePatterns,
    Collection classifications,
    Collection specifications,
    Collection externalIdentifiers,
    Collection externalLinks
  ) throws JAXRException;

  BulkResponse findServices(Key orgKey,
    Collection findQualifiers,
    Collection namePatterns,
    Collection classifications,
    Collection specifications
  ) throws JAXRException;

  BulkResponse findServiceBindings(
    Key serviceKey,
    Collection findQualifiers,
    Collection classifications,
    Collection specifications
  ) throws JAXRException;

  BulkResponse findClassificationSchemes(

    Collection findQualifiers,

    Collection namePatterns,
    Collection classifications,
    Collection externalLinks
  ) throws JAXRException;

  ClassificationScheme findClassificationSchemeByName(String namePattern)
                       throws JAXRException;
```

```
    BulkResponse findConcepts(Collection findQualifiers,
                              Collection namePatterns,
                              Collection classifications,
                              Collection externalIdentifiers,
                              Collection externalLinks)
            throws JAXRException;

    Concept findConceptByPath(String path) throws JAXRException;

    BulkResponse findRegistryPackages(Collection findQualifiers,
                              Collection namePatterns,
                              Collection classifications,
                              Collection externalLinks)
            throws JAXRException;
}
```

`RegistryService` contains two objects that enable us to read information from the registry: `BusinessQueryManager` and `DeclarativeQueryManager`.

`BusinessQueryManager` is composed entirely of `findXXX()` methods. These methods all have almost identical parameters, with the exception of some additional parameters for specific `findXXX()` methods. Here are the definitions of these parameters, from the JavaDocs:

- `findQualifiers` - A `Collection` of find qualifiers as defined by the `FindQualifier` interface. It specifies qualifiers that effect string matching, sorting, and boolean predicate logic, and so on.

- `namePatterns` - A `Collection` of `Strings`. Each `String` is a partial or full name pattern with wildcard searching as specified by the SQL-92 LIKE specification. Unless otherwise specified in `findQualifiers`, this is a logical OR and a match on any name qualifies as a match for this criteria.

  For those not familiar with SQL-92 LIKE, it is enough to know that the "`%`" symbols acts as a wildcard. Thus, adding a `String` containing "`%wrox press%`" would return any organizations whose name contains the words "`wrox press`" at any place in the name.

- `classifications` - A `Collection` of `Classifications` that classify the object. This is analogous to `categoryBag` in UDDI. Unless otherwise specified in `findQualifiers`, this is a Logical AND, and matching on ALL specified `Classifications` qualifies as a match for this criteria.

- `specifications` - A `Collection` of `RegistryObjects` that represent (proxy) a technical specification. This is analogous to `tModelBag` in UDDI. Unless otherwise specified in `findQualifiers`, this is a logical AND, and matching on ALL specified `Specifications` qualifies as a match for this criteria.

- `externalIdentifiers` - A `Collection` of external identifiers that provide an external identifier for the object using an identification scheme such as DUNS. This is analogous to `identifierBag` in UDDI. Unless otherwise specified in `findQualifiers`, this is a logical AND, and matching on ALL specified `Classifications` qualifies as a match for this criteria.

❑ externalLinks - A Collection of ExternalLinks that link the object to content outside the registry. This is analogous to overviewDoc in UDDI. Unless otherwise specified in findQualifiers, this is a Logical AND, and matching on ALL specified ExternalLinks qualifies as a match for this criteria.

You can substitute any parameter for null if you don't want to search based on that parameter.

Some of these findXXX() methods may not make any sense at present because you're not familiar with the objects they find. We will cover these objects a little later. To see the BusinessQueryManager in action, let's revisit a code snippet from our first use case:

```
// obtain the BusinessQueryManager
BusinessQueryManager businessQueryManager =
        registryService.getBusinessQueryManager();

// build the objects necessary to make a query
Collection names = new LinkedList();
names.add("WROX Press");

// execute the query
BulkResponse bulkResponse = businessQueryManager.findOrganizations(
                            null, names, null, null, null, null);
```

DeclarativeQueryManager

```
public interface DeclarativeQueryManager extends QueryManager {
    Query createQuery(int queryType, String queryString)
            throws InvalidRequestException, JAXRException;
    public BulkResponse executeQuery(Query query) throws JAXRException;
}
```

The other method for obtaining information from a registry is using the DeclarativeQueryManager object. Its use is straightforward: first, create a Query object using:

```
Query createQuery(int queryType, String queryString)
        throws InvalidRequestException, JAXRException;
```

The queryType parameter is populated by a constant value from the Query interface. At the moment, only SQL queries are allowed. The queryString parameter is the actual SQL query. Once generated, the Query should be passed to this method:

```
public BulkResponse executeQuery(Query query) throws JAXRException;
```

The syntax for creating SQL style statements for use against registries is provided in this document:

ebXML Registry Information Model
http://www.oasis-open.org/committees/regrep/documents/2.0/specs/ebrim.pdf

Here's a code example for using `DeclarativeQueryManager`, taken (and reformatted) from the JAXR 0.7 source code:

```
DeclarativeQueryManager dqm = registryService.getDeclarativeQueryManager();
Query query = dqm.createQuery(Query.QUERY_TYPE_SQL,
                    "SELECT FROM RegistryObject WHERE objectType =
                    \'BusinessListing\' AND name LIKE \'%Acme%\'");
BulkResponse bulkResponse = dqm.executeQuery(query);
```

BusinessLifeCycleManager

```
public interface BusinessLifeCycleManager extends LifeCycleManager {
    BulkResponse saveOrganizations(Collection organizations) throws JAXRException;
    BulkResponse saveServices(Collection services) throws JAXRException;
    BulkResponse saveServiceBindings(Collection bindings) throws JAXRException;
    BulkResponse saveConcepts(Collection concepts) throws JAXRException;
    BulkResponse saveClassificationSchemes(Collection schemes)
            throws JAXRException;
    BulkResponse saveAssociations(Collection associations, boolean replace)
            throws JAXRException;
    BulkResponse deleteOrganizations(Collection organizationKeys)
            throws JAXRException;
    BulkResponse deleteServices(Collection serviceKeys) throws JAXRException;
    BulkResponse deleteServiceBindings(Collection bindingKeys) throws JAXRException;
    BulkResponse deleteConcepts(Collection conceptKeys) throws JAXRException;
    BulkResponse deleteClassificationSchemes(Collection schemeKeys)
            throws JAXRException;
    BulkResponse deleteAssociations(Collection schemeKeys) throws JAXRException;
}
```

`BusinessLifeCycleManager` enables you to modify the registry. Once an object is obtained from the registry using one of the `QueryManagers`, such as an `Organization` or a `Service`, the object can be mutated and then saved by passing the object to one of the `saveXXX()` methods. Deleting the underlying information an object represents can be accomplished in much the same manner using the `deleteXXX()` methods, with the exception that `Keys` are used for deleting. Key objects are obtained using the `getKey()` method of `RegistryObject`. `RegistryObject` is an interface which all of the JAXR data objects implement.

As with the `QueryManagers`, the results of `BusinessLifeCycleManager` transactions are returned in `BulkResponse` objects. The `Keys` of those objects successfully updated are the results of `BusinessLifeCycleManager saveXXX()` and `deleteXXX()` methods.

Additional JAXR Objects

So far, we've looked at the key JAXR objects used for manipulated registries. Now, we're going to take briefer looks at some of the smaller objects in the JAXR API. These objects are wrappers for registry data but don't perform functionality on their own.

We've seen `Organization` in the use case code examples. We'll define it more completely here and provide information on the objects that it contains.

- ❏ `Organization` – Intuitively enough, this represents an organization that has an entry in the repository. The interface provides methods to get and set the services associated with the organization, as well as the organization's postal address, phone numbers, contact, and users. An organization can also have children organizations, such as autonomous business divisions.

- ❏ `User` – User objects represent those users registered with the XML registry. `User` objects are used to contain other objects, including: parent `Organization`, `PostalAddress`, `PersonName`, and a `Collection` of `TelephoneNumbers`.

- ❏ `PostalAddress` – Used to contain the various attributes of a postal address. It can also be configured to use custom address attributes.

- ❏ `TelephoneNumber` – Used to contain the various attributes of a telephone number.

Service, ServiceBinding, and SpecificationLink

An `Organization` also contains services, which are represented by these objects:

- ❏ `Service` – Represents a web service. The interface allows us to access the `ServiceBindings` associated with the service, and to get the organization to which the service belongs.

- ❏ `ServiceBindings` – Contains the service's URI, a target `ServiceBinding` in case of a redirection, and a collection of `SpecificationLink` objects . An accessor is also provides that returns the `Service` associated with the `ServiceBinding`.

- ❏ `SpecificationLink` – Container for description of how to use a service as well as a `Collection` of the service's parameters.

Summary

The examples and explanations in this chapter demonstrate how to use JAXR to query XML registries for information, and how to authenticate against an XML registry and update its information. There's certainly more depth to the JAXR API than has been covered here (the specification is over 100 pages long), and it's likely to change in some potentially significant ways before it sees a 1.0 release.

To read the latest JAXR specification, see http://java.sun.com/xml/jaxr/. To track JAXR as it nears completion, visit http://www.jcp.org/jsr/detail/93.jsp.

When completed, JAXR will be a good way of searching for web services in a programmatic, automated fashion, or even writing your own XML registry client for end-users to view or change a UDDI, ebXML, or other registry.

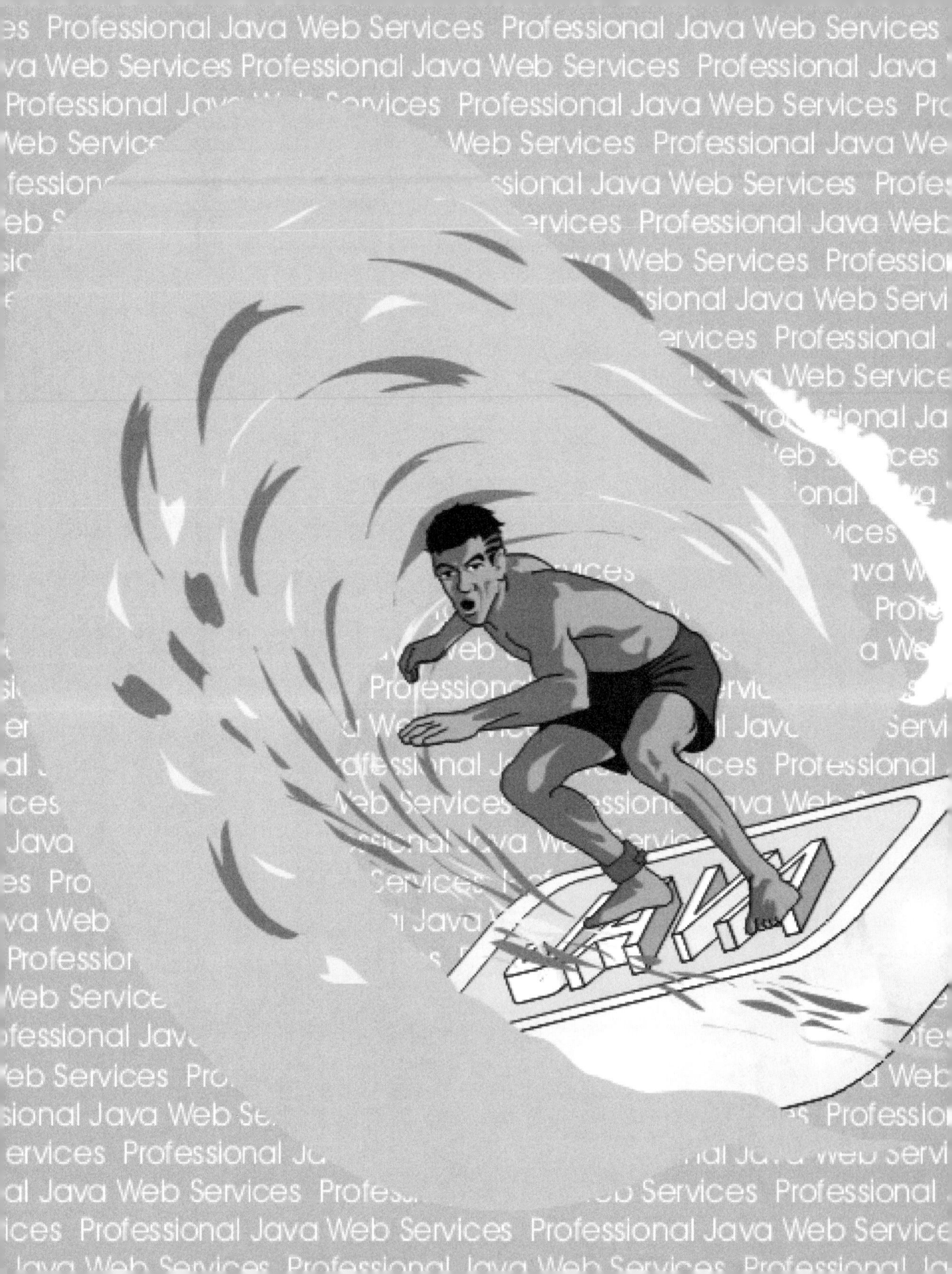
Professional Java Web Services

Introduction to Sun ONE

On February 5, 2001 Sun Microsystems announced the **Sun Open Network Environment**, abbreviated as **Sun ONE**, or simply **ONE** (often pronounced Oh En Ee). ONE represents yet another step towards Sun's ultimate vision of 'the network is the computer'. Having said that, Sun's positioning of ONE has been confusing. On the one hand, ONE appears to be a pure specification that describes a roadmap to creating a service-driven network based on open standards. Yet on the other hand, Sun in most of its discussion about ONE mentions its Forte integrated development environment (IDE) and the iPlanet family of directory, application, web, commerce, and communication servers.

I would like to think that ONE is really the former (that is, pure specification) with Sun simply setting an example (and making some money at the same time) with its own products of how its vision could be implemented with an integrated toolset. After all, Sun does believe in open standards and open specifications. Based on this assumption (that ONE is a *specification*), we will not be going into a discussion on how to use the Forte IDE or how to deploy web services in the iPlanet application server. Instead, we will focus on ONE as the specification and the vision.

Not too long ago most corporate IT departments were faced with a challenge: integrating their monolithic applications to streamline their operations. Now they are faced with another, even bigger challenge: integrating business processes across corporate and geographic boundaries. To help corporate IT departments meet this challenge, Sun has proposed the notion of **Services on Demand**. The notion of Services of Demand goes beyond simply encapsulating business functionality in the form of web services.

Rather, the promise of Services on Demand is to facilitate the delivery of anytime computing, anywhere, to anyone, using any device, and to quickly evolve to include support for emerging service and peer-to-peer application standards. The key point to bear in mind is that Services on Demand are based on open standards that can easily traverse partners, customers, and suppliers with no change in the quality of each service's capabilities. The only prerequisite for creating such Services on Demand is that you have correctly identified the four key elements of your business processes that you wish to expose as services. These elements are:

- ❑ The **data** that the process uses
- ❑ The **applications** that manipulate the data
- ❑ The **reports** that get created as a result of the process
- ❑ The **transactions** that occur within the process during execution

To help remember these four elements (and prerequisites) for creating Services on Demand, Sun has created an acronym, **DART**, short for Data, Applications, Reports, and Transactions.

We can all probably agree with the overall vision of Services on Demand, but a vision by itself can only take you so far. Fortunately, Sun goes beyond the hype and provides an end-to-end architecture that supports the creation of and migration to Services on Demand. This architecture enables customers to support their existing application needs while allowing them to build a solid foundation for web services of the future. As you should have guessed by now, this architecture is ONE, which is an open stack with the ability to be integrated into an already existing architecture, designed to create and deploy Services on Demand and emerging web services.

The ONE Architecture

The ONE architecture is based on open standards (we'll see which ones shortly) and attempts to provide a clear and simple set of practices to build and deploy web services based on technologies available today. An analogy that comes to mind is that of the J2EE Blueprints, which provide best practices for creating high-performance, robust, and scalable J2EE applications. Similarly, the ONE architecture describes how best to take these technologies and fit them together to build web services.

These best practices are universal regardless of which vendor's J2EE application server is used, just as the ONE architecture can be universally applied with or without Sun tools. In fact later on in this chapter, we will create and deploy a web service in WebLogic and invoke it using a Java client that will use a proxy generated by IBM's Web Services Toolkit (which in turn uses Apache's implementation of SOAP). In doing so, we will use many of the key technologies specified in the ONE architecture.

The Concept of Smart Web Services

If you've read anything at all about ONE, especially anything released by Sun, you can't help but have come across the concept of **smart web services**, or **smart services**. That is because smart services are at the core of Sun's vision of the future of the Web. Therefore, it is important that you understand what Sun means by smart web services.

Today's services are fairly simple, struggling with even the basics of security and scalability. These are what Sun refers to as just *plain* web services that is, not *smart*. However, these simplistic services will eventually evolve, providing significantly greater value, a much richer user interface, and be customizable (or even personalizable, that is, customizable per user). These are smart web services.

So how does Sun think this will happen? The answer lies in three characteristics that smart services have, which services today do not:

❑ A shared context

❑ Multinet capabilities

❑ Quality of Service (QoS) metrics

Let's take a look at each of these characteristics in turn.

Shared Context

A distinguishing characteristic of a smart web service is that it always knows the answers to the classic 'who, what, when, where, and why' journalism questions. The answers to these questions form the **context** within which the web service operates. Context provides information to the service about a variety of different aspects of the user, such as where the user is located, what role the user is playing, the identity of the user, the security, privacy, and business preferences of the user, past history of interactions, service-level agreements between the user and the service provider, and so on.

For example, consider a smart travel-booking service. Such a service would base its travel suggestions on aspects such as your budget, where you've been before, activities that your children might enjoy (if you have any children, that is), and so on. Instead of it having to ask you all this information, it would obtain this from the context within which it operates.

How does the web service know so much about you, the user? There is any number of ways that this information could be obtained. These range from simple techniques such as cookies and registration processes, to more complex activities such as tracking the user's web site navigation and accessing a public database. A smart web service uses the context to better satisfy user needs. This is actually being done today by sophisticated CRM (Customer Relationship Management) systems such as provided by Siebel. The ability to work in a context is in fact the foundation of CRM.

In the above discussion, we mentioned several different ways that a smart web service could obtain contextual information. There are many more ways that this could be done. Having so many different options for getting contextual information is actually more of a hurdle to overcome than a blessing to enjoy.

We can all probably agree that for any but the simplest requests, no one service will be able to completely satisfy user needs. In fact, this should be evident from the definition of a web service (see Chapter 1). Rather, each user request will be satisfied by a well-orchestrated *group* of services. This means that downstream services will have to obtain their contextual information from those upstream. Hence the term **shared context**.

The reason so many ways of obtaining contextual information exist today is that there is no standard for web services to share something even as simple as user identity. In fact, there is not even an agreement on what this user identity should be, let alone sharing it. As we've seen earlier though, user identity is only part of the shared context that smart web services need.

The challenge is that before Sun's vision of transparent, dynamic, and seamless interaction of widely distributed web services can occur, the issues of the *what* and *how* of shared context must be resolved, not by a single vendor, but by the software community as a whole. Most importantly, such a solution should be based on open standards.

Multinet Capabilities

As more and more functionality starts to be exposed as web services, it follows that more and more people will want to use web services. It also follows that people will want to be able to access these web services on a variety of different devices that work over a variety of different networks.

For example, I may want to book tickets to a late night symphony and obtain directions to get there, all from my PDA while standing in line to renew my driver's license. Enter ONE's **multinet capabilities**.

Multinet capabilities recognizes that the Web is only one of many networks and refers to the fact that a smart web service should be available across multiple network types. Such networks include, but are not limited to, IP networks, telephony networks, cellular networks, and so on. The reason that multiple network types must be supported is straightforward. Simply stated, as technology continues to advance (see below) and the popularity (and feasibility) of web services continues to grow, people will want to be able to invoke the use of the many web services available to them from a variety of different devices, most of which will probably not work over the Web as we know it today. The ticket-booking example was one of the many millions of possibilities and uses of web services in the future. However, the challenge actually goes beyond just beating the technology barriers to aesthetic and presentation issues as well, for example, adjusting to different screen sizes. If you have ever tried reading the Wall Street Journal on your PDA or reading a map on your cell phone, you will know what I mean.

*How Fast **Does** Technology Advance?*

The pace at which technology advances has been accurately captured by three laws over the past several decades. So far these laws have held up against the test of time:

Moore's law, which predicts that the number of transistors on a microprocessor doubles approximately every 18 months.

Gilder's law, which predicts that the total bandwidth of communication systems will triple every 12 months and that eventually the cost of communicating will drop to next to nothing.

Metcalfe's law, which estimates that the value of a network scales as the square of the number of people connected to it.

Quality of Service (QoS) Metrics

If web services are ever to become mainstream, this is one of the most important characteristics. All the classic 'abilities' are included here, such as reliability, availability, scalability, and so on. Security is also important. QoS specifies that a user can specify the level of these metrics that they desire. For example, the user might desire a high level of reliability and security for services used to transfer money from the US to offshore accounts, but can live with much lower values of these while using a mapping service or a stock quote service. QoS takes on a new dimension when business partners start using web services. In such cases, QoS becomes part of a service-level agreement (SLA) that is contractually and legally enforced. In such cases, not only must the QoS characteristics be configurable, but they must be independently measurable and verifiable as well.

Of all the QoS characteristics, none is as tricky and perhaps as critical as that of security. Not surprisingly, this is also the QoS metric where web services today lack the most. Perhaps the most glaring reason for this is that there is no standard and universally accepted way of handling security. Note that security means a lot of different things to different people, but at the very least it includes the basic concepts of authentication, authorization, non-repudiation, and integrity.

There are many initiatives currently underway by different industry groups in an attempt to be the first to 'standardize' web service security. Here are three of the most prominent efforts:

1. Efforts based on XML and submitted to the W3C for consideration include the **XML Key Management Specification** (**XKMS**) and **XML Signature**. For more information on XKMS and XML Signature initiatives. visit http://www.w3.org/TR/xkms/ and http://www.w3.org/Signature/ respectively.

2. **Microsoft** has made its **Passport** service publicly available for web service authentication. Passport is a non-intrusive service in that when a user/client accesses a web service, they are redirected to the passport site where they are asked to authenticate themselves. Once authenticated, they are then redirected back to the web service. Once a user is authenticated by Passport, any service that uses Passport for authentication will recognize that the user has already been authenticated. Thus, Passport enables **single sign-on** (SSO) capability across web services using Passport. For more information about Passport visit the official Passport web site at http://www.passport.com/.

3. An industry consortium known as the **Liberty Alliance Project** has been recently formed. Members include Sun, Nokia, NTT DoCoMo, and the Apache Software Foundation among others. This seems to be a direct response to Microsoft and its Passport initiative, as its primary goal appears to be to provide a more 'open' alternative to Passport. For more information on the Liberty Alliance Project visit http://www.projectliberty.org/.

Another important QoS characteristic that web services severely lack today is the inability to enforce a transactional context across web services. As discussed earlier, the real power of web services is harnessed when multiple web services work in concert to produce a joint result. To achieve these results in a way that does not compromise the atomicity, isolation, consistency, or durability (in other words, the ACIDity) of any of the data that these web services operate upon, the entire operation spanning multiple web services must be carried out in the context of a transaction. This transaction must propagate or flow from one web service to another. Currently, no standard facility (or known initiative) for doing so exists, which as explained earlier, is a significant impediment in the road for the successful business use of web services.

Two Views of ONE

Some readers are probably familiar with the **Rational Unified Process**, also called RUP (http://www.rational.com/products/rup/index.jsp). One of the key features of this process is the different views of an architecture. These views include *four* core views:

- ❑ **Logical** (or **Design**)
- ❑ **Process**
- ❑ **Development** (or **Component** or **Implementation**)
- ❑ **Physical** (or **Deployment**)

There is also a *fifth* view called the **Use Case** view, which ties the four prior views together. This is known as the 4+1 view of architecture.

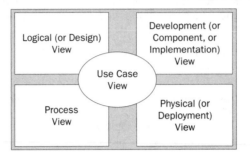

Our discussion of ONE will be based on a similar approach, but with only two views. The two views of ONE include a technology view and a functional view.

A Technology Perspective of ONE

At its very core, ONE is based upon three families of standards. These are summarized in the following table:

Family	Standard/Technology
XML	Core W3C Recommendations such as XML, XML Namespaces, XLink, XPointer, XPath, XSLT, XML Schemas, and DOM.
	Other XML Standards such as SAX.
	Presentation formats such as XHTML, WML, and VoiceXML.
	Messaging formats such as XML-RPC, SOAP, and ebXML Messaging.
	Registries and repositories such as UDDI and ebXML registries.
	Description languages such as WSDL and WSFL.
	B2B frameworks such as ebXML.
Java	Platforms: J2EE, J2SE, and J2ME.
	APIs for XML processing such as JAXP, JAXR, JAXB, JAXM, and JAX/RPC.
	APIs for devices such as the Java Card API, Java TV API, and Java Telephony API.
Infrastructure	Directory access protocols such as LDAP.
	Security protocols such as SSL.
	Information transfer protocols such as HTTP.

ONE provides the architectural *glue* that ties the technologies listed in the above table together. This is shown in the figure at the end of this section.

474

At this point in the book you certainly know that the foundation of web services is XML. XML provides a platform and language-independent, lightweight communication mechanism for describing web content, thus easing interoperability. The three cornerstones of web services, SOAP, WSDL, and UDDI registries, are all based on XML technologies. For a refresher on these, refer to Chapters 2 (SOAP), 4 (WSDL), and 5 (UDDI). With no intentions of reinventing the wheel, ONE has based its smart web services on XML as well.

ONE relies on the family of Java technologies to leverage existing and future functionality that will eventually lead to its vision of smart web services. More importantly though, enough mature Java technologies and platforms such as J2EE, J2SE, and J2ME, exist to allow the creation of sophisticated web services, even today.

The most common scenario today is for a web service to be exposed as a URL on the Web. More than likely, these web services are created using the J2EE platform (in the context of Java). The web tier for these services is a Java servlet in all likelihood (as opposed to JSP which is more suited to visual components). A client sends a SOAP (XML) request to the front-end, which then processes it and calls one or more EJBs to perform the actual business logic for that request. Although JavaBeans could be used to process requests, EJBs provide several benefits over JavaBeans. For example, EJBs are hosted in application servers that provide many value added services such as pooling (instance reuse), resource management, distributed transactions, and declarative transaction and security configuration to name just a few. These are all services that are critical for enterprise-level applications and web services because these services result in much of the scalability and performance of such applications.

The EJB components may process data from relational databases, such as Oracle, accessed via JDBC and a variety of other Enterprise Information Systems (EIS), such as SAP, Seibel, and so on, possibly using adapters based on the J2EE connector technology. The ultimate result of all this processing is then returned back to the client in the form of a SOAP response.

Note that the request/response could be over any protocol such as HTTP, FTP, or POP. HTTP is one of the popular protocols since most firewalls are configured to allow HTTP traffic (this actually acts as a double-edged sword by enabling security threats, but that is beyond the scope of this chapter).

So, how did the client find the service (and its endpoint JSP or servlet) in the first place? The answer is through the WSDL description of the service registered at a well-known UDDI registry. Once again, for a refresher on these we defer to previous chapters.

One interesting API, or rather family of APIs is the JAX pack, including JAXP, JAXM, JAXB, JAXR, or JAX-RPC. Almost all Java developers are familiar with JAXP, which is the **Java API for XML Parsing**. This API abstracts both SAX and DOM-based XML parsers, thus allowing developers to program to a set of standard interfaces defined by JAXP and the actual parser being used is configured at run-time.

It is a concept that has been well embraced by Java developers. The success of JAXP has been the foundation of all the other JAX APIs. Most of these are still in the specification stage at the time of this writing, with the exception of JAXM, the **Java API for XML-based Messaging**, for which there is a beta implementation available from Sun. From a web services developer's standpoint though, both the JAXR and JAX-RPC APIs are very exciting.

JAXR, which is the **Java APIs for XML Registries**, provides a generic API for accessing any XML-based registry, which includes UDDI registries, so you can rely less on those complex UDDI API calls. The **Java API for XML-based RPC**, or JAX-RPC is also very interesting. It shields you from the specifics of sending requests and receiving responses using XML-based protocols, such as SOAP, XML RPC, or XMLP (or SOAP 1.2). For example, currently there are a variety of Java-based SOAP implementations available, the most notable being Apache SOAP. JAX-RPC provides a uniform layer, or a façade, above all of them, thus allowing you to keep your code clean of any implementation-specific details and giving you greater flexibility at runtime.

Another interesting API that ONE includes support for, but sometimes gets ignored in all the talk about SOAP, WSDL, and UDDI, is **ebXML**. The ebXML initiative is sponsored by an international group established by the United Nations (UN/CEFACT) and OASIS to research, develop, and promote global standards for the implementation of XML to exchange electronic business data. The ebXML architecture begins with a business process and information model, maps the model to XML documents, and defines requirements for applications that process the documents and exchange them among trading partners. The ebXML group works to promote the creation of a global e-business market place through the exchange of XML documents and messages, regardless of geographic or political boundaries.

In a nutshell, the ebXML architecture defines:

❑ Business processes and their associated messages and content

❑ A registry and discovery mechanism for publishing business process sequences with related message exchanges

❑ Company profiles

❑ Trading partner agreements

❑ A uniform message transport layer (mapped to SOAP with multipart MIME attachments)

The initiative is intended to allow businesses to find each other using the registry, define trading partner agreements, and exchange XML messages in support of business operations. The goal is to allow all of these things to be performed automatically, without human intervention, over the Internet. There are many similarities between ebXML and SOAP/WSDL/UDDI, and some level of convergence is already taking place with the recent adoption of SOAP in the ebXML transport specification.

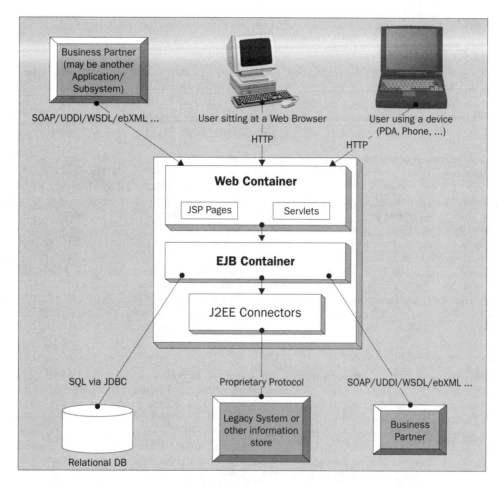

The figure above illustrates a *micro-level* view of ONE, but there is a higher-level view as well. This leads us to our next topic, the second view of the ONE architecture, the functional perspective of ONE.

A Functional Perspective of ONE

The following figure depicts the major components of the ONE web services architecture:

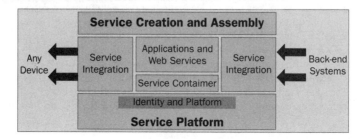

Let's take a brief look at each one of these components to see how they all fit together.

Service Creation and Assembly

This part of the model represents the service developer's toolbox that is used to develop systems based on the ONE architecture. An example of such tools includes the Enterprise Edition of Forte for Java by Sun. Other tools include the Web Services Toolkit by IBM or special compiler extensions provided by WebLogic that make standard J2EE components such as EJBs available as web services. Mastering any of these tools can make the life of a service based system creator much more productive.

There are two types of services in the ONE architecture. **Micro services** are discrete services that specialize in doing a specific function or set of cohesive functions very well. They are created using IDEs, code generators, XML editors, and other authoring tools. Micro services however, are not typically meant to be exposed directly to the end users. Rather, they are composed into, or aggregated by, the second type of services known as macro or composite services.

Macro services are created by service assemblers using tools that allow workflow and business process modeling. While there are many sophisticated tools that allow the creation of micro services (some of them named above), the tools for creating macro services are still in their infancy. Examples of these tools today include Microsoft's Biztalk 2000 and webMethods. In the future, expect to see more tools based on ebXML, Web Services Flow Language (WSFL), and Business Process Modeling Language (BPML). To find out more about WSFL and BPML visit http://www-4.ibm.com/software/solutions/webservices/pdf/WSFL.pdf and http://www.bpmi.org/ respectively.

Application and Web Services

This part of the model represents deployed web services. Examples of Sun-provided services based on ONE are iPlanet's Commerce and Communications portfolios. The iPlanet Commerce portfolio provides services for the most common business transactions. Functions such as buying, selling, billing, and auctioning have been collected into a suite of software. The iPlanet Communications portfolio provides basic services that enable communication via standard protocols such as HTTP, and is extensible enough to accommodate additional communications channels and protocols, such as Short Messaging Service (SMS) and instant messaging. Open standards allow seamless transaction integration with whatever services support open standard communications protocols.

Web services are deployed on a specific platform and live and execute within the context of a service container. That naturally takes us to the next part of the model described below.

Service Container

As mentioned above, a web service is deployed and executed within some type of service container, such as a web or application server. Examples of such servers include the Apache Tomcat web server, BEA's WebLogic application server, IBM's WebSphere application server, and Sun's iPlanet Application, Web, and Process Manager servers, to name a few.

The service container fulfills the important purpose of providing a runtime environment for the service. The relationship between a service and the container is similar to that of a process and operating system. Some of the key facilities provided by the container include security and transaction management, resource management, persistence and state management, and application management.

The type of container used depends on the platform hosting the service. For example, on a server machine, such a container would be a J2EE application server; all the examples above are in this category. If on the other hand, the host platform is a device (such as a wireless phone, a PDA, a television, or a variety of other consumer and embedded devices) then the service container should be based on J2ME. A popular example is the Mobile Information Device Profile (MIDP) for phones and PDAs.

iPlanet Application Server

As mentioned above, Sun provides the iPlanet Application Server as one of the containers for hosting services. In most services, the business logic exists as EJBs and other J2EE components, which reside in the iPlanet Application Server. The application server provides a scalable, available, robust, J2EE standard execution environment for these J2EE components. In addition to providing a J2EE technology standard implementation of the runtime environment and libraries that programmers can rely on, the application server also provides for redundant replication of state information through software clustering. This provides high availability to service components even in the event of hardware failure. The application server also manages pools of reusable resources, such as execution threads and database connections, making business logic easier to write and more scalable. The application server is often used in conjunction with an integration server, which we will describe in the section on *Service Delivery*.

iPlanet Web Server

As mentioned above, Sun also provides the iPlanet Web Server as one of the containers for hosting services. Don't let the name fool you. The iPlanet Web Server is more than just a simple HTTP server. It is actually a mini application server topped off with a Java technology-enabled, automatic, report-generation package. The web server not only allows you to create and serve static pages, augmented by simple routines written to the Common Gateway Interface (CGI) protocol, but also completely dynamically create complex, customized documents with up-to-the second information using JSPs and Java servlet technology. By providing a stable environment for running Java components, the iPlanet Web Server effectively functions as a lightweight application server, providing an execution environment and resource pooling to the components that implement reporting logic. Using these facilities, content can be shared seamlessly across multiple web server machines, allowing unparalleled scalability.

In addition, the extensibility of the web server allows it to adopt new protocols as they are finalized and approved. SOAP and XML are being accommodated as new releases of the protocol specifications emerge. This not only protects the web server investment from obsolescence, it also provides a facility for transcoding content from a base XML form to a device-specific form.

Service Delivery

Just as a service can be hosted on a variety of different platforms, it can be accessed from a variety of different types of device platforms as well. Therefore, the ONE architecture supports a variety of different device-specific presentation formats. Examples of such presentation formats include HTML for browser clients, Wireless Markup Language (WML) for WAP-compliant wireless devices, and VoiceXML for telephony devices.

iPlanet Portal Server

Sun's iPlanet Portal Server is an example of a product that targets this layer of the architecture. There are two main parts to the iPlanet Portal Server:

❑   content aggregation and customization

❑   secure remote access

There are also a number of auxiliary parts, which include the Instant Collaboration Pack, Personalized Knowledge Access Pack, Access Pack (includes a WAP server), and Secure Remote Access Pack. The auxiliary packages provide additional functionality to the iPlanet Portal Server, including a flexibly configurable search engine, a WAP server, and transcoding services for converting content for presentation on a variety of devices, including HTML/XML to WML.

The content aggregation component allows for the aggregation of any HTML or XML-encoded content as well as virtually any application that can be run on any major server OS, including X Windows-based applications running on the UNIX operating system. In addition, the content aggregation component includes Java clients for standard Internet operations, such as mail and file transfer.

The secure remote access component uses a Java technology-based virtual private network (VPN) client that can run on any Java technology-enabled web browser. This technology is called the **Netlet technology**. A user/client at their web browser anywhere on the Internet can download the Netlet and all further communications (such as mail, internal enterprise web sites, and custom applications regardless of what native protocol they use) between that browser and the enterprise will be tunneled through an encrypted Secure Sockets Layer (SSL) connection (port 443 usually).

Service Integration

Most services will probably rely on other resources to complete the function they perform. This is the purpose of the service integration part of the model. This part provides the facilities that allow the service to access other services and resources such as databases, files, directories, and legacy applications.

As an example, consider a service that needs information from an Oracle database and a SAP system. Facilities provided by the service integration layer to accomplish this may include an Oracle JDBC driver and a J2EE SAP Connector.

iPlanet Integration Server

Sun provides the iPlanet Integration Server as part of its implementation of the ONE platform. The primary function of the integration server is to enhance/supercharge the capabilities of an application server (namely Sun's iPlanet Application Server). Sun's integration server comes in two flavors:

❑   The iPlanet Integration Server, EAI Edition (formerly the Forte Fusion product)

❑   The iPlanet Integration Server, B2B Edition (formerly iPlanet ECXpert)

The EAI Edition provides a framework for integrating a variety of legacy applications such as SAP and PeopleSoft (using available connectors), and defining workflows that create single services from a variety of functions that cross services. For example, you could wire up the integration server to retrieve information from both a human resources (HR) system and a separate legacy enterprise resource planning (ERP) system to optimize and automate staffing of projects. The prime benefit of using an integration server is that it allows an enterprise to integrate all of its internal services and make them available for use as services.

The B2B Edition provides a facility for secure document exchange between business partners. Similar to the EAI Edition, the B2B Edition also allows for integration of an enterprise's internal services, but also goes a step beyond and allows for integration of information between enterprises. That is, it facilitates both intra and inter-enterprise information integration. As part of its framework, the B2B Edition provides for mapping document data from one enterprise to another and a mechanism for securely exchanging that data using EDI or XML protocols.

Service Platform

The entire environment, that is all the other layers, run on the service platform. The service platform provides access to local operating system services, such as file management and hardware resources such as storage and networks. The service platform also includes identity and policy facilities that manage the environment and ensure security. A service platform can be anything from a mainframe to a personal computer to a smart card. Examples of platforms include Sun's Solaris, the various implementations of Linux, and Microsoft's Windows NT and 2000. Service platforms also include auxiliary servers such as Sun's iPlanet Directory Server.

iPlanet Directory Server

Web services are a medium for making enterprise information available to other entities and partners both inside and outside the enterprise. Before web services can expose any information though, the information must first be created. The iPlanet Directory Server is a tool that can be used to transform the raw data about the company assets into an informational directory. It is the core of an LDAP-based, multi-purpose directory framework that acts as both an information repository and a policy management infrastructure. As a result, it not only provides enterprise-wide and extranet-wide access to information about the supported communities and information assets, it also provides authentication, authorization, non-repudiation, metering, rating (pricing), and billing support.

The iPlanet Directory Server suite of software includes *four* auxiliary tools to fulfill this central role. These are:

- ❑ **iPlanet Meta-Directory** – A software framework and a set of adaptors and connectors to provide bi-directional integration between the master LDAP directory and all of the special purpose directories throughout an enterprise (such as PeopleSoft, SAP, Microsoft Active Directory, and so on).

- ❑ **iPlanet Certificate Management System** – A digital certificate management system for producing, signing, and distributing the digital tokens that implement a typical chain-of-trust authentication and authorization mechanism.

- ❑ **iPlanet Policy Server** – A framework for defining access and authorization rights for the enterprise, including constituent-based rights, resources-based rights, and delegated administration.

- ❑ **iPlanet Directory Access Router** – A load-balancing mechanism for examining and re-directing LDAP requests to appropriate servers, and an invaluable aid to scaling and distributing directory resources.

An Example

Now that we have an understanding of the theory behind ONE, let's look at an example web service that is based on the ONE architecture. A logical question at this point is what it means for a web service to be based on the ONE architecture.

To answer this question, we'll map the tools and technologies used in the example with the two views (technology and functional) of the ONE architecture. However, before we do that exercise, let's first create, deploy, and test the service.

> **This example will only work with WebLogic version 6.1.**

Creating the Web Service

We will be implementing a stock quote service. As the name suggests, this service retrieves delayed stock quotes of a list of stock symbols provided to the service. The service itself is implemented as a stateless session bean called `StockQuoteService`.

As all J2EE programmers know, all EJBs need a home interface. Our `StockQuoteService` bean, which is no exception to the rule, has the following home interface:

```
package wrox.webservices;

import java.rmi.RemoteException;
import javax.ejb.CreateException;
import javax.ejb.EJBHome;

public interface StockQuoteServiceHome extends EJBHome {
    public StockQuoteService create() throws RemoteException, CreateException;
}
```

Per the EJB specification for stateless session beans, the home interface has no argument for the `create()` method.

Another requirement for EJBs (except for the message-driven beans introduced in EJB 2.0) is a remote interface, which defines the set of methods that are visible (accessible) to clients of the beans. The `StockQuoteService` has one remotely accessible method called `getQuotes()`. This method accepts a space-delimited list (string) of stock symbols and returns a space-delimited list (string) of stock quotes. For example, if the input string was:

```
CLRS IBM MSFT SUNW RADS INTC ORCL CSCO DELL CPQ
```

then the output would be:

```
CLRS=7.24 IBM=99.95 MSFT=57.05 SUNW=11.45 RADS=9.56 INTC=27.96 ORCL=12.21
CSCO=16.33 DELL=21.38.
```

The remote interface for our `StockQuoteService` bean is defined as follows:

```
package wrox.webservices;

import java.rmi.RemoteException;
import javax.ejb.EJBObject;

public interface StockQuoteService extends EJBObject {
    public String getQuote(String stocksymbols) throws RemoteException;
}
```

Now let's turn our attention to the actual bean implementation itself. All stateless session beans must implement the SessionBean interface, which defines a set of methods used by the EJB container to control the bean's lifecycle. In addition to this, the bean must contain all the business methods defined in the remote interface (see above). It is very important to note that the bean *does not* implement the remote interface due to the fact you do not want the bean class accessed directly (not through the container) by client code. It simply defines the methods again in its implementation with the exact same signature and return type.

Here's a basic shell of the StockQuoteService bean:

```java
package wrox.webservices;

import java.io.*;
import java.net.*;
import javax.ejb.CreateException;
import javax.ejb.SessionBean;
import javax.ejb.SessionContext;
import javax.ejb.SessionSynchronization;
import javax.xml.parsers.DocumentBuilder;
import javax.xml.parsers.DocumentBuilderFactory;
import javax.xml.parsers.ParserConfigurationException;
import javax.naming.InitialContext;
import org.w3c.dom.*;
import org.xml.sax.*;

public class StockQuoteServiceEJB implements SessionBean {
  private SessionContext context;

  // No argument constructor required by container.
  public StockQuoteServiceEJB() { }

  // Create method specified in EJB 2.0
  public void ejbCreate() { }

  // Methods required by SessionBean Interface. EJB 2.0
  public void setSessionContext(SessionContext context){
    this.context = context;
  }

  public void ejbActivate() { }
  public void ejbPassivate() { }
  public void ejbRemove() { }

  public String getQuote(String stocksymbols) {
    // Business Logic goes here
    // Discussed in the next few pages
  }
```

Note the default no-argument constructor and the no-argument ejbCreate() method, which corresponds to the create() method in the home interface. The only thing remaining to finish the bean implementation is implementing the getQuote() method from the remote interface.

We will implement two ways to get the stock quotes. The way of obtaining the quotes is configurable by means of a J2EE environment property. This property is specified in the EJB deployment descriptor, which we will see in the next section.

The first way is to go straight to the Yahoo quotes server. The Yahoo quotes server returns a comma-separated list of details for each stock symbol, which we then parse to extract the stock symbol and the stock quote to send back to the user. All this logic is buried in the private `getYahooQuotes()` method shown below:

```java
private String getYahooQuotes(String stocksymbols) {
  String urlString = "http://quote.yahoo.com/d/quotes.csv?s=";
  java.util.StringTokenizer st =
    new java.util.StringTokenizer(stocksymbols, " ");
  boolean first = true;
  while (st.hasMoreTokens()) {
    if (first) {
      urlString += st.nextToken().trim();
      first = false;
    } else {
      urlString += ("+" + st.nextToken().trim());
    }
  }
  urlString += "&f=sl1d1t1c1ohgvj1pp2owern&e=.csv";

  System.out.println("**** [StockQuoteService] URL: " + urlString);

  String response = "";
  String symbol = "";
  String quote = "";
  try {
    URL url = new URL(urlString);
    BufferedReader in =
      new BufferedReader(new InputStreamReader(url.openStream()));
    String s = null;
    while ((s = in.readLine()) != null) {
      s = s.trim();
      symbol = s.substring(1, s.indexOf("\"", 1));
      quote = s.substring(s.indexOf(",") + 1,
                          s.indexOf(",", s.indexOf(",") + 1));
      response += (symbol + "=" + quote + " ");
    }
    in.close();
  } catch (Exception e) {
    e.printStackTrace();
  }
  return response.trim();
}
```

The gist of the `getYahooQuotes()` method is as follows:

1. Create the URL based on the stock symbols passed in. For example, if SUNW and IBM are the stock symbols passed in then the URL created will be
http://quote.yahoo.com/d/quotes.csv?s=SUNW+IBM&f=sl1d1t1c1ohgvj1pp2owern&e=.csv

2. Open a connection and get the input stream from it.

3. The Yahoo quotes server returns a comma-delimited string for each stock symbol. Thus, we will get back two of these (one for SUNW and one for IBM) and these will be separated by the newline character.

4. Extract the stock symbol and quote from each comma-delimited string.

5. Return a space-separated string of stock symbols and quotes back to the caller.

The second way of retrieving stock quotes is to go to the XmlToday quotes server. This server itself goes to the Yahoo server just as we did above, but it converts the information into a neatly packaged XML document and returns this XML to us (that is, the user).

Our implementation parses and extracts the stock symbols and quotes from this XML document and returns the information back to the caller in the form of the space-delimited string. This entire logic is encapsulated in the private `getXmlTodayQuotes()` method, shown below:

```java
private String getXmlTodayQuotes(String stocksymbols) {
  String urlString =
    "http://www.xmltoday.com/examples/stockquote/getxmlquote.vep?s=";
  java.util.StringTokenizer st =
    new java.util.StringTokenizer(stocksymbols, " ");
  boolean first = true;
  while (st.hasMoreTokens()) {
    if (first) {
      urlString += st.nextToken().trim();
      first = false;
    } else {
      urlString += ("+" + st.nextToken().trim());
    }
  }

  System.out.println("**** [StockQuoteService] URL: " + urlString);

  String response = "";
  String symbol = "";
  String quote = "";
  try {
    URL url = new URL(urlString);
    BufferedInputStream bis = new BufferedInputStream(url.openStream());

    DocumentBuilderFactory fact = DocumentBuilderFactory.newInstance();
    DocumentBuilder db = fact.newDocumentBuilder();
    Document doc = db.parse(new InputSource(bis));
```

```
        NodeList nodes = doc.getElementsByTagName("stock_quote");
        for (int i = 0; i < nodes.getLength(); i++) {
          NodeList nodes1 = nodes.item(i).getChildNodes();
          for (int j = 0; j < nodes1.getLength(); j++) {
            Node n = nodes1.item(j);
            if (n.getNodeType() != Node.ELEMENT_NODE) {
              continue;
            }
            Element e = (Element) n;
            if (e.getNodeName().equals("symbol")) {
              symbol = e.getFirstChild().getNodeValue();
            } else if (e.getNodeName().equals("price")
                    && e.getAttribute("type").equals("ask")) {
              quote = e.getAttribute("value");
            }
          }
          response += (symbol + "=" + quote + " ");
        }
      } catch (Exception e) {
        e.printStackTrace();
      }
      return response.trim();
    }
```

The gist of the `getXmlTodayQuotes()` method is as follows:

1. Create the URL based on the stock symbols passed in. For example, if SUNW and IBM are the stock symbols passed in, then the URL created will be http://www.xmltoday.com/examples/stockquote/getxmlquote.vep?s=SUNW+IBM.

2. Open a connection and get the input stream from it.

3. Parse the XML document returned by the XMLToday quote server. We used the DOM parser to accomplish this along with a `for` loop. This code is obviously designed for readability as opposed to performance. Some of the shortcuts we took are:

We could have used the XPath API to accomplish this more efficiently. If you haven't already noticed, we're concatenating strings without using the `StringBuffer` class. And remember, the quotes are delayed by about 20 minutes anyway (you have to pay money for real-time quotes!), so what's a few more seconds on top of that.

4. Return a space-separated string of stock symbols and quotes back to the caller.

Since all the logic for forming and sending the request for the quotes and receiving and parsing the response from the quote servers is handled by the private methods discussed above, the implementation of the `getQuote()` method becomes extremely simple. It is shown below for reference:

```
    public String getQuote(String stocksymbols) {
      String quoteSource = "Yahoo";
      try {
        InitialContext ic = new InitialContext();
```

```
        quoteSource = (String) ic.lookup("java:/comp/env/QuoteSource");
        System.out.println("**** [StockQuoteService] Quote Source is "
                            + quoteSource);
    } catch (Exception e) {
      e.printStackTrace();
    }

    if (quoteSource.equalsIgnoreCase("Yahoo")) {
      return getYahooQuotes(stocksymbols);
    } else if (quoteSource.equalsIgnoreCase("XML")) {
      return getXmlTodayQuotes(stocksymbols);
    } else {
      return "";
    }
  }
```

The method checks what quote server it is supposed to use by looking up the `QuoteSource` environment variable (all user-defined J2EE environment variables are available in the `/comp/env/` namespace in JNDI). Based on the value of this variable the method invokes one of the two private methods that we discussed above.

Building and Deploying the Service

To get some useful value out of what we just did, we will have to first build and then deploy the `StockQuoteService` onto a J2EE-compliant application server. For this example, we will be using BEA's WebLogic application server version 6.1, which has excellent support for building and deploying web services. Once again, we will not go into the details of installing the application server. BEA already has excellent documentation for this available at http://edocs.bea.com/wls/docs61/install/index.html. On a Windows platform, it basically boils down to downloading the set up program and executing it. The wizards take you through the rest of the process. The default configuration will work fine for this example. Also make sure that you install the examples (you do not need to do this if you are comfortable using WebLogic).

To simplify the build and deployment process, we create a simple batch file, `build.bat`, that sets up the environment and kicks off the actual build process using Ant, which is included in WebLogic 6.1. Ant is a great little build utility targeted at providing an XML-based replacement for the much revered make utility. Ant is part of the Apache Jakarta project and is therefore freely available under the Apache Open Source License. The batch file and XML build files follow:

```
@echo off
@echo Setting Environment Variables...
set WL_HOME=C:\bea\wlserver6.1
set JAVA_HOME=C:\bea\jdk131
set
CLASSPATH=%JAVA_HOME%\lib\tools.jar;%WL_HOME%\lib\weblogic_sp.jar;%WL_HOME%\lib\we
blogic.jar
set PATH=%WL_HOME%\bin;%JAVA_HOME%\bin;%PATH%
@echo Done
ant
```

The above batch file, `build.bat`, assumes that WebLogic is installed in the
`C:\bea\wlserver6.1` directory.

We will now look at the `build.xml` file. Refer to the Ant documentation at
http://jakarta.apache.org/ant/manual/index.html for information about the specifics of the
`build.xml` file:

```xml
<project name="StockQuoteService" default="all">
  <property file="build.properties"/>
  <property name="src" value="."/>
  <property name="build" value="${src}/build"/>
  <property name="jarfile" value="${build}/${PROJECT}.jar"/>
  <property name="earfile" value="${build}/${PROJECT}.ear"/>
  <property name="deployment" value=
                          "${WL_HOME}/config/${DOMAIN}/applications"/>

  <target name="all" depends="clean, init, compile, jar, ejbc, copy"/>

  <target name="clean">
    <delete dir="${build}"/>
    <delete dir="ejbcgen"/>
    <delete file="${src}/temp.jar"/>
  </target>

  <target name="init">
    <mkdir dir="${build}"/>
    <mkdir dir="${build}/META-INF"/>
    <copy todir="${build}/META-INF">
      <fileset dir="${src}">
        <include name="ejb-jar.xml"/>
        <include name="weblogic-ejb-jar.xml"/>
      </fileset>
    </copy>
  </target>

  <target name="compile">
    <javac srcdir="${src}" destdir="${build}"
      includes="${SRCFILES}"/>
  </target>

  <target name="jar" depends="compile">
    <jar jarfile="${src}/temp.jar"
      basedir="${build}">
    </jar>
  </target>

  <!-- Run ejbc to create the deployable jar file -->
  <target name="ejbc" depends="jar">
    <java classname="weblogic.ejbc" fork="yes">
      <sysproperty key="weblogic.home" value="${WL_HOME}"/>
      <arg line="-compiler javac ${src}/temp.jar ${build}/${PROJECT}.jar"/>
      <classpath>
        <pathelement path=
 "${WL_HOME}/lib/weblogic_sp.jar;${WL_HOME}/lib/weblogic.jar"/>
      </classpath>
    </java>
    <delete file="${src}/temp.jar"/>
  </target>
```

```
<target name="wsgen">
  <wsgen destpath="${earfile}" context="/webservice">
    <rpcservices path="${jarfile}">
    <rpcservice bean="${PROJECT}" uri="/${PROJECT}"/>
    </rpcservices>
  </wsgen>
</target>

<target name="copy" depends="wsgen">
  <copy file="${earfile}" todir="${deployment}"/>
</target>

</project>
```

At a higher level though, the file has seven targets:

- ❏ clean – Deletes the build directory to ensure a fresh start.

- ❏ init – Creates the build directory structure and copies the XML deployment descriptors (discussed below) there.

- ❏ compile – Compiles the StockQuoteService classes.

- ❏ jar – Creates a temporary JAR file to feed into the ejbc target.

- ❏ ejbc – Generates and compiles the proxy/stub code to make the EJBs accessible. This code is combined with the JAR file created in the jar step to create the actual EJB JAR file.

- ❏ wsgen – Generates and compiles the JSPs and servlets (that is, the web application) that expose the EJB as a web service. This WAR file is combined with the JAR file created as the output of the ejbc step to create the EAR file, which is the file that is deployed. This target uses a custom Ant task wsgen, which is provided with WebLogic 6.1, and is responsible for exposing the StockQuoteService bean as a web service.

- ❏ copy – Deploys the web service. For the WebLogic application server this is as simple as copying the EAR file to the right directory.

The build process depends on some external information that is encapsulated in the build.properties file. The contents of this file are shown below:

```
# set to your Weblogic Application Server Install Directory
WL_HOME=C:/bea/wlserver6.1

# WebLogic Domain Name
# This determines where the application is deployed.
# The default is examples.
DOMAIN=examples

# Project Name
# Must be the same as the value of the <ejb-name> tag in ejb-jar.xml
PROJECT=StockQuoteService

# Source Java Files to compile
SRCFILES=*.java
```

The only property that you must make sure is correct is WL_HOME. This must be set to the directory where you installed WebLogic. In addition, if you chose *not* to install the examples during the WebLogic installation process, you must change the value of the DOMAIN property to an existing WebLogic domain. The default domain is examples.

Now let's look at the XML deployment descriptors. There are two XML deployment descriptor files: the first one, ejb-jar.xml, is the standard EJB deployment descriptor and the other one, weblogic-ejb-jar.xml, is WebLogic-specific. Here is the ejb-jar.xml descriptor file:

```xml
<?xml version="1.0"?>

<!DOCTYPE ejb-jar PUBLIC '-//Sun Microsystems, Inc.//DTD Enterprise JavaBeans
2.0//EN' 'http://java.sun.com/dtd/ejb-jar_2_0.dtd'>

<ejb-jar>
  <enterprise-beans>
    <session>
      <ejb-name>StockQuoteService</ejb-name>
      <home>wrox.webservices.StockQuoteServiceHome</home>
      <remote>wrox.webservices.StockQuoteService</remote>
      <ejb-class>wrox.webservices.StockQuoteServiceEJB</ejb-class>
      <session-type>Stateless</session-type>
      <transaction-type>Container</transaction-type>
      <env-entry>
        <env-entry-name>QuoteSource</env-entry-name>
        <env-entry-type>java.lang.String</env-entry-type>
        <env-entry-value>XML</env-entry-value>
      </env-entry>
    </session>
  </enterprise-beans>
  <assembly-descriptor>
    <container-transaction>
      <method>
        <ejb-name>StockQuoteService</ejb-name>
          <method-intf>Remote</method-intf>
          <method-name>*</method-name>
      </method>
      <trans-attribute>Required</trans-attribute>
    </container-transaction>
  </assembly-descriptor>
</ejb-jar>
```

We will not go into the details of all the standard deployment information contained within ejb-jar.xml. However, there is one piece of information to be pointed out, and that is the <env-entry> section. This section defines the environment variables accessible to the StockQuoteService. We have defined one such variable, QuoteSource, which tells us where to get the quotes from. The two legal values of this variable are Yahoo and XML. We've already seen how the getQuote() method accesses and uses this variable to call the correct private method.

Here is the `weblogic-ejb-jar.xml` descriptor file:

```xml
<?xml version="1.0"?>

<!DOCTYPE weblogic-ejb-jar PUBLIC '-//BEA Systems, Inc.//DTD WebLogic 6.0.0
EJB//EN' 'http://www.bea.com/servers/wls600/dtd/weblogic-ejb-jar.dtd'>

<weblogic-ejb-jar>
  <weblogic-enterprise-bean>
    <ejb-name>StockQuoteService</ejb-name>
    <jndi-name>webservices.StockQuoteService</jndi-name>
  </weblogic-enterprise-bean>
</weblogic-ejb-jar>
```

The WebLogic-specific file serves the important purpose of mapping the `StockQuoteService` with its JNDI name, `webservices.StockQuoteService`. The `StockQuoteService` cannot be used unless this is done. For a complete reference to what else can be done in the WebLogic-specific descriptor, refer to http://edocs.bea.com/wls/docs61/ejb/reference.html#1053093.

We can now deploy the service using the simple command:

```
>build.bat
```

Using the Service

To verify that the `StockQuoteService` is really deployed, start the WebLogic server. If you haven't changed the domain property in the `build.properties` file then your application will be deployed in the examples domain (which is what we did). Starting the server in this case is a simple matter of going to the `%WL_HOME%\config\examples` directory, where `%WL_HOME%` is the directory you installed WebLogic, and executing the `startExamplesServer.bat` batch file or shell script. Windows users can also access the same functionality through the following sequence; Start | Program | BEA WebLogic E-Business Platform | WebLogic Server 6.1 | Examples | Start Examples Server.

Now point your browser to the following URL http://localhost:7001/webservice/. You should see a web page with a link to our web service. Click on it and you'll get another page with two links, one to a `client.jar` file and another to a WSDL file. The `client.jar` file can be downloaded to write Java client code. We won't be creating our client that way. We are however interested in the WSDL that describes the service, so right click on that link, select Save As, and save the file to your file system. (For this example, we save it as `StockQuoteService.wsdl` in a folder called `client` under the `StockQuoteService` code).

The generated WSDL is shown below for reference:

```xml
<?xml version="1.0"?>

<definitions
  targetNamespace="java:wrox.webservices"
  xmlns="http://schemas.xmlsoap.org/wsdl/"
  xmlns:xsi="http://www.w3.org/1999/XMLSchema-instance"
  xmlns:xsd="http://www.w3.org/1999/XMLSchema"
```

```
    xmlns:soap="http://schemas.xmlsoap.org/wsdl/soap/"
    xmlns:tns="java:wrox.webservices"
>

<types>
  <schema
    targetNamespace='java:wrox.webservices'
    xmlns='http://www.w3.org/1999/XMLSchema'>
  </schema>
</types>

<message name="getQuoteRequest">
  <part name="arg0" type="xsd:string" />
</message>
<message name="getQuoteResponse">
  <part name="return" type="xsd:string" />
</message>

<portType name="StockQuoteServicePortType">
  <operation name="getQuote">
    <input message="tns:getQuoteRequest"/>
    <output message="tns:getQuoteResponse"/>
  </operation>
</portType>

<binding
  name="StockQuoteServiceBinding"
  type="tns:StockQuoteServicePortType">
  <soap:binding style="rpc"
    transport="http://schemas.xmlsoap.org/soap/http/"/>
  <operation name="getQuote">
    <soap:operation soapAction="urn:getQuote"/>
    <input>
      <soap:body use="encoded" namespace='urn:StockQuoteService'
                   encodingStyle=
                       "http://schemas.xmlsoap.org/soap/encoding/"/>
    </input>
    <output>
      <soap:body use="encoded" namespace='urn:StockQuoteService'
        encodingStyle="http://schemas.xmlsoap.org/soap/encoding/"/>
    </output>
  </operation>
</binding>

<service name="StockQuoteService">
  <documentation>todo</documentation>
  <port name="StockQuoteServicePort" binding="tns:StockQuoteServiceBinding">
    <soap:address
      location="http://localhost:7001/webservice/StockQuoteService"/>
  </port>
</service>

</definitions>
```

Open the WSDL file and find the following line (shown in **bold** in the above listing):

```
<soap:binding style="rpc"
  transport="http://schemas.xmlsoap.org/soap/http/"/>
```

Remove the trailing slash (/) behind `http` from the URL, so that the line now looks like this:

```
<soap:binding style="rpc"
  transport="http://schemas.xmlsoap.org/soap/http"/>
```

This is a quirk in the WSDL generated by WebLogic. Expect to see quirks like this in almost any tool you use until at least a few releases of each tool.

For the remainder of this exercise you will need IBM's Web Services Toolkit. You can download this from IBM's DeveloperWorks web site for free at http://www.alphaworks.ibm.com/tech/webservicestoolkit and then install it (which I've done in the directory `C:\wstk-2.4\`).

Now open a command prompt in the directory where you saved the WSDL file and run the following:

```
>proxygen StockQuoteService.wsdl
```

`proxygen` is a batch file located in the `bin` directory in your IBM Web Services Toolkit installation, and this directory is in my `PATH`.

This will create and compile a class called `webservices_StockQuoteServiceBinding` in a package called `java_wrox`. Take a look at the Java code for this class, which is listed below for reference:

```java
package java_wrox;
/** Proxy object  "java_wrox.webservices_StockQuoteServiceBinding" */

public class webservices_StockQuoteServiceBinding
{
  public static java.net.URL[] _KnownServiceLocations= null;
  private org.apache.soap.rpc.Call
          call=new org.apache.soap.rpc.Call();
  private java.net.URL _____url= null;
  private java.lang.String SOAPActionURI = "";
  private org.apache.soap.encoding.SOAPMappingRegistry smr =
          call.getSOAPMappingRegistry();
  static
  {
    try{
    _KnownServiceLocations= new java.net.URL[]{
      new java.net.URL("http://localhost:7001/webservice/StockQuoteService")
    };
    }catch(java.net.MalformedURLException e ){_KnownServiceLocations=
                                        new java.net.URL[0];};
  }
  public webservices_StockQuoteServiceBinding(java.net.URL endPointURL)
  {
```

```
                _____call.setTargetObjectURI("urn:StockQuoteService");
                _____call.setEncodingStyleURI(
                    "http://schemas.xmlsoap.org/soap/encoding/");
        this._____url = endPointURL;
        this.SOAPActionURI = "urn:getQuote";
    }
    public synchronized java.lang.String getQuote (java.lang.String arg0)
                        throws  org.apache.soap.SOAPException
    {
        if(_____url == null) throw new
    org.apache.soap.SOAPException(org.apache.soap.Constants.FAULT_CODE_CLIENT,
    "A URL must be specified \"webservices_StockQuoteServiceBinding\"." );
        this._____call.setMethodName("getQuote");
        java.util.Vector _____parms  = new java.util.Vector(1);
        _____parms.addElement( new org.apache.soap.rpc.Parameter("arg0",
                            java.lang.String.class, arg0, null));
        this._____call.setParams(_____parms);
        org.apache.soap.rpc.Response _____resp =
            this._____call.invoke(_____url, SOAPActionURI);
        if(_____resp.generatedFault())
        {
            org.apache.soap.Fault _____fault = _____resp.getFault();
            throw new
                org.apache.soap.SOAPException(_____fault.getFaultCode(),
                _____fault.getFaultString());
        }
        return (java.lang.String)_____resp.getReturnValue().getValue();
    }
}
```

If you have ever used Apache SOAP, this code will look very familiar. If you are not familiar with Apache SOAP, then please refer to Chapter 3 for details on this implementation of SOAP.

Creating a client for the service now is simple. Need proof? Let's look at the code:

```
import java_wrox.*;

public class Client {
  public static void main(String[] args) throws Exception {
    if (args.length == 0) {
      System.out.println("Usage: java Client <stock symbols>");
      System.exit(0);
    }

    String symbols = "";
    for (int i = 0; i < args.length; i++) {
      symbols += (args[i] + " ");
    }

    // Create an instance of the Service Proxy
    webservices_StockQuoteServiceBinding quoteService =
      new webservices_StockQuoteServiceBinding(
        webservices_StockQuoteServiceBinding._KnownServiceLocations[0]);
```

```
       String quotes = quoteService.getQuote(symbols);
    java.util.StringTokenizer st = new java.util.StringTokenizer(quotes, " ");
      while (st.hasMoreTokens()) {
        System.out.println(st.nextToken().trim());
      }
    }
  }
```

Most of the code deals with creating the input space-delimited stock symbol string and then parsing the result string and displaying the quotes. The actual code for using and invoking the StockQuoteService is limited to the following two lines:

```
webservices_StockQuoteServiceBinding quoteService =
  new webservices_StockQuoteServiceBinding(
    webservices_StockQuoteServiceBinding._KnownServiceLocations[0]);

String quotes = quoteService.getQuote(symbols);
```

To ease the process of compiling and running the client, we have created two batch files, compile.bat and run.bat. Here is compile.bat:

```
call C:\wstk-2.4\bin\wstkenv.bat
C:\jdk1.3\bin\javac -classpath .;C:\jdk1.3\lib\tools.jar;%WSTK_CP% *.java
```

and now run.bat:

```
call C:\wstk-2.4\bin\wstkenv.bat
java -cp .;C:\jdk1.3\lib\tools.jar;%WSTK_CP% Client %1 %2 %3 %4 %5 %6 %7 %8 %9
```

The results will look something like the following:

```
run CLRS IBM MSFT SUNW RADS INTC ORCL CSCO DELL CPQ

call C:\wstk-2.4\bin\wstkenv.bat
CLRS=7.24
IBM=99.95
MSFT=57.05
SUNW=11.45
RADS=9.56
INTC=27.96
ORCL=12.21
CSCO=16.33
DELL=21.38


run CLQQ

call C:\wstk-2.4\bin\wstkenv.bat
CLQQ=0.00
```

495

If you get a `java.net.UnknownHostException`, then chances are that you are behind a firewall/proxy server. To verify this, go to a console and try pinging the XmlToday server; type and execute:

```
>ping www.xmltoday.com
```

If you do not get a response or get a message such as:

```
Unknown Host www.xmltoday.com
```

then you are definitely behind a firewall/proxy server. Going through the steps for configuring WebLogic to work with proxy servers is beyond the scope of this chapter, but here is a link to get you started: http://e-docs.bea.com/wls/docs61/adminguide/http_proxy.html#112653.

Summarizing the Example

OK, so now let's take a step back and review what we have done in the example, and how it maps to the ONE architecture.

How the Example Maps to the Technology View of ONE

The `StockQuoteService` web service itself is implemented as a stateless session bean. The front-end of the web service is a Java servlet that expects to get a SOAP request message from a client and sends back a SOAP response. We've used WSDL to describe the service, which was made available to anyone interested.

Although we did not publish our service and its WSDL in a UDDI registry, it is not a long shot to imagine how easily that could have been done. Now, take a look at the second diagram in the chapter again and you cannot help but see that our example maps perfectly to it.

How the Example Maps to the Functional Perspective of ONE

To help speed up the development of the service, I used Forte as an IDE. To then help speed up the compilation and deployment, we used Ant. Together, these map to the service creation and assembly part of the second diagram. The web service itself along with the Yahoo Quotes server and the XmlToday server maps to the applications and services section.

The service was deployed on BEA's WebLogic application server (which includes a web server). This maps to the service container part of the diagram. The web server also served as our service delivery vehicle. Our service did not need to integrate with any EIS systems. Finally, Windows 2000 provided the service platform in our case.

So, based on the above mapping, we can see that we have created a ONE-based service using all the tools and technologies available today. However, note that we haven't exploited all the facilities of the ONE architecture, the most notable of those being the shared context that leads to the creation of a *smart* web service. While we could have used a homegrown mechanism for this, we're going to wait for some standards to be defined! This is actually in agreement with Sun's roadmap for ONE, which is described in the next section.

The Sun ONE Road Map

First Wave – Early 2001

This wave helps early adopter companies start experimenting with web services technologies while solving their immediate and ongoing platform needs. Developers can manually create and assemble basic web services through SOAP support across various products. This includes the ability to develop and assemble existing technologies as basic web services through standards-based integration. These first-generation services basically equate to providing a new face to existing applications and business models.

Second Wave – Year end 2001

This wave helps companies start deploying their services to explore code-sharing and new business models based on exchanged services. Developers can begin deploying web services on the J2EE platforms of the web and application servers. Developers can take their assembled basic web services and register them in a central directory for broader code availability.

Third Wave – 2002 and beyond

This wave helps companies get a head start providing cutting-edge services based on their unique market value, while helping early majority companies understand the possibilities for capitalizing on web services. Developers can create web services that incorporate the ability to act on a user's context, traverse different IP-connected devices, and utilize any other web services built on open standards.

As you look through the road map, it should have become very obvious to you that our example web service fits squarely into the *second wave* of web services. Given the state of standards and technology available today, this is an expected result.

Microsoft .NET

By now you are well versed in ONE architecture, having looked at both theory and practice. However, ONE is not the only web services architecture out there. There are many players in the market, each trying to get their piece of the pie. Probably one of the most significant contenders in the web services arena is Microsoft. Throughout the past decade, Microsoft has always stood alone with its own suite of technologies. Microsoft is definitely a formidable player in the web services arena with its huge ownership of the PC operating system market.

Remember OLE that evolved into ActiveX and then into COM/DCOM? MTS was then thrown into the mix to create COM+. In the middle of 2000, Microsoft announced yet another significant change in strategy and direction with the .NET platform.

.NET Architecture – The 30,000 Foot View

.NET is Microsoft's vision and implementation of a web services-centric platform. Over the past decade, Microsoft has continuously evolved its technologies to meet/beat the changing needs of software. The path from OLE to COM+ was long and to Microsoft's credit, the results have been good. Most important of all though, programmers were left with a clear migration path. Not so with .NET.

Yes, it's true that .NET can interoperate with (legacy) COM, but in our opinion eventually Microsoft hopes that people will just rewrite everything in .NET. The truth of the matter is that the .NET platform is a rather radical and brute-force change in the way Microsoft programmers will design solutions in the future.

The .NET platform consists of the following five parts:

- ❑ The **.NET framework**. We'll be talking more about this in a moment.

- ❑ An IDE, **Visual Studio.NET**. To support developers who wish to use .NET, Microsoft has updated its Visual Studio IDE and released it as Visual Studio.NET. Using this IDE, developers can create .NET solutions using any combination of VB.NET (the version of Visual Basic for .NET), Managed C++ (Microsoft's extensions to C++ for the .NET environment), and C# (C Sharp), which is Microsoft's replacement for Java and is the flagship language of .NET.

- ❑ A **server infrastructure** that includes MSMQ (a message queuing product similar to JMS products or MQ Series), COM+ (a component services model similar to EJBs), Active Directory (an LDAP implementation), and IIS (a web server).

- ❑ A suite of building block XML web services called **.NET My Services** (**Hailstorm**). Some .NET My Services services will be available for free and some on a subscription basis. The most notable and well known of these today is the Passport service for user authentication (this is also a service available for free). The Passport service provides a shared user identity context to other .NET My Services services that can use this information in their dealings with the user. Other services in this suite include myProfile, myAddress, myWallet, myNotifications, myCalendar, myInbox, myContacts, myProfile, myApplicationSettings, myDevices, myDocuments, myLocation, and myFavoriteWebsites.

- ❑ A set of **.NET servers** such as Microsoft SQL Server 2000, Microsoft Biztalk server 2000, and any other Microsoft server products with 2000 or 2001 in their name. Once again, we will not discuss any of these server products in this chapter. Refer to the Microsoft web site if you are interested in learning more about these.

Now let's talk about the most interesting (and possibly most significant) part of the .NET platform, namely the .NET framework. The .NET framework itself consists of the following five concepts:

- ❑ **The Common Language Runtime (CLR)**
  This is the foundation of the .NET framework. This is the piece that hosts all .NET code and provides core services such as memory management, thread management, and remoting. It also enforces the safety and accuracy of the code. If this reminds you of the Java Virtual Machine (VM), you are right. Code that runs within a CLR is referred to as 'managed' code, while code that does not, such as legacy COM code, is referred to as 'unmanaged' code.

- ❑ **The Common Type System (CTS)** and **the Common Language Specification (CLS)**
  The CTS fully defines all possible data types supported by the runtime, how those types can interact, and how these types are represented as meta data (discussed later). The CLS is a proper subset of the CTS and must be supported by all .NET languages, such as VB.NET and C#. Thus, as long as .NET programs use data types from within the CLS, they are guaranteed to work with any .NET runtime, no matter who the vendor or what the operating system is.

- ❑ **The Base Class Libraries**
  This is a comprehensive, object-oriented collection of reusable classes that are used by .NET developers. The class libraries consist of classes for all kinds of .NET applications, ranging from simple command-line applications to web applications and web services. The base class libraries are organized into a series of assemblies.

❑ **Microsoft Intermediate Language (MSIL)**
All code written in a .NET-compliant language compiles to a truly platform-neutral code called Microsoft Intermediate Language (MSIL). This should remind you of Java byte code.

❑ **Assemblies**
An assembly is the fundamental unit of deployment, version control, reuse, activation, and security. Think of it as a JAR file on steroids. While the Java Platform allows for class execution without the need for it to be in a JAR, all classes in .NET must be part of an assembly to be any use. Also, there are two distinct types of assemblies:

> 1) private assemblies used only by the application that owns them and are contained within the application directory

> 2) public assemblies which have a unique (strong) name, are shared, and are located in a special area in the file system called the Global Assembly Cache (GAC).

On the surface, assemblies appear just like any other Windows DLL or EXE file because of the way their name ends with a `.dll` or `.exe`, but that's where the similarity ends. Assemblies do not contain native Windows-executable code. Rather they contain meta data describing the assembly and its contents, and the MSIL that will be executed by the CLR. The .NET framework comes with many assemblies of its own, which contain the base class libraries discussed above. For example, the `System.Xml` assembly (`System.Xml.dll`) contains the .NET classes that help in XML manipulation (parsing, transforming, and so on).

Comparing .NET and ONE

So now that we've given you a quick overview of the .NET platform, how does it compare to the ONE platform? Since both are fairly complex platforms, we'll do a comparison from seven different angles:

❑ Industry support and platform-independence

❑ Legacy support

❑ Platform maturity

❑ Standards support (with respect to web services)

❑ Language support

❑ Tool support

❑ Availability today

Now let's take a look at each one.

Industry Support and Platform-Independence

.NET is a 'one-company standard'. True, Microsoft has submitted the CLR and C# specifications to ECMA, but the truth remains that Microsoft defines and implements .NET (at least today and the foreseeable future). Today, the fact remains that .NET is a one-vendor solution, which is definitely something to think about, no matter how strong and stable the vendor is.

Another interesting point to ponder is that even though Microsoft touts the CLR and MSIL cornerstones of .NET as proof that .NET can be ported to other platforms, how likely is that to happen? How committed will Microsoft be to those efforts? Even if Microsoft does the port of .NET to other platforms itself and then sells it as a product, it would still have a direct negative impact on its sales of Windows operating systems.

Now let's assume that .NET does turn out to be a great platform to create web services and there is a huge demand in the Linux world to make it available on Linux. Technically, the port of .NET to other operating systems is not that straightforward. For example, .NET relies on COM+ for all its enterprise services, such as transaction support, object pooling, resource pooling, just-in-time activation, and so on. So that means COM+ would have to be ported as well, but COM+ is heavily tied to the Windows operating system, and that too is limited to only some versions of Windows. Anyone see the problem?

On the other hand, the Java Platform upon which ONE is built is a widely accepted standard/specification and there are (today) many compliant commercial and open source web and application servers available in the market. The benefit of this is that your business is less likely to be 'married' to a particular vendor, which provides flexibility/options to switch vendors as business needs dictate.

Legacy Support

Microsoft has always enjoyed the unique (and possibly enviable) position of not having to provide 100 percent (or less than optimal) legacy support. The same continues with .NET. For example, VB.NET has many incompatibilities with Visual Basic 6.0, which is the last released version of Visual Basic and has been used for several years to create many millions of lines of code.

Another legacy support issue is the support for COM components that .NET components use via a Remote Callable Wrapper (RCW). Microsoft is already talking about porting legacy COM components into .NET. It also provides tools to help to do that. While that may be useful, it may be a sign of not wishing to support legacy COM later.

Platform Maturity

.NET is not a rewrite of COM/DCOM or COM+. It is not the next version of these either. It is a completely new 'product' that implements Microsoft's strategy for the Web that relies partially on COM+. The truth is that, though Microsoft as a company has quite a bit of maturity and that maturity will be evident in .NET, .NET itself lacks maturity as far as real world, highly distributed, highly scalable, and high performance systems having been built on it go. In fact, at the time of this writing, it is still in beta 2.

ONE on the other hand is based completely on the Java Platform, which has proven itself over several years. And as mentioned above in *Industry Support and Platform-Independence*, there are many excellent implementations of the Java Platform by many leading industry vendors including Sun, BEA, and IBM to name a few.

Standards Support (with Respect to Web Services)

Both .NET and ONE have pledged their support to Web Service standards such as SOAP, WSDL, and UDDI. In fact, Microsoft was instrumental in creating SOAP along with IBM, DevelopMentor, and others (Sun was not involved). Microsoft with IBM and Ariba also created UDDI. WSDL evolved from Microsoft's SDL.

Language Support

.NET has taken language-neutrality/independence to a completely new level. Both COM and CORBA were language-independent, right? Yes, in both platforms you could call a component written in one language (such as C) from a component written in another language (such as Java or J++ in Microsoft's case). However, with .NET you can create a component in one language such as C# or J# and then create a completely new component that extends (that is, inherits from) the component in VB.NET. Thus, we could create a commercial .NET class library that interfaces with TVs (type values) in C# and it could be used by .NET programmers regardless of which .NET supported language they used. In addition, there are .NET versions of COBOL, Smalltalk, Python, and many others either already available or in development. All of these can be plugged into the Visual Studio.NET IDE and gain support of all the IDE features, such as debug support, and so on. The availability of so many languages means that developers can program in the language they're most comfortable in and the one that makes sense for the task at hand. It also means that companies do not have to spend lots of money in retraining.

ONE on the other hand is limited to just one language, Java. While most developers who already know Java do not consider this a limitation, it does serve as a significant barrier to entry. After all, Java is not an easy language to master.

Tool Support

Visual Studio.NET is a very well designed, well thought out IDE that is also extremely easy and intuitive to use. It provides a common environment for all .NET languages and seamless cross-language debugging. It also includes support (wizards) for building installation programs, performing stress testing, and a host of other capabilities.

Availability Today

.NET as of this writing is still in beta 2. The beta proves that Microsoft has something to back its claims about .NET, but it does not mean that enterprises should immediately start using .NET in their products. As we've mentioned above, .NET is still 'immature'.

ONE on the other hand has an edge over .NET simply because it is not a complete rewrite or reinvention of a way of creating solutions, but a new way of packaging existing technologies and a vision of the future of this integrated package.

The Bottom Line

Based on the above comparison, .NET is a clear winner in its tool and language support. ONE on the other hand, is a clear winner in industry and interoperability support. ONE also has a short-term edge over .NET in terms of availability and maturity. Legacy and standards support are good in both. So who wins? There is no clear winner. As long as both support standards such as SOAP, WSDL, and UDDI this should pose no problem at all to either side.

Summary

In this chapter, we took a look at ONE, which is Sun's exciting new architectural framework for creating the next generation of today's web applications using today's technologies. ONE is an architectural framework that supports web services today and lays the foundation for the smart web services of tomorrow. Sun's vision is that smart web services will provide a high level of customization and personalization, well beyond the generic web services of today. This will be achieved through the addition of context awareness, multinet capabilities, and quality of service (meeting user needs with the least amount of effort invested by the user). While ONE lays the foundation for achieving the lofty goal of smart web services, there exist undefined gray areas as well. One such gray area is the management of a shared context, which is key to creating smart web services. This is because there is no standard for managing shared context across web services today. That leads us to the next salient feature of ONE, which is the fact that it is based completely on well-accepted industry standards. The ubiquitous nature of web services almost demands that a solution/architecture be based upon open and universally accepted standards if it is to be successful in gaining complete industry support.

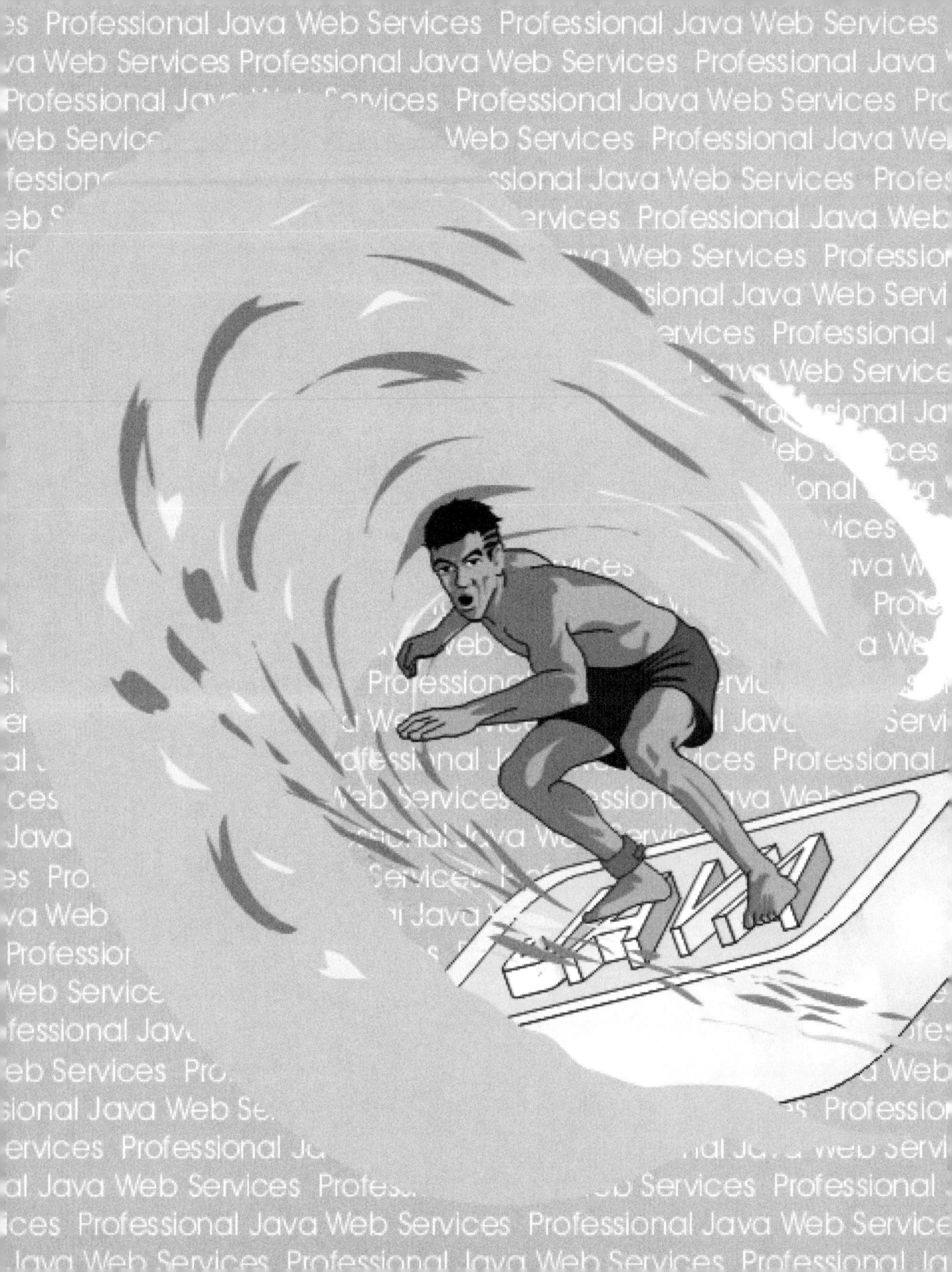
Professional Java Web Services

Introduction to Axis

The **A**pache e**X**tensible **I**nteraction **S**ystem (**Axis**) has evolved from the process to re-architect the design of SOAP implementation based on configurable **chains** of messages and **Handler objects**. Axis is currently in alpha 3 release, and is an ongoing project by Apache to provide many features that are not present in the current Apache SOAP implementation.

Axis is the project name for version 3.0 of Apache SOAP and the goal of Axis is to extend the functionality of Apache SOAP v2.0 in the following ways:

❑ Define a **message processing node** that can be packaged for use by service requestors (clients), service providers, and intermediaries. The Axis message processing node is a service provider or service requestor engine that facilitates manipulation of XML messages.

❑ Support the **XML Protocol**, which is an ongoing work at the W3C working group by re-designing the current Apache SOAP implementation to allow pluggable message protocol layers.

❑ Provide a **pluggable framework** for the components like transport Listener, Router, Serializer/De-serializer, Dispatcher, and Handler objects. A transport listener receives incoming messages in a specific transport protocol format and converts them into input sources, and a dispatcher is the component responsible for invoking the target web service. We will be discussing these components in detail in the *Architecture* section.

A web service is deployed into an Axis message processing node using a deployment descriptor known as a **W**eb **S**ervice **D**eployment **D**escriptor (**WSDD**). The WSDD describes how the various components installed in the Axis node are to be 'chained' together to process incoming and outgoing messages to the service. These chain definitions are 'compiled' and made available at runtime through registries. At runtime, the SOAP request flows through chains of handlers that potentially alter the message (add/remove headers, manipulate the body, and so on). We will be looking in detail the chains, registries, and WSDD in subsequent sections.

> *At the time of writing, Axis was in alpha 3 version, so the details are based on this release. More information on Axis can be found at* http://xml.apache.org/axis

Key Features of Axis

Axis provides the following features and advantages:

❑   **Speed** – The parsing mechanism used in the early implementation of Apache SOAP was based on DOM (the **D**ocument **O**bject **M**odel), which takes more time than a SAX (the **S**imple **A**PI for **XML**) implementation to parse large XML documents, resulting in low performance. As DOM also reads the entire XML file into memory before it begins the parsing, it results in huge memory consumption with very large XML files. For more information on DOM, refer to http://www.w3c.org/dom/.

Axis uses SAX-based parsing to achieve significantly greater speed than SOAP. The SAX implementation is based on an event-based model and operates at a lower level than DOM. For more information on SAX, visit http://www.megginson.com/SAX/.

❑   **Flexibility** – Axis provides features to facilitate insertion of new extensions into the engine for custom header processing and system management. To achieve this, Axis provides a deployment descriptor for describing various components like services, `Handler` objects, serializers/de-serializers, and so on. The deployment descriptor (WSDD) is used by the client application to deploy a web service. We will be discussing more on this in the coming sections.

❑   **Component-oriented deployment** – Axis introduces the concept of **chainables** and **handlers** for implementing common patterns of processing for applications. A handler is responsible for some specific processing associated with the input, output, and fault flows. A chainable is an abstract concept that describes an object's ability to participate in a chain that contains an ordered collection of handlers. We will be discussing more on this in the following section.

❑   **Transport framework** – Axis provides a transport framework by providing senders and listeners for SOAP over various protocols such as SMTP, FTP, and so on.

Architecture

Though Apache SOAP lays the foundation for the architecture of Axis, Axis contains many features that are not present in Apache SOAP. We will start looking into the core components and look in detail at the communication between each core component.

In order to understand the remainder of the chapter you should have read the Apache SOAP chapter. If in doubt, please refer to Chapter 3 for more information.

We begin by looking at how the flow of communication happens between the base components using the following diagram:

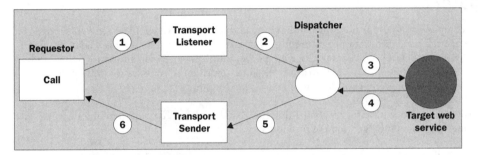

The processing of a SOAP service is done by passing a **message context** between each component. A message context is a structure that contains a request message, a response message, and a bag of properties (such as SOAP header attributes).

The steps for processing an incoming request to the target web service are shown below:

1. The requestor builds a SOAP request using a `Call` object by specifying the target URI, details of the service (such as service name, method name, and input parameters) and encoding style and so on. Then, the request message is sent to the Axis message processing node at the transport listener. The request message, at this point, will be in a wire protocol-specific format.

2. The transport listener converts the incoming message into a `Message` object (`org.apache.axis.Message`), and puts it into a `MessageContext` object. The transport listener also loads various properties like SOAP attributes (for example, the SOAP `Action` header) and sets the `transportName` property on the `MessageContext`. This `transportName` can be `http`, `smtp`, or `ftp`, based on the protocol used for the transport mechanism. Then the message is sent to the dispatcher.

3. The dispatcher is responsible for forwarding the request to the target web service.

4. The target web service executes the method and returns the response to the dispatcher.

5. The dispatcher forwards the response to the transport sender.

6. The transport sender, in collaboration with the transport context object, sends the XML message back over the wire protocol to the requestor. The transport context object encapsulates the details of transport listener, the context related to the request initiator and the destination of the message response/fault, the session details, and so on.

Transport Listener

The transport listener encapsulates details of networking protocols. This component sits on the receiving end to receive HTTP messages. The transport listener prepares the incoming message as an input source for XML parsing. It also creates a transport context to reference protocol-specific details of the request message.

Dispatcher

This component is responsible for invoking the target web service. The target web service can be implemented using different programming languages. A service can be a Java Bean or an EJB or a COM component. Axis facilitates describing different dispatchers for different types of web services in the WSDD. A WSDD is an XML structure used to describe the services for deployment. We will be discussing more on WSDD in the later parts of this chapter.

A **provider** is responsible for implementing the actual backend logic of invoking the service. Axis provides the following two kinds of providers:

❑ RPCProvider – The RPCProvider is the provider for all RPC services. The provider class, org.apache.axis.providers.java.RPCProvider, gets the class name from the WSDD and invokes the service object. The RPCProvider uses the SOAP RPC convention for determining the method to call, and makes sure the types of the incoming XML-encoded arguments match the types of the required parameters of the resulting method.

❑ MsgProvider – The MsgProvider is the provider for messaging services. This also reads the details of the implementation class from the WSDD to invoke the service object.

Transport Sender

The transport sender encapsulates details of networking protocols. This component is responsible for sending HTTP messages to the transport layer of the network by obtaining the configuration properties from transport context, which encapsulates the details of the transport layer for a message.

The above depicts the flow of request and response in an abstract view. We will drill down to one more level to understand the communication between transport listener, dispatcher, and transport sender. Axis provides various Handler objects to carry out different activities. A handler is responsible for some specific processing associated with an input, output, or fault flow. Handlers can be used to encrypt/decrypt message headers and the message body, to process digital signature headers, and so on.

As shown below, both the transport listener and transport sender chains consist of handlers that help in processing the request/response message:

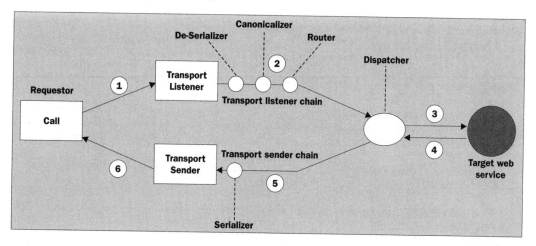

Let's first discuss the transport listener chain. As shown above, the transport listener is configured with the following chain of handlers:

- ❑ **De-Serializer** – This handler parses the InputStream into XML and uses various decoding schemes to convert XML into a format native to the programming language underlying the Axis processing node.

- ❑ **Canonicalizer** – This handler is responsible for getting the AxisContext object from the Axis node and creating a TransportContext object including information on where/how to return the response message. The canonicalizer handler creates the output message to be forwarded to the dispatcher.

- ❑ **Router** – This handler determines the service details like the service name and operation from the incoming request message. This information is used as a key to look up in the deployed service registry. The deployed service registry contains chainables for all services deployed to the Axis node.

The transport sender chain consists of a single handler:

- ❑ **Serializer** – This handler is responsible for converting a message into an XML stream by encapsulating the details of the messaging protocol

Apart from the above components, the Axis engine also contains input, output, and fault chains. These chains can be service-specific or global chains as shown in the following section.

Chains

Axis provides a **chainable generator** for deploying chainables from the WSDD description. A chainable is an abstract concept that describes an object's ability to participate in a chain. Chain container, chain, and handler are all chainables. The chainable generator uses the WSDD utility classes to parse the WSDD and interpret the chain container, chain, and handler structure to generate the chainable for the target of the WSDD, which may be a web service or a chainable component. Typically the chainable is then inserted into the deployed service registry or the chainable registry.

The deployed service registry contains the chainables for all services deployed to the Axis node. This registry provides a key-value mapping between service and chainable where the key is the service/operation name and the value is a chainable that has been deployed for that service.

The chainable registry contains the chainables corresponding to all the deployed handlers, chain types, and the chainable types deployed to the Axis node.

A chain is associated with the input, output, and fault flows for a deployed web service, and contains an ordered collection of handlers.

These chains are placed in a **chain container**. A chain container is a container for the chains associated with a deployed web service. A deployed web service has several chains like input, output, and several fault chains deployed for the service. The chain container groups these chains together.

The SOAP request message is processed by the engine global input chain and service-specific input chain. Similarly, the response message is processed by the engine global output chain and service-specific output chain as shown below:

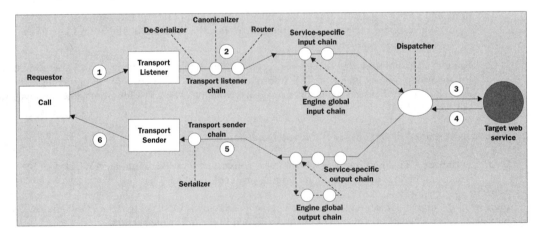

Web Services Deployment Descriptor (WSDD)

Axis defines an XML-based Web Services deployment descriptor (WSDD) for defining services, handlers and `Transport` objects to deploy into the Axis engine. The format of this description is based on the deployment descriptor format defined in SOAP v2.0. The WSDD at the root level contains the elements `<deployment>` to notify the Axis engine that it is to deploy a service/handler or the `<undeployment>` element to tell the Axis engine that it is to undeploy a particular service or handler.

The WSDD can be used on the clientside as well on the serverside. The client uses the WSDD to deploy/undeploy a particular service or `Handler` object. We will discuss more on using the WSDD on the clientside while developing the sample Axis service.

The serverside, there will be a default descriptor for notifying the Axis engine to deploy the basic required services and handlers. When we deploy a service on Tomcat servlet engine, using the deployment descriptor, the Axis engine generates the server configuration file (`server-config.wsdd`), which is placed at `%TOMCAT_HOME%\webapps\axis\WEB_INF`, where `%TOMCAT_HOME%` represents the installation directory for Tomcat.

The complete structure of the `server-config.wsdd` is as shown below. I have also provided the `server-config.wsdd` file in `javawebservices\Ch14` for your reference.

The root element of the deployment document, which tells the Axis engine that this is for deploying services and handlers, is specified in the descriptor:

```
<?xml version="1.0" encoding="UTF-8"?>
<deployment xmlns="http://xml.apache.org/axis/wsdd/"
            xmlns:java="http://xml.apache.org/axis/wsdd/providers/java">
```

The `globalConfiguration` element describes properties and handlers that are available for all services:

```
<globalConfiguration>
  <parameter name="adminPassword" value="admin"/>
  <parameter name="sendXsiTypes" value="true"/>
  <parameter name="sendMultiRefs" value="true"/>
  <parameter name="sendXMLDeclaration" value="true"/>
```

The WSDD defines a `<handler>` element to define `Handler` objects. You can define handlers for `requestFlow`, `responseFlow`, and `faultFlow` to perform a specific task on the request message, response message, and fault message respectively, of a deployed web service:

```
<requestFlow>
  <handler type="java:org.apache.axis.handlers.JWSHandler"/>
</requestFlow>
</globalConfiguration>
```

The default handlers used by the Axis engine for processing the services are shown next.

The `URLMapper` handler attempts to use the extra path info of this request as the service name. For example, the `URLMapper` handler maps a URL like http://localhost/axis/services/AdminService to the `AdminService`:

```
<handler name="URLMapper"
         type="java:org.apache.axis.handlers.http.URLMapper"/>
```

Axis provides a default handler for authentication purpose. The `SimpleAuthenticationHandler` object authenticates the user by validating the username and password. The user credentials are specified in a file called `users.list` located in the `%TOMCAT_HOME%\webapps\axis\WEB_INF` directory. We could also provide a custom `Handler` object to authenticate the user as per the requirement in the real applications:

```
<handler name="Authenticate"
         type="java:org.apache.axis.handlers.SimpleAuthenticationHandler"/>
<handler name="LocalResponder"
         type="java:org.apache.axis.transport.local.LocalResponder"/>
```

The `MessageDispatcher` handler is to handle the message-based SOAP services and is implemented by the class `java:org.apache.axis.providers.java.MsgProvider`:

```
<handler name="MsgDispatcher"
         type="java:org.apache.axis.providers.java.MsgProvider"/>
```

Similarly, the `RPCDispatcher` handler is for handling SOAP services of type RPC and is implemented by the Java class `java:org.apache.axis.providers.java.RPCProvider`:

```
<handler name="RPCDispatcher"
         type="java:org.apache.axis.providers.java.RPCProvider"/>
```

The `<service>` element is used to describe the services to be deployed. We can define the details like class name, method name, and scope using the `parameter` attribute:

```
<service name="AdminService" provider="java:MSG">
  <parameter name="methodName" value="AdminService"/>
  <parameter name="enableRemoteAdmin" value="false"/>
  <parameter name="className" value="org.apache.axis.utils.Admin"/>
</service>
<service name="JWSProcessor" provider="Handler">
  <parameter name="handlerClass"
             value="org.apache.axis.handlers.JWSProcessor"/>
</service>
<service name="EchoService" provider="Handler">
  <parameter name="handlerClass"
             value="org.apache.axis.handlers.EchoHandler"/>
</service>
```

The WSDD contains a `<transport>` element to define a transport on the serverside, which is invoked when an incoming SOAP request arrives. The `<transport>` element may define `<requestFlow>` and/or `<responseFlow>` elements to specify handlers/chains, which should be invoked during the request (in other words, the incoming message) or response (in other words, the outgoing message) portion of processing. The `HTTPAuthHandler` is a utility class to provide simple authentication facility. This class sets the username and password properties of `MessageContext` by extracting from the HTTP header:

```
<transport name="http">
  <requestFlow>
    <handler type="URLMapper"/>
    <handler type="java:org.apache.axis.handlers.http.HTTPAuthHandler"/>
  </requestFlow>
</transport>
<transport name="local">
  <responseFlow>
    <handler type="java:org.apache.axis.transport.local.LocalResponder"/>
  </responseFlow>
</transport>
</deployment>
```

The Web Services deployment description used in the present implementation (Axis alpha 3) may be subject to changes in terms of adding new elements, renaming some of the existing elements, and so on in the next versions (beta version).

Deployment of Components

In this section, we will look at the architecture of components used for deploying chainable objects, handlers, and services.

Axis provides the following two types of services for deploying the chainables:

❏ Handlers

❏ Services

Chainable Deployment Service

The Axis message processing node provides a web service to deploy/redeploy or undeploy a chainable from the chainable registry.

This service accepts the WSDD and generates the newly deployed chainable in the chainable registry. If the WSDD is for redeploying the chainable, then the service updates the deployment of an existing chainable in the chainable registry. The chainable deployment service provides functionality to remove or undeploy a chainable and to get the list of chainables that are currently deployed in the chainable registry.

The above scenarios are depicted in the following diagram:

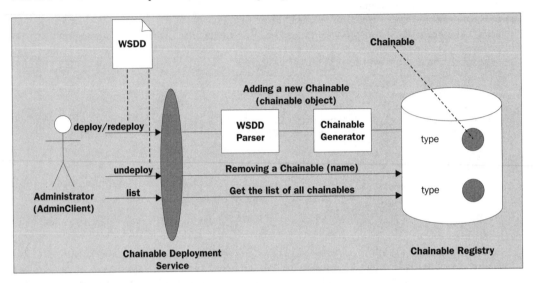

As shown above, to register a new chainable, the Axis administrator invokes the deploy operation on the chainable deployment service by passing the deployment descriptor (WSDD). This results in the deployment of new chainable object by making the registration of a new entry in the chainable registry, keyed by chainable 'type'. The value in the chainable registry is the chainable generated from the chainable generator after processing the deployment descriptor.

Web Service Deployment Service

The Axis message processing node also provides a web service to deploy/redeploy or undeploy a web service from the deployed service registry. The web service deployment service also accepts the WSDD and generates a newly deployed web service in the deployed service registry. The service also provides functionality to update (redeploy) the deployment of an existing web service, undeploy a web service, and get the list of all deployed web services from the deployment service registry.

Let's discuss this with reference to the following diagram:

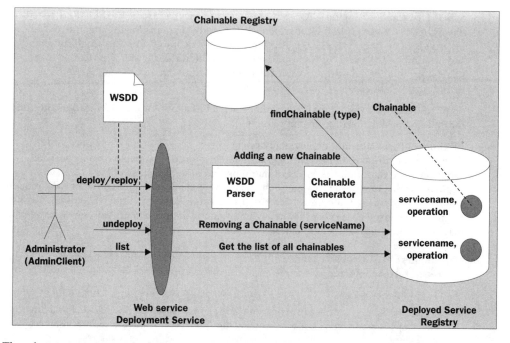

The administrator passes the WSDD to the web service deployment service by specifying the services (such as class name, operations, and methods), and request and response handlers specific to the service. The deployment service uses WSDD helper classes to parse the descriptor. The chainable generator checks the instance of chainable in the chainable registry by passing the chain type to the findChainable functionality. If it is not found in the registry, then the chainable generator creates a new chainable object. These chainables are built from the components registered in the chainable registry.

As shown in the diagram, the chainable is registered in the Deployed Service Registry by making the Service/Operation name the key for the mapping.

Features Available in Alpha 3

Apart from providing SOAP 1.1 features, Axis provides many other features.

Please note that the features described are based on alpha 3 release and are likely to change in the subsequent releases. Hence, for the current list of features, refer to the document section of the latest AXIS version at http://xml.apache.org/axis/.

The following is a list of features available for **general SOAP systems**:

- ❑ **SOAP 1.1-compliant engine** – Axis supports most of the features of the SOAP1.1 specification like SOAP **Envelope**, SOAP **Header**, and SOAP **Body** elements for defining the SOAP message, SOAP `encodingStyle` attribute, and the encoding rules for serialization and de-serialization, SOAP `mustUnderstand` attribute to indicate whether the Header entry is mandatory or optional for the recipient (receiver of SOAP request), and SOAP **Fault** element including the fault codes to describe the error messages.

  Some of the features like SOAP actor of Section 5 in the SOAP 1.1 specification and support for multidimensional arrays are yet to be implemented

- ❑ **Flexible configuration and deployment system** – Axis provides an easily configurable descriptor file, the WSDD, for configuring handler objects, chainable objects, services, serializers, and de-serializers for bean mapping and other provider objects. A service is deployed with a unique service name that is used by the Axis engine to tie an RPC request to a SOAP service. The deployment descriptor contains a `scope` parameter to define the lifetime of the service instance serving the invocation request. In the current Axis version, the scope may have one of the following values:

  - ❑ `Request` – A service instance with `Request` scope is available for the duration of the request. Hence the request scope ensures isolation of successive calls.

  - ❑ `Session` – A service instance with `Session` scope is available for the entire session.

  - ❑ `Application` – A service instance with `Application` scope is available for all invocations. This scope is used when all users accessing the Axis server share the service instance.

  We will see more on specifying the scope of a service while developing the sample service application in the later part of the chapter.

- ❑ **Support for 'drop-in' deployment of SOAP services** – Axis provides easy drop-in deployment of a service. A Java file can be deployed as a web service by merely modifying the file extension from `.java` to `.jws` to make it accessible from the client application on HTTP. For example, if we deployed a greeting service implemented by `GreetingService.java` using the JWS option, then this service could be accessed directly from the client program using the following URL value as the endpoint of the service, assuming that the service was deployed on Tomcat using the default port (8080):

  http://localhost:8080/axis/GreetingService.jws

  The Apache SOAP implementation doesn't provide the above mentioned kind of drop-in deployment of a SOAP service. Axis introduced this unique feature for easy deployment of a Java class as a SOAP service. We will be looking into more details of the drop-in deployment while developing the sample service in the later part of the chapter. Though JWS provides an easy drop-in deployment, we require the source file for this drop-in kind of deployment. Hence, this feature could not be used if we have only the class files. For such cases, Axis provides an alternative way of deploying a service using the WSDD.

❑ **Automatic serialization and de-serialization mechanism** – Axis provides support for all the basic types. The types supported by Axis are:

> ❑ Built-in data types
>
> ❑ Enumeration
>
> ❑ Array of bytes
>
> ❑ Complex type (Java Bean Mapping)
>
> ❑ Arrays (using SOAP encoding)
>
> ❑ Arrays (WSDL derivation style)
>
> ❑ Arrays (SOAP derivation style)
>
> ❑ Sequence/all attribute support
>
> ❑ Multi-reference object support (run-time)

To define the type mapping of custom data types, Axis defines a WSDD for automatic serialization/de-serialization of Java beans. We will be looking in more detail into serialization and de-serialization of custom specific bean types in the example service that we will be developing in the later part of the chapter. The Axis engine comes with many default serializers such as `ArraySerializer` to handle serializing and de-serializing SOAP arrays, `EnumSerializer` to serializer an `enum` object, a `MapSerializer` to serialize and de-serialize maps using the `SOAP-ENC` encoding style, and `VectorDeserializer` to handle deserializing SOAP vectors.

❑ **Support for SOAP messages with attachments** – Axis supports sending SOAP messages with attachments based on the W3C guidelines given at http://www.w3c.org/TR/SOAP-attachments.

The multi-purpose Internet mail extension (MIME) message with content type multipart/related was incorporated into the SOAP standard as SOAP message with attachments. The MIME multipart message may contain many parts where each part may specify the type of content it contains. Axis uses the JavaBeans Activation Framework (JAF) specification from Sun. The JAF specification is part of the Glasgow JavaBeans specification and provides features to determine the MIME data type, to determine the commands available on that data. JAF provides two very simple JAF-aware viewer beans:

> ❑ A text viewer
>
> ❑ An image viewer

These handle data with the content type set to text/plain or image/gif respectively. More details on JAF can be obtained from the link http://java.sun.com/beans/glasgow/jaf.html.

An attachment may be created as a JAF `DataHandler` object. The `DataHandler` object may then be treated as any other complex type object being sent. For the serialization/de-serialization of the content that the `DataHandler` references as an attachment, Axis provides a serializer, `org.apache.axis.encoding.JAFDataHandlerSerializer` and a de-serializer factory, `org.apche.axis.encoding.JAFDataHandlerDeserializerFactory`. We need to register both the serializer and de-serializer in the deployment descriptor for sending/receiving the SOAP messages with attachments.

We will be looking more into SOAP messages with attachments while developing the sample service in later part of chapter. We will be writing a service that accepts attachments and a client application for sending the attachments to the service.

And now we have the features available to **containers and services systems**:

❑ **Providers for RPC and message-based SOAP services** – Axis comes with the providers for handling RPC and message-based SOAP services. Axis provides two handlers:

 ❑ RPCDispatcher – Handling RPC services

 ❑ MsgDispatcher – Handling message-based services

We discussed these in the *Architecture* section.

❑ **HTTP servlet-based transport** – Similar to the Apache SOAP implementation, Axis also provides a servlet-based transport mechanism. The AxisServlet provided by Axis is similar to RPCRouterServlet provided by the Apache SOAP implementation. Axis also provides AxisHttpSession for HTTP servlet-based session implementation.

❑ **Standalone version of the HTTP server** – Axis comes with a standalone HTTP server known as the SimpleAxisServer. This is a single-threaded implementation of an HTTP server for processing SOAP requests. The server can be used for demos, debugging, and performance profiling. The server can be run from the command prompt as shown below:

> **java org.apache.axis.transport.http.SimpleAxisServer**

Once the server is up and running, we can access the deployed services using SOAP on HTTP. The SimpleAxisServer also supports HTTP basic authentication.

❑ **EJB provider for accessing EJBs as web services** – Axis provides an EJB provider (org.apache.axis.providers.java.EJBProvider) for accessing EJBs as web services.

The details of the EJB that needs to be deployed are specified in the WSDD, which we have seen in the *Web Services Deployment Descriptor (WSDD)* section, earlier in the chapter. For example, to deploy a sample stateless session bean called SampleEJBServiceBean in the service-config.wsdd file as shown below, we specify the following required parameters:

 ❑ allowedMethods – Methods that a client can access from the service. Use * for all methods or a space-separated list for multiple methods.

 ❑ beanJndiName – JNDI name of the EJB intended to be looked up (for example SampleEJBService or java:comp/env/ejb/SampleEJBService).

 ❑ homeInterfaceName – Class name of the stateless session EJB's home interface (for example, SampleEJBServiceHome).

and the following optional parameters:

- jndiContextClass – The bean's JNDI context class.
- jndiURL – The bean's JNDI URL.
- jndiUser – The bean username. This user ID is mapped to the property java.naming.security.principal in InitialContext
- jndiPassword – The bean's JNDI password, which maps to the property java.naming.security.credentials in InitialContext.

The values are described in the service-config.wsdd shown below:

```
<service name="SampleEJBService" provider="java:EJB">
  <parameter name="allowedMethods" value="*"/>
  <parameter name="beanJndiName"
          value="java:comp/env/ejb/SampleEJBService"/>
  <parameter name="homeInterfaceName" value="SampleEJBServiceHome"/>
  <parameter name="jndiContextClass" value="allaire.ejipt.ContextFactory"/>
  <parameter name="jndiURL" value="ejipt://localhost:2323"/>
  <parameter name="jndiUser" value="AxisUser"/>
  <parameter name="jndiPassword" value="AxisPassword"/>
</service>
```

- **Log4J for logging/debugging** – Axis uses the **Log4J API** for all logging and debugging information. Log4J is an open source project at Apache. It provides a Java API with logging and debugging features. The API is fully configurable and has three main components:

  - **Categories**
  - **Appenders**
  - **Layouts**

  to enable developers to log messages according to message type and priority, and to control at run-time how these messages are formatted, where they are reported, and so on.

  For more information on Log4J please visit http://jakarta.apache.org/log4j/.

- **Preliminary security extensions** – Axis provides a basic version of a security provider, known as SimpleSecurityProvider, for basic user authentication. A security provider for servlets, known as ServletSecurityProvider, is also included in Axis. The ServletSecurityProvider allows the standard servlet security mechanisms (isUserInRole(), and so on) to integrate with Axis's access control mechanism.

  Axis also allows authentication handlers to use an extensible security provider interface, which should allow easy integration with existing security providers such as those provided by application servers.

❑ **Automatic WSDL generation from deployed services** – Axis provides a tool (`org.apache.axis.wsdlgen.Java2Wsdl`) to support WSDL generation that can be used for generating the proxy classes. For example, you can directly view the WSDL file of an Axis service by appending ?wsdl to the service endpoint URL, like this:
http://localhost:8080/axis/services/myservice?wsdl.

Here, myservice is the name of the deployed service. Alternatively, you could also generate the WSDL by passing the service class to the Java2Wsdl tool at the command prompt as shown below:

```
> java org.apache.axis.wsdlgen.Java2Wsdl <ServiceClassName>
```

We will be discussing more on generating WSDL documents while developing our sample Axis service later.

❑ **Wsdl2java tool for building stubs and skeletons** – Axis also provides a utility tool, `org.apache.axis.wsdl.Wsdl2java`, for generating stubs and skeleton Java classes. We need to pass the WSDL file to the Wsdl2java tool to generate the stub and skeleton classes. We could also give the URL mentioned in the above section to the Wsdl2java tool.

We will be discussing more about the tool while generating stubs and skeletons for our sample service.

Developing a Sample Axis Service

Now we will develop, deploy, and access a sample Axis service. The steps involved are as follows:

❑ Software requirements

❑ Developing the Axis service

❑ Types of deployment provided by Axis

❑ Naming the input parameters

❑ Passing custom type input parameters

❑ Adding handlers to the Greeting service

❑ Sending a SOAP message with attachments

❑ Generating the WSDL document for the service

❑ Generating stubs and skeletons using Wsdl2java

❑ Using the Axis TCP monitor (tcpmon)

Software Requirements

In this section, we will go through the software required to execute the sample service.

Tomcat

We will be deploying the service on Tomcat server version 3.2.x. You can download Tomcat from http://jakarta.apache.org/tomcat/.

If you are using Tomcat 4.0.x, you need to edit the `catalina.bat` file in the bin directory (`%TOMCAT_HOME%\bin\catalina.bat`) by changing:

```
set CLASSPATH=%CP%
```

to:

```
set CLASSPATH=%CLASSPATH%;%CP%
```

This edit needs to be made in the *Set Up The Runtime Classpath* section of the batch file. The `%CLASSPATH%` refers to the system `CLASSPATH`.

Axis

Next you need to download Axis from http://xml.apache.org/axis/. At the time of writing, the latest Axis version available was alpha 3, hence this version has been used for the sample service. You may find a later version by the time you read this chapter.

Once the download and installation of the tomcat is complete, copy the `axis` directory located at `%AXIS_HOME%\webapps\` to `%TOMCAT_HOME%\webapps\`.

Make sure that the `CLASSPATH` has an entry of the working directory for the sample service, which is `javawebservices\Ch14`. Also to access the Axis framework, we need to make the `CLASSPATH` entry for the JAR files (`axis.jar`, `clutil.jar`, `log4j-core.jar`, `wsdl4j.jar`) located in `%AXIS_HOME%\lib`.

XML Parser Classes

You need to download XML parser classes that are complaint with JAXP1.1 for the XML parsing functionality. For this, download `xalan.jar` and `xerces.jar` from http://java.sun.com/xml/xml_jaxp.html. Once the download is completed, make a `CLASSPATH` entry for the JAR files. Also, add the JAR files to the `lib` directory located at `%TOMCAT_HOME%\webapps\axis\WEB-INF\lib\`.

> *Alternatively you could also download the `xerces.jar` (v1.4.4) file from the link http://xml.apache.org/dist/xerces-j/ for XML parsing functionality.*

Java Activation Framework

We will be using the **Java Activation Framework** (JAF 1.0.1) in the sample service for building a `DataHandler` object by reading the contents from a file. This is used for sending SOAP messages with attachments. Hence, we need `activation.jar`. This JAR file contains the classes that make up JavaBeans Activation Framework. The JAR file can be downloaded from http://java.sun.com/products/javabeans/glasgow/jaf.html.

Once the download is complete, make sure `activation.jar` is in the system `CLASSPATH`.

Developing the Axis Service

For our demonstration, we will develop a greeting service. The service is implemented as a JavaBean and contains a single method called `sayHello()`, which accepts the first name and last name of a customer and returns a message of greeting. The Java file is located in the `\javawebservices\Ch14` directory.

```
public class GreetingService {

  // This method accepts the first name and last name and
  // returns a greeting.
  public String sayHello(String firstName, String lastName) {
    return "Hi "+firstName+"."+lastName+"! Have a Good Day!!";
  }
}
```

Now we will deploy the above functionality as a web service.

Types of Deployment Provided by AXIS

Axis provides two ways of deploying a service. The first one is by deploying the Java file with a `.jws` extension and the second is using a deployment descriptor. Let's see both the options in detail. We will also look into the advantages and disadvantages of each method.

Instant Deployment in the Form of JWS (Java Web Service) Files

This is the simplest kind of deployment provided by Axis. We will use the Tomcat 3.2.x server for deploying our greeting service. To deploy our service, we need to place the `GreetingService.java` file in the `axis` directory under `webapps` in `%TOMCAT_HOME%`. Assuming that the `jakarta-tomcat-3.2.x` is the `%TOMCAT_HOME%`, the location of the Java file will be `c:\jakarta-tomcat-3.2.3\webapps\axis\GreetingService.java`.

Rename the Java file as `GreetingService.jws` and that's it. We have finished the deployment. Now the service is available as a Axis service at the URL http://localhost:8080/axis/GreetingService.jws.

When you start the Tomcat server and access the above service at the URL, Axis automatically locates the file, compiles the class, and converts SOAP calls correctly into Java invocations of your service class.

Though we could deploy a service using the JWS option, we cannot use this system in every scenario. The JWS way of deploying a service requires the sourcecode of the service. Hence, if we want to expose a pre-existing compiled class without sourcecode, we cannot use JWS option to deploy the service. Also, in the JWS way of deployment, there is no way to configure a service using application-specific type mappings and custom handlers. Hence, for such scenarios where we have only class files and where we want to configure a service and describe handlers, we need to go for the other option of deploying a service using a deployment descriptor described in the next section.

A Client Application to Access the Greeting Service

Let's develop the client application to access the Axis service. The Java file, called `AxisClient.java`, for the client program is located in `\javawebservices\Ch14`.

The `endpointURL` string refers the target service, which is the greeting service deployed on the local host on Tomcat's default port 8080.

Here is the code for `AxisClient.java`:

```
import org.apache.axis.client.Call;
import org.apache.axis.client.Service;
import org.apache.axis.encoding.XMLType;

public class AxisClient {
  public static void main(String[] args) {

    try {
      String endpointURL = "http://localhost:8080/axis/GreetingService.jws";
      String methodName = "sayHello";
```

The `Service` class is a factory class and is capable of returning a `javax.xml.rpc.Call`. The `javax.xml.rpc.Call` interface provides support for dynamic invocation of a service port. The `org.apache.axis.client.Call` object implements the `javax.xml.rpc.Call` interface:

```
      Service service = new Service();
      Call call = (Call) service.createCall();
```

Once a `Call` instance is created, the setter methods are used to set the endpoint URL of target service port, operation, and encoding style specified as a namespace URI, Name, type, and mode (IN, INOUT, or OUT) of the parameters and the return type as shown below:

```
      call.setTargetEndpointAddress(new java.net.URL(endpointURL));
      call.setOperationName(methodName);
      call.setProperty(Call.NAMESPACE, "urn:greetingService");
      call.addParameter("firstName", XMLType.XSD_STRING, Call.PARAM_MODE_IN);
      call.addParameter("lastName", XMLType.XSD_STRING, Call.PARAM_MODE_IN);
```

Then, we invoke the service using the `Call` object by passing the first name and last name of the customer as input parameters. The service returns a response message of type `String`:

```
      String response = (String) call.invoke(new Object[] {
        "Stephen", "Mitchell"
      });

      // Print the response on console
      System.out.println("The Resonse:");
      System.out.println(response);
    } catch (Exception e) {
      System.out.println(e);
    }
  }
}
```

Now you need compile and run the `AxisClient.java` file to access the service. You will get a greeting message from the `GreetingService` as shown below:

```
> javac AxisClient.java

> java AxisClient
The Response:
Hi Stephen.Mitchell! Have a Good Day!!
```

Naming the Input Parameters

Here, I would like to discuss how Axis allows the user to name the input parameters explicitly.

If you notice the from the client code, we have added the input parameters to the `Call` object by explicitly defining their data type as shown below:

```
call.addParameter("firstName", XMLType.XSD_STRING, Call.PARAM_MODE_IN);
call.addParameter("lastName", XMLType.XSD_STRING, Call.PARAM_MODE_IN);
```

This feature of naming the parameters provided by Axis becomes very handy for developers, since if you look at the SOAP request message given below, the input parameters are reflected by their actual names instead of the names assigned by the Axis engine.

SOAP Request

Here is the SOAP request message:

```
POST /axis/GreetingService.jws HTTP/1.0
Content-Length: 520
Host: localhost
Content-Type: text/xml; charset=utf-8
SOAPAction: "urn:greetingService/sayHello"

<?xml version="1.0" encoding="UTF-8"?>
<SOAP-ENV:Envelope SOAP-
ENV:encodingStyle="http://schemas.xmlsoap.org/soap/encoding/" xmlns:SOAP-
ENV="http://schemas.xmlsoap.org/soap/envelope/"
xmlns:xsd="http://www.w3.org/2001/XMLSchema"
xmlns:xsi="http://www.w3.org/2001/XMLSchema-instance">
  <SOAP-ENV:Body>
    <ns3:sayHello xmlns:ns3="urn:greetingService">
        <firstName xsi:type="xsd:string">Stephen</firstName>
        <lastName xsi:type="xsd:string">Mitchell</lastName>
    </ns3:sayHello>
  </SOAP-ENV:Body>
</SOAP-ENV:Envelope>
```

We could directly pass the input parameters in the `invoke()` method without explicitly adding the parameters to the `Call` object using `addParameter()`. In such a case, the SOAP request will generate the parameter names in the order they are passed to the invoke method. The parameter part in the body of the SOAP request will look like the following:

```
<SOAP-ENV:Body>
  <ns3:sayHello xmlns:ns3="urn:greetingService">
    <arg0 xsi:type="xsd:string">Stephen</arg0>
    <arg1 xsi:type="xsd:string">Mitchell</arg1>
  </ns3:sayHello>
</SOAP-ENV:Body>
```

Similarly, Axis allows us to explicitly specify the data type of the return value from within the SOAP response. This is done by setting the data type of the return value to the `Call` object as shown below:

```
call.setReturnType( org.apache.axis.encoding.XMLType.XSD_STRING );
```

This method will tell the Axis client that, if the return element is not typed then it should act as if the return value has an `xsi:type` attribute set to the predefined SOAP `String` type.

Custom Deployment

The alternative is to carry out a custom deployment using a deployment descriptor. The deployment descriptor captures the service information, the handlers, and chainable objects to make them available to the Axis engine. The deployment descriptor for our greeting service is given in `deploy.wsdd` file as shown overleaf and is located in the directory `\javawebservices\Ch14`:

```
<deployment xmlns="http://xml.apache.org/axis/wsdd/"
            xmlns:java="http://xml.apache.org/axis/wsdd/providers/java">
  <service name="urn:greetingService" provider="java:RPC">
    <parameter name="className" value="GreetingService"/>
    <parameter name="methodName" value="sayHello"/>
  </service>
</deployment>
```

The outermost element, `<deployment>`, tells the engine that this is a deployment. The other options available are `<undeployment>` to undeploy a web service and `<list>` to list the deployed services.

The `<deployment>` service element defines the `java` namespace. The `<service>` element specifies the service name and provider for handling the service. We have discussed in the *Architecture* section that a service is a targeted chain and may contain any/all of a request handler, a pivot handler (which for a service is called a **provider**), and a response handler.

Since `GreetingService` is of type RPC, the provider is `java:RPC`, which is pre-defined to indicate the Java RPC service. The Java RPC service is implemented in the Axis engine by the class `org.apache.axis.providers.java.RPCProvider`. As we discussed earlier, the other type of provider available in the Axis engine for handling message type of services is `MsgDispatcher`, which is implemented by the `org.apache.axis.providers.java.MsgProvider` class.

To make sure that the RPC service should instantiate and call the correct class, the `<service>` element contains the `<parameter>` element to specify the class name. You can see that the method name to be invoked is also specified using the `<parameter>` element. If the service has more than one method, all methods will be specified with whitespace or a comma as the delimiter. Alternatively, we could also use `*` to include all methods with a public access modifier.

We can also define the scope of a particular web service in the deployment descriptor as shown below:

```
<service>
  <parameter name="scope" value="(Session||Request||Application)"/>
</service>
```

As mentioned above, the scope of a service instance with respect to a client can be of type `Session`, `Request`, or `Application`. The default scope, `Request`, keeps the instance values until the request is fulfilled and `Session` scope means the instance values are maintained until the session is active. The `Application` scope is used to share the values throughout the application.

Using AdminClient to Deploy a Service Using deploy.wsdd

Axis provides a utility service, `org.apache.axis.client.AdminClient`, to deploy a service using the deployment descriptor. Run the `AdminClient` class file by passing the `deploy.wsdd` file as the input parameter from the command prompt as shown below:

```
> java org.apache.axis.client.AdminClient deploy.wsdd
Processing file deploy.wsdd
<Admin>Done processing</Admin>
```

We have successfully deployed our greeting service. Before accessing the service, we need to modify the Java code for the client. We use the modified Java file, called `AxisClient1.java` to access the service. Since this time the service is deployed with the name `urn:greetingService`, the URL will be referring to this instead of the JWS file, as shown below. The rest of the client code remains exactly same.

```java
import org.apache.axis.client.Call;
import org.apache.axis.client.Service;
import org.apache.axis.encoding.XMLType;

public class AxisClient1 {
  public static void main(String[] args) {

    try {
      String endpointURL =
        "http://localhost:8080/axis/services/urn:greetingService";
      String methodName = "sayHello";
      Service service = new Service();
      Call call = (Call) service.createCall();
      call.setTargetEndpointAddress(new java.net.URL(endpointURL));
      call.setOperationName(methodName);
      call.setProperty(Call.NAMESPACE, "urn:greetingService");
      call.addParameter("firstName", XMLType.XSD_STRING,
                        Call.PARAM_MODE_IN);
      call.addParameter("lastName", XMLType.XSD_STRING, Call.PARAM_MODE_IN);
      String response = (String) call.invoke(new Object[] {
        "John", "Myers"
      });

      // Print the response on console
      System.out.println("The Response:");
      System.out.println(response);
    } catch (Exception e) {
      System.out.println(e);
    }
  }
}
```

We are set to access the service now. Compile the Java file, run it, and a greeting message will be displayed on the console:

```
> javac AxisClient1.java

> java AxisClient1
The Response:
Hi John.Myers! Have a Good Day!!
```

Here also, we could access the service by specifying the following URL value for the `endpointURL`:

```
String endpointURL = "http://localhost:8080/axis/servlet/AxisServlet/urn:greetingS
ervice";
```

This is because if you look at the web.xml file located at %TOMCAT-HOME%\webapps\axis\WEB-INF, the servlet mapping for both the patterns point to the same servlet, which is the AxisServlet as shown below:

```
    .
    .
    .
<servlet-mapping>
  <servlet-name>AxisServlet</servlet-name>
  <url-pattern>servlet/AxisServlet</url-pattern>
</servlet-mapping>
    .
    .
    .
<servlet-mapping>
  <servlet-name>AxisServlet</servlet-name>
  <url-pattern>/services/*</url-pattern>
</servlet-mapping>
    .
    .
    .
```

Let's look into what has happened behind the scenes when we deployed the service. Whenever a new Axis service is deployed using the deployment descriptor, an entry of the service is made in the server-config.wsdd located at %TOMCAT-HOME%\webapps\axis\WEB-INF. When we access any service, the Axis engine checks the service entry in server-config.wsdd, and reads the details of class name, method name, and so on. If you look at the server-config.wsdd file, you will notice the following entry for the greeting service.

```
  </service>
   <service name="urn:greetingService" provider="java:RPC">
    <parameter name="methodName" value="sayHello"/>
    <parameter name="className" value="GreetingService"/>
   </service>
```

The above code snippet is similar to the service description that we specified in the deploy.wsdd file. When we undeploy the service, the entry will be deleted from the server-config.wsdd file.

To make sure that the service is undeployed properly, we will undeploy the service and then access it. The descriptor to undeploy the greeting service is provided in undeploy.wsdd as shown below. The descriptor is very simple and contains the <undeployment> element to indicate the AdminClient that it is to undeploy a web service. The service name is included using the name attribute in the <service> element:

```
<undeployment xmlns="http://xml.apache.org/axis/wsdd/">
  <service name="urn:greetingService"/>
</undeployment>
```

Let's undeploy the greeting service using `undeploy.wsdd` and `AdminClient`, and then try to access the service using `AxisClient1` class as shown below:

```
> java org.apache.axis.client.AdminClient undeploy.wsdd
Processing file undeploy.wsdd
<Admin>Done processing</Admin>

> java AxisClient1
The AXIS engine could not find a target service to invoke!  targetService is
urn:greetingService
```

You can see that when we try to access the service, the Axis server returns a fault message saying that it could not find the target service.

Passing Custom Type Input Parameters

At present, the `sayHello()` method in `GreetingService.java` accepts first name and last name of customer as input parameters of type `java.lang.String`. In real-life the scenarios though, it is often required to pass application-specific data types. In real-life projects, the input parameters of methods of service classes may be objects of JavaBean classes like, for example, passing the credit card information as a JavaBean object to the credit card validation service. We will now look at passing such an application-specific or custom type JavaBean object to represent the customer name for our greeting service.

The JavaBean `Customer` contains attributes for first name and last name with setter and getter methods. The complete code for `Customer` is given below:

```java
public class Customer {

  String firstName = null;
  String lastName = null;

  public void setFirstName(String firstName) {
    this.firstName = firstName;
  }

  public void setLastName(String lastName) {
    this.lastName = lastName;
  }

  public String getFirstName() {
    return firstName;
  }

  public String getLastName() {
    return lastName;
  }
}
```

And the greeting service is modified so that the `sayHello()` method now accepts an object of type `Customer` as the input parameter as shown below:

```
public class GreetingService1 {

  public String sayHello(Customer customer) {
    return "Hi " + customer.getFirstName() + " " + customer.getLastName()
          + ", have a Good Day!!";
  }
}
```

The deployment descriptor for the greeting service, `deploy1.wsdd`, is modified accordingly to define the mappings for the `Customer` class. The service name this time is `urn:greetingService1`. Actually we could have used `urn:greetingService` as the service name. A new service name is given only to assist the reader to run different versions of the greeting service at one time.

```
<deployment xmlns="http://xml.apache.org/axis/wsdd/"
            xmlns:java="http://xml.apache.org/axis/wsdd/providers/java">
  <service name="urn:greetingService1" provider="java:RPC">
    <parameter name="className" value="GreetingService1"/>
    <parameter name="methodName" value="sayHello"/>

    <beanMapping qname="myNS:customer" xmlns:myNS="urn:greetingService1"
                 languageSpecificType="java:Customer"/>
  </service>
</deployment>
```

As shown above, the `<beanMapping>` element defines a namespace and the actual class for the input parameter. The attribute `qname` defines a qualified name based on namespaces in XML specification. Axis internally uses objects of the `javax.xml.rpc.namespace.QName` class to map the value of `qname` attribute. When the namespace is used later in the document, the `customer` is used as a prefix to the element used to identify the namespace it belongs to.

The client program needs to be modified to include a serializer and de-serializer for the `Customer` class.

The first part of defining endpoint and method details remains same as shown below:

```
import org.apache.axis.client.Call;
import org.apache.axis.client.Service;
import org.apache.axis.encoding.BeanSerializer;
import org.apache.axis.encoding.XMLType;
import javax.xml.rpc.namespace.QName;

public class AxisClient2 {
  public static void main(String[] args) {

    try {
      String endpointURL =
        "http://localhost:8080/axis/services/urn:greetingService1";
      String methodName = "sayHello";
```

The code requires the first name and last name to be passed as parameters at the command prompt:

```
if (args.length == 0) {
    System.out.println("usage: java AxisClient <firstName> <lastName>");
    System.exit(1);
}
```

An instance of the `Call` class is obtained from `Service` and the endpoint URL of the target service. The method name and namespace are set using the setter methods:

```
Service service = new Service();

// Create a Call object and set the parameters
Call call = (Call) service.createCall();
call.setTargetEndpointAddress(new java.net.URL(endpointURL));
call.setOperationName(methodName);
call.setProperty(Call.NAMESPACE, "urn:greetingService1");
```

Then we create an object of type `Customer` and set the first name and last name:

```
// Create the customer object to set first and last names
Customer customer = new Customer();
customer.setFirstName(args[0]);
customer.setLastName(args[1]);
```

Now, we define a qualified name object for the `Customer` object and add `BeanSerializer` to the `Call` object:

```
// register the Customer class
QName qn = new QName("urn:greetingService1", "customer");
Class cls = Customer.class;
call.addSerializer(cls, qn, new BeanSerializer(cls));
```

Then we set the customer instance as the input parameter by setting the `Qname` object as shown below:

```
// Set the input parameter to Call object
call.addParameter("arg1", new XMLType(qn), Call.PARAM_MODE_IN);
```

That's it. We are set. Now we will invoke the service by passing the `customer` object as the input parameter:

```
// Invoke the service to get the response message as String object
String response = (String) call.invoke(new Object[] {
    customer
});

System.out.println("The Resonse:");
System.out.println(response);
} catch (Exception e) {
System.out.println(e);
}
}
}
```

Let's deploy the service using `deploy1.wsdd` deployment descriptor and access the service from the client, `AxisClient2`:

> **javac Customer.java**

> **javac GreetingService1.java**

> **java org.apache.axis.client.AdminClient deploy1.wsdd**
Processing file deploy1.wsdd

> **javac AxisClient2.java**

Adding Handlers to the Greeting Service

As said earlier, a handler is intended to perform specific processing on the input, output, and fault flow. We will write a handler class called `EventRecorder` to record the number of times that the greeting service has been called.

All application-specific handlers are required to extend the base class `BasicHandler`. The `BasicHandler` class is a utility class that implements the `Handler` interface to provide functionality to generate WSDL, to get the list of options and add more options to the service descriptor, get deployment information of the handler, and so on:

```
import java.io.*;
import java.util.Date;
import org.apache.axis.*;
import org.apache.axis.handlers.BasicHandler;

public class EventRecorder extends BasicHandler {
```

We define a static variable called `count` to record the number of times the service is accessed:

```
    static int count = 1;
```

All the handlers are required to implement the `invoke()` and `undo()` methods of the `Handler` interface. The Axis engine invokes the `invoke()` method by passing the context information. The `MessageContext` object contains the handler for the greeting service. We will get the file name, `greetingService.log`, from the service handler using the `getOption()` method provided by `BasicHandler`:

```
    public void invoke(MessageContext msgContext) throws AxisFault {
      try {
        Handler serviceHandler = msgContext.getServiceHandler();
        String filename = (String) getOption("filename");
```

If the file is not present, an exception is thrown to indicate to the user that it could not find the `greetingService.log` file. The `org.apache.axis.AxisFault` class maps an exception to SOAP fault:

```
if ((filename == null) || (filename.equals(""))) {
    throw new AxisFault("Server.NoLogFile", "Could not find log file",
                        null, null);
}
```

Then, we open an output stream to write the log information including the date, the name of the target service, and its access count to the log file:

```
FileOutputStream fos = new FileOutputStream(filename, true);

PrintWriter writer = new PrintWriter(fos);

String logMsg = new Date() + ": service "
                + msgContext.getTargetService() + " accessed "
                + count + " time(s).";

writer.println(logMsg);
count++;
writer.close();
} catch (Exception e) {
    throw new AxisFault(e);
}
}
```

All subclasses need to implement the `undo()` method. This method will be called when a fault occurs to 'undo' whatever the 'invoke' did:

```
public void undo(MessageContext msgContext) {}
}
```

The deployment descriptor is modified to include the details of the handler, and is named `deploy2.wsdd`.

The `<handler>` element defines a handler to be used in the service. The class attribute specifies the handler implementation class. The optional element, `<parameter>`, is provided to specify the file name for logging the information. The `<parameter>` element could be used to specify any other information required by the handler class. The name attribute of the `<handler>` element is used to add the handler object to the greeting service. The element `<requestFlow>` tells the Axis engine to direct all requests to the handler class before passing them to the service.

```
<deployment xmlns="http://xml.apache.org/axis/wsdd/"
            xmlns:java="http://xml.apache.org/axis/wsdd/providers/java">

  <handler name="track" type="java:EventRecorder">
    <parameter name="filename" value="greetingService.log"/>
  </handler>
```

```
    <service name="urn:greetingService1" provider="java:RPC">
      <requestFlow>
        <handler type="track"/>
      </requestFlow>
      <parameter name="className" value="GreetingService1"/>
      <parameter name="methodName" value="sayHello"/>

      <beanMapping qname="myNS:customer" xmlns:myNS="urn:greetingService1"
                   languageSpecificType="java:Customer"/>
    </service>
  </deployment>
```

Let's compile the `EventRecorder.java` file, deploy the service using `AdminClient` and the `deploy2.wsdd` deployment descriptor, and access the greeting service that we have deployed with the service name `urn:greetingService1` using `AxisClient2` as shown below:

```
> javac EventRecorder.java

> java org.apache.axis.client.AdminClient deploy2.wsdd
Processing file deploy2.wsdd

> java AxisClient2 James Bond
The Response:
Hi James.Bond! Have a Good Day!!

> java AxisClient2 Jackie Chan
The Response:
Hi Jackie.Chan! Have a Good Day!!
```

If you open the `greetingService.log` file, there will be an entry for the service with the access count as shown below:

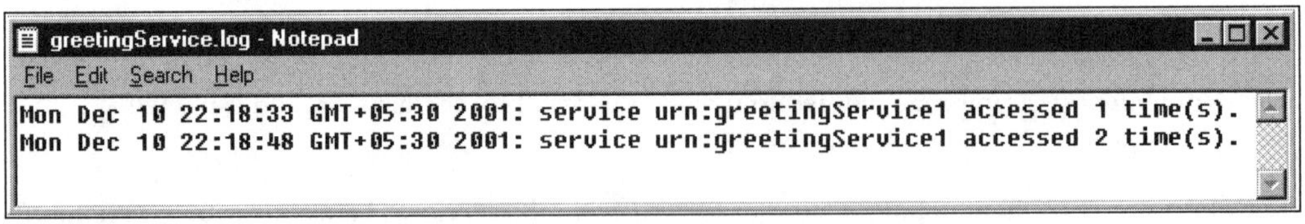

```
greetingService.log - Notepad
File  Edit  Search  Help
Mon Dec 10 22:18:33 GMT+05:30 2001: service urn:greetingService1 accessed 1 time(s).
Mon Dec 10 22:18:48 GMT+05:30 2001: service urn:greetingService1 accessed 2 time(s).
```

Sending a SOAP Message with Attachments

As mentioned in the earlier section of the *Features Available in alpha 3* section, Axis provides support for sending SOAP messages with attachments. We will modify the greeting service so that the `sayHello()` method can accept an object of type `DataHandler`. The `javax.activation.DataHandler` class encapsulates a `Data` object, and provides methods that act on that data. It provides a handle to the operations and data available on a data element.

Let us look into the `GreetingSevice2` class. The `sayHello()` method accepts an object of type `DataHandler` as input parameter:

```java
import java.net.URL;
import java.io.*;
import java.util.StringTokenizer;
import javax.activation.DataHandler;

public class GreetingService2 {

  public String sayHello(DataHandler dhandler) {

    String firstName = null;
    String lastName = null;
```

Then, we create an `InputStreamReader` object from the `DataHandler` object. This stream has the contents that are received from the client application. A `BufferedReader` object is created for reading the contents as a string:

```java
try {
  // Create the data for the attached file.
  InputStreamReader isr =
    new InputStreamReader(dhandler.getInputStream());
  BufferedReader br = new BufferedReader(isr);
  String line = null;
```

Then using the `StringTokenizer` class, we parse the string to get the values. Since the client application we are going to look at next sends the content in the format `firstname=somename;lastname=somename` after finishing with the service class, we loop through the tokenizer accordingly, to fetch the values shown below:

```java
      StringTokenizer sToken = new StringTokenizer(line, "=;");
      while (sToken.hasMoreTokens()) {

        // The content format: firstname=Billy;lastname=Bob
        sToken.nextToken();                        // This will be firstname
        firstName = sToken.nextToken().trim();     // This will be Billy
        sToken.nextToken();                        // This will be lastname
        lastName = sToken.nextToken().trim();      // This will be Bob
      }
    }
  } catch (IOException e) {
    System.out.println(e);
  }
```

Then we return the `String` object to the client application as we did in the other versions of the greeting service:

```java
    return "Hi " + firstName + "." + lastName + "!, Have a Good Day!!";
  }
}
```

We are done with the service. Let's look into the deployment descriptor for the greeting service, `deploy3.wsdd`. The initial part is to define the namespace. The service is described using the `<service>` element and the `parameter` attributes:

```
<deployment xmlns="http://xml.apache.org/axis/wsdd/"
            xmlns:java="http://xml.apache.org/axis/wsdd/providers/java">

  <service name="urn:greetingService2" provider="java:RPC" >
    <parameter name="className" value="GreetingService2"/>
    <parameter name="methodName" value="sayHello"/>
```

Then, we define the bean type mapping for the `DataHandler` object. Axis provides a `JAFDataHandlerSerializer` class for the serialization and a `JAFDataHandlerDeserializer` class for the de-serialization functionality:

```
<typeMapping
deserializer="org.apache.axis.encoding.JAFDataHandlerDeserializer$Factory"
  languageSpecificType="java:javax.activation.DataHandler"
  qname="ns1:DataHandler"
  serializer="org.apache.axis.encoding.JAFDataHandlerSerializer"
  xmlns:ns1="urn:greetingService2"/>
</service>
</deployment>
```

Before deploying the service, let's look at the client program. On the clientside, the client application passes the user information in a file as an attachment. Hence we will create a properties file called `user.properties` by specifying the first name as `Billy` and last name as `Bob`:

```
firstname=Billy;lastname=Bob
```

Now we can move on to the client application, `AxisClient3`. We create an object of type `DataHandler` by passing the file `user.properties` through a `FileDataSource` in the constructor:

```
import org.apache.axis.AxisFault;
import org.apache.axis.client.Call;
import org.apache.axis.client.Service;
import org.apache.axis.encoding.XMLType;
import org.apache.axis.encoding.JAFDataHandlerSerializer;
import org.apache.axis.encoding.JAFDataHandlerDeserializer;
import javax.activation.DataHandler;
import javax.activation.FileDataSource;
import javax.xml.rpc.namespace.QName;

import java.net.URL;

public class AxisClient3 {

  public static void main(String[] args) {

    try {

      // Create the data for the attached file.
      String fileName = "user.properties";
      DataHandler dhandler = new DataHandler(new FileDataSource(fileName));
```

Then, we define the endpoint URL for the target service and the method name:

```
String endpointURL =
   "http://localhost:8080/axis/services/urn:greetingService2";
String methodName = "sayHello";
```

Now we create a `Call` object and set the values, like target endpoint address, operation name, and so on:

```
Service service = new Service();

// Create a Call object and set the parameterss
Call call = (Call) service.createCall();
call.setTargetEndpointAddress(new java.net.URL(endpointURL));
call.setOperationName(methodName);
call.setProperty(Call.NAMESPACE, "urn:greetingService2");
```

Then we define a qualified name called qname of type `javax.xml.rpc.namespace.QName` for the `DataHandler` object:

```
QName qname = new QName("urn:greetingService2", "DataHandler");
```

Axis provides a serializer known as `JAFDataHandlerSerializer` for handling the serialization of `DataHandler` objects. It also has a factory method called `getFactory()` that returns a `DeserializerFactory` for the de-serialization of `DataHandler` objects:

```
call.addSerializer(DataHandler.class, qname,
                   new JAFDataHandlerSerializer());

call.addDeserializerFactory(qname, DataHandler.class,
                            JAFDataHandlerDeserializer.getFactory());
```

Now add the parameter to the `Call` object. The qualified name is added as an XML data type:

```
call.addParameter("source", new XMLType(qname), Call.PARAM_MODE_IN);
```

And finally invoke the service by passing the `DataHandler` object and print the response on the console:

```
   String response = (String) call.invoke(new Object[] {
      dhandler
   });
   System.out.println("The Response:");
   System.out.println(response);
 } catch (AxisFault fault) {
   System.out.println(fault.toString());
 } catch (Exception e) {    // Any IO Exception
   System.out.println(e);
 }
   }
}
```

537

Now we compile the `GreetingService2.java` file and deploy it using `deploy3.wsdd` and `AdminClient`. Compile the `AxisClient3.java` file for the client and run the class file. You can see that the service returns a greeting message to Billy Bob is displayed in the console by the client application:

```
> javac GreetingService2.java

> java org.apache.axis.client.AdminClient deploy3.wsdd
Processing file deploy3.wsdd
<Admin>Done processing</Admin>

> javac AxisClient3.java

> java Axisclient3
The Response:
Hi Billy.Bob! Have a Good Day!!
```

Generating a WSDL Document for the Service

The WSDL document can be obtained by appending `"?WSDL"` to the end of URL of the deployed service.

For example, the WSDL document for the `GreetingService` that is deployed as `.jws` can be obtained by entering the following URL in any browser http://localhost:8080/axis/GreetingService.jws?wsdl.

And for the greeting service, `urn:greetingService`, that we deployed using the deployment descriptor, `deploy.wsdd`, the URL for generating the WSDL document is http://localhost:8080/axis/services/urn:greetingService?wsdl.

If you access the service URL in a browser, you'll see a message indicating that the endpoint is an Axis service, and that you should usually access it using SOAP. However, if we append `?wsdl` to the end of the URL, Axis will automatically generate a service description for the deployed service, and return it as XML in your browser.

The WSDL document may be saved or used as input to proxy generation. Axis also provides a utility tool to generate Java proxy classes for the service. You can find the complete WSDL document in the file `greetingService.wsdl` at `\javawebservices\Ch14`.

Generating Stubs and Skeletons with Wsdl2java

Axis provides the tool `org.apache.axis.wsdl.Wsdl2java` to generate proxy classes in Java from a WSDL document. Hence, the service requestors (clients) can access a service provided by the service provider by reading the WSDL file and generating the proxy classes dynamically. The `Wsdl2java` tool also generates a test case class for testing the web service. We can also generate the skeleton classes from a given WSDL document of a web service.

The basic invocation to use the tool looks like this:

```
> java org.apache.axis.wsdl.Wsdl2java (url-to-wsdl-file)
```

Let's see more details on generating the Java classes using the `Wsdl2java` tool.

Generating Stubs

A **stub** is a Java class that has the same interface as that of a remote web service. It stands in as a proxy for the remote service, letting us call it exactly as if it were a local object. The generated stub class contains the endpoint URL, namespace, or parameter arrays, which are involved in dynamic invocation via the `Service` and `Call` classes.

We will generate the stub classes for the greeting service as shown below. The `-v` option is provided for verbose output and `-o` is to specify the output directory. We will create a sub directory called `stubs` in `\javawebservices\Ch14` to place all the stub classes. By default, the `Wsdl2java` tool creates a directory called `localhost` and places all the generated classes as shown below:

The `Wsdl2java` tool generates the following classes:

- ❑ `GreetingService.java` – This interface represents the port type. There will be an interface for each referenced `PortType` in the WSDL. These interfaces are the ones you will actually use to call the remote methods, as they contain the operations described in the WSDL.

- ❑ `UrnGreetingServiceSoapBindingStub.java` – This stub class implements the interface, and contains the code that turns the method invocations into SOAP calls using the `Service` and `Call` classes.

- ❑ `UrnGreetingServiceService.java` - This service class serves as a factory for obtaining the stub instance. The `Service` class will by default make a `Stub`, which points to the endpoint URL that is described in the WSDL file.

The client program to access the greeting service by using the stub classes is shown below. The Java file, `Client.java` is located in `\javawebservices\Ch14\stubs`:

```java
public class Client {

  public static void main(String [] args) throws Exception
  {
    // Make a service (PortType factory)
    localhost.UrnGreetingServiceService service = new
                              localhost.UrnGreetingServiceService();

    // Now use the service to get a PortType that we can call.
    localhost.GreetingService port = service.getUrnGreetingService();

    // Make the actual call
    String ret = port.sayHello("Mike", "Myers");

    System.out.println("Response is : " + ret);
  }
}
```

Before running the `Client` class, we need to compile the stub classes generated by `Wsdl2java` utility tool. Let's compile the Java code for the stub classes and client application and run the `Client` class as shown below:

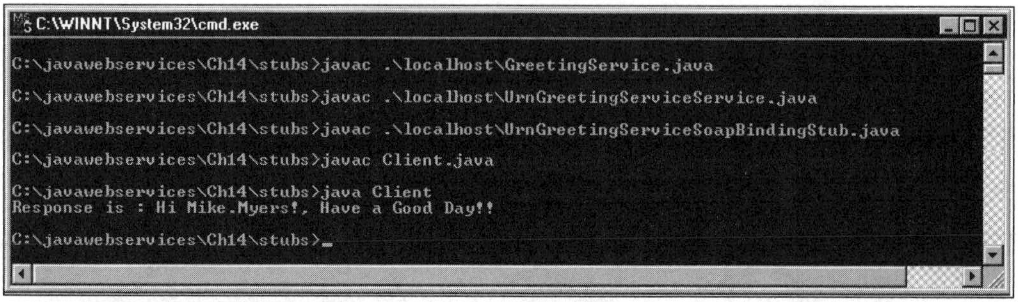

```
C:\WINNT\System32\cmd.exe

C:\javawebservices\Ch14\stubs>javac .\localhost\GreetingService.java

C:\javawebservices\Ch14\stubs>javac .\localhost\UrnGreetingServiceService.java

C:\javawebservices\Ch14\stubs>javac .\localhost\UrnGreetingServiceSoapBindingStub.java

C:\javawebservices\Ch14\stubs>javac Client.java

C:\javawebservices\Ch14\stubs>java Client
Response is : Hi Mike.Myers!, Have a Good Day!!

C:\javawebservices\Ch14\stubs>_
```

Generating Skeleton Classes

A **skeleton class** represents the server-side framework. You'd want to make a skeleton if you had a WSDL description of a service, which you'd like to implement. To make skeleton classes, we just specify the `--skeleton` option to `Wsdl2java`. For instance, to replicate the greeting service, the command will be as shown below:

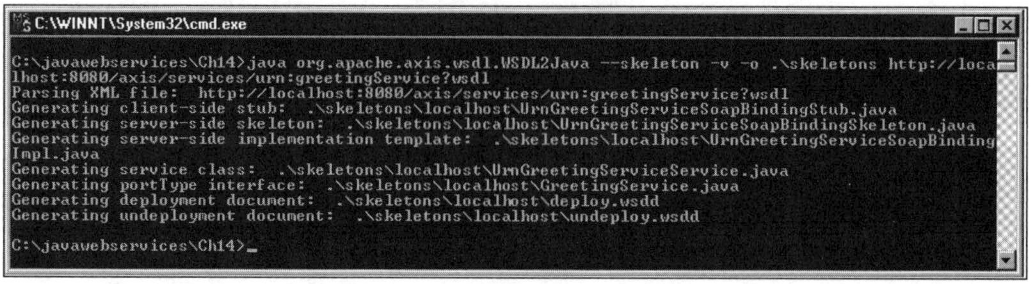

```
C:\WINNT\System32\cmd.exe

C:\javawebservices\Ch14>java org.apache.axis.wsdl.WSDL2Java --skeleton -v -o .\skeletons http://loca
lhost:8080/axis/services/urn:greetingService?wsdl
Parsing XML file:  http://localhost:8080/axis/services/urn:greetingService?wsdl
Generating client-side stub:  .\skeletons\localhost\UrnGreetingServiceSoapBindingStub.java
Generating server-side skeleton:  .\skeletons\localhost\UrnGreetingServiceSoapBindingSkeleton.java
Generating server-side implementation template:  .\skeletons\localhost\UrnGreetingServiceSoapBinding
Impl.java
Generating service class:  .\skeletons\localhost\UrnGreetingServiceService.java
Generating portType interface:  .\skeletons\localhost\GreetingService.java
Generating deployment document:  .\skeletons\localhost\deploy.wsdd
Generating undeployment document:  .\skeletons\localhost\undeploy.wsdd

C:\javawebservices\Ch14>_
```

There are a number of classes produced by the skeleton generator we need to look into as shown below:

These classes are located at `\javawebservices\Ch14\skeletons\localhost`:

❑ `UrnGreetingServiceSoapBindingSkeleton.java` – This is the class that we need to deploy as an Axis service

❑ `UrnGreetingServiceSoapBindingImpl.java` – This is the framework class (base interface for the service) that will be implemented by the service classes

❑ `deploy.wsdd` – The deployment descriptor required for the `AdminClient` to deploy the service

❑ `undeploy.wsdd` – The deployment descriptor required for the `AdminClient` to undeploy the service

Using the Axis TCP Monitor (tcpmon)

Axis provides a utility class known as tcpmon for monitoring messages flowing through the Axis engine by acting as a TCP router. This is similar to TCPTunnelGui provided by the Apache SOAP implementation. tcpmon allows us to see the TCP messages move between the client and server. This tool allows us to examine the SOAP on-the-wire protocol and even check various SOAP implementations for compatibility.

Start Tomcat server by executing the startup.bat batch file located at %TOMCAT_HOME%\bin. Tomcat starts up on port 8080 by default. Then, start the utility in a separate window by running the class file from the command prompt as shown below:

```
> java org.apache.axis.utils.tcpmon
```

You will see a window with the title, TCPMonitor. By default the Listener radio button is selected. The other option, Proxy, is used to specify the details of a HTTP proxy server. Enter the values of Listen Port #, Target Hostname, and Target Port # for the listener as shown in the following screenshot. tcpmon will monitor for incoming requests on the listen port, the target host is where it will forward such connections, and the target port is the port number on the target machine which should be 'tunneled' to.

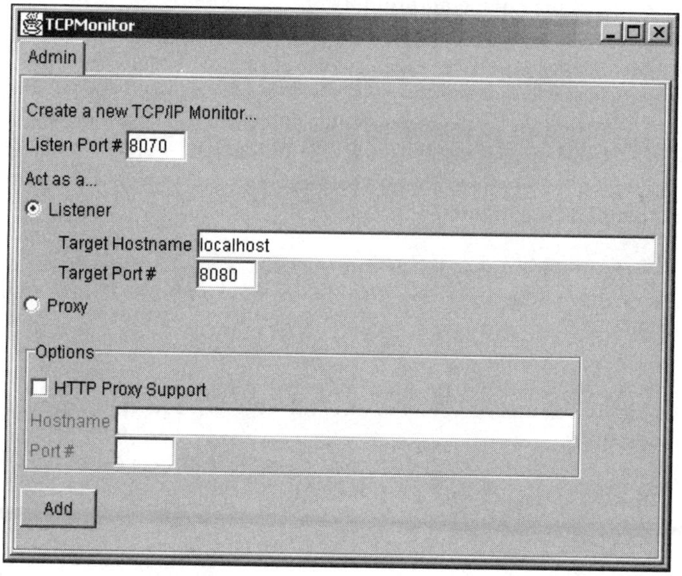

Then click on the Add button. A new window will be displayed with a new additional tab titled Port 8070. Click on the tab and a window appears showing the monitor listening for requests on the specified port:

You could also come to this window directly by passing the values of the listening port, target host name, and target port from the command prompt:

```
> java org.apache.axis.utils.tcpmon 8070 localhost 8080
```

At this point, the monitor is acting as an intermediary between the client and port 8080, waiting for requests on port 8070. Once it receives a request, it will pass it on to the listener at port 8080. If you see that the request and response windows are one on the top on another in the window, you can click on the **Switch Layout** button at the bottom.

The client we are going to test the monitor with is `AxisClient4.java`, and is basically the same as `AxisClient3.java`, except the `endpointURL`. This refers to port 8070 instead of the Tomcat default port of 8080.

We have changed the port number to 8070 to direct the SOAP request to `tcpmon` which is listening for TCP requests on port 8070.

```
String endpointURL =
    "http://localhost:8070/axis/services/urn:greetingService2";
```

Now we will run the client by passing the values of first name and last name as `Mike` and `Myers`:

Now, each time the client invokes the greeting service, a SOAP connection to the local port is made. The SOAP request appears in the Request panel, and the response from the server is in the Response panel. tcpmon keeps a log of all request-response pairs, and allows you to view any particular pair by selecting an entry in the top panel. You may also remove selected, or all, entries, or choose to save to a file for later viewing.

The left-hand pane shows the outgoing SOAP request comprising a standard HTTP header followed by an XML document that represents the client service invocation and the right-hand pane shows the resulting SOAP response consisting of a standard HTTP header followed by an XML document that is the server response.

The Resend button will re-send the request you are currently viewing, and record a new response. This is particularly handy in that you can edit the XML in the request window before re-sending the SOAP request, and we can use this feature for testing the effects of different XML on SOAP servers.

The tcpmon tool also has features for specifying the HTTP proxy. It accepts the hostname and port of the proxy server as shown in the first diagram in this section. This feature is very handy in HTTP tunneling scenarios.

Features Expected in the Next Versions

In this closing section to our introduction to Axis, we will look at the features that will be implemented in newer versions, since this chapter was based on alpha 3. We can expect to see features such as:

❑ **Full support for SOAP with attachments specification** – Though the alpha 3 version of Axis provides basic support for SOAP messages with attachments, support for base 64 transfer encoding and quoted printable types is not yet provided.

❑ **Support for multi-dimensional arrays** – Support for sparse arrays is not yet implemented. In a sparse array, each element representing a member value contains a enc:position attribute that indicates its position with in the array. For more details on sparse arrays, refer to *Section 4.4.2.2* of *SOAP Version 1.2 Part 2: Adjuncts* at http://www.w3.org/TR/2001/WD-soap12-part2-20011002/.

❑ **Support for the SOAP actor attribute** – Axis version alpha 3 doesn't support the SOAP actor attribute. For information on SOAP actor please refer to *Section 2.2* of *SOAP Version 1.2 Part 1: Messaging Framework* at http://www.w3.org/TR/2001/WD-soap12-part1-20011002/.

❑ **WSDL support** – Though the current version of Axis supports generation of WSDL documents, the support for generating complex type definitions in WSDL is not yet provided.

❑ **Support for SMTP protocol** – Axis alpha 3 provides an implementation of SOAP over the HTTP protocol. The SOAP implementation over the SMTP protocol is not yet implemented.

Summary

We started discussing Axis by looking into some of the key features. Then we discussed the features available in the current release at this time, alpha 3. We have discussed the architecture and flow of components. We looked into WSDDs and their usage in chainable and web service deployment services.

Then, we developed a simple web service to demonstrate the various features provided by Axis. In the course of the example, we discussed the following features:

❑ Deploying a service as a JWS service

❑ Deploying a service using AdminClient and a deployment descriptor

❑ Naming the input parameters and explicitly specifying the return type of a method

❑ Passing custom data type input parameters

❑ Defining a Handler object for the service

❑ Sending a SOAP message with attachments

❑ Generating a WSDL for the deployed service

❑ Generating stubs and skeletons for the service using Wsdl2java tool

❑ Using tcpmon to monitor the request and response messages for the sample service

And finally we looked into the features that are expected in the next releases of Axis.

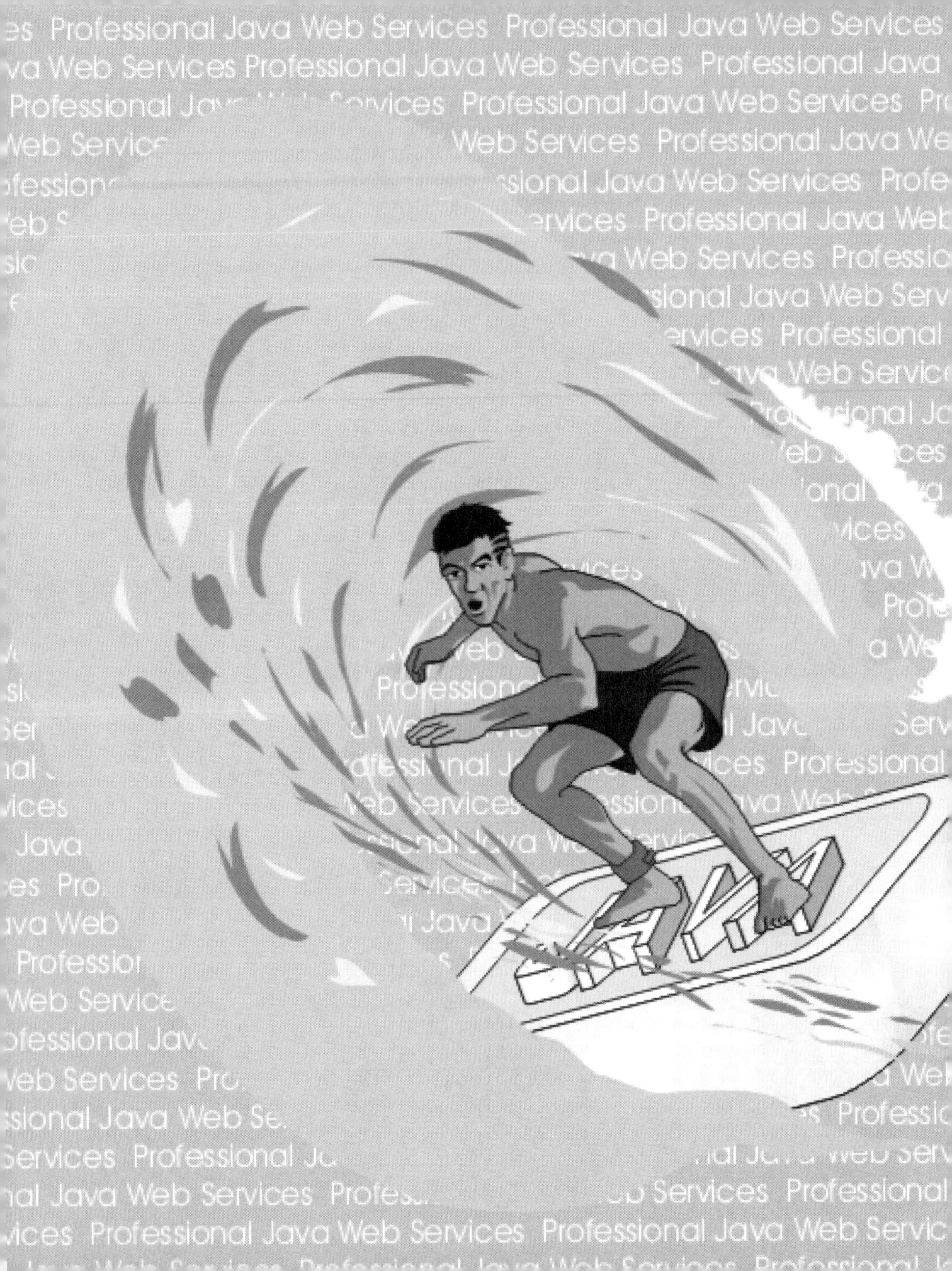
Professional Java Web Services

Installing CapeConnect Three

In this appendix, we will install CapeClear's CapeConnect Three and integrate it with WebLogic server 6.1.

Here are the steps and the accompanying screens for each step in the installation process.

❑ **Download Information**
To download the free evaluation installation for CapeConnect Three, go to
http://www.capeclear.com/products/download/index.shtml and follow the instructions for
downloading it.

❑ **Running the Installation Program**
Double click the self-running installation program that you downloaded from the above site.

Step 1 – Introduction Screen

The first step in the installation program brings up the information screen as shown below. Click on the
Next button.

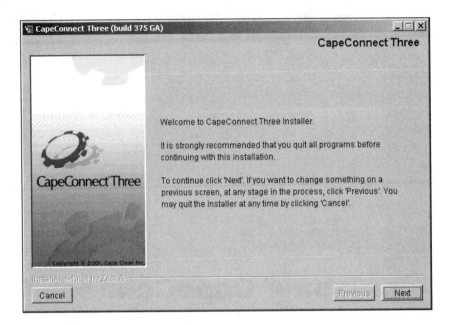

Step 2 – License Agreement

Accept the terms of the License Agreement and click on Next button.

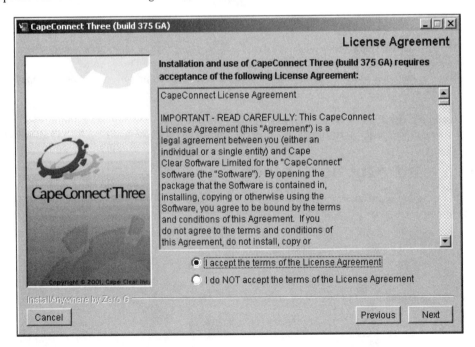

Step 3 – Choose the Installation Directory

Select the directory in which you want to install CapeConnect Three. We have selected
`c:\CapeClear\CapeConnectThree`.

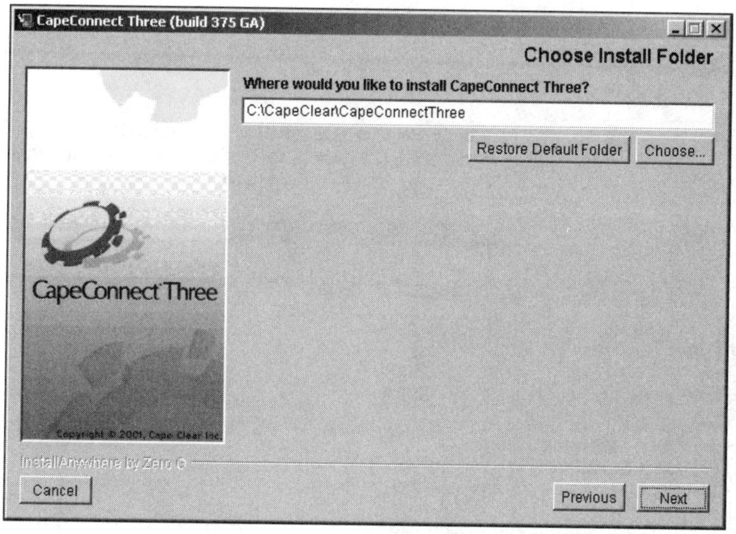

Step 4 – Choose Shortcut Location

CapeConnect Three can create a **program group** in which useful shortcuts are placed, in order to start
the CapeConnect Server, amongst other things. Select a new Program Group CapeConnect Three as
shown below. Click on the Next button to continue.

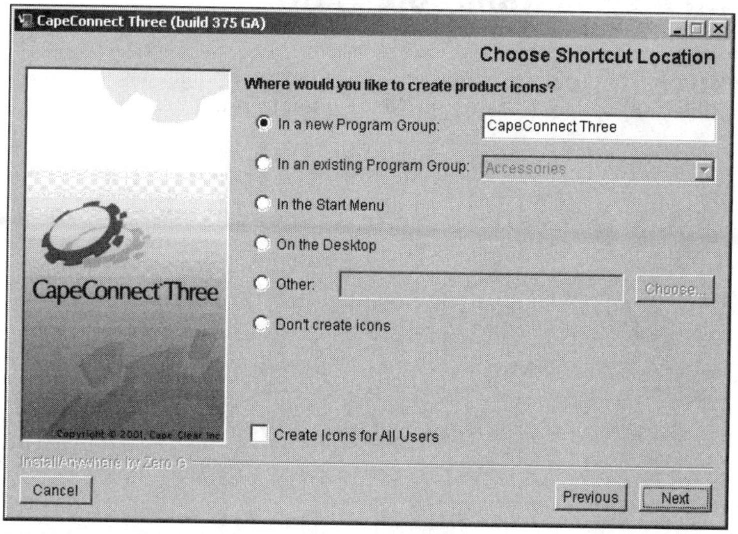

Step 5 – Choose Java Virtual Machine

CapeConnect Three requires that a **Java Virtual Machine** be installed on your computer. As shown below, the installation program detects all the JVMs present on your machine. You can select a valid JVM and then click on the Next button to continue.

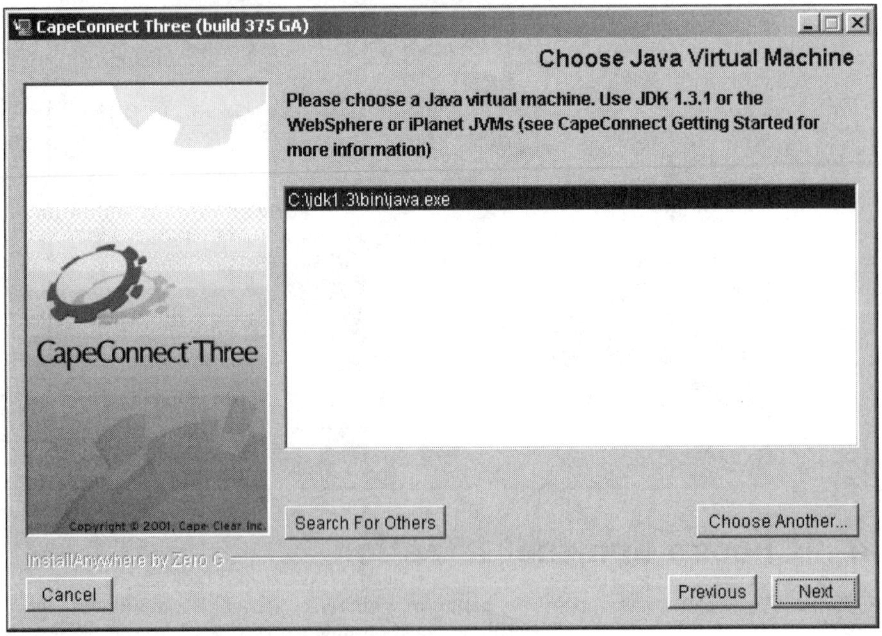

Step 6 – Choose Installation Option

In this dialog, you can decide which particular components of the CapeConnect Three platform you wish to install. If you are planning on running everything on a single machine, it is advisable to select the Full Install (default) option. Click on the Next button to continue.

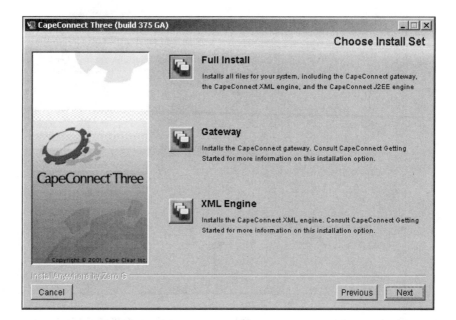

Step 7 – Select Application Server to Integrate with

CapeConnect Three integrates with several popular J2EE Application Servers such as BEA WebLogic, IBM Websphere, and iPlanet, amongst others. You should select Integrate with WebLogic 6.1 since we will be using CapeConnect Three in conjunction with WebLogic 6.1 in Chapter 8. Click on the Next button to continue.

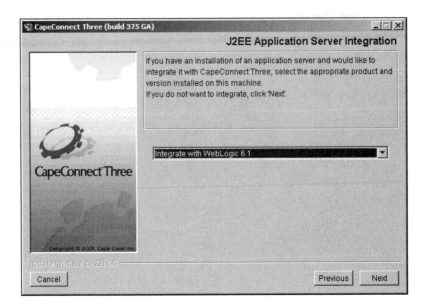

Step 8 – Select the Home Directory for BEA WebLogic 6.1

Since we selected the option of installing CapeConnect Three with WebLogic 6.1, we need to provide CapeConnect Three with the home directory in which WebLogic 6.1 installation has been done. By default the WebLogic 6.1 installation will be done in `C:\bea\wlserver6.1` directory. Provide this directory name or the appropriate home directory for the WebLogic 6.1 installation on your machine. Click on the **Next** button.

Step 9 – CORBA Integration

CapeConnect Three also provides integration with CORBA. Since we are not using this feature, do not select this option. Click on the **Next** button to continue.

Step 10 – UDDI Host

CapeConnect Three also provides a local UDDI implementation for use with your Web Services. In this option, it asks you for the hostname of your UDDI server. You can leave this as **localhost** and click on the **Next** button to continue.

Step 11 – Select UDDI Password

To access the UDDI implementation, especially when you are using the publishing functions of UDDI, you need to select a password to access the UDDI server. Provide a password of your choice here. Click on the Next button to continue.

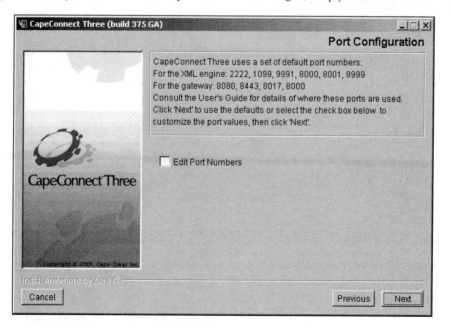

Step 12 – Port Configuration

CapeConnect Three consists of several servers such as the Log Server, the XMLEngine, and the Gateway, amongst others. For this it needs to use certain ports on your machine. The default ports that it uses are shown below. If you feel that some of these ports are in use by other programs on your machine, then you may wish to change the port numbers by selecting the **Edit Port Numbers** option and clicking on **Next**. If you wish to leave the port numbers unchanged, simply click on **Next**.

Step 13 – Final Confirmation

As a final check, the CapeConnect Three installation program displays the list of options that you selected, such as the installation directory, the JVM, and the port numbers. If you wish to change any of these parameters, click on the Previous button to return to previous stages in the installation process. If everything looks good, then click on the Install button.

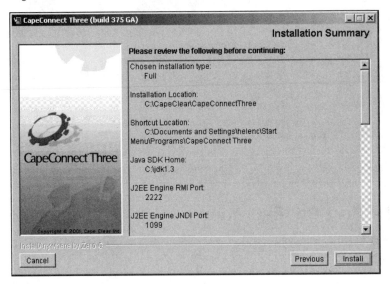

Step 14 – Copying Files

Finally, the CapeConnect Three installation program copies the files and sets up the program.

Setting Up CapeConnect with WebLogic

Before we configure CapeConnect and WebLogic to work with each other, it is necessary to establish which directories these products are already installed in:

For the purposes of our example, the root directory for CapeConnect Three is `C:\CapeClear\CapeConnectThree`, and the root directory for WebLogic Server 6.1 is `C:\bea\wlserver6.1`.

Configure WebLogic

❑   Modify the `StartWeblogic.cmd` file in the `C:\bea\wlserver6.1\config\mydomain` directory so that the `capeconnect.jar` and `common.jar` files are in the WebLogic classpath. Alter the `StartWeblogic.cmd` file as shown below:

```
set CCTHREE_HOME=C:\CapeClear\CapeConnectThree

set CLASSPATH=.;%CCTHREE_HOME%\lib\capeconnect.jar;%CCTHREE_HOME%\lib\common.jar;
.\lib\weblogic_sp.jar;.\lib\weblogic.jar;.\samples\eval\cloudscape\lib\cloudscape.
jar;C:\javawebservices\Chap08\wroxcuisine\xml-jars\jdom.jar;C:\javawebservices\
Chap08\wroxcuisine\xml-jars\xalan.jar; C:\javawebservices\Chap08\wroxcuisine\xml-
jars\xerces.jar
```

Configure CapeConnect

When you install CapeConnect, it asks you if you want to integrate with a particular application server. If you select WebLogic, it will complete the necessary steps for communicating with WebLogic. You can then skip the next section on *Setting up WebLogic Integration Manually* and proceed to *Identifying the WebLogic Server to CapeConnect Three*.

Setting Up WebLogic Integration Manually

However, if you did not select the option of integration of WebLogic and you decide that you need to configure CapeConnect Three for communication with WebLogic 6.1, you will need to perform the following steps:

Make the following entry in the `C:\CapeClear\CapeConnectThree\console\conf\console.properties` file:

```
com.capeclear.capeconnect.console.env.WL_HOME=C:\\bea\\wlserver6.1
```

Now, add the following permissions to the `C:\CapeClear\CapeConnectThree\xmlengine\conf\server.policy`.

> *These Java security permissions will enable the CapeConnect software to be assigned appropriate rights to communication to the WebLogic Server instance, which is assumed to be running between the ports of 1-9000. Note that if you had selected the option of integrating WebLogic 6.1 with CapeConnect Three during the installation process, you would not need to follow these steps.*

```
grant codeBase "file:${WL_HOME}/-" {
permission java.io.FilePermission "${WL_HOME}${/}-", "read,write,delete,execute";
permission java.net.SocketPermission "localhost:1-9000",
"connect,accept,listen,resolve";
permission java.net.SocketPermission "localhost", "connect,accept,listen,resolve";
permission java.awt.AWTPermission "accessClipboard";
permission java.awt.AWTPermission "accessEventQueue";
permission java.awt.AWTPermission "showWindowWithoutWarningBanner";
permission java.io.SerializablePermission "enableSubclassImplementation";
permission java.io.SerializablePermission "enableSubstitution";
permission java.lang.RuntimePermission "accessClassInPackage.*";
permission java.lang.RuntimePermission "accessDeclaredMembers.*";
permission java.lang.RuntimePermission "createClassLoader";
permission java.lang.RuntimePermission "createSecurityManager";
permission java.lang.RuntimePermission "defineClassInPackage.*";
permission java.lang.RuntimePermission "exitVM";
permission java.lang.RuntimePermission "getClassLoader";
permission java.lang.RuntimePermission "createClassLoader";
permission java.lang.RuntimePermission "getProtectionDomain";
permission java.lang.RuntimePermission "loadLibrary.*";
permission java.lang.RuntimePermission "modifyThread";
permission java.lang.RuntimePermission "modifyThreadGroup";
permission java.lang.RuntimePermission "readFileDescriptor";
permission java.lang.RuntimePermission "setContextClassLoader";
permission java.lang.RuntimePermission "setFactory";
permission java.lang.RuntimePermission "setIO";
permission java.lang.RuntimePermission "setProtectionDomain";
permission java.lang.RuntimePermission "setSecurityManager";
permission java.lang.RuntimePermission "writeFileDescriptor";
permission java.lang.reflect.ReflectPermission "suppressAccessChecks";
permission java.net.NetPermission "requestPasswordAuthentication";
permission java.net.NetPermission "setDefaultAuthenticator";
permission java.security.SecurityPermission "getPolicy";
permission java.security.SecurityPermission "setPolicy";
permission java.util.PropertyPermission "*", "read,write";
};
```

Finally, add the following line to the `start-capeconnect.bat` file in the
`C:\CapeClear\CapeConnectThree\bin` directory:

```
set SYSLIB=%SVRHOME%\\lib
set DRIVERLIB=%SYSLIB%\\drivers
set WL_HOME=C:\bea\wlserver6.1
```

Identifying the WebLogic Server to CapeConnect Three

When you deploy your Enterprise JavaBeans in the WebLogic Server, CapeConnect needs to have information about your WebLogic Server. More specifically, it needs to know how to look up the EJBs in WebLogic Server (for instance, using the JNDI lookup).

So you need to identify your WebLogic Server instance to CapeConnect by adding a `<server>` element in the `servermap.xml` file in the `C:\CapeClear\CapeConnectThree\xmlengine\conf` directory as shown below:

```
<!-- Registered servers -->
<servers>

    <server name="weblogic_1" type="weblogic61" >
    <!-- JNDI lookup properties for this server -->
    <lookup>
        <property name="java.naming.factory.initial"
          value="weblogic.jndi.WLInitialContextFactory"/>
        <property name="java.naming.provider.url"
          value="t3://localhost:7001"/>
    </lookup>
    </server>
    ...
```

Make sure that this entry is present in the `servermap.xml` file, since we will be using this server value to configure our `WroxCuisineService` web service. If you have WebLogic Server running on another port, please modify the port value `7001` appropriately.

Verifying the Installation

Please restart your WebLogic Server to set the CapeConnect JARs in the `CLASSPATH`. To start the CapeConnect Platform, we need to first start the CapeConnect Console Program. The CapeConnect Console Program can be used to do a variety of tasks like

❑ Starting the CapeConnect services like Log Server, Gateway Server and so on

❑ Invoking the Deployment Wizard to configure your Web Services within CapeConnect

To start the CapeConnect Three Console Program, first start the **CapeConnect Console Server** from the start up menu.

Once the CapeConnect Console Server has started successfully, start the CapeConnect Console Program from the Program Group.

You will see the CapeConnect console window as shown below:

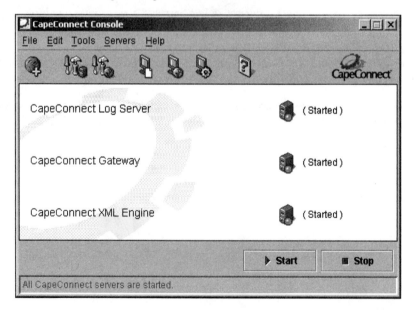

Click on the Start button, this will start the Log Server, the Gateway, and the CapeConnect XML Engine. Make sure that all the lights are green (started) as shown below:

At this moment, it is vital to check that CapeConnect Three has been configured correctly with WebLogic 6.1. To check this, click on **Servers/XML Engine Status**. This will bring up a status window as shown below. Notice that the log window indicates that it detected a version of WebLogic at the `WL_HOME` directory that was specified in the `console/conf/console.properties` file. If the logs indicate that no WebLogic installation has been found, please check the configuration settings as described in the previous section.

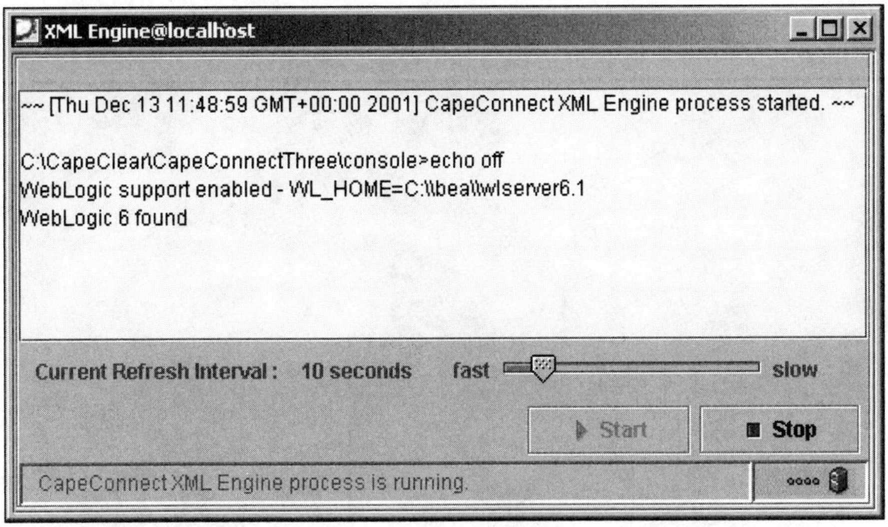

The message **WebLogic 6 found** is not inaccurate, even though we have integrated it with WebLogic 6.1 Server. Congratulations, you have now configured CapeConnect Three to run with WebLogic 6.1!

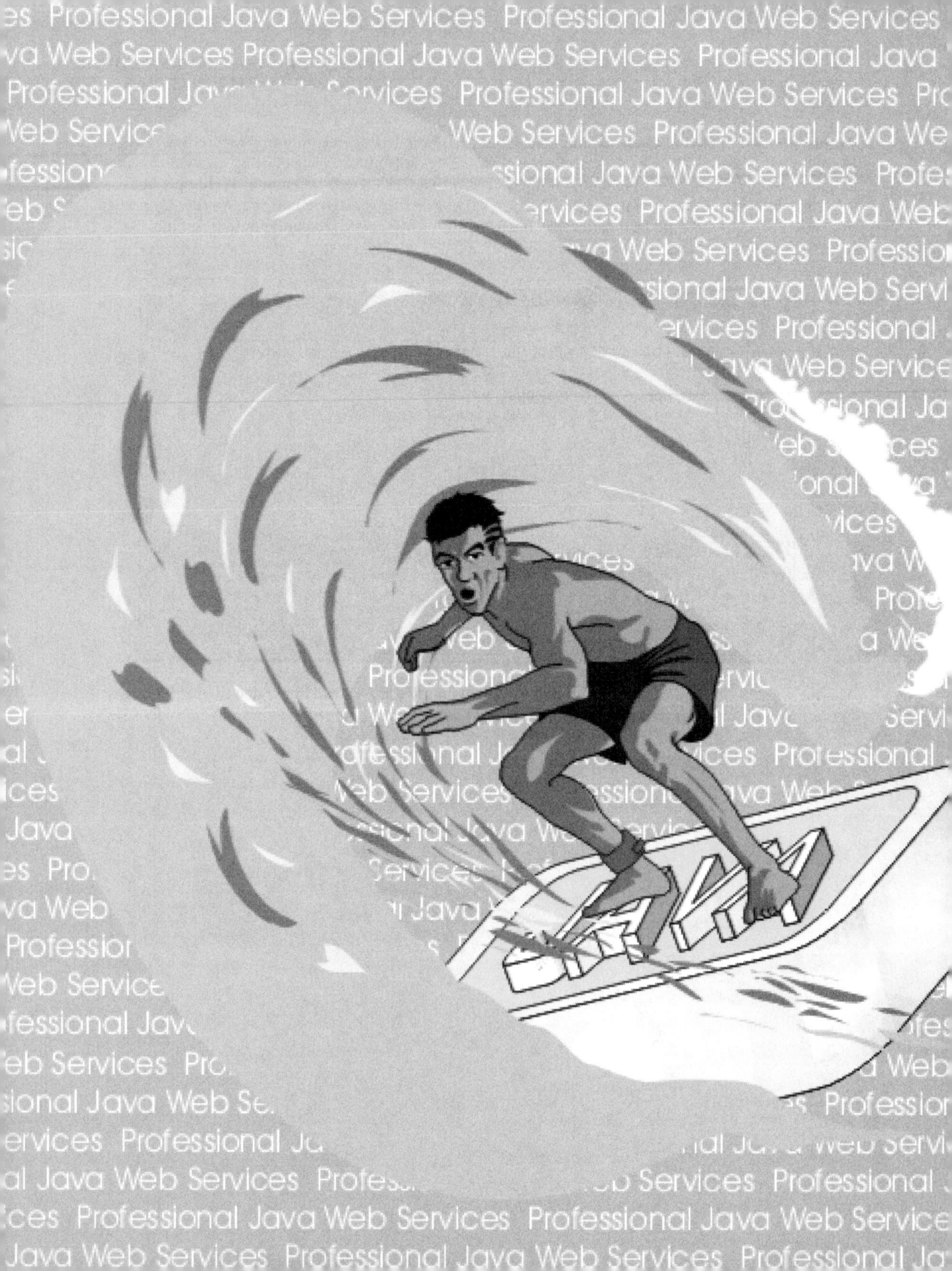
Professional Java Web Services

Installing CapeStudio 1.1

This appendix demonstrates how to download and set up CapeStudio 1.1.

❑ **Download Information**
To download the installable for CapeStudio 1.1, go to
http://www.capeclear.com/products/download/capestudio/index.shtml and follow the instructions
for downloading it.

❑ **Running the Installation Program**
Double click the self-running installation program that you downloaded from the above site.

Given below are the steps and the accompanying screens at each step in the installation process.

Step 1 - Introduction Screen

The first step in the installation program brings up the information screen as shown below. Click on the
Next button.

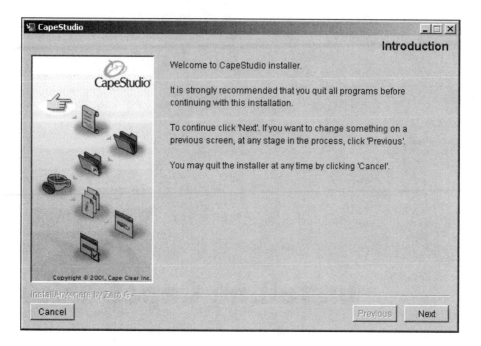

Step 2 – License Agreement

Accept the terms of the License Agreement and click on the Next button.

Step 3 – Choose the Installation Directory

Select the directory in which you want to install CapeStudio. We have selected
`c:\CapeClear\CapeStudio`.

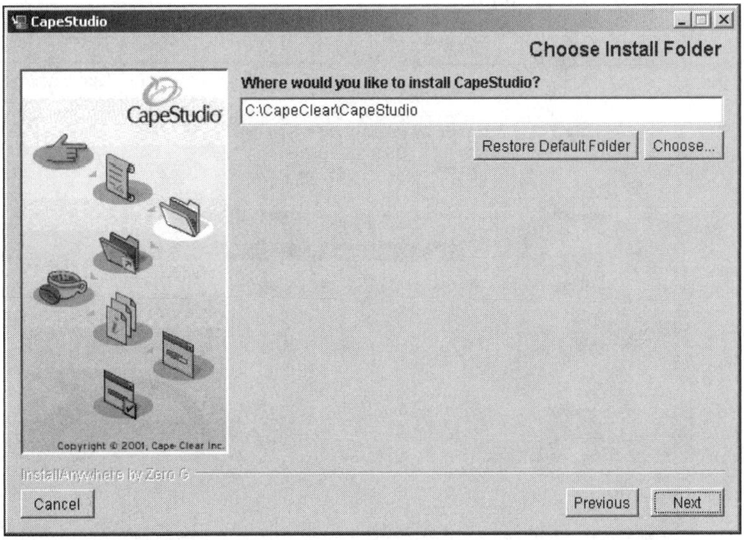

Step 4 – Choose Shortcut Location

CapeStudio can create a program group in which the shortcut to start CapeStudio is placed. Select the existing **CapeConnect Three** as shown below. Click on the **Next** button to continue.

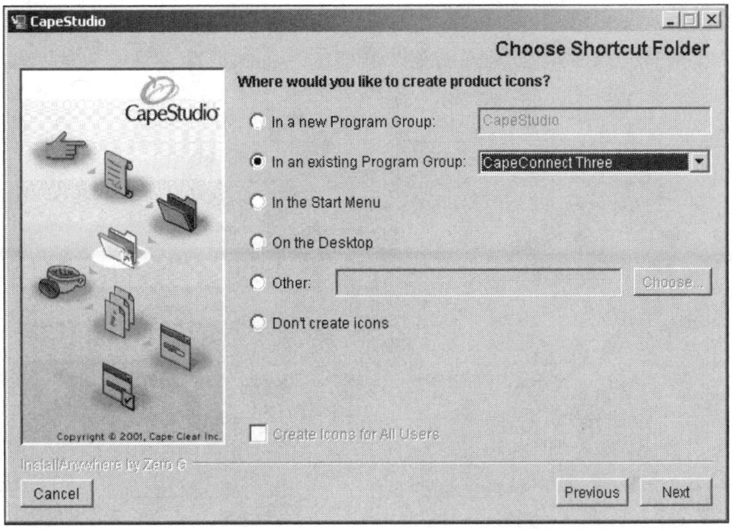

Step 5 – Choose Java Virtual Machine

CapeStudio requires that a Java Virtual Machine be installed on your computer. As shown below, the installation program detects all the JVMs present on your machine. You can select a valid JVM and then click on the Next button to continue.

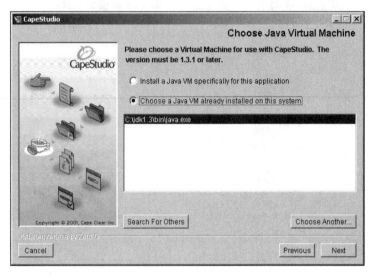

Step 6 – Final Confirmation

As a final check, CapeStudio installation program displays a list of options that you have selected, such as the installation directory, and the JVM. If you wish to change any of these parameters, click on the Previous button to reach the previous steps of the installation process. If everything looks fine, click on the Install button.

Step 7 – Copy Files

Finally the CapeStudio installation program copies the files into the appropriate directories.

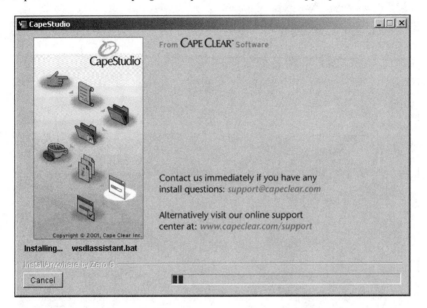

It displays a message if the installation completed successfully.

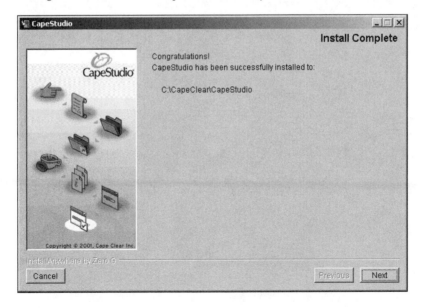

Note that it reminds you about certain environment entries that might have changed. You are advised to take appropriate action as shown below:

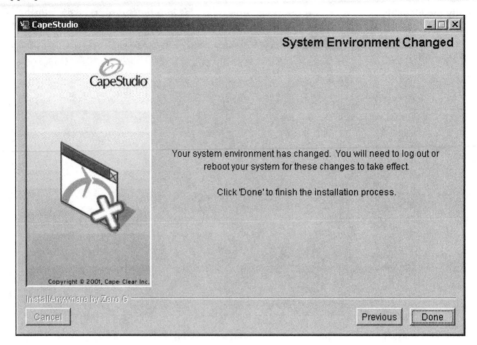

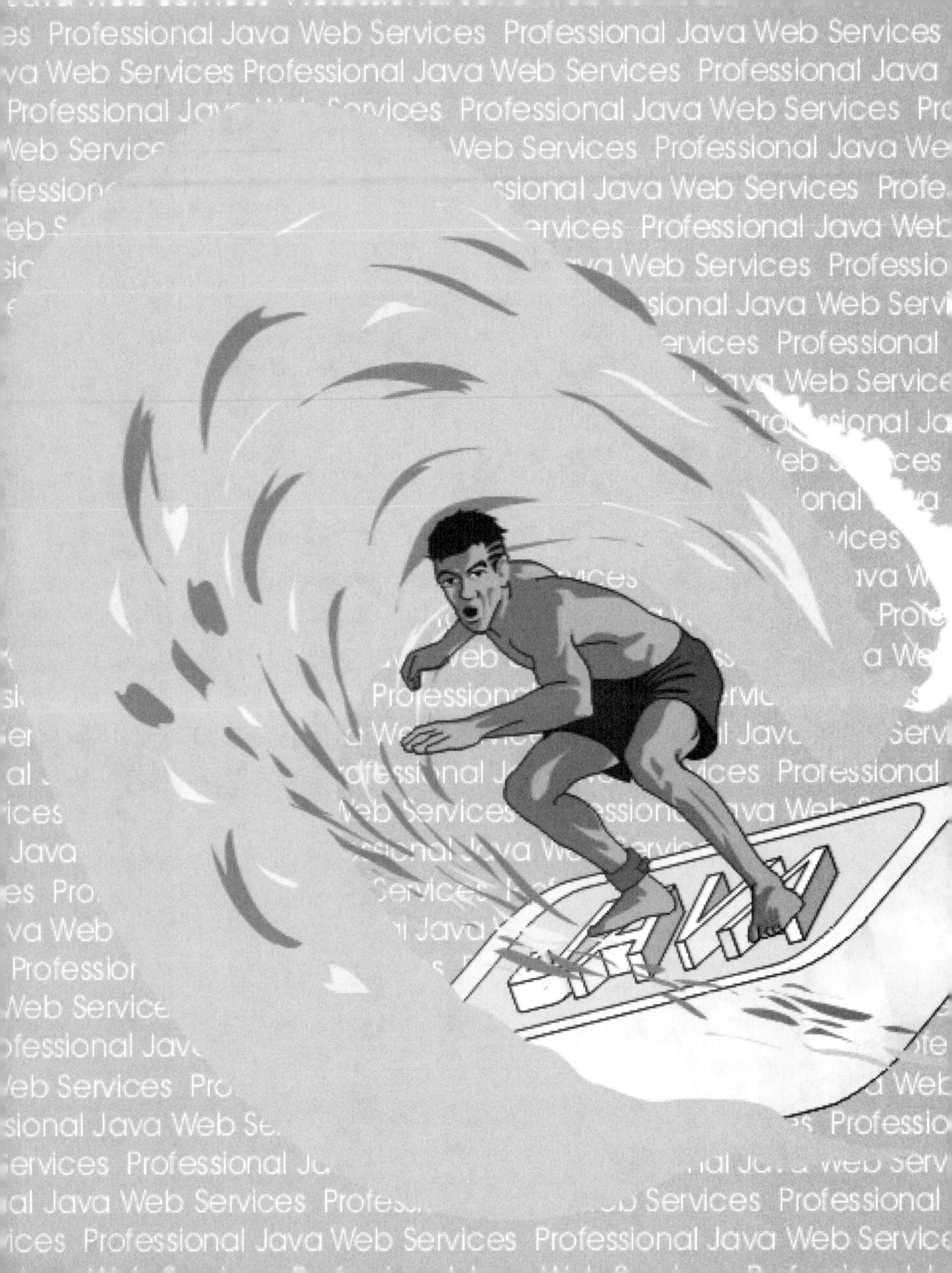
Professional Java Web Services

Index

A Guide to the Index

The index is arranged hierarchically, in alphabetical order, with symbols preceding the letter A. Most second-level entries and many third-level entries also occur as first-level entries. This is to ensure that users will find the information they require however they choose to search for it.

H

I

Notes

Notes

Notes

Notes

Notes

Notes

Notes

Notes

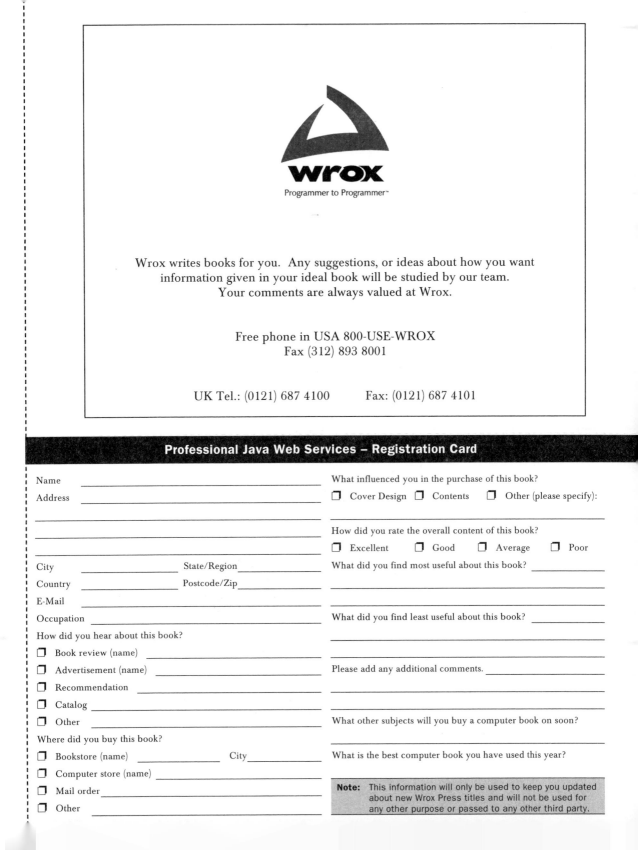

wrox

Programmer to Programmer™

Wrox writes books for you. Any suggestions, or ideas about how you want information given in your ideal book will be studied by our team.
Your comments are always valued at Wrox.

Free phone in USA 800-USE-WROX
Fax (312) 893 8001

UK Tel.: (0121) 687 4100   Fax: (0121) 687 4101

Professional Java Web Services – Registration Card

Name _____

Address _____

_____

_____

City _____ State/Region _____

Country _____ Postcode/Zip _____

E-Mail _____

Occupation _____

How did you hear about this book?

❑ Book review (name) _____

❑ Advertisement (name) _____

❑ Recommendation _____

❑ Catalog _____

❑ Other _____

Where did you buy this book?

❑ Bookstore (name) _____ City _____

❑ Computer store (name) _____

❑ Mail order _____

❑ Other _____

What influenced you in the purchase of this book?

❑ Cover Design   ❑ Contents   ❑ Other (please specify):

_____

How did you rate the overall content of this book?

❑ Excellent   ❑ Good   ❑ Average   ❑ Poor

What did you find most useful about this book? _____

_____

What did you find least useful about this book? _____

_____

Please add any additional comments. _____

_____

What other subjects will you buy a computer book on soon?

_____

What is the best computer book you have used this year?

_____

Note: This information will only be used to keep you updated about new Wrox Press titles and will not be used for any other purpose or passed to any other third party.

wrox

Programmer to Programmer™

Note: If you post the bounce back card below in the UK, please send it to:

Wrox Press Limited, Arden House, 1102 Warwick Road,
Acocks Green, Birmingham B27 6HB. UK.

Computer Book Publishers